ATLA BIBLIOGRAPHY SERIES
edited by Dr. Kenneth E. Rowe

1. *A Guide to the Study of the Holiness Movement*, by Charles Edwin Jones. 1974.
2. *Thomas Merton: A Bibliography*, by Marquita E. Breit. 1974.
3. *The Sermon on the Mount: A History of Interpretation and Bibliography*, by Warren S. Kissinger. 1975.
4. *The Parables of Jesus: A History of Interpretation and Bibliography*, by Warren S. Kissinger. 1979.
5. *Homosexuality and the Judeo-Christian Tradition: An Annotated Bibliography*, by Thom Horner. 1981.
6. *A Guide to the Study of the Pentecostal Movement*, by Charles Edwin Jones. 1983.
7. *The Genesis of Modern Process Thought: A Historical Outline with Bibliography*, by George R. Lucas, Jr. 1983.
8. *A Presbyterian Bibliography*, by Harold B. Prince. 1983.
9. *Paul Tillich: A Comprehensive Bibliography . . .*, by Richard C. Crossman. 1983.
10. *A Bibliography of the Samaritans*, by Alan David Crown. 1984.
11. *An Annotated and Classified Bibliography of English Literature Pertaining to the Ethiopian Orthodox Church*, by Jon Bonk. 1984.
12. *International Meditation Bibliography, 1950 to 1982*, by Howard R. Jarrell. 1984.

An Index to
English Periodical Literature
on the Old Testament
and
Ancient Near Eastern Studies

Volume II

Compiled and Edited by

William G. Hupper

ATLA Bibliography Series, No. 21

When you help scholars, you gain a share in their learning.
... Nachman of Bratslav

The American Theological Library Association, and
The Scarecrow Press, Inc.
Metuchen, NJ, & London 1988

Title page illustration from a freehand sketch by Joyce Lozzi

Library of Congress Cataloging-in-Publication Data
(Revised for vol. 2)

Hupper, William G.
 An index to English periodical literature on
the Old Testament and ancient Near Eastern
studies

 (ATLA bibliography series; no. 21)
 Includes bibliographies.
 1. Bible. O.T.--Periodicals--Indexes.
2. Middle East--Periodicals--Indexes. 3. Bible. O.T.--
Bibliography. 4. Middle East--Bibliography.
I. American Theological Library Association.
II. Title   III. Series.
Z7772.A1.H86 1987 [BS1171.2] 16.221   86-31448
ISBN 0-8108-1984-8 (v. 1)
ISBN 0-8108-2126-5 (v. 2)

Table of Contents

iii

Table of Contents

Preface

The increase in periodical literature over the past 17 years has exploded beyond all expectations. Recent discussions with the periodicals librarian at Andover-Harvard only serves to underscore this point. When *IEPLOT* was started in 1970, the library was subscribing to approximately 900 periodicals. Today, that number is over 1500, and there are still many titles which they do not carry!

It is against this backdrop that Volume II is presented. Hopefully it will allow users access to a great deal of retroactive material which has been published over the last two centuries. While it is still too early to expect reviews of Volume I to have been published, initial reaction to this work has been most favorable. Work is continuing as fast as humanly possible to produce the remaining volumes, though the subject and author index will not be attempted until all the volumes are complete. At this writing, 90% of Volume III has been input into the computer and proofreading of it has begun. Volume IV has been completely input to the computer and work on Volume V has been started. Volumes IV and V are anticipated by the editor to be the high point of the series, consisting of the articles dealing directly with the Hebrew Scriptures, both critically and exegetically.

With the advent of computers and word processing in today's world of "hi-tech" rather than speak of "word count", it is perhaps more appropriate to talk in terms of "megabytes". Volume I contains 123,836 words, which is equivalent to 1.6 megabytes. Likewise, Volume II contains 1.5 megabytes. This will be more understandable for the computer literate. It shall be left to readers to acertain the magnitude of the input.

Continued thanks go to the two proof-readers, Florence Hall and Norman Anderson, who fortunately, considering their mundane task, are as excited about the project as the editor.

Fortunately the schema for this work has some overlapping in classification. This has allowed some articles which were inadvertantly missed in the first volume to be picked up later. Eg.:

* James G. Williams, "The Prophetic 'Father': A Brief Explanation of the term 'Sons of the Prophets'," *JBL* 85 (1966) 344-348.

This article should have been included under §50 *Schools of the Prophets*" as noted in the "Corrections and Additions" Section, but will also be listed later under *Hebrew Word Studies*. While all the "Corrections and Additions" will be brought together in the final Author and Subject Index volume, those that have been discovered by the editor in Volume I are being issued by the publisher in a separate booklet which can be inserted into the flyleaf. This list should decrease proportionately with each succeeding volume.

Section 167 is an alphabetical listing of places within Israel (Palestine). While some cross references are listed, because there still remains some question as to exact locations,[1] this has been kept to a minimum. Places with the prefix "Tel" or "Tel el", etc. will be located under the last word in the name (eg. Tel ed-Duweir is located under Duweir). Names beginning with Khirbet, "Wadi" or "Wady" on the other hand are located under *K* and *W* respectively.

October, 1987

---

1. See Volume I, p. xxix for a complete discussion.

Periodical Abbreviations*

A

A&A   *Art and Archaeology; the arts throughout the ages*
(Washington, DC, Baltimore, MD, 1914-1934)

A/R   *Action/Reaction* (San Anselmo, CA, 1967ff.)

A&S   *Antiquity and Survival* (The Hague, 1955-1962)

AA   *Acta Archaeologica* (Copenhagen, 1930ff.)

AAA   *Annals of Archaeology and Anthropology*
(Liverpool, 1908-1948; Suspended,
1916-1920)

AAAS   *Annales archéologiques arabes de Syriennes*
(Damascus, 1951ff.) [Volumes 1-15 as:
Les Annales archéologiques de Syrie)

AAASH   *Acta Antiqua Academiae Scientiarum Hungaricae*
(Budapest, 1951ff.)

AAB   *Acta Archaeologica* (Budapest, 1951ff.)

AAI   *Anadolu Arastirmalari Istanbul Üniversitesi
Edebiyat Fakültesi eski Önasya Dilleri ve
Kültürleri Kürsüsü Tarafindan Čikarilir*
(Istanbul, 1955ff.) [Supersedes: *Jahrbuch
für Kleinasiatische Forschungen*]

AAOJ   *American Antiquarian and Oriental Journal*
(Cleveland, Chicago 1878-1914)

AASCS   *Antichthon. The Australian Society for Classical
Studies* (Sydney, 1967ff.)

ABBTS   *The Alumni Bulletin [of] Bangor Theological Seminary*
(Bangor, ME; 1926ff.)

ABenR   *The American Benedictine Review* (St. Paul,
1950ff.)

ABR   *Australian Biblical Review* (Melbourne, 1951ff.)

Abr-N   *Abr-Nahrain, An Annual Published by the Department
of Middle Eastern Studies, University of
Melbourne* (Melbourne, 1959ff.)

*All the journals indexed are listed in the Periodical Abbreviations even though no specific citation may appear in the first volume. Although the titles of many foreign language journals have been listed, only English Language articles are included in this index (except as noted). Articles from Modern Hebrew Language Journals are referred to by their English summary page.

Periodical Abbreviations

ACM   *The American Church Monthly* (New York, 1917-1939)
[Volumes 43-45 as: *The New American Church Monthly*]

ACQ   *American Church Quarterly* (New York, 1961ff.)
[Volume 7 on as: *Church Theological Review*]

ACQR   *The American Catholic Quarterly Review* (Philadelphia, 1876-1929)

ACR   *The Australasian Catholic Record* (Sydney, 1924ff.)

ACSR   *American Catholic Sociological Review* (Chicago, 1940ff.)
[From Volume 25 on as: *Sociologial Analysis*]

ADAJ   *Annual of the Department of Antiquities of Jordan* (Amman, 1957ff.) [Volume 14 not published - destroyed by fire at the publishers]

AE   *Annales d'Ethiopie* (Paris, 1955ff.)

AEE   *Ancient Egypt and the East* (New York, London, Chicago, 1914-1935; Suspended, 1918-1919)

Aeg   *Aegyptus: Rivista Italiana di Egittologia e di Papirologia* (Milan,1920ff.)

AER   *American Ecclesiastical Review* (Philadelphia, New York, Cincinnati, Baltimore, 1889ff.) [Volumes 11-19 as: *Ecclesiastical Review*]

AfER   *African Ecclesiastical Review: A Quartlerly for Priests in Africa* (Masaka, Uganda, 1959ff.)

Aff   *Affirmation* (Richmond, VA, 1966ff.) [Volume 1 runs from 1966 to 1980 inclusive]

AfO   *Archiv für Orientforschung: Internationale Zeitschrift für Wissenschaft vom Vorderen Orient* (Berlin, 1923ff.)

AfRW   *Archiv für Religionswissenschaft* (Leipzig, 1898-1941)

AHDO   *Archives d'histoire du droit oriental et Revue internationale des droits de l'antiquité* (Brussels, 1937-38, 1947-1951, *N.S.*, 1952-53)

AIPHOS   *Annuaire de l'institut de philologie et d'histoire orientales et slaves* (Brussels, 1932ff.)

AJ   *The Antiquaries Journal. Being the Journal of the Society of Antiquaries of London* (London, 1921ff.)

AJA   *The American Journal of Archaeology* (Baltimore, 1885ff.) [Original Series, 1885-1896 shown with *O. S.*; Second Series shown without notation]

AJBA   *The Australian Journal of Biblical Archaeology* (Sydney, 1968ff.) [Volume 1 runs from 1968 to 1971 inclusive]

Periodical Abbreviations

AJP   *The American Journal of Philology* (Baltimore, 1880ff.)

AJRPE   *The American Journal of Religious Psychology and
            Education* (Worcester, MA, 1904-1911)

AJSL   *The American Journal of Semitic Languages and
            Literatures* (Chicago, 1884-1941) [Volumes
            1-11 as: *Hebraica*]

AJT   *American Journal of Theology* (Chicago, 1897-1920)

AL   *Archivum Linguisticum: A Review of Comparative
            Philology and General Linguistics* (Glasgow,
            1949-1962)

ALUOS   *The Annual of the Leeds University Oriental Society*
            (Leiden,1958ff.)

Amb   *The Ambassador* (Wartburg Theological Seminary,
            Dubuque, IA, 1952ff.)

AmHR   *American Historical Review* (New York, Lancaster, PA,
            1895ff.)

AmSR   *American Sociological Review* (Washington, DC, 1936ff.)

Anat   *Anatolica: Annuaire International pour les Civilisations
            de l'Asie Anterieure* (Leiden, 1967ff.)

ANQ   *Newton Theological Institute Bulletin* (Newton, MA,
            1906ff.) [Title varies as: *Andover-Newton
            Theological Bulletin; Andover-Newton Quarterly,
            New Series,* beginning 1960ff.]

Anthro   *Anthropos; ephemeris internationalis ethnologica et
            linguistica* (Salzburg, Vienna, 1906ff.)

Antiq   *Antiquity: A Quarterly Review of Archaeology*
            (Gloucester, England, 1927ff.)

Anton   *Antonianum. Periodicum Philosophico-Theologicum
            Trimestre* (Rome, 1926ff.)

AO   *Acta Orientalia ediderunt Societates Orientales Bœtava
            Donica, Norvegica* (Lugundi Batavorum, Havniæ,
            1922ff.)

AOASH   *Acta Orientalia Academiae Scientiarum Hungaricae*
            (Budapest, 1950ff.)

AOL   *Annals of Oriental Literature* (London, 1820-21)

APST   *Aberdeen Philosophical Society, Transactions* (Aberdeen,
            Scotland, 1840-1931)

AQ   *Augustana Quarterly* (Rock Island, IL, 1922-1948)

AQW   *Anthropological Quarterly* (Washington, DC, 1928ff.)
            [Volumes 1-25 as: *Primitive Man*]

AR   *The Andover Review* (Boston, 1884-1893)

Arch   *Archaeology* (Cambrige, MA, 1948ff.)

Periodical Abbreviations

Archm   *Archaeometry. Bulletin of the Research Laboratory for Archaeology and the History of Art, Oxford University* (Oxford,1958ff.)

ARL   *The Archæological Review* (London, 1888-1890)

ArOr   *Archiv Orientální. Journal of the Czechoslovak Oriental Institute, Prague* (Vlašska, Czechoslovakia,1929ff.)

AS   *Anatolian Studies: Journal of the British Institute of Archaeology at Ankara* (London, 1951ff.)

ASAE   *Annales du service des antiquités de l'Égypte* (Cairo, 1899ff.)

ASBFE   *Austin Seminary Bulletin. Faculty Edition* (Austin, TX; begins with volume 71 /sic/, 1955ff.)

ASR   *Augustana Seminary Review* (Rock Island, IL, 1949-1967) [From volume 12 on as: *The Seminary Review*]

ASRB   *Advent Shield and Review* (Boston, 1844-45)

ASRec   *Auburn Seminary Record* (Auburn, NY, 1905-1932)

ASSF   *Acta Societatis Scientiarum Fennicae* (Helsinki, 1842-1926) [Suomen tideseura]

ASTI   *Annual of the Swedish Theological Institute (in Jerusalem)* (Jerusalem, 1962ff.)

ASW   *The Asbury Seminarian* (Wilmore, KY, 1946ff.)

AT   *Ancient Times: A Quarterly Review of Biblical Archaeology* (Melbourne, 1956-1961)

ATB   *Ashland Theological Bulletin* (Ashland, OH, 1968ff.)

ATG   *Advocate for the Testimony of God* (Richmond, VA, 1834-1839)

AThR   *The American Theological Review* (New York, 1859-1868) [*New Series* as: *American Presbyterian and Theological Review*; 1863-1868]

'Atiqot   *'Atiqot: Journal of the Israel Department of Antiquities* (Jerusalem, 1955ff.)

ATJ   *Africa Theological Journal* (Usa River, Tanzania, 1968ff.)

ATR   *Anglican Theological Review* (New York, Lancaster, Pa; 1918ff.)

AubSRev   *Auburn Seminary Review* (Auburn, NY, 1897-1904)

Aug   *Augustinianum* (Rome, 1961ff.)

AULLUÅ   *Acta Universitatis Lundensis. Lunds Universitets Årsskrift. Första Avdelningen. Teologi, Juridik och Humanistika Ämnen* (Lund, 1864-1904; *N. S.*, 1905-1964)

Periodical Abbreviations

Periodical Abbreviations

BIES   *Bulletin of the Israel Exploration Society* (Jerusalem, 1937-1967) [*Yediot* - **ארץ־ישראל** **ידיעות** **החברה ועאיקותיה לחקירת** - Begun as: *Bulletin of the Jewish Palestine Exploration Society* through volume 15. English summaries discontinued from volume 27 on as translations published in: *Israel Exploration Journal*]

BIFAO   *Bulletin de l'institut français d'archéologie orientale au Caire* (Cairo, 1901ff.)

BJ   *Biblical Journal* (Boston, 1842-1843)

BJRL   *Bulletin of the John Rylands Library* (Manchester, 1903ff.)

BM   *Bible Magazine* (New York, 1913-1915)

BMB   *Bulletin du Musée de Byrouth* (Paris, 1937ff.)

BN   *Bible Numerics: a Periodical Devoted to the Numerical Study of the Scriptures* (Grafton, MA; 1904)

BO   *Bibliotheca Orientalis* (Leiden, 1944ff.)

BofT   *Banner of Truth* (London, 1955ff.)

BOR   *The Babylonian and Oriental Record: A Monthly Magazine of the Antiquities of the East* (London, 1886-1901)

BQ   *Baptist Quarterly* (Philadelphia, 1867-1877)

BQL   *Baptist Quarterly* (London, 1922ff.)

BQR   *Baptist Quarterly Review* (Cincinnati, New York, Philadelphia,1879-1892)

BQRL   *The British Quarterly Review* (London, 1845-1886)

BR   *Biblical Review* (New York, 1916-1932)

BRCM   *The Biblical Review and Congregational Magazine* (London, 1846-1850)

BRCR   *The Biblical Repository and Classical Review* (Andover, MA,1831-1850) [Title varies as: *Biblical Repository; The Biblical Repository and Quarterly Observer; The American Biblical Repository*]

BRec   *Bible Record* (New York, 1903-1912) [Volume 1, #1-4 as: *Bible Teachers Training School, New York City, Bulletin*]

BRes   *Biblical Research: Papers of the Chicago Society of Biblical Research* (Amsterdam, Chicago, 1956ff.)

BS   *Bibliotheca Sacra* (New York, Andover, Oberlin, OH; St. Louis, Dallas, 1843, 1844ff.)

Periodical Abbreviations

BSAJB   *British School of Archaeology in Jerusalem, Bulletin*
        (Jerusalem, 1922-1925)

BSOAS   *Bulletin of the School of Oriental and African Studies.*
        University of London (London, 1917ff.)

BSQ   *Bethel Seminary Quarterly* (St. Paul, MN; 1952ff.)
        [From Volume 13 on as: *Bethel Seminary*
        Journal]

BT   *Biblical Theology* (Belfast, 1950ff.)

BTF   *Bangalore Theological Forum* (Bangalore, India, 1967ff.)

BTPT   *Bijdragen Tijdschrift voor philosophie en theologie*
        (Maastricht,1938ff.) [Title varies as: *Bijdragen.*
        Tijdschrift voor filosofie entheologie]

BTr   *Bible Translator* (London, 1950ff.)

BUS   *Bucknell University Studies* (Lewisburg, PA; 1941ff.)
        [From Volume 5 on as: *Bucknell Review*]

BW   *Biblical World* (Chicago, 1893-1920)

BWR   *Bible Witness and Review* (London, 1877-1881)

BWTS   *The Bulletin of the Western Theological Seminary*
        (Pittsburgh, 1908-1931)

BZ   *Biblische Zeitschrift* (Paderborn, 1903-1939; *New*
        Series, 1957ff.) [*N.S.* shown without notation]

C

C&C   *Cross and Crown. A Thomistic Quarterly of Spiritual*
        Theology (St. Louis, 1949ff.)

CAAMA   *Cahiers archéologiques fin de l'antiquité et moyen age*
        (Paris, 1961ff.)

CAAST   *Connecticut Academy of Arts and Sciences, Transactions*
        (New Haven, 1866ff.)

Carm   *Carmelus. Commentarii ab instituto carmelitano editi*
        (Rome, 1954ff.)

CBQ   *Catholic Biblical Quarterly* (Washington, DC; 1939ff.)

CC   *Cross Currents* (West Nyack, NY; 1950ff.)

CCARJ   *Central Conference of American Rabbis Journal*
        (New York,1953ff.)

CCBQ   *Central Conservative Baptist Quarterly* (Minneapolis,
        1958ff.) [From volume 9, #2 on as: *Central Bible*
        Quarterly]

Periodical Abbreviations

CCQ	*Crisis Christology Quarterly* (Dubuque, IA, 1943-1949) [Volume 6 as: *Trinitarian Theology*]
CD	*Christian Disciple* (Boston, 1813-1823) [Superseded by: *Christian Examiner*]
CdÉ	*Chronique d'Égypte* (Brussels, 1925ff.)
CE	*Christian Examiner* (Boston, New York, 1824-1869)
Cent	*Centaurus. International Magazine of the History of Science and Medicine* (Copenhagen, 1950ff.)
Center	*The Center* (Atlanta, 1960-1965)
CFL	*Christian Faith and Life* (Columbia, SC, 1897-1939) [Title varies: Original Series as: *The Bible Student and Relgious Outlook,* volume 1 & 2 as: *The Religious Outlook;* New Series as: *The Bible Student;* Third Series as: *The Bible Student and Teacher;* Several Volumes as: *Bible Champion*]
ChgoS	*Chicago Studies* (Mundelein, IL; 1962ff.)
CJ	*Conservative Judaism* (New York, 1945ff.)
CJL	*Canadian Journal of Linguistics* (Montreal, 1954ff.)
CJRT	*The Canadian Journal of Religious Thought* (Toronto, 1924-1932)
CJT	*Canadian Journal of Theology* (Toronto, 1955ff.)
ClR	*Clergy Review* (London, 1931ff.)
CM	*The Clergyman's Magazine* (London, 1875-1897)
CMR	*Canadian Methodist Review* (Toronto, 1889-1895) [Volumes 1-5 as: *Canadian Methodist Quarterly*]
CNI	*Christian News from Israel* (Jerusalem, 1949ff.)
CO	*Christian Opinion* (New York, 1943-1948)
Coll	*Colloquium. The Australian and New Zealand Theological Review* (Auckland, 1964ff.) [Volume 1 through Volume 2, #1 as: *The New Zealand Theological Review*]
CollBQ	*The College of the Bible Quarterly* (Lexington, KY, 1909-1965) [Break in sequence between 1927 and 1937, resumes in 1938 with volume 15 duplicated in number]
ColTM	*Columbus Theological Magazine* (Columbus, OH; 1881-1910)
CongL	*The Congregationalist* (London, 1872-1886)
CongML	*The Congregational Magazine* (London, 1818-1845)
CongQB	*The Congregational Quarterly* (Boston, 1859-1878)
CongQL	*The Congregational Quarterly* (London, 1923-1958)
CongR	*The Congregational Review* (Boston, Chicago, 1861-1871) [Volumes 1-6 as: *The Boston Review*]

Periodical Abbreviations

CongRL	*The Congregational Review* (London, 1887-1891)
ConstrQ	*The Constructive Quarterly. A Journal of the Faith, Work, and Thought of Christendom* (New York, London, 1913-1922)
Cont	*Continuum* (St. Paul, 1963-1970)
ContextC	*Context (Journal of the Lutheran School of Theology at Chicago)* (Chicago, 1967-1968)
ContR	*Contemporary Review* (London, New York, 1866ff.)
CovQ	*The Covenant Quarterly* (Chicago, 1941ff.) [Volume 1, #1 as: *Covenant Minister's Quarterly*]
CQ	*Crozer Quarterly* (Chester, PA; 1924-1952)
CQR	*Church Quarterly Review* (London, 1875-1968)
CR	*The Church Review* (New Haven, 1848-1891) [Title varies; Volume 62 not published]
CraneR	*The Crane Review* (Medford, MA; 1958-1968)
CRB	*The Christian Review* (Boston, Rochester; 1836-1863)
CRDSB	*Colgate-Rochester Divinity School Bulletin* (Rochester, NY;1928-1967)
Crit	*Criterion* (Chicago, 1962ff.)
CRP	*The Christian Review: A Quarterly Magazine* (Philadelphia, 1932-1941)
CS	*The Cumberland Seminarian* (McKenzie, TN; Memphis; 1953-1970)
CSQ	*Chicago Seminary Quarterly* (Chicago, 1901-1907)
CSQC	*The Culver-Stockton Quarterly* (Canton, MO; 1925-1931)
CSSH	*Comparative Studies in Society and History: An International Quarterly* (The Hague, 1958ff.)
CT	*Christian Thought* (New York, 1883-1894)
CTJ	*Calvin Theological Journal* (Grand Rapids, 1966ff.)
CTM	*Concordia Theological Monthly* (St. Louis, 1930ff.)
CTPR	*The Christian Teacher [and Chronicle]* (London, 1835-1838; *N.S.,* 1838-1844 as: *A Theological and Literary Journal*) [Continues as: *The Prospective Review; A Quarterly Journal of Theology and Literature*)
CTSB	*Columbia Theological Seminary Bulletin* (Columbia, SC; Decatur, GA; 1907ff.) [Title varies]
CTSP	*Catholic Theological Society, Proceedings* (Washingon, DC; Yonkers, NY; 1948ff.)
CTSQ	*Central Theological Seminary Quarterly* (Dayton, OH; 1923-1931)
CUB	*Catholic University Bulletin* (Washington, DC;1895-1914) [Volumes 1-20 only]

D

DDSR   *Duke Divinity School Review* (Durham, NC; 1936ff.)
              [Volumes 1-20 as: *The Duke School of Religion
              Bulletin;* Volumes 21-29 as: *Duke Divinity School
              Bulletin*]
DG   *The Drew Gateway* (Madison, NJ; 1930ff.)
DI   *Diné Israel. An Annual of Jewish Law and Israeli Family
              Law* דיני ישואל שנתון למשט עברי ולדיני
              משחח ביראל   (Jerusalem, 1969ff.)
DJT   *Dialogue: A Journal of Theology* (Minneapolis, 1962ff.)
DQR   *Danville Quarterly Review* (Danville, KY; Cincinnati;
              1861-1864)
DownsR   *Downside Review* (Bath, 1880ff.)
DR   *Dublin Review* (London, 1836-1968) [Between 1961 and
              1964 as: *Wiseman Review*]
DS   *Dominican Studies. A Quarterly Review of Theology and
              Philosophy* (Oxford, 1948-1954)
DSJ   *The Dubuque Seminary Journal* (Dubuque, IA;
              1966-1967)
DSQ   *Dubuque Seminary Quarterly* (Dubuque, IA; 1947-1949)
              [Volume 3, #3 not published]
DTCW   *Dimension: Theology in Church and World* (Princeton,
              NJ; 1964-1969) [Volumes 1 & 2 as: *Dimension*;
              New format beginning in 1966 with full title,
              beginning again with Volume 1]
DTQ   *Dickinson's Theological Quarterly* (London, 1875-1883)
              [Superseded by *John Lobb's Theological Quarterly*]
DUJ   *The Durham University Journal* (Durham, 1876ff.; *N.S.,*
              1940ff.) [Volume 32 of *O.S.* = Volume 1 of *N.S.*]
DUM   *Dublin University Magazine* (Dublin, London, 1833-1880)
DunR   *The Dunwoodie Review* (Yonkers, NY; 1961ff.)

Periodical Abbreviations

E

EgR   *Egyptian Religion* (New York, 1933-1936)

EI   *Eretz-Israel. Archaeological, Historical and Geographical Studies* (Jerusalem, 1951ff.) מחקרים

        ארץ־ישראל בידיעת הארץ ועתיקותיה

        [English Summaries from Volume 3 on]

EJS   *Archives européennes de Sociologie / European Journal of Sociology / Europäisches Archiv für Soziologie* (Paris, 1960ff.)

EN   *The Everlasting Nation* (London, 1889-1892)

EQ   *Evangelical Quarterly* (London, 1929ff.)

ER   *Evangelical Review* (Gettysburg, PA; 1849-1870) [From Volume 14 on as: *Evangelical Quarterly Review*]

ERCJ   *Edinburgh Review, or Critical Journal* (Edinburgh, London, 1802-1929)

ERG   *The Evangelical Repository: A Quarterly Magazine of Theological Literature* (Glasgow, 1854-1888)

ERL   *The English Review, or Quarterly Journal of Eccesiastical and General Literature* (London, 1844-1853) [Continues *British Critic*]

ESS   *Ecumenical Study Series* (Indianapolis, 1955-1960)

ET   *The Expository Times* (Aberdeen, Edinburgh, 1889ff.)

ETL   *Ephemerides Theologicae Lovanienses* (Notre Dame, 1924ff.)

Eud   *Eudemus. An International Journal Devoted to the History of Mathematics and Astronomy* (Copenhagen, 1941)

Exp   *The Expositor* (London, 1875-1925)

Exped   *Expedition* (Philadelphia, 1958ff.) [Continues: *The University Museum Bulletin*]

Periodical Abbreviations

F

F&T	*Faith and Thought* (London, 1958ff.) [Supersedes: *Journal of the Transactions of the Victoria Institute, or Philosophical Society of Great Britain*]
FBQ	*The Freewill Baptist Quarterly* (Providence, London, Dover, 1853-1869)
FDWL	*Friends of Dr.Williams's Library (Lectures)* (Cambridge, Oxford, 1948ff.)
FLB	*Fuller Library Bulletin* (Pasadena, CA; 1949ff.)
FO	*Folia Orientalia* (Kraków, 1960ff.)
Focus	*Focus. A Theological Journal* (Willowdale, Ontario, 1964-1968)
Folk	*Folk-Lore: A Quarterly Review of Myth, Tradition, Institution & Custom being the Transactions of the Folk-Lore Society And Incorporating the Archæological Review and the Folk-Lore Journal* (London, 1890ff.)
Found	*Foundations (A Baptist Journal of History and Theology)* (Rochester, NY; 1958ff.)
FUQ	*Free University Quarterly* (Amsterdam-Centrum, 1950-1965)

G

GBT	*Ghana Bulletin of Theology* (Legon, Ghana; 1957ff.)
GJ	*Grace Journal* (Winona Lake, IN; 1960ff.)
GOTR	*Greek Orthodox Theological Review* (Brookline, MA; 1954ff.)
GR	*Gordon Review* (Boston; Beverly Farms, MA; Wenham, MA; 1955ff.)
GRBS	*Greek, Roman and Byzantine Studies* (San Antonio; Cambridge, MA; University, MS; Durham, NC; 1958ff.) [Volume 1 as: *Greek and Byzantine Studies*]

Periodical Abbreviations

J

JAAR   *Journal of the American Academy of Religion*
(Wolcott, NY; Somerville, NJ; Baltimore;
Brattleboro, VT) [Volumes 1-4 as: *Journal of the
National Association of Biblical Instructors;*
Volumes 5-34 as: *Journal of Bible and Religion*]

JANES   *Journal of the Ancient Near Eastern Society of Columbia
University* (New York, 1968ff.)

Janus   *Janus; Archives internationales pour l'Histoire de la
Médecine et pour la Géographie Médicale*
(Amsterdam; Haarlem; Leiden; 1896ff.)

JAOS   *Journal of the American Oriental Society* (Baltimore,
New Haven, 1843ff.)

JAOSS   *Journal of the American Oriental Society, Supplements*
(Baltimore, New Haven, 1935-1954)

JARCE   *Journal of the American Research Center in Egypt*
(Gluckstadt, Germany; Cambridge, MA; 1962ff.)

JASA   *Journal of the American Scientific Affiliation*
(Wheaton, IL, 1949ff.)

JBL   *Journal of Biblical Literature* (Middletown, CT; New
Haven; Boston; Philadelphia; Missoula, MT; 1881ff.)

JC&S   *The Journal of Church and State* (Fresno, CA; 1965ff.)

JCP   *Christian Philosophy Quarterly* (New York, 1881-1884)
[From Volume 2 on as: *The Journal of Christian
Philosophy*]

JCS   *Journal of Cuneiform Studies* (New Haven; Cambridge,
MA;1947ff.)

JCSP   *Journal of Classical and Sacred Philology* (Cambridge,
England, 1854-1857)

JEA   *Journal of Egyptian Archaeology* (London, 1914ff.)

JEBH   *Journal of Economic and Business History* (Cambridge,
MA;1928-1932)

JEOL   *Jaarbericht van het Vooraziatisch-Egyptisch Gezelschap
Ex Oriente Lux* (Leiden, 1933ff.)

JES   *Journal of Ethiopian Studies* (Addis Ababa, 1963ff.)

JESHO   *Journal of the Economic and Social History of the Orient*
(Leiden, 1958ff.)

JHI   *Journal of the History of Ideas. A Quarterly Devoted to
Intellectual History* (Lancaster, PA; New York;
1940ff.

Periodical Abbreviations

Periodical Abbreviations

JTALC   *Journal of Theology of the American Lutheran Conference* (Minneapolis, 1936-1943) [Volumes 1-5 as: *American Lutheran Conference Journal;* continued from volume 8, #3 as: *Lutheran Outlook* (not included)]

JTC   *Journal for Theology and the Church* (New York, 1965ff.)

JTLC   *Journal of Theology: Church of the Lutheran Confession* (Eau Claire, WI; 1961ff.)

JTS   *Journal of Theological Studies* (Oxford, 1899-1949; *N.S.,* 1950ff.)

JTVI   *Journal of the Transactions of the Victoria Institute, or Philosophical Society of Great Britain* (London, 1866-1957) [Superseded by *Faith & Thought*]

Jud   *Judaism. A Quarterly Journal of Jewish Life and Thought* (New York, 1952ff.)

JWCI   *Journal of the Warburg and Courtauld Institutes* (London,1937ff.)

JWH   *Journal of World History - Cahiers d'Histoire Mondiale - Cuadernos de Historia Mundial* (Paris, 1953ff.)

K

Kêmi   *Kêmi. Revue de philologie et d'archéologie égyptiennes et coptes* (Paris, 1928ff.)

Klio   *Klio. Beiträge zur alten Geschichte* (Leipzig, 1901ff.)

Kobez   *Kobez (Qobeş);* קובץ החברה העברית לחקירת

ארץ־ישראל   ועתיקותיה (Jerusalem, 1921-1945)

KSJA   *Kedem; Studies in Jewish Archaeology* (Jerusalem, 1942, 1945)

Kuml   *Kuml. Årbog for Jysk Arkæologisk Selskab* (Århus, 1951ff.)

Kush   *Kush. Journal of the Sudan Antiquities Service* (Khartoum, Sudan, 1953-1968)

KZ   *Kirchliche Zeitschrift* (St. Louis; Waverly, IA; Chicago; Columbus; 1876-1943)

KZFE   *Kadmos. Zeitschrift für vor-und frühgriechische Epigraphik* (Berlin, 1962ff.)

Periodical Abbreviations

L

L	*Levant (Journal of the British School of Archaeology in Jerusalem)* (London, 1969ff.)
Lang	*Language. Journal of the Linguistic Society of America* (Baltimore, 1925ff.)
LCQ	*Lutheran Church Quarterly* (Gettysburg, PA; 1928-1949)
LCR	*Lutheran Church Review* (Philadelphia, 1882-1927)
Lĕš	*Lĕšonénu. Quarterly for the Study of the Hebrew Language and Cognate Subjects* לשוננו (Jerusalem, 1925ff.) [English Summaries from volume 30 onward]
LIST	*Lown Institute. Studies and Texts* (Brandies University. Lown School of Near Eastern and Judaic Studies. Cambridge, MA; 1963ff.)
Listen	*Listening* (Dubuque, IA; 1965ff.) [Volume numbers start with "zero"]
LofS	*Life of the Spirit* (London, 1946-1964)
LQ	*The Quarterly Review of the Evangelical Lutheran Church* (Gettysburg, PA; 1871-1927; revived in 1949ff.) [From 1878 on as: *The Lutheran Quarterly*]
LQHR	*London Quarterly and Holborn Review* (London, 1853-1968)
LS	*Louvain Studies* (Louvain, 1966ff.)
LSQ	*Lutheran Synod Quarterly* (Mankato, MN, 1960ff.) [Formerly *Clergy Bulletin* (Volume 1 of *LSQ* as *Clergy Bulletin,* Volume 20, #1 & #2)
LTJ	*Lutheran Theological Journal* (North Adelaide, South Australia, 1967ff.)
LTP	*Laval Theologique et Philosophique* (Quebec, 1945ff.)
LTQ	*Lexington Theological Quarterly* (Lexington, KY; 1966ff.)
LTR	*Literary and Theological Review* (New York; Boston, 1834-1839)
LTSB	*Lutheran Theological Seminary Bulletin* (Gettysburg, PA; 1921ff.)
LTSR	*Luther Theological Seminary Review* (St. Paul, MN; 1962ff.)
LWR	*The Lutheran World Review* (Philadelphia, 1948-1950)

Periodical Abbreviations

M

Man	*Man. A Monthly Record of Anthropological Science* (London,1901-1965; *N. S.,* 1966ff.) [Articles in original series referred to by *article* number not by *page* number - New Series subtitled: *the journal of the Royal Anthropological Institute*]
ManSL	*Manuscripta* (St. Louis, 1957ff.)
MB	*Medelhavsmuseet Bulletin* (Stockholm, 1961ff.)
MC	*The Modern Churchman* (Ludlow, England; 1911ff.)
McQ	*McCormick Quarterly* (Chicago, 1947ff.) [Volumes 1-13 as: *McCormick Speaking*]
MCS	*Manchester Cuneiform Studies* (Manchester, 1951-1964)
MDIÄA	*Mitteilungen des deutsches Instituts für ägyptische Altertumskunde in Kairo* (Cairo, 1930ff.)
Mesop	*Mesopotamia* (Torino, Italy, 1966ff.)
MH	*The Modern Humanist* (Weston, MA; 1944-1962)
MHSB	*The Mission House Seminary Bulletin* (Plymouth, WI; 1954-1962)
MI	*Monthly Interpreter* (Edinburgh, 1884-1886)
MidS	*Midstream (Council on Christian Unity)* (Indianapolis, 1961ff.)
Min	*Ministry. A Quarterly Theological Review for South Africa* (Morija, Basutolan, 1960ff.)
Minos	*Minos. Investigaciones y Materiales Para el Estudio de los Textos Paleocretenses Publicados Bajo la Direccion de Antonio Tovar y Emilio Peruzzi* (Salamanca, 1951ff.) [From Volume 4 on as: *Minos Revista de Filologia Egea*]
MIO	*Mitteilungen des Instituts für Orientforschung [Deutsche Akademie der Wissenschaften zu Berlin Institut für Orientforschung]* (Berlin, 1953ff.)
Miz	*Mizraim. Journal of Papyrology, Egyptology, History of Ancient Laws, and their Relations to the Civilizations of Bible Lands* (New York, 1933-1938)
MJ	*The Museum Journal. Pennsylvania University* (Philadelphia,1910-1935)

Periodical Abbreviations

MMBR   *The Monthly Magazine and British Register* (London,
             1796-1843) [*1st Ser.*, 1796-1826, Volumes 1-60;
             N.S., 1826-1838, Volumes 1-26; *3rd Ser.*, 1839-
             1843, Volumes 1-9, however, Volumes 7-9 are
             marked 95-97 */sic/*]

ModR   *The Modern Review* (London, 1880-1884)

Monist   *The Monist. An International Quarterly Journal of
             General Philosophical Inquiry* (Chicago; La Salle,
             IL; 1891ff.)

Mosaic   *Mosaic* (Cambridge, MA; 1960ff.)

MQ   *The Minister's Quarterly* (New York, 1945-1966)

MQR   *Methodist Quarterly Review (South)* (Louisville,
             Nashville,1847-1861; 1879-1886; 1886-1930)
             [*3rd Ser.* as: *Southern Methodist Review;*
             Volume 52 (1926) misnumbered as 53;
             Volume 53 (1927) misnumbered as 54;
             and the volume for 1928 is also marked as 54]

MR   *Methodist Review* (New York, 1818-1931) [Volume 100
             not published]

MTSB   *Moravian Theological Seminary Bulletin* (Bethlehem, PA;
             1959-1970) [Volume for 1969 apparently not
             published]

MTSQB   *Meadville Theological School Quarterly Bulletin*
             (Meadville, PA;1906-1933) [From Volume 25
             on as: *Meadville Journal*]

Muséon   *Le Muséon. Revue d'Études Orientales* (Louvain,
             1882-1915;1930/32ff.)

MUSJ   *Mélánges de l'Université Saint-Joseph. Faculté orientale*
             (Beirut, 1906ff.)

Mwa-M   *Milla wa-Milla. The Australian Bulletin of Comparative
             Religion* (Parkville, Victoria, 1961ff.)

N

NB   *Blackfriars. A Monthly Magazine* (Oxford, 1920ff.)
             [From Volume 46 on as: *New Blackfriars*]

NBR   *North British Review* (Edinburgh, 1844-1871)

NCB   *New College Bulletin* (Edinburgh, 1964ff.)

NEAJT   *Northeast Asia Journal of Theology* (Kyoto, Japan,
             1968ff.)

Periodical Abbreviations

NEST	*The Near East School of Theology Quarterly* (Beirut, 1952ff.)
Nexus	*Nexus* (Boston, 1957ff.)
NGTT	*Nederduitse gereformeerde teologiese tydskrif* (Kaapstad, N.G., Kerk-Uitgewers, 1959ff.)
NOGG	*Nihon Orient Gakkai geppo* (Tokyo, 1955-1959) [Being the *Bulletin of the Society for Near Eastern Studies in Japan* - Continued as: *Oriento*]
NPR	*The New Princeton Review* (New York, 1886-1888)
NOP	*New Orient* (Prague, 1960-1968)
NQR	*Nashotah Quarterly Review* (Nashotah, WI; 1960ff.)
NT	*Novum Testamentum* (Leiden, 1955ff.)
NTS	*New Testament Studies* (Cambridge, England; 1954ff.)
NTT	*Nederlandsch Theologisch Tijdschrift* (Wageningen, 1946ff.)
NTTO	*Norsk Teologisk Tidsskrift* (Oslo, 1900ff.)
Numen	*Numen: International Review for the History of Religions* (Leiden, 1954ff.)
NW	*The New World. A Quarterly Review of Religion, Ethics and Theology* (Boston, 1892-1900)
NYR	*The New York Review. A Journal of The Ancient Faith and Modern Thought (St. John's Seminary)* (New York, 1905-1908)
NZJT	*New Zealand Journal of Theology* (Christchurch, 1931-1935)

O

OA	*Oriens Antiquus* (Rome, 1962ff.)
OBJ	*The Oriental and Biblical Journal* (Chicago, 1880-1881)
OC	*Open Court* (Chicago, 1887-1936)
ONTS	*The Hebrew Student* (Morgan Park, IL; New Haven; Hartford;1881-1892) [Volumes 3-8 as: *The Old Testament Student;* Volume 9 onwards as: *The Old and New Testament Student*]
OOR	*Oriens: The Oriental Review* (Paris, 1926)
OQR	*The Oberlin Quarterly Review* (Oberlin, OH; 1845-1849)
Or	*Orientalia commentarii de rebus Assyri-Babylonicis, Arabicis, and Aegyptiacis, etc.* (Rome 1920-1930)

Periodical Abbreviations

Or. N.S.   *Orientalia: commentarii, periodici de rebus orientis antiqui* (Rome, 1932ff.)

Oriens   *Oriens. Journal of the International Society of Oriental Research* (Leiden, 1948ff.)

Orient   *Orient. The Reports of the Society for Near Eastern Studies in Japan* (Tokyo, 1960ff.)

Orita   *Orita. Ibadan Journal of Religious Studies* (Ibadan, Nigeria, 1967ff.)

OrS   *Orientalia Suecana* (Uppsala, 1952ff.)

OSHTP   *Oxford Society of Historical Theology, Abstract of Proceedings* (Oxford, 1891-1968 [Through 1919 as: *Society of Historical Theology, Proceedings*]

Osiris   *Osiris* (Bruges, Belgium; 1936-1968) *[Subtitle varies]*

OTS   *Oudtestamentische Studiën* (Leiden, 1942ff.)

OTW   *Ou-Testamentiese Werkgemeenskap in Suid-Afrika, Proceedings of die* (Pretoria, 1958ff.) [Volume 1 in Volume 14 of: *Hervormde Teologiese Studies*]

P

P   *Preaching: A Journal of Homiletics* (Dubuque, IA; 1965ff.)

P&P   *Past and Present* (London, 1952ff.) *[Subtitle varies]*

PA   *Practical Anthropology* (Wheaton, IL; Eugene, OR; Tarrytown, NY; 1954ff.)

PAAJR   *Proceedings of the American Academy for Jewish Research* (Philadelphia, 1928ff.)

PAOS   *Proceedings of the American Oriental Society* (Baltimore, New Haven; 1842, 1846-50, 1852-1860) [After 1860 all proceedings are bound with *Journal*]

PAPA   *American Philological Association, Proceedings* (Hartford, Boston, 1896ff.) [*Transactions* as: *TAPA, Transactions* and *Proceedings* combine page numbers from volume 77 on]

PAPS   *Proceedings of the American Philosophical Society* (Philadelphia, 1838ff.)

PBA   *Proceedings of the British Academy* (London, 1903ff.)

Periodical Abbreviations

PEFQS   *Palestine Exploration Fund Quarterly Statement* (London, 1869ff.) [From Volume 69 (1937) on as: *Palestine Exploration Quarterly*]

PEQ   *Palestine Exploration Quarterly* [See: *PEFQS*]

PER   *The Protestant Episcopal Review* (Fairfax, Co., VA; 1886-1900) [Volumes 1-5 as: *The Virginian Seminary Magazine*]

Person   *Personalist . An International Review of Philosophy, Religion and Literature* (Los Angeles, 1920ff.)

PF   *Philosophical Forum* (Boston, 1943-1957; *N.S.*, 1968ff.)

PHDS   *Perspectives. Harvard Divinity School* (Cambridge, MA; 1965-1967)

PIASH   *Proceedings of the Israel Academy of Sciences and Humanities* (Jerusalem, 1967ff.)

PIJSL   *Papers of the Institute of Jewish Studies, London* (Jerusalem, 1964)

PJT   *Pacific Journal of Theology* (Western Samoa, 1961ff.)

PJTSA   *Jewish Theological Seminary Association, Proceedings* (New York, 1888-1902)

PP   *Perspective* (Pittsburgh, 1960ff.) [Volumes 1-8 as: *Pittsburgh Perspective*]

PQ   *The Presbyterian Quarterly* (New York, 1887-1904)

PQL   *The Preacher's Quarterly* (London, 1954-1969)

PQPR   *The Presbyterian Quarterly and Princeton Review* (New York, 1872-1877)

PQR   *Presbyterian Quarterly Review* (Philadlephia, 1852-1862)

PR   *Presbyterian Review* (New York, 1880-1889)

PRev   *The Biblical Repertory and Princeton Review* (Princeton, Philadelphia, New York, 1829-1884) [Volume 1 as: *The Biblical Repertory, New Series;* Volumes 2-8 as: *The Biblical Repertory and Theological Review*]

PRR   *Presbyterian and Reformed Review* (New York, Philadelphia, (1890-1902)

PSB   *The Princeton Seminary Bulletin* (Princeton, 1907ff.)

PSTJ   *Perkins School of Theology Journal* (Dallas, 1947ff.)

PTR   *Princeton Theological Review* (Princeton, 1903-1929)

PUNTPS   *Proceedings of the University of Newcastle upon the Tyne Philosophical Society* (Newcastle-upon-Tyne, 1967ff.)

Q

QCS	*Quarterly Christian Spectator* (New Haven, 1819-1838) */1st Series* and *New Series* as: *Christian Spectator/*
QDAP	*The Quarterly of the Department of Antiquities in Palestine* (Jerusalem, 1931-1950)
QRL	*Quarterly Review* (London, 1809-1967)
QTMRP	*The Quarterly Theological Magazine, and Religious Repository* (Philadelphia, 1813-1814)

R

R&E	*/Baptist/ Review and Expositor* (Louisville, 1904ff.)
R&S	*Religion and Society* (Bangalore, India, 1953ff.)
RAAO	*Revue d'Assyriologie et d'Archéologie Orientale* (Paris, 1886ff.)
RdQ	*Revue de Qumran* (Paris, 1958ff.)
RChR	*The Reformed Church Review* (Mercersburg, PA; Chambersburg, PA; Philadelphia; 1849-1926) [Volumes 1-25 as: *Mercersburg Review;* Volumes 26-40 as: *Reformed Quarterly Review;* *4th Series* on as: *Reformed Church Review*]
RCM	*Reformed Church Magazine* (Reading, PA; 1893-1896) [Volume 3 as: *Reformed Church Historical Magazine*]
RDSO	*Rivista degli Studi Orientali* (Rome, 1907ff.)
RÉ	*Revue Égyptologique* (Paris, 1880-1896; *N.S.,* 1919-1924)
RÉg	*Revue d'Égyptologie* (Paris, 1933ff.)
RefmR	*The Reformation Review* (Amsterdam, 1953ff.)
RefR	*The Reformed Review. A Quarterly Journal of the Seminaries of the Reformed Church in America* (Holland, MI; New Brunswick, NJ; 1947ff.) [Volumes 1-9 as: *Western Seminary Bulletin*]
RelM	*Religion in the Making* (Lakeland, FL; 1940-1943)
Resp	*Response—in worship—Music—The arts* (St. Paul, 1959ff.)

Periodical Abbreviations

RestQ   *Restoration Quarterly* (Austin, TX; Abeline, TX; 1957ff.)

RFEASB   *The Hebrew University / Jerusalem: Department of Archaeology. Louis M. Rabinowitz Fund for the Exploration of Ancient Synagogues, Bulletin* (Jerusalem, 1949-1960)

RHA   *Revue Hittite et Asianique* (Paris, 1930ff.)

RIDA   *Revue internationale des droits de l'antiquité* (Brussels, 1948ff.)

RJ   *Res Judicatae. The Journal of the Law Students' Society of Victoria* (Melbourne, 1935-1957)

RL   *Religion in Life* (New York, 1932ff.)

RO   *Rocznik Orjentalistyczny. (Wydaje Polskie towarzystwo orjentalisyczne)* (Kraków, Warsaw, 1914ff.)

RP   *Records of the Past* (Washington, DC; 1902-1914)

RR   *Review of Religion* (New York, 1936-1958)

RS   *Religious Studies* (London, 1965ff.)

RTP   *Review of Theology and Philosophy* (Edinburgh, 1905-1915)

RTR   *Recueil de travaux relatifs à la philologie et à l'archéologie egyptiennes et assyriennes* (Paris, 1870-1923)

RTRM   *The Reformed Theological Review* (Melbourne, 1941ff.)

S

SAENJ   *Seminar. An Annual Extraordinary Number of the Jurist* (Washington, DC; 1943-1956)

SBAP   *Society of Biblical Archæology, Proceedings* (London, 1878-1918)

SBAT   *Society of Biblical Archæology, Transactions* (London, 1872-1893)

SBE   *Studia Biblica et Ecclesiastica* (Oxford, 1885-1903) Volume 1 as: *Studia Biblica*]

SBFLA   *Studii (Studium) Biblici Franciscani. Liber Annuus* (Jerusalem, 1950ff.)

SBLP   *Society of Biblical Literature & Exegesis, Proceedings* (Baltimore, 1880)

Periodical Abbreviations

SBO	*Studia Biblica et Orientalia* (Rome 1959) [Being Volumes 10-12 respectively of *Analecta Biblica. Investigationes Scientificae in Res Biblicas*]
SBSB	*Society for Biblical Studies Bulletin* (Madras, India, 1964ff.)
SCO	*Studi Classici e Orientali* (Pisa, 1951ff.)
Scotist	*The Scotist* (Teutopolis, IL; 1939-1967)
SCR	*Studies in Comparative Religion* (Bedfont, Middlesex, England, 1967ff.)
Scrip	*Scripture. The Quarterly of the Catholic Biblical Association* (London, 1944-1968)
SE	*Study Encounter* (Geneva, 1965ff.)
SEA	*Svensk Exegetisk Årsbok* (Uppsala-Lund, 1936ff.)
SEAJT	*South East Journal of Theology* (Singapore, 1959ff.)
Sefunim	*Sefunim (Bulletin)* [היפח] סינים (Haifa, 1966-1968)
SGEI	*Studies in the Geography of Eretz-Israel* (Jerusalem, מחקרים בגיאוגרפיה של ארץ-ישראל 1959ff.) [English summaries in Volumes 1-3 only; continuing the *Bulletin of the Israel Exploration Society (Yediot)*]
SH	*Scripta Hierosolymitana* (Jerusalem, 1954ff.)
Shekel	*The Shekel* (New York, 1968ff.)
SIR	*Smithsonian Institute Annual Report of the Board of Regents* (Washington, DC; 1846-1964; becomes: *Smithsonian Year* from 1965 on]
SJH	*Seminary Journal* (Hamilton, NY; 1892)
SJT	*Scottish Journal of Theology* (Edinburgh, 1947ff.)
SL	*Studia Liturgica. An International Ecumenical Quarterly for Liturgical Research and Renewal* (Rotterdam, 1962ff.)
SLBR	*Sierra Leone Bulletin of Religion* (Freetown, Sierra Leone;1959-1966)
SMR	*Studia Montes Regii* (Montreal, 1958-1967)
SMSDR	*Studi e Materiali di Storia Delle Religioni* (Rome, Bologna, 1925ff.
SO	*Studia Orientalia* (Helsinki, 1925ff.)
SOOG	*Studi Orientalistici in Onore di Giorgio Levi Della Vida* (Rome, 1956)
Sophia	*Sophia. A Journal for Discussion in Philosophical Theology* (Parkville, N.S.W., Australia, 1962ff.)
SP	*Spirit of the Pilgrims* (Boston, 1828-1833)

Periodical Abbreviations

SPR	*Southern Presbyterian Review* (Columbia, SC; 1847-1885)
SQ/E	*The Shane Quarterly* (Indianapolis, 1940ff.) [From Volume 17 on as: *Encounter*]
SR	*The Seminary Review* (Cincinnati, 1954ff.)
SRL	*The Scottish Review* (London, Edinburgh, 1882-1900; 1914-1920)
SS	*Seminary Studies of the Athenaeum of Ohio* (Cincinnati, 1926-1968) [Volumes 1-15 as: *Seminary Studies*]
SSO	*Studia Semitica et Orientalia* (Glasgow, 1920, 1945)
SSR	*Studi Semitici* (Rome, 1958ff.)
ST	*Studia Theologica* (Lund, 1947ff.)
StEv	*Studia Evangelica* (Berlin, 1959ff.) [Being miscellaneous volumes of: *Text und Untersuchungen zur Geschichte der altchristlichen Literatur*, beginning with Volume 73]
StL.J	*The Saint Luke's Journal* (Sewanee, TN; 1957ff.) [Volume 1, #1 as: *St. Luke's Journal of Theology*]
StMR	*St. Mark's Review: An Anglican Quarterly* (Canberra, N.S.W., Australia, 1955ff.)
StP	*Studia Patristica* (Berlin, 1957ff.) [Being miscellaneous volumes of: *Text und Untersuchungen zur Geschichte der altchristlichen Literatur*, beginning with Volume 63]
StVTQ	*St. Vladimir's Theological Quarterly* (Crestwood, NY; 1952ff. [Volumes 1-4 as: *St. Vladimir's Seminary Quarterly*]
Sumer	*Sumer. A Journal of Archaeology in Iraq* (Bagdad, 1945ff.)
SWJT	*Southwestern Journal of Theology* (Fort Worth, 1917-1924; *N.S.*, 1950ff.)
Syria	*Syria, revue d'art oriental et d'archéologie* (Paris, 1920ff.)

T

T&C	*Theology and the Church / SÎN-HÂK kap kàu-Hōe (Tainan Theological College)* (Tainan, Formosa, 1957ff.)
T&L	*Theology and Life* (Lancester, PA; 1958-1966)

Periodical Abbreviations

TAD   *Türk tarih, arkeologya ve etnoğrafya dergisi* (Istanbul, 1933-1949; continued as: *Türk arkeoloji Dergisi,* (Ankara, 1956ff.)

TAPA   *American Philological Society, Transactions* (See: *PAPA*)

TAPS   *Transactions of the American Philosophical Society* (Philadelphia, 1789-1804; *N.S.,* 1818ff.)

Tarbiz   *Tarbiz. A quarterly review of the humanities:* תרביץ רעזן למדעי היהדות. שנת (Jerusalem, 1929ff.) [English Summaries from Volume 24 on only]

TB   *Tyndale Bulletin* (London, 1956ff.) [Numbers 1-16 as: *Tyndale House Bulletin*]

TBMDC   *Theological Bulletin: McMaster Divinity College* (Hamilton, Ontario, 1967ff.)

TE   *Theological Education* (Dayton, 1964ff.)

Tem   *Temenos. Studies in Comparative Religion* (Helsinki, 1965ff.)

TEP   *Theologica Evangelica. Journal of the Faculty of Theology, University of South Africa* (Pretoria, 1968ff.)

Text   *Textus. Annual of the Hebrew University Bible Project* (Jerusalem, 1960ff.)

TF   *Theological Forum* (Minneapolis, 1929-1935)

TFUQ   *Thought . A Quarterly of the Sciences and Letters* (New York, 1926ff.) [From Volume 15 on as: *Thought. Fordham University Quarterly*]

ThE   *Theological Eclectic* (Cincinnati; New York, 1864-1871)

Them   *Themelios, International Fellowship of Evangelical Students* (Fresno, CA; 1962ff.)

Theo   *Theology; A Journal of Historic Christianity* (London, 1920ff.)

ThSt   *Theological Studies* (New York; Woodstock, MD; 1940ff.)

TLJ   *Theological and Literary Journal* (New York, 1848-1861)

TM   *Theological Monthly* (St. Louis, 1921-1929)

TML   *The Theological Monthly* (London, 1889-1891)

TPS   *Transactions of the Philological Society* (London, 1842ff.) [Volumes 1-6 as: *Proceedings*]

TQ   *Theological Quarterly* (St. Louis, 1897-1920)

Tr   *Traditio. Studies in Ancient and Medieval History, Thought and Religion* (New York, 1943ff.)

Trad   *Tradition, A Journal of Orthodox Jewish Thought* (New York, 1958ff.)

TRep   *Theological Repository* (London, 1769-1788)

Periodical Abbreviations

TRFCCQ   *Theological Review and Free Church College Quarterly*
          (Edinburgh, 1886-1890)
TRGR   *The Theological Review and General Repository*
          of Religious and Moral Information,
          Published Quarterly (Baltimore, 1822)
TRL   *Theological Review: A Quarterly Journal of Religious*
          Thought and Life (London, 1864-1879)
TT   *Theology Today* (Lansdown, PA; 1944ff.)
TTCA   *Trinity Theological College Annual* (Singapore,
          1964-1969) [Volume 5 apparently never
          published]
TTD   *Teologisk Tidsskrift* (Decorah, IA; 1899-1907)
TTKB   *Türk Tarih Kurumu Belleten* (Ankara, 1937ff.)
TTKF   *Tidskrift för teologi och kyrkiga frågor (The Augustana*
          Theological Quarterly) (Rock Island, IL;
          1899-1917)
TTL   *Theologisch Tijdschrift* (Leiden, 1867-1919)
          [English articles from Volume 45 on only]
TTM   *Teologisk Tidsskrift* (Minneapolis, 1917-1928)
TUSR   *Trinity University Studies in Religion* (San Antonio,
          1950ff.)
TZ   *Theologische Zeitschrift* (Basel, 1945ff.)
TZDES   *Theologische Zeitschrift (Deutsche Evangelische Synode*
          des Westens. North America) (St. Louis,
          1873-1934) [Continued from Volumes 22 through
          26 as: *Magazin für Evangel. Theologie und Kirche;*
          and from Volume 27 on as: *Theological Magazine*]
TZTM   *Theologische Zeitblätter, Theological Magazine*
          (Columbus,1911-1919)

U

UC   *The Unitarian Christian* (Boston, 1947ff.)
          [Volumes 1-4 as: *Our Faith*]
UCPSP   *University of California Publications in Semitic Philology*
          (Berkeley, 1907ff.)
UF   *Ugarit-Forschungen. Internationales Jahrbuch für die*
          Altertumskunde Syrien-Palästinas (Neukirchen,
          West Germany; 1969ff.)

Periodical Abbreviations

ULBIA   *Univeristy of London. Bulletin of the Institute of Archaeology* (London, 1958ff.)

UMB   *The University Museum Bulletin (University of Pennsylvania* (Philadelphia, 1930-1958)

UMMAAP   *University of Michigan. Museum of Anthropology. Anthropological Papers* (Ann Arbor, 1949ff.)

UPQR   *The United Presbyterian Quarterly Review* (Pittsburgh, 1860-1861)

UQGR   *Universalist Quarterly and General Review* (Boston, 1844-1891)

UnionR   *The Union Review* (New York, 1939-1945)

URRM   *The Unitarian Review and Religious Magazine* (Boston, 1873-1891)

USQR   *Union Seminary Quarterly Review* (New York, 1945ff.)

USR   *Union Seminary Review* (Hampton-Sidney, VA; Richmond; 1890-1946) [Volumes 1-23 as: *Union Seminary Magazine*]

UTSB   *United Theological Seminary Bulletin* (Dayton, 1905ff.) [Including: *The Bulletin of the Evangelical School of Theology; Bulletin of the Union Biblical Seminary*, later, *Bonebrake Theological Bulletin*]

UUÅ   *Uppsala Universitets Årsskrift* (Uppsala, 1861-1960)

V

VC   *Virgiliae Christianae: A Review of Early Christian Life and Language* (Amsterdam, 1947ff.)

VDETF   *Deutsche Vierteljahrsschrift für englisch-theologische Forschung und Kritik / herausgegeben von M. Heidenheim* (Leipzig, Zurich, 1861-1865) [Continued as: *Vierteljahrsschrift für deutsch-englisch- theologische Forschung und Kritik...* 1866-1873]

VDI   *Vestnik Drevnei Istorii. Journal of Ancient History* (Moscow, 1946ff.) [English summaries from 1967 on only]

VDR   *Koinonia* (Nashville, 1957-1968) [Continued as: *Vanderbilt Divinity Review*, 1969-1971]

Periodical Abbreviations

VE   *Vox Evangelica. Biblical and Historical Essays by the Members of the Faculty of the London Bible College* (London, 1962ff.)

Voice   *The Voice* (St. Paul, 1958-1960) [Subtitle varies]

VR   *Vox Reformata* (Geelong, Victoria, Australia, 1962ff.)

VT   *Vetus Testamentum* (Leiden, 1951ff.)

VTS   *Vetus Testamentum, Supplements* (Leiden, 1953ff.)

W

Way   *The Way. A Quarterly Review of Christian Spirituality* (London, 1961ff.)

WBHDN *The Wittenberg Bulletin (Hamma Digest Number)* (Springfield, OH; 1903ff.) [Volumes 40-60 (1943-1963) only contain *Hamma Digest Numbers*]

WesTJ *Wesleyan Theological Journal. Bulletin of the Wesleyan Theological Society* (Lakeville, IN; 1966ff.)

WLQ   *Wisconsin Lutheran Quarterly* (Wauwatosa, WI; Milwaukee;1904ff.) [Also entitled: *Theologische Quartalschrift*]

WO   *Die Welt des Orients. Wissenschaftliche Beiträge zur Kunde des Morgenlandes* (Göttingen, 1947ff.)

Word   *Word: Journal of the Linguistic Circle of New York* (New York, 1945ff.)

WR   *The Westminster Review* (London, New York, 1824-1914)

WSQ   *Wartburg Seminary Quarterly* (Dubuque, IA; 1937-1960) [Volumes 1-9, #1 as: *Quarterly of the Wartburg Seminary Association*]

WSR   *Wesleyan Studies in Religion* (Buckhannon,WV; 1960-1970) [Volumes 53-62 only /sic/]

WTJ   *Westminster Theological Journal* (Philadelphia, 1938ff.)

WW   *Western Watch* (Pittsburgh, 1950-1959) [Superseded by: *Pittsburgh Perspective*]

WZKM *Wiener Zeitschrift für die Kunde des Morgenlandes* (Vienna, 1886ff.)

Periodical Abbreviations

Y

YCCAR	*Yearbook of the Central Conference of American Rabbis* (Cincinnati, 1890ff.)
YCS	*Yale Classical Studies* (New Haven, 1928ff.)
YDQ	*Yale Divinity Quarterly* (New Haven, 1904ff.) [Volumes 30-62 as: *Yale Divinity News*, continued as: *Reflections*]
YR	*The Yavneh Review. A Religious Jewish Collegiate Magazine* (New York, 1961ff.) [Volume 2 never published]

Z

Z	*Zygon. Journal of Religion and Science* (Chicago, 1966ff.)
ZA	*Zeitschrift für Assyriologie und verwandte Gebiete* (Leipzig, Strassburg, Berlin, 1886ff.)
ZAS	*Zeitschrift für ägyptische Sprache und Altertumskunde* (Leipzig, Berlin, 1863ff.)
ZAW	*Zeitschrift für die alttestamentliche Wissenschaft* (Giessen, Berlin, 1881ff.)
ZDMG	*Zeitschrift der Deutschen Morgenländischen Gesellschaft* (Leipzig, Wiesbaden, 1847ff.)
ZDPV	*Zeitschrift des Deutschen Palästina-Vereins* (Leipzig, Wiesbaden, 1878ff.) [English articles from Volume 82 on only]
Zion	*Zion. A Quarterly for Research in Jewish History, New Series* ציון סדרה חדשה רבעון לחקר תולדות ישראל (Jerusalem, 1935ff.) [English summaries from Volume 3 on only]
ZK	*Zeitschrift für Keilschriftforschung* (Leipzig, 1884-1885)
ZNW	*Zeitschrift für die neutestamentliche Wissenschaft und die Kunde des Urchristentums (... Kunde der älteren Kirche, 1921—) (Giessen, Berlin, 1900ff.)*
ZS	*Zeitschrift für Semitistik und verwandte Gebiete* (Leipzig, 1922-1935)

§139   *2.4   Ancient Near Eastern History - General Studies*
   [See also: Historiography §54 ←]

Anonymous, "The Ancient World and Its Inhabitants," *BRCM* 4
   (1847-48) 137-138.

G. B., "Remarks on Certain Passages in Ancient Assyrian and Median
   History," *JSL, 3rd Ser.*, 10 (1859-60) 136-154.

G. H. E., "Rawlinson's Herodotus: The Ancient Empires," *UQGR* 18
   (1861) 77-97. *(Review)*

Anonymous, "Rawlinson's Ancient Monarchies of the East," *NBR* 44
   (1866) 331-362. *(Review)*

†Anonymous, "Rawlinson's Ancient Monarchies," *ERCJ* 125 (1867)
   108-154. *(Review)*

†Anonymous, "Rawlinson's Ancient Monarchies of the East,"
   BQRL 49 (1869) 349-391. *(Review)*

G[eorge] Rawlinson, "Early Oriental History," *ContR* 14 (1870)
   80-100.

A. H. Sayce, "The Synchronous History of Assyria and Babylonia,"
   SBAT 2 (1873) 119-145.

H. Rassam, "Biblical Nationalities, Past and Present," *SBAP* 6
   (1883-84) 33.

H. Rassam, "Biblical Nationalities, Past and Present," *SBAT* 8
   (1883-84) 358-385.

J. F. McCurdy, "Contemporaneous History: Josiah to Ezra," *BW* 11
   (1898) 369-381.

Walter M. Patton, "Pre-Semitic Populations in Semitic Lands,"
   MR 86 (1904) 106-110.

Martin L. Rouse, "The Bible Pedigree of the Nations of the World,
   *as attested and expanded by ancient Records and Traditions,
   and by early and long-lasting national Names,*" *JTVI* 38
   (1906) 123-150. (Discussion, pp. 151-153)

*Percy E. Newberry, "To what Race did the Founders of Sais belong?" *SBAP* 28 (1906) 68-75.

M[artin] L. Rouse, "The Pedigree of the Nations. No. II," *JTVI* 39 (1907) 83-101.

*G. Frederick Wright, "Solar Eclipses and Ancient History," *RP* 7 (1908) 275-281.

*A. H. Sayce, "Notes on Assyrian and Egyptian History. An Aramaic Ostracon," *SBAP* 30 (1908) 13-19.

*G. Frederick Wright, "Solar Eclipses and Ancient History," *CFL, 3rd Ser.,* 10 (1909) 101-105.

Owen C. Whitehouse, "The Condition of Egypt and Western Asia 1700-1200 B.C.," *ICMM* 6 (1909-10) 128-138, 316-327, 414-422; 7 (1910-11) 80-87, 205-216.

T. Eric Peet, "Are we justified in speaking of a Megalithic Race?" *AAA* 5 (1912-13) 112-128.

James Henry Breasted, "The Ancient History of the Near East (with remarks on Western Asia, by Daniel David Luckenbill)," *AJSL* 30 (1913-14) 125-137.

Felix v. Luschan, "The Early Inhabitants of Western Asia," *SIR* (1914) 553-577.

*William Mitchell Ramsay, "The Intermixture of Races in Asia Minor: Some of its Causes and Effects," *PBA* 7 (1915-16) 359-422.

*L[uther] T. Townsend, "Cretans and other Prehistoric Peoples: Their Bearing on the Theory of Evolution," *CFL, 3rd Ser.,* 25 (1919) 89-93.

*W. J. Phythian-Adams, "Pre-Philistine Inhabitants of Palestine," *PEFQS* 53 (1921) 170-172.

*H. R. Hall, "The Caucasian Relations of the Peoples of the Sea," *Klio* 22 (1928-29) 335-344.

*S. Yeivin, "A New Egyptian Source for the History of Palestine and Syria," *JPOS* 14 (1934) 194-239.

*G. A. Wainwright, "Some Sea-Peoples and Others in the Hittite Archives," *JEA* 25 (1939) 148-153.

*W[illiam] F[oxwell] Albright, "How well can we know the Ancient Near East?" *JAOS* 56 (1936) 121-144.

*G. R. Gair, "The Races and Peoples of the Early Hebrew World," *JTVI* 68 (1936) 194-209, 212. (Discussion, pp. 209-212)

*Henry L. F. Lutz, "The Eighth Century B.C. and Its Religious Significance," *KZ* 64 (1940) 463-474.

*C. J. Mullo Weir, "Problems of Western Asiatic Pre-History," *GUOST* 13 (1947-48) 44-48. [Pre-Literate Peoples; The Sumerians; The Semites; The Indo-Europeans; (Elamites, Gutians, Kassites, Hurrians, Urartians, and Khatti)]

*Burr C. Brundage, "The Ancient Near East as History," *AmHR* 54 (1948-49) 530-547.

*A[braham] Malamat, "Cushan Rishathaim and the Decline of the Near East Around 1200 B.C.," *JNES* 13 (1954) 231-242.

*D. E. Derry, "The Dynastic Race in Egypt," *JEA* 42 (1956) 80-85.

G. Ernest Wright, "The Problem of the Transition between the Chalcolithic and Bronze Ages," *EI* 5 (1958) 37*-45*.

Christo Danov, "Thracian penetration into the Greek cities on the West coast of the Black Sea," *Klio* 38 (1960) 75-80.

James Mellaart, "Early Cultures of the South Anatolian Plateau," *AS* 11 (1961) 159-184.

James Mellaart, "Early Cultures of the South Anatolian Plateau, II. The Late Chalcolithic and Early Bronze Ages in the Konya Plain," *AS* 13 (1963) 199-236.

*K[enneth] A. Kitchen, "Byblos, Egypt and Mari in the Early Second Millennium B.C.," *Or, N.S.,* 36 (1967) 39-54.

*Michael C. Astour, "The Partition of the Confederacy of Mukiš-Nuḫafšše-Nii by Šuppiluliuma. A Study in Political Geography of the Amarna Age," *Or., N.S.,* 38 (1969) 381-414.

§140 *2.4.1 Biographical Studies of Ancient Near Eastern
Persons (not necessarily mentioned in the
Old Testament) - General Studies*

†Anonymous, "Ancient Egyptian Kings and their Monuments,"
WR 14 (1831) 405-419.

*F. L. Griffith, "Notes on some Royal Names and Families. *Ameni;
Menthuhotep;* The Cartouche of the Ebers Calendar," *SBAP* 14
(1887-88) 39-44.

*E. de Bunsen, "The Pharaohs of Moses according to Hebrew and
Egyptian Chronology," *SBAP* 12 (1889-90) 157-166.

*W. Spiegelberg, "The Viziers of the New Empire," *SBAP* 15
(1892-93) 522-526.

*James Henry Breasted, "Ramses II and the Princes in the Karnak
Reliefs of Seti I," *ZÄS* 37 (1899) 130-139.

Seymour de Ricci, "The Praefects of Egypt," *SBAP* 22 (1900) 347-383.

Seymour de Ricci, "The Praefects of Egypt. II," *SBAP* 24 (1902)
56-67, 97-107.

*F. Legee, "The Kings of Abydos," *SBAP* 26 (1904) 125-144.
[1. Ka; 2. Ro; 3. Zeser; 4. Narmer; 5. Sma; 6. Aha; 7. Zer;
8. Zet; 9. Merneit; 10. Den; 11. Azab; 12. Mersekha; 13. Qa]

H. F. Pelham, "The Early Roman Emperors," *QRL* 202 (1905)
521-545. *(Review)*

J. Hunt Cook, "Some Contemporaries of Moses," *R&E* 2 (1905)
362-370. [Kanro; Ramses; Beka; Ani]

James T. Dennis, "New Officials of the IVth to Vth Dynasties,"
SBAP 27 (1905) 32-34. *[Egyptian]*

*Louis H. Gray, "The Kings of Early Iran according to the Sidrā
Rabbā," *ZA* 19 (1905-06) 272-287.

Joseph Offord, "Aegyptiaca. The Queens of Egypt," *AAOJ* 31 (1909)
91-93. *(Review)*

S. Richard Fuller, "The Value of Historic Personality in Archaeological Interest," *AJA* 18 (1914) 83.

*Anonymous,   "Kings   of   Kish,"   *RP*   13   (1914)   43.

George A. Reisner, "The Viceroys of Ethiopia," *JEA* 6 (1920) 28-55, 73-88.

M. A. Murray, "Maqrizi's Names of the Pharaohs," *AEE* 9 (1924) 51-55.

[W. M.] Flinders Petrie, "The Royal Officials," *AEE* 10 (1925) 11-18.

[W. M.] Flinders Petrie, "The Rulers," *AEE* 10 (1925) 79-88.

*G. A. Frank Knight, "The Identification of the Pharoahs of the Pentateuch," *JTVI* 59 (1927) 96-112, 119-120. [(Discussion, pp. 112-117) (Communications by J. A. Fleming, pp. 117-118; G. B. Michell, pp. 118-119)]

*P[atrick] P. McKenna, "Transjordania and its Rulers after the Birth of Christ," *IER, 5th Ser.*, 41 (1933) 277-288.

Nabia Abbott, "Pre-Islamic Arab Queens," *AJSL* 58 (1941) 1-22.

M. F. Laming Macadam, "A Royal Family of the Thirteenth Dyansty," *JEA* 37 (1951) 20-28.

T. Robert S. Broughton, "Notes on Roman Magistrates," *HJAH* 2 (1953-54) 209-213. [The Augaurates of Two Marci Antonii; Marius and the Mater Magna; C. Cosconius C. f., Proconsul of Macedonia]

*Henry G. Fischer, "Four Provincial Administrators at the Memphite Cemeteries," *JAOS* 74 (1954) 26-34.

*Lionel Pearson, "Real and Conventional Personalities in Greek History," *JHI* 15 (1954) 136-145.

Kathleen M. T. Atkinson, "The Governors of the Province Asia in the Reign of Augustus," *HJAH* 7 (1958) 300-330.

Labbib Habachi, "The First Two Viceroys of Kush and their Family," *Kush* 7 (1959) 45-62.

*Keith C. Seele, "Ramesses VI and the Medinat Habu Procession of the Princes," *JNES* 19 (1960) 184-204.

*W[illaim] F[oxwell] Albright, "The Eighteenth-Century Princes of Byblos and the Chronology of Middle Bronze," *BASOR* #176 (1964) 38-46.

*Alan R. Schulman, "The Berlin 'Trauerrelief' (No. 12411) and Some Officials of Tut'ankhamūn and Ay," *JARCE* 4 (1965) 55-68.

O. W. Reinmuth, "A Working List of the Prefects of Egypt: 30 B.C. - 299 A.D. Their Names, Terms of Office, and References to them which appeared since A. Stein, *Die Praefekten von Aegypten,* 1950," *BASP* 4 (1967) 75-128. [Addenda, *BASP* 5 (1968) pp. 105-106]

§141 *2.4.1.1. Alphabetical Listing of Persons*

A

Aah-hetep

Percy E. Newberry, "The Parentage of Queen Aah-hetep," *SBAP* 24 (1902) 285-289.

Aat-shet

*Percy E. Newberry, "Extracts from my Notebooks V.," *SBAP* 24 (1902) 244-252. [38. Queen Aat-shet, p. 251]

Abba-AN

*Anne Draffkorn, "Was King Abba-AN of Yamḫad a Vizier for the King of Ḫattuša?" *JCS* 13 (1959) 94-97.

Accroupi

*J. R. Harris, "The name of the scribe in the Louvre—a note," *JEA* 41 (1955) 122-123. *[Kai(?); Accroupi(?)]*

Adad-nirair III

*Stephanie Page, "Adad-nirair III and Semiramis: The Stelae of Saba'a and Rimah," *Or, N.S.,* 38 (1969) 457-458.

Adiebis

*J[aroslav] Černý, "Philological and Etymological notes (II)," *ASAE* 42 (1943) 341-350. [5. King 'Adiebis', pp. 348-350]

Aeschylus

*Stuart Piggott, "Iron, Cimmerians and Aeschylus," *Antiq* 38 (1964) 300-303.

Agathobulus

G. M. FitzGerald, "The Rhodian Potter Agathobulus," *JPOS* 8 (1928) 7-11.

Agathocles

*P. Maas, "Oenathe's Husbands," *JEA* 31 (1945) 74. *[Agathocles]*

Ahmes

H. W. Fairman, "A Statue from the Karnack Cache," *JEA* 20 (1934) 1-4. *[Ahmes, son of Smendes]*

Aḥmes-sa-pa-àr

A. Wiedemann, "The King Aḥmes-sa-pa-àr," *SBAP* 8 (1885-86) 220-225. *[Egyptian]*

Ahmose

Anonymous, "A Lost Statue of the Seventeenth Dynasty," *JEA* 10 (1924) 203. *[Ahmose, son of Seḳenenrē' Ta'o II.]*

Ain-Rimmon

*Philip J. Baldensperger, "The Identification of Ain-Rimmon with Ain-Urtas (Artas)," *PEFQS* 44 (1912) 209-211.

Ain-Urtas (Artas)

*Philip J. Baldensberger, "The Idenification of Ain-Rimmon with Ain-Urtas (Artas)," *PEFQS* 44 (1912) 209-211.

Akhamenru

Miriam Lichtheim, "The High Steward Akhamenru," *JNES* 7 (1948) 163-179.

Akhenaton [see also: Amenhotep (Amenophis) IV]

*Alfred C. Bryant and F. W. Read, "Akhuenaten and Queen Tii," *SBAP* 17 (1895) 246-250.

Anonymous, "A Bergsonian Pharaoh," *HR* 69 (1915) 23.

F. Ll. Griffith, "The Jubilee of Akhenaton," *JEA* 5 (1918) 61-63.

*T. Eric Peet, "The Problem of Akhenaton," *JMUEOS* #9 (1921) 39-48.

*Nora Griffith, "Akhenaten and the Hittites," *JEA* 9 (1923) 78-79.

N. de G. Davies, "Akhenaten at Thebes," *JEA* 9 (1923) 132-152.

*R. B. Henderson, "Akhnaton and Moses," *CQR* 97 (1923-24) 109-131.

*D[ouglas] E. Derry, "Notes on the Skeleton hitherto believed to be that of King Akhenaten," *ASAE* 31 (1931) 115-119.

*John Robert Towers, "Was Akhenaten a Monotheist Before His Accession?" *AEE* 16 (1931) 97-100.

*R. Engelbach, "A limestone head of King Akhenaten in the Cairo Museum," *ASAE* 38 (1938) 95-108.

Akhenaten concluded

*P. Ghalioungui, "A medical study of Akhenaten," *ASAE* 47 (1947) 29-46.

S. G. F. Brandon, "Akhenaten: The Heretic King of Egypt," *HT* 12 (1962) 622-631.

Alexander the Great

†Anonymous, "Sir R. Clayton on Alexander the Great," *BDQTR* 3 (1794) 510-517, 620-629. *(Review)*

†Anonymous, "Alexander the Great," *ERCJ* 105 (1857) 305-341. *(Review)*

Justin Perkins, "Notice of a Life of Alexander the Great, translated from the Syriac," *JAOS* 4 (1853-54) 357-440. (With Extracts from the Same, by Theodore D. Woolsey)

Henry Elliott Malden, "Alexander in Afgahanistan," *JP* 12 (1883) 271-277.

*Alfred Emerson, "The Portraiture of Alexander the Great: A Terracotta Head in Munich (I)," *AJA, O.S.,* 2 (1886) 408-413.

*E. A. Wallis Budge, "Alexander the Great and Gog and Magog," *ZA* 6 (1891) 357-358.

*Alfred Emerson, "The Portraiture of Alexander the Great: A Terracotta Head in Munich (II)," *AJA, O.S.,* 3 (1887) 243-260.

*H. B. Swete, "Requests and Replies," *ET* 3 (1891-92) 300. *[Alexander's visit to Jerusalem in Josephus & the Prophecies of Daniel]*

B. Perrrin, "Genesis and Growth of the Alexander-myth," *TAPA* 26 (1895) 56-68.

*A. H. Godbey, "The Influence of Alexander's Conquest upon Jewish Life," *BW* 38 (1911) 171-184.

*Cuthbert Lattey, "Alexander the God," *Exp, 8th Ser.,* 5 (1913) 97-115.

Alexander the Great continued

D. G. Hogarth, "Alexander in Egypt and some Consequences," *JEA* 2 (1915) 53-60.

*Roger S. Loomis, "Treatment in Art of Alexander the Great's Celestial Journey," *AJA* 20 (1916) 80-81.

*Sidney Smith, "The Deaths of Alexander the Great and Philip Arrhidæus," *JRAS* (1928) 618-621.

Andrew Runni Anderson, "Alexander at the Caspian Gates," *TAPA* 59 (1928) 130-163.

*J. G. Milne, "Alexander and Ammon," *AEE* 14 (1929) 74-78.

R. G. Burton, "Alexander the Great and the Indian Frontier," *ERCJ* 250 (1929) 50-64.

C. A. Robinson Jr., "When Did Alexander Reach the Hindu Kush?" *AJP* 51 (1930) 22-31.

C. A. Robinson Jr., "Two Notes on the History of Alexander the Great," *AJP* 53 (1932) 353-359.

*W. W. Tarn, "Alexander the Great and the Unity of Mankind," *PBA* 19 (1933) 123-166.

*M. H. Fisch, "Alexander and the Stoics, Part I," *AJP* 58 (1937) 59-82.

*M. H. Fisch, "Alexander and the Stoics (Cont.)," *AJP* 58 (1937) 129-151.

C. A. Robinson Jr., "Alexander's Plans," *AJP* 61 (1940) 402-412.

Luitpold Wallach, "Alexander the Great and the Indian Gymnosophists in Hebrew Tradition," *PAAJR* 11 (1941) 47-83.

*C. A. Robinson Jr., "Alexander's Deification," *AJP* 64 (1943) 286-301.

*C. A. Robinson Jr., "Alexander the Great and Parmenio," *AJA* 49 (1945) 422-424.

Alexander the Great cont.

Henry M. de Mauriac, "Alexander the Great and the Politics of 'Homonoia'," *JHI* 10 (1949) 104-114.

J. P. V. D. Balsdon, "The 'Divinity' of Alexander," *HJAH* 1 (1950) 363-388.

C. A. Robinson Jr., "Alexander's Brutality," *AJA* 56 (1952) 169-170.

George Cary, "Alexander the Great in Mediaeval Theology," *JWCI* 17 (1954) 98-114.

*Philip Merlan, "Isocrates, Aristotle and Alexander the Great," *HJAH* 3 (1954-55) 60-81.

Lionel Pearson, "The Diary and the Letters of Alexander the Great," *HJAH* 3 (1954-55) 429-455.

C. A. Robinson Jr., "The Extraordinary Ideas of Alexander the Great," *AmHR* 62 (1956-57) 326-344.

K. Czeglédy, "The Syriac Legend Concerning Alexander the Great," *AOASH* 7 (1957) 231-249.

*E. Badian, "Alexander the Great and the Unity of Mankind," *HJAH* 7 (1958) 425-444.

E. Badian, "Alexander the Great and the Creation of an Empire," *HT* 8 (1958) 369-376, 494-502. [I: The Hellenic Crusade; II: The New Empire]

Truesdell S. Brown, "A Megasthenes Fragment on Alexander and Mandanis," *JAOS* 80 (1960) 133-135.

John R. Krueger, "A Note on Alexander's Arabic Epithet," *JAOS* 81 (1961) 426-427.

*Arthur Darby Nock, "Sapor I and the Apollo of Bryaxis," *AJA* 66 (1962) 307-310. *[Alexander]*

*R. D. Milns, "Alexander's Pursuit of Darius Through Iran," *HJAH* 15 (1966) 256.

Alexander the Great concluded

Eugene N. Borza, "Alexander and the Return from Siwah," *HJAH* 16 (1967) 369.

A. S. Shofman, "The Idea of World Domination in Alexander of Macedon's Plans of Conquest," *VDI* (1969) #4, 111-112.

*C. H. R. Martin, "Alexander and the High Priest," *GUOST* 23 (1969-70) 102-114.

Alexander IV

*Nathaniel Reich, "A Notary of Ancient Thebes," *MJ* 14 (1923) 22-25. *[Alexander IV, Son of Alexander the Great]*

*Sidney Smith, "The Chronology of Philip Arrhidaeus, Antigonus and Alexander IV," *RAAO* 22 (1924) 179-197.

Alexander Midas

Ernest A. Fredericksmeyer, "Alexander Midas, and the Oracle at Gordium," *AJA* 64 (1960) 184.

Alumbiumu

W. F. Leemans, "King Alumbiumu," *JCS* 20 (1966) 48-49.

Alyattes

*George Huxley, "A War between Astyages and Alyattes," *GRBS* 6 (1965) 201-206.

Aman-ḥatpe

W[illiam] F[oxwell] Albright, "Aman-ḥatpe, governor of Palestine," *ZÄS* 62 (1927) 63-64.

Amarpal

Daniel   Hy.   Haigh,   "Amarpal,"   *ZÄS*   12   (1874)   53.

Amasis

*Richard A. Parker, "The Length of Reign of Amasis and the Beginning of the Twenty-Sixth Dynasty," *MDIÄA* 15 (1957) 208-212.

Amen Neb-uenenef

*Percy E. Newberry, "Egyptian Historical Notes. III," *SBAP* 36 (1914) 168-174. [15. Cube of Limestone Bearing the Name of the;

 *High   Priest   of   Amen*

Neb-uenenef, p. 169]

Amenemḫab

*Nina M. Davies, "Amenemḫab encountering a Hyena. *From the tomb of Amenemḫab at Thebes* (no. 85)," *JEA* 26 (1940) 82.

Amenemhat-Sebekhetep

*Percy E. Newberry, "Extracts from my Notebooks V.," *SBAP* 24 (1902) 244-252. [34. A New King of the Thirteenth Dynasty, (*Amenemhat-Sebekhetep*), p. 250]

*Percy E. Newberry, "Extracts from my Notebooks VI.," *SBAP* 25 (1903) 130-138. [43. King Amenemhat-Sebekhetep, p. 135]

Amenemhet I

H. F. Lutz, "Was King Amenemhet I Assassinated?" *AJSL* 41 (1924-25) 192-193.

H[ermann] R[anke], "A Contemporary of Queen Hatshepsut," *UMB* 8 (1939-40) #1, 29-30 *[Amenemhet]*

Amenemhet III

*W. M. F[linders] P[etrie], "The Portraits," *AEE* 1 (1914) 48. *[Amenemhet III]*

Amenemhat-senb-ef

Percy E. Newberry, "Note on a new King of the XIIIth Dynasty," *SBAP* 21 (1899) 282-283. *[Amenemhat-senb-ef]*

Amenemapet

*Percy E. Newberry, "Extracts from my Notebooks. VII.," *SBAP* 25 (1903) 357-362. [54. The Princess Amenemapet, pp. 360-361]

Amenemone

*G. A. Gaballa and K. A. Kitchen, "Ramesside Varia I," *CdE* 43 (1968) 259-270. [2. Amenemone, pp. 263-269]

Amenemopě

Hellmut Brunner, "An Honoured Teacher of the Ramesside Period," *JEA* 45 (1959) 3-5. *[Amenemopě]*

Amenhetep

*Percy E. Newberry, "Extracts from my Notebooks. VII.," *SBAP* 25 (1903) 357-362. [50. A Prince Amenhetep of the Seventeenth Dynasty, p. 358]

Amenhetep II

F. Ll Griffith, "The Length of the Reign of Amenhotp */sic/* II," *SBAP* 31 (1909) 42-43.

H. R. Hall, "The Reign of Amenhetep II: A Criticism of a Theory," *SBAP* 34 (1912) 107-108.

H. R. Hall, "A Note on the Reign of Amenhetep II," *SBAP* 34 (1912) 143-144.

Amenhetep II concluded

*Yohanan Aharoni, "Some Geographical Remarks Concerning the Campaigns of Amenhotep II," *JNES* 19 (1960) 177-183.

*Abraham Malamat, "Campaigns of Amenhotep II and Thutmose IV to Canaan," *SH* 8 (1961) 218-231.

Amenhetep III

Percy E. Newberry, "Extracts from my Note-Books. V.," *SBAP* 24 (1902)244-252.[31. The Family of Amenhetep III, pp. 246-248]

Percy E. Newberry, "Note on the Parentage of Amenhetep III," *SBAP* 25 (1903) 294-295.

F. J. Giles, "Amenhotpe/sic/*, Ikhnaton and the succession," *Aeg* 32 (1952) 293-310.

Amenhotep IV

*L. Lund, "The Epoch of Joseph: Amenhotep IV as the Pharaoh of the Famine," *SBAP* 4 (1881-82) 96-102. (Remarks by H. Villiers Stuart, pp. 95-96; by St. Vioncent Beechey, p. 102; by Samuel Birch, p. 102)

Anonymous, "A Heretic Pharaoh," *BH* 4 (1968) 75-76. /*Amenhotep IV*/

J. Murtagh, "The Heretic Pharaoh," *Scrip* 19 (1967) 74-81. /*Amenhotep/Akhenaton*/

Amenemmēs III

*Charles Ricketts, "Head of Amenemmēs III in Obsidian, from the Collection of the Rev. W. MacGregor, Tamworth," *JEA* 4 (1916) 71-73.

*Charles Ricketts, "Head in Serpentine of Amenemmēs III in the possession of Oscar Raphael, Esq.," *JEA* 4 (1916) 211-212.

*P[ercy] E. Newberry, "Co-regencies of Ammenemes III, IV, and Sebknofru," *JEA* 29 (1943) 74-75.

Amenophis

⁺R. W. Dawson, "Amenophis the son of Hapu," *Aeg* 7 (1926) 113-138.

J. A. Paine, "A Criticism of Professor Maspero's identification of Amenophis I. among the royal mummies of Daïr el-Baharî," *JAOS* 14 (1890) cxcii-cxciii.

Amenophis II

Cyril Aldred, "The Second Jubilee of Amenophis II," *ZÄS* 94 (1967) 1-6.

⁺Donald B. Redford, "The Coregency of Tuthmosis III and Amenophis II," *JEA* 51 (1965) 107-122.

Amenophis III

⁺S. R. K. Glanville, "Some Notes on Material for the Reign of Amenophis III," *JEA* 15 (1929) 2-8.

Ammenemes I

⁺Battiscombe Gunn, "Notes on Ammenemes I," *JEA* 27 (1941) 2-6.

Ammenemes IV

⁺P[ercy] E. Newberry, "Co-regencies of Ammenemes III, IV, and Sebknofru," *JEA* 29 (1943) 74-75.

Amraphel

⁺W[illiam] F[oxwell] Albright, "Shinar-Šangār and Its Monarch Amraphel," *AJSL* 40 (1923-24) 125-133.

⁺Hugo Radau, "Hammurabi and Amraphel," *OC* 17 (1903) 705-707.

Amraphel concluded

*W. T. Pilter, "Eastern and Western Semitic Personal Names. The Equivalence of Hammurapi and Amrāphel," *SBAP* 35 (1913) 171-186. (Supplementary Note, pp. 244-245)

*Charles Marston, "Correspondence," *PEFQS* 68 (1936) 230. *[Amraphel]*

Amūn

*Cyril Aldred, "The Carnarvon, Statuette of Amūn," *JEA* 42 (1956) 3-7.

Amunezeh

*Percy E. Newberry, "Egyptian Historical Notes. I," *SBAP* 35 (1913) 156-158. [1. The Royal Herald Amunezeh, p. 156]

Amūn-mes

*A. Hamada, "Statue of the Fan-bearer ꜗꜳ," *ASAE* 47 (1947) 15-21. *[Amūn-mes]*

'Ankhkheprurē'

Percy E. Newberry, "Akhenaten's Eldest Son-in-law 'Ankhkheprurē'," *JEA* 14 (1928) 3-9.

'Ankhu

*J. V. Beckerath, "Notes on the Viziers 'Ankhu and 'Iymeru in the Thirteenth Egyptian Dynasty," *JNES* 17 (1958) 263-268.

Anmanila

*Theophilus G. Pinches, "A New Babylonian King of the Period of the First Dynasty of Babylon; with Incidental References to Immerum and Anmanila," *SBAP* 21 (1899) 158-163.

Antef

'Alan H. Gardiner, "The Name of King Sankhere," *SBAP* 26 (1904) 75-76. *[Antef]*

*Alan H. Gardiner, "The Tomb of a much-travelled Theban Official," *JEA* 4 (1916) 28-38. *[Antef]*

Antef Nub-kheper-RA

M. A. Murray, "A Pharaoh of the Old Kingdom," *AEE* 15 (1930) 8-10. *[Antef Nub-kheper-RA]*

Antiochus Epiphanes

*Shailer Mathews, "Antiochus Epiphanes and the Jewish State," *BW* 14 (1899) 13-26.

*Edward M. Merrins, "The Deaths of Antiochus IV., Herod the Great, and Herod Agrippa I," *BS* 61 (1904) 548-562.

Thomas Hodgkin, "Antiochus Epiphanes and the Maccabees. A Study in Two Parts. Part I—Antiochus Epiphanes," *ICMM* 3 (1906-07) 273-284.

Barry Phillips, "Antiochus IV. Epiphanes," *JBL* 29 (1910) 126-138.

Wallace N. Stearns, "The Land of Judah and Antiochus Epiphanes," *IJA* #50 (1917) 42-48.

R. B. Townshend, "Antiochus Epiphanes, the Brilliant Madman," *HJ* 11 (1912-13) 819-829.

E. Badian, "Antiochus Epiphanes and the Rebirth of Judaea," *HT* 9 (1959) 415-423.

*T. C. Skeat, "Notes on Ptolemaic Chronology," *JEA* 47 (1961) 107-109. [II. 'The Twelfth Year which is also the First': The Invasion of Egypt by Antiochus Epiphanes']

*Yitzhak Baer, "The Persecution of Monotheistic Religion by Antiochus Epiphanes," *Zion* 33 (1968) #3/4 I-II.

Antigonus

*Sidney Smith, "The Chronology of Philip Arrhidaeus, Antigonus and Alexander IV," *RAAO* 22 (1924) 179-197.

Mark Antony (Marcus Antonius)

Otto J. Brendel, "The Iconography of Marc Antony," *AJA* 65 (1961) 186-187.

Anukis

*L[ibib] Habachi, "Was Anukis considered as the wife of Khnum or as his daughter?" *ASAE* 50 (1950) 501-507.

Apries

F. W. Read, "Was Apries of Royal Blood?" *AEE* 8 (1923) 57-59.

Arad

*Menahem Naor, "The Problem of Biblical Arad," *PAAJR* 36 (1968) 95-105.

Arad-Sin

W. T. Pilter, "The Reign of "Arad-Sin,' King of Larsa," *SBAP* 33 (1911) 204-212.

Arioch

*Edgar J. Banks, "Who was the Biblical Arioch of the Days of Abraham?" *OC* 28 (1914) 557-559.

*E. H., "Arioch and Belshazzar," *JSL, 3rd Ser.*, 14 (1861-62) 398-420.

*(   ) G., "Arioch and Belshazzar," *JSL, 4th Ser.*, 1 (1862) 452-453.

Aristophanes

†Anonymous, "Aristophanes," *QRL* 158 (1884) 334-373. *(Review)*

Aristotle

Anonymous, "Characteristics of Aristotle," *WR* 116 (1881) 1-41. *(Review)*

*†Anonymous, "Aristotle and the Athenian Constitution," *ERCJ* 173 (1891) 470-494. *(Review)*

*Philip Merlan, "Isocrates, Aristotle and Alexander the Great," *HJAH* 3 (1954-55) 60-81.

Philip Arrhidaeus

*Sidney Smith, "The Chronology of Philip Arrhidaeus, Antigonus and Alexander IV," *RAAO* 22 (1924) 179-197.

*Sidney Smith, "The Deaths of Alexander the Great and Philip Arrhidæus," *JRAS* (1928) 618-621.

Artas

*Philip J. Baldensperger, "The Identification of Ain-Rimmon with Ain-Urtas (Artas)," *PEFQS* 44 (1912) 209-211.

Artaxerxes

*G. B., "Ahasuerus and Artaxerxes," *JSL, 3rd Ser.,* 6 (1857-58) 171.

G. B., "Dr. Carl Auberlen and Artaxerxes Longimanus," *JSL, 3rd Ser.,* 6 (1857-58) 418-425.

*J. W. Bosanquet, "Chronological Remarks on the History of Esther and Ahasuerus, or 'Atossa and Tanu-Axares," *SBAT* 5 (1876-77) 225-292.

Artaxerxes concluded

*Malcolm MacLaren Jr., "Xenophon and Themistogenes," *TAPA* 65 (1934) 240-247. *[Artaxerxes]*

*Arno Poebel, "The King of the Persepolis Tablets: The Nineteenth Year of Artaxerxes I," *AJSL* 56 (1939) 301-304.

Julia Neuffer, "The accession of Artaxerxes I," *AUSS* 6 (1968) 60-87.

Artayctes

Ye. A. Monchadskaya, "Artayctes the 'Chorasmian' (From the history of the Greco-Persian Wars, 480-478 B.C.)," *VDI* (1968) #2, 106.

Artystone

George G. Cameron, "Darius' Daughter and Persepolis Inscriptions," *JNES* 1 (1942) 214-218. *[Artystone]*

Ases-Kaf

*C. W. Goodwin, "King Semempses and King Ases-Kaf," *ZÄS* 5 (1867) 82-85.

Asher-nasir-pal

A. T. Olmstead, "The Calculated Frightfulness of Asher Nasir Apal," *JAOS* 38 (1918) 209-263.

Ashmodai

*Alexander Haggerty Krappe, "Solomon and Ashmodai," *AJP* 54 (1933) 260-268.

Ashurbanipal

*†D[aniel] H[y.] Haigh, "To the Editor," *ZÄS* 6 (1868) 80-83. *[Ashurbanipul, pp. 80-81]*

Ashurbanipal concluded

*George Smith, "Egyptian campaigns of Esarhaddan and Assur-bani-pul," *ZÄS* 6 (1868) 93-99, 113-122.

Dean A. Walker, "The Assyrian King Ašhurbanipal," *ONTS* 8 (1888-89) 57-62, 96-101.

*C. H. W. Johns, "The Chronology of Asurbanipal's reign. I," *SBAP* 24 (1902) 235-241.

*C. H. W. Johns, "The Chronology of Asurbanipal's Reign B.C. 668-626. II," *SBAP* 25 (1903) 82-89.

*C. H. W. Johns, "The Chronology of Asurbanipal's Reign B.C. 668-626. III," *SBAP* 27 (1905) 92-100.

*C. H. W. Johns, "The Chronology of Asurbanipal's Reign B.C. 668-626. IV. The 'Forecast' Tablets," *SBAP* 27 (1905) 288-296.

*C. H. W. Johns, "The Chronology of Asurbanipal's Reign B.C. 668-626. V," *SBAP* 29 (1907) 74-84.

*C. H. W. Johns, "The Chronology of Asurbanipal's Reign. VI," *SBAP* 36 (1914) 181-187.

John A. Maynard, "Recent Historical Material on Ashurbanipal," *JSOR* 6 (1922) 99-105.

John A. Maynard, "New Historical Material on Ashurbanipal," *JSOR* 7 (1923) 21-26.

*Sidney Smith, "Dating by Ashurbanipal and Kandalanu," *JRAS* (1928) 622-626.

*S. Ahmed, "Ashurbanipal and Shamash-shum-ukin During Esarhaddon's Reign," *Abr-N* 6 (1965-66) 53-62.

Assis (?)

Arthur E. P. Weigall, "Upper-Egyptian Notes," *ASAE* 9 (1908) 105-112. [12. The Name of an unknown King, p. 110] *[Assis(?)]*

Astyages

*Anonymous, "The Possible Identification of the Ahasuerus of Esther with Astyages," *RP* 8 (1909) 170.

*George Huxley, "A War between Astyages and Alyattes," *GRBS* 6 (1965) 201-206.

*Robert Drews, "The Fall of Astyages and Herodutus' Chronology of the Eastern Kingdoms," *HJAH* 18 (1969) 1-11.

Atanah-Samas

Kurt Jartitz, "The Kassite King Atanah-Samas," *JSS* 2 (1957) 321-326.

Ateas

D. P. Kallistov, "Strabo on the Scythian King Ateas," *VDI* (1969) #1, 130.

Augustus

*Lily Ross Taylor, "The Worship of Augustus in Italy during His Lifetime," *TAPA* 51 (1920) 116-133.

Ronald Syme, "The Spanish War of Augustus (26-25 B.C.)," *AJP* 55 (1934) 293-317.

*Meriwether Stuart, "A Faience Head of Augustus," *AJA* 48 (1944) 171-175.

*Colin N. Edmonson, "Augustus, Actium and Nicopolis," *AJA* 73 (1969) 235.

*Harold Ingholt, "On the Prima Porta Statue of Augustus," *AJA* 73 (1969) 237-238.

Authŷ

*Percy E. Newberry, "Miscellanea," *JEA* 14 (1928) 109-111. [III. A new Vizier of the Nineteenth Dynasty, p. 110] *[Authŷ]*

Ay

Percy E. Newberry, "King Ay, the successor of Tut'ankhamūn," *JEA* 18 (1932) 50-52.

*Keith C. Seele, "King Ay and the Close of the Amarna Age," *JNES* 14 (1955) 168-179.

B

Bagoas

C. C. Torrey, "The Two Persian Officers Named Bagoas," *AJSL* 56 (1939) 300-301.

Bahman

*Anonymous, "The History of the Reign of Bahman, and of the Second Desolation of Jerusalem; by Persian and Oriental Writers," *MMBR* 28 (1809-10) 449-450. *[Grandson of (Gushtasp) Darius Hystapes]*

Bakennifi

*Libib Habachi, "A Statue of Bakennifi, Nomarch of Athribis during the Invasion of Egypt by Assurbanipul," *MDIÄA* 15 (1957) 68-77.

Bay

Jaroslav Černý, "A Note on the Chancellor Bay," *ZÄS* 93 (1966) 35-39.

Bebi

*Percy E. Newberry, "Miscellanea," *JEA* 14 (1928) 109-111. [II. A new Vizier of the Eleventh Dynasty, p. 109] *[Bebi]*

Bēl-Kabi

*Stephen Langdon, "The Derivation of *šabattu* and other notes,"
ZDMG 62 (1908) 29-32. [*Bēl-Kabi* contemporary of *Sinmubaliṭ*,
pp. 30-31]

Belshazzar

*G. B., "Belshazzar and Cyrus the Persian," *JSL*, *3rd Ser.*, 1 (1855)
157-184.

*E. H., "Arioch and Belshazzar," *JSL*, *3rd Ser.*, 14 (1861-62)
398-420.

*(   ) G., "Arioch and Belshazzar," *JSL*, *4th Ser.*, 1 (1862) 452-453.

G. H. Rouse, "Belshazzar," *ET* 5 (1893-94) 41.

Owen C. Whitehouse, "Belshazzar," *ET* 5 (1893-94) 69.

William Hayes Ward, "Light on Scriptural Texts from Recent
Discoveries. XII. Belshazzar," *HR* 27 (1894) 27-29.

John D. Davis, "Belshazzar's Ancestry," *CFL, O.S.,* 3 (1899)
270-273.

John D. Davis, "Belshazzar in Public Life," *CFL, O.S.,* 3 (1899)
309-314.

*John D. Davis, "Belshazzar and the Fall of Babylon," *CFL, O.S.,* 3
(1899) 349-352.

*Theophilus Pinches, "Babylonian Inscriptions referring to
Belshazzar," *GUOST* 2 (1901-07) 14-15.

*Robert Dick Wilson, "Belshazzar and Darius the Mede,"
CFL, 3rd Ser., 6 (1906) 83-93.

A. T. Clay, "Current Notes and News. The Rehabilitation of
Belshazzar," *A&A* 3 (1916) 180.

*Joseph Offord, "Archaeological Notes. X. *Notes*," *PEFQS* 48 (1916)
94-97. [*Belshazzar*]

Belshazzar concluded

*Joseph Offord, "Archaeological Notes on Jewish Antiquities. XIX. *Belshazzar and Gobryas the Median,*" *PEFQS* 48 (1916) 147-148.

*H. H. Rowley, "The Beshazzar of Daniel and of History," *Exp, 9th Ser.,* 2 (1924) 182-195, 255-272.

*P. E Kretzmann, "Nabonidus—Belshazzar," *CTM* 3 (1932) 215.

*Michael J. Gruenthaner, "The Last King of Babylon," *CBQ* 11 (1949) 406-427. *[Belshazzar]*

G. G. Garner, "*Writing and the Bible:* Belshazzar the King," *AT* 2 (1957-58) #3, 8-10.

Bener-mert

*Percy E. Newberry, "Egyptian Historical Notes. III," *SBAP* 36 (1914) 168-174. [16. A Paint-Grinder of the;

 *Superintendent of all the Works of the King Bener-mert,* p.169]

Ben-Hadad

*Theo. G. Pinches, "The name Ben-Hadad," *SBAP* 5 (1882-83) 71-74. (Remarks by George Bertin, pp. 75-76)

*J. F McCurdy, "Light on Scriptural Texts from Recent Discoveries. Bible Personages. II. Benhadad and Hazael," *HR* 36 (1898) 23-26.

*Anonymous, "Inscription Referring to Ben-Hadad," *RP* 7 (1908) 211.

*D. D. Luckenbill, "Benhadad and Hadadezer," *AJSL* 27 (1910-11) 267-284.

Ben-Hadad concluded

*Stephen Langdon, "Pir-idri (Ben-Hadad) King of Syria," *ET* 23 (1911-12) 68-69.

*Anonymous, "Benhadad," *ET* 29 (1917-18) 156-160.

*John D. Davis, "Hadadezer or Ben-Hadad," *PTR* 17 (1919) 173-183.

Bu-du-ilu

Morris Jastrow Jr., "Note on the proper name Bu-du-ilu," *JAOS* 13 (1889) cxlvi-cxlvii. *[Ammonite King]*

C

Cadmus

*John Day, "The Letters of Cadmus," *AJA* 42 (1938) 125.

"Cæsar"

†Anonymous, "The History of Julius Cæsar," *BQRL* 41 (1865) 495-538. *(Review)*

†Anonymous, "Froude's Cæsar," *ERCJ* 150 (1879) 498-523. *(Review)*

†Anonymous, "The Tragedy of the Cæsars," *ERCJ* 178 (1893) 55-82. *(Review)*

R. S. Conway, "Julius Cæsar: Man or Superman?" *QRL* 261 (1933) 21-38. *(Review)*

*E. T. Salmon, "Catiline, Crassus, and Caesar," *AJP* 56 (1935) 302-316.

*John H. Collins, "Caesar and the Corruption of Power," *HJAH* 4 (1955) 445-465.

"Cæsar" concluded

Peter Green, "Imperial Caesar," *HT* 10 (1960) 678-685.

S. Usher, "Julius Caesar and his Commentaries," *HT* 15 (1965) 651-658.

Cambyses

*Waldo H. Dubberstein, "The Chronology of Cyrus and Cambyses," *AJSL* 55 (1938) 417-419.

*K. M. T. Atkinson, "The Legitimacy of Cambyses and Darius as Kings of Egypt," *JAOS* 76 (1956) 167-177.

Jes P. Asmussen, "Iranica. A) *The Death of Cambyses*," *AO* 31 (1968) 9-14.

Catiline

*†Anonymous, "Objects of the Catilinarian Conspiracy," *WR* 21 (1834) 89-102. *[Catiline]*

*E. T. Salmon, "Catiline, Crassus, and Caesar," *AJP* 56 (1935) 302-316.

Chabrias

*J. K. Anderson, "The Statue of Chabrias," *AJA* 67 (1963) 411-413.

Chedorlaomer

J. A. Selbie, "Chedorlaomer," *ET* 8 (1896-97) 272.

Joseph Offord, "Chedorlaomer," *SBAP* 21 (1899) 256.

*C[laude] R. Conder, "The Alleged Mention of Chedarlaomer on a Babylonian Tablet," *PEFQS* 36 (1904) 80-83.

Cheops

Anonymous, "Africa:—Egypt," *RP* 2 (1903) 286. *[Portrait of Cheops]*

Chosroes II

Selah Merrill, "Notes by Dr. Selah Merrill. Was Chosroes II ever in Palestine?" *PEFQS* 23 (1891) 76.

Chu-en-iten

*A. Wiedemann, "On a Monument of the Time of King Chu-en-iten," *SBAP* 7 (1884-85) 200-203.

Cicero

*J. Wells, "Cicero and the Conquest of Gaul," *QRL* 230 (1918) 361-379. *(Review)*

E. Badian, "Cicero: Words and Illustrations," *HT* 9 (1959) 13-21.

Cleopatra

H. A. Dick, "Cleopatra. A Biographical Sketch," *DUM* 79 (1872) 229-240, 317-330.

Edwin W. Bowen, "Cleopatra, the Ill-Starred Queen of Egypt," *RChR, 4th Ser.*, 20 (1916) 64-82.

Cleopatra VI

J. P. Mahaffy, "Cleopatra VI," *JEA* 2 (1915) 1-4.

Cleopatra VII

J. Gwyn Griffiths, "The Death of Cleopatra VII," *JEA* 47 (1961) 113-118.

Cleopatra VII concluded

*T. C. Skeat, "Notes on Ptolemaic Chronology," *JEA* 48 (1962) 100-105. [III. 'The First Year which is also the third' A date in the reign of Cleopatra VII]

B. Baldwin, "The Death of Cleopatra VII," *JEA* 50 (1964) 181-182.

J. Gwyn Griffiths, "The death of Cleopatra VII: a rejoinder and a postscript," *JEA* 51 (1965) 209-211.

Comanus

C. B. Welles, "The Problem of Comanus," *BSAP* 2 (1964-65) 93-104.

Crassus

*E. T. Salmon, "Catiline, Crassus, and Caesar," *AJP* 56 (1935) 302-316.

Croesus

Molly Miller, "The Herodotean Croesus," *Klio* 41 (1963) 58-94.

Cushan-Rishathaim

*J. W. Jack, "Cushan-Rishathaim (רִשְׁעָתַיִם   כּוּשַׁן)," *ET* 35 (1923-24) 426-428.

Eugen Taeubler, "Cushan-Rishathaim," *HUCA* 20 (1947) 137-142.

*A[braham] Malamat, "Cushan-Rishathaim and the Decline of the Near East Around 1200 B.C.," *JNES* 13 (1954) 231-242.

Cyrus

†M. M., "Death of Cyrus," *MMBR* 43 (1817) 311-312.

Cyrus cont.

†Richard Faber, "Mr. Faber on the Death of Cyrus," *MMBR* 43 (1817) 499-503; 44 (1817-18) 27-29, 121-124; 45 (1818) 206-208.

M. M., "Death of Cyrus," *MMBR* 45 (1818) 396.

*H. M. G., "On the Identity of Cyrus and the Times of Daniel," *JSL, 2nd Ser.,* 6 (1854) 435-465; 7 (1854-55) 364-381.

*G. B., "Belshazzar and Cyrus the Persian," *JSL, 3rd Ser.,* 1 (1855) 157-184.

*G. B., "Xenophon as an Historian, and as a Writer of the Anabasis," *JSL, 3rd Ser.,* 5 (1857) 438-439. *[Cyrus]*

*J. W. Bosanquet, "Darius and Cyrus the Great," *JSL, 3rd Ser.,* 6 (1857-58) 163-167.

*G. B., "Xenophon and Cyrus the Great," *JSL, 3rd Ser.,* 6 (1857-58) 170-171.

G. B., "Cyrus the Great," *JSL, 3rd Ser.,* 8 (1858-59) 184-186.

*Anonymous, "Sacred Chronology," *JSL, 3rd Ser.,* 11 (1860) 459-460. *[Cyrus]*

*J. W. Bosanquet, "Cyrus the Second. *Concerning Cyrus, son of Cambyses king of Persia and of Mandane daughter of Astyages, who overthrew Babylon and released the Jews: as distinguished from Cyrus father of Cambyses, who conquered Astyages, and founded the Empire of the Medes and Persians,"* *SBAT* 1 (1872) 183-262.

*Theophilus G. Pinches, "On an Cuneiform Tablet relating to the Capture of Babylon by Cyrus and the Events which preceded and led to it," *SBAP* 2 (1879-80) 39-42.

†F[rancis] Brown, "Cyrus the Great, in the Bible and in the cuneiform inscriptions," *SBLP* (June, 1880) 16.

*T[errien] de Lacouperie, "Did Cyrus Introduce Writing into India?" *BOR* 1 (1886-87) 58-64.

Cyrus cont.

*Owen C. Whitehouse, "Cyrus and the Capture of Babylon," *ET* 4 (1892-83) 396-402.

*J. A. Selbie, "Cyrus and Deutero-Isaiah," *ET* 9 (1897-98) 407-408.

*J. A. Selbie, "The Date of the Capture of Babylon by Cyrus, etc.," *ET* 10 (1898-99) 119-120.

J. F. McCurdy, "Light on Scriptural Texts from Recent Discoveries. Bible Personages — Cyrus," *HR* 37 (1899) 23-26.

*Martin Sprengling, "Chronological Notes from the Aramaic Papryi. The Jewish Calendar. Dates of the Achaemenians (Cyrus-Darius II)," *AJSL* 27 (1910-11) 233-266.

*Theophilus G. Pinches, "The Latest Discoveries in Babylonia," *JTVI* 46 (1914) 167-192, 196. {(Discussion, pp. 192-196.) [The Capture of Babylon by Cyrus, 539 B.C., pp. 186-190]}

Percy Sykes, "Cyrus the Great," *ContR* 130 (1926) 447-452.

*R[obert] D[ick] Wilson, "Foreign Words in the Old Testament as an Evidence of Historicity," *PTR* 26 (1928) 177-247. [Excursus on the Name "Cyrus", pp. 246-247]

†F[rancis] Brown, "Cyrus the Great, in the Bible and in the cuneiform inscriptions," *JBL* 49 (1930) xxxvii-xxxviii. *[Reprint of the Proceedings of the first meeting of SBL (may be bound separately)]*

A. William Ahl, "'Cyrus,' in the Light of Recent Research," *PAPA* 63 (1932) xli-xlii.

*Malcolm MacLaren Jr., "Xenophon and Themistogenes," *TAPA* 65 (1934) 240-247. *[Cyrus]*

*Carroll E. Simcox, "The *Rôle* of Cyrus in Deutero-Isaiah," *JAOS* 57 (1937) 158-171.

*Waldo H. Dubberstein, "The Chronology of Cyrus and Cambyses," *AJSL* 55 (1938) 417-419.

Cyrus concluded

Joseph E. Fontenrose, "Cyrus the Great and the Cyrus-Legend,"
PAPA 71 (1940) xxxiv-xxxv.

Cyrus II

*J. W. Bosanquet, "Cyrus the Second. *Concerning Cyrus, son of
Cambyses king of Persia and of Mandane daughter of
Astyages, who overthrew Babylon and released the Jews:
as distinguished from Cyrus father of Cambyses, who
conquered Astyages, and founded the Empire of the
Medes and Persians,*" *SBAT* 1 (1872) 183-262.

D

Daddu

*Anonymous, "The Statue of King Daddu, the Oldest in the World,"
MQR, 3rd Ser., 31 (1905) 387-389.

*George A. Barton, "The names of two Kings of Adab," *JAOS* 33
(1913) 295-296. *[Daddu]*

Daduša

*Hildegard Lewy, "The Synchronism Assyria—Ešnunna—Babylon,"
WO 2 (1954-59) 438-453. [1. Šamši-Adad and Daduša,
pp. 438-445]

Danel

*George A. Barton, "Danel, a Pre-Israelite Hero of Galilee," *JBL* 60
(1941) 213-225.

W[illiam] F[oxwell] Albright, "The Traditional Home of the Syrian
Daniel," *BASOR* #130 (1953) 26-27. *[Dan'el]*

Darius

*Anonymous, "Who was Darius the Median in the Book of Daniel?"
BRCM 1 (1846) 25-38.

B[ourchier] W[rey] Savile, "Darius the Mede and Darius Hystapes,"
JSL, 3rd Ser., 5 (1857) 163-170.

G. B., "Darius the Mede," *JSL, 3rd Ser.,* 5 (1857) 431-434.

*G. B., "Xenophon as an Historian, and as a Writer of the Anabasis,"
JSL, 3rd Ser., 5 (1857) 438-439. *[Darius]*

*J. W. Bosanquet, "Darius and Cyrus the Great," *JSL, 3rd Ser.,* 6
(1857-58) 163-167.

Bourchier Wrey Savile, "The Darius of Scripture," *JSL, 3rd Ser.,* 6
(1857-58) 408-418.

I. */sic/* W. Bosanquet, "The Darius of Scripture," *JSL, 3rd Ser.,* 7
(1858) 183-189.

B[ourchier] W[rey] Savile, "Darius the Mede," *JSL, 3rd Ser.,* 7 (1858)
458-460.

G. B., "The Darius of Scripture," *JSL, 3rd Ser.,* 7 (1858) 449-458.

*J. W. Bosanquet, "Chronology of the Medes, from the Reign of
Dieoces to the Reign of Darius, the Son of Hystaspes, or Darius
the Mede," *JRAS* (1860) 39-69.

G. B., "The Two Dariuses (?)," *JSL, 5th Ser.,* 2 (1867-68) 192-200.

*Buchanan Blake, "Darius the Mede, and the Seventy Weeks of
Daniel," *ET* 5 (1893-94) 479.

Andrew Gray, "Darius the Mede," *ET* 5 (1893-94) 563-564.

J. E. H. Thomson, "Who was Darius the Mede?" *ET* 7 (1895-96) 235.

Parke P. Flournoy, "Who was 'Darius the Median?'—New Light from
Babylonian Tablets," *PQ* 14 (1900) 602-612.

Darius cont.

John Urquhart, "'Darius the Median'," *CFL, 3rd Ser.,* 3 (1905) 219-223.

*Robert Dick Wilson, "Belshazzar and Darius the Mede," *CFL, 3rd Ser.,* 6 (1906) 83-93.

W. S. Auchincloss, "Darius the Median," *BS* 66 (1909) 536-538.

Edward J. Kassane, "Darius the Mede," *ITQ* 14 (1919) 43-57.

*Andrew Craig Robinson, "Darius the Median and the Cyropaedia of Xenophon in the Light of the Cuneiform Inscriptions," *JTVI* 54 (1922) 1-30.

*Robert Dick Wilson, "Darius the Mede," *PTR* 20 (1922) 177-211.

*Leon Legrain, "Darius and Pseudo Smerdis. A Green Jade Relief. CBS. 14543," *MJ* 14 (1923) 200-203.

*A.T. Olmstead, "Darius as Lawgiver," *AJSL* 51 (1934-35) 247-249.

*Arno Poebel, "Chronology of Darius' First Year of Reign," *AJSL* 55 (1938) 142-165, 285-314.

*A.T. Olmstead, "Darius and His Behistun Inscription," *AJSL* 55 (1938) 392-416.

*George G. Cameron, "Darius and Xerxes in Babylonia," *AJSL* 58 (1941) 314-325.

Richard A. Parker, "Darius and His Egyptian Campaign," *AJSL* 58 (1941) 373-377.

Richard T. Hallock, "Darius I, the King of the Persepolis Tablets," *JNES* 1 (1942) 230-232.

Herbert Owen, "The Enigma of Darius the Mede: A Way to Its Final Solution," *JTVI* 74 (1942) 72-87, 94-98. [(Written Discussions, by Frederic Kenyon, pp. 87-88; by W. E. Leslie, pp. 88-89; by E. B. W. Chappelow, pp. 89-91; by H. S. Curr, pp. 91-92; by C. C. O. van Lennep, pp. 92-93; by H. B Clarke, p. 93; by J. Barcroft Anderson, p. 98) (Correction, *JTVI* 75 (1943) p. vi)]

Darius concluded

W. Arndt, "An Attack on the Reliability of the Scriptures," *CTM* 14 (1943) 58-59. *[Darius the Mede]*

*K. M. T. Atkinson, "The Legitimacy of Cambyses and Darius as Kings of Egypt," *JAOS* 76 (1956) 167-177.

*Richard T. Hallock, "The 'One Year' of Darius I," *JNES* 19 (1960) 36-39.

*Patrick T. Brannan, "Herodotus and History: The Constitutional Debate Preceding Darius' Accession," *Tr* 19 (1963) 427-438.

*R. D. Milns, "Alexander's Pursuit of Darius through Iran," *HJAH* 15 (1966) 256.

Darius II

*Martin Sprengling, "Chronological Notes from the Aramaic Papyri. The Jewish Calendar. Dates of the Achaemanians (Cyrus-Darius II)," *AJSL* 27 (1910-11) 233-266.

Decebalus

Robert Gordon Latham, "On the Name and Nation of the Dacian King Decebalus, with Notices of the Agathyrsi and Alani," *TPS* (1854) 109-113.

Demd-âb-taui Uatijkara

H. R. Hall, "King Demd-âb-taui Uatijkara," *SBAP* 34 (1912) 290-292.

Demetrius I

W. Rees, "Demetrius I, King of Syria, 162-150 B.C.," *Scrip* 4 (1949-51) 107-114.

Dhutihetep

*Percy E. Newberry, "Miscellanea," *JEA* 14 (1928) 109-111. [VII. The High Priest Dhutihetep, p. 111]

Dido

R. S. Conway, "The Place of Dido in History," *QRL* 234 (1920) 73-88.

Dieoces

*J. W. Bosanquet, "Chronology of the Medes, from the Reign of Dieoces to the Reign of Darius, the Son of Hystaspes, or Darius the Mede," *JRAS* (1860) 39-69.

Diogenes

Charles Seltman, "Diogenes: The Original Cynic," *HT* 6 (1956) 110-115.

Dja'u

Alan H. Gardiner, "Was the Vizier Dja'u one of the six like-named brothers?" *ZÄS* 79 (1954) 95-96.

Dudu

Naji al-Asil, "Dudu, the Sumerian Scribe," *Sumer* 5 (1949) 131-132.

Fuad Safar, "The Identification of Dudu," *Sumer* 5 (1949) 133-135.

E

Enentarzi

*Ferris J. Stephens, "Notes on some Economic Texts of the Time of Urukagina," *RAAO* 49 (1955) 129-136. [1. Who was Urukagina's Predecessor? pp. 129-131] *[Enetarzi?]*

Entemena

*S[tephen] Langdon, "Assyriological Note," *JRAS* (1931) 421-424. *[Lugal-ki-GUB-ni-dú-dú Contemporary of Entemena?]*

Epaninondas

*James Wiseman, "Epaninondas and the Theban Invasions," *Klio* 51 (1969) 177-199.

Epicurus

Charles Seltman, "The Garden of Epicurus," *HT* 6 (1956) 181-187.

Ergamenes

Bryan G. Haycock, "Towards a Date for King Ergamenes," *Kush* 13 (1965) 264-266.

Esarhaddon

†*D[aniel] H[y.] Haigh, "To the editor," *ZÄS* 6 (1868) 80-83. *[Esarhaddon, p. 81]*

*George Smith, "Egyptian campaigns of Esarhaddon and Assur-bani-pul," *ZÄS* 6 (1868) 93-99, 113-122.

*E. H. Plumptre, "Assyrian Inscriptions in Their Bearing on Old Testament History. XVII. Esarhaddon," *Exp, 2nd Ser.*, 4 (1882) 448-461.

Esarhaddon concluded

*Cyrus Adler, "On the death of Sennacherib and the accession of Esarhaddon," *JAOS* 13 (1889) ccxxxv-ccxxxviii.

*Christopher Johnston, "Šamaš-šum-ukîn the eldest son of Esarhaddon," *JAOS* 25 (1904) 79-83.

C. H. W. Johns, "Fresh Light on the History of Esarhaddon," *SBAP* 37 (1915) 47-49.

*S. Ahmed, "Ashurbanipal and Shamashu-shum-ukin During Esarhaddon's Reign," *Abr-N* 6 (1965-66) 53-62.

Esarhaddon II

Arthur Amiaud, "Esarhaddon II," *BOR* 2 (1887-88) 197-201.

Ēse

*Jaroslav Černý, "Queen Ēse of the Twentieth Dynasty and Her Mother," *JEA* 44 (1958) 31-37.

Euhemerus

*Truesdell S. Brown, "Euhemerus and the Historians," *HTR* 39 (1946) 259-274.

Eurydice

*Grace H. Macurdy, "Queen Eurydice and the Evidence for Woman-Power in Early Macedonia," *AJP* 48 (1927) 201-214.

F

Flamininus

*Frederic M. Wood Jr., "The Military and Diplomatic Campaign of
T. Quinctius Flamininus in 198 B.C.," *AJP* 62 (1941) 277-288.

G

Gaddaš

Theo. G. Pinches, "Babylonian Notes. I. Gaddaš, an early Babylonian
King," *BOR* 1 (1886-87) 54.

Theo. G. Pinches, "Additional Note on the name of the Babylonian
King Gaddaš," *BOR* 1 (1886-87) 78.

C. Sulpicius Galba

*James H. Oliver, "C. Sulpicius Galba, Procounsul of Achaia," *AJA* 46
(1942) 380-388.

Genubath

*H. G. Tomkins, "The Name Genubath," *SBAP* 10 (1887-88) 372.
(Remarks by P. le Page Renouf, pp. 373-376. [גנבת]

Gobryas

*Joseph Offord, "Archaeological Notes on Jewish Antiquities. XIX.
Belshazzar and Gobryas the Median," *PEFQS* 48 (1916)
147-148.

Albert T. Clay, "Gobryas, governor of Babylonia," *JAOS* 41 (1921)
466-467.

Gudea

*W. St. Chad Boscawen, "Statue of Gudea as 'The Architect'," *BOR* 6 (1892-93) 282-283.

*S[tephen] Langdon, "Statuette of Gudea," *JRAS* (1927) 765-768.

*L[eon] L[egrain], "The Museum's Gudea," *UMB* 6 (1935-37) #6, 6-8.

*Selim [J.] Levy, "A Statue of Gudea in the Iraq Museum in Bagdad," *AfO* 11 (1936-37) 151-152.

*M. Tsevat, "A Reference to Gudea of Lagash in an Old Mari Text," *OA* 1 (1962) 9-10.

H

Habadilat

*Jaroslav Černý, "Queen Ēse of the Twentieth Dynasty and Her Mother," *JEA* 44 (1958) 31-37. *[Habadilat; Hmdrt; Hblda(n)t]*

Hadadezer

*D. D. Luckenbill, "Benhadad and Hadadezer," *AJSL* 27 (1910-11) 267-284.

*D. D. Luckenbill, "Hadadezer, King of Syria," *ET* 23 (1911-12) 282-284.

*John D. Davis, "Hadadezer or Ben-Hadad," *PTR* 17 (1919) 173-183.

Hadrian

*Joseph Offord, "Archaeological Notes on Jewish Antiquities. LV. *Fresh Light on Hadrian's Jewish War*," *PEFQS* 51 (1919) 37-38.

Haikar

*John P. Brown, "The History of the Learned Haikar, Vizir /sic/ of
Sennacherib the King, and of Nadan, son of Haikar's Sister,
translated from the Arabic," *JAOS* 8 (1866) lvi.

Hammurabi

Anonymous, "Hammurabi," *MR* 83 (1901) 642-643.

*J. A. Selbie, "Moses and Hammurabi," *ET* 14 (1902-03) 363-364.

[Stephen D. Peet], "Hammurabi, the Ancient Law-Giver," *AAOJ* 25
(1903) 207-209.

Paul Carus, "Hammurabi," *OC* 17 (1903) 274-280.

*Constantine Grethenbach, "Hammurabi and Abraham," *OC* 17
(1903) 760.

*Hugo Radau, "Hammurabi and Amraphel," *OC* 17 (1903) 705-707.

J. W. McGarvey, "Hammurabi and the Critics," *CFL, 3rd Ser.*, 1
(1904) 674-676.

*Anonymous, "Hammurabi and Moses," *MR* 86 (1904) 132-136.

*C. M. Cobern, "Moses and Hammurabi and Their Laws," *MR* 86
(1904) 697-703.

*Claude R. Conder, "Notes on New Discoveries," *PEFQS* 41 (1909)
266-275. [Hammurabi, pp. 266-267]

*J. Dyneley Prince, "The name Hammurabi," *JBL* 29 (1910) 21-23.

*M. G. Kyle, "Hammurabi, Abraham, and the Reviewers," *BS* 70
(1913) 528-531.

*W. T. Pilter, "Eastern and Western Semitic Personal Names. The
Equivalence of Hammurapi and Amrāphel," *SBAP* 35 (1913)
171-186. (Supplementary Note, pp. 244-245)

*D. D. Lukenbill, "The Name Hammurabi," *JAOS* 37 (1917) 250-253.

Hammurabi concluded

*W[illiam] F[oxwell] Albright, "The Amorite Form of the Name Hammurabi," *AJSL* 38 (1921-22) 140-141.

*O. E. Ravn, "The Rise of Marduk," *AO* 7 (1928-29) 81-90. *[The attitude of Hammurabi (Marked as "continued" but never was)]*

*Charles Marston, "Correspondence," *PEFQS* 68 (1936) 230. *[Hammurabi]*

*Roger T. O'Callaghan, "Notes on Mesopotamian History," *CBQ* 12 (1950) 132-135. [2. Hammurabi, pp. 133-134]

*M. B. Rowton, "*Ṭuppu* and the Date of Hammurabi," *JNES* 10 (1951) 184-204.

M. B. Rowton, "The Date of Hammurabi," *JNES* 17 (1958) 97-111.

*J. J. Finkelstein, "The Genealogy of the Hammurapi Dynasty," *JCS* 20 (1966) 95-118. [BM 80328]

Clifford Wilson, "Hammurabi: New Light on His Genealogy," *BH* 3 (1967) #3, 26-28.

*W. G. Lambert, "Another Look at Hammurabi's Ancestors," *JCS* 22 (1968-69) 1-2.

Josef Klíma, "Their Lord was Hammurabi—the Powerful King, the Sun of Babylon, the King who Brings the Four Quarters of the World to Obedience," *NOP* 7 (1968) 114-117.

Hannibal

†Anonymous, "Hannibal's Passage of the Alps," *ERCJ* 43 (1825-26) 163-197.

†Anonymous, "Hannibal's Passage of the Alps," *QRL* 123 (1867) 191-220. *(Review)*

Hapata

Dows Dunham and M. F. Laming Macadam, "Names and Relationships of the Royal Family of Hapata," *JEA* 35 (1949) 139-149.

Hapu

*Percy E. Newberry, "Extracts from my Notebooks (III).," *SBAP* 22 (1900) 142-154. [18. A Statue of Hapu, father of Thothmes IInd's Vezîr, Hapu-senb, pp. 148-150]

*R. H. Dawson, "Amenophis the son of Hapu," *Aeg* 7 (1926) 113-138.

Hapu-senb

*Percy E. Newberry, "Extracts from my Notebooks (III).," *SBAP* 22 (1900) 142-154. [18. A Statue of Hapu, father of Thothmes IInd's Vezîr, Hapu-senb, pp. 148-150]

Ḥaremḥab / Horemḥēb

*James Henry Breasted, "King Harmhab and his Sakkara tomb," *ZÄS* 38 (1900) 47-50.

*H. E. Winlock, "A Statue of Horemhab before his Accession," *JEA* 10 (1924) 1-5.

*Keith C. Seele, "Ḥawrûn-em-Ḥab or Haremhab?" *JNES* 4 (1945) 234-239.

*Keith C. Seele, "Ḥawrûn-Harmachis: A Comment on Posener's 'Houroun'," *JNES* 4 (1945) 243-244.

*Alan [H.] Gardiner, "The Coronation of King Ḥaremḥab," *JEA* 39 (1953) 13-31.

*Alan R. Schulman, "The Berlin 'Trauerrelief' (No. 12411) and Some Officials of Tut'ankhamūn and Ay," *JARCE* 4 (1965) 55-68. [II. The "General" and *RPT* Ḥoremḥēb, pp. 58-61]

J. R[endell] Harris, "How Long was the Reign of Ḥoremḥeb?" *JEA* 54 (1968) 95-99.

Hasmonaeans

*E. G. Sihler, "The Hasmonaeans and Herod the Idumaean," *BR* 10 (1925) 197-222.

*Joshua Efron, "The Psalms of Solomon, The Hasmonean Decline, and Christianity," *Zion* 30 (1965) #1/2, I-II.

Hathor-nofer-hotep

*A. H. Sayce, "Hieroglyphic Inscription at How, containing the Name of a New King," *SBAP* 7 (1884-85) 185-187. *[Hathor-nofer-hotep]*

Hatshepsut

A. H. Sayce, "Queen Hatshepsu," *ET* 15 (1903-04) 370.

C. H. S. Davis, "Hatshepsu," *AAOJ* 28 (1906) 293-294.

*H. R. Hall, "A New Portrait Head of Tuthmosis III (?) at Berlin, and the Portraits of Hatshepsut," *JEA* 15 (1929) 78-79.

G. H. Lang, "An Ancient Egyptian Queen," *EQ* 29 (1957) 206-217. *[Hatshepsut]*

*J. Vercoutter, "Editorial Notes: Hatshepsut, Tuthmosis III or Amenophis II? (Khartoum Museum statue no. 30)," *Kush* 5 (1957) 5-7.

Charles F. Nims, "The date of the dishonoring of Hatsheput," *ZÄS* 93 (1966) 97-100.

Ḥawrûm-em-Ḥab

*Keith C. Seele, "Ḥawrûn-em-Ḥab or Haremhab?" *JNES* 4 (1945) 234-239.

*Keith C. Seele, "Ḥawrûn-em-Ḥab or Haremhab?" *JNES* 4 (1945) 234-239.

*Keith C. Seele, "Ḥawrûn-Harmachis: A Comment on Posener's 'Houroun'," *JNES* 4 (1945) 243-244.

Ḥȝty-ꜥ n Kpn

*Percy E. Newberry, "Miscellanea," *JEA* 14 (1928) 109-111. [I. A Middle Kingdom Mayor of Byblos, p. 109] *[Ḥȝty-ꜥ n Kpn]*

Hekaib

*Labib Habachi, "Hekaib: The Deified Governor of Elephantine," *Arch* 9 (1956) 8-15.

Hen Hekht

C. S. Meyrs, "The Bones of Hen Nekht, an Egyptian King of the Third Dynasty," *Man* 1 (1901) #127.

Ḥenenu

William C. Hayes, "Career of the Great Steward Ḥenenu under Nebḥepetre Mentuḥotpe," *JEA* 35 (1949) 43-49.

Herakles

Burr C. Brundage, "Herakles the Levantine: A Comprehensive View," *JNES* 17 (1958) 225-236.

Hermogenes

*Francis W. Schehl, "The Date of Hermogenes the Architect," *AJA* 55 (1951) 152.

Herod (and the Herodian Family)

A. B., "Herod 'the Great,' or Herod 'the Elder'," *JSL, 1st Ser.,* 5 (1850) 221-223.

John D. Keiley, "The Herodian Family [FROM THE GERMAN OF BILFINGER]," *MQR* 9 (1855) 229-235.

Anonymous,   "Herod   the   Great,"   *CongR*   4   (1864)   15-38.

Herod (and the Herodian Family) cont.

W. S. Hooper, "When was Herod made King of Judea?" *MR* 61 (1879) 546-555.

A. C. Zenos, "The Herods," *CFL, N.S.,* 2 (1900) 29-32, 89-94, 150-156.

*Edward M. Merrins, "The Deaths of Antiochus IV., Herod the Great, and Herod Agrippa I," *BS* 61 (1904) 548-562.

Anonymous, "The House of Herod in History and Art," *ERCJ* 215 (1912) 291-317.

*E. G. Sihler, "The Hasmonaeans and Herod the Idumaean," *BR* 10 (1925) 197-222.

Rudolph M. Rosenthal, "Herod—A Literary Biography," *JIQ* 5 (1928-29) #2, 10-23.

Thomas Corbishley, "The Chronology of Herod the Great," *JTS* 36 (1935) 22-32.

Pat E. Harrell, "The Smallness and Greatness of Herod," *RestQ* 1 (1957) 79-91.

*W. Wirgin, "Two Notes," *IEJ* 11 (1961) 151-154. [II. On King Herod's Messianism, p.153-154]

*E. G. Sihler, "The Hasmonaeans and Herod the Idumaean," *BR* 10 (1925) 197-222.

S. G. F. Brandon, "Herod the Great: Judaea's most able but most hated king," *HT* 12 (1962) 234-242.

*Harald Ingholt, "Colossal Head in Boston, Severan or Augustan?" *AJA* 67 (1963) 213. *[Herod the Great(?)]*

*Harald Ingholt, "A Colossal Head from Memphis, Severan or Augustan?" *JARCE* 2 (1963) 125-145. *[Herod the Great(?)]*

Solomon Zeitlin, "Herod," *JQR, N.S.,* 54 (1963-64) 1-27.

*Menahem Stern, "The Politics of Herod and Jewish Society towards the End of the Second Commonweatlh," *Tarbiz* 35 (1965-66) #3, III.

Herod (and the Herodian Family) concluded

W. E. Filmer. "The Chronology of the Reign of Herod the Great," *JTS, N.S.,* 17 (1966) 283-298.

T. D. Barnes, "The Date of Herod's Death." *JTS, N.S.,* 19 (1968) 204-209.

Herod Agrippa

*Edward M. Merrins, "The Deaths of Antiochus IV., Herod the Great, and Herod Agrippa I," *BS* 61 (1904) 548-562.

Herod Antipas

F. F. Bruce, "Herod Antipas, Tetrach of Galilee and Peraea," *ALUOS* 5 (1963-65) 6-23.

Herodotus

*G. B. Grundy, "Herodotus the Historian," *QRL* 210 (1909) 115-140. *(Review)*

*Truesdell S. Brown, "Herodotus and His Profession," *AmHR* 59 (1953-54) 829-843.

Russell Meiggs, "Herodotus," *HT* 7 (1957) 729-738.

*Molly Miller, "Herodotus as a Chronographer," *Klio* 46 (1966) 109-128.

Hesiod

Peter Green, "A Peasant of Helicon: A Study of Hesiod and His Society," *HT* 9 (1959) 729-735.

Hieronymus

Truesdell S. Brown, "Hieronymus of Cardia," *AmHR* 52 (1946-47) 684-696.

Hieronymus concluded

*Robert A. Hadley, "Hieronymus of Cardia and Early Seleucid Mythology," *HJAH* 18 (1969) 142-152.

Hippodamus

*R. E. Wycherley, "Hippodamus and Rhodes," *HJAH* 13 (1964) 135-139.

Hiram

C. Clermont-Ganneau, "Hiram, King of Tyre," *PEFQS* 12 (1880) 174-181.

William Hayes Ward, "Light on Scriptural Texts from Recent Discoveries. Hiram, King of Tyre," *HR* 30 (1895) 124-126.

Charles C. Torrey, "Concerning Hiram ('Huram-abi'), the Phoenican Craftsman," *JBL* 31 (1912) 151-155.

J. Liver, "On the Chronology of Hiram King of Tyre," *BIES* 17 (1952-53) #3/4, I.

*H. J. Katzenstein, "Is There any Synchronism Between the Reigns of Hiram and Solomon?" *JNES* 24 (1965) 116-117.

Homer

*T. B. Browne, "Troy and Homer," *ContR* 12 (1869) 481-499.

*W. E. Gladstone, "The Place of Homer in History and in Egyptian Chronology," *ContR* 24 (1874) 1-22, 175-200.

*Anonymous, "Homer Illustrated by Recent Discovery," *CQR* 7 (1878-79) 392-421.

*T. B. L. Webster, "Homer and the Mycenaean Tablets," *Antiq* 29 (1955) 10-14.

*L. R. Palmer, "Homer and Mycenae: I Heroic Greek Society," *HT* 7 (1957) 367-372.

Homer concluded

*A. R. Campbell, "Homer and Ugaritic Literature," *Abr-N* 5 (1964-65) 29-56.

Humbaba

A. T. Clay, "The Early Amorite King Humbaba," *ET* 34 (1922-23) 38-42.

Ḥwdfȝ

Hans Goedicke, "King *Ḥwdfȝ?*" *JEA* 42 (1956) 50-53.

Ḥwny-r-ḥr

John A. Wilson, "The descendants of *ḥwny-r-ḥr,*" *ZÄS* 68 (1932) 56-57.

Hyrcanus

A. Schalit, "Has Hyrcanus been appointed 'Brother of the King'?" *BIES* 6 (1938-39) #3, IV.

*D[aniel] Sperber, "A Note on Hasmonean Coin-Legends. Heber and Rosh-Heber," *PEQ* 97 (1965) 85-93. *[Jochanan Hyrcanus I]*

Hyspaosines

*Terrien de Lacouperie, "Hyspaosines, Kharacenian king, on a Babylonian Tablet dated 127 a.c. and the Arsacian era, 248 a.c.," *BOR* 4 (1889-90) 136-144.

Hystaspes

*Roland G. Kent, "The Name Hystaspes," *Lang* 21 (1945) 55-58.

I

Iasmaḫ-Adad

*Hildegard Lewy, "The Synchronism Assyria—Ešnunna—Babylon," *WO* 2 (1954-59) 438-453. [2. Iasmaḫ-Adad and Ibal-pî-El, pp. 445-453]

i(?)-b(?)

A. H. Sayce, "The Name of the Ethiopian King, Found at Basa," *SBAP* 31 (1908) 268. [⌐ i(?)-b(?)]

Ibal-pî-El

*Hildegard Lewy, "The Synchronism Assyria—Ešnunna—Babylon," *WO* 2 (1954-59) 438-453. [2. Iasmaḫ-Adad and Ibal-pî-El, pp. 445-453]

Ibi-Sin

*Leon Legrain, "Reconstructing Ancient History," *MJ* 11 (1920) 169-180. [I Portrait of a King Who Reigned 4130 Years Ago, (Ibi-Sin), pp. 169-175]

*S[tephen] Langdon, "Ibi-Sin and the fall of the kingdom of Ur," *RAAO* 20 (1923) 49-51. (Correction, *RAAO* 21 (1924), pp. 37-38)

*Edmond Sollberger, "Selected Texts from American Collections," *JCS* 10 (1956) 11-31. [4-5. Texts Relating to Ibbi-Sîn's Coronation, pp. 18-20 (Emory University No. 38 and No. 55)]

Ikhnaton

*Leslie A. White, "Ikhnaton: The Great Man *vs.* the Culture Process," *JAOS* 68 (1948) 91-114.

*William F. Edgerton, "'The Great Man': a Note on Methods," *JAOS* 68 (1948) 192-193. *[Ikhnaton]*

Ikhnaton concluded

Leslie A. White, "Reply to Professor Edgerton," *JAOS* 68 (1948) 193. *[Ikhnaton]*

*F. J. Giles, "Amenhotpe, Ikhnaton and the succession," *Aeg* 32 (1952) 293-310.

Immerum

*Theophilus G. Pinches, "A New Babylonian King of the Period of the First Dynasty of Babylon; with Incidental References to Immerum and Anmanila," *SBAP* 21 (1899) 158-163.

Ina Bit Saggil tuklat

*W. St. C[had] B[oscawen], "Note.— A Daughter of Nabonidus," *BOR* 4 (1889-90) 144. (Additional Note by T[errian] d[e] L[acouperie], p. 168) *[Ina Bit Saggil tuklat(?)]*

Ini-teśub

R. D. Barnett and J[aroslav] Černý, "King Ini-teśub of Carchemish in an Egyptian document," *JEA* 33 (1947) 94.

ipi

Ludlow S. Bull, "A New Vizier of the Eleventh Dynasty," *JEA* 10 (1924) 15. [𓏞𓂧𓀾]

Ira

*Moshe Aberbach, "The Relation between Ira the Jarite and King David according to Talmudic Legend," *Tarbiz* 33 (1963-64) #4, III.

Isis

*Percy E. Newberry, "Egyptian Historical Notes. I," *SBAP* 35 (1913) 156-158. [5. Amenhetep IIIrd's Daughter Isis, p. 158]

Isocrates

*Philip Merlan, "Isocrates, Aristotle and Alexander the Great," *HJAH* 3 (1954-55) 60-81.

Iterty

Alan [H.] Gardiner, "The Personal Name of King Serpent," *JEA* 44 (1958) 38-39. *[Iterty]*

'Iymeru

*J. V. Beckerath, "Notes on the Viziers 'Ankhu and 'Iymeru in the Thirteenth Egyptian Dynasty," *JNES* 17 (1958) 263-268.

J

Alexander Jannaeus

B. Kanael, "Notes on Alexander Jannaeus' Campaigns in the Coastal Region," *Tarbiz* 24 (1954-55) #1, III.

*C. Rabin, "Alexander Jannaeus and the Pharisees," *JJS* 7 (1956) 3-12.

*John M. Allegro, "*Thrakidan*, The 'Lion of Wrath' and Alexander Jannaeus," *PEQ* 91 (1959) 47-51.

Manaḥem Stern, "*Trachides*—Surname of Alexander Yannai*[sic]* in Josephus and Syncellus," *Tarbiz* 29 (1959-60) #3, II.

*Solomon Zeitlin, "Queen Salome and King Jannaeus Alexander," *JQR, N.S.,* 51 (1960-61) 1-33.

Manaḥem Stern, "The Political Background of the Wars of Alexander Jannai," *Tarbiz* 33 (1963-64) #4, I.

Jareb

*A. H. Sayce, "Was Jareb the Original Name of Sargon?" *BOR* 2 (1887-88) 18-22.

A. H. Sayce, "Jareb," *BOR* 2 (1887-88) 145-146.

J. A. Selbie, "Who was King Jareb?" *ET* 9 (1897-98) 364.

Juba II

Stanislav Segert, "Juba II, the Writer King," *NOP* 4 (1965) 11-12.

Judas (of Galilee)

J. Spencer Kennard Jr., "Judas of Galilee and His Clan," *JQR, N.S.,* 36 (1945-46) 281-286.

K

Kai

*J. R. Harris, "The name of the scribe in the Louvre—a note," *JEA* 41 (1955) 122-123. *[Kai(?); Accroupi(?)]*

K₃i-'pr

Henry G. Fischer, "A Scribe of the Army in a Saqqara Mastaba of the Early Fifth Dynasty," *JNES* 18 (1959) 233-272. *[K₃i-'pr]*

Kai-Khosiu

*( ) G., "Kai-Khosiu and Ahasuerus," *JSL, 3rd Ser.,* 11 (1860) 385-416.

Kalamis

Anton E. Raubitschek, "A Possible Signature of Kalamis," *AJA* 45 (1941) 90.

Ka-mes

*Percy E. Newberry, "Extracts from my Notebooks (IV.)," *SBAP* 23 (1901) 218-224. [21. Statue of a Fan-bearer of the Body-guard of Amenhetep III (*Ka-mes*), pp. 218-219]

Kandalanu

*Sidney Smith, "Dating by Ashurbanipal and Kandalanu," *JRAS* (1928) 622-626.

Kandaules

A. H. Sayce, "Notes on—(4) Kandaules of Lydia," *SBAP* 23 (1901) 113.

Kha-em-maat

*Percy E. Newberry, "Egyptian Historical Notes. I.," *SBAP* 35 (1913) 156-158. [4. An Official of the Royal Barge of Amenhetep III, pp. 157-158 *(Kha-em-maat)*]

Kha-nefer-Ra

*Percy E. Newberry, "Extracts from my Notebooks VII.," *SBAP* 25 (1903) 357-362. [49. The Queen of Kha-nefer-Ra Sebek-hetep III, p. 358]

Khasekhmui

*F. Legge, "Was Khasekhmui called Mena?" *SBAP* 31 (1909) 128-132.

Khảŷ

*Percy E. Newberry, "Extracts from my Notebooks (II).," *SBAP* 22 (1900) 59-66. [7. The Vezîr Khảŷ, p. 62]

*Percy E. Newberry, "Extracts from my Notebooks. VIII.," *SBAP* 27 (1905) 101-105. [58. The Vezîr Khaŷ, p. 101]

Khentybau

W. K. Simpson, "The non-existence of a vizier Khentybau in the Middle Kingdom," *JEA* 41 (1955) 129-130.

Kheper-ka-Ra

M. A. Murray, "A Statue of Kheper-ka-Ra," *AEE* 13 (1928) 105-109.

Khnems

*Percy E. Newberry, "Extracts from my Notebooks (IV).," *SBAP* 23 (1901) 218-224. [26. Khnems, Vezîr of Sekhem-ka-Ra, pp. 222-223]

Khnum

*L[abib] Habachi, "Was Anukis considered as the wife of Khnum or as his daughter?" *ASAE* 50 (1950) 501-507.

Khnumḥotep

W. A. Ward, "The Nomarch Khnumḥotep at Pelusium," *JEA* 55 (1969) 215-216.

Khonsu

F. W. Read, "A Statuette of Khonsu," *AEE* 4 (1917) 120-121.

Khuenaten

Colin Campbell, "Inscribed Slab with a portrait of Khuenaten," *SBAP* 28 (1906) 156.

Kleon

*Malcolm F. McGregor, "The Last Campaign of Kleon and the Athenian Calendar in 422/1 B.C.," *AJP* 59 (1938) 145-168.

Kyniska

*Alfred Emerson, "The Case of Kyniska," *AJA* 15 (1911) 60.

L

Leon

C. Bradford Welles, "Leon the Toparch," *JARCE* 5 (1966) 65-68.

Lilul-dannum

Selim J. Levy, "A New King of the Akkadian Dynasty," *AfO* 10 (1935-36) 281. *[Lilul-dannum]*

Livia

*David M. Robinson, "A New Bust of the Empress Livia in the Robinson Collection," *AJA* 60 (1956) 181.

Lugalanda

*Ferris J. Stephens, "Notes on some Economic Texts of the Time of Urukagina," *RAAO* 49 (1955) 129-136. [1. Who was Urukagina's Predecessor? pp. 129-131] *[Lugalanda?]*

Lugal-ki-GUB-ni-dú-dú

*S[tephen] Langdon, "Assyriological Note," *JRAS* (1931) 421-424. *[Lugal-ki-GUB-ni-dú-dú Contemporary of Entemena?]*

Lysander

W. K. Prentice, "The Character of Lysander," *AJA* 38 (1934) 37-42.

M

Maccabees [Maccabeans]

Thomas H. Gill, "The Maccabees," *CongL* 6 (1877) 193-207.

Wallace N. Stearns, "The Rise of the Maccabees," *IJA* #51 (1917) 52-55.

H. G. Bevenot, "Prolegomena to the Maccabees," *BS* 81 (1924) 480-492.

*A. A. Bevan, "The Origin of the Name Maccabee," *JTS* 30 (1928-29) 191-193.

B. Maisler, "Topographical Researches," *BIES* 8 (1940-41) #3, II. [II. The place of origin of the Maccabeans]

*Sidney B. Hoeing, "Maccabees, Zealots and Josephus," *JQR, N.S.,* 49 (1958-59) 75-80.

Thomas Hodgkin, "Antiochus Epiphanes and the Maccabees. A Study in Two Parts. Part II—The Maccabees," *ICMM* 3 (1906-07) 423-441.

Judas Maccabaeus

[R. Gordon] Nicol, "Judas Maccabaeus," *APST* 4 (1900-10) 1-19.

Henry F. Henderson, "Judas Maccabaeus," *IJA* #6 (1906) 10-11.

(Miss) L. Hands, "The Character of Judas Maccabaeus," *IJA* #19 (1909) 17-19.

*Wallace N. Stearns, "Judas Maccabaeus as a Military Strategist," *IJA* #47 (1916) 54-53.

Simon (Maccabaeus)

H. F. B. Compston, "Simon (Maccabaeus) surnamed Thassi," *IJA* #29 (1912) 22-23.

Manamaltel

*Theophilus G. Pinches, "A New Babylonian King of the Period of the First Dynasty of Babylon; with Incidental References to Immerum and Anmanila," *SBAP* 21 (1899) 158-163. *[Manamaltel]*

Manetho

Gustav Seyffarth, "Manetho's Autograph in the Royal Museum at Turin," *JAOS* 8 (1866) xxix.

G. C. Lentulus Marcellinus

*Otto J. Brendel, "A Diademed Roman? *For Richard Krautheimer,*" *AJA* 71 (1967) 407-409. *[Gnaeus Cornelius Lentulus Marcellinus(?)]*

Marduk

*O. E. Ravn, "The Rise of Marduk," *AO* 7 (1928-29) 81-90. *[Marked as "to be continued" but never was]*

Marduk-bel-zeri

A. H. Sayce, "Marduk-bel-zeri King of Babylon," *Baby* 7 (1913-23) 242.

*Albert T. Clay, "A new king of Babylonia," *JAOS* 41 (1921) 313. *[Marduk-bêl-zêri]*

Mauramai Batita

C. W. Goodwin, "On the name of a King of the Rabu (Libyans)," *ZÄS* 6 (1868) 39. *[Mauramai Batita]*

May

Donald B. Redford, "The Identity of the High-priest of Amun at the Beginning of Akhenaten's Reign," *JAOS* 83 (1963) 240-241. *[May]*

Mayer

*Alan R. Schulman, "The Berlin 'Trauerrelief' (No. 12411) and Some Officials of Tut'ankhamūn and Ay," *JARCE* 4 (1965) 55-68. [IV. The Overseer of the Treasury, Mayer, pp. 66-67]

Meannesi

Faraj Basmachi and Dietz Otto Edzard, "Statue of a Son of Enannatum I in the Iraq Museum," *Sumer* 14 (1958) 109-113. *[Meannesi(?)]*

Meleager

*Edmund von Mach, "The Statue of Meleager in the Fogg Museum of Harvard University," *AJA* 5 (1901) 29-30.

Memnon

Anonymous, "On the Memnonium," *MMBR* 59 (1825) 493-496. *[Statue of Memnon]*

Mena

*F. Legge, "Was Khasekhmui called Mena?" *SBAP* 31 (1909) 128-132.

Menes

*Ernest de Bunsen, "The Date of Menes and the Date of Budda," *SBAP* 3 (1880-81) 96.

*W[illiam] F[oxwell] Albright, "Menes and Narâm-Sin," *JEA* 6 (1920) 89-98.

*W[illiam] F[oxwell] Albright, Stephen Langdon, A. H. Sayce, and [Alan H. Gardiner], "Communications I: Menes and Naram-Sin," *JEA* 6 (1920) 295-296.

*W[illiam] F[oxwell] Albright, "Magan, Meluḫa, and the Synchronism between Menes and Narâm-Šin," *JEA* 7 (1921) 80-86.

Menes concluded

A. J. Arkell, "Was King Scorpion Menes?" *Antiq* 37 (1963) 31-35.

Menkaura

W. M. Flinders Petrie, "A Portrait of Menkaura," *AEE* 8 (1923) 1-2. *[Bust of Menkaura]*

Menkheperrē'senb

*H. R. Hall, "The Statues of Sennemut and Menkheperrē'senb in the British Museum," *JEA* 14 (1928) 1-2.

Menophres

*M. B. Rowton, "Mesoptamian Chronology and the 'Era of Menophres'," *Iraq* 8 (1946) 96-110.

Menteḥetef

Jac. J. Janssen, "Vizier Menteḥetef," *JEA* 53 (1967) 163-164.

Menṭhotpe

Alan [H.] Gardiner, "The First King Menṭhotpe of the Eleventh Dynasty," *MDIÄA* 14 (1956) 42-51.

Mentuhetep

*Percy E. Newberry, "Extracts from my Notebooks. VIII.," *SBAP* 27 (1905) 101-105. [62. A *post*-XIIth Dynasty King Mentuhetep, p. 103]

*Alan H. Gardiner, "The Name of King Sankhere," *SBAP* 26 (1904) 75-76. *[Mentuhotep]*

Merenptah

*A[ngus] C[rawford], "Archæological Notes," *PER* 5 (1891-92) 363-365. [Etruscan Inscription and Merenptah, p. 363]

Merenptah concluded

*[George H. Schodde], "Biblical Research Notes," *ColTM* 17 (1897) 117-121. [Mer-en-ptah and His Inscriptions, p. 121]

*D. R. Fotheringham, "Merenptah and the Exodus. I.," *ET* 20 (1908-09) 141.

*Wm. Fisher, "Merenptah and the Exodus. II.," *ET* 20 (1908-09) 142.

*Anonymous, "The Pharaoh of the Exodus Identified with Menephtah," *CFL, 3rd Ser.,* 13 (1910) 222-223. *(Editorial Note)*

John Urquhart, "The Traditional View of the Death of Menephtah," *CFL, 3rd Ser.,* 13 (1910) 224-227.

*Anonymous, "Mummy of the Red Sea Pharaoh," *RP* 9 (1910) 343. *[Meneptah]*

Ed. Naville, "Did Menephtah invade Syria?" *JEA* 2 (1915) 195-201.

Merenra

[W. M. Flinders Petrie], "The Portraits," *AEE* 1 (1915) 48. *[Prince/King Merenra]*

Merodach Baladan

*G. B., "The Dial of Ahaz and the Embassy from Merodach Baladan," *JSL, 3rd Ser.,* 2 (1855-56) 163-179.

T. H. Bindley, "Merodach-Baladan," *TML* 6 (1891) 73-78.

J. F. McCurdy, "Light on Scriptural Texts from Recent Discoveries. Bible Personages.—Merodach-baladan," *HR* 36 (1898) 413-416.

*J. A. Brinkman, "Elamite Military Aid to Merodach-Baladan," *JNES* 24 (1965) 161-166.

Anonymous, "Merodach-Baladan—A Scheming King," *BH* 3 (1967) #1, 5-7.

Merynar

*S. Yeivin, "Further Evidence of Narmar at 'Gat'," *OA* 2 (1963) 205-213. *[Merynar(?)]*

Meryt-Amon

M. A. Murray, "Queen Meryt-Amon," *AEE* 15 (1930) 55.

Mesannepadda

*Edmund I. Gordon, "Mesilim and Mesannepadda—Are They Identical?" *BASOR* #132 (1953) 27-30.

Mêshitug

*George A. Barton, "The Names of Two Kings of Adab," *JAOS* 33 (1913) 295-296. *[Mêshitug]*

Mesilim

*Edmund I. Gordon, "Mesilim and Mesannepadda—Are They Identical?" *BASOR* #132 (1953) 27-30.

Mesha

*J. Liver, "The Wars of Mesha, King of Moab," *PEQ* 99 (1967) 14-31.

Messalla

Arthur E. Gordon, "Potitius Valerius Messalla, Consul Suffect in 29 B.C.," *AJA* 58 (1954) 145-146.

Min-nekht

*Percy E. Newberry, "Extracts from my Notebook (III).," *SBAP* 22 (1900) 142-154. [19. A Statue of Min-nekht, Superintendent of the Granaries under Thothmes III, pp. 150-152]

*Percy E. Newberry, "Extracts from my Notebooks V.," *SBAP* 24 (1902) 244-252. [29. A Statuette of Min-nekht, pp. 245-246]

Minos

*William Ridgeway, "Minos the Destroyer rather than the Creator of the so-called 'Minoan' Culture of Cnossus," *PBA* 4 (1909-10) 97-129.

Mithradates I

David M. Robinson, "A Graeco-Parthian Portrait Head of Mithradates I," *AJA* 31 (1927) 338-344.

Mukiš-Nuḫafšše-Nii

*Michael C. Astour, "The Partition of the Confederacy of Mukiš-Nuḫafšše-Nii by Šuppiluliuma. A Study in Political Geography of the Amarna Age," *Or, N.S.,* 38 (1969) 381-414.

Mursilis

Philo H. J. Houwink ten Cate, "Mursilis' North-Western Campaigns — A Commentary," *Anat* 1 (1967) 44-61.

Mutnedjemet

*Elizabeth Thomas, "Was Queen Mutnedjemet the owner of Tomb 33 in the Valley of the Queens?" *JEA* 53 (1967) 161-163.

N

Nabonassar

Daniel Hy. Haigh, "Nabonassar," *ZÄS* 10 (1872) 46-48.

Nabonidus

*W. St. C[had] B[oscawen], "Note.—A Daughter of Nabonidus," *BOR* 4 (1889-90) 144. (Additional Note by T[errian] d[e] L[acouperie], p. 168)

*Raymond P. Dougherty, "Nabonidus in Arabia," *JAOS* 42 (1922) 305-316.

Nabonidus concluded

*Leon Legrain, "King Nabonidus and the Great Walls of Babylon,"
MJ 14 (1923) 282-287.

W[illiam] F[oxwell] Albright, "The Conquests of Nabonidus in Arabia,"
JRAS (1925) 293-295.

*Sidney Smith, "Assyriological Notes," *JRAS* (1925) 508-513.
[Nabonidus' Sickness, p. 511]

*P. E. Kretzmann, "Nabonidus—Belshazzar," *CTM* 3 (1932) 215.

*Michael J. Gruenthaner, "The Last King of Babylon," *CBQ* 11 (1949)
406-427. *[Nabonidus]*

*J. M. Wilkie, "Nabonidus and the Later Jewish Exiles," *JTS, N.S.,* 2
(1951) 36-44.

*Berta Segall, "The Arts and King Nabonidus," *AJA* 59 (1955)
315-318.

Nabopolassar

Edw. Hincks, "Letter from Dr. Hincks, in reply to Colonel Rawlinson's
Note on the Successor of Sennacherib," *JRAS* (1855) 402-403.

Nabû-shum-libur

*L. W. King, "Nabû-shum-libur, king of Babylon," *SBAP* 29 (1907)
221.

Nadan

John P. Brown, "The History of the Learned Haikar, Vizir/sic/* of
Sennacherib the King, and of Nadan, son of Haikar's Sister,
translated from the Arabic," *JAOS* 8 (1866) lvi.

Nakht

*Jean Capart, "Some Remarks on the Sheikh el-Beled," *JEA* 6 (1920)
225-233. *[Nakht]*

Nakhtmin

Alan R. Schulman, "Excursus on the 'Military Officer' Nakhtmin," *JARCE* 3 (1964) 124-126.

*Alan R. Schulman, "The Berlin 'Trauerrelief' (No. 12411) and Some Officials of Tut'ankhamūn and Ay," *JARCE* 4 (1965) 55-68. [III. The Military Officer Nakhtmin, pp. 61-66]

Naram-Sin

*†John P. Peters, "Date of Naram-Sin, Son of Sargon," *SBAP* 8 (1885-86) 142.

*W[illiam] F[oxwell] Albright, "Menes and Narâm-Sin," *JEA* 6 (1920) 89-98.

*W[illiam] F[oxwell] Albright, Stephen Langdon, A. H. Sayce, and [Alan H. Gardiner], "Communications I: Menes and Naram-Sin," *JEA* 6 (1920) 295-296.

*W[illiam] F[oxwell] Albright, "Magan, Meluḫa, and the Synchronism between Menes and Narâm-Šin," *JEA* 7 (1921) 80-86.

Nâr-Ba-Thai

*Vladimir Vikentiev, "Nâr-Ba-Thai," *JEA* 17 (1931) 67-80.

[I. Nâr-Mertha or Nâr-Ba-Thai? pp. 67-71 (🕮)]

Narmar

*S. Yeivin, "Further Evidence of Narmar at 'Gat'," *OA* 2 (1963) 205-213. *[Narmar; Merynar(?)]*

William A. Ward, "The supposed Asiatic campaign of Narmer," *MUSJ* 45 (1969) 203-221.

Nâr-Mertha

*Vladimir Vikentiev, "Nâr-Ba-Thai," *JEA* 17 (1931) 67-80.

[I. Nâr-Mertha or Nâr-Ba-Thai? pp. 67-71 (🝔⌐ 🜋)]

Nb(·i)-k3(·i)

J[aroslav] Černý, "Name of the King of the unfinished pyramid at Zawiyet el-Aryân," *MDIÄA* 16 (1958) 25-29. *[Nb(·i)-k3(·i)]*

Neb-Ḥepet-Rē' Mentu-Ḥotpe

H. E. Winlock, "Neb-Ḥepet-Rē' Mentu-Ḥotpe of the Eleveth Dynasty," *JEA* 26 (1940) 116-119.

Labib Habachi, "King Nebhepetre Menthuhotp: His Monuments, Place in History, Deification and Unusual Representations in the Form of Gods," *MDIÄA* 19 (1963) 16-52.

Nebopolassar

*Morris Jastrow Jr., "Nebopolassar and the Temple to the Sun-God at Sippar," *AJSL* 15 (1898-99) 65-86.

Nebt-ant

*Percy E. Newberry, "Extracts from my Notebooks VIII.," *SBAP* 27 (1905) 101-105. [59. The Queen of Sebekhetep III (*Nebt-ant*), pp. 101-102]

Nebt-nenat

*Percy E. Newberry, "Extracts from my Notebooks. VII.," *SBAP* 25 (1903) 357-362. [51. Queen Nebt-nenat, pp. 358-359]

Nebuchadnezzer

A. Sayce, "Nebuchadnezzer and his Subjects," *JSL, 4th Ser.*, 9 (1866) 180-193.

Nebuchadnezzer cont.

*G. B., "On the Accession of Nebuchadnezzer and the Eclipse of B.C. 585," *JSL, 5th Ser.,* 2 (1867-68) 455-457.

*J. W. Bosanquet, "On the Date of the Fall of Nineveh and the Beginning of the Reign of Nebuchadnezzer at Babylon, B.C. 581," *SBAT* 2 (1873) 147-178.

John P. Peters, "Nebuchadrezzer I," *AJSL* 2 (1885-86) 171-173.

William Hayes Ward, "Light on Scriptural Texts from Recent Discoveries. Nebuchadnezzer in Egypt," *HR* 29 (1895) 221-223.

John P. Peters, "Notes on the Old Testament," *JBL* 15 (1896) 106-117. [3. The Nebuchadnezzars of Daniel, pp. 111-114]

P. Thomson, "Nebuchadnezzar's Conquest of Egypt. confirmed from a contemporary Hieroglyphic Inscription," *Exp., 1st Ser.,* 10 (1879) 397-403.

*J. A. Selbie, "Was Tyre Taken by Nebuchadrezzer?" *ET* 10 (1898-99) 378-379.

*A. H. Sayce, "The Capture of Tyre by Nebuchadrezzer," *ET* 10 (1898-99) 430.

*J. A. Selbie, "Nebuchadrezzer and the Siege of Tyre," *ET* 10 (1898-99) 475.

*Fritz Hommel, "Was Tyre Taken by Nebuchadrezzer?" *ET* 10 (1898-99) 520.

Francis R. Harper, "Nebuchadnezzar, King of Babylon (604-561 B.C.)," *BW* 14 (1899) 3-12.

Anonymous, "Asia:—Babylonia," *RP* 3 (1904) 123. *[Discovery of the first cylinder bearing the inscription of Nebuchadrezzar]*

*Edward M. Merrins, "The Abasement of Nebuchadnezzar," *BS* 62 (1905) 601-625.

Edward J. Young, "The Folly of Nebuchadnezzar," *CO* 4 (1946-47) 19-24.

Nebuchadnezzer concluded

*A[braham] Malamat, "A New Record of Nebuchadrezzar's Palestinian Campaigns," *IEJ* 6 (1956) 246-256.

J. Philip Hyatt, "New Light on Nebuchadrezzar and Judean History," *JBL* 75 (1956) 277-284.

*Jack Finegan, "Nebuchadnezzar and Jerusalem," *JAAR* 25 (1957) 203-205.

*Werner E. Lemke, "'Nebuchadrezzar, My Servant'," *CBQ* 28 (1966) 45-50.

*Thomas W. Overholt, "King Nebuchadnezzar in the Jeremiah Tradition," *CBQ* 30 (1968) 39-48.

*George Telcs, "Jeremiah and Nebuchadnezzar, King of Justice," *CJT* 14 (1969) 122-130.

Nebuchadnezzar III

*Theophilus G. Pinches, "A new fragment of the History of Nebuchadnezzer III," *SBAP* 1 (1878-79) 12-14.

*Theophilus G. Pinches, "A New Fragment of the History of Nebuchadnezzer III," *SBAT* 7 (1880-82) 210-225.

*Arno Poebel, "The Duration of the Reign of Smerdis, the Magian, and the Reigns of Nebuchadnezzar III and Nebuchadnezzar IV," *AJSL* 56 (1939) 121-145.

Nebuchadnezzar IV

*Arno Poebel, "The Duration of the Reign of Smerdis, the Magian, and the Reigns of Nebuchadnezzar III and Nebuchadnezzar IV," *AJSL* 56 (1939) 121-145.

Necho

Anonymous, "Pharaoh Necho," *BH* 5 (1969) 81.

Necho

Anonymous,   "Pharaoh   Necho,"   *BH*   5   (1969)   81.

Necho II

L. E. Binns, "The Syrian Campaign of Necho II," *JTS* 18 (1916-17) 36-47.

Nectanebus

B. E. Perry, "The Egyptian Legend of Nectanebus," *TAPA* 97 (1966) 327-333.

Mahmud Abd el-Razik, "Study on Nectanebo Ist in Luxor Temple and Karnak," *MDIÄA* 23 (1968) 156-159.

Neferkerē'

*Giuseppe Botti, "Who succeeded Ramesses IX—Neferkerē'?" *JEA* 14 (1928) 48-51.

Cyril Aldred, "A Statue of King Neferkerē' Ramesses IX," *JEA* 41 (1955) 3-8.

Nefer-Sma-Āa

M. A. Murray, "Statue of Nefer-Sma-Āa," *AEE* 4 (1917) 146-148.

Neferurē'

K. A. Kitchen, "A Long-lost Portrait of Princess Neferurē' from Deir El-Baḥri," *JEA* 49 (1963) 38-40.

Nekht

Percy E. Newberry, "Egyptian Historical Notes. I," *SBAP* 35 (1913) 156-158. [4. An Official of the Royal Barge of Amenhetep III, pp. 157-158 *(Nekht)*]

Neotera

*Arthur Darby Nock, "Neotera, queen or goddess?" *Aeg* 33 (1953) 283-296.

Nes-Ames

*E. A. Wallis Budge, "The Mummy and Coffin of Nes-Ames, Prophet of Ames and Chonsu," *SBAP* 8 (1885-86) 106-108.

Nesnebneteru

Rosalind Moss, "The Statue of an Ambassador to Ethiopia at Kiev," *Kush* 8 (1959) 269-271. *[Nesnebneteru]*

ʿnḫ-n.ś-Ppy

Henry George Fischer, "A Daughter of the Overlords of Upper Egypt in the First Intermediate Period," *JAOS* 76 (1956) 99-110. *[ʿnḫ-n.ś-Ppy]*

Nicosthenes

*Stephen Bleeker Luce, "Nicosthenes: His Activity and Affiliations," *AJA* 29 (1925) 38-52.

Nitocris

Percy E. Newberry, "Queen Nitocris of the Sixth Dynasty," *JEA* 29 (1943) 51-54.

Hildegard Lewy, "Nitokris-Naqîʾa," *JNES* 11 (1952) 264-286.

*Livio C. Stecchini, "Rhodopis," *AJA* 59 (1955) 177. *[Rhodopis of Naucratis - Nitocris]*

H. S. K. Bakry, "Nitōcris the God's Wife," *ASAE* 59 (1966) 9-13.

Nub-χās

A. Wiedemann, "On a Relative of Queen Nub-χās," *SBAP* 9 (1886-87) 190-193.

Nyneter

*W. K. Simpson, "A Statuette of Nyneter," *JEA* 42 (1956) 45-49.

Ny-Swtḥ

Hans Goedicke, "The Pharaoh *Ny-Swtḥ*," *ZÄS* 81 (1956) 18-24.

O

Oenanthe

*P.   Maas,   "Oenanthe's   Husbands,"   *JEA*   31   (1945)   74.
[Agathocles and Theogenes]

Oltos

Franklin   P.   Johnson,   "Oltos,"   *AJA*   42   (1938)   124.

Onias III

*M. Stern, "The Death of Onias III," *Zion* 25 (1960) #1, I.

Orontids

Cyril Toumanoff, "A Note on the Orontids," *Muséon* 72 (1959) 1-36.

P

Pa-Ramessu

*R. Engelbach, "The Sarcophagus of Pa-Ramessu from Gurob. Was He
the Heir of Seti I?" *AEE* 7 (1922) 9-13. (Note by [W. M.]
F[linders] P[etrie], p. 13)

Parmenio

*C. A. Robinson Jr., "Alexander the Great and Parmenio," *AJA* 49
(1945) 422-424.

Paser

*Percy E. Newberry, "Extracts from my Notebooks (II).," *SBAP* 22 (1900) 59-66. [8. The Vezîr Paser, pp. 62-63; 11. An Ushabti Figure of Paser, Mayor of Thebes, pp. 64-65]

Pedeamūn-nebnesuttaui

*H. S. K. Bakry, "A Statue of Pedeamūn-nebnesuttaui," *ASAE* 60 (1968) 15-25.

Pedeēset

*Georg Steindorff, "The Statuette of an Egyptian Commissioner in Syria," *JEA* 25 (1939) 30-33. *[Pedeēset]*

Pedubast

Alan R. Schulman, "A Problem of Pedubasts," *JARCE* 5 (1966) 33-41.

Peisistratus

Charles Seltman, "Peisistratus of Athens," *HT* 5 (1955) 438-445.

Charles Seltman, "Peisistratus: II," *HT* 5 (1955) 507-515.

Pekersala

A. Wiedemann, "The Queen Pekersala, of the beginning of the Saitic period," *SBAP* 8 (1885-86) 31-35.

Pelops

*T. B. Mitford, "Ptolemy son of Pelops," *JEA* 46 (1960) 109-111.

Pepi (Pepy)

R. Engelbach, "Statuette of Pepy from Saqqâra," *AEE* 17 (1932) 13.

*Hans Goedicke, "An Approximate Date for the Harem Investigation under Pepy I," *JAOS* 74 (1954) 88-89.

Pepi (Pepy) concluded

Hans Goedicke, "The Abydene Marriage of Pepi I," *JAOS* 75 (1955) 180-183.

Hans Goedicke, "The Alleged Military Campaign in Southern Palestine in the Reign of Pepi I (VIth Dynasty)," *RDSO* 38 (1963) 187-197.

Pericles

*A. E. Raubitschek, "The Peace Policy of Perikles," *AJA* 69 (1965) 174.

Stephen Usher, "Architects of the Athenian Empire II: Pericles," *HT* 17 (1967) 402-408.

Philadelphos

Dorothy Burr Thompson, "A Portrait of Arsinoe Philadelphos," *AJA* 59 (1955) 199-206.

Pheidon

Donald W. Bradeen, "The Lelantine War and Pheidon of Argos," *TAPA* 78 (1947) 223-241.

Philetairos

*Karl Lehmann-Hartleben, "Some Ancient Portraits," *AJA* 46 (1942) 198-216. [I. Philetairos, pp. 198-204]

Piankhi

*Henry Howorth, "Was Piankhi a Synonym for Sabako?" *BOR* 2 (1887-88) 233-236.

Pontius Pilate

*E. Bammel, "Syrian Coinage and Pilate," *JJS* 2 (1950-51) 108-110.

Pontius Pilate concluded

E. Mary Smallwood, "The Date of the Dismissal of Pontius Pilate from Judea," *JJS* 5 (1954) 12-21.

S. G. F. Brandon, "Pontius Pilate in History and Legend," *HT* 18 (1968) 523-530.

Pisistratus

M. V. Skrzhinskaya, "The Oral Tradition about Pisistratus," *VDI* (1969) #4, 95-96.

Plato

Anonymous, "Plato," *CRB* 24 (1859) 187-213.

Anonymous, "Plato and his Times," *WR* 114 (1880) 389-419. *(Review)*

Anonymous, "Plato as a Reformer," *WR* 115 (1881) 28-70 *(Review)*

F. C. Schiller, "Plato and his Predecessors," *QRL* 204 (1906) 62-88. *(Review)*

Pliny

Peter Green, "Two Gentlemen of Rome: The Elder and the Younger Pliny," *HT* 6 (1956) 266-273.

Pollio

Louis H. Feldman, "Asinius Pollio and His Jewish Interests," *TAPA* 84 (1953) 73-80.

Polybius

†Anonymous, "Polybius and his Times," *QRL* 148 (1879) 186-222. *(Review)*

S[tephen] Usher, " Polybius," *HT* 13 (1963) 267-274.

Polykates

Mary E. White, "The Duration of the Samian Tyranny," *AJA* 55 (1951) 151. */Polykates/*

Pompeius

H. A. Ormerod, "The Distribution of Pompeius' Forces in the Campaign of 67 B.C.," *AAA* 10 (1923) 46-51.

Pompey

*Kurt von Fritz, "Pompey's Policy before and after the Outbreak of the Civil War of 49 B.C.," *TAPA* 73 (1942) 145-180.

Psammetic-Neith

†Joseph Offord, "Portrait Statue of Psammetic-Neith," *SBAP* 21 (1899) 80.

Psammetikh II (Psammētichus II)

*Arthur E. P. Weigall, "A Report on some Objects recently found at Sebakh and other Diggings," *ASAE* 8 (1907) 39-50. [Stele of Psammetikh II from Shellal, pp. 39-42]

*H. S. K. Bakry, "Psammētichus II and his Newly-Found Stela at Shellâl," *OA* 6 (1967) 225-244.

Psusennes II

*J. W. Jack, "Recent Biblical Archaeology," *ET* 51 (1939-40) 420-423. [Mummy of Solomon's Father-in-Law (Psusennes II), p. 423]

Ptah-Hotep

Hiram H. Rice, "Ptah-Hotep. The Radical of Ancient Egypt," *OC* 6 (1892) 3033-3035.

Ptahmose

Alan H. Gardiner, "A statuette of the High Priest of Memphis, Ptahmose," *ZÄS* 43 (1906) 55-59.

Ptah-neferu

*Percy E. Newberry, "Extracts from my Notebooks. VII.," *SBAP* 25 (1903) 357-362. [52. Princess Ptah-neferu, p. 359]

Ptolemaeus Apion

*Otto [J.] Brendel, "A Diademed Roman?" *AJA* 70 (1966) 184. *[Ptolemaeus Apion(?)]*

*Otto J. Brendel, "A Diademed Roman? *For Richard Krautheimer,*" *AJA* 71 (1967) 407-409. *[Ptolemaeus Apion(?)]*

Ptolemy(s)

[W. M. Flinders Petrie], "The Portraits," *AEE* 3 (1916) 95-96. *[The Ptolemys]*

*T. C. Skeat, "The Reigns of the Ptolemies. With Tables for Converting Egyptian Dates to the Julian System," *Miz* 6 (1937) 7-40.

Dorothy B. Thompson, "Faience Portraits of Ptolemaic Kings," *AJA* 69 (1965) 177.

*Oswyn Murray, "Aristeas and Ptolemaic Kingship," *JTS, N.S.,* 18 (1967) 337-371.

Ptolemy I

M. A. Murray, "Sculpture of Ptolemy I," *AEE* 4 (1917) 167-169.

*T. B. Mitford, "Ptolemy son of Pelops," *JEA* 46 (1960) 109-111.

Ptolemy II

W. W. Tarn, "Ptolemy II," *JEA* 14 (1928) 246-260.

*W. W. Tarn, "Ptolemy II and Arabia," *JEA* 15 (1929) 9-25.

P[hilippus] M[iller], "A Granite Relief of Ptolemy II," *UMB* 7 (1937-39) #1, 25-26.

*Frank J. Frost, "A Friend of Ptolemy at Halicarnassus," *AJA* 71 (1967) 187. *[Ptolemy II]*

Ptolemy Epiphanes (Ptolemy V)

*F. W. Walbank, "The Accession of Ptolemy Epiphanes: A Problem in Chronology," *JEA* 22 (1936) 20-34.

*Charles F. Nims, "Notes on University of Michigan Demotic Papyri from Philadelphia," *JEA* 24 (1938) 73-82. [1. The Chronology of the Early Years of Ptolemy Epiphanes, pp. 73-74]

Ptolemy VI

*Brunilde Sismondo Ridgway, "A Head of Ptolemy VI in Providence," *AJA* 72 (1968) 171.

Ptolemy Eupator

Joseph Offord, "Aegyptiaca. Ptolemy Eupator, King of Egypt," *AAOJ* 34 (1912) 282-283.

Pudu-ḥepa

*I. J. Gelb, "Queen Pudu-ḥepa," *AJA* 41 (1937) 289-290.

Pul (See also: Tiglath-Pileser III)

Francis Brown, "Pul, King of Assyria," *PR* 3 (1882) 400-401.

*Joseph Horner, "Pul, Jereb, Tiglath-pileser — A Chronologico-Historical Study," *MR* 76 (1894) 928-935.

Pul concluded

*Robert W. Rogers, "'Pul, Jareb, Tiglath-pileser'," *MR* 77 (1895) 129-130.

*Joseph Horner, "Pul, Jareb, Tiglath, and the Corrections," *MR* 77 (1895) 298-300.

*Robert W. Rogers, "Pul, Jareb, Tiglath-pileser III — A Reply," *MR* 77 (1895) 301-302.

Py

Richard A. Parker, "King *Py,* a Historical Problem," *ZÄS* 93 (1966) 111-114.

Pythagoras

Charles Seltman, "Pythagaros: Artist,   Scholar,   Statesman, Philosopher," *HT* 6 (1956) 522-527, 592-597. [I. Pythagoras in Samos; II. Pythagoras in Italy]

R

Ra-*aa-peh-ti*

*John Campbell, "The Pharaoh of Joseph," *SBAP* 3 (1880-81) 87. /Ra-*aa-peh-ti*/

Rāhotep

P. le Page Renouf, "An Ambassador Royal of Rameses the Great," *SBAP* 14 (1891-92) 163-165. /Rāhotep/

[W. M. Flinders Petrie], "The Portraits," *AEE* 3 (1916) 48. /Prince Rahotep/

Ramessenakht

*Jaroslav Černý, "Two King's Sons of Kush of the Twentieth Dynasty," *Kush* 7 (1959) 71-75. /Ramessenakht/

Ramesses I

Anonymous, "A Head of King Ramesses I from his Temple at Abydos," *JEA* 10 (1924) 79.

Ramesses II

*Henry George Tomkins, "The Campaign of Rameses II in his fifth year against Kadesh on the Orontes," *SBAT* 7 (1880-82) 390-406.

†H[enry] G[eorge] Tomkins, "The Campaign of Rameses II in his fifth year against Kadesh on the Orontes," *SBAP* 4 (1881-82) 6-7. (Remarks by William Wright, pp. 8-9)

*C[laude] R. Conder, "Conquests of Rameses in Galilee," *PEFQS* 22 (1890) 310.

*James Henry Breasted, "Ramses II and the Princes in the Karnak Reliefs of Seti I," *ZÄS* 37 (1899) 130-139.

George W. Gilmore, "The Pharaoh of the Oppression," *HR* 87 (1924) 139. *[Rameses II]*

Philippus Miller, "A Statue of Ramesses II in the University Museum, Philadelphia," *JEA* 25 (1939) 1-7.

Mostafa El-Amir, "A statue of Ramesses II," *ASAE* 42 (1943) 359-363.

*M. B. Rowton, "Manetho's Date for Ramesses II," *JEA* 34 (1948) 57-73. (With Appendix by Professor H. Kees, pp. 73-74)

*K[enneth] A. Kitchen, "Some New Light on the Asiatic Wars of Ramesses II," *JEA* 50 (1964) 47-70.

*G. A. Gaballa and K[enneth] A. Kitchen, "Ramesside Varia I," *CdÉ* 43 (1968) 259-270. [1. The Ancestry of Ramesses II, pp. 259-263]

*K[enneth] A. Kitchen and G. A. Gaballa, "Ramesside Varia II," *ZÄS* 96 (1969-70) 14-28. [1. The Second Hittite Marriage of Ramesses II, pp. 14-18]

Ramesses III

*Hans Goedicke, "Was Magic used in the Harem Conspiracy against Ramesses III?" *JEA* 49 (1963) 71-92.

*William F. Edgerton, "The Strikes in Ramses III's Twenty-ninth Year," *JNES* 10 (1951) 137-145.

Elizabeth Thomas, "Ramesses III: notes and queries," *JEA* 45 (1959) 101-102.

Ramesses VI

*Keith C. Seele, "Ramesses VI and the Medinat Habu Procession of the Princes," *JNES* 19 (1960) 184-204.

Ramesses IX

*Giuseppe Botti, "Who succeeded Ramesses IX — Neferkerē'?" *JEA* 14 (1928) 48-51.

Ramesses X

Richard A. Parker, "The Length of Reign of Ramses X," *RÉg* 11 (1957) 163-164.

Ramose

*Cyril Aldred, "Two Theban Notables During the Later Reign of Amenophis III," *JNES* 18 (1959) 113-120. [II. The Southern Vizier Ramose, pp. 116-120]

Ra-Nafer

*Anonymous, "Mummy of Ra-Nafer," *RP* 9 (1910) 226.

[W. M. Flinders Petrie], "The Portraits," *AEE* 1 (1914) 192. *[Ranefer]*

Renï

*Percy E. Newberry, "Extracts from my Notebooks V.," *SBAP* 24 (1902) 244-252. [28. A Statuette of Renï, Mayor of El Kab, pp. 244-25]

Rhodopis

*Livio C. Stecchini, "Rhodopis," *AJA* 59 (1955) 177. *[Rhodopis of Naucratis = Nitocris]*

Rîm-Sin

W. T. Pilter, "The Reign of 'Rîm-Sin' and the Conquest of Isin," *SBAP* 34 (1912) 6-16, 41-51.

*S[tephen] Langdon, "I. Rim-Sin a Contemporary of Samsuiluna," *SBAP* 40 (1918) 131-133.

Rynty

*Geoffrey T. Martin, "A Ruler of Byblos of the Second Intermediate Period," *Bery* 18 (1969) 81-83. *[Rynty]*

S

Sabako

*Henry Howorth, "Was Piankhi a Synonym for Sabako?" *BOR* 2 (1887-88) 233-236.

Salome

*Solomon Zeitlin, "Queen Salome and King Jannaeus Alexander," *JQR, N.S.,* 51 (1960-61) 1-33.

Samou

*G. Legrain, "The King Samou or Seshemou and the Enclosures of El-Kab," *SBAP* 27 (1905) 106-111.

Samsu-iluna

*C. H. W. Johns, "The First Year of Samsu-iluna," *SBAP* 30 (1908) 70-71.

*S[tephen] Langdon, "I. Rim-Sin a Contemporary of Samsuiluna," *SBAP* 40 (1918) 131-133.

Sanduarri

H. F. Lutz, "Sanduarri, king of Kundi and Sizû," *JAOS* 42 (1922) 201-202.

Sankhere

*Alan H. Gardiner, "The Name of King Sankhere," *SBAP* 26 (1904) 75-76. *[Mentuhotep; Antef; (?)]*

Sapor I

*Arthur Darby Nock, "Sapor I and the Apollo of Bryaxis," *AJA* 66 (1962) 307-310. *[Alexander(?)]*

Sargon

E. H., "Chronology of the Reigns of Sargon and Sennacherib," *JSL, 2nd Ser.,* 6 (1854) 393-410.

*J. W. Bosanquet, "Chronology of the Reigns of Tiglath Pileser, Sargon, Shalmanezer, and Sennacherib, in connexion with the Phenomenon seen on the Dial of Ahaz," *JRAS* (1855) 277-296.

*J. W. Bosanquet, "Synchronous History of the Reigns of Tiglath-Pileser.. and .. Azariah. Shalmanezer .. and .. Jotham. Sargon .. and .. Ahaz. Sennecherib .. and .. Hezekiah," *SBAT* 3 (1874) 1-82.

Sargon cont.

John P. Peters, "The Date of Sargon of Akkad," *AJSL* 2 (1885-86) 173-174.

*†John P. Peters, "Date of Naram-Sin, Son of Sargon," *SBAP* 8 (1885-86) 142.

*†Theo. G. Pinches, "Assyriological Notes," *SBAP* 8 (1885-86) 240-245. [The Name of Sargon of Agadé, pp. 242-244]

*A. H. Sayce, "Was Jareb the Original Name of Sargon?" *BOR* 2 (1887-88) 18-22.

W. St. C[had] Boscawen, "Shen-nung, and Sargon," *BOR* 2 (1887-88) 208-209.

*Joseph Horner, "Hezekiah, Sargon, and Sennecherib— A Chronological Study," *MR* 75 (1893) 74-89.

*L. W. King, "Sargon I, King of Kish, and Shar-Gani-sharri, King of Akkad," *SBAP* 30 (1908) 238-242.

Theophilus G. Pinches, "Sargon of Assyria in the Lake Region of Van and Urmia, 714 B.C.," *ET* 24 (1912-13) 398-401, 460-464.

A. H. Sayce, "The Northern Campaigns of Sargon of Akkad," *SBAP* 38 (1916) 201.

W[illiam] F[oxwell] Albright, "The Epic of the King of Battle: Sargon of Akkad in Cappadocia," *JSOR* 7 (1923) 1-20.

*W[illiam] F[oxwell] Albright, "A Babylonian Geographical Treatise on Sargon of Akkad's Empire," *JAOS* 45 (1925) 193-245.

*Hans G. Güterbock, "Sargon of Akkad Mentioned by Ḫattušili I of Hatti," *JCS* 18 (1964) 1-6.

Anonymous, "A New Stele of The Assyrian King Sargon: Villagers Uncover Historic Relief," *BH* 3 (1967) #2, 9.

Sargon II

W. St. C[had] Boscawen, "Campaign of Sargon II. (B.C. 712) against Judea," *BOR* 4 (1889-90) 118-120.

T[heophilus] G. Pinches, "Sargon's Eighth Campaign," *JRAS* (1913) 612-613.

W[illiam] F[oxwell] Albright, "The Eighth Campaign of Sargon," *JAOS* 36 (1916) 226-232.

Horace Abram Rigg Jr., "Sargon's 'Eighth Military Campaign'," *JAOS* 62 (1942) 130-138.

Edwin M. Wright, "The Eighth Campaign of Sargon II of Assyria (714 B.C.)," *JNES* 2 (1943) 173-186.

*H[yim] Tadmor, "Sargon's Campaigns against Ashdod," *BIES* 18 (1953-54) #3/4, III-IV.

H[yim] Tadmor, "The 'Sin of Sargon'," *EI* 5 (1958) 93*.

Hyim Tadmor, "The Campagins of Sargon II of Assur: A Chronological-Historical Study," *JCS* 12 (1958) 22-40, 77-100.

*G. L. Ginsberg, "Reflexes of Sargon in Isaiah after 715 B.C.E.," *JAOS* 88 (1968) 47-53.

*Michael Ford, "The Contradictory Records of Sargon II of Assyria and the Meaning of *palû*," *JCS* 22 (1968-69) 83-84.

Sargon-Yareb

A. Neubauer, "Sargon-Yareb," *ZA* 3 (1888) 103.

Sat-aah

*Percy E. Newberry, "Extracts from my Notebooks VI.," *SBAP* 25 (1903) 357-362. [48. Sat-aah, Queen of Thotmes III, p. 357]

Sat-aah concluded

*Percy E. Newberry, "Egyptian Historical Notes. III," *SBAP* 36 (1914) 168-174. [11. A Pebble inscribed with the name of the

p. 168]

Sebek-hetep III

*Percy E. Newberry, "Extracts from my Notebooks VII.," *SBAP* 25 (1903) 357-362. [49. The Queen of Kha-nefer-Ra Sebek-hetep III, p. 358]

*Percy E. Newberry, "Extracts from my Notebooks VIII.," *SBAP* 27 (1905) 101-105. [59. The Queen of Sebekhetep III (*Nebt-ant*), pp. 101-102]

Sebekḥotpe

*R. Englebach, "Statuette-Group from Kîmân Faris, of Sebekḥotpe and his womenfolk," *ASAE* 35 (1935) 203-205.

*P[ercy] E. Newberry, "Co-regencies of Ammenemes III, IV, and Sebknofru," *JEA* 29 (1943) 74-75.

Sehetepibre Pedubastis

*Labib Habachi, "Three Monuments of the Unknown King Sehetepibre Pedubastis," *ZÄS* 93 (1966) 69-74.

Sekhemka(-Ra[?])

*Percy E. Newberry, "Extracts from my Notebooks (IV.)," *SBAP* 23 (1901) 218-224. [26. Khnems, Vezîr of Sekhem-ka-Ra, pp. 222-223]

*T. G. H. James, "The Northampton Statue of Sekhemka," *JEA* 49 (1963) 5-12.

Semempses

C. W. Goodwin, "On the King Semempses of the 1st Dynasty," *ZÄS* 5 (1867) 34-36.

*C. W. Goodwin, "King Semempses and King Ases-Kaf," *ZÄS* 5 (1867) 82-85.

Semeramis

*A. H. Sayce, "Notes on Assyrian and Egyptian History. An Aramaic Ostracon," *SBAP* 30 (1908) 13-19. [II. Semeramis = Šammu-ramat, p. 16]

*Stephanie Page, "Adad-nirair III and Semiramis: The Stelae of Saba'a and Rimah," *Or, N.S.,* 38 (1969) 457-458.

Semti

H. R. Hall, "King Semti," *SBAP* 33 (1911) 15-18.

F. Legge, "Mr. Hall's 'King Semti'," *SBAP* 33 (1911) 68-71.

H. R. Hall, "The Question of King Semti," *SBAP* 33 (1911) 127.

Senb-hena-es

*Percy E. Newberry, "Extracts from my Notebooks V.," *SBAP* 24 (1902) 244-252. [39. Queen Senb-hena-es, pp. 251-252]

Senïŷ

*Percy E. Newberry, "Extracts from my Notebooks (IV).," *SBAP* 23 (1901) 218-224. [27. The Vezîr Senïŷ, pp. 223-224]

Sen-mut

Percy E. Newberry, "Extracts from my Notebooks (II).," *SBAP* 22 (1900) 59-66. [9. Hapshepsut's Favourite Minister and Architect, Sen-mut, p. 63]

Sen-mut concluded

Alan R. Schulman, "Some Remarks on the Alleged 'Fall' of Senmūt," *JARCE* 8 (1969-70) 29-48.

Sen-nefer

Percy E. Newberry, "Extracts from my Notebooks (II).," *SBAP* 22 (1900) 59-66. [5. Sen-nefer, Mayor of Thebes under Amenhetep II, pp. 59-61]

Percy E. Newberry, "Extracts from my Notebooks (II).," *SBAP* 22 (1900) 59-66. [6. Sen-nefer, Treasurer of Hatshepsut and Thothmes III, pp. 61-62]

Sennacherib

E. H., "Chronology of the Reigns of Sargon and Sennacherib," *JSL, 2nd Ser.,* 6 (1854) 393-410.

*J. W. Bosanquet, "Chronology of the Reigns of Tiglath Pileser, Sargon, Shalmanezer, and Sennacherib, in connexion with the Phenomenon seen on the Dial of Ahaz," *JRAS* (1855) 277-296.

*George Smith, "Assyrian History.   Sennacherib," *ZÄS* 8 (1870) 34-40.

*J. W. Bosanquet, "Synchronous History of the Reigns of Tiglath-Pileser. . and . . Azariah. Shalmanezer . . and . . Jotham. Sargon . . and . . Ahaz. Sennacherib . . and . . Hezekiah," *SBAT* 3 (1874) 1-82.

*Cyrus Adler, "On the death of Sennacherib and the accession of Esarhaddon," *JAOS* 13 (1889) ccxxxv-ccxxxviii.

*Joseph Horner, "Hezekiah, Sargon, and Sennacherib— A Chronological Study," *MR* 75 (1893) 74-89.

*William Hayes Ward, "Light on Scriptural Texts from Recent Discoveries.   Sennacherib and the Destruction of Nineveh," *HR* 30 (1895) 505-506.

Sennacherib cont.

*C. H. W. Johns, "Sennacherib's Murder," *ET* 7 (1895-96) 238-239.

J. A. Selbie, "The Murderer(s) of Sennacherib," *ET* 9 (1897-98) 363-364

J. F. McCurdy, "Light on Scriptural Texts from Recent Discoveries. Bible Personages. — III. Sennacherib," *HR* 36 (1898) 123-126, 314-317.

*C. H. W. Johns, "The Biblical Account of Sennacherib's Murder," *SBAP* 21 (1899) 174-175.

*J. V. Prášek, "Sennacherib's Second Expedition to the West, and the Siege of Jerusalem," *ET* 12 (1900-01) 225-229, 405-427.

*J. V. Prášek, "Sennacherib's Second Expedition to the West, and the Date of His Siege of Jerusalem," *ET* 13 (1901-02) 326-328.

Stephen Langdon, "Evidence for an Advance on Egypt by Sennacherib in the Campaign of 701-700 B.C.," *JAOS* 24 (1903) 265-274.

Willis J. Beecher, "A Few Notes on the Sennacherib Invasion," *CFL, 3rd Ser.,* 2 (1905) 458-461.

*G. A. Smith, "Sennacherib and Jerusalem," *Exp, 6th Ser.,* 12 (1905) 215-233.

Kemper Fullerton, "The Invasion of Sennacherib," *BS* 63 (1906) 577-634.

*Theophilus G. Pinches, "Sennacherib's Campaigns on the North-West and his Work at Nineveh," *JRAS* (1910) 387-411.

*I. G. Matthews, "Sennacherib's Invasion and Its Religious Significance," *BW* 37 (1911) 115-119.

G. H. Richardson, "The Most Important Event in Ancient History," *BW* 44 (1914) 45-48. *[Sennacherib]*

*Joseph Offord, "Archaeological Notes on Jewish Antiquities. XLIII. *The Assassination of Sennacherib*," *PEFQS* 50 (1918) 88-90.

Sennacherib concluded

Charles Boutflower, "Sennacherib's Invasion of Judah, *701* B.C.," *JTVI* 60 (1928) 194-213, 219-220. [(Discussion, pp. 214-218) (Communication by W. R. Rowlatt Jones, pp. 218-219)]

R. P. Dougherty, "Sennacherib and the Walled Cities of Judah," *JBL* 49 (1930) 160-171.

Emil G. Kraeling, "The Death of Sennacherib," *JAOS* 53 (1933) 335-346.

E. B. W. Chappelow, "The Assassination of Sennacherib," *JTVI* 75 (1943) 116-124.

*David Diringer, "Sennacherib's Attack on Lachish: New Epigraphical Evidence," *VT* 1 (1951) 134-136.

*Siegfried H. Horn, "Did Sennacherib Campaign Once or Twice Against Hezekiah?" *AUSS* 4 (1966) 1-28.

Sennemut

*H. R. Hall, "The Statues of Sennemut and Menkheperrē'senb in the British Museum," *JEA* 14 (1928) 1-2.

*William C. Hayes, "Varia from the Time of Hatshepsut," *MDIÄA* 15 (1957) 78-90. [4. The Naville Statuette of Sennemut, pp. 88-89]

Senusert I

*[W. M. Flinders Petrie], "The Portraits," *AEE* 1 (1914) 144. [Senusert I]

*[W. M. Flinders Petrie], "The Portraits," *AEE* 2 (1915) 192. [Senusert I]

Senusert II

*[W. M. Flinders Petrie], "The Portraits," *AEE* 1 (1914) 144. [Senusert II]

Senusert III

R. Engelbach and Ismail Shehab, "A Portrait Head of Senuset III, from Karnak," *AEE* 14 (1929) 17.

Seshemou

*G. Legrain, "The King Samou or Seshemou and the Enclosures of El-Kab," *SBAP* 27 (1905) 106-111.

Sesostris

*Anonymous, "Who was Sesostris?" *MMBR* 23 (1807) 560-562.

*G. A. Wainwright, "The Attempted Sacrifice of Sesostris," *JEA* 27 (1941) 138-143.

Sesostris III

A. M. Blackman, "An Indirect Reference to Sesostris III's Syrian Campaign in the Tomb-Chapel of *Dḥwty-ḥtp* at El-Bersheh," *JEA* 2 (1915) 13-14.

H. R. Hall, "A Portrait-Statuette of Sesostris III," *JEA* 15 (1929) 154.

Set

Percy E. Newberry, "The Set Rebellion of the IInd Dynasty," *AEE* 7 (1922) 40-46.

Sethos I

R. O. Faulkner, "The Wars of Sethos I," *JEA* 33 (1947) 34-39.

Sethos II

*G. A. Gaballa and K[enneth] A. Kitchen, "Ramesside Varia I," *CdÉ* 43 (1968) 259-270. [3. Fragment of a Stela of Sethos II, pp. 269-270]

Seti I

*R. Engelbach, "The Sarcophagus of Pa-Ramessu from Gurob. Was He the Heir of Seti I?" *AEE* 7 (1922) 9-13. (Note by [W. M.] F[linders] P[etrie], p. 13)

Severus Alexander

*Harald Ingholt, "A Colossal Head from Memphis, Severan or Augustan?" *JARCE* 2 (1963) 125-145. [Severus Alexander (?)]

*Harald Ingholt, "Colossal Head in Boston, Severan or Augustan?" *AJA* 67 (1963) 213. [Severus Alexander (?)]

Shabaka

R. Engelbach, "A Head of King Shabaka," *ASAE* 29 (1929) 15-18.

Shalmaneser II

*Joseph Horner, "The Chronology of Israel and Assyria in the Reign of Shalmaneser II," *MR* 71 (1889) 711-724.

*Robert W. Rogers, "Shalmaneser," *ET* 23 (1911-12) 237-238. *[Shalmaneser II]*

Shalmaneser III

*J. W. Bosanquet, "Chronology of the Reigns of Tiglath Pileser, Sargon, Shalmanezer, and Sennacherib, in connexion with the Phenomenon seen on the Dial of Ahaz," *JRAS* (1855) 277-296.

*J. W. Bosanquet, "Synchronous History of the Reigns of Tiglath-Pileser.. and .. Azariah. Shalmanezer .. and .. Jotham. Sargon .. and .. Ahaz. Sennacherib .. and .. Hezekiah," *SBAT* 3 (1874) 1-82.

*Robert W. Rogers, "Shalmaneser," *ET* 23 (1911-12) 237-238. *[Shalmaneser III]*

A. T. Olmstead, "Shalmaneser III and the Establishment of the Assyrian Power," *JAOS* 41 (1921) 345-382.

Shalmaneser III concluded

*J. V. Kinnier Wilson, "The Kurba'il Statue of Shalmaneser III," *Iraq* 24 (1962) 90-115.

Šamši-Adad

Jack M. Sasson, "A King of Early Assyria: Shamsi-Adad," *HT* 18 (1968) 794-801.

*Hildegard Lewy, "The Synchronism Assyria—Ešnunna—Babylon," *WO* 2 (1954-59) 438-453. [1. Šamši-Adad and Daduša, pp. 438-445]

Šamaš-šum-ukîn

*Christopher Johnston, "Šamaš-šum-ukîn the eldest son of Esarhaddon," *JAOS* 25 (1904) 79-83.

*S[ami S.] Ahmed, "Ashurbanipal and Shamash-shum-ukin During Esarhaddon's Reign," *Abr-N* 6 (1965-66) 53-62.

Sami S. Ahmed, "The Causes of Shamash-shum-ukin's uprising 652-651 B.C.," *ZAW* 79 (1967) 1-13.

Shar-Gani-sharri

*L. W. King, "Sargon I, King of Kish, and Shar-Gani-sharri, King of Akkad," *SBAP* 30 (1908) 238-242.

Sharu

A. H. Sayce, "A New Egyptian King; the predecessor of Kheops," *SBAP* 21 (1899) 108-110. *[Sharu]*

A. H. Sayce, "The Egyptian King Sharu," *SBAP* 26 (1904) 93.

Shashanq Heqa-Kheper-Re

Guy Brunton, "Some notes of the burial of Shashanq Heqa-Kheper-Re," *ASAE* 39 (1939) 541-547.

Shashu

*G. A. Wainwright, "Shekelesh or Shashu?" *JEA* 50 (1964) 40-46.

Sheba (Queen of)

William Hayes Ward, "Light on Scriptural Texts from Recent Discoveries. The Queen of Sheba," *HR* 27 (1894) 408-410.

[Paul Carus], "The Queen of Sheba According to the Tradition of Axum," *OC* 19 (1905) 31-34.

Edward Ullendorff, "The Queen of Sheba," *BJRL* 45 (1962-63) 486-504.

*Harold M. Parker Jr., "Solomon and the Queen of Sheba," *IR* 24 (1967) #3, 17-24.

*Anonymous, "Trade Routes, Fortresses and The Queen of Sheba. Interesting and Enlightening Background Material from Archaeological Research," *BH* 4 (1968) 45-49.

Shekelesh

*G. A. Wainwright, "Shekelesh or Shashu?" *JEA* 50 (1964) 40-46.

Sheshonq

*[W. M.] Flinders Petrie, "The Shishak Migration," *AEE* 13 (1928) 101-104. *[Sheshonq]*

Shishak I

F. W. Read, "Notes and Queries. *Shishak I and Palestine History*," *PEFQS* 48 (1916) 211.

*[W. M.] Flinders Petrie, "The Shishak Migration," *AEE* 13 (1928) 101-104. *[Sheshonq]*

B. Mazar (Maisler), "The campaign of Pharaoh Shiskhak to Palestine," *VTS* 4 (1957) 57-66.

Shoshenk

A. M. Blackman, "The Stela of Shoshenk, Great Chief of the Meshwesh," *JEA* 27 (1941) 83-95.

Shulgi (of Ur)

*Samuel Noah Kramer, "Shulgi of Ur: A Royal Hymn and Divine Blessing," *JQR, 75th* (1967) 369-380.

Samuel Noah Kramer, "Shulgi of Ur: Portrait of the Ideal King," *AJA* 70 (1966) 192.

Siamon

*Siegried H. Horn, "Who was Solomon's Father-in Law?" *BRes* 12 (1967) 3-17. *[Siamon]*

Si-Mut

*Cyril Aldred, "Two Theban Notables During the Later Reign of Amenophis III," *JNES* 18 (1959) 113-120. [I. The Fourth Prophet of Amun, Si-Mut, pp. 113-116]

Sinkashid

Saadi al-Ruweshdi, "The King Sinkashid," *Sumer* 22 (1966) 107-110.

Sinmubaliṭ

*Stephen Langdon, "The Derivation of *šabattu* and other notes," *ZDMG* 62 (1908) 29-32. [*Bēl-Kabi* contemporary of *Sinmubaliṭ*, pp. 30-31]

Sinsariskun

*L. W. King, "Sinsariskun and his rule in Babylon," *ZA* 9 (1884-85) 396-440.

Siptaḥ

*Alan [H.] Gardiner, "Only One King Siptaḥ and Twosre not His Wife," *JEA* 44 (1958) 12-22.

*J. von Beckerath, "Queen Twosre as Guardian of Siptaḥ," *JEA* 48 (1962) 70-74.

Cyril Aldred, "The Parentage of King Siptaḥ," *JEA* 49 (1963) 41-48.

Sipylos

*R. W. Hutchison, "Sipylos and *S-P-L-L*," *ASAE* 41 (1942) 159-160. *[Šuppiluliuma]*

Sisera

*A. H. Sayce, "Recent Biblical Archaeology. Note on the Name Sisera," *ET* 10 (1898-99) 203.

Smenkhkerê'

*D[ouglas] E. Derry, "Notes on the Skeleton hitherto believed to be that of King Akhenaten," *ASAE* 31 (1931) 115-119. *[Smenkhkerê']*

H. R. Hall, "A Portrait of Smenkhkerē'(?) and other Amarnah Fragments in the British Museum," *JEA* 17 (1931) 165.

Smenkhu-ptah

W. M. F[linders] P[etrie], "An Early Portrait," *AEE* 5 (1920) 18. *[Smenkhu-ptah]*

Smerdis

*Arno Poebel, "The Duration of the Reign of Smerdis, the Magian, and the Reigns of Nebuchadnezzer III and Nebuchadnezzar IV," *AJSL* 56 (1939) 121-145.

(Pseudo) Smerdis

*Leon Legrain, "Darius and Pseudo Smerdis. A Green Jade Relief
CBS. 14543," *MJ* 14 (1923) 200-202.

Snofru

*Battiscombe Gunn, "Notes on two Egyptian Kings," *JEA* 12 (1926)
250-253. [1. Concerning King Snefru, pp. 250-251]

Jaroslav Černý, "The True Form of the Name of King Snofru,"
RDSO 38 (1963) 89-92.

So

S. Yeivin, "Who was Šō' the King of Egypt?" *VT* 2 (1952) 164-168.

Hans Goedicke, "The End of 'So, King of Egypt'," *BASOR* #171 (1963)
64-66.

W[illaim] F[oxwell] Albright, "The Elimination of King 'So',"
BASOR #171 (1963) 66.

Sobkemḥēt

William K. Simpson, "Sobkemḥēt, A Vizier of Sesostris III," *JEA* 43
(1957) 26-29.

Sophocles

†Anonymous, "Sophocles," *QRL* 170 (1890) 415-442. *(Review)*

Herbert T. Warren, "Sophocles and Greek Genius," *QRL* 198 (1903)
307-335. *(Review)*

Strabo

William E. Gwatkin Jr., "The Father of Pompey the Great," *PAPA* 71
(1940) xxxvii-xxxviii. *[Strabo]*

Strabo concluded

*Lawrence Waddy, "Did Strabo Visit Athens?" *AJA* 67 (1963) 296-300.

Sulla

*Rhys Carpenter, "The 'Hellenistic Ruler' of the Terne Museum," *AJA* 31 (1927) 160-168. */Sulla/*

Rhys Carpenter, "The Identity of the Ruler," *AJA* 49 (1945) 353-357. */Sulla/*

Sumu-yamūtbāl

Albrecht Goetze, "Sumu-yamūtbāl, a Local Ruler of the Old-Babylonian Period," *JCS* 4 (1950) 65-72.

Šuppiluliuma

*R. W. Hutchison, "Sipylos and *S-P-L-L*," *ASAE* 41 (1942) 159-160. */Šuppiluliuma/*

Albrecht Goetze, "The Predecessors of Šuppiluliumaš of Ḫatti," *JAOS* 72 (1952) 67-72.

Suzub

C. P. Tiele, "Suzub the Babylonian, and Suzub the Chaldean, Kings of Babylon," *AJSL* 2 (1885-86) 218-220.

T

Ta-āath

*Margaret A. Murray, "The Coffin of Ta-āath in the Brassey Institute at Hastings," *SBAP* 30 (1908) 20-24.

Taharqa (Tirhaka)

*Samuel Birch, "Monuments of the Reign of Tirhaka," *SBAP* 2 (1879-80) 60. *(Taharqa)*

Richard A. Parker, "The Length of Reign of Taharqa," *Kush* 8 (1959) 267-269.

Ta-usert-em-suten-pa

*G. Elliot Smith, "An Account of the Mummy of a Priestess of Amen, supposed to be Ta-usert-em-suten-pa (With which is incorporated a detailed account of the wrappings by M. A. C. Mace and some archæological notes by M. Georges Daressy)," *ASAE* 7 (1906) 155-182.

*E. R. Ayrton, "The position of Tausert in the XIXth Dynasty," *SBAP* 28 (1906) 185-186.

Tany

W. K. Simpson, "The Hyksos Princess Tany," *CdE* 34 (1959) 233-239.

Tarḳû-timme

*Theo. G. Pinches, "The Name of the City and Country over which Tarḳû-timme Ruled," *SBAP* 7 (1884-85) 124-127.

Tarqumuwa

W[illiam] F[oxwell] Albright, "Tarqumuwa King of Mera," *AfO* 4 (1927) 137-138.

Tarzîa

Theo. G. Pinches, "Babylonian Notes. II. Tarzîa, 'king of Babylon and Countries'," *BOR* 1 (1886-87) 54-55.

Tattenai

A. T. Olmstead, "Tattenai, Governor of 'Across the River'," *JNES* 3 (1944) 46.

Teb-ket

*Percy E. Newberry, "Extracts from my Notebooks V.," *SBAP* 24 (1902) 244-252. [40. Prince Teb-ket, p. 252]

Teta-em-re

*Percy E. Newberry, "Egyptian Historical Notes. I.," *SBAP* 35 (1913) 156-158. {3. An Official of Hatshepsut. p. 157.

Tety-shery

H. E. Winlock, "On Queen Tetisheri, Grandmother of Ahmose I," *AEE* 6 (1921) 14-16.

M. A. Murray, "Queen Tety-shery," *AEE* 19 (1934) 6, 65-69.

Teumman

*Paul Haupt, "The Disease of King Teumman of Elam," *JSOR* 1 (1917) 88-91.

Thaa

*Percy E. Newberry, "Extracts from my Notebooks. VII.," *SBAP* 25 (1903) 357-362. [53. Princess Thaa, pp. 359-360]

Themistocles

Stephen Usher, "Architects of the Athenian Empire. I: Themistocles,"
    HT 17 (1967) 285-292.

Themistogenes

*Malcolm MacLaren Jr., "Xenophon and Themistogenes," *TAPA* 65
    (1934) 240-247.

Theogenes

*P. Maas, "Oenanthe's Husbands," *JEA* 31 (1945) 74. *[Theogenes]*

Thucydides

P. A. Brunt, "Thucydides: The Compassionate Scientist," *HT* 7 (1957)
    820-828.

A. Andrewes, "Thucydides and the Perisans," *HJAH* 10 (1961) 1-18.

Thutmose III

James Henry Breasted, "The Length and Season of Thutmose III.'s
    First Campaign," *ZÄS* 37 (1899) 123-129.

Thutmose IV

G. Elliot Smith, "Notes sur la momie de Thoutmôsis IV: §II. Report
    on the physical Characters," *ASAE* 4 (1903) 112-115.

*Abraham Malamat, "Campaigns of Amenhotep II and Thutmose IV
    to Canaan," *SH* 8 (1961) 218-231.

*Raphael Giveon, "Thutmosis IV and Asia," *JNES* 28 (1969) 54-59.

Tidal

A. H. Sayce, "Was Tidal. King of Nations, a Hittite?" *ET* 19 (1907-08) 283.

Tiglath-pileser I

A. T. Olmstead, "Tiglath-pileser I and His Wars," *JAOS* 37 (1917) 169-185.

Tiglath-pileser II

*George Smith, "The annals of Tiglath Pileser II," *ZÄS* 7 (1869) 9-19.

*George Smith, "Assyrian History. Additions to history of Tiglath Pileser II," *ZÄS* 7 (1869) 92-100.

Tiglath-pileser III (See also: Pul ←)

*J. W. Bosanquet, "Chronology of the Reigns of Tiglath Pileser, Sargon. Shalmanezer, and Sennacherib, in connexion with the Phenomenon seen on the Dial of Ahaz," *JRAS* (1855) 277-296.

*J. W. Bosanquet, "Synchronous History of the Reigns of Tiglath-Pileser.. and .. Azariah. Shalmanezer .. and .. Jotham. Sargon .. and .. Ahaz. Sennacherib .. and .. Hezekiah," *SBAT* 3 (1874) 1-82.

*Joseph Horner, "Pul, Jereb, Tiglath-pileser — A Chronologico-Historical Study," *MR* 76 (1894) 928-935.

*Robert W. Rogers, "'Pul, Jareb, Tiglath-pileser'," *MR* 77 (1895) 129-130.

*Joseph Horner, "Pul, Jareb, Tiglath, and the Corrections," *MR* 77 (1895) 298-300.

*Robert W. Rogers, "Pul, Jareb, Tiglath-pileser III — A Reply," *MR* 77 (1895) 301-302.

Tiglath-pileser III concluded

J. F. McCurdy, "Light on Scriptural Texts from Recent Discoveries. Tiglath-pileser III," *HR* 32 (1896) 27.

*Howell M. Haydin, "Azariah of Judah and Tiglath-pileser III," *JBL* 28 (1909) 182-199.

Tii

*Alfred C. Bryant and F. W. Read, "Akhuenaten and Queen Tii," *SBAP* 17 (1895) 246-250.

Tirhakah

*Samuel Birch, "Monuments of the Reign of Tirhakah," *SBAT* 7 (1880-82) 193-203.

*Joseph Offord, "Archaeological Notes on Jewish Antiquities. XLVIII. *A Statue of Tirhakah*," *PEFQS* 50 (1918) 135-136.

Tobiads

*C. C. McCown, "The 'Araq el-Emir and the Tobiads," *BA* 20 (1957) 63-76. [VI. Position of Tobiad Family in Transjordan, pp. 71-72; VIII. The Last Tobiads, pp. 74-76]

B[enjamin] Mazar, "The Tobiads," *IEJ* 7 (1957) 137-145, 229-238.

Tutankhamen

Mitchell Carroll, "The Story of Tutankhamen," *A&A* 15 (1923) 187-192.

Dudley S. Corlett, "Art on the Screen; or the Film of Tutankhamen," *A&A* 16 (1923) 231-240.

William E. Barton, "The Human Side of Tut-Ankh-Aton," *OC* 37 (1923) 193-209.

Tutankhamen concluded

Maria Mogensen, "A Tut-Ankh-Amon Portrait at the Ny Carlsberg Glyptothek," *AEE* 10 (1925) 40.

*A. H. Sayce, "What happened after the death of Tut'ankhamūn," *JEA* 12 (1926) 168-170.

*Battiscombe Gunn, "Notes on two Egyptian Kings," *JEA* 12 (1926) 250-253. [2. The Name Tut'ankhamūn, pp. 251-253]

R. Engelbach, "A hitherto unknown statue of King Tut'Ankhamûn," *ASAE* 38 (1938) 23-28.

R. Engelbach, "A hitherto unknown statue of King Tut'Ankhamûn —further remarks," *ASAE* 39 (1939) 199-201.

*Ambrose Lansing, "A Head of Tut'ankhamūn," *JEA* 37 (1951) 3-4.

W. K. Simpson, "The Head of a Statuette of Tut'ankhamūn in the Metropolitan Museum," *JEA* 41 (1955) 112-114.

Tuthmosis

*Percy E. Newberry, "Miscellanea," *JEA* 14 (1928) 109-111. [VI. An Official of King Horemheb, p. 111] *[Tuthmosis]*

Tuthmosis I

*H. E. Winlock, "Notes on the Reburial of Tuthmosis I," *JEA* 15 (1929) 56-68.

Tuthmosis III

*H. R. Hall, "A New Portrait Head of Tuthmosis III (?) at Berlin, and the Portraits of Hatshepsut," *JEA* 15 (1929) 78-79.

*R. O. Faulkner, "The Euphrates Campaign of Tuthmosis III," *JEA* 32 (1946) 39-42.

Tuthmosis III concluded

*Giuseppe Botti, "A Fragment of the Story of a Military Expedition of Tuthmosis III to Syria (P. Turin 1940-1941)," *JEA* 41 (1955) 64-66.

*Donald B. Redford, "The Coregency of Tuthmosis III and Amenophis II," *JEA* 51 (1965) 107-122.

Tuthmosis IV

Percy E. Newberry, "The Sons of Tuthmosis IV," *JEA* 14 (1928) 82-85.

Twosre

*Alan [H.] Gardiner, "Only One King Siptaḥ and Twosre not His Wife," *JEA* 44 (1958) 12-22.

*J. von Beckerath, "Queen Twosre as Guardian of Siptaḥ," *JEA* 48 (1962) 70-74.

U

Udy-mu (Den)

*Percy E. Newberry and G. A. Wainwright, "King Udy-mu (Den) and the Palermo Stone," *AEE* 1 (1914) 148-155.

Urdamani

*†D[aniel] H[y.] Haigh, "To the editor," *ZÄS* 6 (1868) 80-83. *[Urdamani, p. 81-82]*

Ur-Engur

*C. J. Gadd, "Notes on Some Babylonian Rulers," *JRAS* (1922) 389-396. [1. 𒌨𒂗𒄖 (Ur-Engur), pp. 389-391]

Ur-Ningirus

*C. J. Gadd, "Notes on Some Babylonian Rulers," *JRAS* (1922) 389-396. [2. Ur-Ningirus, Governor of Lagash, pp. 391-394]

Ursaggina

Terrien de Lacouperie, "An Unknown King of Lagash, from a lost inscription of 6000 years ago," *BOR* 4 (1889-90) 181-187, 193-208. *[Ursaggina]*

Urukagina

*Ferris J. Stephens, "Notes on some Economic Texts of the Time of Urukagina," *RAAO* 49 (1955) 129-136. [1. Who was Urukagina's Predecessor? pp. 129-131]

*I. M. Diaknoff, "Some Remarks on the 'Reforms' of Urukagina," *RAAO* 52 (1958) 1-15.

User

*Percy E. Newberry, "Extracts from my Notebook (I).," *SBAP* 21 (1899) 303-308. [4. A Statue of User, Vezîr of Upper Egypt under Thothmess III, pp. 306-308]

User-Maota-Ra Uapet

[W. M.] Flinders Petrie, "The Ethiopian Revival," *AEE* 10 (1925) 1-2. *[Stela of King User-Maota-Ra Uapet]*

W

Wadjkarē'

William C. Hayes, "King Wadjkarē' of Dynasty VII," *JEA* 34 (1948) 115-116.

Wadjmose

A[lan] H. Gardiner, "A Priest of King Tuthmosis III and Prince Wadjmose," *Or, N.S.*, 6 (1937) 358-359.

Wateh-ben-Hazel

*Paul Haupt, "Wateh-ben-Hazel, Prince of the Kedarenes about 650 B.C.," *AJSL* 1 (1884-85) 217-231.

Weha'u

William Kelly Simpson, "The vizer Weha'u in Papyrus Lythgoe and Ostr. Moscow 4478," *JEA* 49 (1963) 172.

Weni

Hans Goedicke, "Comment on a passage in Weni's Biography," *REg* 10 (1955) 92.

Wentawat

*Jaroslav Černý, "Two King's Sons of Kush of the Twentieth Dynasty," *Kush* 7 (1959) 71-75. *[Wentawat]*

Wepemnofret

*William Stevenson Smith, "The Stela of Prince Wepemnofret," *Arch* 16 (1963) 2-13.

X

Xenophon

*G. B., "Xenophon and Cyrus the Great," *JSL, 3rd Ser.*, 6 (1857-58) 170-171.

Xenophon concluded

C[harles] D. Morris, "The Age of Xenophon at the Time of the Anabasis," *PAPA* 6 (1874) 25. *[Bound with Transactions, but paged separately]*

Charles D. Morris, "On the Age of Xenophon at the Time of the Anabasis," *TAPA* 5 (1874) 82-95.

*Charles A. Robinson Jr., "Topographical Notes on Perachora, with Special Reference to Xenophon's Account of the Corinthian War, 390 B.C.," *AJA* 31 (1927) 96.

*Malcolm MacLaren Jr., "Xenophon and Themistogenes," *TAPA* 65 (1934) 240-247.

S[tephen] Usher, "Xenophon and his Times," *HT* 12 (1962) 496-505.

Albert Eustance, "Xenophon: A Correspondence," *HT* 12 (1962) 667. (Reply by S. Usher, p. 667)

E. D. Frolov, "Xenophon and the Later Tyranny," *VDI* (1969) #1, 124.

Xerxes

Anonymous, "Cornucopia," *MMBR* 43 (1817) 519. *[Xerxes]*

V. Lesný, "On the date of Xerxes' accension," *ArOr* 10 (1938) 433-436.

*George G. Cameron, "Darius and Xerxes in Babylonia," *AJSL* 58 (1941) 314-325.

W. Kendrick Pritchett, "Xerxes' Fleet at the 'Ovens'," *AJA* 67 (1963) 1-6.

*Arthur Ferrill, "Herodotus and the Strategy and Tactics of the Invasion of Xerxes," *AmHR* 72 (1966-67) 102-115.

Y

Yamu-Nedjeḥ

*W. C. Hayes Jr., "A Statue of the herald Yamu-Nedjeḥ in the Egyptian Museum, Cairo, and some biographical notes on its owner," *ASAE* 33 (1933) 6-16.

Yarim-Lim

Sidney Smith, "Yarim-Lim of Yamḫad," *RDSO* 32 (1957) 155-184.

Ŷ-meru

*Percy E. Newberry, "Extracts from my Notebooks VII.," *SBAP* 25 (1903) 357-362. [55. The Vezîr Ŷ-meru, p. 361]

Ŷm-hetep

*Percy E. Newberry, "Extracts from my Notebooks V.," *SBAP* 24 (1902) 244-252. [33. The Vezîr Ŷm-hetep, p. 250]

Yuía

H. R. Hall, "Yuia the Syrian," *SBAP* 35 (1913) 63-65.

Z

Zarathustra

*S. G. F. Brandon, "Zarathustra and the Dualism of Iran," *HT* 13 (1963) 250-259.

Zāriqum

William W. Hallo, "Zāriqum," *JNES* 15 (1956) 220-225.

Zenon (of Caunus)

W. L. Westermann, "Notes and Suggestions. Ephraim Beanland and Zenon of Caunus: a historical comparison," *AmHR* 47 (1941-42) 64-72.

Zêt

W. M. F[linders] P[etrie], "The Mysterious Zêt," *AEE* 1 (1914) 32.

F. W. Read, "King Zêt of the XXIIIrd Dynasty," *AEE* 3 (1916) 150.

§142 *2.4.1 Nations, Peoples and Their History*
(not necessarily mentioned in the Old
Testament) [Alphabetical Listing]

A

Abyssinians

*[J.] Rendel Harris, "Egypt and Abyssinia. A Prehistoric Study," *HJ* 35 (1936-37) 250-253.

Achaeans

William K. Prentice, "The Achaeans," *AJA* 33 (1929) 206-218.

J[ohn] F[ranklin] D[aniel], "The Achaeans at Kourion," *UMB* 8 (1939-40) #1, 3-14.

Akkadians

A. Sayce, "The Casdim and the Chaldees," *JSL, 4th Ser.*, 4 (1863-64) 165-171. *[Akkadians]*

*O. D. Miller, "Accadian or Sumerian?" *OBJ* 1 (1880) 105-111.

C[laude] R. Conder, "Early Akkadians in Lebanon," *PEFQS* 23 (1891) 184-185.

D. D. Luckenbill, "Akkadian Origins," *AJSL* 40 (1923-24) 1-13.

Amalekites

*(Miss) Fanny Corbaux, "The Rephaim, and Their Connexion with Egyptian History," *JSL, 2nd Ser.*, 1 (1851-52) 151-172, 363-394; 2 (1852) 55-91, 303-340; 3 (1852-53) 87-116, 279-307. [Chap. 12 - The Amalekites, 2 (1852) pp. 89-91]

*John P. Peters, "Miscellaneous Notes," *AJSL* 1 (1884-85) 115-119. [The Amalekites, p. 115]

Amorites (Amurru)

A. H. Sayce, "The White Race of Ancient Palestine," *Exp, 3rd Ser.*, 8 (1888) 48-57. *[Amorites]*

Anonymous, "The Amurru," *MR* 92 (1910) 481-483.

A. H. Sayce, "The Amorites:—Their Place in History," *CFL, 3rd Ser.*, 10 (1909) 338-342.

George W. Gilmore, "The Empire of the Amorites," *HR* 78 (1919) 99-101. *(Review)*

Emil G. H. Kraeling, "Biblical Aspects of the 'Amurru' Theory," *LCR* 38 (1919) 237-245.

A. H. Sayce, "Who were the Amorites?" *AEE* 9 (1924) 72-75.

*A. B. Miller, "The Relation of the Ancient Amorites to the Historicity of the Old Testament," *SWJT* 8 (1924) 36-44.

George A. Barton, "The Place of the Amorites in the Civilization of Western Asia," *JAOS* 45 (1925) 1-38.

Albert T. Clay, "A Rejoinder to Professor George A. Barton," *JAOS* 45 (1925) 119-151.

George A. Barton, "A Correction," *JAOS* 45 (1925) 323.

*Albert T. Clay, "The Early Civilization of Amurru—The Land of the Amorites—Showing Amorite Influence on Biblical Literature," *JTVI* 57 (1925) 88-104. (Discussion and Communications by [T. G. Pinches] pp. 104-105; William Theodore Roberts, p. 106; William Dale, pp. 106-107; W. Hoste, pp. 107-108; W. E. Leslie, pp. 108-109; G. B. Mitchell, pp. 108-111]

H. Tur-Sinai (Torczyner), "The Amorite and the Amurru of the Inscriptions," *JQR, N.S.*, 39 (1948-49) 249-258.

*Sabatino Moscati, "*Israel's Predecessors:* A Re-Examination of Certain Current Theories," *JAAR* 24 (1956) 245-254. *[Amorites]*

Amorites concluded

George M. Landes, "The Material Civilization of the Ammorites,"
    BA 24 (1961) 66-86.

*Julius   Lewy,   "Amurritica,"   *HUCA*   32   (1961)   31-74.

*John C. L. Gibson, "Observations on Some Important Ethnic Terms
    in the Pentateuch," *JNES* 20 (1961) 217-238. [Amorites, pp.
    220-224]

*M. B. Rowton, "The Abu Amurrim," *Iraq* 31 (1969) 68-73.

'Amu

*S. Yeivin, "Topographical and Ethnic Notes," *'Atiqot* 2 (1959)
    155-164. [C. The 'Amu, pp. 163-164]

Anakim

*(Miss) Fanny Corbaux, "The Rephaim, and Their Connexion with
    Egyptian History," *JSL, 2nd Ser.,* 1 (1851-52) 151-172,
    363-394; 2 (1852) 55-91, 303-340; 3 (1852-53) 87-116,
    279-307. [2 (1852) Chap. 13 - The Anakim, pp. 303-323; Chap.
    15 - Final Wars of the Anakim with Egypt, pp. 329-340]

Arabs

*G. Seyffarth, "Three Lectures on Egyptian Antiquities, &c.,
    delivered at the Stuyvesant Institute, New York, May 1856,"
    ER 8 (1856-57) 34-104. [XXIII. The Arabians, pp. 103-104]

Anonymous,   "The   Arabs,"   *PQR*   9   (1860-61)   177-203.

*A. Sprenger, "The Ishmaelites, and the Arabic Tribes
    who Conquered Tribes who conquered their Country,"
    JRAS (1872-73) 1-19.

C. Clermont-Ganneau, "The Arabs in Palestine," *PEFQS* 7 (1875)
    199-214.

Anonymous, "Note on M. Ganneau's Paper, 'The Arabs in Palestine',"
    PEFQS 8 (1876) 8.

Arabs concluded

Henry Field, "The Ancient and Modern Inhabitants of Arabia," *OC* 46 (1932) 847-872.

*A. Guillaume, "The Habiru, The Hebrews, and the Arabs," *PEQ* 78 (1946) 64-85.

*A. Guillaume, "The Ḫābiru, The Hebrews, and the Arabs," *Man* 47 (1947) #77.

*W[illiam] F[oxwell] Albright, "The Chronology of the Minaean Kings of Arabia," *BASOR* #129 (1953) 20-24.

*David Neiman, "*Urbi* = 'Irregulars' or 'Arabs'," *JQR, N.S.,* 60 (1969-70) 237-258.

Arameans

*A. H. Sacye, "Miscellaneous Notes," *ZA* 4 (1889) 382-393. [25. The origin of the name of Armenia, pp. 386-387]

*Raymond A. Bowman, "Arameans, Aramaic, and the Bible," *JNES* 7 (1948) 65-90.

*John C. L. Gibson, "Observations on Some Important Ethnic Terms in the Pentateuch," *JNES* 20 (1961) 217-238. [Arameans, pp. 229-234]

*Benjamin Mazar, "The Aramean Empire and Its Relations with Israel," *BA* 25 (1962) 98-120.

Argives

*J. P. Mahaffy, "On the Date of the Capture of Mycenæ by the Argives," *Herm* 3 (1877-79) 60-66.

Aryans

John Gibb, "The Original Home of the Aryans," *BQRL* 80 (1884) 377-389. *(Review)*

Aryans concluded

[A. H.] Sayce, "The Primitive Home of the Aryans," *TPS* (1885-87) 678-690.

A. H. Sayce, "The Primitive Home of the Aryans," *ContR* 56 (1889) 106-119.

A. H. Sayce, "Primitive Home of the Aryans," *SIR* (1890) 475-487.

J. S. Stuart-Glennie, "Aryan Origins," *ContR* 62 (1892) 833-848.

William F. Warren, "Creed and Home of the Earliest Aryans," *MR* 76 (1894) 76-81.

G. D. Gurley, "The Aryan Race," *RChR* 42 (1895) 331-350.

A. J. Heller, "The Origin of the Aryans," *RChR, 4th Ser.,* 1 (1897) 214-235.

*G. Sergi, "The Aryans and the Ancient Italians. A Page of Primitive History," *Monist* 8 (1897-98) 161-182.

Chas. W. Super, "The Original Home of the Aryans," *AAOJ* 20 (1898) 353-357.

A. H. Sayce, "The Aryan Problem—fifty years later," *Antiq* 1 (1927) 204-215.

Assyrians

*T. M. Dickinson, "An Inquiry into the Fate of the Ten Tribes of Israel after the Fall of Samaria; with a View of the History of the Assyrian Empire at that period, as derived from a comparison of what is recorded on the Subject in the Histories of the Jews, the Greeks, and the Persians," *JRAS* (1837) 217-253.

*George Smith, "The annals of Tiglath Pileser II," *ZÄS* 7 (1869) 9-19.

George Smith, "Assyrian History. Additions to the history of Tiglath Pileser II," *ZÄS* 7 (1869) 92-100. [Shalmaneser; Sargon; Chronology of the 40 years from B.C. 745-705]

Assyrians concluded

George Smith, "Assyrian History (Continuation)," *ZÄS* 7 (1869) 106-112.

*George Smith, "Assyrian History. Sennecharib," *ZÄS* 8 (1870) 34-40.

W. St. Chad Boscawen, "The Assyrians in Eastern Palestine and Syria Deserta /sic/," *PEFQS* 13 (1881) 224-229.

Claude R. Conder, "The Assyrians in Syria," *PEFQS* 27 (1895) 191-192.

J. F. McCurdy, "Light on Scriptural Texts from Recent Discoveries. Dissolution of the Assyrian Empire," *HR* 33 (1897) 314-316.

*Fritz Hommel, "Assyriological Notes," *SBAP* 19 (1897) 78-90. [§26 *Untitled*, pp. 82-87] /*Assyrian History*/

Lewis Bayles Paton, "Assyria and Prussia: An Historical Parallel," *HJ* 15 (1916-17) 97-112.

Theresa Howard Carter, "Early Assyrians in the Sinjar," *Exped* 7 (1964-65) #1, 34-42.

Robert Drews, "Assyria in Classical Universal History," *HJAH* 14 (1965) 129-142.

P. Artzi, "The First Stage in the Rise of the Middle-Assyrian Empire: EA 15," *EI* 9 (1969) 134. /*English Summary*/

Athenians

D. B. Thompson, "Are Tanagras Athenians?" *AJA* 56 (1952) 177.

G. E. M. de St. Croix, "The Character of the Athenian Empire," *HJAH* 3 (1954-55) 1-41.

Donald W. Bradeen, "The Popularity of the Athenian Empire," *HJAH* 9 (1960) 257-269.

*H. D. Westlake, "Athenian Aims in Sicily 427-424 B.C. *A Study in Thucydidean Motivation*," *HJAH* 9 (1960) 385-402.

Athenians concluded

*Sterling Dow, "Some Athenians in Aristophanes," *AJA* 73 (1969) 234-235. [IG II^2 2343]

B

Babylonians

F. A. Gast, "The Pre-Semitic Babylonians," *RChR* 32 (1885) 22-46.

*G. Bertin, "The Babylonians at Home," *ContR* 49 (1886) 212-218.

William Hayes Ward, "Light on Scriptural Texts from Recent Discoveries. II. The Early Babylonians in Palestine," *HR* 25 (1893) 220-222.

Henry H. Howorth, "Some Unsolved Difficulties in Babylonian History: A Series of Queries.—Part I.," *BOR* 8 (1895-1900) 212-215.

James A. Craig, "The Earliest Chapter of History," *Monist* 11 (1900-01) 481-499. *(Review)*

Anonymous, "The Oldest Library in the World," *MQR, 3rd Ser.,* 29 (1903) 377-382. *[Babylonian History]*

*William Hayes Ward, "The Origin of Babylonian Civilization and Art," *AJA* 9 (1905) 77-79.

N. H. Winchell, "Migration of the Early Babylonian Civilization," *RP* 7 (1908) 176.

Albert T. Clay, "The Antiquity of Babylonian Civilization," *JAOS* 41 (1921) 241-263.

Sami [S.] Ahmed, "The Babylonian Struggle for Independence 630-626 B.C.," *IR* 24 (1967) #2, 35-42.

Badarians

*V. G. Childe, "Capsians and Badarians," *AEE* 13 (1928) 6-7.

Bedouins

[John Lewis] Burckhardt, "Notes on the Bedouins," *BRCR* 4 (1834) 711-766.

John Zeller, "The Bedawin. (*A Lecture delivered at Jerusalem*.)," *PEFQS* 33 (1901) 185-203.

W. E. Jennings-Bramley, "The Bedouin of the Sinaitic Peninsula," *PEFQS* 38 (1906) 23-33, 103-109, 197-205, 250-258.

Henry Field, "Among the Beduins of North Arabia," *OC* 45 (1931) 577-595.

S. Hillelson, "Notes on the Bedouin Tribes of Beersheba District," *PEQ* 69 (1937) 242-252.

S. Hillelson, "Notes on the Bedouin Tribes of Beersheba District, II," *PEQ* 70 (1938) 55-63.

S. Hillelson, "Notes on the Bedouin Tribes of Beersheba District, III," *PEQ* 70 (1938) 117-126.

E. Epstein, "Bedouin of the Negeb," *PEQ* 71 (1939) 59-73.

Walter Dostal, "The Evolution of Bedouin Life," *SSR* 2 (1959) 11-34.

C

Canaanites

*(Miss) Fanny Corbaux, "The Rephaim, and Their Connexion with Egyptian History," *JSL, 2nd Ser.,* 1 (1851-52) 151-172, 363-394; 2 (1852) 55-91, 303-340; 3 (1852-53) 87-116, 279-307. [Chap. 3 - Geographical Distribution of the Canaanites and Rephaim, 1 (1851-52) pp. 162-169]

John Walter Lea, "The Canaanites in the Time of Deborah," *JSL, 4th Ser.,* 8 (1865-66) 200-202.

Canaanites cont.

C. H. Toy, "Remarks on J. G. Mueller's Die Semiten," *BS* 31 (1874) 355-365. */Canaanites/*

*A. E. Simpson, "The Speech and Culture of Canaan," *DTQ* 6 (1880) 605-622.

Claude R. Conder, "The Canaanites," *PEFQS* 19 (1887) 149, 227-231.

*Charles A. Hobbs, "The Alleged Cruelty of God to the Canaanites," *BQR* 14 (1892) 455-496.

George S. Goodspeed, "A Sketch of Canaanitish History to About the Year 1000 B.C.," *BW* 7 (1896) 459-471.

C[laude] R. Conder, "On the Canaanites," *JTVI* 24 (1890-91) 33-66, 81-82. [(Discussion, pp. 66-78) (Remarks by Isaac Taylor, p. 79; G. W. Leitner, p. 79; G. Bertin, pp. 79-80)]

C[laude] R. Conder, "Light from Exploration on Canaanite Civilization," *HR* 42 (1901) 483-487.

L[ewis] B[ayles] Paton, "The Civilization of Canaan in the Fifteenth Century B.C.," *BW* 20 (1902) 25-30, 113-122.

C. F. Burney, "Old Testament Notes. III. Who Were the hosts of the Egyptian Sinuhe?" *JTS* 10 (1908-09) 587-589. */Canaanites/*

*Stephen Langdon, "Franz Böhl, *Kanaanäer und Hebräer*," *Baby* 6 (1912) 54-55. *(Review)*

B[enjamin] Maisler, "Canaan and the Canaanites," *BASOR* #102 (1946) 7-12.

*Sabatino Moscati, "*Israel's Predecessors:* A Re-Examination of Certain Current Theories," *JAAR* 24 (1956) 245-254. */Canaanites/*

*A. van Selms, "The Canaanites in the Book of Genesis," *OTS* 12 (1958) 182-213.

Canaanites concluded

*John C. L. Gibson, "Observations on Some Important Ethnic Terms in the Pentateuch," *JNES* 20 (1961) 217-238. [Canaanites, pp. 217-220]

*A[nson] F. Rainey, "Ugarit and the Canaanites Again," *IEJ* 14 (1964) 101.

[Clifford Wilson], "Another Look at the Canaanites," *BH* 3 (1967) #3, 16.

*Donald R. Rouse, "God's Judgment on the Canaanites," *CCBQ* 10 (1967) #4, 34-46.

Caphtorim

A. Hallen, "The Caphtorim. Who were These People and Where was Their Original Home?" *ONTS* 6 (1886-87) 243-245.

Cappadocians

J. R. S. Sterrett, "The Cappadocian Troglodytes," *AJA* 4 (1900) 167.

Capsians

*V. G. Childe, "Capsians and Badarians," *AEE* 13 (1928) 6-7.

Chaldeans

W. St. C[had] Boscawen, "Beginnings of Chaldean Civilization," *BOR* 7 (1893-94) 1-8, 25-30.

*William Hayes Ward, "Light on Scriptural Texts from Recent Discoveries. Chaldea and the Chaldeans," *HR* 30 (1895) 220-222. [Criticism by John D. Sands, p. 378]

A. T. Olmstead, "Chaldaeans and Chaldians in Armenia," *AJSL* 18 (1900-01) 250-253.

Chaldaeans concluded

*T. G. P[inches], "Chaldean Princes on the Throne of Babylon," *JRAS* (1904) 367-368.

*T. G. P[inches], "The Chaldeans of the Book of Daniel," *JRAS* (1904) 368-369.

*A. T. Olmstead, "The Chaldean Dynasty," *HUCA* 2 (1925) 29-55.

Cherethites

*W[illiam] F[oxwell] Albright, "A Colony of Cretan Mercenaries on the Coast of the Negeb," *JPOS* 1 (1920-21) 187-194. *[Cherethites]*

*L. M. Muntingh, "The Cherethites and Pelethites," *OTW* 3 (1960) 43-53.

Cilicians

Albrecht Goetze, "Cilicians," *JCS* 16 (1962) 48-58.

Cimmerians

J. B. Bury, "The Homeric and the historic Kimmerians," *Klio* 6 (1906) 79-88.

*H. H. von der Osten, "Additions to 'Oriental Institute Publications,' Volume VI," *AJSL* 47 (1930-31) #1, Part 1, 53-55. *[Cimmerians, pp. 54-55]*

Tadeusz Sulimirski, "The Cimmerian Problem," *ULBIA* 2 (1959) 45-64.

*Stuart Piggott, "Iron, Cimmerians and Aeschylus," *Antiq* 38 (1964) 300-303.

Cretans

*Anonymous, "Crete and the Cretans," *CE* 82 (1867) 244-246. *(Review)*

*J. Rendel Harris, "Crete, the Jordan, and the Rhône," *ET* 21 (1909-10) 303-306. *[The Cretans, Their Linguistic Influence]*

*L[uther] T. Townsend, "Cretans and other Prehistoric Peoples: Their Bearing on the Theory of Evolution," *CFL, 3rd Ser.*, 25 (1919) 89-93.

*W[illiam] F[oxwell] Albright, "A Colony of Cretan Mercenaries on the Coast of the Negeb," *JPOS* 1 (1920-21) 187-194.

Colchians

*Patrick T. English, "Cushites, Colchians, and Khazars," *JNES* 18 (1959) 49-53.

Cushites

C. H. Toy, "On the Kushites," *JAOS* 11 (1885) cviii-cix.

T[errien] de Lacouperie, "The Kushites—Who Were They?" *BOR* 1 (1886-87) 25-31.

*Patrick T. English, "Cushites, Colchians, and Khazars," *JNES* 18 (1959) 49-53.

S. Yeivin, "Topographic and Ethnic Notes, II," *'Atiqot* 3 (1961) 176-180. [E. The Five Kushite Clans in Canaan]

Cuthites

*M. Eliash, "The Cuthites and Psalm 74," *JPOS* 5 (1925) 55-57.

Cypriotes

Lawrence Angel, "The First Cypriotes," *AJA* 54 (1950) 261.

D

Dorians

S. Casson, "The Dorian Invasion reviewed in the light of some new evidence," *Man* 21 (1921) #39.

*John Franklin Daniel, "The Dorian Invasion: The Setting," *AJA* 52 (1948) 107-110.

*Oscar Broneer, "The Dorian Invasion: What Happened at Athens," *AJA* 52 (1948) 111-114.

*H. T. Wade-Gery, "The Dorian Invasion: What Happened in Pylos?" *AJA* 52 (1948) 115-118.

Druse

Edward Robinson, "The Druzes of Mount Lebanon," *BS* (1843) 205-253.

E

Edomites

*Anonymous, "Genealogy of the Edomites," *SBAP* 8 (1885-86) 41.

Charles C. Torrey, "The Edomites in Southern Judah," *JBL* 17 (1898) 16-20.

T. K. Cheyne, "Dr. Torrey on the Edomites," *JBL* 17 (1898) 207-208.

Nelson Glueck, "The Civilization of the Edomites," *BA* 10 (1947) 77-84.

*J. R. Bartlett, "The Edomite King-List of Genesis XXXVI. 31-39 and I Chron. I. 43-50," *JTS, N.S.*, 16 (1965) 301-314.

Egyptians

†Anonymous, "Wilkinson— *On the Ancient Egyptians*," *ERCJ* 68 (1838-39) 315-337. *(Review)*

†Anonymous, "Egypt's Place in the History of the World," *CTPR, 3rd Ser.*, 2 (1846) 1-32. *(Review)*

*Anonymous, "Egyptian Chronology and History," *CTPR, 3rd Ser.*, 6 (1850) 193-211. *(Review)*

†Anonymous, "Egypt Under the Pharaohs," *BQRL* 13 (1851) 92-124. *(Review)*

Anonymous, "Ancient Egypt Under the Pharaohs," *CTPR, 3rd Ser.*, 7 (1851) 1-24. *(Review)*

*(Miss) Fanny Corbaux, "The Rephaim, and Their Connexion with Egyptian History," *JSL, 2nd Ser.*, 1 (1851-52) 151-172, 363-394; 2 (1852) 55-91, 303-340; 3 (1852-53) 87-116, 279-307. [Chap. 10 - The Wars of Emim with Egypt, 2 (1852) pp. 67-80; Chap. 15 - Final Wars of the Anakim with Egypt, pp. 329-340]

*Anonymous, "Ancient Egypt, its Literature and People," *ER* 4 (1852-53) 35-57.

Anonymous, "*Egypt's Place in Universal History: An Historical Investigation*," *LQHR* 5 (1855-56) 1-30. *(Review)*

*G. Seyffarth, "Three Lectures on Egyptian Antiquities, &c., delivered at the Stuyvesant Institute, New York, May 1856," *ER* 8 (1856-57) 34-104. [XVII. The History of Egypt, pp. 87-90]

*†D[aniel] H[y.] Haigh, "To the Editor," *ZÄS* 6 (1868) 80-83. *[Egyptian History]*

*[Daniel Hy.] Haigh, "Assyrica," *ZÄS* 7 (1869) 3-5. *[Egyptian History]*

*Daniel Hy. Haigh, "Assyrio-Aegyptiaca," *ZÄS* 9 (1871) 112-117.

Anonymous, "The Ancient Egyptians," *CQR* 2 (1876) 338-385. *(Review)*

Egyptians cont.

†Anonymous, "Brugsch's Egypt under the Pharaohs," *ERCJ* 150 (1879) 77-111. *(Review)*

P. le Page Renouf, "The Priestly Character of the Earliest Egyptian Civilization," *SBAP* 12 (1889-90) 355-362.

Oscar Montélius, "The Age of Bronze in Egypt," *SIR* (1890) 499-515.

Anonymous, "Egyptian Beginnings according to Maspero and Lockyer," *BOR* 7 (1893-94) 239-240.

W. St. C[had] Boscawen, "The Threshold of History," *BOR* 7 (1893-94) 285-288. *[Egyptian origins]*

Robert W. Rogers, "The Origin of Egyptian Culture," *MR* 76 (1894) 51-63.

James Henry Breasted, "Sketch of Egyptian History," *BW* 7 (1896) 438-458.

James Henry Breasted, "Sketch of Egyptian History from the Fall of the Native Kings to the Persian Captivity. (Illustrated)," *BW* 9 (1897) 413-428.

*W. M. McPheeters, "Light on Early Egyptian History," *CFL, O.S.,* 3 (1899) 151-153.

Grant Bey, "An Introduction to Ancient Egyptian History," *APST* 3 (1890-1900) 1-30.

M. B. Chapman, "Origin of Egyptian Civilization," *MQR, 3rd Ser.,* 26 (1900) 671-677.

*Arthur Keith, "Were the Ancient Egyptians a Dual Race?" *Man* 6 (1906) #2.

Edouard Naville, "The Origin of Egyptian Civilization," *SIR* (1907) 549-564.

Anonymous, "Ancient Inhabitants of Egypt," *RP* 7 (1908) 258.

Egyptians cont.

*Arthur E. P. Weigall, "Religion and the Empire in Ancient Egypt," *QRL* 210 (1909) 44-66. *(Review)*

Percy E. Newberry, "Notes on Some Egyptian Nome Ensigns and Their Historical Significance," *AEE* 1 (1914) 5-8. (Note by [W. M.] F[linders] P[etrie], p. 8)

D. G. Hogarth, "Egyptian Empire in Asia," *JEA* 1 (1914) 9-17.

W. M. Flinders Petrie, "The Stone Age in Egypt," *AEE* 2 (1915) 59-76, 122-135.

*V. Giuffrida-Ruggeri, "Were the Pre-Dynastic Egyptians Libyans or Ethiopians?" *Man* 15 (1915) #32.

G. Elliot Smith, "Professor Giuffrida-Ruggeri's Views on the Affinities of the Egyptians," *Man* 15 (1915) #41.

*V. Giuffrida-Ruggeri, "A Few Notes on the Neolithic Egyptians and the Ethiopians," *Man* 16 (1916) #55.

*G. Elliot Smith, "The Influence of Ancient Egyptian Civilization in the East and in America," *BJRL* 3 (1916-17) 48-77.

*T. Eric Peet, "The Antiquity of Egyptian Civilization being a plea for some attempt to formulate the laws which should form the basis of archaeological argument," *JEA* 8 (1922) 5-12.

[W. M.] Flinders Petrie, "The Antiquity of Egyptian Civilization," *JEA* 9 (1923) 153-156.

H. Idris Bell, "A Greek Adventurer in Egypt," *ERCJ* 243 (1926) 123-138. *[Egyptian Life in 3rd Century B.C.]*

J. Grafton Milne, "Egyptian Nationalism under Greek and Roman Rule," *JEA* 14 (1928) 226-234.

Guy Brunton, "The Beginnings of Egyptian Civilization," *Antiq* 3 (1929) 456-467.

[W. M.] Flinders Petrie, "The Peoples of Egypt," *AEE* 16 (1931) 77-85.

Egyptians cont.

Henry L. F. Lutz, "Saitic Myths in Arabic Tradition," *UCPSP* 10 (1931-46) 305-312. *[Egyptian History (Myth) after the Exodus]*

Samuel A. B. Mercer, "The So-called First and Second Civilizations," *EgR* 1 (1933) 73-75.

Samuel A. B. Mercer, "The Civilization of the North and the South," *EgR* 1 (1933) 76-77.

George S. Duncan, "The Antiquity of Egyptian Civilization," *AJA* 38 (1934) 190.

*[W. M.] Flinders Petrie, "Copper or Bronze?" *AEE* 20 (1935) *Supplement,* p. 148. *[Egyptian History]*

*[J.] Rendel Harris, "Egypt and Abyssinia. A Prehistoric Study," *HJ* 35 (1936-37) 250-253.

*Warren R. Dawson, "The First Egyptian Society," *JEA* 23 (1937) 259-260.

‡G. A. Wainwright, "N. de G. Davies, A. N. Dakin, M. F. L. Macadam, I. E. S. Edwards, P. C. Smither, H. W. Fairman, R. O. Faulkner, and R. W. Sloley, "Bibliography: Pharaonic Egypt (1938)," *JEA* 25 (1939) 188-214.

*Hermann Ranke, E. A. Speiser, W. Norman Brown, and Carl W. Bishop, "The Beginnings of Civilization in the Orient. A Symposium at the Meetings of the American Oriental Society, Baltimore, April 13, 1939," *JAOSS* #4 (1939) 3-61. [The Beginnings of Civilization in Egypt, pp. 3-16(R)]

*Kurt Pfluger, "The Private Funerary Stelae of the Middle Kingdom and Their Importance for the Study of Ancient Egyptian History," *JAOS* 67 (1947) 127-135.

*Leslie A. White, "Ikhnaton: The Great Man *vs.* the Culture Process," *JAOS* 68 (1948) 91-114.

*William F. Edgerton, "'The Great Man': a Note on Methods," *JAOS* 68 (1948) 192-193. *[Ikhnaton]*

Egyptians concluded

*H[enri] Frankfort, "The Ancient Egyptians and the Hamites," *Man* 49 (1949) #130.

[V.] Gordon Chile, "Terminology in Egyptian Prehistory," *Antiq* 26 (1952) 149-150.

Elise J. Baugartel, "Some Notes on the Origins of Egypt," *ArOr* 20 (1952) 278-287.

*Keith C. Seele, "King Ay and the Close of the Amarna Age," *JNES* 14 (1955) 168-179.

*D. E. Derry, "The Dynastic Race in Egypt," *JEA* 42 (1956) 80-85.

*E. Badian, "Egypt under the Ptolemies," *HT* 10 (1960) 451-459.

*Z[byněk] Žába, "The Development of Primitive and Class Societies in Ancient Egypt," *NOP* 3 (1962) 35-40, 60.

*K[enneth] A. Kitchen, "On the Chronology and History of the New Kingdom," *CdÉ* 39 (1964) 310-322.

C. J. Bleeker, "The Pattern of Ancient Egyptian Culture," *JWH* 9 (1965-66) 107-113.

*Jana Siegelová, "The Hittites and Egypt," *NOP* 5 (1966) 76-79.

*K[enneth] A. Kitchen, "Further Notes on New Kingdom Chronology and History," *CdÉ* 43 (1968) 313-324.

Elamites

*Edith Porada, "Iranian Art and Archaeology: A Report of the Fifth International Congress, 1968," *Arch* 22 (1969) 54-65. [The Elamites, p. 58]

Max Mallowan, "Elamite Problems," *PBA* 55 (1969) 255-284.

Emim

*(Miss) Fanny Corbaux, "The Rephaim, and Their Connexion with Egyptian History," *JSL, 2nd Ser.,* 1 (1851-52) 151-172, 363-394; 2 (1852) 55-91, 303-340; 3 (1852-53) 87-116, 279-307. [2 (1852) Chap. 9 - The Emim, pp. 55-67; Chap. 10 - The Wars of Emim with Egypt, pp. 67-80]

Ethanites

*T. K. Cheyne, "From Isaiah to Ezra. A Study of Ethanites and Jerahmeelites," *AJT* 5 (1901) 433-444.

Ethiopians

Anonymous, "The Kings of Ethiopia," *AEE* 5 (1920) 39.

*V. Giuffrida-Ruggeri, "Were the Pre-Dynastic Egyptians Libyans or Ethiopians?" *Man* 15 (1915) #32.

*V. Giuffrida-Ruggeri, "A Few Notes on the Neolithic Egyptains and the Ethiopians," *Man* 16 (1916) #55.

A. H. Sayce, "The Ethiopian Sovereigns at Meroe," *AEE* 5 (1920) 70-73.

*Frank M. Snowden Jr., "Some Greek and Roman Observations on the Ethiopian," *Tr* 16 (1960) 19-38.

Etruscans

*R. [L.] Ellis, "On the probable Connexion of the Rhœtians and Etruscans with the Thracian stock of nations," *JCSP* 1 (1854) 1-20, 169-185.

Robert P. Keep, "Mr. Isaac Taylor's 'Etruscan Researchs'," *PAPA* 6 (1874) 29-31. *[Bound with Transactions, but paged separately]*

*Anonymous, "The Etruscans and their Language," *BQRL* 62 (1875) 405-437. *(Review)*

Etruscans concluded

Alexander S. Murray, "The Etruscans," *ContR* 26 (1875) 716-734.

*Claude R. Conder, "Hittites and Etruscans," *PEFQS* 19 (1887) 136-143.

James D. Butler, "Light on Etruscan Darkness," *AAOJ* 14 (1892) 106-107.

Salomon Reinach, "Lydian Origin of the Etruscans," *BOR* 6 (1892-93) 85-90.

*Joseph Offord, "Archaeological Notes on Jewish Antiquities. LX. *The Double-Headed Eagle and the Etruscans and Hittites,*" *PEFQS* 52 (1920) 41-42.

D[avid] Randall-McIver, "The Etruscans," *Antiq* 1 (1927) 159-171.

D[avid] Randall-McIver, "Forerunners of the Romans," *Antiq* 2 (1928) 26-36, 133-146. *[Etruscans]*

*Edith Hall Dohan, "Archaeological Evidence for an Etruscan Invasion of Italy," *AJA* 46 (1942) 119.

David Randall-McIver, "Who Were the Etruscans?" *AJA* 47 (1943) 91-94.

*George M. A. Hanfmann, "The Evidence of Architecture and Sculpture," *AJA* 47 (1943) 94-100.

*G. A. Wainwright, "The Teresh, the Etruscans and Asia Minor," *AS* 9 (1959) 197-213.

Clark Hopkins, "The Geometric Period in Etruscan History," *AJA* 69 (1965) 169-170.

F

Fellahhen

(Mrs.) E. A. Finn, "The Fallahhen of Palestine. Notes on their Clans, Warfare, Religion, and Laws," *PEFQS* 11 (1879) 33-48.

(Mrs.) E. A. Finn, "The Fallahhen of Palestine. Notes on the Chief Traits in their Character, their Faults, and their Virtues," *PEFQS* 11 (1879) 72-87.

F. A. Klein, "Life, Habits, and Customs of the Fellahin of Palestine," *PEFQS* 13 (1881) 110-118, 297-304; 15 (1883) 41-48.

G

Galileans

*Arie Rubinstein, "The Appellation 'Galileans' in Ben Kosebah's Letter to Ben Galgola," *JJS* 6 (1955) 26-34.

Gibeonites

*H. C., "The Origin and History of the Sacred Slaves of Israel in Hivitia, Mount Se'yr, and the Hivite Tetrapolis," *JSL, 3rd Ser.,* 10 (1859-60) 266-283. [Chap. III.—The History of the Gibeonites, in and after the time of Joshua, pp. 276-283]

*M. Haran, "The Gibeonites, the Nethinim and the sons of Solomon's Servants," *VT* 11 (1961) 159-169.

*I. M. Grintz, "The Treaty with the Gibeonites," *Zion* 26 (1961) #2, I.

*Jehoshua M. Grintz, "The Treaty of Joshua with the Gibeonites," *JAOS* 86 (1966) 113-126.

Greeks

Anonymous, "The Lycæum of Ancient Literature.—No. II. of the Life, Age, and Country of Homer," *MMBR* 23 (1807) 44-48.

John W. Donaldson, Herodotus and the Athenians," *TPS* 1 (1842-44) 161-167.

†Anonymous, "Ancient Greece—Its Constitutional History," *BQRL* 1 (1845) 413-435. *(Review)*

*I. B. Trautmann, "The Hellenes, Romans, and Israelites. Their Position, Secular and Religious, in the History of the World," *CRB* 16 (1851) 96-105.

*[Henry] Malden, "On the Amphictyonic League, and the meaning of the term *Amphictyones,*" *TPS* 6 (1852-53) 51-58.

*G. Seyffarth, "Three Lectures on Egyptian Antiquities, &c., delivered at the Stuyvesant Institute, New York, May 1856," *ER* 8 (1856-57) 34-104. [XX. The History of the Greeks and Romans, pp. 94-96]

Anonymous, "The Greeks," *CE* 72 (1862) 403-422. *(Review)*

*E. F. Rockwell, "Superiority of the Greeks in Literature, and the Fine Arts," *SPR* 15 (1862-63) 198-204.

Fisk P. Brewer, "Inaccuracies of Grote's Narrative of the Retreat of the Ten Thousand," *PAPA* 3 (1871) 4-5. *[Bound with Transactions, but paged separately]*

†Anonymous, "Finlay's *History of the Servitude of Greece,*" *ERCJ* 148 (1878) 232-262. *(Review)*

A. H. Sayce, "The age of Homer," *JP* 12 (1883) 36-42.

Goldwin Smith, "The Age of Homer," *AmHR* 7 (1901-02) 1-10.

*Joseph Clark Hoppin, "The Greek Colonial Movement as a Commercial Factor," *AJA* 7 (1903) 80-81.

J. Murphy, "Prehistoric Greece and the Aegean Civilization," *ACQR* 38 (1913) 109-135.

Greeks cont.

W. Rhys Roberts, "Greek Civilization as a Study for the People," *PBA* 7 (1915-16) 505-517.

S. A. Steel, "The Old Greeks," *MQR, 3rd Ser.,* 47 (1921) 99-109.

*William Linn Westermann, "New Historical Documents in Greek and Roman History," *AmHR* 35 (1929-30) 14-32.

Allen Brown West, "The Tribute Lists and Non-Tributary Members of the Delian League," *AmHR* 35 (1929-30) 267-275.

J. Penrose Harland, "The Contributions of the Helladic Bronze Age," *AJA* 38 (1934) 189.

*William Wallace, "The Egyptian Expedition and the Chronology of the Decade 460-450 B.C.," *TAPA* 67 (1936) 252-260. *[Greek History]*

Vincent M. Scramuzza, "Notes and Suggestions. Greek and English Colonization," *AmHR* 44 (1938-39) 303-315.

Michael I. Rostovtzeff., "The Greeks in South Russia," *AJA* 43 (1939) 308.
C. Bradford Welles, "The Greeks in Egypt," *AJA* 43 (1939) 308.

John V. A. Fine, "The Background of the Social War of 220-217 B.C.," *AJP* 61 (1940) 129-165.

*John Franklin Daniel, "The Dorian Invasion: The Setting," *AJA* 52 (1948) 107-110.

*Oscar Broneer, "The Dorian Invasion: What Happened at Athens," *AJA* 52 (1948) 111-114.

*H. T. Wade-Gery, "The Dorian Invasion: What Happened in Pylos?" *AJA* 52 (1948) 115-118.

*J. L. Angel, "Health and Society in Greece," *AJA* 52 (1948) 373.

M. D. W. Jeffreys, "The Greek Race," *Man* 49 (1949) #43.

J. G. Koumaris, "The Greek Race," *Man* 49 (1949) #186.

Greeks cont.

P. A. Brunt, "The Hellenic League against Persia," *HJAH* 2 (1953-54) 135-163. *[Greek History, 480-479 B.C.]*

*John Barns, "Cimon and the first Athenian Expedition to Cyprus," *HJAH* 2 (1953-54) 163-176.

Cs. Töttössy, "The Name of the Greeks in Ancient India," *AAASH* 3 (1955) 301-318.

S. Perlman, "Isocrates' 'Philippus' — A Reinterpretation," *HJAH* 6 (1957) 306-317.

R. H. Simpson, "Antigonus, Polyperchon and the Macedonian Regency," *HJAH* 6 (1957) 371-373.

*Howard Becker, "Culture Case Study and Greek History: Comparison Viewed Sociologically," *AmSR* 23 (1958) 489-504.

*M. I. Finley, "Was Greek Civilisation based on Slave Labor?" *HJAH* 8 (1959) 145-164.

Chester G. Starr, "The Decline of the Early Greek Kings," *HJAH* 10 (1961) 129-138.

W. Kendrick Pritchett, "Herodotos */sic/* and the Themistokles Decree," *AJA* 66 (1962) 43-47.

A. M. Snodgrass, "Iron Age Greece and Central Europe," *AJA* 66 (1962) 408-410.

*John Alexander, "Greeks, Italians and the Earliest Balkan Iron Age," *Antiq* 36 (1962) 123-130.

M. I. Finley, "Athenian Demagogues," *P&P* #21 (1962) 3-24.

*Patrick T. Brannan, "Herodotus and History: The Constitutional Debate Preceeding Darius' Accession," *Tr* 19 (1963) 427-438.

A. H. M. Jones, "The Hellenistic Age," *P&P* #27 (1964) 3-22.

E. Ferenczy, "The Rise of the Patrician—Plebeian State," *AAASH* 14 (1966) 113-139.

Greeks concluded

D. Hegyi, "The Historical Background of the Ionian Revolt," *AAASH* 14 (1966) 285-302.

*Robert Bierstedt, Gregory Vlastos, and Lewis A. Coser, "Review Symposium: Alvin W. Gouldner. *Enter Plato: Classical Greece and the Origins of Social Theory,*" *AmSR* 31 (1966) 548-550.

T. D. Zlatkovskaya, "The South-Thracian Tribal Federation in the Sixth and Fifth Centuries B.C.," *VDI* (1967) #2, 158.

Charles W. Fornara, "The Value of Themistocles Decree," *AmHR* 73 (1967-68) 425-433. *[Greek History]*

Ernst Grumach, "The Coming of the Greeks," *BJRL* 51 (1968-69) 73-103, 400-430.

Thomas Kelly, "The Traditional Enmity between Sparta and Argos: The Birth and Development of a Myth," *AmHR* 75 (1969-70) 971-1003.

H

Habiru (see: *The Habiru / Hebrew Question S61* ←)

Hamites

*Morris Jastrow Jr., "The Hamites and Semites in the Tenth Chapter of Genesis," *PAPS* 43 (1904) 173-207.

*Edouard Naville, "The Land of Punt and the Hamites," *JTVI* 57 (1925) 190-203. (Discussion, pp. 203-207)

(Lord) Raglan, "Dr. Frankfort and the Hamites," *Man* 49 (1949) #61, #176.

*H[enri] Frankfort, "The Ancient Egyptians and the Hamites," *Man* 49 (1949) #130.

Hethites (see: Hittites)

Hittites (Hethites)

*Claude R. Conder, "Notes from the Memoir," *PEFQS* 8 (1876) 149-151, 167-171; 9 (1877) 20-30, 85-89, 137-142, 178-183; 10 (1878) 18-22, 76-77. [The Hittites, p. 138]

Anonymous, "The Empire of the Hittites," *PEFQS* 12 (1880) 118-124.

(   ) A., "The Empire of the Hittites," *PR* 1 (1880) 369-370.

W. St. C[had] Boscawen, "The Hittites," *PEFQS* 13 (1881) 281-223. (Note by Dunbar Isidore Heath, pp. 223-224)

*W. Wright, "The Hittites and the Bible," *BQRL* 76 (1882) 53-78.

J. F. Riggs, "The Hittites," *CT* 2 (1884-85) 368-400.

A. H. Sayce, "The Empire of the Hittites," *ONTS* 4 (1884-85) 32-34.

A. H. Sayce, "The Hittite Empire," *ONTS* 4 (1884-85) 227-228.

T. K. Cheyne, "Rev. Dr. Cheyne and the 'Hittites'," *ONTS* 4 (1884-85) 424-425. *[with Editorial Notes]*

†W. H. Summers, "Communication with W. H. Summers," *SBAP* 7 (1884-85) 179. *[Hittites]*

Isaac Taylor, "The Hittites," *BQRL* 81 (1885) 112-116. *(Review)*

†Robert Brown Jr., "Notes on the Hittites," *SBAP* 8 (1885-86) 125-126.

Francis Brown, "The Hittites," *PR* 7 (1886) 277-303.

William Wright, "The Empire of the Hittites," *JTVI* 21 (1886-87) 55-64. [(Discussion, pp. 65-70) (Note, pp. 71-72)]

*H. B. Tristram, "Canaan, Ancient and Modern, with references to the Light thrown by recent Research on the Movements of the Hittites," *JTVI* 21 (1886-87) 73-76.

Angus Crawford, "A Lost Empire Restored," *CR* 50 (1887) 129-145. *[Hittites]*

Hittites cont.

Claude R. Conder, "The Hittites," *PEFQS* 19 (1887) 133-136.

*Claude R. Conder, "Hittites and Etruscans," *PEFQS* 19 (1887) 136-143.

Claude R. Conder, "The Criticism of the Hittites," *PEFQS* 19 (1887) 143-148.

R. Lovett, "Fresh Light on the Hittite Problem," *CongRL* 1 (1887-88) 570-577.

W. W. Moore, "The Hittite Empire," *PQ* 1 (1887-88) 433-453.

*C[laude] R. Conder, "Notes on the *Quarterly Statement*," *PEFQS* 20 (1888) 39-41. [The Hittites, pp. 39-40]

C[laude] R. Conder, "Recent Notes on the Hittites," *PEFQS* 21 (1889) 30-32.

Claude R. Conder, "Notes by Major Conder, R.E. I. Professor Sayce on the Hittites," *PEFQS* 21 (1889) 82-85.

Richard Chandler, "The Sons of Heth," *EN* 2 (1890) 213-219, 264-268, 309-311, 355-359.

C[laude] R. Conder, "Rev. C. de Cara and the Hittites," *PEFQS* 22 (1890) 182.

W. St. C[had] B[oscawen], "The Hittites," *BOR* 6 (1892-93) 144.

William Hayes Ward, "Light on Scriptural Texts from Recent Discoveries. Who Were the Hittites?" *HR* 28 (1894) 210-212.

Anonymous, "The Hittites," *MR* 77 (1895) 137-140.

Chas. W. Super, "Who were the Hittites (Hethites)?" *MR* 81 (1899) 260-264.

A. H. Sayce, "Hittite Notes," *SBAP* 21 (1899) 194-223.

J. N. Fradenburgh, "The Problem of the Hittites," *AAOJ* 22 (1900) 185-187.

Hittites cont.

Geo. H. Schodde, "Biblical Finds and Recent Discussions," *ColTM* 20 (1900) 170-183. [The Biblical Hittites, pp. 179-181]

William Hayes Ward, "Light from Archaeology on the Hittites of the Old Testament," *HR* 39 (1900) 111-115.

C[laude] R. Conder, "Recent Hittite Discoveries," *SRL* 36 (1900) 62-80.

G[eorge] H. Schodde, "The Biblical Hittites," *ColTM* 21 (1901) 58-60.

A. H. Sayce, "The Hittites, or the Story of a Forgotten Empire," *HR* 41 (1901) 387-391.

*Walter M. Patton, "Hittites and Semites," *MQR, 3rd Ser.,* 28 (1902) 722-728.

Leopold Messerschmidt, "The Ancient Hitties," *SIR* (1903) 681-703.

A. H. Sayce, "Were There Hitties in Southern Palestine?" *ET* 15 (1903-04) 280-285, 474.

Anonymous, "The Hittites," *MQR, 3rd Ser.,* 30 (1904) 184-186.

J. H. Stevenson, "The Hittites," *MQR, 3rd Ser.,* 30 (1904) 251-261.

James Henry Breasted, "When Did the Hittites Enter Palestine?" *AJSL* 21 (1904-05) 153-158.

Albert T. Clay, "Discovery of the Lost Hittite Empire," *CFL, 3rd Ser.,* 6 (1907) 354.

Anonymous, "Hittite Discoveries," *RP* 6 (1907) 302-303.

A. H. Sayce, "The Hittite Invasion of Babylonia," *ET* 19 (1907-08) 379.

A. H. Sayce, "Hittite Discoveries," *R&E* 5 (1908) 169-180.

George E. White, "Hittites Near Marsovan, Asia Minor," *RP* 7 (1908) 267-274.

Hittites cont.

A. H. Sayce, "The Latest Hittite Discoveries," *BW* 33 (1909) 367-381.

Francis Isabel Dodd, "Most Recent Hittite Discoveries," *RP* 8 (1909) 247-248.

George Frederick Wright, "The Hittites," *RP* 8 (1909) 308-310.

Anonymous, "Sayce on the Hittites," *RP* 8 (1909) 317.

Anonymous, "M. Fossey on the Hittites," *RP* 8 (1909) 321.

*E. G. Harmer, "The Bible and the Latest Research in the Hittite Lands," *CFL, 3rd Ser.,* 13 (1910) 159-161.

Anonymous, "Hittite Research," *HR* 59 (1910) 26.

Anonymous, "Indications of Hittites in Greece," *RP* 9 (1910) 122.

*D. G. Hogarth, "Hittite Problems and the Excavations of Carchemish," *PBA* 5 (1911-12) 361-375.

Anonymous, "The Hittites," *MR* 94 (1912) 307-311.

A. H. Sayce, "The Solution of the Hittite Problem," *SBAP* 34 (1912) 217-226, 269-273. [I. The Cilician Empire in Syria; II. The Herakleid Dynasty of Lydia; III. The Midas-City]

D. D. Luckenbill, "The Hittites," *AJT* 18 (1914) 24-58.

*A. H. Sayce, "What We Now Know About the Hittites, and Its Bearing on the Hittites of Genesis," *ET* 26 (1914-15) 89-91.

*George W. Gilmore, "Hittite Civilization at Carchemish," *HR* 67 (1914) 438-441.

W. M. Flinders Petrie, "The End of the Hittites," *AEE* 3 (1916) 32-33.

James Hope Moulton, "New Light on the Hittite Problem," *ET* 28 (1916-17) 106-109. (Correction p. 284)

*G[eorge] W. Gilmore, "Boghaz-Köi and the Hittites," *HR* 73 (1917) 485-486.

Hittites cont.

*L[uther] T. Townsend, "Prehistoric Babylon, Nineveh and the Hittite Empire; their Bearing on the Theory of Evolution," *CFL, 3rd Ser.,* 25 (1919) 45-49.

*Joseph Offord, "Archaeological Notes on Jewish Antiquities. LX. *The Double-headed Eagle and the Etruscans and Hittites,"* *PEFQS* 52 (1920) 41-42.

*W. J. Phythian-Adams, "Hittite and Trojan Allies," *BSAJB* #1 (1922) 3-7.

*Nora Griffith, "Akhenaten and the Hittites," *JEA* 9 (1923) 78-79.

George A. Barton, "Current Notes and Comments. The Hittites," *A&A* 17 (1924) 286.

*William W. Everts, "Statements Concerning the Hittites Affirmed by the Scriptures Confirmed by the Monuments," *BS* 81 (1924) 18-27.

*Samuel A. B. Mercer, "The Hittites, Mitanni and Babylonia in the Tell el-Amarna Letters," *JSOR* 8 (1924) 13-28.

*L. A. Mayer and J. Garstang, "Kizzuwadna and other Hittite States," *JEA* 11 (1925) 23-35.

George A. Barton, "The Present Status of the Hittite Problem," *PAPS* 65 (1926) 232-243.

J. Rendel Harris, "Further Traces of Hittite Migration," *BJRL* 11 (1927) 57-76.

W. J. Rutherford, "Note on the Hittites in Laconia," *BJRL* 12 (1928) 11-12.

W. J. Rutherford, "The Hittites in Laconia," *BJRL* 12 (1928) 302-303.

*A. H. Sayce, "The Original Home of the Hittites and the Site of Kussar," *JRAS* (1928) 257-264.

Hittites cont.

B. Hrozny, "The Coming of the Hittites into Asia," *EO* 2 (1930) 120-126.

*H. H. von der Osten, "Additions to 'Oriental Institute Publications,' Volume VI," *AJSL* 47 (1930-31) #1, Part 1, 53-55. *[Hittites, p. 54]*

*A. H. Sayce, "Hittite and Moscho-Hittite," *RHA* 1 (1930-32) 1-8.

*N. D. Mironov, "Aryan Vestiges in the Near East of the Second Millenary B.C.," *AO* 11 (1932-33) 140-217. [V. The Hittites, pp. 205-215]

E. O. Forrer, The Hittites in Palestine. I," *PEFQS* 68 (1936) 190-203.

E. O. Forrer, The Hittites in Palestine. II," *PEFQS* 69 (1937) 100-115.

Edward A. Cerny, "Archaeological Corner. Hittites (Hethites)," *CBQ* 2 (1940) 71-73.

Robert S. Hardy, "The Old Hittite Kingdom — A Political History," *AJSL* 58 (1941) 177-216.

*Albrecht Goetze, "The Problem of Chronology and Early Hittite History," *BASOR* #122 (1951) 18-25.

M. I. Maksimova, "Hittites in the Black Sea Region," *JNES* 10 (1951) 74-81.

A[lbrecht] Goetze, "Hittite Courtiers and their titles," *RHA* 12 (1952) 1-14.

*J. O'Connell, "A Recent Work on the Hittites," *ITQ* 21 (1954) 68-74. *(Review)*

Hans Gustav Güterbock, "The Hurrian Element in the Hittite Empire," *JWH* 2 (1954-55) 383-394.

*John C. L. Gibson, "Observations on Some Important Ethnic Terms in the Pentateuch," *JNES* 20 (1961) 217-238. [Hittites, pp. 224-227]

Hittites concluded

*Jana Siegelová, "The Hittites and Egypt," *NOP* 5 (1966) 76-79.

*Hans G[ustav] Güterbock, "The Hittite Conquest of Cyprus Reconsidered," *JNES* 26 (1967) 73-81.

*Harry A. Hoffner Jr., "Some Contributions of Hittitology to Old Testament Study," *TB* #20 (1969) 27-55. [A. Who were the 'Hittites' of the Old Testament? pp. 28-37]

*G. G. Giorgadze, "Hittites and Hurrians in Old Hittite Texts," *VDI* (1969) #1, 85.

Hivites

*H. C., "The Origin and History of the Sacred Slaves of Israel in Hivitia, Mount Se'yr, and the Hivite Tetrapolis," *JSL, 3rd Ser.,* 10 (1859-60) 266-283. [Chap. I.—The Hivites of Lebanon, and the colony conducted by Se'yr to the south of Canaan, pp. 266-272; Chap. II.—The History of the Hivites in Mount Se'yr, pp. 272-276]

*C[laude] R. Conder, "Notes on the Antiquities of the Book of Joshua," *PEFQS* 31 (1899) 161-162. *[The Hivites]*

*K. V. Mathew, "Ancient Religions of the Fertile Crescent—and the Sanathana Drama," *IJT* 8 (1959) 83-90. [Hivites (Gen. 10:16), pp. 85-86]

I. H. Eybers, "Who were the Hivites?" *OTW* 2 (1959) 6-14.

Homonadeis

T. R. S. Broughton, "Some Notes on the War with the Homonadeis," *AJP* 54 (1933) 134-144.

Horites

*A. Benisch, "Correspondence," *JSL, 1st Ser.,* 3 (1849) 168-170. *[The Horites]*

Horites concluded

*Anonymous, "Genealogy of the Horites," *SBAP* 8 (1885-86) 41.

E[ugen] Täubler, "Kharu, Horim, Dedanim," *HUCA* 1 (1924) 97-124. *[Horites]*

*Cyrus H. Gordon, "Biblical Customs and the Nuzu Tablets," *BA* 3 (1940) 1-12. [Hebrews and Horites, p. 12]

Hurrians

*Robert H. Pfeiffer, "Nuzi and the Hurrians: The excavations at Nuzi (Kirkuk, Iraq) and their contribution to our knowledge of the history of the Hurrians," *SIR* (1935) 535-558.

C. J. Mullo Weir, "The Place of the Hurrites in Early Near-Eastern History," *GUOST* 9 (1938-39) 23-25.

Edward Cerny, "Archaeological Corner.   Hurrians," *CBQ* 2 (1940) 179-181.

John   Paterson,   "The   Hurrians,"   *SSO*   2   (1945)   95-115.

*E[phraim] A. Speiser, "'Hurrians and Subarians'," *JAOS* 68 (1948) 1-13.

*Sidney Smith, "On Hurrians and Subarians': A Review Article," *PEQ* 81 (1949) 117-126. *(Review)*

*Ephraim A. Speiser, "The Hurrian Participation in the Civilizations of Mesopotamia, Syria and Palestine," *JWH* 1 (1953-54) 311-327.

*I. J. Gelb, "New Light on Hurrians and Şubarians," *SOOG* 1 (1956) 378-392.

*Warren C. Benedict, "Urartians and Hurrians," *JAOS* 80 (1960) 100-104.

*John C. L. Gibson, "Observations on Some Important Ethnic Terms in the Pentateuch," *JNES* 20 (1961) 217-238. [Hurrians, pp. 227-229]

Hurrians concluded

*R. North, "Some Links between the Hurrians and the Language of the Exodus," *AAI* 2 (1965) 343-357.

*G. G. Giorgadze, "Hittites and Hurrians in Old Hittite Texts," *VDI* (1969) #1, 85.

Hyksos

*(Miss) Fanny Corbaux, "The Rephaim, and Their Connexion with Egyptian History," *JSL, 2nd Ser.,* 1 (1851-52) 151-172, 363-394; 2 (1852) 55-91, 303-340; 3 (1852-53) 87-116, 279-307. [Chap. 6 - Wars of the Hyksos and Thebans, 1 (1851-52) pp. 367-375]

*Joseph P. Thompson, "Notes on Egyptology," *BS* 26 (1869) 184-191, 577-585. [Data for the Hyksos Period, pp. 581-585]

*A. Wiedemann, "Notes on the Cult of Set and on the Hyksos-Kings," *SBAP* 8 (1885-86) 92-95.

*G. Willoughby Fraser, "El Kab and Gebelen," *SBAP* 15 (1892-93) 494-500. [III. The Hyksos, p. 500]

*W. W. Moore, "The Hyksos and the Hebrews," *USR* 8 (1896-97) 263-266.

A. H. Sayce, "Notes on—(1) The Hyksos," *SBAP* 23 (1901) 95-98.

A. H. Sayce, "The Hyksos," *BW* 21 (1903) 347-355.

W. M. Flinders Petrie, "The Hyksos," *Man* 6 (1906) #75.

W. M. Flinders Petrie, "The Hyksos," *RP* 5 (1906) 286-288.

Melvin Grove Kyle, "The 'Dark Ages' in Egypt," *CFL, 3rd Ser.,* 7 (1907) 14-16. *(Editorial Note) [The Hyksos Period]*

Anonymous, "A Hint as to Who the Hyksos Were," *CFL, 3rd Ser.,* 9 (1908) 359-360. *(Editorial Note)*

*E. W. Hollingworth, "The Hyksos and the Twelfth Dyansty," *SBAP* 30 (1908) 155-158.

Hyksos concluded

M[elvin] G[rove] Kyle, "The Hyksos at Heliopolis," *JBL* 32 (1913) 155-158.

*Battiscombe Gunn and Alan H. Gardiner, "New Renderings of Egyptian Texts," *JEA* 5 (1918) 36-56. [II. The Expulsion of the Hyksos]

George W. Gilmore, "Light on the Hyksos," *HR* 77 (1919) 390-391.

Anonymous, "The Hyksos," *MR* 102 (1919) 297-303.

*[W. M.] Flinders Petrie, "The Shepherd Kings of Palestine. Excavations at Beth-pelet, II," *AEE* 14 (1929) 1-16. *[Hyksos]*

*N. D. Mironov, "Aryan Vestiges in the Near East of the Second Millenary B.C.," *AO* 11 (1932-33) 140-217. [II. The Hyksos, pp. 150-170]

Sidney Smith, "The Hyksos Reconsidered. A Review," *PEQ* 72 (1940) 64-74. *(Review)*

T. Säve-Söderbergh, "The Hyksos Rule in Egypt," *JEA* 37 (1951) 53-71.

Hyrnathians

W. R. Halliday, "The Alleged Existence of a Hyrnathian Tribe at Epidauras," *AAA* 10 (1923) 27-33.

I

Indo-Europeans

Jarl Charpentier, "The Original Home of the Indo-Europeans," *BSOAS* 4 (1926-28) 147-170.

*Basil F. C. Atkinson, "The Indo-European Peoples of Genesis X," *EQ* 1 (1929) 121-129.

Indo-Europeans concluded

*C. J. Mullo Weir, "Problems of Western Asiatic Pre-History," *GUOST* 13 (1947-48) 44-48. [The Indo-Europeans, p. 48]

*R. A Crossland, "Indo-European Origins: The Linguistic Evidence," *P&P* #12 (1957) 16-46.

Indo-Iranians

W[illiam] F[oxwell] Albright, "New Light on the History of Western Asia in the Second Millennium B.C.," *BASOR* #78 (1940) 23-31. [The Earliest Historical Appearance of the Indo-Iranians, pp. 30-31]

Indians

*J. J. Crowley, "The Indus and the Pentateuch: A Study of the Indus Civilization," *NB* 27 (1946) 264-269.

Ionians

James Hadley, "On Recent Discussion and Opinion respecting the Ionian Migration," *JAOS* 8 (1866) xx-xxi.

*A. H. Sayce, "The Ionians in the Tel el-Amarna Tablets," *SBAP* 24 (1902) 10-13.

Iranians

*Geo Widengren, "Iran and Israel in Parthian Times with Special Regard to the Ethiopic Book of Enoch," *Tem* 2 (1966) 139-177.

T. Cuyler Young Jr., "The Iranian Migration into the Zagros," *Iran* 5 (1967) 11-34.

Ishmaelites

*A. Sprenger, "The Ishmaelites, and the Arabic Tribes who conquered their Country," *JRAS* (1872-73) 1-19.

Italians

*G. Sergi, "The Ayrans and the Ancient Italians. A Page of Primitive History," *Monist* 8 (1897-98) 161-182.

*John Alexander, "Greeks, Italians and the Earliest Balkan Iron Age," *Antiq* 36 (1962) 123-130.

K

Kasdim

A. H. Sayce, "The Kasdim," *ET* 17 (1905-06) 214-216.

Kassites

*N. D. Mironov, "Aryan Vestiges in the Near East of the Second Millenary B.C.," *AO* 11 (1932-33) 140-217. [I. The Kassites, pp. 142-149]

*A[lbrecht] Goetze, "The Kassites and Near Eastern Chronology," *JCS* 18 (1964) 97-101.

Keftiu-People

G. A. Wainwright, "The Keftiu-People of the Egyptian Monuments," *AAA* 6 (1913-14) 24-83.

Kenites

*(Miss) Fanny Corbaux, "The Rephaim, and Their Connexion with Egyptian History," *JSL, 2nd Ser.,* 1 (1851-52) 151-172, 363-394; 2 (1852) 55-91, 303-340; 3 (1852-53) 87-116, 279-307. [Chap. 11 - The Kenites, 2 (1852) pp. 80-89]

*Nelson Glueck, "Kenites and Kenizzites," *PEQ* 72 (1940) 22-24.

R. H. Altus, "The Kenites," *AusTR* 14 (1943) 84-90.

*F. Charles Fensham, "Did a Treaty Between the Israelites and the Kenites Exist?" *BASOR* #175 (1964) 51-54.

Kenizzites

*Nelson Glueck, "Kenites and Kenizzites," *PEQ* 72 (1940) 22-24.

Khabiri (see: *The Habiru / Hebrew Question* §61 ←)

Khazars

*Patrick T. English, "Cushites, Colchians, and Khazars," *JNES* 18 (1959) 49-53.

Khapiru

*Albrecht Goetze, "The City of Khalbi and the Khapiru People," *BASOR* #79 (1940) 32-34.

Kimmerians (See: Cimmerians)

Kushites (see: Cushites)

L

Libyans (See also: "Sea-Peoples" →)

Max Müller, "Notes on the 'Peoples of the Sea' of Merenptah," *SBAP* 10 (1887-88) 147-154. *[Libyans]*

Max Müller, "Supplementary Notes to 'Notes on the Peoples of the Sea' etc.," *SBAP* 10 (1887-88) 287-289. *[Libyans]*

P. le Page Renouf, "Who were the Libyans?" *SBAP* 13 (1890-91) 599-603.

*V. Giuffrida-Ruggeri, "Were the Pre-Dynastic Egyptians Libyans or Ethiopians?" *Man* 15 (1915) #32.

John A. Wilson, "The Libyans and the End of the Egyptian Empire," *AJSL* 51 (1934-35) 73-82.

M

Macedonians

John Van Antwerp Fine, "The Problem of Macedonian Holdings in Epirus and Thessaly in 221 B.C.," *TAPA* 63 (1932) 126-155.

Medes

*C[harles] C[utler] Torrey, "Concerning the Medes and the Persians," *JBL* 55 (1936) xi.

*Charles C[utler] Torrey, "'Medes and Persians'," *JAOS* 66 (1946) 1-15.

Meshwesh

G. A. Wainwright, "The Meshwesh," *JEA* 48 (1962) 89-99.

Mesopotamians

M. E. L. Mallowan, "A Mesopotamian Trilogy," *Antiq* 13 (1939) 159-70. *(Review)*

*Hermann Ranke, E. A. Speiser, W. Norman Brown, and Carl W. Bishop, "The Beginnings of Civilization in the Orient. A Symposium at the Meetings of the American Oriental Society, Baltimore, April 13, 1939," *JAOSS* #4 (1939) 3-61. [The Beginnings of Civilization in Mesopotamia, pp. 17-31(S)]

E[phraim] A. Speiser, "The Beginnings of Civilization in Mesopotamia," *Antiq* 15 (1941) 162-175.

*Josef Klíma, "The Periphery of Mesopotamian Culture," *NOP* 4 (1965) 17-19.

Minaeans

F. V. Winnett, "The Place of the Minaeans in the History of Pre-Islamic Arabia," *BASOR* #73 (1939) 3-9.

Minoans

*(Mrs.) Harriet Boyd Hawes, "Minoans and Mycenaeans: A Working Hypothesis for the Solution of Certain Problems of Early Mediterranean Race and Culture," *AJA* 11 (1907) 57-58.

Minyans

J. Penrose Harland, "The Minyan Migration," *AJA* 26 (1922) 77-78.

Miši

Thomas O. Lambdin, "The *Miši-* People of the Byblian Amarna Letters," *JCS* 7 (1953) 75-77.

Mitanni

'N. D. Mironov, "Aryan Vestiges in the Near East of the Second Millenary B.C.," *AO* 11 (1932-33) 140-217. [IV. The Mitanni, pp. 186-205]

Mizraim

*(Miss) Fanny Corbaux, "The Rephaim, and Their Connexion with Egyptian History," *JSL, 2nd Ser.,* 1 (1851-52) 151-172, 363-394; 2 (1852) 55-91, 303-340; 3 (1852-53) 87-116, 279-307. [Chap. 2 - Geographical Distribution of the Mizraim, 1 (1851-52) pp. 157-162]

Mnṯyw

S. Yeivin, "Who were the *Mnṯyw* ?" *JEA* 51 (1965) 204-206.

Moabites

Nelson Glueck, "The Civilization of the Moabites," *AJA* 38 (1934) 212-218.

Mycenaeans

T[errien] de L[acouperie], "On the Chronology of the Mycenian civilisation," *BOR* 6 (1892-93) 192.

*(Mrs.) Harriet Boyd Hawes, "Minoans and Mycenaeans: A Working Hypothesis for the Solution of Certain Problems of Early Mediterranean Race and Culture," *AJA* 11 (1907) 57-58.

*Bedřich Hrozný, "New Contribution to Knowledge of the Religious, Social and Public Conditions on the Peloponnesus (E. L. Benett, The Pylos Tablets, Preliminary Transcription)," *JJP* 6 (1952) 11-13. *[The Mycenaeans]*

*Emily Townsend Vermeule, "The Mycenaeans in Achaia," *AJA* 62 (1958) 227.

*Sara A. Immerwahr, Mycenaean Trade and Colonization," *Arch* 13 (1960) 4-13.

(Miss) Nancy [K.] Sandars, "The Last Mycenaeans and the European Late Bronze Age," *Antiq* 38 (1964) 258-262.

N

Nabataeans

Anonymous, "The Nabataeans and Professor Chwolson," *JSL, 4th Ser.*, 1 (1862) 103-115.

*Nelson Glueck, "Nabataean Syria," *BASOR* #85 (1942) 3-8.

Jean Starcky, "The Nabataeans: A Historical Sketch," *BA* 18 (1955) 84-106. (Introduction by Frank M. Cross Jr., pp. 82-83) [1. The Nabataeans and the Land of Edom; 2. The Early Kings; 3. The Golden Age at Petra, 50 B.C.-A.D. 70; 4. The End of the Nabataean Kingdom and the Province of Arabia]

*Crystal M. Bennett, "The Nabataeans in Petra," *Arch* 15 (1962) 233-243.

Nabataeans concluded

Yigael Yadin, "The Nabataean Kingdom, Provincia Arabia, Petra and En-geddi in the Documents from Naḥal Ḥever," *JEOL* #17 (1963) 227-241.

*P. J. Parr, "The Nabataeans and North-West Arabia," *ULBIA* 8&9 (1968-69) 250-252.

Natufians

Dorothy A. E. Garrod, "The Natufian Culture: The Life and Economy of a Mesolithic People in the Near East," *PBA* 43 (1957) 211-227.

Nubians

*N. M. Davies, "Nubians in the Tomb of Amunedjeḥ," *JEA* 28 (1942) 50-52.

*Hans-Åke Nordström, "A-Group and C-Group in Upper Nubia," *Kush* 14 (1966) 63-68. *[Nubians]*

H. S. Smith, "The Nubian B-Group," *Kush* 14 (1966) 69-124.

P

Parthians

Neilson C. Debovoise, "Parthian Problems," *AJSL* 47 (1930-31) 73-82.

*Józef Wolski, "The Decay of the Iranian Empire of the Seleucids and the Chronology of the Parthian Beginnings," *Bery* 12 (1956-58) 35-52.

Sami S. Ahmed, "Early Parthians—Philhellenism as Evidenced in the Figurines from Seleucia on the Tigris Level III," *AAAS* 17 (1967) 85-90.

G. A. Koshelenko, "Problems of Early Parthian History," *VDI* (1968) #1, 71.

Pelethites

*L. M. Muntingh, "The Cherethites and Pelethites," *OTW* 3 (1960) 43-53.

Persians

†Anonymous, "Persian Monarchy," *MMBR* 53 (1822) 400-401.

†Anonymous, "On the Ancient History of Persia," *MMBR* 55 (1823) 515-518; 56 (1823-24) 18-20.

H. H. Howorth, "The Beginnings of Persian History," *JRAS* (1892) 372-375.

S. Krauss, "The Duration of the Persian Empire," *JQR* 10 (1897-98) 725-726.

George S. Goodspeed, "The Persian Empire from Darius to Artaxerxes," *BW* 14 (1899) 251-257.

*W. M. Flinders Petrie, "The Peoples of the Persian Empire," *Man* 8 (1908) #71.

Stanley Casson, "The Vita Miltiadis of Cornelius Nepos," *Klio* 14 (1914-15) 69-90. *[The Persian Wars]*

*C[harles] C[utler] Torrey, "Concerning the Medes and the Persians," *JBL* 55 (1936) xi.

*Charles C[utler] Torrey, "'Medes and Persians'," *JAOS* 66 (1946) 1-15.

*A. E. Wardmann, "Tactics and the Tradition of the Persian Wars," *HJAH* 8 (1959) 49-60.

*A. Andrewes, "Thucydides and the Persians," *HJAH* 10 (1961) 1-18.

A[nson] F. Rainey, "The Satrapy 'Beyond the River'," *AJBA* 1 (1968-71) #2, 51-78.

Philistines

*(Miss) Fanny Corbaux, "The Rephaim, and Their Connexion with Egyptian History," *JSL, 2nd Ser.,* 1 (1851-52) 151-172, 363-394; 2 (1852) 55-91, 303-340; 3 (1852-53) 87-116, 279-307. [Chap. 14 - The Philistines, 2 (1852) pp. 323-329]

John Campbell, "The Philistines," *BFER* 26 (1877) 477-511.

*Claude R. Conder, "Notes on New Discoveries," *PEFQS* 41 (1909) 266-275. [The Philistines, pp. 268-269]

*Anonymous, "The Philistines and Steel," *RP* 10 (1911) 295.

Robert C. Horn, "The Philistines and Ancient Crete—Caphtor, Keftiu, Crete," *RP* 12 (1913) 119-122.

Anonymous, "The Philistines," *MR* 96 (1914) 805-809.

Anonymous, "The Philistines," *RP* 13 (1914) 58.

George Jackson, "Were the Philistines 'Philistines'?" *LQHR* 136 (1921) 16-30.

*John Garstang, "Askalon Reports. *The Philistine Problem,*" *PEFQS* 53 (1921) 162-163.

Anonymous, "The Mystery of the Philistines," *HR* 84 (1922) 282-283.

W. J. Phythian-Adams, "Philistine Origins in the Light of Palestinian Archaeology," *BSAJB* #3 (1923) 20-27.

Redcliffe N. Salaman, "What has become of the Philistines? A Biologist's Point of View," *PEFQS* 57 (1925) 37-45, 68-79.

G. A. Wainwright, "Caphtor, Keftiu, and Cappadocia," *PEFQS* 63 (1931) 203-216. *[Origin of the Philistines]*

Elihu Grant, "The Philistines," *JBL* 55 (1936) 175-194.

N. H. Torczyner, "Plesheth, Philistines," *BIES* 6 (1938-39) #1, V.

Philistines concluded

S. Y[eivin], "On Plesheth—Shephelah," *BIES* 6 (1938-39) #1, v.
   [Philistines]

G. Bonfante, "Who Were the Philistines?" *AJA* 50 (1946) 251-262.

Cyrus H. Gordon, "The Rôle of the Philistines," *Antiq* 30 (1956)
   22-26.

Trude Dothan, "Archaeological Reflections on the Philistine Problem,"
   A&S 2 (1957) #2/3, 151-164.

Trude Dothan, "Philistine Civilization in the Light of Archaeolgical
   Finds in Palestine and Egypt," *EI* 5 (1958) 86*.

Edward F. Campbell Jr., "In Search of the Philistines," *BA* 26 (1963)
   30-32.

Anonymous, "The Philistines," *BH* 1 (1964) #3, 15-19.

*Hanna E. Kassis, "Gath and the Structure of the 'Philistine' Society,"
   JBL 84 (1965) 259-271.

*B. D. Rahtjen, "Philistine and Hebrew Amphictyonies," *JNES* 24
   (1965) 100-104.

Trude Dothan, "New Finds Relating to the Philistine Culture,"
   AJA 70 (1966) 187.

G. Ernest Wright, "Fresh Evidence for the Philistine Story," *BA* 29
   (1966) 70-86.

*B[enjamin] Mazar, "The Philistines and the Rise of Israel and Tyre,"
   PIASH 1 (1967) #7, 1-22.

Gordon H. Lovik, "The Philistines," *CCBQ* 12 (1969) #4, 2-15.

Phoenicians

John Campbell, "The Origin of the Phœnicians," *BFER* 24 (1875)
   425-448.

Phoenicians cont.

A. H. Sayce, "The Phœnicians in Greece," *ContR* 34 (1878-79) 60-76.

S[elah] M[errill], "The Original Seat of the Phœnicians," *AAOJ* 2 (1879-80) 170.

J. Hammond Trumbull, "On Recent Discussions of the Evidence of Phœnician Occupation of America," *JAOS* 10 (1880) cv-cvi.

Selah Merrill, The Original Seat of the Phœnicians," *OBJ* 1 (1880) 16.

[Jens] Lieblein, "The Phoenicians in Egypt," *SBAP* 4 (1881-82) 108-110.

C[laude] R. Conder, "Notes by Major Conder, D.C.L., R.E. II. Phoenician Notes," *PEFQS* 21 (1889) 142-145.

†Anonymous, "Rawlinson's History of Phœnicia," *ERCJ* 174 (1891) 88-121. *(Review)*

H. B. S. W., "Phoenians in Devonshire," *PEFQS* 23 (1891) 77-78. (Note by C[laude] R. Conder, p. 186)

*Hugh Pope, "Phoenicia and Israel," *IER, 4th Ser.,* 2 (1897) 488-499; 3 (1898) 38-59.

John A. Maynard, "Were the Phoenicians a Semitic People?" *JSOR* 5 (1921) 51-55.

Robert Dunlop, "Ireland of the Phœnicians," *ContR* 124 (1923) 749-754.

D. B. Harden, "The Phoenicians on the West Coast of Africa," *Antiq* 22 (1948) 141-150.

Rhys Carpenter, "Phoenicians in the West," *AJA* 62 (1958) 35-53.

W. Culican, "Aspects of Phoenician Settlement in the West Mediterranean," *Abr-N* 1 (1959-60) 36-55.

*Theresa Howard Carter, "Western Phoenicians at Lepcis Magna," *AJA* 69 (1965) 123-132.

Phoenicians concluded

*W. Shanklin and M. Ghantus, "A preliminary report on the anthropology of the Phoenicians," *BMB* 19 (1966) 91-94.

Phrygians

*Machteld J. Mellink, "Mita, Mushki and Phrygians," *AAI* 2 (1965) 317-325.

Q

Qatna Kings

Claire Epstein, "'That Wretched Enemy of Kadesh'," *JNES* 22 (1963) 242-246. *[Qatna Kings]*

Qenites

S.   Abramski,   "The   Qenites,"   *EI*   3   (1954)   VI-VII.

R

Rabbahites

*L. T. Townsend, "King David and the Rabbahites," *CFL, 3rd Ser.,* 19 (1915) 205-206.

Rechabites

Josephus *[sic]*, "Historical Sketch of the Rechabites," *QCS, N.S.,* 2 (1828) 179-186.

Ernest M. Bowden, "The Original Rechabites," *TML* 6 (1891) 166-183.

Rephaim

*(Miss) Fanny Corbaux, "The Rephaim, and Their Connexion with Egyptian History," *JSL, 2nd Ser.,* 1 (1851-52) 151-172, 363-394; 2 (1852) 55-91, 303-340; 3 (1852-53) 87-116, 279-307. [Chap. 1 - State of Palestine during the Patriarchal Period; Chap. 2 - Geographical Distribution of the Mizraim; Chap. 3 - Geographical Distribution of the Canaanites and Rephaim; Chap. 4 - Origin of the Rephaim; Chap. 5 - The Zuzim; Chap. 6. - Wars of the Hyksos and Thebans; Chap. 7 - Geographical Identity of the Zuzim and *shas·u;* Chap. 8 - Cities and Dependencies of the Zuzim; Chap. 9 - The Emim; Chap. 10 - The Wars of Emim with Egypt; Chap. 11 - The Kenites; Chap. 12 - The Amalekites; Chap. 13 - The Anakim; Chap. 14 - The Philistines; Chap. 15 - Final Wars of the Anakim with Egypt; Chap. 16 - Religious System and Pantheon of the Rephaim; Chap. 17 - *(untitled);* Chap. 18 - Costumes of the Rephaim]

*J. W. Jack, "Recent Biblical Archaeology," *ET* 51 (1939-40) 420-423. [The Rephaim, pp. 421-422]

*John Gray, "The Rephaim," *PEQ* 81 (1949) 127-139.

Reten

*D. H. Haigh,  *ZÄS* 13 (1875) 29-32, 60-64. *[Reten]*

Rhœtians

*R. [L.] Ellis, "On the probable Connexion of the Rhœtians and Etruscans with the Thracian stock of nations," *JCSP* 1 (1854) 1-20, 169-185.

Romans

†Anonymous, "Early History of Rome," *QRL* 27 (1822) 273-308. *(Review)*

†Anonymous, "Early Roman History," *QRL* 32 (1825) 67-92. *(Review)*

†Anonymous, "National Character of the Romans," *WR* 16 (1832) 368-390. *(Review)*

†Anonymous, "Niebuhr's *Roman History*," *ERCJ* 56 (1832-33) 267-312. *(Review)*

*†Anonymous, "Objects of the Catilinarian Conspiracy," *WR* 21 (1834) 89-102.

*Albert Smith, "Character and Theology of the Early Romans," *BRCR, N.S.,* 9 (1843) 253-285.

*Albert Smith, "Character and Theology of the Later Romans," *BRCR, N.S.,* 10 (1843) 328-352.

†Anonymous, "The Poetical Element in Roman History," *CTPR, 3rd Ser.,* 2 (1846) 322-337. *(Review)*

†[Henry Holland], "Mr. Merivale's *History of the Roman Empire*," *QRL* 88 (1850-51) 385-416. *(Review)*

*I. B. Trautman, "The Hellenes, Romans, and Israelites. Their Position, Secular and Religious, in the History of the World," *CRB* 16 (1851) 96-105.

Anonymous, "A History of the Romans under the Empire," *DR* 30 (1851) 436-453. *(Review)*

†[Edward Hebert Bunbury], "Lewis *on Early Roman History*," *QRL* 98 (1855-56) 321-352. *(Review)*

Anonymous, "Merivale's History of the Romans," *DUM* 37 (1851) 611-624; 48 (1856) 30-47. *(Review)*

Romans cont.

*G. Seyffarth, "Three Lectures on Egyptian Antiquities, &c., delivered at the Stuyvesant Institute, New York, May 1856," *ER* 8 (1856-57) 34-104. [XX. The History of the Greeks and Romans, pp. 94-96]

†Anonymous, "Sir G. C. Lewis on the Credibility of Early Roman History," *ERCJ* 104 (1856) 1-24. *(Review)*

†Anonymous, "Merivale's *Romans under the Empire*," *ERCJ* 106 (1857) 157-194. *(Review)*

D. B. Monro, "Notes on Roman history," *JP* 2 (1869) 197-205.

†Anonymous, "The Roman Empire," *BQRL* 54 (1871) 1-33. *(Review)*

Goldwin Smith, "The Greatness of the Romans," *ContR* 32 (1878) 321-337.

*Anonymous, "The Provinces of the Roman Empire," *SRL* 12 (1888) 293-330. *(Review)*

*J. P. Mahaffy, "The Slave Wars against Rome," *Herm* 7 (1889-90) 167-182.

Samuel Ball Platner, "The Credibility of Early Roman History," *AmHR* 7 (1901-02) 233-253.

William Ridgeway, "Who Were the Romans?" *PBA* 3 (1907-08) 17-60.

T. E. Peet, "Who Were the Romans? A Note on some Recent Answers," *AAA* 2 (1909) 187-193.

Richard Wellington Husband, "Race Mixture in Early Rome," *TAPA* 40 (1909) 63-81.

F. Haverfield, "Roman History since Mommsen," *QRL* 217 (1912) 323-345. *(Review)*

M. O. B. Caspari, "On some Problems of Roman agrarian history," *Klio* 13 (1913) 184-198.

Romans concluded

Helen M. Tanzer, "The Humanity of the Romans," *PAPA* 57 (1926) xxiii-xxiv.

*William Linn Westermann, "New Historical Documents in Greek and Roman History," *AmHR* 35 (1929-30) 14-32.

Eva Matthews Sanford, "Contrasting Views of the Roman Empire," *AJP* 58 (1937) 437-455.

Walter F. Snyder, "On Chronology in the Imperial Books of Cassius Dio's Roman History," *Klio* 33 (1940) 39-56.

*Frederic M. Wood Jr., "The Military and Diplomatic Campaign of T. Quinctius Flamininus in 198 B.C.," *AJP* 62 (1941) 277-288.

C. E. Stevens, "55 B.C. and 54 B.C.," *Antiq* 21 (1947) 3-9. *[Roman History]*

F. W. Adams, "Some Observations on the Consular Fasti in the Early Empire," *AJA* 55 (1951) 239-241.

E. Badian, "Caepio and Norbanus. *Notes on the Decade 100-90 B.C.*," *HJAH* 6 (1957) 318-346. *[Roman History]*

*P. A. Brunt, "Charges of Provincial Maladministartion under the Early Principate," *HJAH* 10 (1961) 189-227.

E. Badian, "Notes on Roman Senators of the Republic," *HJAH* 12 (1963) 129-143.

*Erich S. Gruen, "Political Persecutions in the 90's B.C.," *HJAH* 15 (1966) 32-64.

*P. A. Brunt, "The Roman Mob," *P&P* #35 (1966) 3-27.

Einar Gjerstad, "Discussions concerning Early Rome, 3," *HJAH* 16 (1967) 257-278. [Parts 1 & 2 published in *Opusc. Rom. III & V]*

S

Samaritans

Anonymous, "The Samaritans, Ancient and Modern," *PRev* 38 (1866) 195-221.

*Albert Lowy, "The Samaritans in Talmudical Writings," *SBAP* 2 (1879-80) 11-13.

George St. Clair, "The Samaritans," *PEFQS* 20 (1888) 50-51.

*A. Cowley, "Samaritan Literature and Religion," *JQR* 8 (1895-96) 562-575.

John R. Sampey, "The Samaritans," *BW* 14 (1899) 188-191.

J. E. H. Thomson, "The Samaritans," *ET* 11 (1899-1900) 375-377.

Jacob, Son of Aaron, "The History and Religion of the Samaritans," *BS* 63 (1906) 385-426. *(Edited by William Eleazer Barton)*

Jacob, Son of Aaron, "Mount Gerizim the One True Sanctuary," *BS* 64 (1907) 489-518. *(Trans. by Abdullah ben Kori; Edited by William E[leazer] Barton)*

Jacob, Son of Aaron, "The Samaritan Sabbath," *BS* 65 (1908) 430-444. *(Trans. by Abdullah ben Kori; Edited by William E[leazer] Barton)*

Anonymous, "The Samaritans," *MR* 102 (1919) 630-636.

*P. P. McKenna, "The Samaritans and Their Pascal Sacrifice," *IER, 5th Ser.,* 32 (1928) 291-299.

Douglas V. Duff, "'Icabod': The Glory Has Departed," *DR* 193 (1933) 231-243. *[Samaritans]*

‡L. A. Mayer, "Outline of a Bibliography of the Samaritans," *EI* 4 (1956) XVI, 252-268.

Samaritans concluded

John Bowman, "Samaritan Studies," *BJRL* 40 (1957-58) 298-327.
[I. The Fourth Gospel and the Samaritans;   II. Faith in
Samaritan Thought; III. Samaritan Law and Liturgy]

John Bowman, "The Importance of Samaritan Researches," *ALUOS* 1
(1958-59) 43-54.

G. Ernest Wright, "The Samaritans at Shechem," *HTR* 55 (1962)
357-366.

*I. H. Eybers, "Relations between Jews and Samaritans in the
Persian Period," *OTW* 9 (1966) 72-89.

R. J. Coggins, "The Old Testament and Samaritan Origins," *ASTI* 6
(1967-68) 35-48.

*B. N. Grakov, "Survivals of Scythian Religion and Epos among the
Samaritans," *VDI* (1969) #3, 72.

Scythians

*(   ) G., "The Scythian Dominion in Asia (as recorded by Herodotus)
in its Connexion with Josiah's Exercise of Sovereign Power in
the Territory of the Ten Tribes," *JSL, 2nd Ser.*, 4 (1853) 1-34.

Reinhold Solger, "On the Ethnological Relations of the Ancient
Scythians," *PAOS*, May (1859) 7-8.

P. S. Nazaroff, "The Scythians," *ERCJ* 250 (1929) 108-122.

G. W. B. Huntingford, "Who were the Scythians?" *Anthro* 30 (1935)
785-795.

*B. N. Grakov, "Survivals of Scythian Religion and Epos among the
Samaritans," *VDI* (1969) #3, 72.

"Sea-Peoples" [See also: Libyans ←]

*J. Offord Jr., "The 'Peoples of the Sea' of Merenptah," *SBAP* 10
(1887-88) 231.

"Sea-Peoples" concluded

*Max Müller, "Notes on the 'Peoples of the Sea' of Merenptah'," *SBAP* 10 (1887-88) 147-154.

*Max Müller, "Supplementary Notes to 'Notes on the Peoples of the Sea', etc.," *SBAP* 10 (1887-88) 287-289.

*H. R. Hall, "The Caucasian Relations of the Peoples of the Sea," *Klio* 22 (1928-29) 335-344.

*G. A. Wainwright, "Some Sea-Peoples and Others in the Hittite Archives," *JEA* 25 (1939) 148-153.

G. A. Wainwright, "Some Sea-peoples," *JEA* 47 (1961) 71-90.

G. A. Wainwright, "Two Groups among the Sea Peoples," *AAI* 2 (1965) 481-489.

Seleucids

*Glanville Downey, "Seleucid Chronology in Malalas," *AJA* 42 (1938) 106-120.

Alfred R. Bellinger, "The End of the Seleucids," *CAAST* 38 (1949) 51-102.

*Józef Wolski, "The Decay of the Iranian Empire of the Seleucids and the Chronology of the Parthian Beginnings," *Bery* 12 (1956-58) 35-52.

K. M. T. Atkinson, "The Seleucids in the Greek Cities of Western Asia Minor," *AASCS* 2 (1968) 32-57.

Semites

*A. H. Sayce, "The Origin of Semitic Civilisation, chiefly upon Philological Evidence," *SBAT* 1 (1872) 294-309.

Thomas Chalmers Murray, "Origin and History of the Shemitic Peoples," *DTQ* 6 (1880) 458-469.

Semites cont.

[Crawford H.] Toy, "The Home of the Primitive Semitic Race," *PAPA* 13 (1881) 6. *[Bound with Transactions, but paged separately]*

Crawford H. Toy, "The Home of the Primitive Semitic Race," *TAPA* 12 (1881) 26-51.

W. Volck, "'The Semites'," *AJSL* 2 (1885-86) 147-161. *(Trans. by D. M. Welton)*

G. Bertin, "The Pre-Akkadian Semites," *JRAS* (1886) 409-436.

Albert A. Isaacs, "The Semitic Race," *EN* 1 (1889) 337-341.

*[Paul Carus], "Accad and the Early Semites," *OC* 9 (1895) 4651-4654.

F[ritz] Hommel, "The Oldest History of the Semites," *ET* 8 (1896-97) 103-109.

Walter M. Patton, "The Home of the Semites," *MQR, 3rd Ser.,* 28 (1902) 34-47.

*Walter M. Patton, "Hittites and Semites," *MQR, 3rd Ser.,* 28 (1902) 722-728.

Hugo Radau, "Semitic Origins," *Monist* 13 (1902-03) 608-617. *(Review)*

*Morris Jastrow Jr., "The Hamites and Semites in the Tenth Chapter of Genesis," *PAPS* 43 (1904) 173-207.

*Stephen Langdon, "Sumerians and Semites in Babylonia," *Baby* 2 (1907-08) 137-161.

A. H. Sayce, "The Semites. Their Origin and Characteristics According to Professor Sayce," *OC* 23 (1909) 238-249.

N. Kolkin, "Early Semitic Adventures and Semitic Lore," *AAOJ* 34 (1912) 114-119.

Semites concluded

*Paul Haupt, "Semites, Hebrews, Israelites, Jews," *OC* 32 (1918) 753-760.

John P. Peters, "The Home of the Semites," *JAOS* 39 (1919) 243-260.

*W. H. Worrell, "Noun Classes and Polarity in Hamitic and their bearing upon the Origin of the Semites," *JPOS* 1 (1920-21) 15-21.

Hilary G. Richardson, "The Semites," *AJSL* 41 (1924-25) 1-10.

Edward Day, "The Early Semite," *AJSL* 46 (1929-30) 150-188.

*Thorkild Jacobson, "The Assumed Conflict between Sumerians and Semites in Early Mesopotamian History," *JAOS* 59 (1939) 485-495.

*C. J. Mullo Weir, "Problems of Western Asiatic Pre-History," *GUOST* 13 (1947-48) 44-48. [The Semites, p. 47]

*Sabatino Moscati, "*Israel's Predecessors:* A Re-Examination of Certain Current Theories," *JAAR* 24 (1956) 245-254. *[Semites]*

Sabatino Moscati, "The Semites: A Linguistic, Ethnic, and Racial Problem," *CBQ* 19 (1957) 412-434.

I. J. Gelb, "The Early History of the West Semitic Peoples," *JCS* 15 (1961) 27-47.

Jehoshua M. Grintz, "On the Original Home of the Semites," *JNES* 21 (1962) 186-206.

Sethites

*W. W. Martin, "The Chronology of the Sethites," *MQR, 3rd Ser.*, 42 (1916) 357-359.

Shasu

*(Miss) Fanny Corbaux, "The Rephaim, and Their Connexion with Egyptian History," *JSL, 2nd Ser.,* 1 (1851-52) 151-172, 363-394; 2 (1852) 55-91, 303-340; 3 (1852-53) 87-116, 279-307. [1 (1851-52) Chap. 5 - The Zuzim, pp. 363-367; Chap. 7 - Geographical Identity of the Zuzim and *shas·u,* pp. 375-384; Chap. 8 - Cities and Dependencies of the Zuzim, pp. 384-392]

*D. H. Haigh. [hieroglyphs], *ZÄS* 13 (1875) 29-32, 60-64. *[S̆asu]*

Daniel Hy. Haigh. "On the Shasu-people," *ZÄS* 14 (1876) 52-57.

Raphael Giveon, "The Shosu of the Late XXth Dyansty," *JARCE* 8 (1969-70) 51-53.

Shuhites

*A. H. Sayce, "An Early Babylonian Document relating to the Shuhites," *SBAP* 21 (1899) 24-25.

Sicilians

Peter Green. "The First Sicilian Slave War," *P&P* #20 (1961) 10-29.

W. G. G. Forrest and T. C. W. Stinton, "Communications: The First Sicilian Slave War," *P&P* #22 (1962) 87-91.

Sinim

Anonymous. "Who were the Sinim?" *BRCM* 2 (1846) 51-53.

†T[errien] de Lacouperie, "The Sinim of Isaiah, not the Chinese," *BOR* 1 (1886-87) 45-48.

Subarians

*E[phraim] A. Speiser, "'Hurrians and Subarians'," *JAOS* 68 (1948) 1-13.

*Sidney Smith, "On Hurrians and Subarians': A Review Article," *PEQ* 81 (1949) 117-126. *(Review)*

*I. J. Gelb, "New Light on Hurrians and Ṣubarians," *SOOG* 1 (1956) 378-392.

Sumerians

*O. D. Miller, "Accadian or Sumerian?" *OBJ* 1 (1880) 105-111.

F. A. Gast, "The Pre-Semitic Babylonians," *RChR* 32 (1885) 22-46. *[Sumerains]*

J. F. McCurdy, "The Sumerian Question," *PRR* 2 (1891) 58-81.

H. V. Hilprecht, "The Early Inhabitants of Babylonia," *ET* 8 (1896-97) 88-89. *[Sumerians]*

J. A. Selbie, "The Sumerian Question," *ET* 10 (1898-99) 71-72.

Morris Jastrow Jr., "A New Aspect of the Sumerian Question," *AJSL* 22 (1905-06) 89-109.

Anonymous, "The Sumerians," *MR* 89 (1907) 137-140.

*Stephen Langdon, "Sumerians and Semites in Babylonia," *Baby* 2 (1907-08) 137-161.

Theophilus G. Pinches, "The Sumerians of Lagas," *SBAP* 35 (1913) 13-36.

*H. R. Hall, "The Discoveries at Ur, and the Seniority of the Sumerian Civilization," *Antiq* 2 (1928) 56-68.

George A. Barton, "Whence Came the Sumerians?" *JAOS* 49 (1929) 263-268.

E. Berrum, "The Sumarians *[sic]*," *TF* 2 (1930) 203-212.

Sumerians cont.

S[tephen] Langdon, "A New Factor in the Problem of Sumerian Origins," *JRAS* (1931) 593-596.

T. Fish, "Aspects of Sumerian Civilisation as Evidenced on Tablets in the John Rylands Library. I About Building in Ur III," *BJRL* 18 (1934) 131-139.

*T. Fish, "Aspects of Sumerian Civilization During the Third Dynasty of Ur. II About Wool," *BJRL* 18 (1934) 315-324.

*T. Fish, "Aspects of Sumerian Civilization During the Third Dynasty of Ur. III Rivers and Canals," *BJRL* 19 (1935) 90-101.

*T. Fish, "Aspects of Sumerian Civilization During the Third Dynasty of Ur. IV Silver," *BJRL* 20 (1936) 121-133.

*T. Fish, "Aspects of Sumerian Civilisation During the Third Dynasty of Ur. V Literature," *BJRL* 20 (1936) 286-296.

*T. Fish, "Aspects of Sumerian Civilisation During the Third Dynasty of Ur. VI The Royal Family," *BJRL* 21 (1937) 157-166.

*Thorkild Jacobson, "The Assumed Conflict between Sumerians and Semites in Early Mesopotamian History," *JAOS* 59 (1939) 485-495.

Samuel N[oah] Kramer, "A New Heroic Age and Its Archaeological Implications," *AJA* 50 (1946) 285. *[Sumerians]*

E. Douglas Van Buren, "A New Book on Sumerian Culture," *Or., N.S.,* 16 (1947) 403-413. *(Review)*

*C. J. Mullo Weir, "Problems of Western Asiatic Pre-History," *GUOST* 13 (1947-48) 44-48. [The Sumerians, pp. 45-47]

Samuel Noah Kramer, "New Light on the Early History of the Ancient Near East," *AJA* 52 (1948) 156-164. *[Sumerians]*

E[phraim] A. Speiser, "The Sumerian Problem Reviewed," *HUCA* 23 (1950-51) Part 1, 339-355.

Sumerians concluded

*S[amuel] N[oah] Kramer, "Sumerian Historiography," *IEJ* 3 (1953) 217-232.

T. Fish, "One Aspect of the Sumerian Character," *Sumer* 10 (1954) 113-115.

William W. Hallo, "A Sumerian Amphictyony," *JCS* 14 (1960) 88-114.

*E[velyn] Brandt, "Early Sumerian Art and Culture," *NOP* 2 (1961) 165-168.

J[osef] Klíma, "Sumerian Origins—the First Steps of Mankind's History," *NOP* 3 (1962) 153-157.

Syrians

*N. M. Davies and N. de G. Davies, "Syrians in the Tomb of Amunedjeḥ," *JEA* 27 (1941) 96-98.

James B. Pritchard, "Syrians as Pictured in the Paintings of the Theban Tombs," *BASOR* #122 (1951) 37-41.

T

Teresh

*G. A. Wainwright, "The Teresh, the Etruscans and Asia Minor," *AS* 9 (1959) 197-213.

Thebans

*(Miss) Fanny Corbaux, "The Rephaim, and Their Connexion with Egyptian History," *JSL, 2nd Ser.,* 1 (1851-52) 151-172, 363-394; 2 (1852) 55-91, 303-340; 3 (1852-53) 87-116, 279-307. [Chap. 6 - Wars of the Hyksos and Thebans, 1 (1851-52) pp. 367-375]

Trojans

Henry M. Baird. "Schliemann's Trojan Researches," *MR* 60 (1878) 426-447. *(Review)*

J. B. Bury. "The Trojan War," *QRL* 226 (1916) 1-20. *(Review)*

*W. J. Phythian-Adams, "Hittite and Trojan Allies," *BSAJB* #1 (1922) 3-7.

U

Urartians

*Warren C. Benedict, "Urartians and Hurrians," *JAOS* 80 (1960) 100-104.

X

χaru

*D. H. Haigh. *ZÄS* 13 (1875) 29-32, 60-64. */χaru/*

Z

Zuzim

*(Miss) Fanny Corbaux, "The Rephaim, and Their Connexion with Egyptian History," *JSL, 2nd Ser.,* 1 (1851-52) 151-172, 363-394; 2 (1852) 55-91, 303-340; 3 (1852-53) 87-116, 279-307. [1 (1851-52) Chap. 5 - The Zuzim, pp. 363-367; Chap. 7 - Geographical Identity of the Zuzim and *shas·u,* pp. 375-384; Chap. 8 - Cities and Dependencies of the Zuzim, pp. 384-392]

§143 *2.4.2 Chronology of the Ancient Near East*
       - General Studies [See also: Date Formulae,
       Regnal Years, etc. §118 ←]

*†Anonymous, "The Chronology of the Sieges of Nineveh rectified,"
    MMBR 10 (1800) 5-7.

*†Anonymous, "Ancient Chronology," *BCQTR, 4th Ser.*, 12 (1832)
    120-141. *(Review)*

*†Anonymous, "Chronology," *WR* 16 (1832) 327-341. *(Review)*

*Anonymous, "Restoration of the Chronology of Josephus,"
    JSL, 1st Ser., 5 (1850) 60-81.

S. W., "Armenian Translation of Eusebius. On the Historical
    Advantage to be Derived from the Armenian Translation of
    the Chronicle of Eusebius," *JSL, 2nd Ser.*, 4 (1853) 263-297.
    [Chronology]

(   ) G., "Niebuhr and Eusebius," *JSL, 2nd Ser.*, 5 (1853-54)
    489-508.

J. F., "To the Editor of 'The Journal of Sacred Literature',"
    JSL, 3rd Ser., 4 (1856-57) 177-178. *[Chronology of Herodotus]*

*J. F., "Did Josephus Adopt the Long or Short Chronology?"
    JSL, 3rd Ser., 7 (1858) 178-181.

*G. B., "Date of the Capture of Larissa," *JSL, 3rd Ser.*, 7 (1858)
    192-193.

*E[dward] Hincks, "On the Rectifications of Sacred and Profane
    Chronology, which the Newly Discovered Apis Steles Render
    Necessary," *JSL, 3rd Ser.*, 8 (1858-59) 126-139.

(   ) G., "The Prince of Persia; The Law of the Medes and the
    Persians; and the Chronology of the Jewish Writer Demetrius,"
    JSL, 3rd Ser., 12 (1860-61) 446-456; 13 (1861) 153-175.

*R. E. Trywhitt, "Ptolemy's Chronology of Babylonian Reigns conclusively vindicated; and the date of the Fall of Nineveh ascertained; with Elucidations of Connected points in Assyrian, Scythian, Median, Lydian, and Israelite History," *JRAS* (1861) 106-149.

I./sic/W. Bosanquet, "The Prince of Grecia, the Prince of Persia, and Michael, One of the Chief Princes, in connexion with the Chronology of Demetrius," *JSL, 3rd Ser.,* 13 (1861) 416-429.

*Henry Fox Talbot, "On an Ancient Eclipse," *SBAT* 1 (1872) 13-19. (Addition on pp. 348-354)

*George Smith, "On Fragments of an Inscription giving part of the Chronology from which the Canon of Berosus was copied," *SBAT* 3 (1874) 361-379.

*W. St. Chad Boscawen, "Babylonian Dated Tablets, and the Canon of Ptolemy," *SBAT* 6 (1878-79) 1-78. (Discussion, pp. 79-133)

*Theo. G. Pinches, "Notes upon Babylonian Contract Tablets and the Canon of Ptolemy," *SBAT* 6 (1878-79) 484-493.

*John B. Wood, "The Antiquity of Man," *CR* 46 (1885) 159-170. *[Chronology]*

*O. D. Miller, "Zodiacal Chronology," *AAOJ* 12 (1890) 313-328.

*Fritz Hommel, "The Ten Patriarchs of Berosus," *SBAP* 15 (1892-93) 243-246.

*J. F. Hewitt, "The History of the Week as a Guide to Historic Chronology," *WR* 148 (1897) 8-22, 126-149, 237-250.

Lewis Bayles Paton, "Recent Investigations in Ancient Oriental Chronology," *BW* 18 (1901) 13-30.

W. F. Harvey, "Primitive Chronology," *WR* 157 (1902) 295-299.

Anonymous, "The Age of Buried Cities—Miscalculations," *CFL, 3rd Ser.,* 8 (1908) 273-274.

P. Boylan, "New Dates in Oriental History," *ITQ* 3 (1908) 186-208. *(Review)*

*Anonymous, "M. de Morgan on the Date of the Neolithic Age in Western Asia," *RP* 8 (1909) 267-268.

*F. Legge, "New Light on Sequence-Dating," *SBAP* 35 (1913) 101-113.

Anonymous, "The Reaction in Archaeological Chronology," *HR* 67 (1914) 196.

*W[illiam] F[oxwell] Albright, "Menes and Narâm-Sin," *JEA* 6 (1920) 89-98. *[Synchronism of Chronology]*

*W[illiam] F[oxwell] Albright, "Magan, Meluḫa, and the Synchronism between Menes and Narâm-Šin," *JEA* 7 (1921) 80-86.

*John Garstang, Louis Vincent, W[illiam] F[oxwell] Albright, and W. J. Phythian-Adams, "A New Chronological Classification of Palestinian Archaeology," *BASOR* #7 (1922) 9.

A. T. Olmstead, "Near-East Problems in the Second Pre-Christian Millenium," *JEA* 8 (1922) 223-232.

*G. B. Michell, "The Comparative Chronology of Ancient Nations in its Bearing on Holy Scripture," *JTVI* 59 (1927) 65-81, 91-95. [(Discussion, pp. 81-90) (Communication by H. Biddulph, pp. 90-91)]

W[illiam] F[oxwell] Albright, "A Note on the Chronology of the Second Millennium B.C.," *BASOR* #126 (1952) 24-26.

W[illiam] F[oxwell] Albright, "Further Observations on the Chronology of the Early Second Millennium B.C.," *BASOR* #127 (1952) 27-30.

*W[illiam] F[oxwell] Albright, "The Chronology of the Minaean Kings of Arabia," *BASOR* #129 (1953) 20-24.

W[illiam] F[oxwell] Albright, "Stratigraphic Confirmation on the Low Mesopotamian Chronology," *BASOR* #144 (1956) 26-30.

Albrecht Goetze, "On the Chronology of the Second Millennium B.C.," *JCS* 11 (1957) 53-61, 63-73.

*Jerome D. Quinn, "Alcaeus 48 (B 16) and the Fall of Ascalon (604 B.C.)," *BASOR* #164 (1961) 19-20.

*James William Johnson, "Chronological Writing: Its Concepts and Development," *H&T* 2 (1962-63) 124-145.

*Henri de Contenson, "A Further Note on the Chronology of Basal Ras Shamra," *BASOR* #175 (1964) 47-48.

*W[illiam] F[oxwell] Albright, "The Eighteenth-Century Princes of Byblos and the Chronology of Middle Bronze," *BASOR* #176 (1964) 38-46.

*Ben Zion Wacholder, "How Long Did Abram Stay in Egypt? A Study in Hellenistic, Qumran and Rabbinic Chronology," *HUCA* 35 (1964) 43-56.

*A[lbrecht] Goetze, "The Kassites and Near Eastern Chronology," *JCS* 18 (1964) 97-101.

F. E. Zeuner, "Soils and Shorelines as Aids to Chronology," *ULBIA* 4 (1964) 233-250. [Arab's Gulf, Northern Egypt, pp. 238-240; Northern Arabia, pp. 244-245]

*Carl Nylander, "Old Persian and Greek Stonecutting and the Chronology of Achaemenian Monuments. Achaemenian Problems I," *AJA* 69 (1965) 49-55.

*Homer L. Thomas, "Near Eastern Aegean and European Chronology," *AJA* 69 (1965) 176.

Henry de Contenson, "Notes on the Chronology of Near Eastern Neolithic," *BASOR* #184 (1966) 2-6.

*W[illiam] F[oxwell] Albright, "Remarks on the Chronology of Early Bronze IV - Middle Bronze IIA in Phoenicia and Syria-Palestine," *BASOR* #184 (1966) 26-35.

*C[arl] Nylander, "Clamps and chronology (Achaemenian Problems II)," *IA* 6 (1966) 130-146.

*Molly Miller, "Herodotus as Chronographer," *Klio* 46 (1966) 109-128.

*K[enneth] A. Kitchen, "Byblos, Egypt and Mari in the Early Second Millennium B.C.," *Or, N.S.,* 36 (1967) 39-54.

Edith Porada, Donald P. Hansen, and J. R. V. von Beckerath, "Chronologies in Old World Archaeology. Archaeological Seminar at Columbia University 1966-1967. Summary of Contributions," *AJA* 72 (1968) 301-305.

George F. Dales, "A Review of the Chronology of Afganistan, Baluchistan and the Idus Valley," *AJA* 72 (1968) 305-307.

Robert H. Dyson Jr., "Annotations and Corrections of the Relative Chronology of Iran, 1968," *AJA* 72 (1968) 308-313.

*Ruth Amiran, "Chronological Problems of the Early Bronze Age; Early Bronze I-II: The City of Arad; Early Bronze III: The Khirbet Kerak Ware," *AJA* 72 (1968) 316-318.

Maurtis Van Loon, "New Evidence from Inland Syria for the Chronology of the Middle Bronze Age," *AJA* 73 (1969) 276-277.

*Donald P. Hansen, "Some Remarks on the Chronology and Style of Objects from Byblos," *AJA* 73 (1969) 281-284.

*T. Cuyler Young Jr., "The Chronology of the Late Third and Second Millennia in Central Western Iran as Seen from Godin Tepe," *AJA* 73 (1969) 287-291.

A. Negev, "The Chronology of the Middle Nabatean Period," *PEQ* 101 (1969) 5-14.

§144   *2.4.2.1 Biblical (and Hebrew) Chronology*

*†Anonymous, "Chronological Remark on Genesis," *MMBR* 2 (1796)
    686-687.

*Anonymous, "Chronological Remark on the Time of Solomon, &c.,"
    MMBR 3 (1797) 9-10.

†F.   W.,   "Chronology,"   *MMBR*   3   (1797)   252-253.

*†J. Woodhouse, "The Antediluvian Year," *MMBR* 3 (1797) 343-344.

†Anonymous, "Reply to Chronological Remarks," *MMBR* 3 (1797)
    421.

*Anonymous, "Chronological Remarks on the Time of Daniel,"
    MMBR 4 (1797) 258-259.

*Anonymous, "Chronological Remarks on the Book of Ezra," *MMBR* 4
    (1797) 334-335.

Philologus, "The Hebrew Chronology, Established Against the Cavils
    of Volney," *CongML* 2 (1819) 218-221.

*Anonymous, "Comparison of Biblical and Egyptian Chronologies,"
    QCS, 3rd Ser., 9 (1837) 193-212.

J. D. Michaelis, "The Antediluvian Chronology of the Bible.
    *A Discourse delivered before the Royal Society of Göttingen,
    July 5, 1768,*" *BRCR, N.S.,* 6 (1841) 114-139. [Note by the
    Editor, pp. 114-115] *(Trans. by Stephen Chase)*

*Ernest Bertheau, "On the Different Computations of the First Two
    Periods in the Book of Genesis, and the Chronological
    Assumptions on which they are Based," *JSL, 1st Ser.,* 2 (1848)
    115-128. *(Trans. by John Nicholson)*

G. B. Winer, "Biblical Chronology (From Winer's Lexicon)," *BS* 6
    (1849) 558-571.

*Daniel Kerr, "Chronology of the Kingdoms of Israel and Judah,"
    JSL, 1st Ser., 4 (1849) 241-257.

*N. Rouse, "Chronology of the Kings of Judah and Israel," *JSL, 2nd Ser.*, 1 (1851-52) 217-220.

*N. Rouse, "Chronology from the Exodus to Solomon," *JSL, 2nd Ser.*, 2 (1852) 211-217.

*I./sic/ W. Bosanquet, "The Dial of Ahaz and Scripture Chronology," *JSL, 3rd Ser.*, 1 (1855) 407-413.

*J. W. Bosanquet, "Chronology of the Reigns of Tiglath Pileser, Sargon, Shalmanezer, and Sennacherib, in connexion with the Phenomenon seen on the Dial of Ahaz," *JRAS* (1855) 277-296.

E[dward] Hincks, "Mr. Bosanquet on Chronology," *JSL, 3rd Ser.*, 3 (1856) 181-184.

I./sic/ W. Bosanquet, "Biblical Chronology," *JSL, 3rd Ser.*, 3 (1856) 426-433.

James Strong, "Aker's Biblical Chronology," *MR* 38 (1856) 448-467. *(Review)*

James Strong, "Table of Biblical Chronology," *MR* 38 (1856) 600-641.

*G. Seyffarth, "Three Lectures on Egyptian Antiquities, &c., delivered at the Stuyvesant Institute, New York, May 1856," *ER* 8 (1856-57) 34-104. [XIX. The Chronology of the Old Testament, pp. 91-94]

*G. B., "The Inscriptions at Persepolis and Scripture Chronology," *JSL, 3rd Ser.*, 4 (1856-57) 138-161.

Edw[ard] Hincks, "On Mr. Bosanquet's Chronological System," *JSL, 3rd Ser.*, 4 (1856-57) 462-466.

Enoch Pond, "The Chronology of the Old Testament," *TLJ* 9 (1856-57) 239-251.

†Anonymous, "Discoveries in Biblical Chronology," *ER* 9 (1857-58) 436-439.

J. W. Bosanquet, "Biblical Chronology," *JSL, 3rd Ser.*, 5 (1857) 172-174, 429-431.

Joseph Packard, "Sacred Chronology," *BS* 15 (1858) 289-300.

*E[dward] Hincks, "On the Rectifications of Sacred and Profane Chronology, which the Newly Discovered Apis Steles Render Necessary," *JSL, 3rd Ser.,* 8 (1858-59) 126-139.

*†Anonymous, "Bunsen's Egypt and the Chronology of the Bible," *QRL* 105 (1859) 382-421. *(Review)*

Anonymous, "Theories of Biblical Chronology," *JSL, 3rd Ser.,* 10 (1859-60) 310-344.

*B. W. Savile, "Confirmation of Bible History," *JSL, 3rd Ser.,* 10 (1859-60) 388-391.

Franke Parker, "Review of Parker's Chronology," *JSL, 3rd Ser.,* 11 (1860) 417-433.

*Anonymous, "Sacred Chronology," *JSL, 3rd Ser.,* 11 (1860) 459-460.

I./sic/ W. Bosanquet, "Scripture Chronology," *JSL, 3rd Ser.,* 12 (1860-61) 174-182.

*(   ) G., "The Prince of Persia; The Law of the Medes and Persians; and the Chronology of the Jewish Writer Demetrius," *JSL, 3rd Ser.,* 12 (1860-61) 446-456; 13 (1961) 153-175.

I./sic/W. Bosanquet, "Biblical Chronology," *JSL, 4th Ser.,* 2 (1862-63) 166-176; 3 (1863) 423-430.

*Anonymous, "Notes on Bishop Colenso's New Book," *JSL, 4th Ser.,* 2 (1862-63) 385-401. *(Review)* [III. The Family of Judah: Marginal Chronology of the Bible, pp. 398-401]

*Anonymous, "The Earlier Chapters of the First Book of Esdras, and the Eleventh Book of the Jewish Antiquities of Josephus," *JSL, 4th Ser.,* 3 (1863) 413-423. *[Chronology]*

B. W. Savile, "Revelation and Science," *JSL, 4th Ser.,* 3 (1863) 155-164. *[Chronology]*

C. G., "Biblical Chronology," *JSL, 4th Ser.,* 3 (1863) 441-443.

Anonymous, "The Chronology of the Septuagint," *CongR* 4 (1864) 142-148.

*J. W. Bosanquet, "Assyrian and Hebrew Chronology compared with a view of showing the extent to which the Hebrew Chronology of Ussher must be modified, in conformity with the Assyrian Canon," *JRAS* (1864-65) 145-180.

E. C. K., "A Rational View of Hebrew Chronology," *JSL, 4th Ser.,* 6 (1864-65) 107-128.

*H. C., "Chronology of the Book of Judges," *JSL, 4th Ser.,* 9 (1866) 217.

Enoch Pond, "Chronology of the Old Testament," *MR* 49 (1867) 389-400.

H. N. Day, "Linguistic Science and Biblical Chronology," *AThR, N.S.,* 6 (1868) 483-506.

G. Q. Samson, "Bible Chronology," *BQ* 4 (1870) 297-316, 431-447.

*Frederic Gardiner, "The Chronological Value of the Genealogy in Genesis V," *BFER* 22 (1873) 566-575.

*Frederic Gardiner, "The Chronological Value of the Genealogy in Genesis V," *BS* 30 (1873) 323-333.

*Francis Roubiliac Conder, "The Comparative Chronology of Palestine, Egypt, and Assyria," *PEFQS* 5 (1873) 31-35.

Anonymous, "The Chronology of the Bible," *DUM* 83 (1874) 720-732.

*J. W. Bosanquet, "Synchronous History of the Reigns of Tiglath-Pileser. . and . . Azariah. Shalmanezer . . and . . Jotham. Sargon . . and . . Ahaz. Sennacherib . . and . . Hezekiah," *SBAT* 3 (1874) 1-82.

*A. H. Sayce, "The Date of the Ethnological Table of Genesis," *TRL* 11 (1874) 59-69.

Jno. H. Mengert, "Chronology of the Hebrew Testament," *LQ* 5 (1875) 1-23, 238-258.

*B. W. Savile, "On the Harmony between the Chronology of Egypt and the Bible," *JTVI* 9 (1875-76) 38-72. [(Discussion, pp. 72-79) (Remarks by S. Birch, pp. 80-83)]

*Victor Rydberg, "Key to the Genealogical Table of the First Patriarchs of Genesis, *and the Chronology of the Septuagint. From L. L. H. Combertigue's French MS. Translation of the Original Swedish Brochure and Notes. By S. M. Drach,*" *SBAT* 5 (1876-77) 65-87.

*J. W. Bosanquet, "Chronological Remarks on the History of Esther and Ahasuerus, or 'Atossa and Tanu-Axares," *SBAT* 5 (1876-77) 225-292.

*Robert Balgarnie, "'*As Old as Methuselah:*'" A Chapter in Antediluvian Chronology. Genesis V," *Exp, 1st Ser.,* 8 (1878) 449-461.

*†Anonymous, "Egypt and Sacred Chronology," *LQHR* 53 (1879-80) 265-310. *(Review)*

*†Hormuzd Rassam, "Excavations and Discoveries in Assyria," *SBAP* 2 (1879-80) 3-4. (Remarks by J. Oppert, pp. 4-6) *[The Chronology of Genesis]*

*Robert Balgarnie, "'*As Old as Methuselah:*'" A Chapter in Postdiluvian Chronology," *Exp, 1st Ser.,* 11 (1880) 215-236.

*W. J. Beecher, "The Chronology of the Kings of Israel and Judah," *PR* 1 (1880) 211-246.

Theo. G. Pinches, "Notes on a New List of Babylonian Kings, *c.* B.C. 1200 to 2000 *[sic],*" *SBAP* 3 (1880-81) 20-22.

*W. Robertson Smith, "The chronology of the Books of Kings," *JP* 10 (1881-82) 209-213.

*Willis J. Beecher, "The Chronology of the Period of the Judges," *ONTS* 3 (1883-84) 129-141.

*H. G. Mitchell, "Chronological," *ONTS* 3 (1883-84) 110-115. *[Chronology of the Kings of Israel and Judah]*

L. F. Badger, "The Assyrian Eponym Canon and the Chronology of the Bible," *ONTS* 5 (1884-85) 388-394.

*Anonymous, "The Chronology of the Kings of Israel and Judah Compared with the Monuments," *CQR* 21 (1885-86) 257-271.

Francis Brown, "Old Testament Chronology," *AJA, O.S.,* 2 (1886) 431-432.

George Dana Boardman, "The Antediluvian Chronology," *ONTS* 6 (1886-87) 175-176.

L. C. Garland, "The Chronology of the Bible," *MQR, 3rd Ser.,* 3 (1887-88) 22-39.

Charles Rufus Brown, "A Biblical Check to Bible Chronology," *ONTS* 7 (1887-88) 259-260.

*William J. Deane, "The Chronology of the Book of Judges," *BFER* 37 (1888) 100-113.

J[acob] Schwartz, "A Newly Discovered Key to Biblical Chronology," *BS* 45 (1888) 52-83, 437-464.

*Joseph Horner, "The Chronology of Israel and Assyria in the Reign of Shalmaneser II," *MR* 71 (1889) 711-724.

*James Orr, "Assyrian and Hebrew Chronology," *PR* 10 (1889) 41-64.

*Jacob Schwartz, "The Pharaoh and Date of the Exodus: *A Study in Comparative Chronology,*" *TML* 1 (1889) 145-166.

*E[rnest] de Bunsen, "The Pharaohs of Moses according to Hebrew and Egyptian Chronology," *SBAP* 12 (1889-90) 157-166.

William Henry Green, "Primeval Chronology," *BS* 47 (1890) 285-303.

*C. W. Gallagher, "Geology and Sacred Chronology," *MR* 72 (1890) 835-852.

*John D. Davis, "The Fourteenth Year of King Hezekiah," *PRR* 1 (1890) 100-105.

*Peter C. York, "Biblical Chronology and Patristic Tradition," *AER* 4 (1891) 360-376.

C[arl] H[einrich] Cornill, "The Literature of the Old Testament Arranged Chronologically, According to the Generally Accepted Views of Advanced Scholars," *ONTS* 13 (1891) 300-304.

*John D. Davis, "The Chronology of the Divided Kingdom," *PRR* 2 (1891) 98-114.

*Benjamin Wisner Bacon, "Chronology of the Account of the Flood in P.—A Contribution to the History of the Jewish Calendar," *AJSL* 8 (1891-92) 79-88.

Nathaniel Schmidt, "Assyrian Aids to Hebrew Chronology," *SJH* 1 (1892) 29-36.

*J. A. Zahm, "The Age of the Human Race according to Modern Science and Biblical Chronology," *ACQR* 18 (1893) 225-248; 19 (1894) 260-272.

*Joseph Horner, "Hezekiah, Sargon, and Sennacherib — A Chronological Study," *MR* 75 (1893) 74-89.

*Joseph Horner, "Pul, Jareb, Tiglath-pileser — A Chronologico-Historical Study," *MR* 76 (1894) 928-935.

Edward L. Curtis, "Requests and Replies," *ET* 6 (1894-95) 251-252. *[Biblical Chronology]*

*John Elsworth, "Historical Setting of the Post-Exilian Period of the Old Testament, Showing the Approximate Place of Zechariah," *ET* 6 (1894-95) 333.

George H. Schodde, "Exploration and Discovery: The Chronology of the Old Testament," *BW* 5 (1895) 290-293.

*Robert Rogers, "'Pul, Jareb, Tiglath-pileser'," *MR* 77 (1895) 129-130.

*Joseph Horner, "Pul, Jareb, Tiglath, and the Corrections," *MR* 77 (1895) 298-300.

*Robert W. Rogers, "Pul, Jareb, Tiglath-pileser III — A   Reply," *MR* 77 (1895) 301-302.

*J. E. Kerschner, "A Review of an Article on the Numbers of Genesis," *RChR* 26 (1897) 434-444.

Anonymous, "Biblical Research and Discovery. 'Ancient Chronology:' A Needed Caution," *CFL, O.S.,* 2 (1898) 71-72.

Julius Oppert, "Noli me Tangere. *A Mathematical Demonstration of the Exactness of Biblical Chronology,"* *SBAP* 20 (1898) 24-47.

J. H. Selwyn, "Note on Biblical Chronology," *SBAP* 20 (1898) 153.

Joseph Horner, "Biblical Chronology," *SBAP* 20 (1898) 235-246.

Anonymous, "Biblical Research and Discovery," *CFL, O.S.,* 3 (1899) 466-469. *[Chronology]*

*E. Elmer Harding, "Judah and Babylon, A Study in Chronology," *ET* 1 (1899-90) 233.

G. Finke, "Old Testament Chronology in the Light of the Monuments," *ColTM* 20 (1900) 114-118.

F. E. Hastings, "Biblical Chronology. The Historical Period. Kings, Judges," *SBAP* 22 (1900) 10-30.

*Henry H. Howorth, "Some Unconventional Views on the Text of the Bible. II. *The Chronology and Order of Events in Esdras A, compared with and preferred to those in the Canonical Ezra,"* *SBAP* 23 (1901) 305-325, 328-330. (Remarks by R. B. Girdlestone, Paul Ruben and M. Gaster, pp. 325-328)

W. W. Moore, "The Passing of Ussher's Chronology," *USR* 13 (1901-02) 73-81.

*Frederick Gard Fleay, "On the Synchronous Chronology of the Kings of Israel and Judah," *JTVI* 36 (1904) 253-274, 282-285. (Discussion, pp. 274-281)

*A. J. Maas, "The Chronology of Genesis," *ACQR* 29 (1904) 417-433.

M[elvin] G[rove] Kyle, "Reckless Chronology," *CFL, 3rd Ser.*, 1 (1904) 295-298.

*William F. McCauley, "Bible Chronology and the Archæologists," *CFL, 3rd Ser.*, 1 (1904) 733-743.

Henry T. Wirgman, "Pre-Abrahamic Chronology — An Investigation," *CFL, 3rd Ser.*, 3 (1905) 346-356.

*G. Macloskie, "The Latest on Old Testament Chronology, and Its Bearing on the Negative Criticism," *LCR* 25 (1906) 115-124.

*N. McConaughy, "Scripture Chronology — How Old is Man?" *CFL, 3rd Ser.*, 6 (1907) 122-128. [I. Comparative Claims of the Chronology of the Hebrew Scriptures and the Septuagint]

Searle Sheldon, "The Biblical Chronology Vindicated," *CFL, 3rd Ser.*, 7 (1907) 96-99. *(Editorial Note)*

Melvin Grove Kyle, "Archaeology Department: The Biblical Chronology," *CFL, 3rd Ser.*, 7 (1907) 246-247. *(Editorial Note)*

*Robert W. Rogers, "'An Important Chronological Discovery With Biblical Bearings'," *CFL, 3rd Ser.*, 7 (1907) 256-259.

Anonymous, "Rev. Dr. Beecher's Latest Book," *CFL, 3rd Ser.*, 9 (1908) 23-27. *(Review) [O.T. Chronology]*

Willis J. Beecher, "The Latest Work on the Biblical Chronology — a Review of Auchincloss," *CFL, 3rd Ser.*, 9 (1908) 301-302. *(Review)*

*A. H. Sayce, "Notes on Assyrian and Egyptian History. An Aramaic Ostracon," *SBAP* 30 (1908) 13-19. [III. *Biblical Chronology,* pp. 16-17]

Eb. Nestle, "Chronology of the Old Testament in the English Bible," *ET* 21 (1909-10) 567-568.

*Martin Sprengling, "Chronological Notes from the Aramaic Papyri. The Jewish Calendar. Dates of the Achaemenians (Cyrus-Darius II)," *AJSL* 27 (1910-11) 233-266.

Eb. Nestle, "Chronology of the Old Testament," *ET* 24 (1912-13) 188.

W. S. Auchincloss, "Amateur Chronology," *CFL, 3rd Ser.*, 19 (1915) 157-158.

*W. W. Martin, "The Chronology of the Sethites," *MQR, 3rd Ser.*, 42 (1916) 357-359.

*Harold M. Wiener, "The Date of the Exodus and the Chronology of Judges," *BS* 74 (1917) 581-609.

*Cuthbert Lattey, "The Chronology of the Pentateuch," *IER, 5th Ser.*, 13 (1919) 1-13.

*Henry Englander, "Problems of Chronology in the Persian Period of Jewish History," *JJLP* 1 (1919) 83-103.

William F[oxwell] Albright, "A Revision of Early Hebrew Chronology," *JPOS* 1 (1920-21) 49-79.

*Willam D. Gray, "The Founding of Aelia Capitolina and the Chronology of the Jewish War under Hadrian," *AJSL* 39 (1922-23) 248-256.

*T. Nicklin, "Two Chronological Enigmas in the Old Testament," *ET* 35 (1923-24) 168-170. [I. Isa. 36:1 // 2 Kings 18:13 ✗ 2 Chron. 32:1; II. Dan. 1:1 and the Reign of Jehoiakim]

*A. T. Richardson, "Time-Measures of the Pentateuch," *ET* 39 (1927-28) 515-519.

*A. T. Richardson, "Time-Measures of the Pentateuch'," *ET* 41 (1929-30) 45-46.

*Dudley Joseph Whitney, "The Chronology of Genesis," *CFL, 3rd Ser.*, 36 (1930) 478-482.

W. Bell Dawson, "Chronology of the Bible," *CFL, 3rd Ser.*, 36 (1930) 649.

William John Chapman, "Palestinian Chronological Data, 750-700 B.C.," *HUCA* 8&9 (1931-32) 151-168.

M[elvin] G[rove] Kyle, "Old Testament Chronology," *BS* 89 (1932) 56-67, 193-208, 334-345.

J. W. Newton, "How Many Years from Adam to Christ?" *CFL, 3rd Ser.,* 38 (1932) 89-90.

*A. G. Shortt, "The Chronology of the Kings of Israel and Judah," *JTVI* 64 (1932) 11-20, 28 [(Discussion, pp. 20-23) (Communications by Norman S. Denham, pp. 23-25; by G. B. Michell, pp. 25-27)]

*Frank Richards, "The Foundations of Bible History," *LQHR* 156 (1932) 307-317. [I. Chronology, pp. 309-312]

*James B. Tannehill, "The Chronology of Genesis V and XI," *CFL, 3rd Ser.,* 39 (1933) 236-239.

*Jacob Z. Lauterbach, "Misunderstood Chronological Statements in the Talmudical Literature," *PAAJR* 5 (1933-34) 77-84.

G. Ernest Wright, "The Chronology of Palestine in the Early Bronze Age," *BASOR* #63 (1936) 12-21.

D. R. Fotheringham, "Bible Chronology," *ET* 48 (1936-37) 234-235.

*Herbert Parzen, "Aspects of the Problems of Chronology of the Two Kingdoms as Treated by Rabbinic Exegesis," *JQR, N.S.,* 18 (1937-38) 305-331.

*G. Ernest Wright, "The Chronology of Palestinian Pottery in Middle Bronze I," *BASOR* #71 (1938) 27-34.

*Edwin R. Thiele, "The Chronology of the Kings of Judah and Israel," *JNES* 3 (1944) 137-186.

*W[illiam] F[oxwell] Albright, "The Chronology of the Divided Monarchy of Israel," *BASOR* #100 (1945) 16-22.

*Walter R. Roehrs, "Recent Studies in the Chronology of the Period of the Kings," *CTM* 18 (1947) 738-746.

*Nelson Glueck, "Go, View the Land," *BASOR* #122 (1951) 14-18. *[Chronology]*

*G. Ernest Wright, "An Important Correlation Between The Palestinian And Syrian Chalcolithic," *BASOR* #122 (1951) 52-55.

*Gus W. Van Beek, "Cypriote Chronology and the Dating of Iron I Sites in Palestine," *BASOR* #124 (1951) 26-29.

N. M. Powell, "'Time Was'—A New Chronology of the Old Testament," *JBL* 70 (1951) xiii.

R. North, "Maccabean Sabbath Years," *B* 34 (1953) 501-515.

*W[illiam] F[oxwell] Albright, "New Light from Egypt on the Chronology and History of Israel and Judah," *BASOR* #130 (1953) 4-11.

*E[dwin] R. Thiele, "Certain Peculiarities in the Chronological Data of the Hebrew Kings," *JBL* 72 (1953) viii.

Alan Rowe, "A Provisional Chronological Table of the Prehistoric and Historic Ages of Palestine," *PEQ* 86 (1954) 76-82.

A. Murtonen, "On the Chronology of the Old Testament," *ST* 8 (1954) 133-137.

*Edwin R. Thiele, "A comparison of the chronological data of Israel and Judah," *VT* 4 (1954) 185-195.

Edwin R. Thiele, "Difficulties Concerning Biblical Chronology and Their Solution," *JASA* 7 (1955) #3, 37-42.

*Martin J. Wyngaarden, "Some Problems of Chronology in Genesis," *JASA* 7 (1955) #3, 43-46.

Alan Rowe, "A Provisional Chronological Table of the Pre-historic and Historic Ages of Palestine: II," *PEQ* 87 (1955) 176-180.

*Edwin R. Thiele, "New Evidence on the Chronology of the Last Kings of Judah," *BASOR* #143 (1956) 22-27.

*Hayim Tadmor, "Chronology of the Last Kings of Judah," *JNES* 15 (1956) 226-230.

Y. Aharoni and Ruth Amiran, "A New Scheme for the Sub-Division of the Iron Age in Palestine," *IEJ* 8 (1958) 171-184.

*G. Ernest Wright, "Israelites, Samaria and Iron Age Chronology," *BASOR* #155 (1959) 13-29.

*R[obert] North, "'Ghassulian' in Palestine Chronological Nomenclature," *SBO* 1 (1959) 407-421.

Anonymous, "Chronology of Israel: Second Millennium B.C.," *BETS* 3 (1960) 67-69. *[Based on Joseph W. Schmidt's dissertation]*

*Stanley M. Horton, "Critical Note: A Suggestion Concerning the Chronology of Solomon's Reign," *BETS* 4 (1961) 3-4.

*George W. Frey, "Pottery and the Study of the Old Testament," *UTSB* 56 (1961-62) #2, 28-36.

W[illiam] F[oxwell] Albright, "The Chronology of the Middle Bronze I (Early Bronze-Middle Bronze)," *BASOR* #168 (1962) 36-42.

*James Meysing, "The Biblical Chronologies of the Patriarchs," *CNI* 13 (1962) #3/4, 26-30; 14 (1963) #1, 22-26.

*Siegfreid H. Horn, "The Chronology of King Hezekiah's Reign," *AUSS* 2 (1964) 40-52.

*Ben Zion Wacholder, "How Long Did Abram Stay in Egypt? A Study in Hellenistic, Qumran and Rabbinic Chronology," *HUCA* 35 (1964) 43-56.

*K[athleen] M. Kenyon, "Megiddo, Hazor, Samaria and Chronology," *ULBIA* 4 (1964) 143-156.

*Alger F. Johns, "Did David Use Assyrian-Type Annals?" *AUSS* 3 (1965) 97-109.

*W[illiam] F[oxwell] Albright, "Remarks on the Chronology of Early Bronze IV - Middle Bronze IIA in Phoenician and Syria-Palestine," *BASOR* #184 (1966) 26-35.

*Alan F. Johnson, "The Interphased Chronology of Jotham, Ahaz, Hezekiah, and Hoshea," *BETS* 9 (1966) 81-90.

*T. Francis Glasson, "The Reckoning of Dates 'from B.C. to A.D.'," *ET* 78 (1966-67) 376.

*Frank N. Egerton III, "The Longevity of the Patriarchs: A Topic in the History of Demography," *JHI* 27 (1966) 575-584.

*Siegfried H. Horn, "The Babylonian Chronicle and the Ancient Calendar of the Kingdom of Judah," *AUSS* 5 (1967) 12-27.

*J. Maxwell Miller, "Another Look at the Chronology of the Early Divided Monarchy," *JBL* 86 (1967) 276-288.

G. Larsson, "Is Biblical Chronology Systematic or Not?" *RdQ* 6 (1967-69) 499-515.

*Henry Morris, "Biblical Chronology and Geological Dating," *SR* 14 (1967-68) #1, 15-30.

Ben Zion Wacholder, "Biblical Chronology in the Hellenistic World Chronicles," *HTR* 61 (1968) 451-481.

*A. Hurvitz, "The Chronological Significance of 'Aramaisms' in Biblical Hebrew," *IEJ* 18 (1968) 234-240.

*Walter R. Wifall Jr., "The Chronology of the Divided Monarchy of Israel," *ZAW* 80 (1968) 319-337.

*W. J. Martin, "'Dechronologized' narrative in the Old Testament," *VTS* 17 (1969) 179-186.

§145 *2.4.2.2 Assyrian Chronology*

E. H., "Chronology of the Reigns of Sargon and Sennacherib," *JSL, 2nd Ser.,* 6 (1854) 393-410.

*J. W. Bosanquet, "Chronology of the Reigns of Tiglath Pileser, Sargon, Shalmanezer, and Sennacherib, in connexion with the Phenomenon seen on the Dial of Ahaz," *JRAS* (1855) 277-296.

*J. W. Bosanquet, "Assyrian and Hebrew Chronology compared with a view of showing the extent to which the Hebrew Chronology of Ussher must be modified, in conformity with the Assyrian Canon," *JRAS* (1864-65) 145-180.

Daniel Hy. Haigh, "Remarks on Assyrian Chronology," *ZÄS* 7 (1869) 117-121.

George Rawlinson, "The Assyrian Canon," *ZÄS* 8 (1870) 55-56.

Daniel Hy. Haigh, "Comparative chronology of Assyria, Egypt and Israel," *ZÄS* 9 (1871) 74-80, 99-103.

*Daniel Hy. Haigh, "The annals of Assurbanipal considered in their relation to the contemporary chronology of Lydia, Egypt and Israel," *ZÄS* 10 (1872) 125-129.

*Francis Roubiliac Conder, "The Comparative Chronology of Palestine, Egypt, and Assyria," *PEFQS* 5 (1873) 31-35.

*George Smith, "On a New Fragment of the Assyrian Canon belonging to the reigns of Tiglath-Pileser and Shalmaneser," *SBAT* 2 (1873) 321-332.

*J. W. Bosanquet, "Synchronous History of the Reigns of Tiglath-Pileser. . and . . Azariah. Shalmanezer . . and . . Jotham. Sargon . . and . . Ahaz. Sennacherib . . and . . Hezekiah," *SBAT* 3 (1874) 1-82.

*Daniel Hy. Haigh, "Chaldæan and Egyptian synchronisms," *ZÄS* 12 (1874) 12-23.

*Daniel Hy. Haigh, "An Assyrio-Egyptian synchronism," *ZÄS* 12 (1874) 67-69.

*Joseph Horner, "The Chronology of Israel and Assyria in the Reign of Shalmaneser II," *MR* 71 (1889) 711-724.

*James Orr, "Assyrian and Hebrew Chronology," *PR* 10 (1889) 41-64.

*Joseph Horner, "Hezekiah, Sargon, and Sennecherib— A Chronological Study," *MR* 75 (1893) 74-89.

*Joseph Horner, "Pul, Jereb, Tiglath-pileser—A Chronologico-Historical Study," *MR* 76 (1894) 928-935.

*Robert Rogers, "'Pul, Jareb, Tiglath-pileser'," *MR* 77 (1895) 129-130.

*Joseph Horner, "Pul, Jareb, Tiglath, and the Corrections," *MR* 77 (1895) 298-300.

*Robert W. Rogers, "Pul, Jareb, Tiglath-pileser III — A Reply," *MR* 77 (1895) 301-302.

*C. H. W. Johns, "The Chronology of Asurbanipal's reign. I," *SBAP* 24 (1902) 235-241.

*C. H. W. Johns, "The Chronology of Asurbanipal's Reign B.C. 668-626. II," *SBAP* 25 (1903) 82-89.

*C. H. W. Johns, "The Chronology of Asurbanipal's Reign B.C. 668-626. III," *SBAP* 27 (1905) 92-100.

*C. H. W. Johns, "The Chronology of Asurbanipal's Reign B.C. 668-626. IV. The 'Forecast' Tablets," *SBAP* 27 (1905) 288-296.

F. A. Jones, "Pre-Sargonic Times. A Study in Chronology," *SBAP* 28 (1906) 264-267.

*Robert W. Rogers, "'An Important Chronological Discovery With Biblical Bearings'," *CFL, 3rd Ser.,* 7 (1907) 256-259. *[Assyrian Chronology]*

*C. H. W. Johns, "The Chronology of Asurbanipal's Reign B.C. 668-626. V," *SBAP* 29 (1907) 74-84.

*C. H. W. Johns, "The Chronology of Asurbanipal's Reign. VI," *SBAP* 36 (1914) 181-187.

*Leon Legrain, "A New Fragment of Chronology: The Dynasty of Agade," *MJ* 12 (1921) 75-77.

*W[illiam] F[oxwell] Albright, "A revision of early assyrian and middle babylonian chronology," *RAAO* 18 (1921) 83-94.

*W[illiam] F[oxwell] Albright, "The Readjustment of Assyro-Babylonian Chronology by the Elimination of False Synchronisms," *JSOR* 8 (1924) 51-59.

*Sidney Smith, "Dating by Ashurbanipal and Kandalanu," *JRAS* (1928) 622-626.

*Waldo H. Dubberstein, "Assyrian-Babylonian Chronology (669-612 B.C.)," *JNES* 3 (1944) 38-42.

*Hillel A. Fine, "Studies in Middle-Assyrian Chronology and Religion," *HUCA* 24 (1952-53) 187-273.

*W[illiam] F[oxwell] Albright, "The New Assyro-Tyrian Synchronism and the Chronology of Tyre," *AIPHOS* 13 (1953) 1-9.

*Hillel A. Fine, "Studies in Middle-Assyrian Chronology and Religion, Part II," *HUCA* 25 (1954) 107-168.

J. Lewy, "Apropos of a Recent Study in Old Assyrian Chronology," *Or, N.S.,* 26 (1957) 12-36.

Joan Oates, "Assyrian Chronology 631-612 B.C.," *Iraq* 27 (1965) 135-159.

§146 *2.4.2.3 Babylonian Chronology*

*Daniel Hy. Haigh, "Chaldæan and Egyptian synchronisms," *ZÄS* 12 (1874) 12-23.

Julius Oppert, "Revised Chronology of the Latest Babylonian Kings," *SBAT* 6 (1878-79) 260-274.

Theo. G. Pinches, "Notes on a New List of Babylonian Kings, *c.* B.C. 1200 to 2000 *[sic!]*," *SBAP* 3 (1880-81) 20-22.

*Theo. G. Pinches, "Notes on a New List of Early Babylonian Kings: being a continuation of the Paper read 7th December, 1880," *SBAP* 3 (1880-81) 37-46.

*Theo. G. Pinches, "Some recent Discoveries bearing on the Ancient History and Chronology of Babylonia," *SBAP* 5 (1882-83) 6-12. (Remarks by J. Oppert, p. 12)

†Theo. G. Pinches, "The Babylonian Kings of the Second Period, about 2232 B.C., to the end of the existence of the Kingdom," *SBAP* 6 (1883-84) 193-204.

*Julius Oppert, "The real Chronology and true History of the Babylonian Dynasties," *BOR* 2 (1887-88) 105-118.

*William Hayes Ward, "Light on Scriptural Texts from Recent Discoveries. IX. The Chronology of the Kings of Babylon and Persia," *HR* 26 (1893) 315-316.

*A. H. Sayce, "The New Babylonian Chronological Tablet," *SBAP* 21 (1899) 10-22.

*E. Elmer Harding, "Judah and Babylon, A Study in Chronology," *ET* 1 (1899-90) 233.

Stanley A. Cook, "Notes and Queries. (3) *Babylonian Chronology,"* *PEFQS* 39 (1907) 318-319.

Anonymous, "New Light on Babylonian Chronology," *RP* 6 (1907) 254-255.

*C. H. W. Johns, "The First Year of Samsu-iluna," *SBAP* 30 (1908) 70-71.

*Hope W. Hogg, "Relative Chronology of First Dynasties of Isin and Babylon," *JMUEOS* #1 (1911) 21-39.

Anonymous, "Important Discovery Concerning Babylonian Chronology," *RP* 11 (1912) 152-153.

A. H. Sayce, "Babylonian Chronology," *SBAP* 34 (1912) 165-172.

*Theophilus G. Pinches, "Early Babylonian Chronology and the Book of Genesis," *ET* 27 (1915-16) 517-521.

C. H. W. Johns, "Notes on the Chronology of the Neo-Babylonian Empire," *SBAP* 38 (1916) 146-148.

*Theophilus G. Pinches, "Some Texts of the Relph Collection, with Notes on Babylonian Chronology and Genesis xiv," *SBAP* 39 (1917) 4-15, 55-72, 89-98.

*W[illiam] F[oxwell] Albright, "A revision of early assyrian and middle babylonian chronology," *RAAO* 18 (1921) 83-94.

*P. Burrows, "Notes on the Ist Dynasty of Kīs," *Or* #6 (1923) 33-40. *[Babylonian Chronology]*

*W[illiam] F[oxwell] Albright, "The Readjustment of Assyro-Babylonian Chronology by the Elimination of False Synchronisms," *JSOR* 8 (1924) 51-59.

*George W. Gilmore, "What One Babylonian Tablet Has Done," *HR* 91 (1926) 135.

O. Neugebauer, "The Chronology of the Hammurabi Age," *JAOS* 61 (1941) 58-61.

*Waldo H. Dubberstein, "Assyrian-Babylonian Chronology (669-612 B.C.)," *JNES* 3 (1944) 38-42.

*Albrecht Goetze, "Additions to Parker and Dubberstein's Babylonian Chronology," *JNES* 3 (1944) 43-46.

*Sidney Smith, "Middle Minoan I-II and Babylonian Chronology," *AJA* 49 (1945) 1-24.

*W[illiam] F[oxwell] Albright, "An Indirect Synchronism Between Egypt and Mesopotamia, cir. 1730 B.C.," *BASOR* #99 (1945) 9-18.

*M. B. Rowton, "Mesopotamian Chronology in the 'Era of Menophres'," *Iraq* 8 (1946) 96-110.

*H. Lewy, "Chronological Notes Relating to a New Volume of Old Babylonian Contracts," *Or, N.S.*, 24 (1955) 275-287.

*Siegfried H. Horn, "The Babylonian Chronicle and the Ancient Calendar of the Kingdom of Judah," *AUSS* 5 (1967) 12-27.

§147 *2.4.2.4 Egyptian Chronology*

*Anonymous, "Comparison of Biblical and Egyptian Chronologies," *QCS, 3rd Ser.*, 9 (1837) 193-212.

†C. W. C., "Chronology of Egyptian History," *WR* 43 (1845) 55-75. *(Review)*

*Anonymous, "Egyptian Chronology and History," *CTPR, 3rd Ser.*, 6 (1850) 193-211. *(Review)*

D. I. H., "Egyptian Chronology," *JSL, 2nd Ser.*, 5 (1853-54) 109-121. *(Review)*

*E[dward] Hincks, "On the Rectifications of Sacred and Profane Chronology, which the Newly Discovered Apis Steles Render Necessary," *JSL, 3rd Ser.*, 8 (1858-59) 126-139.

Edward Hincks, "On Manetho's Chronology of the New Kingdom," *JRAS* (1861) 378-392.

J. W. Bosanquet, "Egyptian Dynasties of Manetho," *JSL, 4th Ser.,* 6 (1864-65) 191-195.

*Daniel Hy. Haigh, "The annals of Assurbanipal considered in their relation to the contemporary chronology of Lydia, Egypt and Israel," *ZÄS* 10 (1872) 125-129.

*Francis Roubiliac Conder, "The Comparative Chronology of Palestine, Egypt, and Assyria," *PEFQS* 5 (1873) 31-35.

*W. E. Gladstone, "The Place of Homer in History and in Egyptian Chronology," *ContR* 24 (1874) 1-22, 175-200.

*Daniel Hy. Haigh, "Chaldæan and Egyptian synchronisms," *ZÄS* 12 (1874) 12-23.

*Daniel Hy. Haigh, "An Assyrio-Egyptian synchronism," *ZÄS* 12 (1874) 67-69.

*B. W. Savile, "On the Harmony between the Chronology of Egypt and the Bible," *JTVI* 9 (1875-76) 38-72. [(Discussion, pp. 72-79) (Remarks by S. Birch, pp. 80-83)]

James Strong, "Egyptian Chronology [First Paper]," *MR* 60 (1878) 197-219.

James Strong, "Egyptian Chronology [Second Paper]," *MR* 60 (1878) 462-479.

*†Anonymous, "Egypt and Sacred Chronology," *LQHR* 53 (1879-80) 265-310. *(Review)*

*Ernest de Bunsen, "The Date of Menes and the Date of Budda," *SBAP* 3 (1880-81) 96.

*Jacob Schwartz, "The Pharaoh and Date of the Exodus: *A Study in Comparative Chronology,*" *TML* 1 (1889) 145-166.

*E[rnest] de Bunsen, "The Pharaohs of Moses according to Hebrew and Egyptian Chronology," *SBAP* 12 (1889-90) 157-166.

Aug. Eisenlohr, "Egyptian Chronology. Warnings," *SBAP* 17 (1895) 280-283.

D. R. Fotheringham, "Some Considerations regarding Professor Petrie's Egyptian Chronology," *SBAP* 18 (1896) 99-102.

Wm. [M.] F. Petrie, "Note on Chronology," *SBAP* 18 (1896) 117.

C[laude] R. Conder, "Egyptian Chronology," *SRL* 29 (1897) 116-127.

Samuel Berwick, "Egyptian Chronology," *AJA, O.S.,* 8 (1893) 171-183.

Anonymous, "Egyptian Chronology and Antiquities," *MR* 82 (1900) 639-642.

*Melvin Grove Kyle, "Professor Breasted on Egyptian Chronology," *CFL, 3rd Ser.,* 5 (1906) 471-472.

*A. H. Sayce, "Notes on Assyrian and Egyptian History. An Aramaic Ostracon," *SBAP* 30 (1908) 13-19. [IV. *Egyptian Chronology,* pp. 17-18]

*W[illiam] F[oxwell] Albright, "Menes and Narâm-Sin," *JEA* 6 (1920) 89-98. *[Synchronism of Chronology]*

*W[illiam] F[oxwell] Albright, "Magan, Meluḫa, and the Synchronism between Menes and Narâm-Šin," *JEA* 7 (1921) 80-86.

*S[tephen] Langdon, "The early Chronology of Sumer and Egypt and the Similarities in their Culture," *JEA* 7 (1921) 133-153.

*G. H. Wheeler, "The Chronology of the Twelfth Dynasty," *JEA* 9 (1923) 196-200.

*[W. M.] Flinders Petrie, "A Revision of History," *AEE* 16 (1931) 1-20. *[Egyptian Chronology]*

*[W. M.] Flinders Petrie, "Copper or Bronze?" *AEE* 20 (1935) Supplement, 148.

*William Wallace, "The Egyptian Expedition and the Chronology of the Decade 460-450 B.C.," *TAPA* 67 (1936) 252-260.

*William F. Edgerton, "On the Chronology of the Early Eighteenth Dyansty (Amenhotep I to Tuthmose III)," *AJSL* 53 (1936-37) 188-197.

*Richard A. Parker, "Persian and Egyptian Chronology," *AJSL* 58 (1941) 285-301.

*William F. Edgerton, "Chronology of the Twelfth Dynasty," *JNES* 1 (1942) 307-314. *[Egyptian]*

*W[illiam] F[oxwell] Albright, "An Indirect Synchronism Between Egypt and Mesopotamia, cir. 1730 B.C.," *BASOR* #99 (1945) 9-18.

*Jaroslav Černý, "Studies in the Chronology of the Twenty-First Dynasty," *JEA* 32 (1946) 24-30.

*M. B. Rowton, "Manetho's Date for Ramesses II," *JEA* 34 (1948) 57-73. (With Appendix by Professor H. Kees, pp. 73-74)

*Hermann Ranke, "The Egyptian Collections of the University Museum," *UMB* 15 (1950) #2/3, 5-109. [A Sketch of Egyptian Chronology p. 5]

*Hans Goedicke, "An Approximate Date for the Harem Investigation under Pepy I," *JAOS* 74 (1954) 88-89.

*Keith C. Seele, "King Ay and the Close of the Amarna Age," *JNES* 14 (1955) 168-179.

*E. E. Knudsen, "On the Chronology of the Middle Eighteenth Dynasty," *AO* 23 (1958-59) 111-118. *[Egyptian]*

*Cyril Aldred, "The Beginning of the El-'Amārna Period," *JEA* 45 (1959) 19-33.

*Donald B. Redford, "Some Observations on 'Amārna Chronology," *JEA* 45 (1959) 34-37.

*H. W. Fairman, "The supposed Year 21 of Akhenaten," *JEA* 46 (1960) 108-109.

*M. B. Rowton, "Comparative Chronology at the Time of Dynasty XIX," *JNES* 19 (1960) 15-22. *[Egyptian]*

Jaroslav Černý, "Note on the supposed beginning of a Sothic period under Sethos I," *JEA* 47 (1961) 150-152.

J. V. Beckerath, "The Date of the End of the Old Kingdom of Egypt," *JNES* 21 (1962) 140-147.

*Eric Young, "Some Notes on the Chronology and Genealogy of the Twenty-first Dynasty," *JARCE* 2 (1963) 99-111.

*K[enneth] A. Kitchen, "On the Chronology and History of the New Kingdom," *CdE* 39 (1964) 310-322.

*Donald B. Redford, "On the Chronology of the Egyptian Eighteenth Dynasty," *JNES* 25 (1966) 113-124.

*M. B. Rowton, "The Material from Western Asia and the Chronology of the Nineteenth Dynasty," *JNES* 25 (1966) 240-258.

*Edward F. Wente, "On the Chronology of the Twenty-first Dynasty," *JNES* 26 (1967) 155-176.

*K[enneth] A. Kitchen, "Byblos, Egypt and Mari in the Early Second Millenium B.C.," *Or, N.S.,* 36 (1967) 39-54.

*K[enneth] A. Kitchen, "Further Notes on New Kingdom Chronology and History," *CdE* 43 (1968) 313-324.

§148 *2.4.2.5 Greek Chronology*

Edward Hincks, "Mr. Parker's Chronology of the Archons," *JSL, 4th Ser.,* 5 (1864) 409-415.

Franke Parker, "The Archons of Demothenes," *JSL, 4th Ser.,* 5 (1864) 158-172; 6 (1864-65) 149-171.

Franke Parker, "The Metonic Cycle and Calippic Period," *JSL, 4th Ser.,* 6 (1864-65) 402-416; 7 (1865) 86-108, 396-407, 438-441.

Edward Hincks, "The Metonic Cycle," *JSL, 4th Ser.,* 7 (1865) 213-217; 8 (1865-66) 186-190.

W. R. A. Boyle, "The Olympiads in connexion with the Golden Age of Greece," *SBAT* 2 (1873) 289-300.

*F. A. Jones, "The Ancient Year and the Sothic Cycle," *SBAP* 30 (1908) 95-106.

J. P[enrose] Harland, "The Bronze Age of Hellas," *AJA* 27 (1923) 60-61.

J. Penrose Harland, "Aegean (Bronze Age) Chronology and Terminology," *AJA* 28 (1924) 69-72.

*Sidney Smith, "The Chronology of Philip Arrhidaeus, Antigonus and Alexander IV," *RAAO* 22 (1924) 179-197.

Saul S. Weinberg, "The Chronology of the Neolithic Period and the Early Bronze Age in the Aegean," *AJA* 46 (1942) 121.

Saul S. Weinberg, "Aegean Chronology: Neolithic Period and Early Bronze Age," *AJA* 51 (1947) 165-182.

N. G. L. Hammond, "Studies in Greek Chronology of the Sixth and Fifth Centuries B.C.," *HJAH* 4 (1955) 371-411.

*W. den Boer, "Political Propaganda in Greek Chronology," *HJAH* 5 (1956) 162-177.

*James Mellaart, "The End of the Early Bronze Age in Anatolia and the Aegean," *AJA* 62 (1958) 9-33.

*John Boardman, "Al Mina and Greek Chronology," *HJAH* 7 (1958) 250.

*Homer L. Thomas, "Near Eastern Aegean and European Chronology," *AJA* 69 (1965) 176.

*Molly Miller, "Herodotus as Chronographer," *Klio* 46 (1966) 109-128.

*Robert Drews, "The Fall of Astyages and Herodotus' Chronology of the Eastern Kingdoms," *HJAH* 18 (1969) 1-11.

§149 *2.4.2.6 Ptolemaic Chronology and the Canon of Ptolemy*

J. W. Bosanquet, "Corrections of the Canon of Ptolemy, required in
    order to place it in harmony with the Solar Eclipses of
    Jan. 11th, *B.C.* 689, and May 28th *B.C.* 585," *JRAS* (1855)
    416-430.

*R. E. Trywhitt, "Ptolemy's Chronology of Babylonian Reigns
    conclusively vindicated; and the date of the Fall of Nineveh
    ascertained; with Elucidations of Connected points in Assyrian,
    Scythian, Median, Lydian, and Israelite History," *JRAS* (1861)
    106-149.

*W. St. Chad Boscawen, "Babylonian Dated Tablets, and the Canon
    of Ptolemy," *SBAT* 6 (1878-79) 1-78. (Discussion, pp. 79-133)

*Theo. G. Pinches, "Notes upon Babylonian Contract Tablets and the
    Canon of Ptolemy," *SBAT* 6 (1878-79) 484-493.

*C. C. Edgar, "On the Dating of Early Ptolemaic Papyri," *ASAE* 17
    (1917) 209-223. [§1.- The Regnal Year of Ptolemy II, pp.
    210-218]

C. C. Edgar, "A further note on early Ptolemaic chronology,"
    ASAE 18 (1918) 58-64.

*F. W. Walbank, "The Accession of Ptolemy Epiphanes: A Problem in
    Chronology," *JEA* 22 (1936) 20-34.

*Charles F. Nims, "Notes on University of Michigan Demotic Papryi
    from Philadelphia," *JEA* 24 (1938) 73-82. [1. The Chronology of
    the Early Years of Ptolemy Epiphanes, pp. 73-74]

*T. C. Skeat, "Notes on Ptolemaic Chronology," *JEA* 46 (1960) 91-94.
    [1. 'The Last Year which is also the First']

*T. C. Skeat, "Notes on Ptolemaic Chronology," *JEA* 47 (1961)
    107-109. [II. 'The Twelfth Year which is also the First': The
    Invasion of Egypt by Antiochus Epiphanes']

*T. C. Skeat, "Notes on Ptolemaic Chronology," *JEA* 48 (1962)
    100-105. [III. 'The First Year which is also the third': A date
    in the reign of Cleopatra VII]

*Alan E. Samuel, "Year 27 = 30 and 88 B.C.," *CdÉ* 40 (1965) 376-400. *[Ptolemaic Chronology]*

§150 *2.4.2.7 Sumerian Chronology*

*Hope W. Hogg, "Relative Chronlogy of First Dynasties of Isin and Babylon," *JMUEOS* #1 (1911) 21-39. *[Sumerian Chronology]*

George T. Molyneux, "A Study in Sumerian Chronology," *JSOR* 4 (1920) 87-90.

*S[tephen] Langdon, "The early Chronology of Sumer and Egypt and the Similarities in their Culture," *JEA* 7 (1921) 133-153.

*Simone Corbiau, "Sumerian Dress Lengths as Chronological Data," *Iraq* 3 (1936) 97-100.

*Samuel Noah Kramer, "Gilgamesh and the First Dynasty of Ur: A New and Unexpected Synchronism in Third Millennium Chronology," *AJA* 61 (1957) 184.

*Albrecht Goetze, "The Chronology of Šulgi Again," *Iraq* 22 (1960) 151-156.

§151 *2.4.2.8 Chronology of Various Nations - Unclassified*

J. W. Bosanquet, "Chronology of the Medes, from the Reign of Deioces to the Reign of Darius, the Son of Hystaspes, or Darius the Mede," *JRAS* (1860) 39-69.

*Daniel Hy. Haigh, "The annals of Assurbanipal considered in their relation to the contemporary chronology of Lydia, Egypt and Israel," *ZÄS* 10 (1872) 125-129.

*J. W. Bosanquet, "Chronological Remarks on the History of Esther and Ahasuerus, or 'Atossa and Tanu-Axares," *SBAT* 5 (1876-77) 225-292.

*William Hayes Ward, "Light on Scriptural Texts from Recent Discoveries. IX. The Chronology of the Kings of Babylon and Persia," *HR* 26 (1893) 315-316.

John L. Myres, "Note on Mycenæan Chronology," *Man* 1 (1901) #139.

*H. Porter, "Another Phoenician Inscription from the Temple of Esmun at Sidon," *PEFQS* 35 (1903) 333-335. *[Phoenician Chronology]*

*G. A. Reisner, "The Meroitic Kingdom of Ethiopia: A Chronological Outline," *JEA* 9 (1923) 34-77.

*G. A. Reisner, "The Meroitic Kingdom of Ethiopia: Additional Note," *JEA* 9 (1923) 157-160.

*Glanville Downey, "Seleucid Chronology in Malalas," *AJA* 42 (1938) 106-120.

W[illam] F[oxwell] Albright, "A Revolution in the Chronology of Ancient Western Asia," *BASOR* #69 (1938) 18-21.

*Waldo H. Dubberstein, "The Chronology of Cyrus and Cambyses," *AJSL* 55 (1938) 417-419.

W[illiam] F[oxwell] Albright, "New Light on the History of Western Asia in the Second Millennium B.C.," *BASOR* #77 (1940) 20-32. [The Chronology of Western Asia before 1500 B.C., pp. 25-30]

*Richard A. Parker, "Persian and Egyptian Chronology," *AJSL* 58 (1941) 285-301.

*O. Neugebauer, "The Chronology of the Aramaic Papryi from Elephantine (Remarks about a new Chronology proposed by A. Kennedy-Hebert)," *Isis* 33 (1941) 575-578.

*W[illam] F[oxwell] Albright, "A Third Revision of the Early Chronology of Western Asia," *BASOR* #88 (1942) 28-36.

*M. Stekelis, "Further Observations on the Chronology of Mughâret Abū Uṣba'," *BASOR* #89 (1943) 22-24.

W[illam] F[oxwell] Albright, "Remarks on Dr. Stekelis Late Prehistoric Chronology," *BASOR* #89 (1943) 24-25.

Elias J. Bickerman, "Notes on Seleucid and Parthian Chronology," *Bery* 8 (1943-44) 73-83.

Hildegard Lewy, "The Genesis of the Faulty Persian Chronology," *JAOS* 64 (1944) 197-214.

*Sidney Smith, "Middle Minoan I-II and Babylonian Chronology," *AJA* 49 (1945) 1-24.

John L. Caskey, "Notes on Trojan Chronology," *AJA* 52 (1948) 119-122.

R. W. Hutchinson, "Notes on Minoan Chronology," *Antiq* 22 (1948) 61-74.

H. StJ. B. Philby, "South Arabian Chronology," *Muséon* 62 (1949) 229-249.

*W[illam] F[oxwell] Albright, "The Chronology of Ancient South Arabia in the Light of the First Campaign of Excavation in Qataban," *BASOR* #119 (1950) 5-15.

*A[lbert] Jamme, "A New Chronology of the Qatabanian Kingdom," *BASOR* #120 (1950) 26-27.

*Albrecht Goetze, "The Problem of Chronology and Early Hittite History," *BASOR* #122 (1951) 18-25.

*Gus W. Van Beek, "Cypriote Chronology and the Dating of Iron I Sites in Palestine," *BASOR* #124 (1951) 26-29.

*G. Ernest Wright, "An Important Correlation Between The Palestinian And Syrian Chalcolithic," *BASOR* #122 (1951) 52-55.

*W[illiam] F[oxwell] Albright, "The New Assyro-Tyrian Synchronism and the Chronology of Tyre," *AIPHOS* 13 (1953) 1-9.

* W[illiam] F[oxwell] Albright, "The Chronology of the Minaean Kings of Arabia," *BASOR* #129 (1953) 20-24.

*J. Liver, "The Chronology of Tyre at the Beginning of the First Millenium B.C.," *IEJ* 3 (1953) 113-120.

Clark Hopkins, "Etruscan Chronology," *AJA* 58 (1954) 146.

R. W. Hutchinson, "Minoan Chronology Reviewed," *Antiq* 28 (1954) 155-164.

A. F. L. Beeston, "Problems of Sabæan Chronology," *BSOAS* 16 (1954) 37-56.

Clark Hopkins, "Oriental Evidence for Early Etruscan Chronology," *Bery* 11 (1954-55) 75-84.

W[illam] F[oxwell] Albright, "A Note on Early Sabaean Chronology," *BASOR* #143 (1956) 9-10.

W[illam] F[oxwell] Albright, "Stratigraphic Confirmation of the Low Mesopotamian Chronology," *BASOR* #144 (1956) 26-30.

*Józef Wolski, "The Decay of the Iranian Empire of the Seleucids and the Chronology of the Parthian Beginnings," *Bery* 12 (1956-58) 35-52.

James Mallaart, "Anatolian Chronology in the Early and Middle Bronze Age," *AS* 7 (1957) 55-88.

A[lbert] Jamme, "On a Drastic Current Reduction of South-Arabian Chronology," *BASOR* #145 (1957) 25-30.

Albrecht Goetze, "Alalaḫ and Hittite Chronology," *BASOR* #146 (1957) 20-26.

W[illam] F[oxwell] Albright, "Further Observations on the Chronology of Alalakh," *BASOR* #146 (1957) 26-34.

Cyril Aldred, "The End of the El-'Amarna Period," *JEA* 43 (1957) 30-41.

*James Mellaart, "The End of the Early Bronze Age in Anatolia and the Aegean," *AJA* 62 (1958) 9-33.

Cyril Aldred, "The Beginning of the El-'Amārna Period," *JEA* 45 (1959) 19-33. [1. The Stela of Kia; 2. The early development of Aten; 3. The jubilees of the Aten; 4. The dates of the jubilees; 5. A Chronology of the co-regency]

Donald B. Redford, "Some Observations on 'Amārna Chronology," *JEA* 45 (1959) 34-37.

Molly Miller, "The earlier Persian dates in Herodotus," *Klio* 37 (1959) 29-52.

*Emmett L. Bennett Jr., "Palaeographical Evidences and Mycenaean Chronology," *AJA* 64 (1960) 182-183.

*Edward F. Campbell Jr., "The Amarna Letters and the Amarna Period," *BA* 23 (1960) 2-22. [The Chronology of the Period, pp. 5-10]

§152 *2.4.2.9 Studies on Various Dynasties of the Ancient Near East (other than Israel & Judah) [For Dynasties of Israel and Judah see Section 46 & 47 ←]*

O. Cockayne, "On the Lydian Dynasty which preceded the Mermnadæ," *TPS* 1 (1842-44) 274-276.

H. M. G., "Egyptian Dynasties," *JSL, 3rd Ser.,* 1 (1855) 75-107.

H. M. G., "Egyptian Dynasties.—No. II," *JSL, 3rd Ser.,* 5 (1857) 305-342.

H. M. G., "Egyptian Dynasties.—No. III," *JSL, 3rd Ser.,* 6 (1857-58) 345-372.

Edward Hincks, "The Egyptian Dynasties of Manetho," *JSL, 4th Ser.,* 2 (1862-63) 333-376. (Additional Note, *JSL, 4th Ser.,* 3 (1863) p. 186)

Edward Hincks, "The Egyptian Dynasties of Manetho, Part II.," *JSL, 4th Ser.,* 4 (1863-64) 421-465.

Daniel Hy Haigh, "Origin of the XXII. dynasty," *ZÄS* 15 (1877) 38-40, 64-71.

(   ) Lauth, "Remarks on the name Šišku," *SBAP* 3 (1880-81) 46-48. (Remarks by Theo. G. Pinches, p. 48-49) *[Babylonian Dynasty]*

*Theo. G. Pinches, "The Early Babylonian King-Lists," *SBAP* 7 (1884-85) 65-71.

*Julius Oppert, "The real Chronology and true History of the Babylonian Dynasties," *BOR* 2 (1887-88) 105-118.

*W. Muss-Arnolt, "The Names of Assyro-Babylonian Months and Their Regents," *JBL* 11 (1892) 72-94, 160-176.

*W. Spiegelberg, "The Viziers of the New Empire," *SBAP* 15 (1892-93) 522-526. *[Egyptian Dynasties]*

*Isaac H. Hall, "On a recently discovered Bronze Statuette now in the Metropolitan Museum of Art, New York," *JAOS* 15 (1893) cii-cvii. *[Phoenician dynasty]*

W. M. Flinders Petrie, "The Arrangement of the XXIst Dynasty," *SBAP* 18 (1896) 56-64.

A. H. Sayce, "The Beginnings of the Egyptian Monarchy," *SBAP* 20 (1898) 96-101.

F. E. Hastings, "The XXIInd Egyptian Dynasty," *SBAP* 21 (1899) 280-281.

W. M. Flinders Petrie, "Notes on the XIXth Dynasty," *SBAP* 24 (1902) 317-319.

W. M. Flinders Petrie, "Notes on the XIXth and XXth Dynasties," *SBAP* 26 (1904) 36-41.

*F. Legge, "The Kings of Abydos," *SBAP* 26 (1904) 125-144. [1. Ka; 2. Ro; 3. Zeser; 4. Narmer; 5. Sma; 6. Aha; 7. Zer; 8. Zet; 9. Merneit; 10. Den; 11. Azab; 12. Mersekha; 13. Qa] *[Egyptian Dynasties]*

W. M. Flinders Petrie, "Notes on the later Egyptian Dynasties," *SBAP* 26 (1904) 238-287.

W. M. F[linders] Petrie, "The Early Monarchy of Egypt," *SBAP* 27 (1905) 279-285.

F. Legge, "' The Early Monarchy of Egypt'," *SBAP* 28 (1906) 14-16.

*E. W. Hollingworth, "The Hyksos and the Twelfth Dynasty," *SBAP* 30 (1908) 155-158.

*E. R. Ayrton, "The position of Tausert in the XIXth Dynasty," *SBAP* 28 (1906) 185-186.

F. Legge, "The First Egyptian Dynasty and Recent Discoveries," *SBAP* 32 (1910) 223-233.

†F. Ll. Griffith, "The Dodecarcy and the XIIth Dynasty," *ZÄS* 47 (1910) 162.

*Hope W. Hogg, "Relative Chronology of First Dynasties of Isin and Babylon," *JMUEOS* #1 (1911) 21-39.

C. H. W. Johns, "The Mananâ-Iapium Dynasty at Kish," *SBAP* 33 (1911) 98-103.

C. H. W. Johns, "Further Notes on the Mananâ-Iapium Dynasty at Kish," *SBAP* 33 (1911) 128-129.

C. H. W. Johns, "Note on the Mananâ-Iapium Dynasty at Kish," *SBAP* 34 (1912) 23-26.

*Anonymous, "Kings of Kish," *RP* 13 (1914) 43.

F. W. Read, "Egyptian Royal Accessions during the Old Kingdom," *SBAP* 36 (1914) 282-288; 37 (1915) 34-41.

C. H. W. Johns, "The Last Years of the Assyrian Monarchy," *SBAP* 38 (1916) 119-128.

C. H. W. Johns, "The Dynasty of Gutium," *SBAP* 38 (1916) 199-200.

A. Mingana, "A New List of Persian Kings," *BJRL* 5 (1918-20) 116-118.

S[tephen] Langdon, "The Dynasties of Sumer and Akkad," *ET* 32 (1920-21) 410-413.

*Leon Legrain, "Reconstructing Ancient History," *MJ* 11 (1920) 169-180. [II. A New List of Kings Who Reigned from 3500 to 3300 B.C., 175-180. (Cat. No. 14220)]

Anonymous, "'Reconstructing Ancient History'," *HR* 81 (1921) 394. *[Babylonain Dynasty]*

*Leon Lagrain, "A New Fragment of Chronology: The Dynasty of Agade," *MJ* 12 (1921) 75-77.

*C. J. Gadd, "Notes on Some Babylonian Rulers," *JRAS* (1922) 389-396. [3. The Eighth or "H" Dynasty in Babylon, pp. 394-396]

*G. H. Wheeler, "The Chronology of the Twelfth Dynasty," *JEA* 9 (1923) 196-200.

*P. Burrows, "Notes on the Ist Dynasty of Kïs," *Or* #6 (1923) 33-40. *[Babylonian Chronology]*

[W. M.] Flinders Petrie, "The Origin of the XIIth Dynasty," *AEE* 9 (1924) 38-42.

*A. T. Olmstead, "The Chaldaean Dynasty," *HUCA* 2 (1925) 29-55.

T. Eric Peet, "The Chronological Problems of the Twentieth Dynasty," *JEA* 14 (1928) 52-73.

*T. J. C. Baly, "The relations of the Eleventh Dynasty and the Heracleopolitans," *JEA* 18 (1932) 173-176.

Percy E. Newberry, "On the Parentage of the Intef Kings of the Eleventh Dynasty," *ZÄS* 72 (1936) 118-120.

*William F. Edgerton, "On the Chronology of the Early Eighteenth Dyansty (Amenhotep I to Tuthmose III)," *AJSL* 53 (1936-37) 188-197.

R. Engelbach, "Material for a revision of the history of the heresy period of the XVIIIth Dynasty," *ASAE* 40 (1940-41) 133-165.

*Lynn H. Wood, "The Kahun Papyrus and the Date of the Twelfth Dynasty (with a Chart)," *BASOR* #99 (1945) 5-9. *[Egyptian]*

Richard A. Parker, "The Duration of the Fifteenth Dynasty according to the Turin Papyrus," *JEA* 28 (1942) 68.

*William F. Edgerton, "The Chronology of the Twelfth Dynasty," *JNES* 1 (1942) 307-314.

*A. Poebel, "The Assyrian King List from Khorsabad," *JNES* 1 (1942) 247-306.

*A. Poebel, "The Assyrian King List from Khorsabad—*Continued*," *JNES* 1 (1942) 460-492.

H. E. Winlock, "The Eleventh Egyptian Dynasty," *JNES* 2 (1943) 249-283.

*A. Poebel, "The Assyrian King List from Khorsabad—*Concluded,*" *JNES* 2 (1943) 56-90.

*Jaroslav Černý, "Studies in the Chronology of the Twenty-First Dynasty," *JEA* 32 (1946) 24-30.

*F. J. Giles, "Amenhotpe, Ikhnaton and the succession," *Aeg* 32 (1952) 293-310.

E. A. Speiser, "Some Factors in the Collapse of Akkad," *JAOS* 72 (1952) 97-101.

*William S. Smith, "Inscriptional Evidence for the History of the Fourth Dynasty," *JNES* 11 (1952) 113-128. *[Egyptian]*

*I. J. Gelb, "Two Assyrian King Lists," *JNES* 13 (1954) 209-230.

*Hildegard Lewy, "The Synchronism Assyria—Ešnunna—Babylon," *WO* 2 (1954-59) 438-453. [1. Šamši-Adad and Daduša, pp. 438-445, 2. Iasmaḫ-Adad and Ibal-pî-El, pp. 445-453]

*Richard A. Parker, "The Length of Reign of Amasis and the Beginning of the Twenty-Sixth Dynasty," *MDIÄA* 15 (1957) 208-212.

Samuel E. Loewenstamm, "The Foundation of the Dynasty of Alalakh," *BIES* 20 (1955-56) #1/2, I.

*E. E. Knudsen, "On the Chronology of the Middle Eighteenth Dynasty," *AO* 23 (1958-59) 111-118. *[Egyptian]*

William W. Hallo, "Oriental Institute Museum Notes No. 10: The Last Years of the Kings of Isin," *JNES* 18 (1959) 54-72.

*M. B. Rowton, "Comparative Chronology at the Time of Dynasty XIX," *JNES* 19 (1960) 15-22. *[Egyptian]*

*M. B. Rowton, "The Date of the Sumerian King List," *JNES* 19 (1960) 156-162.

*Albrecht Goetze, "Early Kings of Kish," *JCS* 15 (1961) 105-111.

*William K. Simpson, "Studies in the Twelfth Eygptian Dynasty: I-II," *JARCE* 2 (1963) 53-63. [The Residence of Itj-Towy, pp. 53-59]

*Eric Young, "Some Notes on the Chronology and Genealogy of the Twenty-first Dynasty," *JARCE* 2 (1963) 99-111.

*Ruth Amiran, "A Preliminary Note on the Sychronisms Between the Early Bronze Strata of Arad and the First Dynasty," *BASOR* #179 (1965) 30-33.

Leonard H. Lesko, "A Little More Evidence for the End of the Nineteenth Dyansty," *JARCE* 5 (1966) 29-32. *[Egyptian]*

*J. J. Finkelstein, "The Genaeology of the Hammurapi Dynasty," *JCS* 20 (1966) 95-118. [B.M. 80328]

R. M. Derricourt, "E. Towry Whyte's List of the Kings of Egypt," *JEA* 52 (1966) 178.

*Donald B. Redford, "On the Chronology of the Egyptian Eighteenth Dynasty," *JNES* 25 (1966) 113-124.

*M. B. Rowton, "The Material from Western Asia and the Chronology of the Nineteenth Dynasty," *JNES* 25 (1966) 240-258.

Sami Ahmed, "The Babylonian Problem and the Establishment of the Chaldaean Dynasty," *IR* 24 (1967) #1, 21-30.

*Edward F. Wente, "On the Chronology of the Twenty-first Dynasty," *JNES* 26 (1967) 155-176.

*Abraham Malamat, "King Lists and the Old Babylonian Period and Biblical Genealogies," *JAOS* 88 (1968) 163-173.

*W. G. Lambert, "Another Look at Hammurabi's Ancestors," *JCS* 22 (1968-69) 1-2. [B.M. 80328]

*Ruth Amiran, "A Second Note on the Synchronism Between Early Bronze Arad and the First Dynasty," *BASOR* #195 (1969) 50-53.

J. A. Brinkman, "The Names of the Last Eight Kings of the Kassite Dynasty," *ZA* 59 (1969) 231-246.

§153 *2.5 Modern Scientific Studies on the
      Ancient Near East & Old Testament*

(   ) P., "Scriptural Notices of Volcanoes and Earthquakes,"
    JSL, 5th Ser., 2 (1867-68) 46-58.

Dugland Campbell, "Analysis of Glass Found in Captain Warren's
    Shafts at Jerusalem," *PEFQS* 4 (1872) 31.

*T. R. Birks, "The Bible and Modern Astronomy," *JTVI* 11 (1877-78)
    402-420, 433-437. {(Letters by: J. Clerk-Maxwell, p. 421; J.
    Challis, p. 421; [William J.] Irons, p. 422;) (Discussion: J. H.
    Titcomb , pp. 422-426; (   ) MacCaul, pp. 426-427; G. Currey,
    p. 427-432; [C. Brooke], pp. 432-433]}

*John R. Jackson, "Notes on Vegetable Remains from the Egyptian
    Tombs," *SBAP* 1 (1878-79) 36-37. (Remarks by Alexander
    Taylor, W. Harry Rylands, and W. F. Birch, p. 37; by George
    Murray, pp. 37-38.) *[Note: pp. 34-35 duplicated in error]*

Oscar Fraas, "The Sulphur of the Valley of Jordan," *PEFQS* 12 (1880)
    246-248.

William Allan, "Dead Sea Water," *PEFQS* 18 (1886) 52-53.

George E. Post, "Narrative of a Scientific Expedition in the
    Trans-Jordan Region in the Spring of 1886," *PEFQS* 20 (1888)
    175-237.

*J. H. Gladstone, "On Copper and Bronze of Ancient Egypt and
    Assyria," *SBAP* 12 (1889-90) 227-234.

*J. H. Gladstone, "On Metallic Copper, Tin, and Antimony from
    Ancient Egypt," *SBAP* 14 (1891-92) 223-227. (Remarks by
    Roberts Austen, pp. 227-228)

M. L. Lortet, "Researches on the Pathogenic Microbes of the Mud of
    the Dead Sea," *PEFQS* 24 (1892) 48-50.

*J. H. Gladstone, "Ancient Metals from Tell-el-Hesy," *SBAP* 16
    (1893-94) 95-99.

*Edward Davies, "Certificate of Analysis," *PEFQS* 28 (1896) 47. *[Water from the Spring of Callirrohe]*

*†J. Herbert Walker, "Analysis of Egyptian Cosmetics," *SBAP* 21 (1899) 79.

A. Lucas, "Analysis of one of the crowns found at Dahshour," *ASAE* 1 (1900) 285.

A. Lucas, "Analysis of bronze and copper objects," *ASAE* 1 (1900) 287-288.

William Ackroyd, "On a Principal Cause of the Saltness of the Dead Sea," *PEFQS* 36 (1904) 64-66.

Augustus H. Gill, "Examination of the Contents of a Mycenaean Vase Found in Egypt," *AJA* 10 (1906) 300-301.

A. Lucas, "Ancient Egyptian Mortars," *ASAE* 7 (1906) 4-7.

Oliver S. Tonks, "Experiments with the Black Glaze on Greek Vases," *AJA* 12 (1908) 417-427.

A. Lucas, "On a Sample of Varnish from the Temple at Deir el-Bahri," *ASAE* 9 (1908) 7.

Anonymous, "Composition of Fatty Matter in Mummies," *RP* 8 (1909) 215.

Oliver S. Tonks, "Experiments with Mycenaean Glaze," *AJA* 14 (1910) 417-421.

W. B. Pollard, "Report on a Sample of liquid from a small jar transmitted by the Antiquities Department," *ASAE* 13 (1914) 253-254.

Nicholas Knight, "Notes and Queries. 1. *Specimen of Rock from Solomon's Quarries*," *PEFQS* 47 (1915) 50-51.

Nicholas Knight, "Notes and Queries. 2. *Specimen of Hard Jewish' Rock from Solomon's Quarries*," *PEFQS* 47 (1915) 51.

A. Lucas, "Efflorescent salt of unusual composition," *ASAE* 17 (1917) 86-88.

A. Lucas, "Mistakes in Chemical Matters frequently made in Archaeology," *JEA* 10 (1924) 128-132.

*A. Lucas, "Damage caused by Salt at Karnak," *ASAE* 25 (1925) 47-54.

*C. Ainsworth Mitchell, "Marking-Ink in Ancient Egypt," *AEE* 12 (1927) 18.

*George W. Morey, "The Mystery of Ancient Glassware," *A&A* 28 (1929) 199-205.

[W. M.] Flinders Petrie, "Recent Analyses," *AEE* 14 (1929) 49. *[Analyses of Metal Objects in Egypt]*

*A. Kenneth Graham, "Scientific Notes on the Finds from Ur," *MJ* 20 (1929) 246-257. [I. Restoration of the Silver; II. Metallurgical Notes; III. The Cosmetics of Queen Shubad (Note by editor, pp. 255-257)]

R. Engelbach, "Ancient Egyptian Woods," *ASAE* 31 (1931) 144.

O. H. Little, "Preliminary report on some geological specimens from the 'Chephren diorite' quarries, Western Desert," *ASAE* 33 (1933) 75-80.

A. Lucas, "Resin from a tomb of the saïte period," *ASAE* 33 (1933) 187-189.

R. W. Wood, "The Purple Gold of Tut'ankhamūn," *JEA* 20 (1934) 62-65.

*E. R. Lacheman, "New Nuzi Texts and a New Method of Copying Cuneiform Tablets," *JAOS* 55 (1935) 429-431.

A. Lucas, "The wood of the third Dynasty Ply-Wood Coffin from Saqqara," *ASAE* 36 (1936) 1-4.

*F. A. Bannister and H. J. Plenderleith, "Physico-Chemical Examination of a Scarab of Tuthmosis IV bearing the name of the God Aten," *JEA* 22 (1936) 3-6.

Howard   Comfort,   Donald   Horton   and   Leonard   C.   Riesch,
"Technological   Analysis   of   Ceramics,   Illustrated   by   Terra
Sigillata," *AJA* 41 (1937) 112-113.

*Donald Horton, "Technological Methods in the Study of Pottery
from Greece and Italy," *AJA* 42 (1938) 128.

*A. Löhnberg, "The Application of Geophysical Measurements to
Archaeological Excavations," *JPOS* 19 (1939-40) 245-252.

*Wayne M. Felts, "A Petrographic Examination of Potsherds from
Ancient Troy," *AJA* 46 (1942) 237-244.

*Dows Dunham and William J. Young, "An Occurrence of Iron in the
Fourth Dynasty," *JEA* 28 (1942) 57-58.

*Dows Dunham, "Notes on Copper-Bronze in the Middle Kingdom,"
JEA 29 (1943) 60-62.

Dows Dunham, "Magnesium in Egyptian Copper-bronze Objects,"
JEA 29 (1943) 76.

Zaki/sic/ Iskandar Hanna, "Liquid found in the sarcophagus of
Ptȝḥ-špss. Saqqara, 1944," *ASAE* 44 (1944) 259-262.

J. L. Kelso, "Some Sixteenth-Century Copper Objects from Tell Beit
Mirsim," *BASOR* #91 (1943) 28-36.

*J. L. Kelso and J. Palin Thorley, "A Ceramic Analysis of
Late-Mycenaean and Other Late-Bronze Vases from Jett in
Palestine," *BASOR* #104 (1946) 21-25.

*Ruth B. Kallner and J. Vroman, "Petrographical Examination of
Pottery," *BIES* 12 (1946) I.

Earle R. Caley, "Results of a Chemical Examination of Some Specimens
of Roman Glaze from Tarsus," *AJA* 51 (1947) 389-393.

*Yigael Sukenik, "On the Technique of Khirbet Kerak Ware,"
BASOR #106 (1947) 9-17.

H. Moore, "Reproduction of an Ancient Babylonian Glaze," *Iraq* 10
(1948) 26-33.

Robert J. Braidwood, Thorkild Jacobsen, Richard A. Parker, Saul S. Weinberg, "Communication: Age Determination of Archaeological Material," *AJA* 54 (1950) 266-267.

*M. W. Lightner, "Analyses of Iron Implements from Tell Beit Mirsim," *BASOR* #119 (1950) 22-24.

J. Paclt, "On the Origin of Ferrous Limestone Coatings in the Plain of Sharon in Israel," *IEJ* 1 (1950-51) 141-145.

*Marie Farnsworth, "Second Century B.C. Rose Madder from Corinth and Athens," *AJA* 55 (1951) 236-239.

*Humphrey Humphreys, "Dental Evidence in Archaeology," *Antiq* 25 (1951) 16-18.

Donald Collier, "New Radiocarbon Method for Dating the Past," *BA* 14 (1951) 25-28. [Samples are Burned; History of Process; Egyptian Boat Plank Used; Test Museum Specimens]

G. Ernest Wright, "Some Radiocarbon Dates," *BA* 14 (1951) 31-32.

*James L. Kelso, "Ancient Copper Refining," *BASOR* #122 (1951) 26-27.

*James L. Kelso, "Ancient Copper Refining," *BASOR* #122 (1951) 26-27.

C. B. M. McBurdey, "Radiocarbon dating results from the Old World," *Antiq* 26 (1952) 35-40.

Zaky Iskander, "Desert Varnish and Mortar of the Rhomboïdal Pyramid at Dahshûr," *ASAE* 52 (1952-54) 271-274.

W. Kendrick Pritchett, "Liquid Rubber for Greek Epigraphy," *AJA* 56 (1952) 118-120.

Norman Herz and W. Kendrick Pritchett, "Marble in Attic Epigraphy," *AJA* 57 (1953) 71-83.

W. Kendrick Pritchett, "Further Notes on Liquid Rubber," *AJA* 57 (1953) 197-198.

R. W. Sloley, "Radiocarbon dating," *JEA* 39 (1953) 115.

G. E[rnest] Wright, "A new Atomic Clock," *BA* 17 (1954) 47.

W. E. S. Turner, "Glass Fagments from Nimrud of the Eighth to the Sixth Century, B.C.," *Iraq* 17 (1955) 57-68.

Ray Winfield Smith, "Technological Research on Ancient Glass," *AJA* 60 (1956) 181.

G. W. Van Beek, "A Radiocarbon Date for Early South Arabia," *BASOR* #143 (1956) 6-9.

M. Dothan, "Radioactive Examination of Archaeological Material from Israel," *IEJ* 5 (1956) 112-114.

Harry Garner, "An Early Piece of Glass from Eridu," *Iraq* 18 (1956) 147-149.

Anonymous, "Radio Carbon Date from Jericho," *AT* 1 (1956-57) #3, 14.

E. V. Sayre and R. W. Dodson, "Neutron Activation Study of Mediterranean Potsherds," *AJA* 61 (1957) 35-41.

*C. F. Cheng, and C. M. Schwitter, "Nickel in Ancient Bronzes," *AJA* 61 (1957) 351-365.

*William L. Reed, "A Recent Analysis of Grain from Ancient Dibon in Moab," *BASOR* #146 (1957) 6-10.

Joseph P. Free, "Radiocarbon Date of Iron Age Level at Dothan," *BASOR* #147 (1957) 36-37.

Anonymous, "Radiocarbon Dating and Archaeology," *Antiq* 32 (1958) 193-194.

Harold Barker, Radio Carbon Dating: Its Scope and Limitations," *Antiq* 32 (1958) 253-263.

Ray Winfield Smith, "Techonological Research on Ancient Glass," *Arch* 11 (1958) 111-116.

C. M. Kraay, "Gold and Copper Traces in Early Greek Silver," *Archm* 1 (1958) 1-5.

Robert M. Cook and John C. Belshé, "Dating by Archaeomagnetism," *Arch* 12 (1959) 158-162.

C. M. Kraay, "Gold and Copper Traces in Early Greek Silver—II.," *Archm* 2 (1959) 1-16.

R. J. Chaleston, "Lead in Glass," *Archm* 3 (1960) 1-4.

Margaret Thompson, "Gold and Copper Traces in Late Athenian Silver," *Archm* 3 (1960) 10-15.

*Henry Field, "Carbon-14 Date for a 'Neolithic' Site in the Rub' al Khali," *Man* 60 (1960) #214.

*Herbert Maryon, "Early Near Eastern Steel Swords," *AJA* 65 (1961) 173-184. [with technical reports by Mr. R. M. Organ, Dr. O. W. Ellis, Dr. R. M. Birch, Dr. R. Sneyers, Dr. E. E. Herzfeld and Dr. F. K. Naumann]

Philip C. Hammond, "The X-Ray Geiger-Counter Spectroscope as an Archaeological Instrument," *AJA* 65 (1961) 305.

Ellen L. Kohler and Elizabeth K. Ralph, "C-14 Dates for Sites in the Mediterranean Area," *AJA* 65 (1961) 357-367.

Arthur Steinberg, "Optical Spectrometry and Etruscan Bronzes," *AJA* 67 (1963) 217.

*Froelich Rainey, "The Applied Science Center for Archaeology," *AJA* 67 (1963) 294-295. *[Radioactive Carbon Dating]*

Curt W. Beck, "Synthetic Elastomers in Epigraphy," *AJA* 67 (1963) 413-416.

W. F. Libby, "The Accuracy of Radiocarbon Dates," *Antiq* 37 (1963) 213-219.

*G. T. Emery, "Dental Pathology and Archaeology," *Antiq* 37 (1963) 274-281.

David Trump, "Carbon, Malta and the Mediterranean," *Antiq* 37 (1963) 302-303.

*R. Knox, "Detection of Iron Carbide Structure in the Oxide Remains of Ancient Steel," *Archm* 6 (1963) 43-45.

*C. A. Key, "Note on the Trace-Element Content of the Artifacts of the Kfar Monash Hoard," *IEJ* 13 (1963) 289-290.

Rutherford J. Gettens, "The Corrosion Products of Metal Antiquities," *SIR* (1963) 547-568.

*Kate C. Lefferts, "Technical Notes on Another Luristan Sword," *AJA* 68 (1964) 59-62.

Arthur Steinberg, "Optical Spectrometry and 'Oriental Bronzes'," *AJA* 68 (1964) 201.

*Marie Fansworth, "Greek Pottery: A Mineralogical Study," *AJA* 68 (1964) 221-228.

*A. Millett, J. B. Pritchard and E. K. Ralph, "A Spectrographic Investigation of Jar Handles Bearing the 'Royal' Stamp of Judah," *Archm* 7 (1964) 67-71.

*G. F. Carter, "Preparation of Ancient Coins for Accurate X-Ray Fluorescene Analysis," *Archm* 7 (1964) 106-113.

*Elizabeth K. Ralph, "The Electronic Detective and the Case of the Missing City," *Exped* 7 (1964-65) #2, 4-8.

*Ora Nebgi, "A Contribution of Mineralogy and Palaeontology to an Archaeological Study of Terracottas," *IEJ* 14 (1964) 187-189.

J. Birmingham, N. F. Kennon and A. S. Malin, "A 'Luristan' Dagger: An Examination of Ancient Metallurgical Techniques," *Iraq* 26 (1964) 44-49.

J. de Heinzelin, "Le Sous-sol du Temple d'Aksha," *Kush* 12 (1964) 102-108. [English Summary - The Sub-Soil of Askha Temple, pp. 109-110]

Jeanette M. Flamm, "Experiments with Rubber Silicon Compounds," *AJA* 69 (1965) 62-63.

*T. C. Yao and F. H. Stross, "The Use of Analysis by X-ray Flourescence in the Study of Coins," *AJA* 69 (1965) 154-156.

*Robert H. Brill and J. Marion Wampler, "Isotope Studies of Ancient Lead," *AJA* 69 (1965) 165-166.

*R. L. Fleischer, P. B. Price and R. M. Walker, "Applications of Fission Tracks and Fission Track Dating to Anthropology," *AJA* 69 (1965) 167-168.

*J. G. D. Clark, "Radiocarbon Dating and the Spread of Farming Economy," *Antiq* 39 (1965) 45-48.

Robert Stuckenrath Jr., "On the Care and Feeding of Radiocarbon Dates," *Arch* 18 (1965) 277-281.

*J. Condamin and M. Picon, "Notes on Diffusion in Ancient Alloys," *Archm* 8 (1965) 110-114.

*M. L. Ryder, "Report on Textiles from Çatal Hüyük," *AS* 15 (1965) 175-176.

*Mahboub al-Chalabi, "Applications of Geo-electrical Methods in Archaeology," *Sumer* 21 (1965) 119-135.

*V. Clain-Stefanelli, "An Application of Physics in Ancient Numismatics: Detection of certain counterfeit Aegina staters through X-ray diffraction analysis," *AJA* 70 (1966) 185.

Julian Whittlesey, "Photogrammetry for the Excavator," *Arch* 19 (1966) 273-276.

*R. Tlalka, "The Applicability of Spectral Analysis for the Purpose of Joining Cuneiform Tablets," *ArOr* 34 (1966) 46-52.

*Henry O. Thompson, "Science and Archaeology," *BA* 29 (1966) 114-125.

Curt W. Beck, "Analysis and Provenience of Minoan and Mycenean Amber, I," *GRBS* 7 (1966) 191-211.

*Joan Crowfoot Payne, "Spectrographic analysis of some Egyptian pottery of the Eighteenth Dynasty," *JEA* 52 (1966) 176-178.

Theresa Howard Carter and Robert Pagliero, "Notes on Mud-Brick Preservations," *Sumer* 22 (1966) 65-76.

*Colin Renfrew, "Cycladic Metallurgy and the Aegean Early Bronze Age," *AJA* 71 (1967) 1-20.

J. A. Charles, "Early Arsenical Bronzes—A Metallurgical View," *AJA* 71 (1967) 21-26.

*Robert H. Brill and J. M. Wampler, "Isotope Studies of Ancient Lead," *AJA* 71 (1967) 63-77.

Lenore O. Keene Congdon, "Metallic Analyses of Three Greek Caryatid Mirrors," *AJA* 71 (1967) 149-153.

V. Bucha and J. Melleart, "Archaeomagnetic Intensity Measurements on Some Neolithic Samples from Çatal Hüyük (Anatolia)," *Archm* 10 (1967) 23-25.

I. M. Blake and J. Cynthia Weber, "Radioactivity of Jericho Bones," *Archm* 10 (1967) 127-128.

*Henry Morris, "Biblical Chronology and Geological Dating," *SR* 14 (1967-68) #1, 15-30.

Robert J. Braidwood, "A Note on the Present Status of Radio Active Carbon Age Determination," *Sumer* 23 (1967) 39-44.

*Curt W. Beck, "The Provenience of Mycenaean Amber Artifacts," *AJA* 72 (1968) 161.

Curt W. Beck, Gretchen C. Southard and Audrey B. Adams, "Analysis and Provenience of Minoan and Mycenaean Amber II. Tiryns," *GRBS* 9 (1968) 5-19.

Elizabeth K. Ralph, "Archaeological Prospecting," *Exped* 11 (1968-69) #2, 14-21.

*Ali M. Dinçol and Faut Baykal, "Petrografik Metodlarla Keramik Incelenmesi," *AAI* 3 (1969) 103-117. [English Summary, pp. 112-113] *[Pottery and Science]*

*Ali M. Dinçol and Yusuf Tekiz, "Maden Eserlerin Incelenmesinde Radyolojik Metodlar," *AAI* 3 (1969) 119-139 [English Summary, p. 126] *[Artifacts and Science]*

*P. Meyers, "Non-Destructive Activation Analysis of Ancient Coins Using Charged Particles and Fast Neutrons," *Archm* 11 (1969) 67-83.

Emanuel Mazor, "The Radio-Activity in the Waters at Jericho," *PEQ* 101 (1969) 46-47.

*Gary A. Wright, "Obsidian Analyses and Prehistoric Near Eastern Trade: 7500 to 3500 B.C.," *UMMAAP* #37 (1969) i-v, 1-92.

*Sönmez Kantman, "A Microanalytic Study of some Ground Stone Artefacts /sic/ from Tilmen Höyük and Gedíklí-Karahöyük (Southeastern Anatolia). Contributions to Functional Typology," *Anat* 3 (1969-70) 139-145.

§154 *2.5.1 Scientific Thought in the Ancient Near East*

*A. Lowy, "On Technological Terms in Ancient Semitic Culture and Foke-lore /sic/," *SBAP* 6 (1883-84) 138-144.

G. T. Plunkett, "The Nilometer of Philoe," *SBAP* 9 (1886-87) 311-313.

Arthur Platt, "Plato and geology," *JP* 18 (1889-90) 134-139.

†Anonymous, "The Alchemists of Egypt and Greece," *ERCJ* 177 (1893) 202-216. *(Review)*

Harold H. Jaochim, "Aristotle's conception of chemical combination," *JP* 29 (1903-04) 72-86.

*Frederic Blass, "Science and Sophistry," *ET* 16 (1904-05) 8-15. [Knowledge and Science; Sophistry; Spread of Sophistry; Distinguishing Marks; Sophistical Science (So-Called) of Religion; Assyriology and the Old Testament; Assyriology—History of Religion and the New Testament] *(Trans. by Margaret D. Gibson)*

T. J. J. See, "On the Temperature, Secular Cooling and Contraction of the Earth, and on the Theory of Earthquakes Held by the Ancients," *PAPS* 46 (1907) 191-299. [IV. On the Theory of Earthquakes Held by the Ancients, pp. 232-298]

H. F. Lutz, "A Nilometer in the Egyptian Collection of the Museum of Anthropology and Ethnology of the University of California," *JAOS* 43 (1923) 49.

Carleton W. Stanley, "Greek Science," *QRL* 249 (1927) 100-115.

*Mabel Lea Hedge, "Biology as Portrayed in Ancient Art," *A&A* 25 (1928) 292-300.

*R. Campbell Thompson and C. J. Gadd, "A Middle-Babylonian Chemical Text," *Iraq* 3 (1936) 87-96. [B.M. 120960]

J. R. Mattingly, "Cosmogony and stereometry in Posidian physics," *Osiris* 3 (1938) 558-583.

Raphael Patai, "The 'Control of Rain' in Ancient Palestine," *HUCA* 14 (1939) 251-286.

Heinrich Gomperz, "Problems and Methods of Early Greek Science," *JHI* 4 (1943) 161-176.

*George G. Cameron, "The Babylonian Scientist and His Hebrew Colleague," *BA* 7 (1944) 21-29, 32-40. [The First Scientific Records; The Babylonian Calendar; Change and Resistance to It; Diseases and their Remedy; Ancient Metallurgy; Sumerian, The 'Dead' Language; Omens and Astronomy; Mathematics and Geometry]

Richard McKeon, "Aristotle's Conception of the Development and the Nature of Scientific Method," *JHI* 8 (1947) 3-44.

*E. F. Sutcliffe, "Clouds as Water-Carriers in Hebrew Thought," *VT* 3 (1953) 99-103.

*V. Gordon Childe, "Science in Preliterate Societies and the Ancient Oriental Civilization," *Cent* 3 (1953-54) 12-23.

*R. J. Forbes, "Metals and Early Science," *Cent* 3 (1953-54) 24-31.

B. Farrington, "The Rise of Abstract Science Among the Greeks," *Cent* 3 (1953-54) 32-37.

Bernard Scully, "Antiquity's View of The Sphericity and Circumference of the Earth," *MH* 10 (Winter, 1953-54) 45-50.

*John W. Wilson, "Egyptian Technology, Science, and Lore," *JWH* 2 (1954-55) 209-213.

Martin Levey, "Evidences of ancient distillation, sublimation and extraction in Mesopotamia," *Cent* 4 (1955-56) 23-33.

*Martin Levey, "Babylonian Chemistry: A Study of Arabic and Second Millenium B.C. Perfumery," *Osiris* 12 (1956) 376-389.

James F. McCue, "Scientific Procedure in Aristotle's 'De caelo'," *Tr* 18 (1962) 1-24.

O. Neugerbauer, "The Survival of Babylonian Methods in Exact Sciences of Antiquity and Middle Ages," *PAPS* 107 (1963) 528-535.

A. L. Oppenheim, "Mesopotamia in the Early History of Alchemy," *RAAO* 60 (1966) 29-45.

Harold J. Johnson, "Three Ancient Meanings of Matter: Democritus, Plato, and Aristotle," *JHI* 28 (1967) 3-16.

§155   *2.5.2 Astrology and Astronomy*

†T. Y., "The Astronomy of the Ancients," *MMBR* 41 (1816) 21-25.

Tayler Lewis, "Astronomical Views of the Ancients," *BRCR, 3rd Ser.*, 5 (1849) 289-316, 528-551.

B. Golding, "The Eclipse of Thales," *JSL, 2nd Ser.*, 6 (1854) 518-519.

*G. Seyffarth, "Three Lectures on Egyptian Antiquities, &c., delivered at the Stuyvesant Institute, New York, May 1856," *ER* 8 (1856-57) 34-104. [VIII. The Astronomy of the Egyptians, pp. 76-78; XII. The Planetary Constellation of Menes, pp. 80-81; XIII. The Planetary Constellations of the Greeks and Romans, pp. 81-82; XIV. The Planetary Constellations of the four Ages of the World, pp. 82-84; XV. The Planetary Constellations in the Alphabet, PP. 84-86; XVI. Defects in the Planetary Tables, pp. 86-87]

Anonymous, "Sir. G. C. Lewis on the Astronomy of the Ancients," *NBR* 36 (1862) 485-513. *(Review)*

*G. B., "On the Accession of Nebuchadnezzer and the Eclipse of B.C. 585," *JSL, 5th Ser.*, 2 (1867-68) 455-457.

†Henry Talbot Fox, "On an Ancient Eclipse," *SBAT* 1 (1872) 13-19. (Addition, pp. 348-354)

*A. H. Sayce, "The Astronomy and Astrology of the Babylonians, with Translations of the Tablets relating to these subjects," *SBAT* 3 (1874) 145-339.

*P. le Page Renouf, "Calendar of Astronomical Observations found in the Royal Tombs of the XXth Dynasty," *SBAT* 3 (1874) 400-421.

*A. H. Sayce, "Revised Translation of a Passage in the Great Astronomical Work of the Babylonians," *SBAT* 4 (1875) 36-37.

*H[enry] Fox Talbot, "Notice of a very Ancient Comet. From a Chaldean Tablet," *SBAT* 4 (1875) 257-262.

J. W. Weddell, "The Heavens of the Hebrews," *ONTS* 1 (1882) 65-67.

*R. V. Foster, "Some Astronomy in the Book of Job," *ONTS* 4 (1884-85) 358-363.

*P. le Page Renouf, "The Eclipse in Egyptian Texts," *SBAP* 7 (1884-85) 163-170.

†*J. Oppert, "Eclipse, Ninety-one Years after the Death of Ahab, King of Israel," *SBAP* 8 (1885-86) 58-59.

*W. St. Chad Boscawen, "Gleanings from Clay Commentaries—No. I.," *BOR* 1 (1886-87) 23-25. *[Astrology]*

*A. H. Sayce, "Miscellaneous Notes," *ZA* 2 (1887) 331-340. [19. Table of Lunar Longitudes, pp. 337-340]

Robt. Brown Jr., "Babylonian Astronomy in the West—The *Aries* or Aratos," *BOR* 1 (1886-87) 33-35.

W.T.Lynn, "Note on Babylonian Astronomy," *BOR* 1 (1886-87) 78-79.

Robt. Brown Jr., "Remarks on Some Euphratean Astronomical Names in the *Lexicon of Hesychois,*" *BOR* 1 (1886-87) 140-143, 148-150.

Joseph Edkins, "When did Babylonian Astrology enter China?" *SBAP* 9 (1886-87) 32-39.

Robert Brown Jr., "On the Eupratean Names of the Constellation *Ursa Major,*" *SBAP* 9 (1886-87) 127-130.

T. de Lacouperie, "The Shifted Cardinal Points.—From Elam to Early China," *BOR* 2 (1887-88) 25-32.

*T[heo.] G. Pinches, "An Astronomical or Astrological table from Babylon," *BOR* 2 (1887-88) 202-207.

†Robert J. Brown, "Names of Stars in Babylonian," *SBAP* 11 (1888-89) 145-151.

*John A. Paine, "The Eclipse of the 7th year of Cambyses," *JAOS* 14 (1890) xc-xciii.

Christopher Johnston Jr., "On the Chaldean Astronomy," *JAOS* 14 (1890) cxl-cxlii.

Robert Brown Jr., "Euphratean Stellar Researches," *SBAP* 14 (1891-92) 280-304.

Fritz Hommel, "Babylonian Astronomy—I. 'The Planets'," *BOR* 6 (1892-93) 169-172.

*(Miss) E[mmeline] M. Plunket, "The Constellation Aries," *SBAP* 15 (1892-93) 237-242.

Robert Brown Jr., "Euphratean Stellar Researches. Part II," *SBAP* 15 (1892-93) 317-342.

Robert Brown Jr., "Euphratean Stellar Researches. Part III," *SBAP* 15 (1892-93) 456-470.

Robert Brown Jr., "Euphratean Stellar Researches, Part IV," *SBAP* 17 (1895) 16-36.

Robert Brown Jr., "Euphratean Stellar Researches, Part V," *SBAP* 17 (1895) 284-303.

Robert Brown Jr., "Euphratean Stellar Researches, Part V (Continued)," *SBAP* 18 (1896) 25-44.

Robert Brown Jr., "On the Origin of the Ancient Northern Constellation-figures," *JRAS* (1897) 205-226.

*E[mmeline] M. Plunkett, "The Median Calendar and the Constellation Taurus," *SBAP* 19 (1897) 229-249. [Note by J[oseph] Offord, pp. 243-245]

*F. W. Read, "A Supposed Eclipse of the Moon under XXIInd Egyptian Dynasty," *SBAP* 21 (1899) 309-310.

(Miss) E[mmeline] M. Plunket, "Ancient Indian Astronomy," *SBAP* 22 (1900) 47-58.

Robert Brown Jr., "A Euphratean Circle of 360°," *SBAP* 22 (1900) 67-71.

*R. Campbell Thompson, "Craig's Astrological-Astronomical Texts," *AJSL* 17 (1900-01) 107-115. [Corr. pp. 111-115] *[Assyrian] (Review)*

R[obert] Brown Jr., "Note on the Heavenly Body ⫣⟊⟊ ⫣⟊⟊," *SBAP* 24 (1902) 126-129.

G. Mackinlay, "Biblical Astronomy," *JTVI* 37 (1905) 122-152, 163-164. [(Discussion, pp. 153-161) (Communications by John Tuckwell, pp. 161-162; A. H. Sayce, p. 162; R. B. Girdlestone, pp. 162-163)]

E. Walter Maunder, "Primitive Astronomy and the Old Testament," *LQHR* 106 (1906) 47-70. *(Review)*

*Edgar L. Larkin, "The Waning of the Light of Egypt," *OC* 20 (1906) 228-242. *[Astronomy & Egyptian Religion]*

(Miss) Emmeline Plunket, "The 'Star of Stars' and 'Dilgan'," *SBAP* 28 (1906) 6-13, 47-53.

*Margaret A. Murray, "The Astrological Character of the Egyptian Magical Wands," *SBAP* 28 (1906) 33-43.

E. Walter Maunder, "The Triad of Stars," *ET* 19 (1907-08) 300-303.

Anonymous, "Babylonian Astronomy," *AAOJ* 30 (1908) 41-42.

William F[airfield] Warren, "The Babylonian Universe Newly Interpreted," *JRAS* (1908) 977-983.

*Morris Jastrow Jr., "The Sign and Name for Planet in Babylonian," *PAPS* 47 (1908) 141-156.

*Morris Jastrow Jr., "Hepatoscopy and Astrology in Babylonian and Assyria," *PAPS* 47 (1908) 646-676.

*George Frederick Wright, "Solar Eclipses and Ancient History," *RP* 7 (1908) 275-281.

*G. Legge, "Is the ⊟ Λ ⌒𝖷 a heliacal rising," *RTR* 31 (1908) 106-112.

Fritz Hommel, "Ancient Babylonian Astrology," *ET* 10 (1908-09) 44.

*George Frederick Wright, "Solar Eclipses and Ancient History,"
  CFL, 3rd Ser., 10 (1909) 101-105.

Franz Cumont, "Astrology and Magic," *OC* 23 (1909) 641-662.
  (Trans. by A. M. Thielen)

Morris Jastrow Jr., "Sun and Saturn," *RAAO* 7 (1909) 163-178.

Morris Jastrow Jr., "Babylonian Orientation," *ZA* 23 (1909) 196-208.
  [Astronomy]

‡William Fairfield Warren, "The Earliest Traceable Astronomy,"
  MR 92 (1910) 642-643.

*Morris Jastrow Jr., "Signs and Names of the Planet Mars," *AJSL* 27
  (1910-11) 64-83.

F. X. Kugler, "Some new lights on Babylonian Astronomy. (Critical
  remarks and positive statements)," *ZA* 25 (1911) 304-320.

E. Walter Maunder, "The Astronomy of the Apocrypha," *IJA* #30
  (1912) 46-52.

E. Walter Maunder, "Jeremias and Astral-Mythology in the Old
  Testament," *LQHR* 118 (1912) 220-237. *(Review)*

*Edward Wesson, "An Assyrian Solar Eclipse," *SBAP* 34 (1912) 53-66.

Edward Wesson, "Some Lunar Eclipses," *SBAP* 34 (1912) 205-211,
  239-246.

*S[tephen] Langdon, "Astronomy and the Early Sumerian Calendar,"
  SBAP 34 (1912) 248-256.

*L. W. King, "A Neo-Babylonian Astronomical Treatise in the British
  Museum, and its bearing on the Age of Babylonian Astronomy,"
  SBAP 35 (1913) 41-46.

Emmeline Plunket, "The Month when the Star Barsag Sets,"
  SBAP 36 (1914) 9-14.

*(Mrs. Walter) Maunder, "Astronomical Allusions in Sacred Books of
  the East," *JTVI* 47 (1915) 181-226, 231-232. [(Discussion, pp.
  226-228) (Communication by F. C. Burkitt, pp. 228-231)]

*Joseph Offord, "Archaeological Notes on Jewish Antiquites. XVIII. *A New Manuscript in Paris concerning Hebrew Astronomy,*" *PEFQS* 48 (1916) 146-147.

Theophilus G. Pinches, "Assyro-Babylonian Astrologers and Their Lore," *ET* 30 (1918-19) 164-168.

*S[tephen] Langdon, "Assyrian Lexicographical Notes," *JRAS* (1920) 325-331. [3. The Babylonian Name of the Milky Way, pp. 329-331]

*G. W. Gilmore, "Astronomy and Egyptian Pyramids and Temples," *HR* 83 (1922) 479.

Peter J. Popoff, "The Bible's Astronomy," *OC* 40 (1926) 363-364.

*Eric Burrows, "Ḫurian Sala(s)," *JRAS* (1927) 318-320. *[Constellation Virgo]*

*G. A. Wainwright, "The Relationship of Amūn to Zeus, and his Connexion with Meteorites," *JEA* 16 (1930) 35-38.

A[lexander] Pogo, "The Astronomical Ceiling-decoration in the Tomb of Senmut (XVIIIth Dynasty)," *Isis* 14 (1930) 301-325.

George Foot Moore, "Jews and Astrology," *TF* 2 (1930) 142-145.

*S[tephen] H. Langdon, "The Star Hêlēl, Jupiter?" *ET* 42 (1930-31) 172-174.

*John Lowel Butler, "Astronomical Solution of Ancient and Modern Climates," *BS* 89 (1932) 86-86.

*A[lexander] Pogo, "The Astronomical Inscriptions on the Coffins of Ḥeny (XIth dynasty?)," *Isis* 18 (1932) 7-13.

[W. M.] Flinders Petrie, "Primitive Astronomy," *AEE* 18 (1933) 111-112.

G. A. Wainwright, "Orion and the Great Star," *JEA* 22 (1936) 45-46.

A. T. Olmstead, "Babylonian Astronomy—Historical Sketch," *AJSL* 55 (1938) 113-129.

*Solomon Gandz, "Studies in Hebrew Mathematics and Astronomy,"
   PAAJR 9 (1938-39) 5-50.

Herbert Chatley, "The lunar mansions in Egypt," *Isis* 31 (1939)
   394-397.

*William Bell Dinsmoor, "Archæology and Astronomy," *PAPS* 80
   (1939) 95-173.

Herbert Chatley, "Egyptian Astronomy," *JEA* 26 (1940) 120-126.

A. Pannekoek, "Some Remarks on the Moon's Diameter and the
   Eclipse Tables in Babylonian Astronomy," *Eud* 1 (1941) 9-22.

*O[tto] Neugebauer, "On a Special Use of the Sign 'Zero' in Cuneiform

   Astronomical Texts," *JAOS* 61 (1941) 213-215. [**2**]

Robert Eisler and [Herbert] Chatley, "Egyptian Astronomy. Letters
   from Dr. Eisler and Dr. Chatley," *JEA* 27 (1941) 149-152.

*O[tto] Neugebauer, "Egyptian Planetary Texts," *TAPS, N.S.,* 32
   (1941-43) 209-250.

*O[tto] Neugebauer, "On Some Astronomical Papyri and Related
   Problems of Ancient Geography," *TAPS, N.S.,* 32 (1941-43)
   251-263.

*Solomon Gandz, "The Zodiacal Light in Semitic Mythology,"
   PAAJR 13 (1943) 1-39.

*George G. Cameron, "The Babylonian Scientist and His Hebrew
   Colleague," *BA* 7 (1944) 21-29, 32-40. [Omens and Astronomy,
   pp. 36-38]

O[tto] Neugebauer, "The History of Ancient Astronomy: Problems
   and Methods," *JNES* 4 (1945) 1-38.

O[tto] Neugebauer, "Studies in Ancient Astronomy. VII. Magnitudes
   of Lunar Eclipses in Babylonian Mathematical Astronomy,"
   Isis 36 (1945-46) 10-15. *[Parts 1-5 published in German;
   Part 6 published in a Festschrift to G. Sarton]*

*B. L. van der Waerden, "On Babylonian Astronomy I. The Venus Tablets of Ammiṣaduqa," *JEOL* #10 (1945-48) 414-424.

*O[tto] Neugebauer, "Studies in Ancient Astronomy. VIII. The Water Clock in Babylonian Astronomy," *Isis* 37 (1947) 37-43.

O[tto] Neugebauer, "A Table of Solstices from Uruk," *JCS* 1 (1947) 143-148. *[Babylonian]*

*O[tto] Neugebauer, "Unusual Writings in Seleucid Astronomical Texts," *JCS* 1 (1947) 217-218.

Homer H. Dubs, "A Canon of Visible Penumbral Lunar Eclipses for the Near East and Egypt from -1400 to -1000," *JNES* 6 (1947) 124-125.

O[tto] Neugebauer, "Solstices and Equinoxes in Babylonian Astronomy During the Selucid Period," *JCS* 2 (1948) 209-222.

A. Sachs, "A Classification of the Babylonian Astronomical Tablets of the Seleucid Period," *JCS* 2 (1948) 271-290.

*Solomon Gandz, "The Origin of the Planetary Week *or* The Planetary Week in Hebrew Literature," *PAAJR* 18 (1948-49) 213-254.

*Hildegard Lewy, "The Babylonian Background of the Kas Kâûs Legend," *ArOr* 17 (1949) Part 2, 28-109. [1. The Astronomers among the Kings of Babylonia, pp. 33-56]

B. L. van der Waerden, "On Babylonian Astronomy II. The Thirty-Six Stars," *JNES* 8 (1949) 6-26.

O[tto] Neugebauer, "The Alleged Babylonian Discovery of the Precession of the Equinoxes," *JAOS* 70 (1950) 1-8.

*P. W. Stoner, "Fifty Years of Development in Astronomy and Its Impact on Scriptural Interpretation," *JASA* 2 (1950) #3, 7-10.

O[tto] Neugebauer, "A Greek Table for the Motion of the Sun," *Cent* 1 (1950-51) 266-270.

Jotham Johnson, "Tell Time by the Stars," *Arch* 4 (1951) 76-82.

B. L. van der Waerden, "On Babylonian Astronomy III. The Earliest Astronomical Computations," *JNES* 10 (1951) 20-34.

O[tto] Neugebauer, "The Babylonian Method for the Computation of the Last Visibilities of Mercury," *PAPS* 95 (1951) 110-116.

A. Sachs, "Sirius Dates in Babylonian Astronomical Texts of the Seleucid Period," *JCS* 6 (1952) 105-114.

A. Sachs, "A Late Babylonian Star Catalog," *JCS* 6 (1952) 146-150.;

O[tto] Neugebauer and A. Sachs, "The 'Dodekatemoria' in Babylonian Astrology," *AfO* 16 (1952-53) 65-66.

O[tto] Neugebauer, "The Rising Times in Babylonian Astronomy," *JCS* 4 (1953) 100-102.

*G. R. Driver, "Two Astronomical Passages in the Old Testament," *JTS, N.S.,* 4 (1953) 208-212. [Amos 5:8-9; Job 38:12-15]

*Maud W. Makemson, "Astronomy in Primitive Religion," *JAAR* 22 (1954) 163-171.

O[tto] Neugebauer, "Babylonian Planetary Theory," *PAPS* 98 (1954) 60-89.

George Sarton, "Chaldaean Astronomy of the Last Three Centuries B.C.," *JAOS* 75 (1955) 166-173.

Asger Aaboe, "On the Babylonian origin of some Hipparchian parameters," *Cent* 4 (1955-56) 122-125.

*G. H. Driver, "Two Astronomical Passages in the O. T.," *JTS, N.S.,* 7 (1956) 1-11. [Job 9:9 (R.V.); Job 38:31-32 (R.V.)]

*Elmer G. Suhr, "The Evolution of the Mesopotamian Cone and Spindle," *AJA* 62 (1958) 226-227. *[Lunar Eclipses]*

*Rudolph E. Siegel, "On the relation between early Greek scientific thought and mysticism: is Hestia, the central fire, an abstract astronomical concept?" *Janus* 49 (1960) 1-20.

*Richard A. Parker, "Two Demotic Astronomical Papyri in the Carlsberg Collection," *AO* 26 (1961-62) 143-147.

‡O[tto] Neugebauer, "Astronomical Papyri and Ostraca: Bibliographical Notes," *PAPS* 106 (1962) 383-391.

George Huxley, "Studies in the Greek Astronomers," *GRBS* 4 (1963) 83-105. [I. Eudoxian Topics; II. A Fragment of Clestratus of Tenedos; III. Friends and Contemporaries of Apollonius of Perge]

David Pingree, "Astronomy and Astrology in India and Iran," *Isis* 54 (1963) 229-246.

*Clark Hopkins, "The Seasonal Drama Illustrated in Phoenican Bowls," *AJA* 68 (1964) 196. *[Eclipse]*

Elmer J. Suhr, "An Interpretation of the Medusa Mask," *AJA* 68 (1964) 202-203. *[Astronomy]*

*A[sger] Aaboe, "A Seleucid Table of Daily Solar (?) Positions," *JCS* 18 (1964) 31-34. [B.M. 37089] *[Babylonian]*

*O[tto] Neugebauer, "Notes on Ethiopic Astronomy," *Or, N.S.,* 33 (1964) 49-71.

‡O[tto] Neugebauer and H. B. Van Hoesen, "Astrological Papyri and Ostraca: Bibliographical Notes," *PAPS* 108 (1964) 57-72.

Asger Aaboe, "On Period Relations in Babylonian Astronomy," *Cent* 10 (1964-65) 213-231.

Owen Gingerich, "Lunar Visibilities in Ancient Babylon," *Isis* 56 (1965) 69.

E. M. Bruins, "Egyptian Astronomy," *Janus* 52 (1965) 161-180.

*Willy Hartner, "The Earliest History of the Constellations in the Near East and the Motif of the Lion-Bull Combat," *JNES* 24 (1965) 1-16.

Asger Aaboe and Abraham Sachs, "Some Dateless Computed Lists of Longitudes of Characteristic Planetary Phenomena from the Late-Babylonian Period," *JCS* 20 (1966) 1-34.

Gerald L. Geison, "Did Conon of Samos Transmit Babylonian Observations?" *Isis* 58 (1967) 398-401.

*O[tto] Neugebauer and A. Sachs, "Some Atypical Astronomical Cuneiform Texts, I," *JCS* 21 (1967) 183-218.

O[tto] Neugebauer, "The Origin of 'System B' of Babylonian Astronomy," *Cent* 12 (1968) 209-214.

P. J. Bicknell, "Did Anaxogoras Observe a Sunspot in 467 B.C.?" *Isis* 59 (1968) 87-90.

Paul Forman, "'The Astrophysics of Berossos the Chaldean'" *Isis* 59 (1968) 91-94. [Comment by J. J. O. Palgen, p. 92; Asger Aaboe, p. 93; Reply by Stephen Toulmin, pp. 93-94] *(Review)*

*O[tto] Neugebauer and A. Sachs, "Some Atypical Astronomical Cuneiform Texts, II," *JCS* 22 (1968-69) 92-113.

*Asger Aaboe and Abraham Sachs, "Two Lunar Texts of the Achaemenid Period from Babylon," *Cent* 14 (1969) 1-22. [B.M. 36822 (=80-6-17, 561) + B.M. 37022 (=80-6-17, 766); B.M. 36599 (=80-6-17, 328 + 444) + 36941 (=80-6-17, 682); B.M. 47912 (=80-11-3, 619)]

Lis Bernsen, "On the Construction of Column B in System A of the Astronomical Cuneiform Texts," *Cent* 14 (1969) 23-28.

Willy Hartner, "Eclipse Periods and Thales' Prediction of a Solar Eclipse.   Historic Truth and Modern Myth," *Cent* 14 (1969) 60-71.

*A. Leo Oppenheim, "Divination and Celestial Observation in the Last Assyrian Empire," *Cent* 14 (1969) 97-135.

Olaf Schmidt, "The Mean Value Principle in Babylonian Planetary Theory," *Cent* 14 (1969) 267-286.

Noel Swerdlow, "Hipparchus on the Distance of the Sun," *Cent* 14 (1969) 287-305.

M. F. Ingham, "The Length of the Sothic Cycle," *JEA* 55 (1969) 36-40.

§156   *2.5.3 Ecological and Meteorological Studies*

*Henricus Ehrenfried Warnekros, "On the Fertility of Palestine, and its Principal Advantages, Compared with those of Egypt," *BibR* 1 (1825) 155-197, 437-446.

H. A. DeForest, "Contributions to the Climatology of Palestine," *BS* 1 (1844) 221-224. *(Communicated by E. Robinson)*

*H. B. Hackett, "Scripture Facts and Illustrations Collected During a Journey in Palestine," *CRB* 18 (1853) 405-424, 517-537. [Fertility of Palestine, pp. 536-537]

G. J. Eldridge, "Meteorological Observations," *PEFQS* 1 (1869) 45. *[Observations for the year 1868]*

James Glaisher and G. J. Eldridge, "Meteorological Observations Taken at Beyrout, Syria. (*Latitude* 33° 54' *N.; longitude* 35° 29' *E. Height above sea level*, 160 *ft.*)," *PEFQS* 1 (1869) 103-107.

James Glaisher, Henry Heald, and G. Jackson Eldridge, "Results of Meteorological Observations Taken at Beyrout, Syria, from the year 1845 to 1854," *PEFQS* 1 (1869) 126-132.

Anonymous, "Note on the Meteorological Observatiosn Published in the 'Quarterly Statement' (First Series, Nos. III., IV., and V.)," *PEFQS* 3 (1871) 119, 156.

Thomas Chaplin, "Remarks on the Climate of Jerusalem. From Observations made by Dr. Thomas Chaplin, for Three Years and Four Months, beginning 1st November, 1863, and ending 28th February, 1867," *PEFQS* 4 (1872) 19-30.

Anonymous, "Returns from Foreign Stations Made to the Scottish Meteorological Society for Quarter Ending June 30, 1871," *PEFQS* 4 (1872) 73.

James Glaisher, "On the Meteorological Observations Taken at Nazareth, Gaza, Beyrout, and Other Places in Syria," *PEFQS* 4 (1872) 92-99.

Thomas Chaplin, "The Climate of Jerusalem," *PEFQS* 5 (1873) 39.

James Glaisher, "On the Meteorology of Various Places in Palestine, At which Observations were taken by the Royal Engineers," *PEFQS* 6 (1874) 210-216.

*Claude R. Conder, "The Fertility of Ancient Palestine," *PEFQS* 8 (1876) 120-132.

*Selah Merrill, "Modern Researches in Palestine," *PEFQS* 11 (1879) 138-154. [Hot Sulphur Springs, pp. 141-142]

Thomas Chaplin, "Observations on the Climate of Jerusalem," *PEFQS* 15 (1883) 8-40.

Edwin W. Rice, "Rainfall in Palestine," *JBL* 6 (1886), Part 1, 69-72.

George E. Post, "Notes on the Meteorology of Syria and Palestine," *JTVI* 20 (1886-87) 279-290, 293-296. (Discussion, pp. 291-293)

James Glaisher, "Meteorological Observations. 1880," *PEFQS* 20 (1888) 167-169.

James Glaisher, "Meteorological Observations. 1881," *PEFQS* 20 (1888) 237-239.

James Glaisher, "Meteorological Observations. Sarona 1882," *PEFQS* 21 (1889) 11-14.

James Glaisher, "Meteorological Observations. Sarona 1883," *PEFQS* 21 (1889) 79-82.

James Glaisher, "Meteorological Observations. Sarona 1884," *PEFQS* 21 (1889) 117-119.

James Glaisher, "Meteorological Observations. Sarona 1885," *PEFQS* 21 (1889) 192-194.

James Glaisher, "Meteorological Observations. Sarona 1886," *PEFQS* 22 (1890) 25-28.

James Glaisher, "Meteorological Observations. Sarona 1887," *PEFQS* 22 (1890) 112-115.

James Glaisher, "Meteorological Observations. Sarona 1888," *PEFQS* 22 (1890) 174-178.

James Glaisher, "Meteorological Observations. Sarona 1889," *PEFQS* 22 (1890) 269-272.

James Glaisher, "Comparision of the Atmospheric Pressure in Palestine and in England in the Ten Years Ending 1889," *PEFQS* 23 (1891) 49-67.

James Glaisher, "Comparison of the Highest and Lowest Temperatures of the Air, and Range of Temperature in Palestine and in England in the Ten Years Ending 1889," *PEFQS* 23 (1891)163-178.

James Glaisher, "Comparison of the Monthly Mean Highest and Monthly Mean Lowest Daily Temperatures of the Air, and Monthly mean Daily Range of Temperatures in Palestine and England in the Ten Years Ending 1889," *PEFQS* 23 (1891) 224-239.

James Glaisher, "On the Monthly and Annual Mean Temperatures of the Air in Palestine and England in the Ten Years Ending 1889," *PEFQS* 23 (1891) 302-309.

Anonymous, "The Climate of Palestine," *EN* 4 (1892) 374-375.

James Glaisher, "On the Fall of Rain, the Amount of Cloud, the Frequency of Cloudless Skies, as Recorded Daily, at 9 a.m. Local Time, by Herr Dreher at Sarona in the Ten Years Ending 1889," *PEFQS* 24 (1892) 50-71.

James Glaisher, "On the Direction of the Wind at Sarona, Recorded Daily by Herr Dreher, in the Ten Years 1880 to 1889," *PEFQS* 24 (1892) 226-250.

James Glaisher, "On the Strength or Pressure of the Wind at Sarona, Recorded Daily by Herr Dreher in the Ten Years 1880 to 1889," *PEFQS* 25 (1893) 43-63, 143-147.

J. E. Hanauer, "Mud Showers and Their effect on Buildings in Palestine," *PEFQS* 25 (1893) 69-70.

J. E. Hanauer, "Letter from Rev. J. E. Hanauer. 3," *PEFQS* 25 (1893) 142. *[Mud Showers in Palestine]*

*George E. Post, "Narrative of a Second Journey to Palmyra. Summary of Barometrical Observations, with Annotations by Professor Robert H. West, M.A.," *PEFQS* 25 (1893) 163-164.

James Glaisher, "Meteorological Report from Jerusalem for Year 1882," *PEFQS* 25 (1893) 242-244.

James Glaisher, "Meteorological Report from Jerusalem for Year 1883," *PEFQS* 25 (1893) 331-334.

James Glaisher, "On the Fall of Rain at Jerusalem in the 32 Years from 1861 to 1892," *PEFQS* 26 (1894) 39-44.

James Glaisher, "Meteorological Report from Jerusalem for Year 1884," *PEFQS* 26 (1894) 44-46.

James Glaisher, "Meteorological Report from Jerusalem for Year 1885," *PEFQS* 26 (1894) 144-146.

James Glaisher, "Results of Meteorological Observations taken at Jerusalem in the Year 1886," *PEFQS* 26 (1894) 266-268.

James Glaisher, "Results of Meteorological Observations taken at Jerusalem in the Year 1887," *PEFQS* 27 (1895) 184-187.

James Glaisher, "Results of Meteorological Observations taken at Jerusalem in the Year 1888," *PEFQS* 27 (1895) 294-296.

James Glaisher, "Results of Meteorological Observations taken at Jerusalem in the Year 1889," *PEFQS* 27 (1895) 368-370.

James Glaisher, "Results of Meteorological Observations taken at Jerusalem in the Year 1890," *PEFQS* 28 (1896) 88-92.

James Glaisher, "Results of Meteorological Observations taken at Tiberias under the Direction of Dr. Torrance in the Year 1890," *PEFQS* 28 (1896) 92-99.

James Glaisher, "Results of Meteorological Observations Taken at Jerusalem in the Year 1891," *PEFQS* 28 (1896) 190-194.

James Glaisher, "Results of Meteorological Observations Taken at Tiberias in the Year 1891," *PEFQS* 28 (1896) 194-199.

James Glaisher, "Results of Meteorological Observations Taken at Jerusalem in the Year 1892," *PEFQS* 28 (1896) 264-268.

James Glaisher, "Results of Meteorological Observations Taken at Tiberias in the Year 1892," *PEFQS* 28 (1896) 268-271.

James Glaisher, "Results of Meteorological Observations Taken at Jerusalem in the Year 1893," *PEFQS* 28 (1896) 350-354.

James Glaisher, "Results of Meteorological Observations Taken at Tiberias in the Year 1893," *PEFQS* 28 (1896) 354-358.

James Glaisher, "Results of Meteorological Observations Taken at Jerusalem in the Year 1894," *PEFQS* 29 (1897) 156-160.

James Glaisher, "Results of Meteorological Observations Taken at Tiberias in the Year 1894," *PEFQS* 29 (1897) 160-163.

James Glaisher, "Results of Meteorological Observations Taken at Tiberias in the Year 1895," *PEFQS* 29 (1897) 231-235.

James Glaisher, "Results of Meteorological Observations Taken at Jerusalem in the Year 1895," *PEFQS* 29 (1897) 235-239.

James Glaisher, "Results of Meteorological Observations Taken at Jerusalem in the Year 1896," *PEFQS* 30 (1898) 66-70.

James Glaisher, "Results of Meteorological Observations Taken at Tiberias in the Year 1896," *PEFQS* 30 (1898) 61-66.

James Glaisher, "On the Pressure of the Atmosphere at Jerusalem," *PEFQS* 30 (1898) 121-134.

James Glaisher, "On the Temperature of the Air at Jerusalem, from Continuous Observations 1882 to 1896, and Comparison with the Temperature of the Air at Sarona, from Simultaneous Observations 1882 to 1889," *PEFQS* 30 (1898) 183-205.

James Glaisher, "Results of Meteorological Observations Taken at Tiberias in the Year 1897," *PEFQS* 31 (1899) 71-76.

James Glaisher, "Results of Meteorological Observations Taken at Jerusalem in the Year 1897," *PEFQS* 31 (1899) 76-80.

James Glaisher, "Results of Meteorological Observations Taken at Jerusalem in the Year 1898," *PEFQS* 31 (1899) 372-376.

James Glaisher, "Results of Meteorological Observations Taken at Tiberias in the Year 1898," *PEFQS* 31 (1899) 376-380.

James Glaisher, "Results of Meteorological Observations Taken at Tiberias in the Year 1899," *PEFQS* 32 (1900) 286-292.

James Glaisher, "Results of Meteorological Observations Taken at Jerusalem in the Year 1899," *PEFQS* 32 (1900) 292-297.

James Glaisher, "Results of Meteorological Observations Taken at Jerusalem in the Year 1900," *PEFQS* 34 (1902) 56-61.

James Glaisher, "Results of Meteorological Observations Taken at Tiberias in the Year 1900," *PEFQS* 34 (1902) 62-65.

George E. Post, "Report on Rainfall at El Meshgharah, a Village of Cœlosyria, *At an elevation of 3,000 feet above the Mediterranean Sea*," *PEFQS* 34 (1902) 65.

James Glaisher, "Results of Meteorological Observations Taken at Jerusalem in the Year 1901," *PEFQS* 34 (1902) 250-255.

James Glaisher, "Results of Meteorological Observations Taken at Tiberias in the Year 1901," *PEFQS* 34 (1902) 255-260.

George E. Post, "Report of Rainfall at el Meshgharah, a Village of Coelosyria," *PEFQS* 32 (1904) 65.

Adolph Datzi, "Meteorological Observations Taken in Jerusalem," *PEFQS* 36 (1904) 161-162; 37 (1905) 151; 38 (1906) 152-153; 39 (1907) 160-161; 40 (1908) 158-159; 41 (1909) 151-152.

J[oseph] Jamal, "Rainfall at Jaffa," *PEFQS* 38 (1906) 70, 316-317.

Rasheed Nassar, "Meteorological Observations Taken at Tiberias in the Years 1904-1906 (under the supervision of Dr. David W. Torrance)," *PEFQS* 39 (1907) 304-306.

Joseph Jamal, "Table Showing the Monthly Means of Meteorological Observations Taken at Jaffa for the Years 1904, 1905, and 1906," *PEFQS* 40 (1908) 329-331.

Rasheed Nassar, "Meteorological Observations Taken in Tiberias," *PEFQS* 40 (1908) 331-332.

Anonymous, "The Climate of Ancient Palestine," *RP* 8 (1909) 140-144.

Rasheed Nassar and Elias [K.] Bisht, "Tables Showing the Monthly Means of Meteorological Observations Taken at Tiberias During 1907 and 1908," *PEFQS* 42 (1910) 69.

Adolph Datzi, "Meteorological Observations taken in Jerusalem," *PEFQS* 42 (1910) 150-151. *[For the year 1909]*

Joseph Jamal, "Rainfall in Jaffa," *PEFQS* 42 (1910) 70.

Adolph Datzi, "Meteorological Observations Taken in Jerusalem, 1910," *PEFQS* 43 (1911) 197-209.

Elias [K.] Bisht, "Table Showing the Monthly Means of Meteorological Observations Taken at Tiberias During 1909," *PEFQS* 42 (1910) 289.

Elias K. Bisht, "Meteorological Observations Taken at Tiberias, 1910," *PEFQS* 44 (1912) 86-87.

*Ellsworth Huntington, "Changes in Climate and History," *AmHR* 18 (1912-13) 213-232.

J[oseph] Jamal, "Table Showing the Amount of Rain Which Fell in Jaffa (Palestine) During the Last Ten Seasons, 1902-3 to 1911-12," *PEFQS* 45 (1913) 45.

Adolph Datzi, "Meteorological Observations Taken in the City of Jerusalem, 1912. Monthly Means," *PEFQS* 45 (1913) 102.

Adolph Datzi, "Meteorological Observations Taken in the City of Jerusalem, 1911. Monthly Means," *PEFQS* 45 (1913) 208.

J[oseph] Jamal, "Rainfall at Jaffa, 1912-1913," *PEFQS* 46 (1914) 48.

Adolph Datzi, "Meteorological Observations Taken in the City of Jerusalem, 1913," *PEFQS* 46 (1914) 89.

*(Miss) Deette Rolfe, "Enviornmental Influences in the Agriculture of Ancient Egypt," *AJSL* 33 (1916-17) 157-168.

*Chester C. McCown, "Climate and Religion in Palestine," *JR* 7 (1927) 520-539.

*Allan Chester Johnson, "Ancient Forests and Navies," *TAPA* 58 (1927) 199-209.

*J. C. Curry, "Climate and Migrations," *Antiq* 2 (1928) 292-307.

*John Lowel Butler, "Astronomical Solution of Ancient and Modern Climates," *BS* 89 (1932) 68-86.

D. Ashbel, "On the Importance of Dew in Palestine," *JPOS* 16 (1936) 316-321.

D. Ashbel, "The Rains in the Winter of 1936-37," *JPOS* 18 (1938) 17-23.

D. Aschbel/sic/*, "The Climate of the Judaean Desert," *BIES* 6 (1938-39) #2, I-II.

*Raphael Patai, "The 'Control of Rain' in Ancient Palestine. A Study in Comparative Religion," *HUCA* 14 (1939) 251-286.

D. Ashbel, "The Very Exceptional Rainy Season of 1937-38 in Palestine and the Near East," *JPOS* 19 (1939-40) 48-58.

*D. Ashbel, "Rain and water conditions in the Negev," *BIES* 8 (1940-41) #2, I.

J. H. J. Barker, "Some Climatological Factors and their Relation to the Bible," *EQ* 13 (1941) 194-201.

Cicely M. Botley, "Climate and Weather in the Bible," *JTVI* 73 (1941) 212-224, 234-235. [(Discussion, 224-228) (Communications by Mrs. Anne S. D. Maunder, pp. 228-230; J. H. J. Barker, pp. 230-232; C. E. P. Brooks, p. 232; H. S. Curr, pp. 232-234)]

C. F. Arden-Close, "The Rainfall of Palestine," *PEQ* 73 (1941) 122-128.

*D. Ashbel, "The Climate of the Negeb," *BIES* 11 (1944-45) #1/2, II.

*M. Rim, "Sand and Soil in the Coastal Plain of Israel. A Study in the Rate of Accumulation," *IEJ* 1 (1950-51) 33-48.

J. Neumann, "Evaporation from the Red Sea," *IEJ* 2 (1952) 153-162.

M. Zohary, "Ecological Studies in the Vegetation of the Near Eastern Deserts," *IEJ* 2 (1952) 201-215.

*R. B. Y. Scott, "Meteorological Phenomena and Terminology in the Old Testament," *ZAW* 64 (1952-53) 11-25.

*E. F. Sutcliffe, "Clouds as Water-Carriers in Hebrew Thought," *VT* 3 (1953) 99-103.

P. L. O. Guy, "Archaeological Evidence of Soil Erosion and Sedimenation in Wadi Musrara," *IEJ* 4 (1954) 77-87.

N. Rosenan and M. Gilead, "Ten Years of Dew Observation in Israel," *IEJ* 4 (1954) 120-123.

D. H. K. Amiran and M. Gilead, "Early Excessive Rainfall and Soil Erosion in Israel," *IEJ* 4 (1954) 286-295.

*G. Orshan, "A Vegetation Map of the Sand Dunes in the Southern Acre Plain," *IEJ* 5 (1955) 109-112.

N. Rosenan, "One-Hundred Years of Rainfall in Jerusalem," *IEJ* 5 (1955) 137-153.

*B. S. J. Isserlin, "Ancient Forests in Palestine: Some Archaeological Indications," *PEQ* 87 (1955) 87-88.

J. Neumann, "On the Incidence of Dry and Wet Years," *IEJ* 6 (1956) 58-63.

D. Nir, "Whirlwinds in Israel in the Winters 1954/55 and 1955/56," *IEJ* 7 (1957) 109-117.

M. Harel, "Reduced Aridity in Eastern Lower Galilee," *IEJ* 7 (1957) 256-261.

D. Sharon, "Physiographic Aspects of the Tuleilat el-'Enab," *SGEI* #1 (1959) V.

*Hans Helbaek, "Ecological Effects of Irrigation in Ancient Mesopotamia," *Iraq* 22 (1960) 186-196.

A. Brosh, "The Soils of Eastern Upper Galilee," *SGEI* #2 (1960) II.

*Stuart A. Harris, "On the land snails of Iraq and their potential use in determining past climatic conditions," *Sumer* 17 (1961) 107-113.

E. Efrat, "Types of Rainfall Years in Israel," *BIES* 26 (1962) #1/2, VII.

E. Efrat, "Types of Rainfall Years in Israel," *SGEI* #3 (1962) VII.

W. M. Levi, "The Dry Winter of 1962/3: a Synoptic Analysis," *IEJ* 13 (1963) 229-241.

A. Bitan-Buttenwieser, "A Comparison of Sixty Years' Rainfall Between Jerusalem and Tel-Aviv," *IEJ* 13 (1963) 242-246.

J. Katsnelson, "The Rainfall Year 1961/62," *IEJ* 13 (1963) 253-255.

J. Katsnelson, "The Rainfall Year 1962/1963," *IEJ* 13 (1963) 255-257.

A. Fahn, Naomi Wachs, and C. Ginzburg, "Dendrochronological Studies in the Negev," *IEJ* 13 (1963) 291-299.

*W[illem] J. van Liere and H[enri] de Contenson, "Holocene Enviroment and Early Settlement in the Levant," *AAAS* 14 (1964) 125-128.

*W. R. Farrand, "Geology, Climate and Chronology of Yabrud Rockshelter I," *AAAS* 15 (1965) #1, 35-50.

D. Sharon, "Variability of Rainfall in Israel. A Map of the Relative Standard Deviation of the Annual Amounts," *IEJ* 15 (1965) 169-176.

J. Katsnelson, "The Rainfall Year 1964/65," *IEJ* 15 (1965) 242-245.

J. Katsnelson, "The Rainfall Year 1963/64," *IEJ* 16 (1966) 265-266.

J. Katsnelson, "The Rainfall Year 1965/66," *IEJ* 16 (1966) 266-267.

*Charles F. Fensham, "An Ancient Tradition of the Fertility of Palestine," *PEQ* 98 (1966) 166-167.

L. Shanan, I. Evenari, and N. H. Tadmor, "Rainfall Patterns in the Central Negev Desert," *IEJ* 17 (1967) 163-183.

*H. E. Wright Jr., "Climatic Change in Mycenaean Greece," *Antiq* 42 (1968) 123-127.

*H. H. Lamb, "Climatic Changes during the Course of Early Greek History," *Antiq* 42 (1968) 231-233.

J. Katsnelson, "The Rainfall Year 1966-1967," *IEJ* 18 (1968) 257-263.

*Alan D. Crown, "Climatic Change, Ecology, and Migrations," *AJBA* 1 (1968-71) #4, 3-22.

J. Katsnelson, "The Rainfall Year 1968/1969," *IEJ* 19 (1969) 253-256.

§157 *2.5.3 Geological Studies*

*Charles A. Lee, "On the Geology of Palestine, and the Destruction of Sodom and Gomorrah," *BRCR, N.S.,* 3 (1840) 324-352.

Anonymous, "1. *General View of the Geology of Scripture.* By George Fairholme, Esq. 2. *Scripture and Geology.* By Rev. Pye Smith, D.D.," *MR* 27 (1845) 198-220. *(Review)*

J. Jay Dana, "The Religion of Geology," *BS* 10 (1853) 505-522.

*E. P. Barrows, "The Mosaic Six Days and Geology," *BS* 14 (1857) 61-98.

*Benjamin F. Hosford, "Geological and Theological Analogies," *BS* 15 (1858) 300-314.

†Anonymous, "Scripture and Geology—Present State of the Question Between Them," *BFER* 10 (1861) 623-641. *(Review)*

(   ) P., "Scriptural Notices of Volcanoes and Earthquakes," *JSL, 5th Ser.,* 2 (1867-68) 46-58.

Robert Hunter, "The Volcanoes and Earthquakes of Scripture," *BFER* 20 (1871) 672-695.

Cl. H. Green, "Note From Mr. Cl. H. Green on the Geological Specimens Sent Home by Lieut. Conder," *PEFQS* 5 (1873) 161-162.

*Selah Merrill, "Modern Researches in Palestine," *PEFQS* 11 (1879) 138-154. [Hot Sulphur Springs, pp. 141-142]

*W. M. Thompson, "Traces of Glacial Action on the Flank of Mt. Lebanon," *JAOS* 10 (1880) 185-188.

Anonymous, "The Bitumen of Judea," *PEFQS* 15 (1883) 242-243.

(   ) Huddleston, "The Geology of Palestine," *PEFQS* 15 (1883) 166-170.

Conrad Schick, "Notes. I. The Stones of Jerusalem," *PEFQS* 19 (1887) 50-51.

*C. W. Gallagher, "Geology and Sacred Chronology," *MR* 72 (1890) 835-852.

Edward Hull, "A New Treatise on the Geology of the Holy Land and the Dead Sea," *PEFQS* 28 (1896) 271-273. *(Review)*

*G. Frederick Wright, "Geological Confirmations of the Biblical History of Israel from Abraham to the Exodus," *CFL, 3rd Ser.,* 2 (1905) 423-430. [Crossing the Red Sea, pp. 423-426; Destruction of Sodom and Gomorrah, pp. 426-430]

Edward Hull, "Lord Kitchener and Palestine Exploration. A Geological Reconnaissance," *PEFQS* 48 (1916) 123-125.

*Alfred Ely Day, "Geology of the Dead Sea," *BS* 81 (1924) 264-270.

*Paul Haupt, "A Cuneiform Description of a Volcanic Eruption," *BAVSS* 10 (1927) Heft 2, 133-136.

*K. S. Sandford, and W. J. Arkell, "The Relation of Palæolithic Man to the History and Geology of the Nile Valley in Egypt," *Man* 29 (1929) #50.

J. W. Gregory, "Geological Researches in the Judean Desert," *PEFQS* 63 (1931) 197-202.

Nelson Glueck, "The Recently Discovered Ore Deposits in Eastern Palestine," *BASOR* #63 (1936) 4-6.

John C. Weaver, "Report on Specimens of Ore and Slag from Eastern Palestine," *BASOR* #63 (1936) 6-8.

L. Picard and P. Solomonica, "On the Geology of the Gaza-Berrsheba District," *JPOS* 16 (1936) 180-223.

L. Picard, "On the Geology of the Central Coastal Plain," *JPOS* 17 (1937) 255-299.

L. Picard, "Synopsis of Stratigraphic Terms in Palestinian Geology," *JPOS* 18 (1938) 254-277.

*C. C. McCown, "Two Years' Achievements in Palestinian Archaeology," *RL* 8 (1939) 97-108. [Paleontology and Prehistory, pp. 97-99]

*M. Avnimelech, "On the Geology and Morphology of the Megiddo Area," *JPOS* 19 (1939-40) 18-37.

*M. Avnimelech, "Contributions to the Geological History of the Palestinian Coastal Plain: Nahariya and its Vicinity," *BIES* 10 (1942-44) #2/3, I.

J. L. Kelso and Alfred R. Powell, "Glance Pitch from Tell Beit Mirsim," *BASOR* #95 (1944) 14-18.

*D. Amiran (Kallner), "The Western Border of the Hebron Mountains," *BIES* 14 (1947-48) #3/4, III-IV.

M. Avnimelech, "Notes on the Geological History of the Yarkon Valley," *BIES* 15 (1949-50) #1/2, I.

*M. Rim, "Sand and Soil in the Coastal Plain of Israel. A Study in the Rate of Accumulation," *IEJ* 1 (1950-51) 33-48.

*M. Avnimelech, "The Geological History of the Yarkon Valley and its Influence on Ancient Settlements," *IEJ* 1 (1950-51) 77-83.

J. Vroman, "The Movement and Solution of Salt Bodies as applied to Mount Sdom /sic/," *IEJ* 1 (1950-51) 185-193.

‡D. H. Kallner-Amiran, "A Revised Earthquake-Catalogue of Palestine — I," *IEJ* 1 (1950-51) 223-246. [Bibliography, pp. 242-246]

J. Bentor, "On Magmatic Phaenomena /sic/ in the Makhtesh Ramon," *BIES* 16 (1951) 1/2, I.

H. E. Wright Jr., "The Geological Setting of Four Prehistoric Sites in Northeastern Iraq," *BASOR* #128 (1952) 11-24.

D. H. K[allner-]Amiran, "A Revised Earthquake-Catalogue of Palestine — II," *IEJ* 2 (1952) 48-62. [with an Appendix 'B' by U. Ben-Horin, pp. 63-65]

A. Loehnberg and E. Loehnberg, "The Buried Structure of Rosh ha-'Ayin in the Central Coastal Plain of Israel," *IEJ* 2 (1952) 145-152.

*W. Rees Williams, "The Origin of the Al Batin in the Al Dibdibba," *Sumer* 8 (1952) 217-218.

J. Paclt, "On a New Subfossil Liptobiolite from the Plain of Sharon in Israel," *IEJ* 3 (1953) 242-245.

D. H. Yaalon, "Calcareous Soils in Israel," *IEJ* 4 (1954) 278-285.

M. Rim, "Interpretation of Polymorphic Profiles in Soils of the Eastern Mediterranean. An Analysis of the Geophysical Factor in Soil Genesis," *IEJ* 4 (1954) 266-277.

M. Rim, "A Quantitative Criterion of Soil Polymorphy, Applicable to Soil in the Eastern Mediterranean," *IEJ* 5 (1955) 103-108.

*H. E. Wright Jr., "Geological Aspects of the Archaeology of Iraq," *Sumer* 11 (1955) 83-90.

N. Shalem, "Seismic Tidal Waves (Tsunamis) in the Eastern Mediterranian," *BIES* 20 (1955-56) #3/4, III.

D. H. K[allner-]Amiran, "Outlines of Geomorphology of Western Palestine North of the Barrsheba Basin," *EI* 4 (1956) II.

*Caesar Voûte, "A Prehistoric Find Near Razzaza (Karbala Liwa). Its Significance for the Morphological and Geological History of the Abu Dibbis Depression and Surrounding Area," *Sumer* 13 (1957) 135-148.

*Stuart A. Harris and Robert M. Adams, "A Note on Canal and Marsh Stratagraphy Near Zubediyah," *Sumer* 13 (1957) 157-162.

Herbert E. Wright Jr., "Geologic Dating in Prehistory," *Arch* 11 (1958) 19-25.

M. Avnimelech, "Remarks on the Geological Features of the Surroundings of Tell Abu Hawam and the Cemetery in the area of the Qishon Mouth," *'Atiqot* 2 (1959) 103-105.

D. Sharon, "Physiographic Aspects of the Tuleilat el-'enab," *BIES* 23 (1959) #3/4, V.

D. Nir and A. Yair, "Geomorphological Studies in the Safed Area," *BIES* 24 (1959-60) #4, I.

A. Brosh, "The Soils of Eastern Upper Galilee," *BIES* 24 (1959-60) #4, II.

D. Safra, "The Abrasion Platform and the Cliff of the Southern Carmel Coast," *BIES* 26 (1962) #1/2, I-II.

Z. Ron, "The Morphographic Configuration of the Western Strip of the Southern Carmel Coast," *BIES* 26 (1962) #1/2, II.

D. Safra, "The Abrasion Platform and the Cliff of the Southern Carmel Coast," *SGEI* #3 (1962) I-II.

*Isaac Schattner, "The Lower Jordan Valley. A Study in the Fluviomorphology of an Arid Region," *SH* 11 (1962) 9-123.

Sheldon Judson, "Stream Changes during Historic Time in East-Central Sicily," *AJA* 67 (1963) 287-289.

A. P. Schick, "The Aviel Depression—A Fossil Sinkhole?" *IEJ* 13 (1963) 224-228.

Henry M. Morris, "Biblical Catastrophes and Geology," *GJ* 4 (1963) #2, 9-14.

*Rhodes W. Fairbridge, "Nile Sedimentation above Wadi Halfa during the last 20,000 years," *Kush* 11 (1963) 96-107.

C. Vita-Finzi, "Observations on the Late Quaternary of Jordan," *PEQ* 96 (1964) 19-33.

*W. R. Farrand, "Geology, Climate and Chronology of Yabrud Rockshelter I," *AAAS* 15 (1965) #1, 35-50.

*Dov Nir, "Geomorphological Map of the Judean Desert Scale 1:100,000 with Explanatory Notes," *SH* 15 (1965) #1, 5-30.

J. de Heinzelin, "Geological observations near Latamne, " *AAAS* 16 (1966) #2, 115-120.

*M. Avnimelech, "Influence of Geological Conditions on the Development of Jerusalem," *BASOR* #181 (1966) 24-31.

D. Sharon, "Microclimatological Studies in the Valley of Sorek, Jerusalem," *IEJ* 16 (1966) 77-78.

Peter Robinson and Gordon W. Hewes, "Comments on the Late Pleistocene Geology of the Wadi Karagan, Murshid District, Northern Province, Sudan," *Kush* 14 (1966) 44-52.

Claudio Vita-Finzi, "The Hasa formation: an alluvial deposition in Jordan," *Man, N.S.*, 1 (1966) 386-390.

Claudio Vita-Finzi, "Late Quaternary alluvial chronology of northern Algeria," *Man, N.S.*, 2 (1967) 205-215.

Claudio Vita-Finzi, "The Hasa formation," *Man, N.S.*, 2 (1967) 133.

M. A. Avnimelech, "A preliminary account of the geological situation of the prehistoric site near Hazorea," *Man, N.S.*, 2 (1967) 457-460.

Leo Picard, The Quaternary in the Northern Jordan Valley," *PIASH* 1 (1967) #4, 1-34.

William G. Dever, "Iron Age Epigraphic Material from the Area of Khirbet El-Kôm," *HUCA* 40&41 (1969-70) 139-204.

§158 *2.5.5 Geographical Studies – General*

†Anonymous, "Rennel on the Geography of Herodotus," *BCQTR* 17 (1801) 592-599; 18 (1801) 136-145, 247-261. *(Review)*

†W. Belsham, "Observations on the Oriental Geography of Ptolemy," *MMBR* 25 (1808) 192-195.

†Anonymous, "Niebuhr's *Geography of Herodotus,*" *WR* 13 (1830) 335-345. *(Review)*

Charles Hall, "Review of Robinson's Biblical Researches," *BRCR, N.S.,* 6 (1841) 419-453. *(Review)*

(   ) L., "Sacred Geography.—Dr. Wilson's 'Lands of the Bible'," *BRCM* 4 (1847-48) 477-492. *(Review)*

*Anonymous, "Geographical Accuracy of the Bible," *CRB* 20 (1855) 451-469.

C. H. B., "Robinson's Later Biblical Researches," *CE* 62 (1857) 161-182. *(Review)*

Edward Robinson, "On Biblical Geography," *PAOS* (October, 1859), 6.

*†Anonymous, "The Geography of Palestine, in Relation to the Historical Truth of the Bible," *BFER* 9 (1860) 253-285. *(Review)*

*C. W. Goodwin, "Topographical notes from Coptic papyri," *ZÄS* 7 (1869) 73-75.

Anonymous, "The Topography of the Bible," *CongL* 4 (1875) 719-725.

*Anonymous, "Topography of the Books of Joshua and Samuel," *CongL* 5 (1876) 109-115.

Philip Schaff, "Disputed Scripture Locations," *PR, 4th Ser.,* 1 (1878) 851-884.

*O. D. Miller, "Symbolical Geography of the Ancients," *AAOJ* 3 (1880-81) 307-319.

Hormuzd Rassam, "The Lands of the Bible, Ancient and Modern," *CT* 1 (1883-84) 129-155. (Remarks by Howard Crosby, pp. 156-158; Francis Brown, pp. 158-160)

Hormuzd Rassam, "A Letter from Mr. Hormuzd Rassam," *CT* 1 (1883-84) 381-384. (Notes by Howard Crosby, p. 384)

Charles G. Hebermann, "The Beginnings of Geography," *ACQR* 9 (1884) 385-411.

*G[eorge] Rawlinson, "Biblical Topography. VI.—Sites connected with the History of Abraham, Harran, Damascus, Hebron," *MI* 6 (1886) 241-252.

*E[dward] Hull, "The Physical Features of Egypt and Syria in Relation to Bible History," *PEFQS* 18 (1886) 53-54. *(Review)*

*Charles W. Warren, "Notes on Arabia Petraea and the Country Lying between Egypt and Palestine," *PEFQS* 19 (1887) 38-46. [The Penninsula of Sinai; The Tih; The Sandy Dunes about the Coast of the Mediterranean and Suez Canal]

Henry George Tomkins, "Notes on the Geography from the Nile to the Euphrates, as known to the ancient Egyptians," *BOR* 2 (1888-89) 92-96, 110-116.

George E. Post, "Essays on the Sects and Nationalities of Syria and Palestine. *The Physical Features, Climate, Soil, Water Supply, Natural History, and Health of Syria and Palestine,*" *PEFQS* 22 (1890) 98-112. (Notes by C. R. Conder, p. 187)

*T. K. Cheyne, "Gleanings in Biblical Criticism and Geography," *JQR* 10 (1897-98) 565-584.

*Henry A. Redpath, "The Geography of the Septuagint," *AJT* 7 (1903) 289-307.

Olaf A. Toffteen, "Notes on Assyrian and Babylonian Geography," *AJSL* 23 (1906-07) 323-357.

F. Hugh Pope, "The Historical Geography of the Greek Bible," *NYR* 3 (1907-08) 686-703.

G. B. F. Hallock, "Geography of Bible Makes Truth Greater," *CFL, 3rd Ser.,* 28 (1922) 265-266.

*S. Tolkowsky, "Aphek. A Study in Biblical Topography," *JPOS* 2 (1922) 145-158.

*Ira Maurice Price, "The Topography of the Gudea Inscriptions," *JAOS* 43 (1923) 41-48.

Albert T. Clay, "The so-called Fertile Crescent and Desert Bay," *JAOS* 44 (1924) 186-201.

*W[illiam] F[oxwell] Albright and R. P. Dougherty, "From Jerusalem to Baghdad Down the Euphrates, II. From Aleppo to Baghdad," *BASOR* #21 (1926) 11-21. [The Mounds of the Balîkah, The Search for Ancient Mari, Among the Mounds of Khana, The Land of the Shuhites]

W. L. Porter, "The Geographic Background of the Bible," *USR* 42 (1930-31) 401-411.

Aubrey Diller, "Geographical Latitudes in Eratosthenes, Hipparchus and Posidonius," *Klio* 27 (1934) 258-269.

George H. T. Kimble, "The Expanse of the Earth as Known in Old Testament Times," *JTVI* 67 (1935) 205-221, 227-230. (Discussion, pp. 221-227)

C. S. Jarvis, "The Desert Yesterday and To-day," *PEQ* 69 (1937) 116-125.

*F. R. Steele, "The Points of the Compass in Hurrian," *JAOS* 61 (1941) 286-287.

*Charles Arden-Close, "Sir Aurel Stein's Explorations of the Roman Frontiers in Iraq and Transjordan," *PEQ* 73 (1941) 18-21.

*O[tto] Neugbauer, "On Some Astronomical Papyri and Related Problems of Ancient Geography," *TAPS, N.S.,* 32 (1941-43) 251-263.

*Carl Eberhard, "Geography of the Bible in Relation to Inspiration (A Conference Paper)," *CTM* 15 (1944) 736-747.

*Steven T. Byington, "Some Bits of Hebrew. I., Topography in Hebrew," *ET* 57 (1945-46) 26-27.

J. Philip Hyatt, "A New Historical Atlas of the Bible," *JAAR* 13 (1945) 106-108. *(Review)*

Jozef M. A. Janssen, "Notes on the Geographical Horizon of the Ancient Egyptians: Aethiopians and Haunebut," *BO* 8 (1951) 213-217.

J. Lewy, "Studies in the Historic Geography of the Ancient Near East. I. Samsi-Adad's Journey from Subat-Enlil to Mari," *Or, N.S.,* 21 (1952) 1-12.

Solomon Gandz, "The Distribution of Land and Sea on the Earth's Surface According to Hebrew Sources," *PAAJR* 22 (1953) 23-53.

*James M. Houston, "The Geographical Background in Old Testament Exegesis," *JTVI* 86 (1954) 62-72, 123. (Discussion, pp. 121-122)

*B. S. J. Isserlin, "Ancient Forests in Palestine: Some Archaeological Indications," *PEQ* 87 (1955) 87-88.

*G. R. Driver, "Geographical Problems," *EI* 5 (1958) 16*-20*.

*A. van Selms, "Amos's Geographical Horizon," *OTW* 7&8 (1964-65) 166-169.

Francis Celoria, "*Delta* as a Geographical Concept in Greek Literature," *Isis* 57 (1966) 385-388.

*Z. Kallai, "The Biblical Geography of Flavius Josephus," *EI* 8 (1967) 77*.

*E. I. Gordon, "The Meaning of the Ideogram ^{d}KASKAL.KUR = 'Underground Water-course' and Its Significance for Bronze Age Historical Geography," *JCS* 21 (1967) 70-88.

*M. B. Rowton, "The Woodlands of Ancient Western Asia," *JNES* 26 (1967) 261-277.

Pinhas Yoeli, "The Globe in Ancient Times," *Sefunim* 2 (1967-68) 28-38.

§159 *2.5.5.1 Maps*

J. F. T., "Map of the Holy Land," *JCSP* 4 (1857-60) 346-348.

Richard Gottheil, "On a Syriac geographical chart," *JAOS* 13 (1889) ccxc-ccxciv.

*A[ngus] Crawford, "Exploration and Discovery," *PER* 12 (1898-99) 149-160. [The Mosaic Map at Madeba, pp. 157-158]

*C. Clermont-Ganneau, "Archaeological and Epigraphic Notes on Palestine. 6. *The Land of Promise, mapped in Mosaic at Madeba,*" *PEFQS* 33 (1901) 235-246.

*John P. Peters, "Palestinian Exploration. *Notes of a Vacation in Palestine in 1902,*" *JBL* 22 (1903) 15-31. [12. Palestine Exploration Fund Map, pp. 29-31]

*A. H. Sayce, "Babylonian Tourist, of the Abrahamic Age, and His Map of the World," *AAOJ* 28 (1906) 334-338.

*A. H. Sayce, "A Babylonian Tourist of the Abrahamic Age and his Map of the World," *ET* 18 (1906-07) 68-73.

S. R. Driver, "On Maps of Palestine Containing Ancient Sites," *ET* 21 (1909-10) 495-497, 562-566.

*W. Ernest Beet, "The Map as an Aid to the Preaching of the Old Testament," *Exp, 8th Ser.,* 11 (1916) 56-66.

S[tephen] H. L[angdon], "An Ancient Babylonian Map," *MJ* 7 (1916) 263-268.

B. Bruyère, "New details for insertion in the Theban 1/1000 scale maps. — I. Deir el-Madina," *ASAE* 25 (1925) 174-177. (Note by R. Engelbach, p. 174)

*N. de G. Davies, "New details for insertion in the Theban 1/1000 scale maps. — II. Sheykh 'Abd el-Qurna and Dira' Abu'l Naga," *ASAE* 25 (1925) 239-241.

*W[illiam] F[oxwell] Albright, "On the Map Found at Nuzi," *BASOR* #42 (1931) 7-10.

*Charles Close, "Note on the Map of the Principal Excavated Sites of Palestine," *PEFQS* 64 (1932) 220.

Eckard Unger, "Ancient Babylonian Maps and Plans," *Antiq* 9 (1935) 311-322.

James Oscar Boyd, "Bible Maps," *EQ* 7 (1935) 287-294.

Theophile J. Meek, "The Orientation of Babylonian Maps," *Antiq* 10 (1936) 223-226.

D. H. Kallner, "Jacotin's Map of Palestine, Surveyed during Napoleon's Campaign in 1799," *PEQ* 76 (1944) 157-163.

J. Shattner, "The Cartography of Palestine," *Kobez* 4 (1945) XII-XIII.

F. W. Adams, "Tabula Imperii Romani. A Map of the Roman Empire based on the Carte Internationale du Monde au Millionième," *AJA* 58 (1954) 45-51.

William H. Stahl, "By Their Maps You Shall Know Them," *Arch* 8 (1955) 146-155.

D. H. Kallner Amiran and N. Kadmon, "Atlas of Israel," *IEJ* 9 (1959) 123-129. *(Review)*

*Donald Trevor, "A Sumerian Plan in the John Rylands Library," *JSS* 7 (1962) 184-190.

*Dov Nir, "Geomorphological Map of the Judean Desert Scale 1:100,000 with Explanatory Notes," *SH* 15 (1965) #1, 5-30.

I. W. J. Hopkins, "Maps and Plans of Bible Lands," *EQ* 40 (1968) 28-33.

Denis Baly, "The Treatment of Geographical Features in Biblical Maps," *BTr* 20 (1969) 56-61.

§160   *2.5.5.2 Demography (Population Studies)*
       [See also Ancient Near Eastern
       Civilization - General Studies S53 ←]

*(   ) Hewlett, "On the Longevity of the Antediluvians," *MR* 4 (1821) 412-413.

[Johann David] Michaelis, "On the Population of Palestine: from Michaelis' Law of Moses," *BibR* 1 (1825) 449-459.

*Luther Halsey, "The Populousness of the ,Antediluvian World Considered," *BibR* 4 (1828) 563-590.

*W. R. French, "Longevity of the Antediluvians," *UQGR, N.S.,* 4 (1867) 227-235.

Hyde Clarke, "On the Pre-Israelite Population of Palestine and Syria, and the Assignment of Archaic Remains," *PEFQS* 3 (1871) 97-101.

S[elah] M[errill], "The Population of Jerusalem During the Siege of Titus," *AAOJ* 2 (1879-80) 166-168.

Anonymous, "A Pecuilarity of Palestine," *ONTS* 2 (1882-83) 175. *[Nomadic Migrations]*

*Anonymous, "The Longevity of the Patriarchs," *ONTS* 15 (1892) 78.

G. Frederick Wright, "The Possible Population of Palestine," *BS* 58 (1901) 740-750.

*William F. McCauley, "Bible Chronology and the Archæologists," *CFL, 3rd Ser.,* 1 (1904) 733-743. [Early Populations, p. 737]

*W. M. Flinders Petrie, "The Census of Israelites," *Exp, 6th Ser.,* 12 (1905) 148-152, 204.

*Franklin Johnson, "A Census of the Early Biblical Population," *CFL, 3rd Ser.,* 6 (1907) 22-26, 83-94. [I. Egypt in the Light of Archaeology and Profane History, pp. 22-26; II. Mesopotamia, Palestine, Syria, in the Light of Archaeology and Profane History, pp. 83-89; III. Confirmations of the Scriptures from the Facts thus Brought to Light, pp. 89-94]

Stephen D. Peet, "The Peopling of the World," *AAOJ* 30 (1908) 225-240.

*Arthur W. Sutton, "From Suez to Sinai," *JTVI* 45 (1913) 249-264. [The Exodus of the Children of Israel. Notes on the Census Numbers, pp. 265-268]

*G. Elliot Smith, "Ships as Evidence of the Migrations of Early Culture," *JMUEOS* #5 (1915-16) 63-102.

*Archy O. Logist/*sic*/, "The Antediluvian 'Span of Life'," *HR* 73 (1917) 83.

*Joseph Offord, "The Vicissitudes of the Population of Palestine as Foretold in the Prophecy of Noah," *PEFQS* 50 (1918) 186-188.

*William Mitchell Ramsay, "The Intermixture of Races in Asia Minor: Some of its Causes and Effects," *PBA* 7 (1915-16) 359-422. [II. Immigrant Races in Ancient Times, pp. 362-374; III. Survival of Ancient Races and Ancient Customs or Law, pp. 374-381]

*E. E. Kellett, "'The Prodigiously Long Ages of the Patriarchs'," *ET* 33 (1921-22) 167-169.

*Edward Chiera, "The Length of the Lives of the Patriarchs," *CQ* 1 (1924) 199-201.

*A. Achtermann, "The Great Age of the Antediluvians," *CFL, 3rd Ser.*, 32 (1926) 114-115.

*J. C. Curry, "Climate and Migrations," *Antiq* 2 (1928) 292-307.

*Dudley Joseph Whitney, "The Antediluvian Earth and its Inhabitants," *CFL, 3rd Ser.*, 34 (1928) 440-445.

Tenney Frank, "Roman Census Statistics from 508 to 225 B.C.," *AJP* 51 (1930) 313-324.

Bessie E. Richardson, "Duration of Life Among the Greeks from Inscriptional Evidence," *AJA* 37 (1933) 115-116.

*John Lowell Butler, "Causes of Antediluvian Longevity," *BS* 90 (1933) 49-69.

*D. Talbot Rice, "Art History as a Key to Racial Migration: A New Field for Research," *Antiq* 10 (1936) 146-153.

*Sherman Leroy Wallace, "Census and Poll-Tax in Ptolemaic Egypt," *AJP* 59 (1938) 418-442.

*Muzaffer Süleyman Şenyürek, "A Craniological Study of the Copper Age and Hittite Populations of Anatolia," *TTKB* 5 (1941) 237-253.

*R. Engelbach, "An essay on the advent of the dynastic race in Egypt and its consequences," *ASAE* 42 (1943) 193-221.

*Dorothy Mackay, "Ancient River Beds and Dead Cities," *Antiq* 19 (1945) 135-144.

*B. Maisler, "The History of Settlement in Ancient Times," *Kobez* 4 (1945) XVII-XVIII.

C. C. McCown, "The Density of Population in Ancient Palestine," *JBL* 66 (1947) v, 425-436.

*George Haddad, "The population of Antioch in the hellenistic-roman period," *AAAS* 1 (1951) 19-31.

Muzaffer Süleyman Şenyürek, "The Longevity of the Chalcolithic and Copper Age Inhabitants of Anatolia," *TTKB* 15 (1951) 447-468.

A.R. Burn, "Hic Breve Vivitur: A Study of the Expectation of Life in the Roman Empire," *P&P* #4 (1953) 2-31.

Finley A. Hooper, "Date from Kom Abou Billou on the Length of Life in Graeco-Roman Egypt," *CdÉ* 31 (1956) 332-340.

*E. A. Speiser, "Census and Ritual Expiation in Mari and Israel," *BASOR* #149 (1958) 17-25.

W. F. Leemans, "The contribution of the nomads to the Babylonian population," *JESHO* 1 (1958) 138-145.

*Glanville Downey, "The Size of the Population of Antioch," *TAPA* 89 (1958) 84-91.

Stephen E. Slocum, "Length of Life," *JASA* 13 (1961) 18-19.

Annabelle Desmond, "How Many People Have Ever Lived on Earth?" *SIR* (1962) 545-565. [Period II—6000 B.C. to 1650 A.D.; The City-Period II; pp. 550-552]

*W[illem] J. van Liere, "Capitals and Citadels of Bronze-Iron Age Syria in Their Relation to Land and Water," *AAAS* 13 (1963) 109-122.

*Frank. N. Egerton III, "The Longevity of the Patriarchs: A Topic in the History of Demography," *JHI* 27 (1966) 575-584.

*Philip Mayerson, "A Note on Demography and Land Use in the Ancient Negeb," *BASOR* #185 (1967) 39-43.

*Alan D. Crown, "Climatic Change, Ecology and Migrations," *AJBA* 1 (1968-71) #4, 3-22.

§161 *2.5.5.3 Studies on Place Names and Town Lists*

†*D[aniel] H[y.] Haigh, "To the editor," *ZÄS* 6 (1868) 80-83. *[Assyrian Place Names of Egyptian Locations]*

*[Daniel Hy.] Haigh, "Assyriaca," *ZÄS* 7 (1869) 3-5. [צער - Place Name, p. 5]

*Daniel Hy. Haigh, "Assyrio-Aegyptiaca," *ZÄS* 9 (1871) 112-117. *[Assyrian Place Names of Egyptian Locations]*

Chs. Sandrezcki, "List of Names East of Jordan," *PEFQS* 4 (1872) 123-150.

George Smith, "Notices of Palestine in the Cuneiform Inscriptions," *PEFQS* 4 (1872) 193-199.

*C. W. Goodwin, "Notes by C. W. Goodwin," *ZÄS* 11 (1873) 12-15. *[Place names]*

*Daniel Hy. Haigh,   *ZÄS* 12 (1874) 55-56, 69-72, 96-100, 130-132. *[χet, χatte]*

Anonymous, "Great Antiquity of the Local Names mentioned in the Bible," *CongL* 5 (1876) 611-617.

*Claude R. Conder, "Samaritan Topography," *PEFQS* 8 (1876) 182-197.

Claude R. Conder, "Christian and Jewish Traditions," *PEFQS* 9 (1877) 30-37. *[Locations]*

*H. G. Tomkins, "Biblical Proper Names, Personal and Local, Illustrated from Sources External to Holy Scripture," *JTVI* 16 (1882-83) 132-147, 166-169. [(Appendix: Lord Bishop of Bath and Wales, pp. 147-148; T. K. Cheyne, pp. 148-149; Robert B. Girdlestone, pp. 149-151; A. Löwy, p. 152) (Discussion, pp. 152-166)]

G. W. Samson, "New Reading of Familiar Texts in the Old Testament. No. II," *HR* 8 (1883-84) 164-165. *[Geographical and Historical Names]*

*Theo. G. Pinches, "The Name of the City and Country over which Tar̲k̲û-timme Ruled," *SBAP* 7 (1884-85) 124-127. *[Ermê or Zumê]*

*A. H. Sayce, "Miscellaneous Notes," *ZK* 2 (1885) 399-405. [11. The Sagartians of the Behistun Inscription, pp. 404-405]

A. Amiaud, "The Various Names of Sumer and Akkad *in the Cuneiform Texts*," *BOR* 1 (1886-87) 120-124, 129-133.

*G. Maspero, "On the Geographical Names of the List of Thothmes III., which may be Referred to Galilee," *JTVI* 20 (1886-87) 308-319. (Discussion and Comments by Henry George Tomkins, p. 320; C. R. Conder, pp. 321-323; Charles Wilson, pp. 323-234; [W. St.] Boscawen, pp. 324-325; W. Wright, pp. 325-326) *(Trans. by Henry George Tomkins)*

*Henry George Tomkins, "On the Topography of Northern Syria, with special reference to the Karnak Lists of Thothmes III," *SBAT* 9 (1886-93) 227-254.

*Henry George Tomkins, "The Karnak Lists of Thothmes III, relating to Northern and Southern Syria," *SBAT* 9 (1886-93) 255-280. (Index to Places in the Lists, pp. 481-484)

Anonymous, "The Karnak Lists of Palestine," *PEFQS* 19 (1887) 149-151.

G. Maspero, "On the Names of the Lists of Thothmes III. which may be assigned to Judea," *JTVI* 22 (1888-89) 76-98. [(Discussion, pp. 98-110) (Remarks by A. H. Sayce, pp. 111-112)] *(Trans. by H. G. Tomkins)*

*A. H. Sayce, "Miscellaneous Notes," *ZA* 4 (1889) 382-393. [24. The Language of the *Su,* pp. 382-384]

Heinrich Brugsch-Bey, "The Land Matâni on the Egyptian Monuments," *JAOS* 14 (1890) cxciv-cxcvii.

*Fritz Hommel, "*Gisgalla-ki*—Babylon. *Ki-nu-nir-ku*—Borsippa," *SBAP* 15 (1892-93) 108-110.

*James Henry Breasted, "Some Egyptian Names in Genesis—A New Inscription of the Oldest Period, etc.," *BW* 2 (1893) 285-288.

*C[laude] R. Conder, "Shishak's Lists," *PEFQS* 25 (1893) 245-246. *[Place Names]*

G. Maspero, "The List of Sheshonq at Karnak," *JTVI* 27 (1893-94) 93-122. [(Discussion, pp. 122, 130-133) (Notes by C. R. Conder, pp. 123-130)] *(Trans. by H. G. Tomkins)*

*F. L. Griffith, "A detail of Geography in the Inscription of Herkhuf," *SBAP* 16 (1893-94) 50-52. *[uḫat = Oasis]*

*Fritz Hommel, "Assyriological Notes," *SBAP* 16 (1893-94) 209-212. [§1. "Sumer and Akkad", pp. 209-210]

*Claude R. Conder, "The City Shelala," *PEFQS* 26 (1894) 82-83.

C[laude] R. Conder, "The Onomasticon," *PEFQS* 28 (1896) 229-245.

Max W. Müller, "The Geographical List of Serreh," *RTR* 19 (1897) 73-74.

*Fritz Hommel, "Assyriological Notes," *SBAP* 19 (1897) 78-90. [§26 *Untitled,* pp. 82-87] *[Assyrian Place Names]*

*T. K. Cheyne, "The N. Arabian Land of Muṣri in Early Hebrew Tradition," *JQR* 11 (1898-99) 551-560.

Joseph Offord, "Yanoem of the Menepthah Stele," *SBAP* 21 (1899) 142.

*T. C. Foote, "The Two Unidentified Geographical Names in the Moabite Stone," *JAOS* 22 (1901) 61-63.

*Joseph Offord, Araza and Aziza, and other Archæological Notes," *SBAP* 23 (1901) 244-247. [*(Kir, or Kerak)*, pp. 246-247]

James Henry Breasted, "A City of Ikhenaton in Nubia," *ZÄS* 40 (1902-03) 106-113.   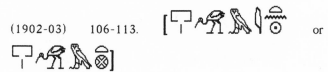   or

*R. A. Stewart Macalister, "Dajun and Beth-Dagon and the Transference of Biblical Place-Names," *PEFQS* 35 (1903) 356-358.

*Charles C. Torrey, "'Yāwān' and 'Hellas' as Designations of the Seleucid Empire," *JAOS* 25 (1904) 302-311. [יָוָן - Javan; היונים]

O. A. Toffteen, "Geographical List to R. F. Harper's 'Assyrian and Babylonian Letters,' Vols. I-VIII," *AJSL* 21 (1904-05) 83-99.

C. H. W. Johns, "Assyriological Notes. II. Some Notes on the Geographical Names in the RFHarper Letters," *AJSL* 22 (1905-06) 228-232.

Joseph Offord, "Miscellaneous Notes," *PEFQS* 37 (1905) 80-81. [1. A New Egyptian Place-List in Northern Syria, p. 80; 2. The Egyptian Name for Canaan and Philistia, p. 81]

*M. G. Kyle, "Some Geographic and Ethnic Lists of Rameses II at the Temple of Luxor," *RTR* 30 (1908) 219-223.

W. E. Crum, "Place-Names in Deubner's *Kosmas und Damian*," *SBAP* 30 (1908) 129-136.

C. F. Burney, "On Certain South-Palestinian Place-Names," *JTS* 13 (1911-12) 83-84.

Oric Bates, "On Some Place-Names in Eastern Libya," *SBAP* 34 (1912) 234-238.

Frederick A. Vanderburgh, "The Babylonian Name of Palestine," *JBL* 32 (1913) 146-150.

*W. Max Müller, "An Egyptian Document for the History of Palestine," *JQR, N.S.*, 4 (1913-14) 651-656. *[Place Names]*

Percy E. Newberry, "*Ta Ṯeḥenu*—'Olive Land'," *AEE* 2 (1915) 97-102. [⌐ | ≏]

Edouard Naville, "Some Geographical Names," *JEA* 4 (1916) 228-233.

W[illiam] F[oxwell] Albright, "A Misunderstood Syrian Place Name—Dana and Tyana," *AJP* 43 (1922) 74-75.

*W[illiam] F[oxwell] Albright, "New Light on Magan and Meluḫa," *JAOS* 42 (1922) 317-322.

*Sidney Smith, "Ḳizzuwadna and Ḳode," *JEA* 8 (1922) 45-47.

A. H. Sayce, "The Geographical Position of Arzawa," *JEA* 8 (1922) 233-234.

*W. J. Pythian Adams, "*Aiguptos:* a Derivation and Some Suggestions," *JPOS* 2 (1922) 94-100.

*John Garstang, "Notes on Hittite Political Geography," *AAA* 10 (1923) 21-25, 172-178. [I. Arzawa; II. Kizzuwadna; III. Gašga]

*David Yellin, "Emek ha-bakha: Bekhaim," *JPOS* 3 (1923) 191-192.

D. D. Luckenbill, "On the Writing of a Few Geographical Names," *AJSL* 40 (1923-24) 288.

*A. H. Sayce, "The Atlas of the Empire of Sargon and Akkad," *AEE* 9 (1924) 1-5. (Note by [W. M.] Flinders Petrie, p. 5)

*Paul Haupt, "Philological and Archaeological Studies," *AJP* 45 (1924) 238-259. [4. The Median Lapis-lazuli Mountain, pp. 245-247]

*Paul Haupt, "Philological and Archaeological Studies," *AJP* 45 (1924) 238-259. [7. The Hittite Name of Troy, pp. 252-255]

W[illiam] F[oxwell] Albright, "The Town of Selle (Zaru) in the 'Amarnah Tablets," *JEA* 10 (1924) 6-8.

*Sidney Smith, "Ḳizzuwadna," *JEA* 10 (1924) 104-115.

W[illiam] F[oxwell] Albright, "Philological Method in the Identification of Anatolian Place-Names," *JEA* 11 (1925) 19-22.

*L. A. Mayer and J. Garstang, "Kizzuwadna and other Hittite States," *JEA* 11 (1925) 23-35.

A. H. Sayce, "Hittite Geography," *OOR* 1 (1926) #2, 21-22.

J. B. Haley, "The Coming of the Greeks: 1. The Geographical Distribution of Pre-Greek Place Names," *AJA* 32 (1928) 141-145.

*Sidney Smith, "Assyriological Notes," *JRAS* (1928) 849-875. [The Three Cities called Tirqan, pp. 868-875]

*Nathaniel Reich, "The Geographical Terms *Mizraim* and *Pathros*," *JSOR* 12 (1928) 43-45.

*T. Canaan, "Studies in the Topography and Folklore of Petra," *JPOS* 9 (1929) 136-218. [IV. Comparative Lists of Place-names, pp. 169-195]

A. H. Sayce, "Notes on Hittite Geographical Names," *JRAS* (1930) 109-111.

*Anonymous, "Developments at Kirkuk," *UMB* 2 (1930-31) 187, 189-190. *[Note of a tablet found at Kirkuk making mention of a place name "Ibla" in Syria]*

G. A. Wainwright, "Keftiu," *JEA* 17 (1931) 26-43.

*H. H. Walker, "Where were Madmenah and the Gebim?" *JPOS* 13 (1933) 90-93.

St. H. Stephen, "Note on the Definite Article in Two Palestinian Place-Names," *JPOS* 13 (1933) 232-237.

R. M. Dawkins, "The Place-Names of Later Greece," *TPS* (1933) 1-45.

Paul Romanoff, "Onomasticon of Palestine," *PAAJR* 7 (1935-36) 147-227.

*M[ichael] Avi-Yonah, "Two Notes on the Jordan Valley," *JPOS* 17 (1937) 252-254. [1. Psittatium; 2. Papyron]

*Ira Maurice Price, "H. De Genouillac on '*Lagash*' and '*Girsu*'," *JAOS* 57 (1937) 309-312.

*J. Braslavski, "Geniza Fragments with Mentions of Dallāta, Kadesh, 'Ammāta and Baneas," *BIES* 5 (1937-38) #4, III.

*M. Hamza, "The correct reading of the place-name

⬜🏠 ⬷ ⌇ ⬷," *ASAE* 38 (1938) 197-208.

E. B. W. Chappelow, "Biblical Sites in the Cuneiform Records of the Later Assyrian Empire," *JTVI* 70 (1938) 263-285.

S. Assaf, Dallata, Kadesh, and Baneas," *BIES* 6 (1938-39) #1, III.

*R[oland] de-Vaux, "The Geographical Location of the Poem of *Krt*," *BIES* 6 (1938-39) #1, IV.

J. Braslawsky, "Futher on Dalata, Kadesh, and Baneas," *BIES* 6 (1938-39) #1, V.

E. R. Lacheman, "Nuzi Geographical Names I," *BASOR* #78 (1940) 18-23.

E. R. Lacheman, "Nuzi Geographical Names II," *BASOR* #81 (1941) 10-15.

Alan H. Gardiner, "The Cow's Belly," *JEA* 27 (1941) 158. *[Place name of the apex of the Nile Delta]*

M. Avi-Yanoh, "Topographical Suggestions," *BIES* 10 (1942-44) #1, I.

Z. Vilnai, "New Identification of Place-Names in Palestine," *BIES* 9 (1941-42) #4, II.

*J. Simons, "Topographical and Archaeological Elements in the Story of Abimelech," *OS* 2 (1943) 35-78.

Battiscombe Gunn, "The Name of the Pyramid-Town of Sesostris II," *JEA* 31 (1945) 106-107. /'nẖ-Snwsrt/

Alan H. Gardiner, "The supposed Athribis of Upper Egypt," *JEA* 31 (1945) 108-111.

*G. A. Wainwright, "Zeberged: The Shipwrecked Sailor's Island," *JEA* 32 (1946) 31-38.

*Selim J. Levy, "Harmal Geographical List," *Sumer* 3 (1947) 50-83.

S. Yeivin, "Zeredah—Zererah—Zarthan," *BIES* 14 (1947-48) #3/4, I-II.

Alan [H.] Gardiner, "The Founding of a New Delta Town in the Twentieth Dynasty," *JEA* 34 (1948) 19-22. /Na-Amen-Rē'/

*G. A. Wainwright, "Zeberged: A Correction," *JEA* 34 (1948) 119.

*Oliver H. Myers, "Zeberged," *JEA* 34 (1948) 119-120.

*H. L. Ginsberg, "The Date of the Town-Lists in Joshua," *JBL* 67 (1948) v.

Emil G. Kraeling, "Two Place Names of Hellenistic Palestine," *JNES* 7 (1948) 199-201.

*Roger T. O'Callaghan, "Notes on Mesopotamian History," *CBQ* 12 (1950) 132-135. [1. Naharin, pp. 132-133]

S. Yeivin, "The Third District in Tuthmosis III's List of Palestino-Syrian Towns," *JEA* 36 (1950) 51-62.

Charles F. Nims, "The Name of the XXIInd Nome of Upper Egypt," *ArOr* 20 (1952) 343-346.

Charles F. Nims, "Another Geographical List from Medinet Habu," *JEA* 38 (1952) 34-45.

A. Honeyman, "The Tributaries of Ugarit, A Toponymic Study," *JKF* 2 (1952-53) 74-87.

Y[ahanan] Aharoni, "The Land of 'Amqi," *IEJ* 3 (1953) 153-161.

*S. H. Horn, "Jericho in a Topographical List of Ramesses II," *JNES* 12 (1953) 201-203. (Comment by B. Maisler, p. 203)

Prescott W. Townsend, "*Bur, Bure,* and *Baris* in Ancient North African Place Names," *JNES* 13 (1954) 52-55.

Zev Vilnay, "Identification of Talmudic Place Names," *JQR, N.S.,* 45 (1954-55) 130-140.

*T. Fish, "Lagash and Umma in Ur III," *MCS* 5 (1955) 56-58.

P. B. S. Andrews, "The Mycenaean name of the Land of the Achaians," *RHA* 13 (1955) 1-19.

W. A. McDonald, "Place Names in the Pylos Area," *AJA* 60 (1956) 180.

*Frank M. Cross Jr. and G. Ernest Wright, "The Boundary and Province Lists of the Kingdom of Judah," *JBL* 75 (1956) 202-226.

*T. Fish, "URÚ.ki," *JSS* 1 (1956) 206-215. *[Quarter of Lagash]*

T. Fish, "A-pi$_4$-sal.ki," *MCS* 6 (1956) 78-84.

T. Fish, "List of CITY/TOWN names on Ur III tablets," *MCS* 6 (1956) 114-130.

B. S J. Isserlin, "Hurrian and Old Anatolian Place Names in the Semitic World: Some Tentative Suggestions," *PEQ* 88 (1956) 141-144.

*Hans Goedicke, "The Route of Sinuhe's Flight," *JEA* 43 (1957) 77-85. *[Place Names]*

T. Fish, "Some Place Names and Their Contexts," *MCS* 7 (1957) 15-24. [KS.ZAL.LU.ki; lú Ka-zal-lu.ki; KIŠ.ki; A-bi/pi-ak; MAR AD.ki; Ka-ma-rí.ki; Ma-hi-li.ki; Bašam lú Simanum.ki]

B. S J. Isserlin, "Israelite and Pre-Israelite Place-Names in Palestine," *PEQ* 89 (1957) 133-144.

D. A. Hester, "Pre-Greek place names in Greece and Asia Minor," *RHA* 15 (1957) 107-119.

Hans G. Güterbock, "Kaneš and Neša: Two Forms of One Anatolian Place Name?" *EI* 5 (1958) 46*-50*. (Correction, p. 82*)

D. M. Dixon, "The Land of Yam," *JEA* 44 (1958) 40-55.

D. M. Dixon, "The extent of *W 3 w 3 t* in the Old Kingdom," *JEA* 44 (1958) 119.

Z. Kallai-Kleinmann, "The Town Lists of Judah, Simeon, Benjamin and Dan," *VT* 8 (1958) 134-160.

William A. McDonald, "Deuro- and Peran-ankalaia," *Minos* 6 (1958-60) 149-155.

*S. Yeivin, "Topographical and Ethnic Notes," *'Atiqot* 2 (1959) 155-164. [D. *HQ3 NISNNWS TYHRS*, p. 164]

S. Yeivin, "Ya'qob'el," *JEA* 45 (1959) 16-18.

Henry G. Fischer, "Some Notes on the Easternmost Names of the Delta in the Old and Middle Kingdoms," *JNES* 18 (1959) 129-142.

Y[ohanan] Aharoni, "The Province-List of Judah," *VT* 9 (1959) 225-246.

D. Leibel, "Two Forgotten Place-Names in the Bible," *BIES* 24 (1959-60) #1, V. *[Goath; Ham]*

Z. Kallai-Kleinmann, "Note on the Town Lists of Judah, Simeon, Benjamin and Dan," *VT* 11 (1961) 223-228.

S. Yeivin, "Topographic and Ethnic Notes. III," *JEA* 48 (1962) 75-80. [Nos. 28-31 in Shoshenḳ I's list of conquered towns]

*Ivan Tracy Kaufman, "A Note on the Place Name *SPR* and the Letter *Samek* in the Samaria Ostraca," *BASOR* #172 (1963) 60-61.

*Henry G. Fischer, "Varia Aegyptiaca," *JARCE* 2 (1963) 17-51. [10. The Land of *Srr*, p. 50]

*Elizabeth Thomas, "*P3 ḤR ḤN' I ḤNW/N HNW ḤN'I*, A Designation of the Valley of the Kings," *JEA* 49 (1963) 57-63.

G. A. Wainwright, "Abimilki's news of Danuna," *JEA* 49 (1963) 175-176.

Michael C. Astour, "Place-Names from the Kingdom of Alalah in the North Syrian List of Thutmose III: A Study in Historical Topography," *JNES* 22 (1963) 220-241.

*Machteld J. Mellink, "Mita, Mushki and Phrygians," *AAI* 2 (1965) 317-325.

S. Talmon, "The Town Lists of Simeon," *IEJ* 15 (1965) 235-241.

David Neiman, "Phoenican Place-Names," *JNES* 24 (1965) 113-115.

Hans Goedicke, "The Location of *Ḥnt-ḥn-nfr*," *Kush* 13 (1965) 102-111.

K[enneth] A. Kitchen, "Thebean Topographical Lists, Old and New," *Or, N.S.,* 34 (1965) 1-9.

Michael C. Astour, "Aegean Place-Names in an Egyptian Inscription," *AJA* 70 (1966) 313-317.

K[enneth] A. Kitchen, "Aegean Place Names in a List of Amenophis III," *BASOR* #181 (1966) 23-24.

*S. Segert, "Some Phoenician Etymologies of North African Toponyms," *OA* 5 (1966) 19-25.

*N. B. Jankowska, "A System of Rotation of Eponyms of the Commerical Association at Kaniš (Asia Minor XIX B.C.," *ArOr* 35 (1967) 524-548.

S. Talmon, "The List of Cities of Simeon," *EI* 8 (1967) 76*.

T. Jacobsen, "Some Sumerian City-names," *JCS* 21 (1967) 100-103. [1. Girsu; 2. Adab/Usab; 3. Lagash]

*G. R. H. Wright, "The Place Name Balāṭah and the Excavations at Shechem," *ZDPV* 83 (1967) 199-202.

Jørgen Laessøe, "The Quest for the Country of *Utûm," *JAOS* 88 (1968) 120-122.

*Hildegard Lewy, "A Contribution to the Historical Geography of the Nuzi Texts," *JAOS* 88 (1968) 150-162.

Miachel C. Astour, "Mesopotamian and the Transtigridian Place Names in the Medinet Habu Lists of Ramses III," *JAOS* 88 (1968) 733-752.

*Edmond Sollberger, "The Problem of Magan and Meluhha," *ULBIA* 8&9 (1968-69) 247-249. (Discussion, p. 250)

*A[braham] Malamat, "Hazor and its Northern Neighbours in New Mari Documents," *EI* 9 (1969) 137. *[English Summary]*

M. E. J. Richardson, "Hebrew Toponyms," *TB* #20 (1969) 95-104.

§162 *2.5.5.4 Studies concerning Boundaries and Borders*

J. F. Thrupp, "On the Borders of the Inheritance of the Tribe of Naphtali; and on the Site of the Cities denounced by Our Saviour in the Gospels," *JCSP* 2 (1855) 290-308.

S. P. Tregelles, "On the Eastern Boundary of Naptali, and the Sites of Bethsaida and Capharnaum," *JCSP* 3 (1856) 141-154.

*C. Clermont-Ganneau, "Notes on Certain New Discoveries at Jerusalem," *PEFQS* 3 (1871) 103-107. [7. Stone of Bohan, p. 105]

Daniel Kerr, "Attempt to Trace the Boundaries of Ephraim, Manasseh, and Issachar," *PEFQS* 9 (1877) 41-50. (Note by Claude R. Conder, pp. 47-50]

Claude R. Conder, "Northern Boundary of Palestine," *PEFQS* 10 (1878) 76.

Trelawney Saunders, "On the River Kanah, the Boundary between Ephraim and Manasseh," *PEFQS* 12 (1880) 224-228.

C[laude] R. Conder, "The Boundary of Ephraim and Manasseh," *PEFQS* 13 (1881) 90-91.

C[laude] R. Conder, "The Northern Border of Zebulon," *PEFQS* 15 (1883) 134-138.

C[laude] R. Conder, "Notes. *Northern Boundary of Israel*," *PEFQS* 15 (1883) 138-139.

C[onrad] Schick, "Boundary between Judah and Benjamin," *PEFQS* 18 (1886) 54-58.

*H. W. Hogg, "Dan to Beersheba: The Origin and Significance of the Phrase," *OSHTP* (1897-98) 31-34.

*H. W. Hogg, "'Dan to Beersheba': The Literary History of the Phrase and the Historical Problems it Raises," *Exp, 5th Ser.,* 8 (1898) 411-421.

*Charles Clermont-Ganneau, "A Newly Discovered Hebrew and Greek Inscription Relating to the Boundary of Gezer," *PEFQS* 31 (1899) 118-127.

C[laude] R. Conder, "Notes on Bible Geography. I. The North Border of the Land of Israel," *PEFQS* 36 (1904) 386-388.

*Caleb Hauser, "Cities in the Negeb, the Tribal Boundaries," *PEFQS* 38 (1906) 213-221.

J. E. Hanauer, "Notes and Queries," *PEFQS* 38 (1906) 238-239. *[Boundary Stone]*

Albert T. Clay, "Babylonian Boundary Stones," *RP* 7 (1908) 39-51.

G. E. White, "Boundary Stones in Asia Minor," *RP* 7 (1908) 149-150.

*A. H. Sayce, "A Boundary Stone," *ET* 19 (1907-08) 497-498. *[Babylonian]*

*Caleb Hauser, "Further Notes on Palestinian Geography," *PEFQS* 42 (1910) 280-286. [4. The boundary of Judah and Benjamin between En-Rogel and Kiriath-Jearim, pp. 282-283]

Anonymous, "A Hittite Boundary Stone," *RP* 9 (1910) 228.

*William F. Albright, "The Administrative Divisions of Israel and Judah," *JPOS* 5 (1925) 17-54.

*E. Power, "Another view on the line of demarcation between the kingdoms of Juda and Israel," *B* 7 (1926) 87-95.

*J. H. Dunbar, "Betwixt Egypt and Nubia," *AEE* 14 (1929) 108-117.

J. W. Phythian-Adams, "The Boundary of Ephraim and Manasseh," *PEFQS* 61 (1929) 228-241.

*M[ichael] Avi-Yonah, "Territorial Boundaries in North-Western Galilee," *JPOS* 14 (1934) 56-60.

C. Mackay, "The North Boundary of Palestine," *JTS* 35 (1934) 22-40.

Stanley A. Cook, "The Confines of Israel and Judah," *PEFQS* 66 (1934) 60-75.

M. Avi-Yonah, "The City Boundaries of Roman Trans-Jordan (with map)," *BIES* 11 (1944-45) #1/2, I.

*B[enjamin] Maisler, "Topographical Researches," *BIES* 12 (1946) VIII-IX. [5. Lebo Hamath and the Northern boundary of Canaan]

*Leo Adler, "The Natural Boundaries of the Aministrative Divisions of Israel under Solomon," *BIES* 16 (1951) #1/2, II.

*Robert North, "Israel's Tribes and Today's Frontier," *CBQ* 16 (1954) 146-153.

*D. H. K. Amiran, "The Geography of the Negev and the Southern Border of Settlement in Israel," *BIES* 20 (1955-56) #3/4, I-II.

*Frank M. Cross Jr. and G. Ernest Wright, "The Boundary and Province Lists of the Kingdom of Judah," *JBL* 75 (1956) 202-226.

Eva Danelius, "The Boundary of Ephraim and Manasseh in the Western Plain," *PEQ* 89 (1957) 55-67.

Yohanan Aharoni, "The Northern Boundary of Judah," *PEQ* 90 (1958) 27-31.

Eva Danelius, "The Boundary of Ephraim and Manasseh in the Western Plain *(Continued)*," *PEQ* 90 (1958) 32-43.

Eva Danelius, "The Boundary of Ephraim and Manasseh in the Western Plain *(Concluded)*," *PEQ* 90 (1958) 122-144.

Yigael Yadin, "The Fourfold Division of Judah," *BASOR* #163 (1961) 6-12.

H. Tadmor, "The Southern Border of Aram," *IEJ* 12 (1962) 114-122.

*Faraj Basmachi, "Miscellania in the Iraq Museum," *Sumer* 18 (1962) 48-50. [Kudurru (A Boundary Stone) (I. M.62269) p.49]

*Cameron Mackay, "The Lebanon Watershed," *CQR* 166 (1965) 278-291. *[Boundaries]*

*J. A. Brinkman, "Remarks on two Kudurrus from the Second Dynasty of Isin," *RAAO* 61 (1967) 70-74.

Ronald S. Stroud, "Tribal Boundary Markers from Corinth," *AJA* 72 (1968) 173.

§163 *2.5.5.5 Caves [See also: §168 for Shindar Cave →]*

*William Simpson, "The Royal Caverns or Quarries, Jerusalem," *PEFQS* 2 (1870) 373-379.

*Philip Schaff, "Disputed Scripture Localities," *PRev* 54 (1878) Part1, 851-884. [The Machphelah, pp. 868-871]

*W. F. Birch, "Notes by Rev. W. F. Birch," *PEFQS* 18 (1886) 26-34. [Cave of Adullum, p. 31]

C[onrad] Schick, "Notes from Jerusalem," *PEFQS* 19 (1887) 151-158, 213-221. [I. 5. Large Caves near Ramleh, 214; II. 6. 218]

C[onrad] Schick, "Recent Discoveries, in Jerusalem," *PEFQS* 21 (1889) 63-68. [III. Notes on the Plans and the Cave East of the Church of the Holy Sepulchre, pp. 67-68]

*G. Schumacher, "Recent Discoveries in Galilee," *PEFQS* 21 (1889) 68-78. [Nazareth—Discovery of Large Cave, pp. 68-74]

J. E. Hanauer, "Curious Cave at Saris," *PEFQS* 21 (1889) 184-185.

Henry Brass, "The Cave of Adullam," *PEFQS* 22 (1890) 180-181.

Selah Merrill, "The Cave of Machpelah," *ONTS* 11 (1890) 327-335.

*W. F. Birch, "The Rock of Etam and the Cave of Adullam," *PEFQS* 27 (1895) 338-341; 28 (1896) 161-164, 261-262. [Notes by C. Clermont-Ganneau, *PEFQS* 28 (1896) pp. 80 & 259; by C. R. Conder, *PEFQS* 28 (1896) pp. 82 & 259]

*Edgar J. Goodspeed, "The City of Herod," *BW* 18 (1901) 88-95. [The Cave of Adullam, pp. 90-92]

*George L. Robinson, "Recent Excavation and Exploration in Palestine," *HTR* 8 (1915) 525-552. [A Visit to the Cave of Machpelah, pp. 551-552]

[W. M.] Flinders Petrie, "The Cave of Macpelah," *AEE* 8 (1923) 105-110.

*M[oshe] Stekelis, "Preliminary Report on Soundings in Prehistoric Caves in Palestine," *BASOR* #86 (1942) 2-10. [Mughâhat al-Waṭat; Mughâret an-Nuqṭah; Mughâret Wâdī Fallâḥ; Mughâret Abū Uṣba'; 'Irâq al-Barûd]

*F. T[urville]-P[etre], "Excavations of Two Palaeolithic Caves in Galilee," *BSAJB* #7 (1925) 99-101. [Addendum: Note on the Galilee Skull, by Arthur Keith, p. 102]

*Alfred Ely Day, "The Rock Shelter of Ksâr 'Aḵil Near the Cave of Anṯilyas," *PEFQS* 58 (1926) 158-160.

*H. J. Orr-Ewing, "The Lion and the Cavern of Bones at Petra," *PEFQS* 59 (1927) 155-156.

*Dorothy A. E. Garrod, "Excavations of a Palaeolithic Cave in Western Judaea," *PEFQS* 60 (1928) 182-185.

*Alexandre Lannes, Sylvester J. Saller, M. Stekelis, "Excavations in Palestine and Trans-Jordan, 1940-1," *QDAP* 11 (1945) 113-118. [Prehistoric caves, pp. 115-118]

*J. du Plat Taylor, M. V. Seton-Williams, and J. Waechter, "The Excavations at Sakce Gözü," *Iraq* 12 (1950) 53-138.

Carleton S. Coon, "The Eastern Cave at Hazer Merd," *Sumer* 6 (1950) 91-92.

C. F. Arden-Close, "The Cave of Machpelah," *PEQ* 83 (1951) 69-77.

*J. Waechter, Sabahat Gögüs, and Veronica Seton-Williams, "The Sakce Gözü Cave Site 1949," *TTKB* 15 (1951) 193-201.

M[oshe] Stekelis and G. Haas, "The Abu Usba Cave (Mount Carmel)," *IEJ* 2 (1952) 15-47.

Carleton S. Coon, "Excavations in the Hotu Cave, Iran, 1951, a Preliminary Report," *PAPS* 96 (1952) 231-249.

*Louis B. Dupree, "The Pleistocene Artifacts of Hotu Cave, Iran," *PAPS* 96 (1952) 250-257.

Ralph S. Solecki, "Notes on a Brief Archaeological Reconnissance of Cave Sites in the Rowanduz District of Iraq," *Sumer* 8 (1952) 37-44.

*Anonymous, "Excavations in Jordan, 1951-1952," *ADAJ* 2 (1953) 82-88. [Qumrân Caves, p. 82]

Ralph S. Solecki, "Dukan Cave, An Occupational Station on the Lesser Zab River in Northeastern Iraq," *Sumer* 10 (1954) 69-72.

Peter J. Parr, "A Cave at Arqub el Dhahr," *ADAJ* 3 (1956) 61-73.

*Dorothy Mackay and E. S. Kennedy, "Report of the Excavation of cave near the mouth of the Dog River. North of Beirut," *BMB* 13 (1956) 53-71.

Y[ehoshua] Ben-Arieh, "The Caves in the Beth-Guvrin Region,"
   BIES 23 (1959) #3/4, IV-V; 24 (1959-60) #4, IV.

Y[ehoshua] Ben-Arieh, "The Caves in the Beth-Guvrin Region,"
   SGEI #1 (1959) IV-V; #2 (1960) IV.

*Andreina Leanza Becker-Colonna, "The Explorations of Mt. Kronion
   Caves and the Finding of Pre-historical Vases," *AJA* 64 (1960)
   182.

E[liezer] Wreschner, M Avnimelech, S. Angress, "The Geulah Caves,
   Haifa: Preliminary Report," *IEJ* 10 (1960) 78-89.

Y[ohanan] Aharoni, "The Caves of Naḥal Ḥever," *'Atiqot* 3 (1961)
   148-162.

*F. E. Zeuner, with the cooperation of I. W. Cornwall and Diana
   Kirkbride, "The Shore-Line Chronology of the Palaeolithic of
   Abri Zumoffen, Adlun Caves, Lebanon," *BMB* 16 (1961) 49-60.

*Avraham Biran, "Archaeological Activities in Israel, 1960/1961,"
   CNI 12 (1961) #1, 15-21. [The Dead Sea Caves; Cave of the Pool;
   The Cave of Dread; Cave of the Treasure; Cave of the Letters;
   Ein Gedi]

Anonymous, "Judean Desert Caves," *IEJ* 11 (1961) 77-81.

*Y[ehoshua] Ben-Arieh, "Caves and Ruins in the Beth Govrin Area,"
   IEJ 12 (1962) 47-61.

*N[ahman] Avigad, "The Expedition to the Judean Desert, 1961.
   Expedition A—Naḥal David," *IEJ* 12 (1962) 169-183.

Y[ohanan] Aharoni, "The Expedition to the Judean Desert, 1961.
   Expedition B—The Cave of Horror," *IEJ* 12 (1962) 186-199.

*P[esah] Bar-Adon, "The Expedition to the Judean Desert, 1961.
   Expedition C—The Cave of Treasure," *IEJ* 12 (1962) 215-226.

*Y[igael] Yadin, The Expedition to the Judean Desert, 1961.
   Expedition D—The Cave of Letters," *IEJ* 12 (1962) 227-257.

Pesah Bar-Adon, "The Cave of the Treasure," *Arch* 16 (1963)
   251-259. *[Naḥal Mishmar]*

E[liezer] Wreschner, "Geulah Cave, Haifa," *IEJ* 13 (1963) 138; 14 (1964) 277-278.

M[oshe] Stekelis, "Kabara Cave," *IEJ* 14 (1964) 277.

*Eliezer Oren, "The Caves of the Palestinian Shephelah," *Arch* 18 (1965) 218-224.

H. Watanabe, "'Amud Cave," *IEJ* 15 (1965) 246.

Y. Shapira, "An Ancient Cave at Bat-Yam," *IEJ* 16 (1966) 8-10.

A[sher] Ovadiah, ". . . 'Elijah's Cave', Mount Carmel," *IEJ* 16 (1966) 284-285.

Thomas W. Jacobsen, "The Franchthi Cave: A Stone Age Site in Southern Greece," *Arch* 22 (1969) 4-9.

§164 *2.5.5.6 Israel (Palestine) – General Geographical Studies [See also: Archaeological Expeditions →]*

Anonymous, "The Land of Hills," *CongML* 20 (1837) 25-32.

Charles Hall, "Review of Robinson's Biblical Researches," *BRCR, N.S.,* 6 (1841) 419-453. *(Review)*

Edward Robinson, "Biblical Researches in Palestine. First Supplement," *BRCR, N.S.,* 8 (1842) 219-243.

Edward Robinson, "Biblical Researches in Palestine," *BS* (1843) 9-88. (Corr. pp. 203-204)

*Edward Robinson, "Notes on Biblical Geography," *BS* (1843) 563-566. [The Exodus, pp. 564-565; Arimathea or Ramah, pp. 565-566; Depression of the Dead Sea, etc., p. 566]

E[dward] Robinson, "Notes on Biblical Geography," *BS* 1 (1844) 217-221. [I. Eleutheropolis, pp. 217-220; II. Legio, Megiddo, Maximianopolis, pp. 220-221]

*E[dward] Robinson, "Notes on Biblical Geography," *BS* 1 (1844) 598-604. [I. Gibeah of Saul, pp. 598-602; II. Rachel's Sepulchre. Ramah of Samuel, pp. 602-604]

Anonymous, "Palestine," *NBR* 2 (1844-45) 515-565.

Samuel Wolcott, "Geographical Notes on Palestine," *BS* 3 (1846) 398-403. [The Coast of the Dead Sea; Masada; Route from Mount Lebanon to Báalbek]

*E[dward] Robinson, "Notes on Biblical Geography," *BS* 4 (1847) 403-409. [I. The Site of Hazor; II. Antiquities on the route from Ba'albek to Hamath and Aleppo; III. The Sabbatical River. Raphanea]

*E[dward] Robinson and G. B. Whiting, "Notes on Biblical Geography," *BS* 5 (1848) 79-97. [I. Abila of Lysanias. The Inscriptions; II. Chalcis; III. Great Inscription at Apamea, Topography of Jerusalem]

E[dward] Robinson, "Notes on Biblical Geography," *BS* 5 (1848) 760-770. [I. Notes on the route from Beirut to Damascus; II. The Dead Sea Expedition]

*E[dward] Robinson, "Notes on Biblical Geography," *BS* 6 (1849) 366-386. [I. The A'waj, the second River of Damascus; II. Natural Bridge of the Lîtâny or Leontes; III. Kedesh of Naphtali and the Hûleh; IV. Kades-Barnea, "in the uttermost border of Edom"; V. Position of the Israelites in Sinai]

W. H. R., "Palestine," *UQGR* 8 (1851) 137-155. *(Review)*

*†Anonymous, "De Saulcy's Dead Sea and Bible Lands," *DR* 35 (1853) 139-172. *(Review)*

*J. W. C., "Late Important Discoveries in Syria and the Holy Land," *DUM* 42 (1853) 364-382.

†Anonymous, "Recent Discoveries in Palestine," *LQHR* 2 (1854) 150-172. *(Review)*

W. M. Thomson, "Notes on Palestine," *BS* 12 (1855) 822-833.

*Anonymous, "Sinai and Palestine," *DUM* 48 (1856) 313-329.

*Anonymous, "Sinai, Palestine, and Mecca," *ERCJ* 104 (1856) 363-399. *(Review)*

*†Anonymous, "Stanley's Sinai and Palestine," *TLJ* 9 (1856-57) 397-411. *(Review)*

Anonymous, "The Holy Land," *CE* 63 (1857) 211-230. *(Review)*

†Anonymous, "Prof. Osborn's Palestine Past and Present," *TLJ* 11 (1858-59) 576-585. *(Review)*

*†Anonymous, "Geography and Biography of the Old Testament," *QRL* 106 (1859) 368-419. *(Review)*

[T. R. G. Peck], "The Present and Past Physical State of Palestine," *SPR* 12 (1859-60) 728-736.

*†Anonymous, "The Geography of Palestine, in Relation to the Historical Truth of the Bible," *BFER* 9 (1860) 153-185. *(Review)*

Lyman Coleman, "Palestine and the Desert, Past and Present," *BS* 21 (1864) 752-786.

*Anonymous, "Recent Researches in Syria and Palestine," *ThE* 3 (1866) 46-48.

†Anonymous, "Recent Researches in Palestine," *BQRL* 46 (1867) 393-429. *(Review)*

Anonymous, "Geography of Palestine," *CE* 82 (1867) 282-299. *(Review)*

*Anonymous, "*The Comparative Geography of Palestine and the Sinaitic Peninsula*," *LQHR* 28 (1867) 404-452. *(Review)*

[Charles Warren], "Heights of One Hundred and Fifty Points to the East of Jordan," *PEFQS* 2 (1870) 307-311.

[Charles Warren], "Positions of Places East of Jordan," *PEFQS* 2 (1870) 381-388.

*A. B. Davidson, "Palestine Exploration of the Moabite Stone," *BFER* 20 (1871) 136-163. *(Review)*

†Anonymous, "The Explorations of Palestine," *BQRL* 53 (1871) 69-103. *(Review)*

†Anonymous, "The Systematic Exploration of the Holy Land,"
LQHR 36 (1871) 1-34. *(Review)*

*Charles Warren, "Approximate Latitutdes, Longitudes, and
Altitudes Above Mean Sea Level of Points in the Plain of
Philistia," *PEFQS* 3 (1871) 162-164.

J. S. Lee, "Recent Explorations of Palestine," *UQGR, N.S.,* 8 (1871)
318-334. *(Review)*

John Eglington Bailey, "Palestine Geography in the Seventeenth
Century," *PEFQS* 4 (1872) 51-57.

*Anonymous, "Recent Travels and Explorations in Syria," *BQRL* 58
(1873) 144-167. *[Palestine] (Review)*

†Anonymous, "The Exploration of Palestine," *LQHR* 45 (1875-76)
277-322. *(Review)*

*Anonymous, "Topography of Books of Joshua and Samuel," *CongL* 5
(1876) 109-115.

*Claude R. Conder, "Proposed Tests for the Survey," *PEFQS* 8 (1876)
66-73. [Enam; Anuath; Bethsarias; Bezek; Netopha; Garob;
Cozeba; Kefr Aziz; Yajur; Choba; Ceperaria; Betooenea;
Fathoura; Salim; Betariph; Hasta; Asor; Betheked] *[Proposed
Idenifications of Various Towns & Cities]*

*Claude R. Conder, "The First Traveller in Palestine," *PEFQS* 8 (1876)
74-88.

*Claude R. Conder, "Palestine Before Joshua, from the Records of
Egyptian Conquest," *PEFQS* 8 (1876) 87-97, 140-148.

*Claude R. Conder, "The Fertility of Ancient Palestine," *PEFQS* 8
(1876) 120-132.

*Claude R. Conder, "Notes from the Memoir," *PEFQS* 8 (1876)
149-151, 167-171; 9 (1877) 20-30, 85-89, 137-142, 178-183;
10 (1878) 18-22, 76-77. *(Identifications of places)* [Ebenezer,
Mizpeh, Aphek, Shen/Hashan, Beth Car; Gibeah, Timnah;
Gederah, Adithaim; Hezron; Ashan; Sharuhen; Adami Nekeb;
Adalah; Jabneel; Nebo Elam, Harim; Neiel; Shihor Libnath;
Zebulon, Hannathon; Mechanum; Ashan; *(continued)*

*Claude R. Conder, "Notes from the Memoir," *PEFQS* 8 (1876)
149-151, 167-171; 9 (1877) 20-30, 85-89, 137-142, 178-183;
10 (1878) 18-22, 76-77. *(continued)* En Gannim; Janua;
Rebbo; Sior; Joshua's Altar at Ebal; Gomorrah; The Early
Christian Ebal and Gerizim; Archi, Ataroth; The Towns of Dan;
Jethlah; Eltekeh; Gibbethon; Baalath; Rakkon; Towns of
Benjamin; Gallaa; "The Valley of Vision," Gehazion; Talmudical
Cities; Suffa; Daroma; El Keniseh; Zion; Millo; Mizpeh; Wady
Mesâ'adet 'Aisa; Ashnah; Aloth; Beth Dagon; Cities of the Plain;
The Cities of the Midbar; Cities of the Negeb; Hormah; Berea;
Janoah; Giloh; Jeshua; Mekaz; Rabbith; Sarid; Tirzah; Zaanaim;
Zanoah; Zereda; Zemaraim; Ailom/Aialon; Beth Rima, En Kushi;
Naarath; Laish; el Mandeseh; Jebel Fureidis; Burjmus; Jami'a
Abu Nejeim; Kabr Hebrun; Ballutet Sebta; Sirah; Hagar's Spring;
Meronoth, Haruph, Lobnah; Talmudic Sites, Ferka, Bekun or
Pekun, Anath, Kefr Likitia, Hamthau, Bethel of Judah,
Keruthim, Yassub, Patris; Early Christian Sites, Cydoessa, Gitta;
Sellem; Jemrurah; Osheh; Tomb of Habakkuk; Hachilah; Geba;
Chasbi; Hawa; Issachar; Sun Dial in the Haram; Sinjil; Kefr Lam;
Scythopolis, Nain, Endor, Jezreel, Shunem, the well Harod,
Bethabara, Megiddo; Gath, Gezer; Jericho; The Hittites; The
Avim; The Cherethites; Ataroth Adar; Eder; Gibbethon; Baalath;
Jabneel; Mount Heres; Shalishar; Meronoth; Pirathon; Melloth;
Saab; Caphrath; Asochis; Aphecos; Beth Rima; Hirieh; Beth Sur;
Megiddo; Gihon; The Stone of Bohan; Shafat; Mountain of
Temptation; Tomb of Micah; Zion; Synagogues; Carmel; 'Athlit;
Samaria; The Feast of Shiloh; Elijah's Fountain;   Neby Lawih;
Tarichoea; Magdiel; Biri; Tor'an; Kustul; Roche Taille; Deidebeh;
Surar; Furn; Bileam, Ibleam; Jeshanah; Joshua's Tomb; Scarioth;
The Nomenclature; The Vale of Siddim; Ataroth Adar; Irpeel;
Valley of Charashim; Nehhalin Bethulia; Elon; Mount Seir; Mount
Jearim; Yemma; Kefr Kama; Saiyadeh; Beth Shearaim; Lachish;
The Tombs of the Patriarchs; Anath; Bethamari; Beidan;
Arimathoea; El Heidhemiyeh; Bir Eyub; Succoth; Abel Mea, Abel
Maula; Surtubeh; Zir; Bornata; Werdeh; El Mineh; The Cities of
the Negeb; Hudhireh; Diblath; Esora, Chusi; Harash; Wady el
Mikteleh]

Anonymous, "Tent Work in Palestine," *BQRL* 68 (1878) 414-441.
    [Palestine] (Review)

†Anonymous, "Recent Explorations in Palestine," *ERCJ* 148 (1878)
    409-436. *(Review)*

Archibald Henderson, "Recent Palestine Exploration," *BFER* 28 (1879) 107-125. *(Review)*

Claude R. Conder, "The Present Condition of Palestine," *PEFQS* 11 (1879) 6-15.

*Selah Merrill, "Modern Researches in Palestine," *PEFQS* 11 (1879) 138-154. [Bridges over the Jordan, p. 138; Water Supply and Irrigation, pp. 138-140; Hot Sulphur Springs, pp. 141-142; Artificial Tels or Mounds, pp. 142-143; The Shittim Plain, pp. 143-144; The Site of Zoar, pp.145-154]

Selah Merrill, "Palestine Explorations," *AAOJ* 2 (1879-80) 155-157.

Selah Merrill, "Palestine Exploration," *OBJ* 1 (1880) 1-3.

Charles Warren, "Eastern Palestine," *PEFQS* 12 (1880) 171-172.

*Charles Warren, "Limits of Error in Latitudes and Longitudes of Places Obtained During the Reconnaissances Made in Palestine," *PEFQS* 12 (1880) 243-246.

Edward E. Hale, "The Holy Land," *URRM* 13 (1880) 97-105.

Joseph A. Seiss, "The Holy Land," *LCR* 1 (1882) 110-125. *(Review)*

Anonymous, "Scenery of Palestine," *ONTS* 2 (1882) 21.

Hugh Macmillan, "The Riviera and Palestine," *BFER* 32 (1883) 135.

G. W. Moorehead, "The Position of Palestine," *ONTS* 3 (1883-84) 122-123.

William Morris Colles, "Palestine West of the Jordan," *BQRL* 79 (1884) 53-83.

C[laude] R. Conder, "Ancient Palestine and Modern Exploration," *ContR* 46 (1884) 856-869.

Anonymous, "Trans-Jordanic Palestine," *CQR* 18 (1884) 111-130.

*Selah Merrill "On Palestinian Archaeology," *JAOS* 11 (1885) xxiii-xxv.

*G[eorge] Rawlinson, "Biblical Topography. VI.—Sites connected with the History of Abraham, Harran, Damascus, Hebron," *MI* 6 (1886) 241-252.

*C[laude] R. Conder, "Notes on 'Across the Jordan'," *PEFQS* 18 (1886) 83-88. *(Review)*

*G. Schumacher, "Across the Jordan. A Reply to C. R. C.'s Notes thereon," *PEFQS* 18 (1886) 168-171.

*H. B. Tristram, "Canaan, Ancient and Modern, with references to the Light thrown by recent Research on the Movements of the Hittites," *JTVI* 21 (1886-87) 73-76.

†Anonymous, "Conder's Syrian Stone-Lore," *ERCJ* 166 (1887) 413-447. *(Review)*

Anonymous, "Recent Explorations in Palestine," *LQHR* 69 (1887-88) 44-57. *(Review)*

Guy le Strange, "Palestine According to the Arab Geographers and Travelers," *PEFQS* 20 (1888) 23-35.

W. M. Flinders Petrie, "Explorations in Palestine," *PEFQS* 22 (1890) 159-166.

W. W. Moore, "Palestine and the Bible," *USR* 3 (1891-92) 282-290.

George Adam Smith, "The Historical Geography of the Holy Land," *Exp., 4th Ser.,* 5 (1892) 139-157, 189-209, 300-317, 417-431; 6 (1892) 48-65, 175-186, 321-342, 464-472. [I. Introductory; II. The Low Hills or Shephelah; III. The Central Range, and the Borders of Judaea; IV. Judaea; V. Samaria; VI. The Strong Places of Samaria; VIII. Esdraelon; VII. The Question of Sychar]

Anonymous, "The Geography of Palestine," *ONTS* 14 (1892) 307.

*Anonymous, "The Shephelah," *ONTS* 14 (1892) 374.

Robert H. West, "Barometrical Determinations of Heights in Lebanon, Anti-Lebanon, and on Hermon," *PEFQS* 24 (1892) 218-226.

Claude R. Conder, "Murray's Guide—Proposed Identifications," *PEFQS* 24 (1892) 206-207. [1. Mahanaim at es Salt; 2. Mizpah Galeed at Suf; 3. Ramoth Gilead at 'Ajlun; 4. Kattath at Khashash; 5. Mishael at Rushmia; 6. Dabbashet/Dabasheh; 7. Ittah Kazin at Kefr Kenna; 8. Remmon Methoar Neah; 9. Hannathon at el Khalladiyeh; 10. Valley of Jiphtah-el at W. el Melek; 11. Bethsaida at el Mes'aidieh; 12. Beteh at Tibuin; 13. Helkath at Yerka; 14. Achshaph at Kala't esh Shukif; 15. Janoah at Hunin]

Haskett Smith, "Identifications Suggested in Murray's 'Handbook'," *PEFQS* 24 (1892) 328-334. [Note by C. R. Conder, *PEFQS* 25 (1893) pp. 78-79]

*Morris Jastrow Jr., "On Palestine and Assyria in the Days of Joshua," *ZA* 7 (1892) 1-7.

W. W. Moore, "The Land of Promise," *USR* 4 (1892-93) 13-26.

J. S. Riggs, "Studies in Palestinian Geography. I. The Land as a Whole," *BW* 4 (1894) 7-13.

C[laude] R. Conder, "Palestine Research—Past and Future," *ContR* 66 (1894) 405-421.

William Hayes Ward, "Early Palestine," *BW* 7 (1896) 401-410.

Edward L. Curtis, "Early Cities of Palestine," *BW* 7 (1896) 411-424.

George Adam Smith, "Buhl's New Geography of Palestine, and Certain Geographical Problems," *Exp, 5th Ser.,* 4 (1896) 401-413.

R[obert] H. West, "Barometrical Determinations of Heights in Lebanon," *PEFQS* 28 (1896) 165-168. [Note by C. Clermont-Ganneau, p. 259-260; by C. R. Conder, p. 341]

J. G. O. Tepper, "Remarks on the Deserts of the Holy Land," *PEFQS* 28 (1896) 187-188.

C[laude] R. Conder, "Mediaeval Topography of Palestine," *PEFQS* 29 (1897) 70-71.

George E. Merrill, "The Hilltops of Palestine (Illustrated.)," *BW* 10 (1897) 333-341.

*A. H. Sayce, "Palestine in the Time of Abraham as Seen in the Light of Archaeology," *HR* 33 (1897) 200-205.

A. H. Sayce, "Light from the Tel-el-Amarna Tablets on Palestine before the Exodus," *HR* 33 (1897) 387-392.

*Joseph Offord, "Pre-Mosaic Palestine," *SBAP* 19 (1897) 7-26.

*W. W. Moore, "Israel's Attitude Towards Canaan During the Egyptian Sojourn," *USR* 9 (1897) 188-193.

Shailer Mathews, "In Elijah's Country," *BW* 12 (1898) 162-168.

[William R. Harper], "The Study of Scriptural Geography," *LCR* 17 (1898) 716-719.

Anonymous, "The Geography of Palestine," *LCR* 17 (1898) 738-745. *(Editorial)*

C[laude] R. Conder, "Palestine Exploration," *HR* 38 (1899) 291-299.

Celvin Haupt, "Some Thoughts on the Topography of Palestine," *LCR* 18 (1899) 121-125.

R. L. Stewart, "Recent Researches in the Holy Land," *CFL, N.S.,* 1 (1900) 44-53.

Anonymous, "Latest Explorations in Palestine," *MR* 82 (1900) 973-976.

*James B. Nies, "Excavations in Palestine and what may be expected from them, and some observations made in 1899, during a series of journeys which covered the greater part of Eastern and Western Palestine," *AJA* 5 (1901) 7-8.

*G. Frederick Wright, "Physical Preparation for Israel in Palestine," *BS* 58 (1901) 360-369.

*C. Clermont-Ganneau, "Archaeological and Epigraphic Notes on Palestine. 6. *The Land of Promise, mapped in Mosaic at Madeba*," *PEFQS* 33 (1901) 235-246.

*S. R. Driver, "Jacob's Route from Haran to Schechem," *ET* 13 (1901-02) 457-460.

A. H. Sayce, "Recent Biblical Archaeology. Discoveries in Eastern Palestine," *ET* 13 (1901-02) 467.

R. L. Stewart, "Pre-Joshuan Palestine," *CFL, N.S.*, 6 (1902) 206-215.

C[laude] R. Conder, "Exploration of Eastern Palestine," *HR* 43 (1902) 291-295.

*J. P. Peters, "Palestinian Exploration. *Notes of a Vacation in Palestine in 1902,*" *JBL* 22 (1903) 15-31. [1. Byblos; 2. Baalbek; 3. Sidon; 4. Gerash-Gerasa; 5. Ta'anuk, ancient Ta'anach, on the Plain of Megiddo; 6. Nejeb; 7. Sandahannah; 8. Gezer; 9. Sites for Excavation; 10. Jerusalem; 11. Jebel 'Osha; 12. Palestine Exploration Fund Map]

A. H. Sayce, "Discoveries in Palestine," *ET* 15 (1903-04) 555-558.

A. H. Godbey, "The Front Door of Palestine," *Monist* 14 (1903-04) 516-522.

*Samuel Ives Curtiss, "Researches in Syria and Palestine Conducted in the Summer of 1903," *BW* 23 (1904) 91-103.

*Anonymous, "Excavations in Palestine," *MR* 86 (1904) 976-979.

C[laude] R. Conder, "The Early Notices of Palestine," *PEFQS* 36 (1904) 168-177.

*Lewis Bayles Paton, "The Results of Recent Archæology for the History of Palestine," *HSR* 15 (1904-05) 175-188.

*Hugh Pope, "Recent Excavations of Biblical Sites in Palestine," *DR* 136 (1905) 27-47.

*G. Buchanan Gray, "The 'Steppes of Moab'," *Exp, 6th Ser.*, 11 (1905) 68-76.

Anonymous, "Notes and Comments. Physical Features of the Holy Land," *ICMM* 1 (1905) 193-194.

*George A. Barton, "Palestine before the Coming of Israel," *BW* 28 (1906) 360-373.

Caleb Hauser, "Notes on the Geography of Palestine," *PEFQS* 38 (1906) 143-146. [I. Abel Cheramim; II. Mattanah; III. Almon Diblathaim (Beth Diblathaim); IV. Jahzah (Jahaz, etc.); V. Atharim (Ha-Atharim); VI. El Meshash; VII. Jazer (Jaazer); VIII. Gemmaruis; IX. Ina; X. Gadora; XI. Salton Bataneos; XII. Canothas; XIII. Zanatha]

Caleb Hauser, "Notes on the Geography of Palestine," *PEFQS* 38 (1906) 301-305. [I. Notes on Some of Ptolemy's Renowned Cities of Arabia Petraea, (1) Thana, (2) Cletharo, (3) Necla, (4) Lydia, (5) Anita, (6) Surattha, (7) Mesada; II. Chananea; III. Jazer; IV. Ramoth-Gilead; V. Camon; VI. Zaphon; VII. Gath]

Llewellyn L. Henson, "Researches in Palestine," *RP* 5 (1906) 39-59.

*Anonymous, "Excavations in Palestine," *MR* 89 (1907) 979-982.

Stanley A. Cook, "Ancient Palestine," *PEFQS* 39 (1907) 56-63, 152-157.

Caleb Hauser, "Notes on the Geography of Palestine," *PEFQS* 39 (1907) 284-290. [I. Mahanaim; II. The Wood of Ephraim; III. Seirah and the Mountain of Ephriam; IV. Mount Halak; V. Bayith; VI. Oboth; VII. Avith; VIII. Shicron; IX. Mokhrath of the Moabite Stone; X. Chesulloth on Egyptian Monuments]

J. O. Kinnaman, "The Topography of Palestine," *AAOJ* 30 (1908) 135-140.

Anonymous, "Palestine as a Study. And Professor George Adam Smith as a Specialist," *HR* 56 (1908) 451-453.

*David G. Lyon, "Recent Excavations in Palestine," *HTR* 1 (1908) 70-96.

*Caleb Hauser, "Notes on the Geography of Palestine," *PEFQS* 40 (1908) 60-64. [XI. Nebaloth; XII. Cosmos; XIII. Pentacomia; XIV. Kalkiliash; XV. On the Topography of the Battle of Mount Gilboa; XVI. Shihor-Libnath; XVII. The Land of Tob; XVIII. Asnah; XIX. Cherith; XX. The Rock Oreb, Orbo]

Caleb Hauser, "From Hazeroth to Mount Hor. Notes on the Topography of the Wilderness," *PEFQS* 40 (1908) 125-133.

*Stanley A. Cook, "Palestine Excavations and the History of Israel,"
   Exp, 7th Ser., 8 (1909) 97-114.

G. A. Barton, "Some Problems in Ancient Palestinian Topography,"
   JBL 28 (1909) 26-33.

*Caleb Hauser, "Notes on the Geography of Palestine," *PEFQS* 41
   (1909) 275-280. (Notes by C. R. Conder, *PEFQS* 42 (1910)
   78-79; Reply by Caleb Hauser, *PEFQS* 42 (1910) 286-288)
   [I. *(Untitled);* II. Minnith; III. Abel-Shittim; IV. Aroer (Josh.
   13:25); V. Jokdeam; VI. Mizpah of Moab; VII. Arubboth
   (2 Kgs. 4:10); VIII. Socoh; IX. Eben Ezer; X. Aphek; XI. Shen;
   XII. Beth Car]

*H. R. Hall, "The Discoveries in Crete and their Relation to the
   History of Egypt and Palestine," *SBAP* 31 (1909) 135-148,
   221-238, 280-285, 311-318.

*D. D. Luckenbill,"The Excavations of Palestine," *BW* 35 (1910)
   21-32, 97-106.

Salvatore Minocchi, "Unknown Palestine," *PEFQS* 42 (1910) 186-196.
   (Trans. by Mary Gurney)

*Caleb Hauser, "Notes on Palestinian Geography," *PEFQS* 42 (1910)
   280-286. [1. Beth-Haccerem; 2. Meronoth; 3. Kiriath-Jearim; 4.
   The boundary of Judah and of Benjamin between En-Rogel and
   Kiriath-Jearim; 5. Gibeah]

*Duncan Mackenzie, "Reports from Dr. Duncan Mackenzie," *PEFQS* 43
   (1911) 8-11. [1. Amman; 2. Madeba; 3. Diban; 4. Rabbath Moab;
   5. The Kerak Region; 6. Petra]

George Frederick Wright, "Palestine and its Transformation," *RP* 10
   (1911) 283-292. *(Review)*

*R. A. S. Macalister, "The Topography of Rachel's Tomb," *PEFQS* 44
   (1912) 74-82.

*Camden M. Cobern, "Most Recent Excavations in Palestine," *HR* 67
   (1914) 94-100.

*George L. Robinson, "Recent Excavation and Exploration in Palestine," *HTR* 8 (1915) 525-552. [Jericho; Samaria; Bethshemesh; Ophel; Mt. Zion; The Standard 'Talent' of the Sanctuary; Balata (Shechem?); Carchemish; The Survey of the Negeb; Discoveries by Natives; An Inscribed Mosaic near Mt. Nebo; A Visit to the Cave of Machpelah]

*Paul Haupt, "Semachontis = Jungled Region," *JBL* 34 (1915) 185-186.

*Anonymous, "Excavations in Palestine, 1907-1914," *HR* 71 (1916) 403.

*George L. Robinson, "Where Archaeological Investigation left off in Palestine and Assyria," *AJA* 21 (1917) 84.

Charles Warren, "The Significance of the Geography of Palestine," *JTVI* 49 (1917) 165-192. (Discussion, pp. 192-198)

Albert T. Clay, "Archaeological Research in Palestine. Editorial," *A&A* 7 (1918) 161-162. *(Editorial)*

Anonymous, "Research in Palestine," *HR* 83 (1922) 394.

William F. Albright, "Palestine in the Earliest Historical Period," *JPOS* 2 (1922) 110-138.

*William J. Hinke, "Recent Excavations in Palestine," *AJA* 27 (1923) 66-67.

W[illiam] F[oxwell] Albright, "Some Archaeological and Topographical Results of a Trip Through Palestine," *BASOR* #11 (1923) 3-14. [The Home of Joshua, Zeredah, Jeroboam's Home, A Philistine Military Base, The Nations of Gilgal, The Coasts of Dor, Some Ancient Mounds, From Tabor to the Jordan, A New Royal Canaanite City]

Anonymous, "Archaeological Notes and Comments. The American School in Jerusalem Expedition," *A&A* 17 (1924) 244.

W[illiam] F[oxwell] Albright, "The Archaeological Results of an Expedition to Moab and the Dead Sea," *BASOR* #14 (1924) 2-12. [Archaeological Survey of the Southern Ghor, The Early Sanctuary of Bab ed-Dra', The Cities of the Plain, Shihan and Ader, The Moabite Capital]

W[illiam] F[oxwell] Albright, "Bronze Age Mounds of Northern
Palestine: The Spring Trip of the School in Jerusalem,"
BASOR #19 (1925) 5-19. [From Jerusalem to Samaria by the
Western Hills, The Ancient Cities of Esdraelon, Northeastern
Galilee, Argob and Bashan, The Bronze Age Mounds of the
Jordan Valley]

*Samuel S. Cohon, "Palestine in Jewish Theology," *HUCA Jubilee
Volume* (1925) 171-210.

Anonymous, "The Expedition to Palestine," *MJ* 16 (1925) 200-201.

Amos I. Dushaw, "Palestine: The Land of Many Sacred Sites," *OC* 39
(1925) 65-71.

*Stanley A. Cook, "Recent Excavations in Palestine," *ET* 37 (1925-26)
487-492.

*J. Walter Johnshoy, "Studies in Biblical Archaeology," *TTM* 9
(1925-26) 116-135. [Palestine, pp. 121-127]

M. B. Hanrahan, "Notes on Palestine for Teachers," *ACR* 3 (1926)
25-33, 134-145, 316-325; 4 (1927) 210-219.

William Foxwell Albright and R. P. Dougherty, "From Jerusalem to
Baghdad down the Euphrates. I. From Jerusalem to Aleppo,"
BASOR #21 (1926) 1-10. [Present Excavations in Northern
Palestine; Archaeological Remains in Southern Phoenicia; The
Irrigation Culture of Northern Phoenicia; Kadesh on the Orontes
and Mishrifeh; Bronze age Mounds near Aleppo]

*W[illiam] F[oxwell] Albright, "The Topography of the Tribe of
Issachar," *ZAW* 44 (1926) 225-236.

Alexis Mallon, "Changes in Palestine," *ACR* 4 (1927) 111-117.

*Anonymous, "Sir Flinders Petrie's Excavations in Palestine,"
Antiq 1 (1927) 348-351.

J. W. Jack, "New Light on Palestine. c. 2000 B.C.," *ET* 39 (1927-28)
329-331.

Anonymous,"New Discoveries in Palestine," *A&A* 27(1929)119-123.

Nelson Glueck, "Recent Archaeological Work in Palestine," *YCCAR* 39 (1929) 265-292. {(Discussion by: Sheldon Blank, pp. 293-296; [Jacob] Singer, p. 296; [Julian] Morgenstern, pp. 296-299; [Ephriam] Frisch, pp. 299-300; [Joseph] Silverman, pp. 300-302; [Edward N.] Calisch, pp. 302-303) (Reply by Nelson Glueck, pp. 303-304)}

P[atrick] P. McKenna, "The Land of Mystery and Symbol," *IER, 5th Ser.*, 36 (1930) 123-135, 346-362. *[Palestine]*

Gerald M. FitzGerald, "Some Stone Age Sites Recently Investigated," *PEFQS* 62 (1930) 85-90.

W[illiam] F[oxwell] Albright, "Recent Progress in the Late Prehistory of Palestine," *BASOR* #42 (1931) 13-15.

P[atrick] P. McKenna, "Palestine: A Land of Invasion and Ruins," *IER, 5th Ser.*, 38 (1931) 591-601.

*Millar Burrows, "Palestinian and Syrian Archaeology in 1931," *AJA* 36 (1932) 64-73 [I. Palestine, pp. 64-70]

W[illiam] F[oxwell] Albright, "The Chalcolithic Age in Palestine," *BASOR* #48 (1932) 10-13.

*Millar Burrows, "Palestinian and Syrian Archaeology in 1931," *AJA* 36 (1932) 64-73. [I. Palestine, pp. 64-70]

A. T. Olmstead, "The Land and Its Past," *OC* 46 (1932) 441-484. *[Palestine]*

*Charles Close, "Note on the Map of the Principal Excavated Sites of Palestine," *PEFQS* 64 (1932) 220.

*‡L. A. Mayer and M. Avi-Yonah, "Concise Bibliography of Excavations in Palestine," *QDAP* 1 (1932) 86-94, 139-149, 163-199.

*Nelson Glueck, "Palestinian and Syrian Archaeology in 1932," *AJA* 37 (1933) 160-172.

Millar Burrows, "Biblical Background in Palestine," *RL* 2 (1933) 212-224.

*W[illiam] F[oxwell] Albright, "Excavations During 1933 in Palestine, Transjordan, and Syria," *AJA* 38 (1934) 191-199.

Dorothy A. E. Garrod, "The Stone Age of Palestine," *Antiq* 8 (1934) 133-150.

*Nelson Glueck, "Explorations in Eastern Palestine and the Negeb," *BASOR* #55 (1934) 3-21.

**S. Yeivin, "A New Egyptian Scource for the History of Palestine and Syria," *JPOS* 14 (1934) 194-239.

*‡Anonymous, "Excavations in Palestine, 1932-3," *QDAP* 3 (1934) 173-187. [Bibliography, pp. 185-187]

*W[illiam] F[oxwell] Albright, "A Summary of Archaeological Research During 1934 in Palestine, Transjordan, and Syria," *AJA* 39 (1935) 137-148.

James L. Kelso, "Locating and Excavating Ancient Palestinian Cities," *BS* 92 (1935) 170-178.

W[illiam] F[oxwell] Albright, "Presidential Address. Palestine in the Earliest Historical Period," *JPOS* 15 (1935) 193-234.

George Adam Smith, "Abel's Geography of Palestine," *PEFQS* 67 (1935) 36-38. *(Review)*

*‡Anonymous, "Excavations in Palestine, 1933-4," *QDAP* 4 (1935) 194-213. [Bibliography, pp. 211-213]

*W[illiam] F[oxwell] Albright, "Archaeological Explorations and Excavation in Palestine and Syria, 1935," *AJA* 40 (1936) 154-167.

*‡Anonymous, "Excavations in Palestine, 1934-5," *QDAP* 5 (1936) 194-212. [Bibliography, pp. 211-212]

*W. F. Albright and Nelson Glueck, "Archaeological Exploration and Excavation in Palestine, Transjordan, and Syria during 1936," *AJA* 41 (1937) 146-153.

G. Ernest Wright, "Palestine in the Chalcolithic Age," *BASOR* #66 (1937) 21-25.

*W. F. Albright, "Further Light on the History of Israel from Lachish and Megiddo," *BASOR* #68 (1937) 22-26.

F. J. Salmon, "The Modern Geography of Palestine," *PEQ* 69 (1937) 33-42.

*P[atrick] P. McKenna, "The Hill Country of Gad," *IER, 5th Ser.,* 50 (1937) 164-173.

*Nelson Glueck, "Archaeological Exploration and Excavation in Palestine, Transjordan, and Syria during 1937," *AJA* 42 (1938) 165-176.

*‡Anonymous, "Excavations in Palestine, 1935-6," *QDAP* 6 (1938) 212-229. [Bibliography, pp. 227-229]

*M. Stekelis, L. Picard, Miss D. M. A. Bate, P. Solomonica, E. Rosenau, Gordon Loud, Miss A. M. Murray, J. Ellis, J. A. Saunders, Nelson Glueck, Lankester Harding, Miss E. W. Gardner, O. Püttrich-Reignard, B[enjamin] Maisler, J. L. Starkey, "Excavations in Palestine and Trans-Jordan, 1936-7," *QDAP* 7 (1938) 45-55. {Jisr Banāt Ya'qūb; Megiddo; Petra; Khirbet et Tannūr; Bethlehem; Khirbet Minya; esh Sheikh Ibreik; Tell ed Duweir; Other Discoveries; *1st July, 1936 to 30th June, 1937,* pp. 56-60. [Corrigendum, to p. 57: *QDAP* 8 (1939) p. 176]}

*‡Anonymous, "Bibliography of Excavations in Palestine and Trans-Jordan, 1936-7," *QDAP* 7 (1938) 61-62.

*D. Aschbel/*sic*/, "The Climate of the Judaean Desert," *BIES* 6 (1938-39) #2, I-II.

*Z. Vilnai, "The Topography of Palestine in the Prophecies of Micah," *BIES* 6 (1938-39) #3, II-III.

*Nelson Glueck, "Archaeological Exploration and Excavation in Palestine, Transjordan and Syria during 1938," *AJA* 43 (1939) 146-157.

Kathleen M. Kenyon, "Archaeology in Palestine," *Antiq* 13 (1939) 171-177.

*E. L. Sukenik, T. J. Colin Baly, O. Püttrich-Reignard, N[elson] Glueck, Gordon Loud, Miss A. M. Murray, E. Mackay, J. L. Starkey, C. H. Inge, P. R. Köppel, J. Waechter, P. L. O. Guy, R. P. Bellermino Bagatti, "Excavations in Palestine and Trans-Jordan, 1937-8," *QDAP* 8 (1939) 157-172. ['Affūle; 'Auja el Ḥafīr; Isbeiṭa; Khalasa; Khirbet Minya; Khirbet et Tannūr; Ma'in; Megiddo; Tell el 'Ajjūl; Tell ed Duweir; Tell el Kheleife; Tell esh Shūhi (Tell el Kudādi); Tuleilāt Ghassūl; Wādi Dhobai; Archaeological Survey of Palestine; 'Ain Kārim; Other Discoveries: *I July 1937 to 30 June 1938,* pp. 173-176]

*‡Anonymous, "Bibliography of Excavations in Palestine and Trans-Jordan, 1937-38," *QDAP* 8 (1939) 177-178.

*C. C. McCown, "Two Years' Achievements in Palestinian Archaeology," *RL* 8 1939) 97-108. [Paleontology and Prehistory; Lachish; History of the Alphabet; Megiddo; The Egyptian Border; Jerusalem; Galilee; Umaiyad Palaces; Transjordan; The Byzantine Period]

*B[enjamin] Maisler, "Topographical Studies: 1. 'From Geba to Beersheba'," *BIES* 8 (1940-41) #1, II.

S. Yeivin, "Topographic Notes (annotations to S. Klein, *The Land of Judah*)," *BIES* 8 (1940-41) #2, II. [1. ᾿Αζώτου ὄρους; 2. The Mount of Olives]

George Ricker Berry, "Some Facts about Palestine," *CQ* 18 (1941) 38-46.

*J. W. Jack, "Recent Biblical Archaeology," *ET* 53 (1941-42) 208-212. [Patriarchal Palestine, pp. 209-210]

*M[oshe] Stekelis, "Preliminary Report on Soundings in Prehistoric Caves in Palestine," *BASOR* #86 (1942) 2-10. [Mughâhat al-Waṭat; Mughâret an-Nuqṭah; Mughâret Wâdī Fallâḥ; Mughâret Abū Uṣba'; 'Irâq al-Barûd]

*O. Püttrich-Reignard, Gordon Loud, B[enjamin] Maisler, Nelson Glueck, P. P. Köppel, Wolfgang Darsow, and Frau Dr. Püttrich, "Excavations in Palestine and Trans-Jordan, 1938-9," *QDAP* 9 (1942) 207-216.

*‡Anonymous, "Bibliography of Excavations in Palestine and Trans-Jordan, 1938-9," *QDAP* 9 (1942) 216-218.

I. Press, "Topographical Essays," *BIES* 10 (1942-44)   #2/3, IV.

*E. L. Sukenik, B[enjamin] Maisler, N[elson] Glueck, "Excavations in Palestine and Trans-Jordan, 1939-40," *QDAP* 10 (1944) 195-200. [Jerusalem, The Third Wall; Kefar Shemaryahu; Esh Sheikh Ibreik; Tell Jerishe; Tell el Kheleife; Other Discoveries: *1 July 1938 to 30 June 1940*, pp. 201-207]

*‡Anonymous, "Bibliography of Excavations in Palestine and Trans-Jordan, 1939-40," *QDAP* 10 (1944) 208-209.

*N. Shalem, "The Desert and the Sown in Judea," *Kobez* 4 (1945) X.

*Alexandre Lannes, Sylvester J. Saller, M. Stekelis, "Excavations in Palestine and Trans-Jordan, 1940-1," *QDAP* 11 (1945) 113-118. [Abu Ghōsh (Qaryat el 'Inab; 'Ain Kārim; Church of St. John the Baptist; Prehistoric caves; Tell esh Shūni, near Tel Aviv]

*‡Anonymous, "Bibliography of Excavations in Palestine and Trans-Jordan, 1940-2," *QDAP* 11 (1945) 119-120.

D. Amiran (Kallner), "The Western Border of the Hebron Mountains," *BIES* 14 (1947-48)   #3/4, III-IV.

R[oland] de Vaux, "Excavations in Palestine, 1943-6," *QDAP* 13 (1948) 166-171. ['Ein el Ma'mudiya and Khirbet ed Deir; Tell el Far'a; Kh. Karak; The Citadel, Jerusalem]

*‡Anonymous, "Bibliography of Excavations in Palestine and Trans-Jordan, 1945-6," *QDAP* 13 (1948) 172.

*Burr C. Brundage, "The Ancient Near East as History," *AmHR* 54 (1948-49) 530-547.

*Kathleen M. Kenyon, "Palestinian Excavations," *Antiq* 24 (1950) 196-200.

M. Rim, "Sand and Soil in the Coastal Plain of Israel. A Study in the Rate of Accumulation," *IEJ* 1 (1950-51) 33-48.

*D. H. Kallner-Amiran, "Geomorphology of the Central Negev Highlands," *IEJ* 1 (1950-51) 107-120.

*Nelson Glueck, "Go, View the Land," *BASOR* #122 (1951) 14-17.

S. Yeivin, "Archaeological News *Near East (Supplement)* Israel, September 1950-October 1951," *AJA* 56 (1952) 141-43.

Y[ohanan] Aharoni and Ruth Amiran, "Researches of the Circle for Historical Geography," *BIES* 17 (1952-53) #1/2, III. [1) Tell en-Najîle; 2) Tell esh-Shar'îe; 3) Tell Abu Hureira; 4) Tell Jemmeh and Tell Far'ah; 5) Kh. Futies; 6) Bir Abu Reqayiq]

Anonymous, "Other Discoveries," *ADAJ* 2 (1953) 89-90. [Um Qeis; Ain Feshkha; Wady el Nar; Howara, Nablus District; Sebastia (Samaria); Bethany]

M. Avi-Yanoh, "Archaeology in Israel," *Antiq* 27 (1953) 97-100.

*Nelson Glueck, "Explorations in Western Palestine," *BASOR* #131 (1953) 6-15.

J. Leibovitch, "Archaeological Activities in Israel," *CNI* 4 (1953) #2/3, 27-31; 5 (1954) #1/2, 24-28; 6 (1955) #1/2, 24-28.

W. C. Lowdermilk, N. Gil, and Z. Rosenzaft, "An Inventory of the Land of Israel," *IEJ* 3 (1953) 162-177.

*Benjamin Maisler (Mazar), "Canaan on the Threshold of the Age of the Patriarchs," *EI* 3 (1954) I-II.

S. Yeivin, "Archaeology in Israel (November 1951-January 1953)," *AJA* 59 (1955) 163-167.

J. Leibovitch [Leibowitz], "Archaeological Activities in Israel, in 1955," *CNI* 6 (1955) #3/4, 31-37.

*B. S. J. Isserlin, "Ancient Forests in Palestine: Some Archaeological Indications," *PEQ* 87 (1955) 87-88.

Y. Karmon, "Geographical Aspects in the History of the Coastal Plain of Israel," *IEJ* 6 (1956) 33-50.

*Z. Kallai-Kleinmann, "Notes on the Topography of Benjamin," *IEJ* 6 (1956) 180-187.

M. Harel, "Stream Piracy in Israel," *BIES* 21 (1957) #3/4, IV.

Anonymous, "Further Explorations in Southern Israel," *AT* 1 (1956-57) #3, 15.

*S. Yeivin, "The Land of Israel and the Birth of Civilization in the Near East," *A&S* 2 (1957) #2/3, 111-120.

M. Avi-Yonah, "Archaeological Activities in Israel in 1956," *CNI* 8 (1957) #1/2, 24-26.

S. Yeivin, "A Year's Work in Israel," *Arch* 11 (1958) 239-245.

*Dov Nir, "The Hydrography of Mount Carmel," *BIES* 22 (1958) #1/2, VI-VII.

*J. Leibovitz, "Archaeological Finds and Activities in Israel, 1957-1958," *CNI* 9 (1958) #1/2, 21-29. [I. The Coastal Region: Shavei Zion; Acre (The Crypt of St. John); Haifa; Benyamina; Caesarea; Ashkelon; Erez; II. The Inland Region: Huqoq; Alumoth (Khirbet Sheikh 'Ali); Hazorea; Kfar Baruch; Tirat Zvi; Beth She'an; Mezer; Azor; Jerusalem; Ajjour; Gath, Areas A, G, & D; Hourvat Ma'on (Nirim)]

*Ruth Amiran, "Palestine, Syria and Cyprus in the MB I Period," *EI* 5 (1958) 84*.

*Peter J. Parr, "Palestine and Anatolia: A Further Note," *ULBIA* 1 (1958) 21-23.

Jean Perrot, "The Dawn of History in Southern Palestine," *Arch* 12 (1959) 8-15.

‡Milka Casutto-Salzmann, "Selected Bibliography: Publications on Archaeological Excavations and Surveys in Israel 1948-1958," *'Atiqot* 2 (1959) 165-183.

*Avraham Biran, "Archaeological Activities in Israel 1958-1959," *CNI* 10 (1959) #1/2, 21-32. [Tell Gath (Tell Sheikh Ahmed el Areini), Area A, Area D, Area F, Area I; Hazor; Safad and Upper Galilee; The Survey of the Negev; Restoration of Negev Cities; Excavation at Karbi by M. W. Prausnitz on behalf of the Department of Antiquities; Akhziv; Azor, Area B, Area C; Makmish; Jaffa; Excavations at Ruhama, 1958; Two Byzantine Churches]

*Y. Karmon, "Geographical Conditions in the Sharon Plain and Their Impact on its Settlement," *SGEI* #1 (1959) I-III.

*D. Sharon, "Physiographic Aspects of the Tuleilat el-'Enab," *SGEI* #1 (1959) V.

M. Harel, "The Canyons of Israel," *BIES* 24 (1959-60) #4, IV.

*Avraham Biran, "Archaeological Activities in Israel, 1959-1960," *CNI* 11 (1960) #2, 16-20. [Bar Kochba Period; 'Avdat; Tel "Gath"]

D. Nir and A. Yair, "Geomorphological Studies in the Safed Area," *SGEI* #2, (1960) I.

M. Harel, "The Canyons of Israel," *SGEI* #2 (1960) IV.

‡Milka Casutto-Salzmann, "Selected Bibliography: Publications on Archaeological Excavations and Surveys in Israel 1959-1960," *'Atiqot* 3 (1961) 188-198.

*Avraham Biran, "Archaeological Activities in Israel, 1960/1961," *CNI* 12 (1961) #1, 15-21. [The Dead Sea Caves; Cave of the Pool; The Cave of Dread; Cave of the Treasure; Cave of the Letters; Ein Gedi]

*Avraham Biran, "Archaeological Activities in Israel, 1960/1961," *CNI* 12 (1961) #2, 13-18. [Ramat Rahel; Caesarea; Antiochus Inscription in the Emek; Hebrew Documents; Azor; Earliest Remains]

D. Safra, "The Abrasion Platform and the Cliff of the Southern Carmel Coast," *BIES* 26 (1962) #1/2 I-II.

*Z. Ron, "The Morphographic Configuration of the Western Strip of the Southern Carmel Coast," *BIES* 26 (1962) #1/2, II.

D. Sharon, "On the Hamada in Israel," *BIES* 26 (1962) #1/2, VI-VII.

*Avraham Biran, "Archaeological Activities in Israel, 1961/62," *CNI* 13 (1962) #1, 16-22. [Part I: Neanderthal Man; Eynan (Ein Mallaha); Nahal Ha-B'sor; Missione Archaeologica Italiana a Cesarea; Finnish Expedition at Kafr Kama; Beth She'an Theatre; Davidic and Solomonic City at Ein Gev]

*Avraham Biran, "Archaeological Activities in Israel, 1961/62: Part II," *CNI* 13 (1962) #2, 14-18. [Early Synagogue at Hamat —Tiberias; Kfar Gil'adi Mausoleum; Hellenistic and Middle Bronze Burials; High school students dig at Ramat Rahel; Work at Jaffa Continues; The Fifth Season at Tell "Gath"; The Mausoleum of Yif'at and Rosh Ha-Ayin; Agricultural Fortress at Tirat Yehuda]

*Z. Ron, "The Morphographic Configuration of the Western Strip of the Southern Carmel Coast," *SGEI* #3 (1962) II.

D. Sharon, "On the Hamada in Israel," *SGEI* #3 (1962) VI-VII.

*William F. Albright, "Recent Advances in Palestinian Archaeology," *Exped* 5 (1962-63) #1, 4-9.

Sylvester J. Saller, "Archaeological Activitiy in the Holy Land in 1962/3," *SBFLA* 13 (1962-63) 323-328. [Jerusalem; Bethlehem and Its Surroudings; Nazareth in Galilee; The Nebo Region; In the Madaba Region; Surface Explorations; The Friends of Archaeology; Government Activity]

Douglas S. Waterhouse, "A Land Flowing with Milk and Honey," *AUSS* 1 (1963) 152-166.

Paul W. Lapp, "Palestine: Known but Mostly Unknown," *BA* 26 (1963) 121-134.

*Avraham Biran, "Archaeological Activities 1962/3," *CNI* 14 (1963) #1, 14-21. [Neolithic Site Near Kfaf Gilada; Nazareth; Chorazin; Hammath-Tiberias; H. Minha (Munhata);The Synagogue of Beit She'an; Beit She'an Theatre; Tel Amal; Ramat Rahel]

*Avraham Biran, "Archaeological Activities 1962/3 (Part II),"
    CNI 14 (1963) #2, 11-16. [Tel Bazul; Yas'ur; Caesarea Synagogue;
    Ashdod; Tel Arad; Ein Gedi; 'Jerusalem' Cave]

A[vraham] Biran, "Archaeological Activities 1963," *CNI* 15 (1964)
    #2/3, 19-32.

A[vraham] Biran, "Archaeological Activities 1964," *CNI* 16 (1965)
    #3, 13-17; #4, 15-20.

A[nson] F. Rainey, "Archaeological News from Israel: Old Testament,"
    JASA 16 (1964) 119-120. [Arad; Ashdod; Achzib; Metsad; Gozal]

Immanuel Ben-Dor, "Recent Archaeological Work in Israel," *AJA* 69
    (1965) 167.

Norman Bentwich, "One Hundred Years of Palestine Archaeology,"
    ContR 206 (1965) 188-191.

A[vraham] Biran, "Archaeological Activities 1965," *CNI* 17 (1966)
    #1, 16-20; #2/3, 22-26. [The Israel Museum; The Archaeological
    Survey; Major Excavations: Masada, Ein Gedi, Arad, Mamshit,
    Ashdod, Gezer; The Smaller Expeditions]

*A[vraham] Biran, "Archaeological Activities 1966," *CNI* 18 (1967)
    #1/2, 24-43 [Tel Dan; Kokhav Hayarden; Horvat Minha;
    Megiddo; Jelemie; Acre; Shikmona; Tel Zeror; Gezer; Lachish;
    Mamshit (Kurnub); Mezad Yaroham; Arad; Prehistoric
    Researches; The Smaller Expeditions and Finds; Tel Barom;
    Tel Kalil; Kibbutz Shamir; Sde Nehemiah; Upper Galilee; Gil-Am;
    Haifa; In the Sharon Area; Jerusaelm; Tel Aviv Area; Ramla;
    Yavne; Ashdod Yam; Ashkelon; Beersheba; Restoration and
    Preservation; Archaeological Survey of Israel]

*A[vraham] Biran, "Archaeological Activities 1967," *CNI* 19 (1968)
    #3/4, 29-48. [The Archaeological Survey of Golan, Samaria,
    Judaea and Sinai; Jerusalem; Tel Dan; Beit Yerah; Ubeidiyeh;
    Horvat Minha (Munhata); Kokhav Hayarden; Tel Amal; Megiddo;
    Me'arat Qedumim; Acre; Shikmona; Tel Megadim; Gezer; Abu
    Ghosh; Gaza; Erez; Beersheba; Arad; Tel Malhata; Mamshit
    (Kurnub); Miscellaneous; Restoration and Preservation]

B[enjamin] Mazar, "The Middle Bronze Age in Palestine," *EI* 8 (1967)
    74*-75*.

*Menaḥem Stern, "The Description of Palestine by Pliny the Elder and the Administrative Division of Judea at the End of the Period of the Second Temple," *Tarbiz* 37 (1967-68) #3, I.

Eugene A. LaVerdiere, "Palestine: The Archaeological Scene," *BibT* #37 (1968) 2577-2584.

B[enjamin] Mazar, "The Middle Bronze Age in Palestine," *IEJ* 18 (1968) 65-97.

‡Milka Cassuto-Salzmann, "Selected Bibliography. Publications on Archaeological Excavations and Surveys in Israel January 1964 —June 1967," *'Atiqot* 8 (1969) Supplement, 1-29, *[paged separately from main entires]*

*A[vraham] Biran, "Archaeological Activities 1968," *CNI* 20 (1969) #3/4, 33-55 [Jerusalem; Tel Dan; Tel Anafa; Hazor; Capernaum; 'En Ha-Shiv'a (Et-Tabgha); Nahariya; Shiqmona; Tel Qedesh; Tel Ta'anach; Tel Megadim; Harvat Tafat; Samaria; Shechem; Tell er-Ras (Mount Gerizim); Khirbet et-Tananir; Ai (Et-Tell); Abu Ghosh; Gezer; Lachish; Tell Aitun; Yavne Yam; Ashdod; Beersheba; Khalit el-Ful; The Smaller Excavations and Accidental Finds; Underwater Archaeology; Preservation and Restoration]

Saul S. Weinberg, "Post-Exilic Palestine. An Archaeological Report," *PIASH* 4 (1969-70) 78-97.

§165   *2.5.5.6.1 Geographical and Archaeological Surveys of Palestine*

*Henry M. Canfield, "Notes on a Surveying Trip from the Phenician *[sic]* Coast to the Euphrates River," *JAOS* 9 (1871) lxv.

George Groves, "Letters on the Survey. I. From Mr. George Groves," *PEFQS* 4 (1872) 1-3.

R. F. Burton, "Letters on the Survey. II. From Captain R. F. Burton," *PEFQS* 4 (1872) 305.

F. W. Holland, "Letters on the Survey. III. From the Rev. F. W. Holland," *PEFQS* 4 (1872) 6-7.

C[harles] F. Tyrwhitt Drake, "Letters on the Survey. Letters from Mr. C. F. Tyrwhitt Drake," *PEFQS* 4 (1872) 7-11.

C[harles] F. Tyrwhitt Drake, "Mr. Tyrwhitt Drake's Reports. I," *PEFQS* 4 (1872) 36-42. [Hadad; Jehud; Bene Berak; Gezer]

*C[harles] F. Tyrwhitt Drake, "Mr. Tyrwhitt Drake's Reports. II," *PEFQS* 4 (1872) 43-47. [The Shephelah]

C[harles] F. Tyrwhitt Drake, "The Survey," *PEFQS* 4 (1872) 77-92.

*Claude R. Conder, "The Survey of Palestine," *PEFQS* 4 (1872) 153-173. [Parts I. & II. *(Untitled)*; III. On the Exploration of Jerusalem—the Second Wall; IV. The Progress of the Survey; V. The Country round Samaria; VI. Rock Indications at Jerusalem]

C[harles] F. Tyrwhitt Drake, "The Survey of Palestine. Mr. Tyrwhitt Drake's Reports," *PEFQS* 4 (1872) 174-193; 5 (1873) 28-31, 55-65; 5 (1873) 99-111.

*Claude R. Conder, "The Survey of Palestine. Lieut. Claude R. Conder's Reports," *PEFQS* 5 (1873) 3-27. [VII. The Plain of Esdraelon; VIII. Progress of the Survey; IX. Explorations in Jerusalem; X. Rock-cut Tombs]

Claude R. Conder, "The Survey of Palestine. Lieut. Claude R. Conder's Reports," *PEFQS* 5 (1873) 43-55. [XI. Winter Work]

Claude R. Conder, "The Survey of Palestine. Lieut. Claude R. Conder's Reports," *PEFQS* 5 (1873) 83-99. [XII. The South Side of Carmel; XIII. Jerusaelm and El Midyeh]

*Claude R. Conder, "The Survey of Palestine. Lieut. Claude R. Conder's Reports," *PEFQS* 5 (1873) 137-154. [XIV. Belad el Jemain Tani beni Sab—Unexplored Country; XV. Jerusalem Topography]

Thomas Chaplin, "The Survey of Palestine. Letters from Dr. Chaplin," *PEFQS* 5 (1873) 155-157.

*C. Clermont-Ganneau, "Letters from M. Clermont-Ganneau," *PEFQS* 6 (1874) 3-10.

Claude R. Conder, "The Survey of Palestine. Lieut. Claude R. Conder's Reports," *PEFQS* 6 (1874) 11-24. [Parts XVI. & XVII. *(Untitled)*]

Charles F. Tyrwhitt Drake, "The Survey of Palestine. Mr. Tyrwhitt Drake's Reports," *PEFQS* 6 (1874) 24-29, 64-79, 187-190; 7 (1875) 27-34.

Claude R. Conder, "The Survey of Palestine. Lieut. Claude R. Conder's Reports," *PEFQS* 6 (1874) 35-64. [XVIII. Gilgal and the Plains of Jericho; XIX. Excursions from Bludan; XX. Gezer, Modin, Gibeah, and Ai]

C. Clermont-Ganneau, "The Jerusalem Researches. Letters from M. Clermont-Ganneau," *PEFQS* 6 (1874) 80-111, 135-178; 261-280.

Claude R. Conder, "The Survey of Palestine. Lieut. Claude R. Conder's Reports," *PEFQS* 6 (1874) 178-187. [Part XXI. *(Untitled)*]

Claude R. Conder, "The Survey of Palestine. A Paper Read before the British Association," *PEFQS* 6 (1874) 248-261.

Claude R. Conder, "The Survey of Palestine. Lieut. Claude R. Conder's Reports," *PEFQS* 7 (1875) 5-27. [Parts XXII. -XXIV *(Untitled)*]

Claude R. Conder, "The Survey of Palestine. Lieut. Claude R. Conder's Reports," *PEFQS* 7 (1875) 63-94. [XXV. Retrospect of the Principal Results of the Survey Work in 1874; XXVI. The Hill Country of Judah—Fifth Campaign; XXVII. The Site of Bethabara; XXVIII. The Survey of Tell Jezer; XXIX. The Muristan; XXX. The Rock Scrap of Zion; XXXI. Mediæval Topography of Palestine]

*Claude R. Conder, "The Survey of Palestine. Lieut. Claude R. Conder's Reports," *PEFQS* 7 (1875) 125-168. [XXXII. The Survey of the Dead Sea Desert, and a Visit to Masada; XXXIII. The Shephalah and Plain of Judah, Beit Jibrin, Gath, Adullam, and Libnah; XXXIV. Ascalon, Ashdod; XXXV. Gaza, Gerar, and Mekkedah]

Claude R. Conder, "The Survey of Palestine. Retrospect for 1875," *PEFQS* 7 (1875) 188-190.

*Claude R. Conder, "Proposed Tests for the Survey," *PEFQS* 8 (1876) 66-73. [Enam; Anuath; Bethsarisa; Bezek; Netopha; Garob; Cozeba; Kefr Aziz; Yajur; Choba; Ceperaria; Betocenea; Fathoura; Salim; Betariph; Hasta; Asor; Betheked] *[Proposed Identifications of Various Towns & Cities]*

H. H. Kitchener, "Lieutenant Kitchener's Reports," *PEFQS* 9 (1877) 70-72, 116-125, 165-178.

H. H. Kitchener, "Journal of the Survey," *PEFQS* 9 (1877) 113-116, 162-164; 10 (1878) 8-15, 62-67.

Claude R. Conder, "The Nomenclature of the Survey," *PEFQS* 9 (1877) 144-148.

W. Hepworth Dixon and Pasha Musurus, "Completion of the Survey," *PEFQS* 10 (1878) 5-8.

H. H. Kitchener, "Survey of Galilee," *PEFQS* 10 (1878) 159-174.

Anonymous, "The Survey of Western Palestine," *PEFQS* 12 (1880) 200-206.

*Charles Warren, "Limits of Error in Latitudes and Longitudes of Places Obtained During the Reconnaissances Made in Palestine," *PEFQS* 12 (1880) 243-246.

Walter Besant, "New Survey of Eastern Palestine," *PEFQS* 13 (1881) 26-33.

*Anonymous, "On Some of the Gains to Biblical Archaeology due to the New Survey," *PEFQS* 13 (1881) 34-49.

‡Anonymous, "Index of Lieut. Conder's Identifications," *PEFQS* 13 (1881) 49-56.

*C[laude] R. Conder, " Lieut. Conder's Reports," *PEFQS* 13 (1881) 158-208, 247-281. [I. Baalbek; Kamu'a el Hirmil; Kadesh; Appendix, Homs, Kalat el Hosn, Tripoli, Marina; II. The Ancient Site of Tyre; The Egyptian Harbour; The Temple of Melkath, Palae Tyrus; III. From Beyrout to Jerusalem; The Road; Khurbert Umm el' Amud; Nakurah; Meselieh; Jacob's Well; En Tappuah; Jufna; Er Ram; Jett; Jerusalem; Siloam; IV. Nablus; Jerusalem; The Mountain of the Scape Goat; V. The Land of Benjamin; VI. Kirjath Jearim; VII. *The Haram, Aceldama, Beth Haccerem, Jerusalem, Emmaus, Muristan;* VIII. Mount Nebo]

C[laude] R. Conder, "Lieut. Conder's Report. No. IX," *PEFQS* 14 (1882) 7-15. [Heshbon and its Cromlechs; Summary of the First Survey Campaign]

*C[laude] R. Conder, "Captain Conder's Reports," *PEFQS* 14 (1882) 69-112. [X. Bamoth Baal and Baal Peor; XI. On Some Arab Folk-lore Tales; XII. 'Amman and 'Arak el Emir]

C[laude] R. Conder, "Notes on Mr. Trelawney Saunders's Introduction," *PEFQS* 14 (1882) 149-154. *[Survey]*

C[laude] R. Conder, "Address by Captain Conder," *PEFQS* 14 (1882) 249-257.

Anonymous, "Palestine Exploration," *ONTS* 2 (1882-83) 116-117.

*[Trelawney Saunders], "The Recent Survey of Western Palestine and its Bearing on the Bible," *JTVI* 17 (1883-84) 15-28. [Remarks by H. A. Stern, p. 29; H. D. Grant, p. 30; A. S. Ayrton, pp. 30-31; S. A. Crowther, p. 31; the Earl of Shaftesbury, pp. 31-32]

A. Socin, "The Survey of Western Palestine," *Exp, 3rd Ser.,* 2 (1885) 241-262.

C[laude] R. Conder, "The English Explorations in Palestine. A Reply to Professor Socin," *Exp, 3rd Ser.,* 3 (1886) 321-335.

*W. F. Birch, "Notes by Rev. W. F. Birch," *PEFQS* 18 (1886) 26-32. [II. Professor Socin's Criticisms, pp. 31-32]

Claude R. Conder, "Captain Conder's Reply to Professor Socin *(From the 'Expositor' of May,* 1886.)," *PEFQS* 18 (1886) 137-142.

C[laude] R. Conder, "Notes by Major Conder, D. C. L., R. E. V. Notes on Nomenclature," *PEFQS* 21 (1889) 146-147.

Putnam Cady, "Exploration of the Wady Mojib from the Dead Sea," *PEFQS* 33 (1901) 44-48 [Note by C. W. Wilson, p. 49]

*John P. Peters, "Palestinian Exploration. *Notes of a Vacation in Palestine in 1902.,*" *JBL* 22 (1903) 15-31. [9. Sites for Excavation, pp. 24-27]

*T. H. Weir, A Survey of Recent Archaeology in Relation to Palestine," *RTP* 8 (1912-13) 1-13.

*S. F. Newcombe, "The Survey of Sinai and South Palestine," *PEFQS* 46 (1914) 128-133.

Arthur Sutton, "Ruined cities of Palestine, east and west of Jordan," *SIR* (1923) 509-518.

*W[illiam] F[oxwell] Albright, "The Archaeological Results of an Expedition to Moab and the Dead Sea," *BASOR* #14 (1924) 2-12. [Archaeological Survey of the Southern Ghor, The Early Sanctuary of Bab ed-Dra', The Cities of the Plain, Shihan and Ader, The Moabite Capital]

*W[illiam] F[oxwell] Albright, "Bronze Age Mounds of Northern Palestine: The Spring Trip of the School in Jerusalem," *BASOR* #19 (1925) 5-19. [From Jerusalem to Samaria by the Western Hills, The Ancient Cities of Esdraelon, Northeastern Galilee, Argob and Bashan, The Bronze Age Mounds of the Jordan Valley]

*Chester C. McCown, "Palestinian Archaeology in 1929," *BASOR* #37 (1930) 2-20. [Tell el-Fâri'; Megiddo; Tell en-Nasbeh; 'Ain Shems; Seilûn; Jerash; Beth Alpha; Monastic Research; Prehistory — Mughâret el-Wâd, Varia]

Charles Close, "The Large Scale Survey of Palestine," *PEFQS* 62 (1930) 162-163.

*Chester C. McCown, "Palestinian Archaeology in 1930," *BASOR* #41 (1931) 2-18. [Tell el-Fâr'ah and Tell el-'Ajjûl; Tell Beit Mirsim; 'Ain Shems; Megiddo; Beisân; Jericho; Transjordan; Petra; 'Ammân; Jerash; Teleilât el-Ghassûl; Prehistory; Maghâret et-Wâd; El-'Aḍeimeh; The Kerâzeh Dolmen Field; Mediaeval Castles; Varia]

*Millar Burrows, "Palestinian and Syrian Archaeology in 1931," *BASOR* #45 (1932) 20-32. [I. Palestine, pp. 20-28]

*Nelson Glueck, "Palestinian and Syrian Archaeology in 1932," *AJA* 39 (1933) 160-172.

*Nelson Glueck, "Explorations in Eastern Palestine and the Negeb," *BASOR* #55 (1934) 3-21.

*T. J. Salmon and T. G. T. McCaw, "The Level and Cartography of the Dead Sea," *PEFQS* 68 (1936) 103-111.

Nelson Glueck, "An Aerial Reconnaissance in Southern Transjordan," *BASOR* #66 (1937) 27-28; #67 (1937) 19-26.

G. E. Kirk, "Archaeological Exploration of the Southern Desert," *PEQ* 70 (1938) 209-233.

*Raymond S. Haupert, "Exploring the Jordan and Dead Sea with the U. S. Navy," *CQ* 22 (1945) 226-241.

A. Reifenberg, "Archaeological Discoveries by Air Photography in Israel," *Arch* 3 (1950) 40-46.

Nelson Glueck, "Explorations in Western Palestine," *BASOR* #131 (1953) 6-15.

Y[ohanan] Aharoni and Ruth Amiran, "Archaeological Surveys: The City Mounds of the Shephelah," *BIES* 19 (1955) #3/4, iii-iv.

*S. Kallai-Kleinmann, "The Judaean Shefelah/*sic*/," *BIES* 19 (1955) #3/4, iv. *[Title page reads: "The Shephelah of Judeah"]*

*Frank M. Cross Jr. and J. T. Milik, "Explorations in the Judaean Buqê'ah," *BASOR* # 142 (1956) 5-17.

Ruth Amiran, "The Tumuli West of Jerusalem. Survey and Excavations, 1953," *IEJ* 8 (1958) 205-227.

J. Aviram, "The Expedition to the Judean Desert, 1960. Introduction," *IEJ* 11 (1961) 3-5.

N. Avigad, "The Expedition to the Judean Desert, 1960. Expedition A," *IEJ* 11 (1961) 6-10.

Y[ohanan] Aharoni, "The Expedition to the Judean Desert, 1960. Expedition B," *IEJ* 11 (1961) 11-24.

P. Bar-Adon, "The Expedition to the Judean Desert, 1960. Expedition C," *IEJ* 11 (1961) 25-35.

Y[igael] Yadin, "The Expedition to the Judean Desert, 1960. Expedition D," *IEJ* 11 (1961) 36-52.

Y. Ben-Arieh, Y. Nashiv, and S. Reichman, "Geographical Survey of the Southern Carmel Coast," *BIES* 26 (1962) #1/2, I.

Y. Ben-Arieh, Y. Nashiv, and S. Reichman, "Geographical Survey of the Southern Carmel Coast," *SGEI* #3 (1962), I.

Anonymous, "The Archaeological Survey of Israel," *IEJ* 15 (1965) 263-264.

§166 *2.5.5.6.2 Levitical Cities and Cities of Refuge*

Anonymous, "Remarks on the Cities of Refuge," *MR* 3 (1820) 453-457.

*George A. Barton, "The Levitical Cities of Israel in the Light of the Excavations at Gezer," *BW* 24 (1904) 167-179.

A. H. Godbey, "The Semitic City of Refuge," *Monist* 15 (1905) 605-625.

*A. Spiro, "Law of Asylum in the Bible," *JBL* 59 (1940) vii-viii.

Charles Lee Feinberg, "The Cities of Refuge," *BS* 103 (1946) 411-417; 104 (1947) 35-48.

B. Dinur, "The Religious Character of the Cities of Refuge and the Ceremony of Admission into Them," *EI* 3 (1954) VII-IX.

Menaḥem Haran, "The Levitical Cities: Utopia and Historical Reality," *Tarbiz* 27 (1957-58) #4, I-II.

*Moshe Greenberg, "The Biblical Concept of Asylum," *JBL* 78 (1959) 125-132.

B[enjamin Mazar, "The cities of the priests and levites," *VTS* 7 (1960) 193-205.

Menaḥem Haran, "Studies in the Account of the Levitical Cities: I. Preliminary Considerations," *JBL* 80 (1961) 45-54.

Menaḥem Haran, "Studies in the Account of the Levitical Cities: II. Utopia and Historical Reality," *JBL* 80 (1961) 156-165.

§167 *2.5.5.6.3 Alphabetical Listing of Specific Cities & Places within Palestine [includes articles on the history of specific places] (See: Volume I Introduction, p. xxii)*

A

Abel-Mehola

*M. Naor, "Jabesh-Gilead, Abel-Mehola and Zaretan," *BIES* 13 (1946-47) #3/4, III.

Abila (of the Decapolis)

Gottieb Schumacher, "Abila of the Decapolis," *PEFQS* 21 (1889) i-iv, 1-51. *[Paged separately; may also be bound separately]*

Field of Abram

M. G. Kyle, "The 'Field of Abram' in the Geographical List of Shoshenq I," *JAOS* 31 (1910-11) 86-91.

James Henry Breasted, "The 'Field of Abram' in the Geographical List of Shoshenq I," *JAOS* 31 (1910-11) 290-295.

Abri Zumoffen

*F. E. Zeuner, with the cooperation of I. W. Cornwall and Diana Kirkbride, "The Shore-Line Chronology of the Palaeolithic of Abri Zumoffen, Adlun Caves, Lebanon," *BMB* 16 (1961) 49-60.

Tel Abu Habil

Henri de Contenson, "Three Soundings in the Jordan Valley," *ADAJ* 4&5 (1960) 12-98. [II. Tel Abu Habil, pp. 31-49]

Tell Abu Hawam

R. W. Hamilton, "Tell Abū Hawām, Interim Report" *QDAP* 3 (1934) 74-80.

R. W. Hamilton, "Excavations at Tell Abū Hawām," *QDAP* 4 (1935) 1-69.

B[enjamin] Maisler, "The Stratification of Tell Abū Huwâm on the Bay of Acre," *BASOR* #124 (1951) 21-25.

E[mmanuel] Anati, "Excavations at the Cemetery of Tell Abu Hawam," *'Atiqot* 2 (1959) 89-102.

E[mmanuel] Anati, "Tell Abu Hawam," *IEJ* 13 (1963) 142-143.

E. Stern, "The Dating of Stratum II at Tell Abu Hawam," *IEJ* 18 (1968) 213-219.

Tell Abu Matar

[M.] J[ean] Perrot, "The Excavations at Tell Abu Matar near Beersheba, (1953-1954)," *BIES* 18 (1953-54) #3/4, II.

[M.] J[ean] Perrot, "The Excavations at Tell Abu Matar near Beersheba," *IEJ* 5 (1955) 17-40, 73-84, 167-189.

Achaia

*Emily Townsend Vermeule, "The Mycenaeans in Achaia," *AJA* 64 (1960) 1-21.

Achzib

M[oshe] W. Prausnitz, "Achzib," *IEJ* 13 (1963) 337-338.

M[oshe] W. Prausnitz, "Tel Achzib," *IEJ* 15 (1965) 256-258.

Acra

*W. F. Birch, "Notes by Rev. W. F. Birch," *PEFQS* 18 (1886) 26-32. [I. Acra South of the Temple, pp. 26-31]

*W. F. Birch, "The City of David and Acra," *PEFQS* 20 (1888) 108.

*W. F. Birch, "Zion (or Acra), Gihon, and Millo. *(All South of the Temple)*," *PEFQS* 25 (1893) 324-330.

*W. F. Birch, "Ancient Jerusalem.—Zion, and Acra, South of the Temple," *PEFQS* 26 (1894) 282-284.

*J. C. Nevin, "Notes on the Topography of Jerusalem," *PEFQS* 38 (1906) 206-213, 278-286. [1. The Site of the Acra, pp. 206-209]

Charles Watson, "The Acra," *PEFQS* 38 (1906) 50-54.

W. F. Birch, "Notes and Queries. 1. *The Acra,*" *PEFQS* 38 (1906) 157.

J. M. Tenz, "Notes and Queries. 2. *Two Places called Acra,*" *PEFQS* 38 (1906) 158.

Charles Watson, "The Site of the Acra," *PEFQS* 39 (1907) 204-214.

J. M. Tenz, "The Acra of the Greeks," *PEFQS* 39 (1907) 290-293.

W. F. Birch, "Notes and Queries. (6.) *The Site of Acra,*" *PEFQS* 40 (1908) 79-82. (Note by J. D. C[race], p. 82)

Acre

Anonymous, "Geography of the Plain of Acre (S.)," *BSAJB* #2 (1922) 10-12.

Asad J. Rustum, "Akka (Acre) and its Defences," *PEFQS* 58 (1926) 143-157.

Adam

R[oland] de Vaux, "Adami Hannekeb," *BIES* 11 (1944-45) #3/4, II-III.

*S. D. Goitein, "The City of Adam in the Book of Psalms?" *BIES* 13 (1946-47) #3/4, II-III.

Ader

W[illiam] F[oxwell] Albright, "Soundings at Ader, a Bronze Age City of Moab," *BASOR* #53 (1934) 13-18.

Admah

*E. Power, "The site of Pentapolis," *B* 11 (1930) 23-62, 149-182. *[Admah]*

Adraha (Dera)

*J. Leslie Porter, "The Old City of Adraha (Dera) and the Roman Road from Gerasa to Bostra," *PEFQS* 13 (1881) 77-79.

Adullam (For Cave of Adullum See: §163 ←)

C. Clermont-Ganneau, "The Site of the City of Adullam," *PEFQS* 7 (1875) 168-177.

*Claude R. Conder, "Notes on Disputed Points," *PEFQS* 12 (1880) 172-174. [Adullam, pp. 173-174]

Aelia Capitolina

*Willam D. Gray, "The Founding of Aelia Capitolina and the Chronology of the Jewish War under Hadrian," *AJSL* 39 (1922-23) 248-256.

Ænon

*William Arnold Stevens, "Ænon near to Salim," *JBL* 3 (1883) 128-141.

'Afula

Eleazer Lipa Sukenik, "Archaeological investigations at Affula [177223]," *JPOS* 21 (1948) 1-79.

M[oshe] Dothan, "The Excavations at 'Afula," *'Atiqot* 1 (1955) 19-70.

Ai (et Tell)

*Charles W. Wilson, "On the Site of Ai and the Position of the Altar which Abram Built between Bethel and Ai," *PEFQS* 1 (1869) 123-126.

H. H. Kitchener, "Site of Ai," *PEFQS* 10 (1878) 74-75.

W. F. Birch, "Ai," *PEFQS* 10 (1878) 132-133; 11 (1879) 103.

T. H. Guest, "On the Site of Ai," *PEFQS* 10 (1878) 194-196.

W. F. Birch, "Varieties. *Ai*," *PEFQS* 14 (1882) 266.

*W. J. Phythian-Adams, "Jericho, Ai and the Occupation of Mount Ephriam," *PEFQS* 68 (1936) 141-149.

J. (=Y.) M. Grintz, "''Ai which is beside Beth-Aven.' A re-examination of the identity of Ai," *B* 42 (1961) 201-216.

Bruce T. Dahlberg, "Ai (et-Tell)," *BA* 28 (1965) 26-30.

Joseph A. Callaway, "The 1964 'Ai (et-Tell) Excavations," *BASOR* #178 (1965) 13-40. [Reports by W. J. A. Power, Robert J. Bull, and Kermit Schoonover]

*Anonymous, "Some Archaeological Notes," *BH* 2 (1965) #3, 16-18. *[Ai (et Tell)]*

G. Herbert Livingston, "Special Report: The Excavation of et-Tell (Ai) in 1966," *ASW* 21 (1967) #2, 31-37.

Anonymous, "Joshua's City of Ai—Another Look At An Archaeological Problem," *BH* 3 (1967) #1, 21-24.

Ai (et Tell) concluded

G. Herbert Livingston, "The Excavation of et-Tell (Ai) in 1968," *ASW* 23 (1969) #3, 20-25.

Joseph A. Callaway, "The 1966 'Ai (et-Tell) Excavations," *BASOR* #196 (1969) 2-16. [Special Reports by Dorothea Harvey, Kermit Schoonover, James M. Ward, Kenneth Vine, and G. Herbert Livingston]

J[oseph] A. Callaway, "Ai (et-Tell)," *IEJ* 19 (1969) 236-239.

W. W. Winter, "Biblical and Archaeological Date on Ai Reappraised," *SR* 16 (1969-70) 73-82.

'Ain el-Feshkhah

*E. W. G. Masterman, "'Ain el-Feshkhah, el-Hajar el Asbah, and Khurbet Ḳumrân," *PEFQS* 34 (1902) 160-167, 297-299.

R[oland] de Vaux, "Excavations at 'Ain Feshkhah," *ADAJ* 4&5 (1960) 7-11.

'Ain en-Nebi

*Diana V. W. Kirkbride, "Short Notices on Some Hitherto Unrecorded Prehistoric Sites in Transjordan," *PEQ* 91 (1959) 52-54. ['Ain en-Nebi, p. 53]

'Ain Shems (See also: Beth-Shemesh)

Duncan Mackenzie, "The Ancient Site of 'Ain Shems, with a Memorandum on the Prospects of Excavation," *PEFQS* 43 (1911) 69-79.

Anonymous, "Doctor Mackenzie's Work at 'Ain/*sic*/ Shems," *RP* 10 (1911) 299. *[Beth-Shemesh]*

Anonymous, "The Excavations at 'Ain-es-Shems," *MR* 94 (1912) 966-969.

'Ain Shems concluded

Duncan Mackenzie, "The Fund's Excavations at 'Ain Shems," *PEFQS* 43 (1911) 139-142, 169-172.

Duncan Mackenzie, "The Excavations at 'Ain Shems, June-July, 1912," *PEFQS* 44 (1912) 171-178.

Anonymous, "Doctor Mackenzie at 'Ain Shems," *RP* 11 (1912) 53-54.

Elihu Grant, "Ain Shems, 1931," *PEFQS* 63 (1931) 167-170.

Tell 'Aitun

Anonymous, "Tell 'Aitun," *IEJ* 18 (1968) 194-195.

Tell el-'Ajjul (See also: Gaza)

*[W. M.] Flinders Petrie, "The Palaces of Ancient Gaza. Tell el Ajjūl," *AEE* 17 (1932) 1-9.

*N. P. Clarke, "Ancient Defences of Tell el Ajjūl," *AEE* 17 (1932) 10-12.

W[illiam] F[oxwell] Albright, "The Chronology of a South Palestinian City, Tell el-'Ajjul," *AJSL* 55 (1938) 337-359.

Olga Tufnell, "The Courtyard Cemetery at Tell El-'Ajjul, Palestine," *ULBIA* 3 (1962) 1-46.

Akra

*W. F. Birch, "The Levelling of Akra," *PEFQS* 35 (1903) 353-355.

Willis A. Shotwell, "The Problem of the Syrian Akra," *BASOR* #176 (1964) 10-19.

'el-'Al

*William L. Reed, "The History of Elealeh ('el-'Al) in Moab," *CollBQ* 42 (1965) #1, 12-16.

Ala Safat

J. d'A. Waechert, "The Excavations at Ala Safat, Transjordan," *JPOS* 21 (1948) 98-103.

Alashiya

A. Jirku, "The Problem of Alashiya," *PEQ* 82 (1950) 40-42.

Alexandrium

Nathaniel Schmidt, "Alexandrium," *JBL* 29 (1910) 77-84.

Tel 'Amal

S. Levy, "Tel 'Amal," *IEJ* 12 (1962) 147.

Amman

G. Lankester Harding, "Excavations on the Citadel, Amman," *ADAJ* 1 (1951) 7-16.

*Anonymous, "Excavations in Jordan, 1953-54," *ADAJ* 3 (1956) 74-87. [Amman, p. 80]

Rudolph H. Dornemann, "Archaeological News. Amman—Theater Consolidation," *ADAJ* 11 (1966) 106.

Ammon

Nelson Glueck, "Explorations in the Land of Ammon," *BASOR* #68 (1937) 13-21.

Tell Amr

Anonymous, "Tell Amr," *BSAJB* #2 (1922) 14-15.

al -'Amuq

*Henri de Contenson, "New Correlations Between Ras Shamra and al-'Amuq," *BASOR* #172 (1963) 35-40.

Tel Anafa

*S[aul] S. Weinberg, "Tel Anafa (Shamir)," *IEJ* 18 (1968) 195-196; 19 (1969) 250-252.

Saul S. Winberg, "The First Season of Excavations at Tel Anafa, Upper Galilee," *AJA* 73 (1969) 246-247.

Anathoth

A. Bergman, "Anathoth?" *BASOR* #63 (1936) 22-23. [Reply by W. F. Albright, p. 23]

A. Bergman, "Soundings at the Supposed Site of Old Testament Anathoth," *BASOR* #62 (1936) 22-26.

Yohanan Aharoni, "Anaharath," *JNES* 26 (1967) 212-215.

Aphek

C[laude] R. Conder, "Aphek," *PEFQS* 15 (1883) 180-181.

*W. T. Pilter, "Aphek and Beth-Dagon," *Exp, 2nd Ser.,* 7 (1884) 303-311.

W. E. Barnes, "The Position of Apheck," *Exp, 5th Ser.,* 2 (1895) 470-472.

*S. Tolkowsky, "Aphek. A Study in Biblical Topography," *JPOS* 2 (1922) 145-158.

William F[oxwell] Albright, "One Aphek or Four?" *JPOS* 2 (1922) 184-189.

W[illiam] F[oxwell] Albright, "The Site of Aphek in Sharon," *JPOS* 3 (1923) 50-53.

Aphek concluded

*R. North, "Ap(h)eq(a) and 'Azeqa," *B* 41 (1960) 41-63.

*A[braham] Eitan, "Tel Aphek (Rosh ha-'Ayin)," *IEJ* 12 (1962) 151-152.

Arab

Z. Vilnay, "Miscellanea," *BIES* 10 (1942-44) #4, III. *[Arab]*

Arabah

*Edward Hull, "Note on Mr. I. C. Russell's Paper on the Jordan Arabah and the Dead Sea," *PEFQS* 21 (1889) 32-34.

*Francis Brown, "Visits to the West Shore of the Dead Sea and the Arabah," *AJA* 13 (1909) 55.

*W. J. Phythian-Adams, "Israel in the Arabah," *PEFQS* 65 (1933) 137-146. *[Ezion-Geber]*

*W. J. Phythian-Adams, "Israel in the Arabah (II)," *PEFQS* 66 (1934) 181-184.

*Nelson Glueck, "The Copper Mines of King Solomon," *AJA* 40 (1936) 125. *[Arabah]*

*Anson F. Rainey, "King Solomon's Mines," *JASA* 16 (1964) 18-19. *[Wadi Timna, Arabah]*

*Beno Rothenberg and Alexandru Lupu, "Excavations in the Early Iron Age Copper Industry at Timna (Wadi Arabah, Israel), May 1964," *ZDPV* 82 (1966) 125-135.

Arad

Y[ohanan] Aharoni and Ruth Amiran, "Tel Arad," *IEJ* 12 (1962) 144-145; 14 (1964) 280-283.

Y[ohanan] Aharoni, "Tel Arad," *IEJ* 13 (1963) 334-337; 15 (1965) 249-251.

Arad cont.

Y[ohanan] Aharoni and Ruth Amiran, "Arad: A Biblical City in Southern Palestine," *Arch* 17 (1964) 43-53.

Anonymous, "Tell Arad and the Bible. Israeli excavations at an apparently insignificant site provide interesting correlations with the Scriptures," *BH* 1 (1964) #4, 14-18.

Y[ohanan] Aharoni and Ruth Amiran, "Excavations at Tel Arad. Preliminary Report on the First Season, 1962," *IEJ* 14 (1964) 131-147.

*Ruth Amiran, "A Preliminary Note on the Sychronisms Between the Early Bronze Strata of Arad and the First Dynasty," *BASOR* #179 (1965) 30-33.

Y[igael] Yadin, "A Note on the Stratigraphy of Arad," *IEJ* 15 (1965) 180.

Ruth Amiran, "The Early Bronze Age City," *IEJ* 15 (1965) 251-252. *[Tel Arad]*

Ruth Amiran, "Arad," *IEJ* 16 (1966) 273-274.

Y[ohanan] Aharoni, "Excavations at Tel Arad: Preliminary Report on the Second Season, 1963," *IEJ* 17 (1967) 233-249.

Y[ohanan] Aharoni, "Arad," *IEJ* 17 (1967) 270-272.

Bernard Boyd, "The Fifth and Final Season of Excavations at Tell Arad," *AJA* 72 (1968) 162.

*Ruth Amiran, "Chronological Problems of the Early Bronze Age: Early Bronze I-II: The City of Arad; Early Bronze III: The Khirbet Kerak Ware," *AJA* 72 (1968) 316-318.

Anonymous, "Findings at Biblical Arad," *BH* 4 (1968) 42.

*Y[ohanan] Aharoni, "Arad: Its Inscriptions and Temple," *BA* 31 (1968) 2-32.

Arad concluded

*Ruth Amiran, "A Second Note on the Synchronism Between Early Bronze Arad and the First Dynasty," *BASOR* #195 (1969) 50-53.

Arair

Anonymous, "Archaeological News. Excavations at Arair 1964," *ADAJ* 11 (1966) 105.

'Arâq el-Emîr

*C. C. McCown, "The 'Araq el-Emir and the Tobiads," *BA* 20 (1957) 63-76. [I. The Elements of the Problem; II. Paths to the Site; III. First Impressions; IV. Caverns and Castle; V. Documentation; VI. Position of Tobiad Family in Transjordan; VII. Nomenclature at 'Araq el-Emir; VIII. The Last Tobiads]

Paul W. Lapp, "Soundings at 'Arâq el-Emîr (Jordan)," *BASOR* #165 (1962) 16-34.

Paul W. Lapp, "The 1961 Excavations at 'Araq el-Emir," *ADAJ* 6&7 (1962) 80-89.

Paul W. Lapp, "The 1962 Excavation at 'Araq el-Emir," *ADAJ* 10 (1965) 37-42.

Paul W. Lapp, "The Second and Third Campaigns at 'Arâq el-Emîr," *BASOR* #171 (1963) 8-39.

Arimathea

*Edward Robinson, "Notes on Biblical Geography," *BS* (1843) 563-566. [Arimathea or Ramah, pp. 565-566]

Arnon

Nathaniel Schmidt, "The River Arnon," *JBL* 24 (1905) 212-220.

A. H. Godbey, "The Site of Arnon," *AJSL* 42 (1925-26) 131.

'Arṭūf

*P. Spyridon Malky, "Eshtaol and 'Arṭūf," *JPOS* 20 (1946) 43-47. [1. The Identification of Eshtaol with 'Arṭūf; 2. The Name of 'Arṭūf]

Aruboth

*Conrad Schick, "Wady 'Arrub, the Aruboth of Scripture," *PEFQS* 30 (1898) 238-241.

Ashdod

*H[ayim] Tadmor, "Sargon's Campaigns against Ashdod," *BIES* 18 (1953-54) #3/4, III-IV.

*M[oshe] Dothan, "The Ancient Harbour of Ashdod," *CNI* 11 (1960) #1, 16-19.

M[oshe] Dothan, "Ashdod," *IEJ* 12 (1962) 147-148; 15 (1965) 259-260.

James L. Swauger, "Use of a Bulldozer in the Excavation of Tell Ashdod, Israel, 1963," *AJA* 68 (1964) 201.

David Noel Freedman, "The Second Season at Ancient Ashdod," *BA* 26 (1963) 134-140.

Frank Cross Moore and David Noel Freedman, "The Name of Ashdod," *BASOR* #175 (1964) 48-50.

M[oshe] Dothan, "Tel Ashdod," *IEJ* 13 (1963) 340-342; 18 (1968) 253-254; 19 (1969) 243-245.

M[oshe] Dothan, "Ashdod: Preliminary Report on the Excavations in Seasons 1962/1963," *IEJ* 14 (1964) 79-95.

Moshe Dothan, "Ashdod: A City of the Philistine Pentapolis," *Arch* 20 (1967) 178-186.

M[oshe] Dothan and David Noel Freedman, "Ashdod: I. The First Season of Excavations 1962," *'Atiqot* 7 (1967) 1-171.

Ashdod-Yam

*J[acob] Kaplan, "Yavneh-Yam and Ashdod-Yam," *IEJ* 17 (1967) 268-269.

J[acob] Kaplan, "The Stronghold of Yamani at Ashdod-Yam," *EI* 9 (1969) 137-138. *[English Summary]*

J[acob] Kaplan, "The Stronghold of Yamani at Ashdod-Yam," *IEJ* 19 (1969) 137-149.

Asher

*(   ) Newbold, "On the Mountainous Country, the portion of Asher, between the Coasts of Tyre and Sidon, and the Jordan," *JRAS* (1850) 348-371.

*A. Saarisalo, "Sites and Roads in Asher and Western Judah," *SO* 28 (1964) #1, 1-30.

Ashkelon

E. B. Pusey, "Ashkelon," *PEFQS* 6 (1874) 30-32.

D. H. Guthe, "The Ruins of Ascalon," *PEFQS* 12 (1880) 182-187.

Duncan Mackenzie, "The Philistine City of Askelon," *PEFQS* 45 (1913) 8-23.

Anonymous, "Philistine City of Askelon," *RP* 12 (1913) 53.

Anonymous, "An Important Discovery at Askelon," *BASOR* #4 (1921) 14.

John Garstang, "The Fund's Excavation of Askalon," *PEFQS* 53 (1921) 12-16.

John Garstang, "The Excavation of Askalon, 1920-1921," *PEFQS* 53 (1921) 73-75.

W. J. Phythian-Adams, "History of Askalon," *PEFQS* 53 (1921) 76-90.

Ashkelon concluded

*John Garstang, "Askalon Reports. *The Philistine Problem*," *PEFQS* 53 (1921) 162-163.

W. J. Phythian-Adams, "Askalon Reports. *Stratigraphical Sections*," *PEFQS* 53 (1921) 163-169.

W. J. Phythian-Adams, "Pre-Philistine Inhabitants of Palestine," *PEFQS* 53 (1921) 170-172. *[Ashkelon]*

W[illiam] F[oxwell] Albright, "The Excavations at Ascalon," *BASOR* #6 (1922) 11-18.

J. Garstang, "The Excavations at Askalon," *PEFQS* 54 (1922) 112-119.

W. J. Phythian-Adams, "Report on the Stratification of Askalon," *PEFQS* 55 (1923) 60-84.

J. Garstang, "Askalon," *PEFQS* 56 (1924) 24-34.

U. Ben Horin, "Lady Hester Stanhope's Excavations at Ascalon in 1815," *BIES* 12 (1946) II.

*Jerome D. Quinn, "Alcaeus 48 (B 16) and the Fall of Ascalon (604 B.C.)," *BASOR* #164 (1961) 19-20.

V. Tsaferis, "Ashkelon-Barnea," *IEJ* 17 (1967) 125-126.

R[am] Gophna, "Ashkelon (Afridar)," *IEJ* 18 (1968) 256.

Asophon

Floyd V. Filson, "Where was Asophon?" *BASOR* #91 (1943) 27-28.

Nelson Glueck, "On the Site of Asophon in the Jordan Valley," *BASOR* #92 (1943) 26-27.

'Aṭaroth

G[eorge] A[dam] Smith, "Notes and Queries. 7. *Callirrhoe; Machaerus; 'Aṭaroth*," *PEFQS* 37 (1905) 170.

'Aṭaroth concluded

*George Adam Smith, "From Machaerus to 'Aṭaroth," *PEFQS* 37 (1905) 357-363.

*Joseph Carson Wampler, "Three Cistern Groups from Tell en-Naṣbeh," *BASOR* #82 (1941) 25-43. *[Ataroth?]*

'Atlīt

C. N. Johns, "Excavations at 'Atlīt (1930-31). The South-Eastern Cemetery," *QDAP* 2 (1933) 41-104.

'Auja Ḥafīr

G. E. Kirk, "Excavations at 'Auja Ḥafīr," *JPOS* 16 (1936) 279-285.

Dunscombe Colt, "Discoveries at Auja Hafia," *PEFQS* 68 (1936) 216-220.

Avdat

Abraham Negev, "Avdat: A Caravan Halt in the Negev," *Arch* 14 (1961) 122-130.

Azekah

*Claude R. Conder, "David and Goliath," *PEFQS* 7 (1875) 191-195. [Azekah, pp. 191-192]

'Azeqa

*R. North, "Ap(h)eq(a) and 'Azeqa," *B* 41 (1960) 41-63.

Ḥ[ayim] Tadmor, "'Azeqa in Judah in a Royal Assyrian Inscription," *BIES* 24 (1959-60) #1, III-IV.

Azor (Tell 'Azūr)

H. J. Orr-Ewing, "Tell 'Azūr," *PEFQS* 59 (1927) 14-17.

M[oshe] Dothan, "Excavations at Azor, 1960," *IEJ* 11 (1961) 171-175.

B

Baal Gad

C[laude] R. Conder, "Baal Gad," *PEFQS* 23 (1891) 251-252.

W. F. Birch, "Baalgad," *PEFQS* 31 (1899) 69.

Mount Baalah

*C[laude] R. Conder, "New Identifications," *PEFQS* 14 (1882) 154-155. [Mount Baalah, p. 154]

Bab edh-Dhra'

Sylvester Saller, "Bab edh-Dhra'," *SBFLA* 15 (1964-65) 137-219.

Paul W. Lapp, "The Cemetery at Bab edh-Dhra', Jordan," *Arch* 19 (1966) 104-111.

Baḥan

G. Edelstein, "Baḥan," *IEJ* 14 (1964) 111.

Bahurim

*C. Clermont-Ganneau, "Notes on Certain New Discoveries at Jerusalem," *PEFQS* 3 (1871) 103-107. [9. Bahurim, pp. 106-107]

Tell Balâṭah (See: Shechem)

Balu'ah

J[oan] W. Crowfoot, "An Expedition to Balu'ah," *PEFQS* 66 (1934) 76-84.

Bashan

J. L. Porter, "The Historico-Geographical Sketch of Bashan," *JSL, 2nd Ser.,* 6 (1854) 281-313.

*J. L. Porter, "Bashan, Ituraea, Kenath," *BS* 13 (1856) 789-808.

L. J. Fletcher, "The Giant Cities of Bashan," *UQGR, N.S.,* 13 (1876) 67-79.

*Claude R. Conder, "Bethany Beyond Jordan," *PEFQS* 9 (1877) 184-187. *[Bashan]*

Selah Merrill, "Notes by Dr. Selah Merrill. Inhabitants of Bashan," *PEFQS* 23 (1891) 76-77.

[George H. Schodde], "Biblical Research Notes," *ColTM* 17 (1897) 117-121. [The Great Cities of Bashan, pp. 120-121]

P[atrick] P. McKenna, "The Ancient Land of Basan," *IER, 5th Ser.,* 38 (1931) 40-51.

Basta

*Diana V. W. Kirkbride, "Short Notes on Some Hitherto Unrecorded Prehistoric Sites in Transjordan," *PEQ* 91 (1959) 52-54. [Basta, p. 52]

Bath Galim

Jar. Petrbok, "Stratigraphical Chronology of the Beds of the Youngest Campaign at Bath Galim in Palestine," *ArOr* 20 (1952) 204-213.

Bath Galim concluded

Josef Skutil, "Bath Galim, a Stone Age Station in Palestine," *ArOr* 20 (1952) 214-221.

Be 'ebēr Hajjardēn

B. Gemser, "Be 'ebēr Hajjardēn: in Jordan's Borderland," *VT* 2 (1952) 349-355.

Beeroth

S. Kallai-Kleinmann, "An Attempt to Determine the Location of Beeroth," *EI* 3 (1954) V-VI.

(Tel) Beersheba

S. R. Driver, "The Wells of Beersheba," *ET* 7 (1895-96) 567-568.

H. Clay Trumbull, "The Wells at Beersheba," *ET* 8 (1896-97) 89.

Lucien Gautier, "The Wells of Beersheba," *ET* 10 (1898-99) 328-329, 429; 12 (1900-01) 478-479.

George L. Robinson, "The Wells of Beersheba," *BW* 17 (1901) 247-255.

Lucien Gautier, "The Wells of Beersheba: A Note," *BW* 18 (1901) 49-52.

George L. Robinson, "Beersheba Revisited," *BW* 31 (1908) 327-335.

*M[oshe] Dothan, "Excavations at Ḥorvat Beter (Beersheba)," *'Atiqot* 2 (1959) 1-42.

R[am] Gophna, "Beersheba," *IEJ* 13 (1963) 145-146.

R. Cohen, "Beersheba," *IEJ* 18 (1968) 130-131.

Y[ohanan] Aharoni, "Tel Beersheba," *IEJ* 19 (1969) 245-247.

Beidha

Diana Kirkbride, "The Excavation of a Neolithic Village at Seyl Aqlat, Beidha, Near Petra," *PEQ* 92 (1960) 136-145.

Diana Kirkbride, "Excavations of the Pre-Pottery Neolithic Village at Seyl Aqlat, Beidha," *ADAJ* 6&7 (1962) 7-12.

Diana Kirkbride, "Beidha: An Early Neolithic Village In Jordan," *Arch* 19 (1966) 199-207.

Diana Kirkbride, "Five Seasons at the Pre-Pottery Neolithic Village of Beidha in Jordan," *PEQ* 98 (1966) 8-72.

Diana Kirkbride, "Beidha 1965: An Interim Report," *PEQ* 99 (1967) 5-13.

Diana Kirkbride, "Beidha 1967: An Interim Report," *PEQ* 100 (1968) 90-96.

Diana Kirkbride, "Beidha: Early Neolithic Village Life South of the Dead Sea," *Antiq* 42 (1968) 263-274.

Beisan (See also: Beth-Shan)

Anonymous, "Current Notes and News. University of Pennsylvania Excavations at Beisan," *A&A* 12 (1921) 279.

Anonymous, "The Excavations at Beisan by the University Museum of Pennsylvania (Season 1922)," *BSAJB* #2 (1922) 17-18.

George J. H. Ovenden, "Notes on the Excavations at Beisan," *PEFQS* 55 (1923) 147-149.

Clarence S. Fisher, "The Expedition to Palestine. Beisan as Seen from the Air: Royal Air Force Photographs," *MJ* 15 (1924) 101-105.

Stanley A. Cook, "The American Excavations at Beisān," *PEFQS* 58 (1926) 29-30.

Alan Rowe, "The Expedition at Beisan," *MJ* 18 (1927) 411-441.

Beisan concluded

Alan Rowe, "The Recent Finds at Beisan," *Antiq* 2 (1928) 192-195.

Alan Rowe, "The 1927 Excavation at Beisan: Final Report," *MJ* 19 (1928) 145-169.

*Alan Rowe, "Excavations at Beisan During the 1927 Season. Two Temples of Thothmes III, etc.," *PEFQS* 60 (1928) 73-90.

Anonymous, "The Beisan Expedition," *UMB* 2 (1930-31) 39-46, 163-166; 5 (1934-35) #1, 8-9; #2, 37-40.

Anonymous, "The New Season at Beisan," *UMB* 3 (1931-32) 66-67.

Anonymous, "The Beisan Report," *UMB* 3 (1931-32) 95-98.

*Anonymous, "The Beisan Expedition and the Beth-Shan Society," *UMB* 4 (1932-33) 144-145.

Beiten

*W. Ross, "Is Beitin the Bethel of Jeroboam?" *PEQ* 73 (1941) 22-27.

*Edward A. Cerny, "Archaeological Corner. Bethel (Beitin)," *CBQ* 4 (1942) 68-71.

*James L. Kelso, "Excavations in Jordan 1960/1961. Condensed Report of the 1960 Beiten Expedition," *ADAJ* 6&7 (1962) 122-123.

Beit Jibrin

A. M. Mantell, "Supposed Village of Jett, Near Beit Jibrîn," *PEFQS* 14 (1882) 164-165.

*Anonymous, "The Tombs of Beit Jibrin," *BASOR* #4 (1921) 5.

*E. W. G. Masterman, "Beit Jibrin and Tell Sandahannah," *PEFQS* 58 (1926) 176-185.

Tell Beit Mirsim (See also: Debir & Kirjath Sepher)

W[illiam] F[oxwell] Albright, "The Excavations at Tell Beit Misrim I & II,"*BASOR* #23 (1926) 2-14.

W[illiam] F[oxwell] Albright, "The Second Campaign at Tell Beit Mirsim (Kiriath-Sepher)," *BASOR* #31 (1928) 1-11.

W[illiam] F[oxwell] Albright, "The Second Campaign at Tell Beit Mirsim," *AfO* 5 (1928-29) 119-120.

W[illiam] F[oxwell] Albright, "The Third Campaign of Excavations at Tell Beit Mirsim," *BASOR* #38 (1930) 9-10; #39 (1930) 1-10.

Ovid R. Sellers, "The 1930 Excavations at Tell Beit Mirsim," *AJA* 35 (1931) 60.

W[illiam] F[oxwell] Albright, "The Third Campaign at Tell Beit Mirsim and its Historical Results," *JPOS* 11 (1931) 105-129. *[pp. 105-116 misnumbered as 21-32]*

W[illiam] F[oxwell] Albright, "The Third Campaign at Tell Beit Mirsim," *AfO* 7 (1931-32) 56-58.

W[illiam] F[oxwell] Albright, "Excavations at Tell Beit Mirsim," *AJA* 36 (1932) 556-564.

M. G. Kyle, "The Fourth Campaign at Tell Beit Mirsim," *BS* 89 (1932) 393-419.

W[illiam] F[oxwell] Albright, "The Fourth Joint Campaign of Excavation at Tell Beit Mirsim," *BASOR* #47 (1932) 3-17.

Anonymous, "Notes and Comments. New Light on Tell Beit Mirsim," *A&A* 34 (1933) 274.

*William F. Stinespring, "Remarks on Biblical Archaeology," *DDSR* 2 (1937) 1-10. [Tell Beit Mirsim, pp. 2-4]

W[illiam] F[oxwell] Albright, "The American Excavations at Tell Beit Mirsim," *ZAW* 47 (1949) 1-17.

*S. Yeivin, "The Western Tower at Tell Beit Mirsim," *BIES* 23 (1959) #1/2, I.

Beit Shelalah

*Claude R. Conder, "The City Shelala," *PEFQS* 26 (1894) 82-83.
[Beit Shelala]

Bekhaim

*Daivd Yellin, "Emek ha-bakha: Bekhaim," *JPOS* 3 (1923) 191-196.

Benei Beraq

J. Kaplan, "Excavations at Benei Beraq, 1951," *IEJ* 13 (1963) 300-312.

Beni Murra

A. S. Kirkbride and [G.] Lankester Harding, "The Seven Wells of Beni Murra," *QDAP* 11 (1945) 37-45.

Benjamin

*[S.] Kallai-Kleinmann, "Notes on the Topography of Benjamin," *IEJ* 6 (1956) 180-187.

Beror-Hail

*C[laude] R. Conder, "New Identifications," *PEFQS* 14 (1882) 154-155. [Beror-Hail, p. 155]

Beşet

A[sher] Ovadiah, "Beşet," *IEJ* 17 (1967) 124-125.

Bethabara/Beth Barah

C[laude] R. Conder, "'Bethabara' and 'Beth Barah'—Some Corrections," *HR* 43 (1902) 567.

Bethany

*Claude R. Conder, "Bethany Beyond Jordan," *PEFQS* 9 (1877) 184-187.

*C[laude] R. Conder, "Bethany and Bethsaida," *PEFQS* 15 (1883) 177.

*W[illiam] F[oxwell] Albright, "New Identifications of Ancient Towns,"*BASOR* #9 (1923) 5-10. [Bethany in the Old Testament, pp. 8-10]

*Auni Dajani, Excavations in Jordan, 1949-1950," *ADAJ* 1 (1951) 44-48. [Bethany, p. 44]

Sylvester Saller, "Excavations in the Ancient Town of Bethany," *SBFLA* 2 (1951-52) 119-162.

Beth-Dagon

*W. T. Pilter, "Aphek and Beth-Dagon," *Exp, 2nd Ser.,* 7 (1884) 303-311.

*R. A. Stewart Macalister, "Dajun and Beth-Dagon and the Transference of Biblical Names," *PEFQS* 35 (1903) 356-358.

M. Naor, "Bet/sic/* Dagon and Gederoth-Kidron, Eltekeh and Ekron," *EI* 5 (1958) 90*-91*.

Bethel

*H. Vogelstein, "Shechem and Bethel," *JQR* 4 (1891-92) 513-532.

W[illiam] F[oxwell] Albright, "A Trail of Excavation in the Mound of Bethel," *BASOR* #29 (1928) 9-11.

W[illiam] F[oxwell] Albright, "The First Month of Excavation at Bethel," *BASOR* #55 (1934) 23-25.

W[illiam] F[oxwell] Albright, "The Kyle Memorial Excavation at Bethel," *BASOR* #56 (1934) 2-15.

Bethel concluded

W[illiam] F[oxwell] Albright, "Observations of the Bethel Report," *BASOR* #57 (1935) 27-30.

James L. Kelso, "Kyle Memorial Excavations at Bethel," *BS* 91 (1934) 415-419.

G. A. Wainwright, "Jacob's Bethel," *PEFQS* 66 (1934) 32-44.

Charles F. Sitterly, "Drew Helps Excavate Bethel," *DG* 6 (1934-35) #2, 1-4.

*William F. Stinespring, "Remarks on Biblical Archaeology," *DDSR* 2 (1937) 1-10. [Bethel, pp. 7-9]

*W. Ross, "Is Beitin the Bethel of Jeroboam?" *PEQ* 73 (1941) 22-27.

*Edward A. Cerny, "Archaeological Corner. Bethel (Beitin)," *CBQ* 4 (1942) 68-71.

James L. Kelso, "The Second Campaign at Bethel," *BASOR* #137 (1955) 5-10.

James L. Kelso, "Excavations at Bethel," *BA* 19 (1956) 36-43.

Anonymous, "Excavations at Bethel," *AT* 1 (1956-57) #1, 9.

James L. Kelso, "The Third Campaign at Bethel," *BASOR* #151 (1958) 3-8.

James L. Kelso, "The Fourth Campagin at Bethel," *BASOR* #164 (1961) 5-19.

Bether

*J. E. Hanauer, "Notes on the Winged Figure at Jaffa, on Bether, &c," *PEFQS* 26 (1894) 148-150. [4. Bether, pp. 149-150]

Bethesda

*C[harles] W. Wilson, "The Sites of Tarichæa and Bethesda," *PEFQS* 9 (1877) 10-13.

Eb. Nestle, "Bethesda," *ET* 13 (1901-02) 332-333.

E. W. G. Masterman, "The Pool of Bethesda," *BW* 25 (1905) 88-102.

Beth Gamul

*Selah Merrill, "The American Expedition. Um el Jemal—the Beth Gamul of Jeremiah?" *PEFQS* 8 (1876) 51-55.

Beth Govrin

*Y. Ben-Arieh, "Caves and Ruins in the Beth Govrin Area," *IEJ* 12 (1962) 47-61.

Beth Horon

*Z. Kallai and H[ayim] Tadmor, "Bīt Ninurta = Beth Horon—On the History of the Kingdom of Jerusalem in the Amarna Period," *EI* 9 (1969) 138. *[English Summary]*

Bethlehem

*Philip Schaff, "Disputed Scripture Localities," *PRev* 54 (1878) Part 1, 851-884. [Bethlehem, pp. 871-873]

Claude R. Conder, "Notes. *Bethlehem*," *PEFQS* 18 (1886) 18-19.

R. L. Stewart, "Bethlehem of Judah," *CFL, N.S.*, 2 (1900) 335-342.

Louise P. Smith, "Bethlehem-Ephrata," *JBL* 67 (1948) xi-xii.

*Anonymous, "Excavations in Jordan, 1953-1954," *ADAJ* 3 (1956) 74-87. [Bethlehem, 1951-1953, pp. 77-79]

Bethlehem concluded

Martin W. Schoenberg, "The Theological Significance of Bethlehem," *BibT* #3 (1962) 153-157.

Ernest Lussier, "Bethlehem," *BibT* #3 (1962) 159-163.

Eugene D. Stockton, "The Stone Age of Bethlehem," *SBFLA* 17 (1967) 129-148.

Sylvester Saller, "Iron Age Remains from the Site of a New School at Bethlehem," *SBFLA* 18 (1968) 153-180.

Beth Mēir

*Julius Jotham Rothschild, "Antiquities in the Mountains of Judah. I. The Khirbet Māsi," *PEQ* 88 (1956) 49-56. *[Beth Mëir]*

Bethsaida

Lyman Abbott, "The Site of Bethsaida," *AAOJ* 3 (1880-81) 234-235.

*C[laude] R. Conder, "New Identifications," *PEFQS* 14 (1882) 154-155. [Bethsaida]

*C[laude] R. Conder, "Bethany and Bethsaida," *PEFQS* 15 (1883) 177.

Beth-Shan (See also: Beisan)

Anonymous, "Excavations at Bethshan," *HR* 83 (1922) 370.

Clarence S. Fisher, "Beth-Shan," *MJ* 13 (1922) 32-45.

Clarence S. Fisher, "Bethshean: Excavations of the University Museum Expedition, 1921-1923," *MJ* 14 (1923) 227-248.

P[hilip] M[auro], "Recent Excavations at Bethshan," *CFL, 3rd Ser.*, 31 (1925) 237-238.

George W. Gilmore, "Bethshan Through the Ages," *HR* 90 (1925) 481.

Beth-Shan cont.

Alan Rowe, "The Discoveries at Beth-Shan During the 1926 Season," *MJ* 18 (1927) 9-45.

Alan Rowe, "Excavations in Palestine. The New Discoveries at Beth-Shan," *PEFQS* 59 (1927) 67-84.

Alan Rowe, "The Discoveries at Beth-Shan—Additional Remarks," *PEFQS* 59 (1927) 148-149.

Alan Rowe, "The Palestine Expedition: Report of the 1928 Season," *MJ* 20 (1929) 37-87. *[Beth-Shan]*

*George P. Hedley, "The 'Temple of Dagon' at Beth-Shan," *AJA* 33 (1929) 34-36.

Alan Rowe, "Palestine Expedition of the Museum of the University of Pennsylvania. Third Report—1928 Season," *PEFQS* 61 (1929) 78-94. *[Beth-Shan]*

G. M. FitzGerald, "Excavations at Beth-Shan in 1930," *PEFQS* 63 (1931) 59-70.

G. M. FitzGerald, "Excavations at Beth-Shan in 1931," *PEFQS* 64 (1932) 138-148.

*Anonymous, "The Beisan Expedition and the Beth-Shan Society," *UMB* 4 (1932-33) 144-145.

G. M. FitzGerald, "Excavations at Beth-Shan in 1933," *PEFQS* 66 (1934) 123-134.

A. Bergman and Ruth Brandsteter, "Exploration in the Valley of Beth-Shan," *BIES* 8 (1940-41) #3, I.

*Robert North, "Beth-shan and Megiddo," *CBQ* 12 (1950) 84-89.

N. Zori, "Beth-Shan Valley," *BIES* 18 (1954) #1/2. VIII.

N. Zori, "The Survey of the Beth-Shan Valley," *BIES* 19 (1954-55) #1/2, IV.

Beth-Shan concluded

N. Tzori, "Neolithic and Chalcolithic Sites in the Valley of Beth-shan," *PEQ* 90 (1958) 44-53.

Francis W. James, "Beth Shan," *Exped* 3 (1960-61) #2, 31-36.

A[braham] Negev, "Beth-Shean," *IEJ* 12 (1962) 151.

N. Zori, "Beth-Shean," *IEJ* 15 (1965) 262.

*Henry O. Thompson, "Tell el-Husn—Biblical Beth-Shan," *BA* 30 (1967) 110-135.

*Andrew Miles, "Beth-Shan—Scythopolis: Part I," *BibT* #41 (1969) 2825-2831.

*Eugene A. LaVerdiere, "Beth-Shan—Scythopolis: Part II," *BibT* #42 (1969) 2926-2931.

Beth Shemesh (See also: 'Ain Shems)

Stanley A. Cook, "The Proposed Excavation of Beth-Shemesh. Notes on the Site and its Environs," *PEFQS* 42 (1910) 220-231.

H. Vincent, "The Archaeological Invocation of a Biblical Site—Notes of a Visit to the Explorations at Beth-Shemesh ('Ain Shems)," *PEFQS* 43 (1911) 143-151.

E. W. G. Masterman, "Bethshemesh and the Recent Excavations of the Palestine Exploration Fund," *BW* 42 (1913) 101-109.

*W[illiam] F[oxwell] Albright, "Among the Canaanite Mounds of Eastern Galilee," *BASOR* #29 (1928) 1-8. [A Visit to Beth-shan, pp. 7-8]

Elihu Grant, "Progress at Beth Shemesh," *BASOR* #31 (1928) 15.

Elihu Grant, "Work at Beth Shemesh in 1928," *PEFQS* 60 (1928) 179-181.

Elihu Grant, "The Haverford College Excavations at Ancient Beth Shemesh," *PEFQS* 61 (1929) 201-210.

Beth Shemesh concluded

*J[oan] W. Crowfoot, "Three Recent Excavations in Palestine," *PEFQS* 62 (1930) 172-177. [2. Beth Shemesh, pp. 174-175]

Elihu Grant, "Beth Shemesh in 1933," *BASOR* #52 (1933) 3-5.

*Elihu Grant, "The Excavations at Old Beth Shemesh, Palestine. See I Samuel VI," *JAAR* 1 (1933) #1, 22.

Elihu Grant, "Beth Shemesh, 1933," *JBL* 53 (1934) ii.

*J. W. Jack, "Recent Biblical Archeology," *ET* 51 (1939-40) 544-548. [Beth-Shemesh ('City of the Sun'). The Hyksos City, The Egyptian City, The Philistine City, The Israelite City, pp. 544-545]

*J. W. Jack, "Recent Biblical Archeology," *ET* 52 (1940-41) 112-115. [Beth-Shemesh (1 Sam. 6), pp. 113-114]

Beth She'arim (See also: Sheikh Abreiq)

B[enjamin] Maisler, "The Second Campaign of Excavations at Beth She'arim, 1937," *BIES* 5 (1937-38) #3, I-II.

S. Klein, "Some Notes on the Papers of Maisler and Schwabe on the Excavations at Beth She'arim (Sheikh Abreiq)," *BIES* 5 (1937-38) #4, I-II.

B[enjamin] Maisler, "The Excavations at Sheikh Ibreiq (Beth She'arim), 1936/7," *JPOS* 18 (1938) 41-49.

B[enjamin] Maisler, "Brief Report on the Third Season's Work at Beth Shearim," *BIES* 6 (1938-39) #2, III-IV.

S. Yeivin, "Notes on the Report of the JPES Excavations at Beth She'arim (Season 1940)," *BIES* 9 (1941-42) #2/3, III.

B[enjamin] Maisler, "The Fourth Campaign at Beth Shearim, 1940 (Preliminary Report)," *BIES* 9 (1941-42) #1, I.

Beth She'arim concluded

S. Yeivin, "Notes on the Report of the JPES Excavations at Beth-She'arim (Season 1940)," *BIES* 10 (1942-44) #1, III. [Additional note by M. Benari under "Miscellany", *BIES* 10 (1942-44) #4, IV]

B[enjamin] Maisler and M. Schwabe, "The Cemetery of Beth-She'arim," *KSJA* 2 (1945) VII.

O. R. Sellers, "Beth She'arim," *BA* 15 (1952) 46-47.

*B[enjamin] Maisler, "Beth She'arim, Gaba, and the Harosheth of the Peoples," *HUCA* 24 (1952-53) 75-84.

N[ahman] Avigad, "The Fifth Season of Excavations at Beth She'arim, 1953. Preliminary Report," *BIES* 18 (1954) #1/2, III-IV.

N[ahman] Avigad, "Excavations at Beth She'arim, 1953. Preliminary Report," *IEJ* 4 (1954) 88-107.

N[ahman] Avigad, "Excavations at Beth She'arim, 1954: Preliminary Report," *IEJ* 5 (1955) 205-239.

B[enjamin] Mazar, "The Eighth Excavation Campaign at Beth She'arim, 1956," *BIES* 21 (1957) #3/4, I-II.

N[ahman] Avigad, "Excavations at Beth She'arim, 1955: Preliminary Report," *IEJ* 7 (1957) 73-92, 239-255.

N[ahman] Avigad, "Excavations at Beth She'arim, 1955," *EI* 5 (1958) 93*-94*.

S. Saphrai, "Beth She'arim in Talmudic Literature," *EI* 5 (1958) 95*.

N[ahman] Avigad, "Excavations at Beth She'arim, 1958: Preliminary Report," *IEJ* 9 (1959) 205-220.

*Anonymous, "Jelemiye, Beth-She'arim, Kafr Yasif," *IEJ* 16 (1966) 283-284.

Bethso

S. Beswick, "The Place Called Bethso," *PEFQS* 12 (1880) 108-109.

Bethul

*C[laude] R. Conder, "New Identifications," *PEFQS* 13 (1881) 89. *[Bethul]*

Beth Yerah

*L. Sukenik, "The Ancient City of Philoteria (*Beth Yerah*)," *JPOS* 2 (1922) 101-109.

B[enjamin] Maisler and M[oshe] Stekelis, "Preliminary Report on the Beth Yerah Excavations," *BIES* 11 (1944-45) #3/4, V.

M[oshe] Stekelis and M[ichael] Avi-Yonah, "Excavations at Beth Yerah (Berl Kaznelson Memorial Expedition) Second Preliminary Report," *BIES* 13 (1946-47) #1/2, V-VII.

*B[enjamin] Maisler, M[oshe] Steklis, and M[ichael] Avi-Yonah, "The Excavations at Beth Yerah (Kirbet el-Kerak), 1944-1946," *IEJ* 2 (1952) 165-173, 218-229.

*P[esah] Bar-Adon, "Sinabri and Beth Yerah in the Light of the Literary Sources and Archaeological Finds," *EI* 4 (1956) V-VI.

Beth-zur (Bethsura)

*C[onrad] Schick, "Reports from Herr Baurath von Schick. 6. *Bethzur,*" *PEFQS* 27 (1895) 37-40.

O. R. Sellers and W[illiam] F[oxwell] Albright, "The First Campaign of Expedition at Beth-Zur," *BASOR* #43 (1931) 2-13. *(Bethsura)*

William F[oxwell] Albright, "The First Campaign of Excavation at Beth-zur (Palestine)," *AJA* 36 (1932) 40.

O. R. Sellers, "The 1957 Campaign at Beth-Zur," *BA* 21 (1958) 71-76.

Robert W. Funk, "The 1957 Campaign at Beth-Zur," *BASOR* #150 (1958) 8-20.

Bezek

C[onrad] Schick, "Adoni-Bezek's City," *PEFQS* 30 (1898) 20-23. *[Bezek]*

*Andrew J. Gregg, "Note on Gibeon, Nob, Bezek and the High-Level Aqueduct to Jerusalem," *PEFQS* 31 (1899) 128-129. [2. Bezek, p. 129]

Bezetha

C[laude] R. Conder, "Bezetha," *PEFQS* 22 (1890) 122-123.

Bīt Ninurta

*Z. Kallai and H[ayim] Tadmor, "Bīt Ninurta = Beth Horon—On the History of the Kingdom of Jerusalem in the Amarna Period," *EI* 9 (1969) 138. *[English Summary]*

Bochim

*C[laude] R. Conder, "Notes on Antiquities of the Book of Judges," *PEFQS* 31 (1899) 162. *[Bochim]*

Buqê 'ah

*Frank M. Cross Jr. and J. T. Milik, "Explorations in the Judean Buqê'ah," *BASOR* #142 (1956) 5-17.

C

Caanan

*Archibald Henderson, "Cana and Megiddo in Tatian's Diatessaron," *PEFQS* 26 (1894) 151.

*W. W. Moore, "Israel's Attitude Towards Canaan During the Egyptian Sojurn," *USR* 9 (1897) 188-193.

*A. H. Sayce, "The Latest Discoveries in Palestine: Canaan Before the Israelites," *BW* 25 (1905) 125-133.

Canaan concluded

*W[illiam] F[oxwell] Albright, "Among the Canaanite Mounds of Eastern Galilee," *BASOR* #29 (1928) 1-8. [The Canaanite Capital of Galilee, The City on the Horns of Ḥaṭṭîn, Chinnereth and Bethsaida, A Visit to Beth-shan]

Caesarea

*G. Schumacher, "Researches in the Plain North of Caesarea," *PEFQS* 19 (1887) 78-90. (Note, p. 151) [(I.) An Excursion to the Crocodile River; (II.) Tiberias and its Vicinity]

*H. Hamburger, "Caesarea Coin-finds and the History of the City," *BIES* 15 (1949-50) #3/4, II.

A. Reifenberg, "Caesarea. A Study of the Decline of a Town," *IEJ* 1 (1950-51) 20-32.

S. Yeivin, "Excavations at Caesarea Maritima," *Arch* 8 (1955) 122-129.

Anonymous, "The 1959 Caesarea Expedition," *AT* 3 (1958-59) #4, 6.

A[braham] Negev, "Caesarea Maritima," *CNI* 11 (1960) #4, 17-22.

A[braham] Negev, "Caesarea," *IEJ* 11 (1961) 81-83.

A. Frova, "Caesarea," *IEJ* 11 (1961) 195-196; 12 (1962) 150-151.

M[ichael] Avi-Yonah and A[braham] Negev, "Caesarea," *IEJ* 13 (1963) 146-148.

Callirrhoe

*George Adam Smith, "Callirrhoe and Machaerus," *PEFQS* 37 (1905) 219-230.

*G[eorge] A[dam] Smith, "Notes and Queries. 7. *Callirrhoe; Machaerus; 'Aṭaroth*," *PEFQS* 37 (1905) 170.

*J. Cropper, "Madeba, M'kaur, and Callirrhoe," *PEFQS* 38 (1906) 292-298.

Cana

*Archibald Henderson, "Cana and Megiddo in Tatian's Diatessaron,"
   PEFQS 26 (1894) 151.

E. W. G. Masterman, "Cana of Galilee," *PEFQS* 46 (1914) 179-183.

Capernaum (See also: Tell Ḥum)

H. B. Hackett, "Biblical Notes. 3. Dispute Respecting Capernaum,"
   BS 23 (1866) 518-519.

S. Graves, "The Site of Capernaum," *AAOJ* 3 (1880-81) 117-121.

Henry Brass, "The Site of Capernaum," *PEFQS* 22 (1890) 178-180.

William Knight, "The Site of Capernaum," *Exp, 7th Ser.,* 2 (1906)
   48-56.

*Edward A. Wicher, "A New Argument for Locating Capernaum at
   Khan Minyeh," *AJA* 20 (1916) 90.

*Joseph Offord, "Archaeological Notes on Jewish Antiquities. XXIV.
   The Site of Capernaum," *PEFQS* 48 (1916) 194.

(Mount) Carmel

Anonymous, "The Lands of Hills. No. II.—Carmel," *CongML* 20
   (1837) 210-220.

Laurence Oliphant, "The Slopes of Carmel," *PEFQS* 15 (1883)
   120-121.

Anonymous, "Carmel," *EN* 4 (1892) 23-25.

P. L. O. Guy, "Mt. Carmel: An Early Iron Age Cemetery near Haifa,
   Excavated September, 1922," *BSAJB* #5 (1924) 47-55.

*M[ichael] Avi-Yonah, "Mount Carmel and the God of Baalbek,"
   IEJ 2 (1952) 118-124.

(Mount) Carmel concluded

J. (I.) Olami, "Prehistoric Survey of Mount Carmel," *BIES* 18 (1954) #1/2, VII; 22 (1958) #3/4, n.p.n.

*S. C. Ylvisaker, "Some Old Testament Difficulties," *WLQ* 54 (1957) 262-264. [Karmel, p. 264] *(Carmel)*

*Dov Nir, "The Hydrography of Mount Carmel," *BIES* 22 (1958) #1/2, VI-VII.

*E. S. Higgs and D. R. Brothwell, "North Africa and Mount Carmel: Recent Developments," *Man* 61 (1961) #166.

Z. Ron, "The Morphographic Configuration of the Western Strip of the Southern Carmel Coast," *BIES* 26 (1962) #1/2, II.

Z. Ron, "The Morphographic Configuration of the Western Strip of the Southern Carmel Coast," *SGEI* #3 (1962) II.

Mt. Casius

M[oshe] Dothan, "Archaeological Survey of Mt. Casius and its Vicinity," *EI* 9 (1969) 135-136. *[English Summary]*

Chephar Haammonai

*Claude R. Conder, "New Identifications," *PEFQS* 12 (1880) 230-231. [Chephar Haammonai, p. 230]

Chephirah

E. W. G. Masterman, "Chephirah of Benjamin," *PEFQS* 39 (1907) 64-65.

Brook Cherith

*Anonymous, "Wady Kelt," *PEFQS* 10 (1878) 119-120. [Brook Cherith]

D

Dahariya

*Sylvester J. Saller, "Ez-Zahiriyye in the light of Ancient Pottery," *SBFLA* 7 (1956-57) 53-63.

Dâjûn

A. M. Mantell, "Dâjûn, Near Sitt Nefîseeh," *PEFQS* 14 (1882) 164.

*R. A. Stewart Macalister, "Dajun and Beth-Dagon and the Transference of Biblical Place-Names," *PEFQS* 35 (1903) 356-358.

Damascus

*G[eorge] Rawlinson, "Biblical Topography. VI.—Sites connected with the History of Abraham—Harran, Damascus, Hebron," *MI* 4 (1886) 241-252. *[Part IV not published]*

(Tel) Dan

Walter Wood, "Dan and Dan-Laish," *Exp, 2nd Ser.,* 3 (1882) 233-240.

B[enjamin] Mazar, "Topographical Studies: VI. The Cities of Dan," *BIES* 24 (1959-60) #1, III.

B[enjamin] Mazar, "The Cities of the Territory of Dan," *IEJ* 10 (1960) 65-77.

A[braham] Biran, "Tel Dan," *IEJ* 16 (1966) 145; 19 (1969) 121-123, 239-241.

Dannaba

*C. Clermont-Ganneau, "Archaeological and Epigraphic Notes on Palestine. 10. *Dannaba and Job's Country,*" *PEFQS* 34 (1902) 10-15.

Daroma

Millar Burrows, ""Daroma," *JPOS* 12 (1932) 142-148.

City of David (See also: Acra)

*W. F. Brich, "The City of David. Zion not at 'Goliath's Castle'," *PEFQS* 27 (1895) 263-264.

*W. F. Birch, "Zion, the City of David. Where was it? How did Joab make his way to it? and who helped him?" *PEFQS* 10 (1878) 129-132, 178-189.

*W. F. Birch, "Zion, the City of David'," *PEFQS* 11 (1879) 104.

*W. F. Birch, "The City and Tomb of David," *PEFQS* 13 (1881) 94-97.

H. B. S. W., "City of David," *PEFQS* 13 (1881) 327-328.

*C[laude] R. Conder, "City of David," *PEFQS* 15 (1883) 194-195.

*W. F. Birch, "Notes by Rev. W. F. Birch," *PEFQS* 18 (1886) 26-32. [I. Acra South of the Temple, pp. 26-31] *(City of David)*

*W. F. Birch, "Zion, the City of David, or Acra, South of the Temple— *continued,*" *PEFQS* 18 (1886) 151-154.

H. B. S. W., "The Size of the 'City of David'," *PEFQS* 19 (1887) 55-57. (Note by Claude R. Conder, pp. 105-106)

H. B. S. W., "The 'City of David' *Not* the Same as the 'City (Jerusalem) of David's Time'," *PEFQS* 19 (1887) 250-252. (Note by Claude R. Conder, *PEFQS* 20 (1888) p. 41)

W. F. Birch, "The City of David," *PEFQS* 20 (1888) 44-46. [III. Zion, South, not North of the Temple, pp. 44-45; IV. Zion not Jerusalem in General in the Historical Books, p. 46]

*W. F. Birch, "The City of David and Acra," *PEFQS* 20 (1888) 108.

*Samuel Gergheim, "The Identification of the City of David—Zion and Millo," *PEFQS* 27 (1895) 120-123.

City of David concluded

*W. F. Birch, "The City of David. Zion not at 'Goliath's Castle'," *PEFQS* 27 (1895) 263-264.

D. Lee Pitcairn, "The Identification of the City of David," *PEFQS* 27 (1895) 342-345. (Correction, *PEFQS* 28 (1896) p. 101)

G. A. Smith, "Sion: The City of David," *Exp, 6th Ser.*, 11 (1905) 1-15.

*J. M. Tenz, "*Notes and Queries.* 3. *Millo, and the City of David,*" *PEFQS* 37 (1905) 165-167.

*Lewis Bayles Paton, "Jerusalem in Biblical Times: IV. The City of David," *BW* 29 (1907) 247-259.

*[Paul Carus], "The City of David," *OC* 23 (1909) 610-618.

*W. F. Birch, "The City and Tomb of David in Ophel (so called)," *PEFQS* 43 (1911) 187-189.

*Gerald M. FitzGerald, "The City of David and the Excavations of 1913-14," *PEFQS* 54 (1922) 8-22.

*F. Garrow Duncan, "Millo and the City of David," *ZAW* 42 (1924) 222-244.

*N[ahman] Avigad, "The Fortification of the City of David," *IEJ* 2 (1952) 230-236.

Dead Sea

*Edward Robinson, "On the Dead Sea, and the Destruction of Sodom and Gomorrah," *BRCR, N.S.*, 3 (1840) 24-39. [Letter from Leopold de Buch and extract from his writings, pp. 31-36; Extract from a paper by N. Hugent, pp. 36-36]

*Edward Robinson, "Notes on Biblical Geography," *BS* (1843) 563-566. [Depression of the Dead Sea, etc., p. 566]

*E[dward] Robinson, "Depression of the Dead Sea and of the Jordan Valley," *BS* 5 (1848) 397-409.

Dead Sea cont.

*Anonymous, "The Jordan and the Dead Sea," *MR* 31 (1849) 633-653. *(Review)*

*†Anonymous, "The River Jordan and the Dead Sea," *NBR* 11 (1849) 494-527. *(Review)*

*†Anonymous, "The Dead Sea," *SPR* 3 (1849-50) 381-410. *(Review)* *[Narrative of the U.S. Expedition]*

*†Anonymous, "United States Expedition to the Jordan and Dead Sea," *TLJ* 2 (1849-50) 288-301. *(Review)*

*T. H. F., "Narrative of the United States Expedition to the River Jordan and the Dead Sea," *MQR, 1st Ser.,* 4 (1850) 15-33. *(Review)*

*Carl Ritter, "On the Explorations of the Jordan River and the Dead Sea," *JSL, 1st Ser.,* 7 (1851) 334-359.

*†Anonymous, "De Saulcy's Dead Sea and Bible Lands," *DR* 35 (1853) 139-172. *(Review)*

Anonymous, "Notice of the Dead Sea," *SPR* 7 (1853-54) 505-522.

Joseph P. Thompson, "Recent Explorations of the Dead Sea," *BS* 12 (1855) 528-559.

J. J. M., "The Dead Sea," *BFER* 19 (1870) 719-734.

*Edward Hull, "Note on Mr. I. C. Russell's Paper on the Jordan Arabah and the Dead Sea," *PEFQS* 21 (1889) 32-34.

W. F. Birch, "The Dead Sea Visible from Jerusalem," *PEFQS* 22 (1890) 170.

J. E. Hanauee,"The Dead Sea Visible from Jerusalem," *PEFQS* 22 (1890) 170.

(Mrs.) E. A. Finn, "Notes by Mrs. Finn, M.R.A.S. I. The Dead Sea Visible from Jerusalem," *PEFQS* 23 (1891) 83.

Gray Hill, "The Dead Sea," *PEFQS* 32 (1900) 273-282.

Dead Sea cont.

C[harles] W. Wilson, "The Dead Sea," *PEFQS* 32 (1900) 365-369. (Note by Charles Warren, p. 369)

E. W. Gurney Masterman, "Observations on the Dead Sea Levels," *PEFQS* 34 (1902) 155-160; 36 (1904) 83-95.

Putnam Cady, "Exploration in the Dead Sea Region," *BW* 21 (1903) 327-346.

E. W. G. Masterman, "Dead Sea Observations," *PEFQS* 35 (1903) 177-178.

E. W. G. Masterman, "Dead Sea Observations. *(Continued),*" *PEFQS* 36 (1904) 163-168, 280-281.

E. W. G. Masterman, "The Physical History of the Dead Sea Valley," *BW* 25 (1905) 249-257.

E. W. G. Masterman, "The Exploration of the Dead Sea Valley," *BW* 25 (1905) 407-417.

E. W. G. Masterman, "Explorations in the Dead Sea Valley," *AAOJ* 27 (1905) 249-258.

E. W. Gurney Masterman, "Dead Sea Observations," *PEFQS* 37 (1905) 158-159; 38 (1906) 69, 232-234; 39 (1907) 302-304; 40 (1908) 160-161; 41 (1909) 68-70; 42 (1910) 290-291; 43 (1911) 59-61, 158-161; 44(1912) 213; 45 (1913) 42-44; 49 (1917) 185-187.

*Nathaniel Schmidt, "The East Shore of the Dead Sea and the Ruins in Wadi Suweil," *JBL* 25 (1906) 82-96.

*Francis Brown, "Visits to the West Shore of the Dead Sea and the Arabah," *AJA* 13 (1909) 55.

E. W. G. Masterman, "Dead Sea Observations: 1908," *PEFQS* 41 (1909) 68-70.

Anonymous, "Causeway Across the Dead Sea," *RP* 9 (1910) 229.

Dead Sea concluded

E. W. G. Masterman, "Three Early Explorers in the Dead Sea Valley. Costigan-Molyneux-Lynch," *PEFQS* 43 (1911) 12-27.

E. W. G. Masterman, "Summary of the Observations on the Rise and Fall of the Level of the Dead Sea, 1900-1913," *PEFQS* 45 (1913) 192-197.

E. W. G. Masterman, "Dead Sea Observations. Spring Visit, 1913," *PEFQS* 45 (1913) 197.

John Gray Hill, "The Dead Sea," *PEFQS* 46 (1914) 23-29.

*T. J. Salmon and T. G. T. McCaw, "The Level and Cartography of the Dead Sea," *PEFQS* 68 (1936) 103-111.

P[atrick] P. McKenna, "By the Shores of the Dead Sea," *IER, 5th Ser.,* 50 (1937) 370-381.

*E. W. G. Masterman, "The Dead Sea and the Lost Cities of the Plain," *JTVI* 69 (1937) 212-223, 228-229. (Discussion, pp. 223-228)

*Raymond S. Haupert, "Exploring the Jordan and Dead Sea with the U. S. Navy," *CQ* 22 (1945) 226-241.

M. Copisarow, "The Ancient Egyptian, Greek and Hebrew concept of the Dead Sea," *VT* 12 (1962) 1-13.

H. W. Underhill, "Dead Sea Levels and the P.E.F. Mark," *PEQ* 99 (1967) 45-53.

Debir (See also: Tell Beit Mirsim & Kirjath Sepher)

Claude R. Conder, "The Royal Canannite and Levitical City of Debir," *PEFQS* 7 (1875) 48-56.

Anonymous, "Debir—A Mound of Ten Cities. The story of a Palestinian city excavated this century considering especially the period from Joshua to Nebuchadnezzar," *BH* 1 (1964) #3, 3-10.

Deir 'Allā

H. J. Franken, "The Excavations at Deir 'Allā in Jordan. with 16 Plates," *VT* 10 (1960) 386-393.

H. J. Franken, "The Excavations at Deir 'Allā in Jordan, 2nd Season. with 23 Plates," *VT* 11 (1961) 361-372.

H. J. Franken, "The Excavations at Deir 'Allā in Jordan, 3rd Season," *VT* 12 (1962) 378-382.

H. J. Franken, "The Excavations at Deir 'Allâ, Season 1964. With X Plates," *VT* 14 (1964) 417-422.

Deir Eban

*C. Clermont-Ganneau, "Deir Eban, The Great Eben, and Eben Ha-ezer," *PEFQS* 9 (1877) 154-156.

Dhahrat el Humraiya

J. Ory, "A Bronze Age Cemetery at Dhahrat el Humraiya," *QDAP* 13 (1948) 75-89.

Diblatham

C[laude] R. Conder, "Diblatham," *PEFQS* 15 (1883) 181-182.

Dibon

Duncan Mackenzie, "Dibon: The City of King Mesa and of the Moabite Stone," *PEFQS* 45 (1913) 57-79.

G. Ernest Wright, "Dibon in Moab," *BA* 15 (1952) 45.

F. V. Winnett, "Excavations at Dibon in Moab, 1950-51," *BASOR* #125 (1952) 7-20.

A. Douglas Tushingham, "Excavations in Dibon in Moab, 1952-53," *BASOR* #133 (1954) 6-26.

Dibon concluded

William L. Reed, The Story of a Biblical City Called Dibon," *LTQ* 2 (1967) 113-122.

Dinhabah

Henry George Tomkins, "Dinhabah. *A New Identification,*" *PEFQS* 23 (1891) 322-323.

*C[laude] R. Conder, "Notes by Major Conder, R.E. III. Notes on Herr Schick's Report, Tell el Hesy Inscriptions, and Dinhabah," *PEFQS* 24 (1892) 46.

Gray Hill, "Dinhabah," *PEFQS* 24 (1892) 47.

Djett

W[illiam] F[oxwell] Albright, "The Late Bronze Town at Modern Djett," *BASOR* #104 (1946) 25-26.

Dor

*B. D. Zaphrir (Frimorgen), "'Even Three Countries'," *BIES* 14 (1947-48) #3/4, II. *[Dor]*

Dothan

Joseph P. Free, "The First Season of Excavation at Dothan," *BASOR* #131 (1953) 16-20.

Joseph P. Free, "The Second Season at Dothan," *BASOR* #135 (1954) 14-20.

Joseph P. Free, "The Third Season at Dothan,"*BASOR* #139 (1955) 3-9.

*Anonymous, "Excavations in Jordan, 1953-1954," *ADAJ* 3 (1956) 74-87. [Dothan, 1954—Wheaton Archaeological Expedition, directed by Joseph P. Free, pp. 79-80]

Dothan concluded

Joseph P. Free, "The Excavation of Dothan," *BA* 19 (1956) 43-48.

Joseph P. Free, "The Fourth Season at Dothan," *BASOR* #143 (1956) 11-17.

Anonymous, "Excavations at Dothan," *AT* 1 (1956-57) #1, 16.

Joseph P. Free, "The Fifth Season at Dothan," *BASOR* #152 (1958) 10-18.

Joseph P. Free, "The Sixth Season at Dothan," *BASOR* #156 (1959) 23-29.

Joseph P. Free, "The Seventh Season at Dothan," *BASOR* #160 (1960) 6-15.

*Joseph P. Free, "Excavations in Jordan 1960/1961. The Seventh Season of Excavations at Dothan," *ADAJ* 6&7 (1962) 117-120.

Tell ed-Duweir

J. L. Starkey, "A Lecture Delivered at the Rooms of the Palestine Exploration Fund, on June 22nd, 1933," *PEFQS* 65 (1933) 190-199. *[Tell ed-Duweir]*

J. L. Starkey, "Excavations at Tell Duweir: Wellcome Archæological Research Expedition, 1933-4," *Man* 34 (1934) #129.

J. L. Starkey, "Excavations at Tell Duweir, 1933-4," *PEFQS* 66 (1934) 164-175.

J. L. Starkey, "Excavations at Tell Duweir, 1934-1935. Wellcome Archaeological Research Expedition to the Near East," *PEFQS* 67 (1935) 198-207.

J. L. Starkey, "Four Season's Work at Tell Duweir. Wellcome Archaeological Research Expedition to the Near East," *PEFQS* 68 (1936) 178-189.

C. H. Inge, "Excavations at Tell ed-Duweir," *PEQ* 70 (1938) 238-256.

Tell ed-Duweir concluded

J. L. Starkey, "Excavations at Tell ed-Duweir. Wellcome Marston Archaeological Research Expedition to the Near East," *PEQ* 69 (1937) 228-241.

*D. Winton Thomas, "The Site of Ancient Lachish. *The Evidence of Ostrakon IV from Tell ed-Duweir*," *PEQ* 72 (1940) 148-149.

Olga Tufnell, "Excavations at Tell Ed-Duweir, Palestine. Directed by the late J. L. Starkey, 1932-1938," *PEQ* 82 (1950) 65-80.

B. S. J. Isserlin and Olga Tufnell, "The City Deposits at Tel Ed-Duweir: A Summary of the Stratification," *PEQ* 82 (1950) 81-91.

E

Mount Ebal

*C[harles] W. Wilson, "Ebal and Gerizim, 1866," *PEFQS* 5 (1873) 66-71.

*C[harles] Wm. Wilson, "Acoustics at Mount Ebal and Gerizim," *PEFQS* 23 (1891) 79.

*Henry A. Harper, "Ebal and Gerizim," *PEFQS* 28 (1896) 85-86.

Eben

*C. Clermont-Ganneau, "Deir Eban, The Great Eben, and Eben Ha-ezer," *PEFQS* 9 (1877) 154-156.

Ebenezer

*C. Clermont-Ganneau, "Deir Eban, The Great Eben, and Eben Ha-ezer," *PEFQS* 9 (1877) 154-156.

W. F. Birch, "Eben-ezer," *PEFQS* 13 (1881) 100-101.

W. F. Birch, "Ebenezer," *PEFQS* 14 (1882) 262-264.

Ebenezer concluded

Thomas Chaplin, "The Site of Ebenezer," *PEFQS* 20 (1888) 263-265. (Note by C. R. Conder, pp. 265-266)

Howard Crosby, "New Exegesis Required by New Discoveries.—No. 2. Ebenezer," *HR* 21 (1891) 460-461.

*Walter Milner, "Kirjath-jearim and Eben-ezer," *PEFQS* 19 (1887) 111.

El-Edhemiyah

*R. A. Stewart Macalister, "El-Edhemiyeh (Jeremiah's Grotto)," *PEFQS* 34 (1902) 129-132.

*J. E. Hanauer, "El-Edhemiyeh (Jeremiah's Grotto)," *PEFQS* 35 (1903) 86-90.

Edom

*Charles W. Wilson, "Recent Investigations in Moab and Edom," *JTVI* 33 (1901) 242-248. (Discussion, pp. 248-252)

G. A. Smith, "The Land of Edom," *Exp, 7th Ser.,* 6 (1908) 325-336, 506-517.

Nelson Glueck, "The Boundaries of Edom," *HUCA* 11 (1936) 141-157.

*Nelson Glueck, "Surface Finds in Edom and Moab," *PEQ* 71 (1939) 188-192.

*John Dayton, "The City of Teima and the Land of Edom," *ULBIA* 8&9 (1968-69) 253-256.

*J. R. Bartlett, "The Land of Seir and the Brotherhood of Edom," *JTS, N.S.,* 20 (1969) 1-20.

Eglon

*Anonymous, "Lachish and Eglon," *ONTS* 11 (1890) 313.

'Ein-Gedi (See Engedi)

'Ein-Gev

Anonymous, "'Ein-Gev," *IEJ* 11 (1961) 192-193.

B[enjamin] Mazar, A[braham] Biran, M[oshe] Dothan, and I[manuel] Dunayevsky, "'Ein-Gev. Excavations in 1961," *IEJ* 14 (1964) 1-49.

Ekron

*S. Kallai-Kleinmann, "Notes on Eltekeh, Ekron and Timnah," *BIES* 17 (1952-53) #1/2, IV.

*M. Naor, "Bet/*sic*/ Dagon and Gederoth-Kidron, Eltekeh and Ekron," *EI* 5 (1958) 90*-91*.

*J. Naveh (Levy), "Khirbet el-Muqanna'—'Eqron," *BIES* 21 (1957) #3/4, III.

*J. Naveh, "Khirbat al-Muqanna'—Ekron," *IEJ* 8 (1958) 87-100, 165-170.

Elah

*Claude R. Conder, "David and Goliath," *PEFQS* 7 (1875) 191-195. [Valley of Elah, pp. 193-194]

Elath (See also: Ezion-Geber)

*Nelson Glueck, "The Topography and History of Ezion-Geber and Elath," *BASOR* #72 (1938) 2-13.

*Nelson Glueck, "Ezion-Geber: Elath, The Gateway to Arabia," *BA* 2 (1939) 37-41.

*Nelson Glueck, "The First Campagin at Tell-Kheleifeh (Ezion-Geber: Elath)," *BASOR* #75 (1939) 8-22.

Elath concluded

*Nelson Glueck, "Ezion-Geber: Elath—City of Bricks and Straw," *BA* 3 (1940) 51-56.

*Y[ohanan] Aharoni, "Tamar and the Roads to Elath," *EI* 5 (1958) 91*.

*Y[ohanan] Aharoni, "Tamar and the Roads to Elath," *IEJ* 13 (1963) 30-42.

Elealeh

*William L. Reed, "The History of Elealeh ('el-'Al) in Moab," *CollBQ* 42 (1965) #1, 12-16.

Eltekeh

*S. Kallai-Kleinmann, "Notes on Eltekeh, Ekron and Timnah," *BIES* 17 (1952-53) #1/2, IV.

*M. Naor, "Bet/sic/ Dagon and Gederoth-Kidron, Eltekeh and Ekron," *EI* 5 (1958) 90*-91*.

Emek

*N. Tzori, "An Ancient Site in Swamp Soil in the Emek (Valley of Jezreel)," *PEQ* 89 (1957) 82-83.

Emek ha-Bakha

*Daivd Yellin, "Emek ha-bakha: Bekhaim," *JPOS* 3 (1923) 191-196.

Emeq Zebulun

*M. Hecker, "The Roman Road and the Swamps in the Emeq Zebulun," *BIES* 8 (1940-41) #3, I.

Endor

*B. C. Zaphrir (Frimorgen), "'Even Three Countries'," *BIES* 14 (1947-48) #3/4, II. [En-dor]

Nehemia Zori, "New Light on Endor," *PEQ* 84 (1952) 114-117.

Z./sic/ Kallai-Kelinmann, "En-Dor," *EI* 5 (1958) 90*.

Engedi

Anonymous, "The Land of Hills. No. III.—Engedi," *CongML* 20 (1837) 554-563.

B[enjamin] Maisler, "A Sounding at En-gedi," *BIES* 15 (1949-50) #1/2, II.

Y[ohanan] Aharoni, "Archaeological Survey of 'Ein-Gedi," *BIES* 22 (1958) #1/2, V-VI.

J. Naveh (Levi), "Chalcolithic Remains at 'Ein-Gedi," *BIES* 22 (1958) #1/2, VI.

*Anonymous, "En-gedi," *IEJ* 11 (1961) 76-77. *(Tell el-Jurn // Tel Goren)*

Anonymous, "En-gedi," *IEJ* 12 (1962) 145-146.

Benjamin Mazar, "Excavations at the Oasis of Engedi," *Arch* 16 (1963) 99-107.

B[enjamin] Mazar and I[manuel] Dunayevsky, "En-Gedi. The Third Sesaon of Excavations. Preliminary Report," *IEJ* 14 (1964) 121-130.

B[enjamin] Mazar and I[manuel] Dunayevsky, "Engeddi," *IEJ* 15 (1965) 258-259.

B[enjamin] Mazar, Trude Dothan, and I[manuel] Dunayevsky, "En-Gedi. The First and Second Seasons of Excavations 1961-1962," *'Atiqot* 5 (1966) 1-100.

En-Gedi concluded

B[enjamin] Mazar and I[manuel] Dunayevsky, "En-Gedi. The Fourth
and Fifth Seasons of Excavations (Preliminary Report)," *IEJ* 17
(1967) 133-143.

En Mishpat

R.   Macgegor,   "En   Mishpat,"   *PEQ*   71   (1939)   204.

T. H. Gaster, "En Mishpat: A Rejoinder," *PEQ* 72 (1940) 61-63.

En-Rogel

*Charles Clermont-Ganneau, "The Stone of Zoheleth, En-Rogel and
the King's Gardens," *PEFQS* 2 (1870) 251-253.

W. F. Birch, "En-rogel, and the Brook that Overflowed," *PEFQS* 21
(1889) 45-52.

G. Dalton, "The Exploration of En-Rogel, or Job's Well," *PEFQS* 55
(1923) 165-173.

R. Macgregor, "The Spring En-Rogel," *PEQ* 70 (1938) 257-258.

Ephes-dammim

*Claude R. Conder, "David and Goliath," *PEFQS* 7 (1875) 191-195.
[Ephes-dammim, p. 192-193]

Ephraim

William F[oxwell] Albright, "The Ephraim of the Old and New
Testaments," *JPOS* 3 (1923) 36-40.

*W. J. Phytian-Adams, "Jericho, Ai and the Occupation of Mount
Ephraim," *PEFQS* 68 (1936) 141-149.

Ephron

C[laude] R. Conder, "Notes. *Mount Ephron,*" *PEFQS* 15 (1883) 102.

W. F. Birch, "Varieties. *Ephron,*" *PEFQS* 15 (1883) 149-150.

Esdraelon

*G. Schumacher, "Reports from Galilee. The Lava Streams of the Plain of Esdraelon," *PEFQS* 32 (1900) 357-359.

Julius J. Rothschild, "The Fortified Zone and the Plain of Esdraelon," *PEQ* 70 (1938) 41-54.

*J[acob] Kaplan, "El-Jarba (Plain of Esdraelon)," *IEJ* 17 (1967) 269-270.

*J[acob] Kaplan, "Ein el Jarba. Chalcolithic Remains in the Plain of Esdraeolon," *BASOR* #194 (1969) 2-39.

Eshtaol

*P. Spyridon Malky, "Eshtaol and 'Arṭūf," *JPOS* 20 (1946) 43-47. [1. The Identification of Eshtaol with 'Arṭūf, pp. 43-45]

Es-Salt

*J. Garrow Duncan, "Es-Salt," *PEFQS* 60 (1928) 28-36, 98-100.

Etam

Anonymous, "The Rock Etam," *PEFQS* 10 (1878) 116-118.

*W. F. Birch, "The Rock of Etam and the Cave of Adullam," *PEFQS* 27 (1895) 338-341. (Notes by C. Clermont-Ganneau, *PEFQS* 28 (1896) p. 80; C. R. Conder, *PEFQS* 28 (1896) p. 82)

*W. F. Birch, "The Rock Etam and the Cave of Adullam," *PEFQS* 28 (1896) 161-164, 261-262. (Notes by C. R. Conder, and C. Clermont-Ganneau, p. 259)

Ezion-Geber (See also: Elath)

*W. J. Phythian-Adams, "Israel in the Arabah," *PEFQS* 65 (1933) 137-146. *[Ezion-Geber]*

*W. J. Phythian-Adams, "Israel in the Arabah (II)," *PEFQS* 66 (1934) 181-188.

Nelson Glueck, "Ezion-Geber," *Antiq* 12 (1938) 345-349.

*Nelson Glueck, "Ezion-Geber: Solomon's Naval Base on the Red Sea," *BA* 1 (1938) 13-16.

Nelson Glueck, "The First Campaign at Tell-Kheleifeh (Ezion-Geber)," *BASOR* #71 (1938) 3-17.

*Nelson Glueck, "The Topography and History of Ezion-Geber and Elath," *BASOR* #72 (1938) 2-13.

*Nelson Glueck, "Ezion-Geber: Elath, The Gateway to Arabia," *BA* 2 (1939) 37-41.

*Nelson Glueck, "The Second Campaign at Tell el-Kheleifeh (Ezion-Geber: Elath)," *BASOR* #75 (1939) 8-22.

*E. A. Cerny, "Archaeological Corner," *CBQ* 1 (1939) 166-168. [Asiongaber (Ezion-geber), pp. 166-167]

*Nelson Glueck, "Ezion-Geber: Elath—City of Bricks and Straw," *BA* 3 (1940) 51-56.

Nelson Glueck, "The Third Season of Excavation at Tell el-Kheleifeh," *BASOR* #79 (1940) 2-18. *[Ezion-Geber]*

*J. W. Jack, "Recent Biblical Archaeology," *ET* 52 (1940-41) 353-357. [Ezion-Geber *(Tell el-Kheleifeh)*, pp. 355-356]

*Nelson Glueck, "The Excavations of Solomon's Seaport: Ezion-Geber," *SIR* (1941) 453-478.

Mary Neely, "Ezion Geber," *AT* 2 (1957-58) #4, 6-7.

Nelson Glueck, "Ezion-Geber," *BA* 28 (1965) 70-87.

Ezion-Geber concluded

*Anonymous, "Ezion-Geber Reconsidered. An excavator takes a new look at his findings at Solomon's seaport on the gulf of Aqabah," *BH* 2 (1965) #4, 17-19, 24.

Nelson Glueck, "Ezion-geber," *BibT* #16 (1965) 1042-1050.

F

Tell El Far'a

*Richard St. Barbe Baker, "The Lost Cities of Judah," *A&A* 33 (1932) 253-258. *[Tell Fara = Shishak]*

G. Ernest Wright, "The Excavation at Tell El-Far'ah," *BA* 12 (1949) 66-68.

*John Gray, "Tell el Far'a by Nablus: A 'Mother' in Ancient Israel," *PEQ* 84 (1952) 110-113.

*R[oland] de Vaux, "The Excavations at Tell El-Far'ah and the Site of the Ancient Tirzah," *PEQ* 88 (1956) 125-140.

Tell el Ful (See: Gibeah)

Fuller's Field

George St. Clair, "The Fuller's Field," *PEFQS* 23 (1891) 189-190.

*W. F. Birch, "The Gutter Not Near the Fuller's Field," *PEFQS* 23 (1891) 254-256.

G

Gaba

*B[enjamin] Maisler, "Topographical Researches (IV)," *BIES* 11 (1944-45) #3/4, III. [Gabaa and Harosheth of the Gentiles]

*B[enjamin] Maisler, "Beth She'arim, Gaba, and the Harosheth of the Peoples," *HUCA* 24 (1952-53) 75-84.

Gabara

*E. W. G. Masterman, "The Galilee of Josephus. The Positions of Gabara, Jotapata and Taricheae," *PEFQS* 42 (1910) 268-280.

Gad

*P[atrick] P. McKenna, "The Hill Country of Gad," *IER, 5th Ser.*, 50 (1937) 164-173.

Gaderah

*J[acob] Kaplan, "Researches in the Gaderah—El-Mughar Area," *BIES* 17 (1952-53) #3/4, VI.

Galilee (includes Sea of)

Anonymous, "Prospectus of a Proposed Expedition to Sea of Galilee," *PEFQS* 10 (1878) 176-178.

Claude R. Conder, "Notes on the Topography of the Sea of Galilee," *PEFQS* 11 (1879) 168-170.

Anonymous, "The Waters of Galilee," *ONTS* 2 (1882-83) 173-174.

C[laude] R. Conder, "Curious Names in Galilee," *PEFQS* 15 (1885) 125-130.

Galilee (includes Sea of) cont.

*G. Maspero, "On the Geographical Names of the List of Thothmes III., which may be Referred to Galilee," *JTVI* 20 (1886-87) 308-319. (Discussion and Comments by Henry George Tomkins, p. 320; C. R. Conder, pp. 321-323; Charles Wilson, pp. 323-234; [W. St.] Boscawen, pp. 324-325; W. Wright, pp. 325-326) *(Trans. by Henry George Tomkins)*

*G. Schumacher, "Recent Discoveries—Notes and News from Galilee," *PEFQS* 19 (1887) 221-226. [1. Zimmarin; 2. Tiberias; 3. Akka; 4. Rushmia; 5. Saida]

*G. Schumacher, "Recent Discoveries in Galilee," *PEFQS* 21 (1889) 68-78. [Nazareth—Discovery of Large Cave; Jâ'uni; Esh-Shejara]

*C[laude] R. Conder, "Conquests of Rameses in Galilee," *PEFQS* 22 (1890) 310.

J. S. Riggs, "Studies in Palestinian Geography. V. Galilee," *BW* 4 (1894) 421-431.

*G. Schumacher, "Reports from Galilee," *PEFQS* 27 (1895) 110-114.

*G. Schumacher, "Reports from Galilee," *PEFQS* 31 (1899) 339-343. (Note by C. Clermont-Ganneau, *PEFQS* 32 (1900) p. 79)

E. W. G. Masterman, "A Three Days' Tour Around the Sea of Galilee," *BW* 26 (1905) 167-183.

Anonymous, "Rise and Fall of the Sea of Galilee, 1904," *PEFQS* 37 (1905) 363.

E. W. G. Masterman, "Lower Galilee," *BW* 32 (1908) 159-168.

E. W. G. Masterman, "Upper Galilee," *BW* 32 (1908) 234-241.

*E. W. G. Masterman, "The Galilee of Josephus. The Positions of Gabara, Jotapata and Taricheae," *PEFQS* 42 (1910) 268-280.

F. Turville Petre, "Prehistoric Galilee," *Antiq* 1 (1927) 299-310.

Galilee (includes Sea of) concluded

*W[illiam] F[oxwell] Albright, "Among the Canaanite Mounds of Eastern Galilee," *BASOR* #29 (1928) 1-8. [The Canaanite Capital of Galilee, The City on the Horns of Ḥaṭṭîn, Chinnereth and Bethsaida, A Visit to Beth-shan]

Aapeli Saarisalo, "Topographical Researches in Galilee," *JPOS* 9 (1929) 27-40.

*M[ichael] Avi-Yonah, "Territorial Boundaries in North-Western Galilee," *JPOS* 14 (1934) 56-60.

*P[atrick] P. McKenna, "Galilee and the Lake of Genesareth," *IER, 5th Ser.,* 48 (1936) 282-294.

*C. C. McCown, "Two Years' Achievements in Palestinian Archaeology," *RL* 8 (1939) 97-108. [Galilee, p. 103]

Augustine Wand, "Along the North Shore of the Sea of Galilee," *CBQ* 5 (1943) 430-444.

Y[ohanan] Aharoni and Ruth Amiran, "Researches in Upper-Galilee," *BIES* 17 (1952-53) #3/4, VI. [1) Tell Hazor (Tell Waqqas); 2) Tell Na'ame; 3) Tell Sheikh Yusur; 4) Kadesh Naptali; 5) Tell Khirbet er-Ruweisa]

*Yohanan Aharoni, "Galilean Survey: Israelite Settlements and their Pottery," *EI* 4 (1956) VI.

D. H. K. Amiran, "Sites of Settlements in the Mountains of Lower Galilee," *IEJ* 6 (1956) 69-77.

Norman Bentwick, "Biblical Archæology in Galilee," *QRL* 296 (1958) 379-389.

The Garrison

W. F. B[irch], "Varieties. 2. *The Garrison,*" *PEFQS* 15 (1883) 150.

Gath

*Claude R. Conder, "David and Goliath," *PEFQS* 7 (1875) 191-195. [Gath, pp. 194-195]

W. F. Birch, "Gath," *PEFQS* 12 (1880) 170-171.

Trelawney Saunders, E. H. Palmers, and Claude R. Conder, "The Site of Gath," *PEFQS* 12 (1880) 211-223.

C[laude] R. Conder, "Notes on Disputed Points. *Gath,*" *PEFQS* 13 (1881) 85-86.

W. F. B[irch], "Varieties. 3. *Gath,*" *PEFQS* 15 (1883) 150.

Henry George Tomkins, "Gath and Its Worthies," *PEFQS* 18 (1886) 200-204.

*J. A. Paine, "Not Lachish, but Gath," *BS* 47 (1890) 682-691.

Anonymous, "Excavations at Gath," *AAOJ* 25 (1903) 177-178.

*W. F. Birch, "Mizpeh and Gath," *PEFQS* 35 (1903) 276.

*Anonymous, "Libnah and Gath," *BASOR* #4 (1921) 6.

*B[enjamin] Mazar, "Gath and Gittaim," *IEJ* 4 (1954) 227-235.

S. Yeivin, "Tel Gath," *IEJ* 11 (1961) 191.

*Hanna E. Kassis, "Gath and the Structure of the 'Philistine' Society," *JBL* 84 (1965) 259-271.

A[nson] F. Rainey, "Gath of the Philistines," *CNI* 17 (1966) #2/3, 30-38; #4, 23-34.

A[nson] F. Rainey, "Gath-Padalla," *IEJ* 18 (1968) 1-14.

Gaza

*Duncan Mackenzie, "The Port of Gaza and Excavations in Philistia," *PEFQS* 50 (1918) 72-87.

Gaza concluded

J. Garstang, "The Walls of Gaza," *PEFQS* 52 (1920) 156-157.

John P. Peters, "Notes and Queries. *The Walls of Gaza*," *PEFQS* 53 (1921) 60-61.

W. J. Phythian-Adams, "Reports on Soundings at Gaza, Etc.," *PEFQS* 55 (1923) 11-17.

W. J. Phythian-Adams, "Second Report on Soundings at Gaza," *PEFQS* 55 (1923) 18-30.

W. J. Phythian-Adams, "The Problem of 'Deserted' Gaza," *PEFQS* 55 (1923) 30-36.

*[W. M.] Flinders Petrie, "The Palaces of Ancient Gaza. Tell el Ajjūl," *AEE* 17 (1932) 1-9.

*N. P. Clarke, "Ancient Defences of Tell el Ajjūl," *AEE* 17 (1932) 10-12. /Gaza/

[W. M.] Flinders Petrie, "Ancient Gaza," *AEE* 17 (1932) 41-46.

[W. M.] Flinders Petrie, "Ancient Gaza, 1933 /sic/," *AEE* 17 (1932) 97-103.

Gebim

W. F. Birch, "Gebim," *PEFQS* 12 (1880) 108.

*H. H. Walker, "Where were Madmenah and the Gebim?" *JPOS* 13 (1933) 90-93.

Gederoth-Kidron

*M. Naor, "Bet /sic/ Dagon and Gederoth-Kidron, Eltekeh and Ekron," *EI* 5 (1958) 90*-91*.

Lake Genesareth

*P[atrick] P. McKenna, "Galilee and the Lake of Genesareth," *IER, 5th Ser.,* 48 (1936) 282-294.

P[atrick] P. McKenna, "By the Shores of Genezareth," *IER, 5th Ser.,* 51 (1938) 272-283.

Gerar

E. W., "Gerar and its Philistine Inhabitants," *JSL, 3rd Ser.,* 11 (1860) 309-319.

Yohanan Aharoni, "The Land of Gerar," *EI* 3 (1954) V.

Y[ohanan] Aharoni, "The Land of Gerar," *IEJ* 6 (1956) 26-32.

Gerasa / Gerash (See also: Jerash)

*John P. Peters, "Palestinian Exploration. *Notes of a Vacation in Palestine in 1902.*," *JBL* 22 (1903) 15-31. [4. Gerash—Gerasa, p. 17]

*Mary I. Hussey, "The Pompeii of Palestine," *A&A* 35 (1934) 3-17. *[Jerash, Gerasa]*

Joshua Starr, "A New Jewish Source for Gerasa," *JBL* 53 (1934) 167-169.

*William L. Reed, "Caravan Cities of the Near East," *CollBQ* 35 (1958) #3, 1-16. [Gerasa-Pearl of the Orient, pp. 8-12]

Mount Gerizim

*C[harles] W. Wilson, "Ebal and Gerizim, 1866," *PEFQS* 5 (1873) 66-71.

*C[harles] Wm. Wilson, "Acoustics at Mounts Ebal and Gerizim," *PEFQS* 23 (1891) 79.

*Henry A. Harper, "Ebal and Gerizim," *PEFQS* 28 (1896) 85-86.

John Bowman, "Pilgrimage to Mount Gerizim," *EI* 7 (1964) 17*-28*.

Geshur

*B[enjamin] Mazar, "Geshur and Maacah," *JBL* 80 (1961) 16-28.

Gezer

C. Clermont-Ganneau, "Discovery of the Royal Canaanite City of Gezer," *PEFQS* 5 (1873) 78-79.

Theodore F. Wright, "Exploration and Discovery: Gezer and its Excavation," *BW* 20 (1902) 388-392.

R. A. Stewart Macalister, "The History and Site of Gezer," *PEFQS* 34 (1902) 227-232.

R. A. Stewart Macalister, "First Quarterly Report of the Excavation of Gezer," *PEFQS* 34 (1902) 317-364. (Plates, pp. 366-375)

E. W. G. Masterman, "The Excavation of Ancient Gezer," *BW* 21 (1903) 407-425; 28 (1906) 176-186.

*John P. Peters, "Palestinian Exploration. *Notes of a Vacation in Palestine in 1902*," *JBL* 22 (1903) 15-31. [8. Gezer, pp. 23-24]

Anonymous, "Excavations at Gezer," *MR* 85 (1903) 306-309.

R. A. Stewart Macalister, "Second Quarterly Report on the Excavation of Gezer," *PEFQS* 35 (1903) 7-50.

R. A. Stewart Macalister, "Third Quarterly Report on the Excavation of Gezer," *PEFQS* 35 (1903) 107-125.

R. A. Stewart Macalister, "Fourth Quarterly Report of the Excavation of Gezer," *PEFQS* 35 (1903) 195-230.

R. A. Stewart Macalister, "Fifth Quarterly Report on the Excavation of Gezer," *PEFQS* 35 (1903) 299-322.

R. A. Stuart*/sic/* Macalister, "The Excavation of Gezer," *RP* 2 (1903) 63-64.

Anonymous, "Palestine," *RP* 2 (1903) 347-348. *[Gezer]*

Gezer cont.

*George A. Barton, "The Levitical Cities of Israel in the Light of the Excavation at Gezer," *BW* 24 (1904)167-179.

Lewis Bayles Paton, "A Visit to the English Excavations at Ancient Gezer," *HR* 48 (1904) 420-426.

R. A. Stewart Macalister, "Sixth Quarterly Report on the Excavation of Gezer," *PEFQS* 36 (1904) 9-26.

R. A. Stewart Macalister, "Seventh Quarterly Report on the Excavation of Gezer," *PEFQS* 36 (1904) 107-128.

R. A. Stewart Macalister, "Eighth Quarterly Report on the Excavation of Gezer," *PEFQS* 36 (1904) 194-228.

R. A. Stewart Macalister, "Ninth Quarterly Report on the Excavation of Gezer," *PEFQS* 36 (1904) 320-354.

R. A. Stewart Macalister, "Supplementary Notes on the Eighth Report," *PEFQS* 36 (1904) 355-357. *[Gezer]*

Anonymous, "Excavations at Gezer," *MR* 87 (1905) 981.

R. A. Stewart Macalister, "Tenth Quarterly Report on the Excavation of Gezer," *PEFQS* 37 (1905) 16-31. (Supplementary Notes on the Ninth Quarterly Report, pp. 31-33)

R. A. Stewart Macalister, "Eleventh Quarterly Report on the Excavation of Gezer," *PEFQS* 37 (1905) 97-115.

R. A. Stewart Macalister, "Twelfth Quarterly Report on the Excavation of Gezer," *PEFQS* 37 (1905) 183-199.

R. A. Stewart Macalister, "Thirteenth Quarterly Report on the Excavation of Gezer," *PEFQS* 37 (1905) 309-327.

E. W. G. Masterman, "The Excavation of Ancient Gezer," *BW* 28 (1906) 176-186.

*R. A. Stewart Macalister, "Gezer and Megiddo," *PEFQS* 38 (1906) 62-66.

Gezer cont.

*R. A. Stewart Macalister, "Gezer and Taanach," *PEFQS* 38 (1906) 115-120.

Hugh [F.] Pope, "The Excavations at Gezer and the Light they throw upon the Bible," *DR* 141 (1907) 296-324.

*S[tanley] A. Cook, "Notes and Queries. 4. *Carthage and Gezer,*" *PEFQS* 38 (1906) 159-160.

R. A. Stewart Macalister, "Fourteenth Quarterly Report on the Excavation of Gezer," *PEFQS* 39 (1907) 184-204.

R. A. Stewart Macalister, "Fifteenth Quarterly Report on the Excavation of Gezer," *PEFQS* 39 (1907) 254-268.

Theodore F. Wright, "Palestine Exploration," *RP* 6 (1907) 157-158. *[Gezer]*

[F.] Hugh Pope, "A Visit to a Modern Excavation," *NYR* 3 (1907-08) 418-428. *[Gezer]*

R. A. Stewart Macalister, "Sixteenth Quarterly Report on the Excavation of Gezer," *PEFQS* 40 (1908) 13-25.

R. A. Stewart Macalister, "Seventeenth Quarterly Report on the Excavation of Gezer," *PEFQS* 40 (1908) 96-111.

R. A. Stewart Macalister, "Eighteenth Quarterly Report on the Excavation of Gezer," *PEFQS* 40 (1908) 200-218. (Correction, *PEFQS* 41 (1909) p. 74)

R. A. Stewart Macalister, "Ninteenth Quarterly Report on the Excavation of Gezer," *PEFQS* 40 (1908) 272-290.

*G. Buchanan Gray, "The Excavations at Gezer and Religion in Ancient Palestine," *Exp, 7th Ser.,*7 (1909) 423-442.

R. A. Stewart Macalister, "Twentieth Quarterly Report on the Excavation of Gezer," *PEFQS* 41 (1909) 13-25.

R. A. Stewart Macalister, "Twenty-First Quarterly Report on the Excavation of Gezer," *PEFQS* 41 (1909) 87-105.

Gezer cont.

R. A. Stewart Macalister, "The Excavation of Gezer: Supplementary Details," *PEFQS* 41 (1909) 183-189.

J. D. Crace, "Work of the Palestine Exploration Fund at Gezer During 1908," *RP* 8 (1909) 78-83.

Wallace Nelson Stearns, "The Story of Gezer," *BS* 75 (1918) 104-117.

*Arthur T. Burbridge, "Caves, Pits, and Sheol," *LQHR* 130 (1918) 75-86. *[Excavations at Gezer]*

E. W. G. Masterman, "Gezer," *PEFQS* 66 (1934) 135-140.

Alan Rowe, "The 1934 Excavations at Gezer," *PEFQS* 67 (1935) 19-33.

*J. W. Jack, "Recent Biblical Archaeology," *ET* 54 (1942-43) 78-82. [1. Gezer, p. 79]

G. Ernest Wright, "A Solomonic City Gate at Gezer," *BA* 21 (1958) 103-104.

Y[igael] Yadin, "Solomon's City Wall and Gate at Gezer," *IEJ* 8 (1958) 80-86.

G. E[rnest] Wright, "Gezer," *IEJ* 15 (1965) 252-253.

Joe D. Seger, "Why We Dig—at Gezer!" *HQ* 7 (1966-67) #4, 19-39.

Wm. G. Dever, "Gezer," *IEJ* 16 (1966) 277-278; 17 (1967) 274-275.

H. Darrell Lance, "Gezer in the Land and in History," *BA* 30 (1967) 34-47.

William G. Dever, "Excavations at Gezer," *BA* 30 (1967) 47-62; 19 (1969) 241-243.

James F. Ross, "Gezer in the Tell el-Amarna Letters," *BA* 30 (1967) 62-70.

Joe D. Seger, "The Hebrew Union College Excavations at Gezer," *AJA* 72 (1968) 172.

Gezer concluded

John S. Holladay Jr., "Excavations at Tell Gezer, 1968," *AJA* 73 (1969) 237.

Dan B. Cole, "Hebrew Union College's Excavation at Gezer," *CCARJ* 16 (1969) #2, 2-9.

W[illiam] G. Dever, "Gezer," *IEJ* 19 (1969) 241-243.

Tell el (Teleilat) Ghassul

*J[oan] W. Crowfoot, "Three Recent Excavations in Palestine," *PEFQS* 62 (1930) 172-177. [1. Teleilat Ghassūl, pp. 172-174]

J. Garrow Duncan, "Pere Mallon's Excavation of Teleilat Ghassul," *AEE* 16 (1931) 65-72.

J. Garrow Duncan, "Pere Mallon's Excavations of Teleilat Ghassūl," *PEFQS* 64 (1932) 71-77.

Edward A. Cerny, "Archaeological Corner. Teleilat Ghassul," *CBQ* 2 (1940) 264-266.

*R[obert] North, "'Ghassulian' in Palestine Chronological Nomenclature," *SBO* 1 (1959) 407-421.

Robert North, "The 1960 Ghassul Excavations," *AJA* 65 (1961) 191.

D. [C.] Baramki, "Preliminary Report on the Excavations at Tell el Ghassil," *BMB* 16 (1961) 87-102.

D. C. Baramki, "Second Preliminary Report on the Excavations at Tell el Ghassil," *BMB* 17 (1964) 47-103.

D. C. Baramki, "Third Preliminary Report of the Excavations at Tell el Ghassil," *BMB* 19 (1966) 29-49.

J. B Hennessy, "Preliminary Report on a First Season of Excavations at Teleilat Ghassul," *L* 1 (1969) 1-24.

Ghrubba

James Mallaart, "The Neolithic Site of Ghrubba," *ADAJ* 3 (1956) 24-40.

Gibbethon

*Anonymous, "Researches of the Circle for Historical Geography,"
BIES 16 (1951) #3/4, VI. *[Gibbethon]*

Gibeah (Tell el Ful)

E[dward] Robinson, "Notes on Biblical Geography. I. Gibeah of Saul,"
BS 1 (1844) 598-602.

Claude R. Conder, "Gibeah of Saul," *PEFQS* 9 (1877) 104-105.

*W. F. Birch, "The Rock Rimmon and Gibeah," *PEFQS* 12 (1880)
236-237.

C[laude] R. Conder, "Notes on Disputed Points. *Gibeah of Saul,"*
PEFQS 13 (1881) 89.

*W. F. Birch, "Varieties," *PEFQS* 14 (1882) 59-61. *[Gibeah]*

*W. F. Birch, "Gibeah of Saul and Zela. The Site of Jonathan's Home
and Tomb," *PEFQS* 43 (1911) 101-109.

*W. F. Birch, "Notes and Queries. 2. *Kh. Adaseh and Gibeah of Saul,"*
PEFQS 43 (1911) 161-162.

W. F. Birch, "Gibeah at Adaseh," *PEFQS* 45 (1913) 38-42.

*E. W. G. Masterman, "Tell el-Ful and Khurbet 'Adāseh," *PEFQS* 45
(1913) 132-137.

W. F. Birch, "The Site of Gibeah," *PEFQS* 46 (1914) 42-44.

Anoymous, "Archaeological Notes and Comments. Excavations of the
American School in Jerusalem at Tell El-Ful," *A&A* 14 (1922)
104.

Anonymous, "Preliminary Reports on Tell El-Ful," *BASOR* #6 (1922)
7-8.

Gibeah concluded

W[illiam] F[oxwell] Albright, "Gibeah of Saul and Benjamin," *BASOR* #6 (1922) 8-11.

Anonymous, "The Excavation at Tell El-Ful," *BASOR* #7 (1922) 7-8.

W[illiam] F[oxwell] Albright, "A New Campaign of Excavation at Gibeah of Saul," *BASOR* #52 (1933) 6-12.

Lawrence A Sinclair, "An Archaeological Study of Gibeah (Tell el-Fûl)," *BA* 27 (1964) 52-64.

Paul W. Lapp, "Tell El-Ful," *BA* 28 (1965) 2-10.

*Anonymous, "Some Archaeological Notes," *BH* 2 (1965) #3, 16-18. [Gibeah (Tell el Ful)]

Gibeon

C[onrad] Schick, "The Waters of Gibeon," *PEFQS* 22 (1890) 23.

*Andrew J. Gregg, "Note on Gibeon, Nob, Bezek and the High-Level Aqueduct to Jerusalem," *PEFQS* 31 (1899) 128-129.

James B. Pritchard, "The First Excavation at Gibeon, 1956," *AJA* 61 (1957) 185.

Anonymous, "Some Important Finds at Gibeon," *AT* 1 (1956-57) #3, 14-15.

James B. Pritchard, "Discovery of Biblical Gibeon," *UMB* 21 (1957) #1, 3-26.

James B. Pritchard, "A Second Excavation at Gibeon," *UMB* 22 (1958) #2, 13-24.

James B. Pritchard, "Gibeon's history in the light of excavation," *VTS* 7 (1960) 1-12.

James B. Pritchard, "The Bible Reports on Gibeon," *Exped* 3 (1960-61) #4, 2-9.

Gibeon concluded

Edward F. Campbell Jr., "Gibeon," *BA* 26 (1963) 27-30.

John Huesman, "'. . . for Gibeon was a Great City' (Jos. 10:2)," *BibT* #12 (1964) 761-767.

Gihon

W. F. Birch, "Gihon," *PEFQS* 22 (1890) 199-200; 23 (1891) 80-82.

Thomas Chaplin, "Gihon," *PEFQS* 22 (1890) 124-125, 331.

*W. F. Birch, "Zion (or Acra), Gihon, and Millo. *(All South of the Temple)*," *PEFQS* 25 (1893) 324-330.

Mount Gilboa

G. J. H. Ovenden, "Mount Gilboa," *PEFQS* 56 (1924) 193-195.

Gil 'Am

E[phraim] Stern, "Gil 'Am," *IEJ* 16 (1966) 281-282.

Gilead

Nelson Glueck, "Some Chalcolithic Sites in Northern Gilead," *BASOR* #104 (1946) 12-20.

Gilgal

Anonymous, "Gilgal," *PEFQS* 10 (1878) 118-119.

James Muilenburg, "The Site of Ancient Gilgal," *BASOR* #140 (1955) 11-27.

C. Umhau Wolf, "The Location of Gilgal," *BRes* 11 (1966) 42-51.

Jack P. Lewis, "In Search of Gilgal," *RestQ* 11 (1968) 137-143.

Gittaim

*B[enjamin] Mazar, "Gath and Gittaim," *IEJ* 4 (1954) 227-235.

Give'at ha-Elohim

*B[enjamin] Mazar, "Topographical Studies III," *BIES* 10 (1942-43) #2/3, III. [Give'at ha-Elohim *(The Hill of God)*]

Gomorrah (For complete listing, see: Sodom)

*George Warington, "The Site of Sodom and Gomorrah," *JSL, 4th Ser.,* 9 (1866) 36-57.

*C. Clermont-Ganneau, "Segor, Gomorrah, and Sodom," *PEFQS* 18 (1886) 19-21.

*John Hogg, "On the Site of Sodom and Gomorrah," *JSL, 4th Ser.,* 10 (1866-67) 185-186.

*Edward Hull, "Requests and Replies," *ET* 6 (1894-95) 420. *[Location of Sodom and Gomorrah]*

*E. Power, "The site of Pentapolis," *B* 11 (1930) 23-62, 149-182. *[Gomorrah]*

*Frederick G. Clapp, "The Site of Sodom and Gomorrah," *AJA* 40 (1936) 323-344.

*P. E. Kretzmann, "The Site of Sodom and Gomorrah," *CTM* 8 (1937) 132-133.

*J. Penrose Harland, "Sodom and Gomorrah: The Location of the Cities of the Plain," *BA* 5 (1942) 17-32. [Evidence from the Bible; Evidence from Greek and Latin Writers; The Pillar of Salt; Water Supply; Evidence from Archaeology; The Rise in Water-Level; The Roman Road; The Location of the Cities of the Plain]

Gomorrah concluded

*J. Penrose Harland, "Sodom and Gomorrah: II. The Destruction of the Cities of the Plain," *BA* 6 (1943) 41-54. [The Biblical Evidence; Evidence of Later Writers; Fire and Brimstone and Geology; The Apple of Sodom; Notes on the Later History of the Plain; Oil in Palestine]

*J. Simons, "Two Notes on the Problem of the Pentapolis," *OTS* 4 (1948) 92-117.

Tel Goren (See: En-gedi ←)

Goshen (in Palestine)

Samuel Daiches, "Goshen in Palestine," *PEFQS* 55 (1923) 91-93.

Gublana

I. Press, "Miscellanea," *BIES* 10 (1942-44) #4, III. *[Gublana]*

The Gutter (Tsinnor)

(Mrs.) E. A. Finn, "The Tsinnor," *PEFQS* 22 (1890) 195-198. [Correction, *PEFQS* 23 (1891) p. 83]

W. F. Birch, "The Gutter (Tsinnor)," *PEFQS* 22 (1890) 330-331.

*W. F. Birch, "The Gutter Not Near the Fuller's Field," *PEFQS* 23 (1891) 254-256.

H

Hadrach

*E. G. H. Kraeling, "Geographical Notes," *AJSL* 41 (1924-25) 193-194. [III. The Location of Hadrach, p. 194]

Haifa

(   ) Dowling, "The Town of Haifa," *PEFQS* 46 (1914) 184-191.

el-Ḥajar

*E. W. G. Masterman, "'Ain el-Feshkhah, el-Ḥajar el-Aṣbaḥ, and Khurbet Ḳumrân, " *PEFQS* 34 (1902) 160-167, 297-299.

Tel Ḥalif

A. Biran and R. Gophna, "Tel Ḥalif," *IEJ* 15 (1965) 255.

Tell el-Ḥammam

Frank Hole, "A Reanalysis of Basal Tabbat al-Hammam, Syria," *Syria* 36 (1959) 149-183.

Tel el-Ḥammeh

Nelson Glueck, "The Archaeological Exploration of el-Ḥammeh on the Yarmuk," *BASOR* #49 (1933) 22-23.

*N. Makhouly, "El Ḥamme. *Discovery of Stone Seats*," *QDAP* 6 (1938) 59-62.

Tell el Harbaj

Anonymous, "Tell el Harbaj," *BSAJB* #2 (1922) 12-14.

Haroseth

*B[enjamin] Maisler, "Topographical Researches (IV)," *BIES* 11 (1944-45) #3/4, III. [Gabaa and Haroseth of the Gentiles]

*B[enjamin] Maisler, "Beth She'arim, Gaba, and the Harosheth of the Peoples," *HUCA* 24 (1952-53) 75-84.

Har Yeruḥam

M[oshe] Kochavi, "Har Yeruḥam," *IEJ* 13 (1963) 141-142.

Hasma

A. S. Kirkbride and Lankester Harding, "Hasma," *PEQ* 79 (1947) 7-26.

Hauran

E. Epstein, "Hauran: Rise and Decline," *PEQ* 72 (1940) 13-21.

Havvoth Jair

*W. Scott Watson, "The References in the Pentateuch to Jair and Havvoth Jair," *PRR* 6 (1895) 323-330.

Hazor

C[laude] R. Conder, "Hazor," *PEFQS* 15 (1883) 181.

J. Garstang, "The Site of Hazor," *AAA* 14 (1927) 35-42.

J. Garstang, "The Site of Hazor," *PEFQS* 59 (1927) 111.

*G. Ernest Wright, "Hazor and the Conquest of Canaan," *BA* 18 (1955) 106-108.

Anonymous, "Excavations at Hazor, 1955," *IEJ* 6 (1956) 120-125. *[Communicated by the Hazor Expedition]*

Yigael Yadin, "Excavations at Hazor," *BA* 19 (1956) 2-11. [The Ruins of Hazor; The Rothschild Expedition; The Enclosure]

Yigael Yadin, "Archaeological Excavations at Hazor," *CNI* 7 (1956) #1/2, 23-30.

Yigael Yadin, "Further Light on Biblical Hazor," *CNI* 7 (1956) #3/4, 18-26.

Hazor concluded

Anonymous, "Excavations at Hazor," *AT* 1 (1956-57) #1, 16.

Anonymous, "Hazor Excavation," *AT* 1 (1956-57) #4, 14-15.

*Yigael Yadin, "Some Aspects of the Material Culture of Northern Israel during the Canaanite and Israelite Periods, in the light of Excavations at Hazor," *A&S* 2 (1957) #2/3, 165-186.

Yigael Yadin, "The Rise and Fall of Hazor," *Arch* 10 (1957) 83-92.

Yigael Yadin, "Further Light on Hazor, Results of the Second Season, 1956," *BA* 20 (1957) 34-47. [Area A; Area B; Area C; Area F]

Yigael Yadin, "Further Light on Biblical Hazor: The City which Joshua Destroyed and Solomon Rebuilt," *CNI* 8 (1957) #3/4, 22-31.

Anonymous, "Excavations at Hazor, 1956—Preliminary Communique," *IEJ* 7 (1957) 118-123.

Anonymous, "Solomonic Gateway at Hazor," *AT* 2 (1957-58) #2, 12.

*Yigael Yadin, "The Third Season of Excavation at Hazor, 1957," *BA* 21 (1958) 30-47. [Area F, An Unexpected "Treasure"; Area H, The Holy of Holies and Cult Furniture of the Temple; Alalakh and the Temple of Solomon, The Tell—The Israelite Cities; Area B; Area G; Area A]

*W[illiam] F[oxwell] Albright, "Recent Progress in Palestine Archaeology: Samaria-Sebaste III and Hazor I," *BASOR* #150 (1958) 21-25.

Yigael Yadin, "The Fourth Season of Excavations at Hazor," *CNI* 9 (1958) #3/4, 21-32.

Y[igael] Yadin, "Excavations at Hazor, 1957—Preliminary Communique," *IEJ* 8 (1958) 1-14.

Mary Neely, "*The Exodus;* The Destruction of Hazor," *AT* 3 (1958-59) #1, 11-14.

Hazor concluded

*Yigael Yadin, "The Fourth Season of Excavations at Hazor," *BA* 22 (1959) 2-20. [Area H - Four Canaanite Temples; Area K; The Mound; Area B; Area A; Conclusion]

Y[igael] Yadin, "Three Years of Excavations at Hazor (1955-1957)," *BO* 16 (1959) 1-11.

Y[igael] Yadin, "Excavations at Hazor, 1958: Preliminary Communique," *IEJ* 9 (1959) 74-88.

*Olga Tufnell, "Hazor, Samaria and Lachish: A Synthesis," *PEQ* 91 (1959) 90-105.

Yigael Yadin, "The Fourth Season of Excavations at Hazor," *SEÅ* 24 (1959) 22-40.

*K[athleen] M. Kenyon, "Megiddo, Hazor, Samaria and Chronology," *ULBIA* 4 (1964) 143-156.

John Gray, "Hazor," *VT* 16 (1966) 26-52.

Yigael Yadin, "The Fifth Season of Excavations at Hazor, 1968-1969," *BA* 32 (1969) 50-71.

*A[braham] Malamat, "Hazor and its Northern Neighbours in New Mari Documents," *EI* 9 (1969) 137. *[English Summary]*

Y[igael] Yadin, "Excavations at Hazor, 1968-1969. Preliminary Communiqué," *IEJ* 19 (1969) 1-19.

Hebron

*G[eorge] Rawlinson, "Biblical Topography. VI.—Sites connected with the History of Abraham—Harran, Damascus, Hebron," *MI* 4 (1886) 241-252. *[Part IV not published]*

Conrad Schick, "Hebron and Its Neighbourhood," *PEFQS* 30 (1898) 232-238.

Anonymous, "Hebron in Tradition and History," *HR* 75 (1918) 399-400.

Hebron concluded

D. Amiran (Kallner), "The Western Border of the Hebron Mountains," *BIES* 14 (1947-48) #3/4, III-IV.

Philip C. Hammond, "The Excavation of Hebron, 1964 Season," *AJA* 69 (1965) 168.

Edward F. Campbell Jr., "Hebron," *BA* 28 (1965) 30-32.

Gerald A. Larue, "The American Expedition to Hebron, 1964," *JAAR* 33 (1965) 337-339.

Philip C. Hammond, "David's First City—The Excavation of Biblical Hebron, 1964," *PSB* 58 (1965) #2, 19-28.

Philip C. Hammond, "The Excavation of Hebron, 1965-1966, *AJA* 71 (1967) 188.

Ḥefṣibah

R[am] Gophna and Efrath Yeivin, "Ḥefṣibah," *IEJ* 19 (1969) 235-236.

(Mount) Hermon

[Charles Warren], "Summit of Hermon," *PEFQS* 2 (1870) 210-215.

William Wright, "Hermon," *Exp, 5th Ser.*, 4 (1896) 351-359.

Herodium

*Edgar J. Goodspeed, "The City of Herod," *BW* 18 (1901) 88-95. *[Herodium]*

G[ideon] Foerster, "Herodium," *IEJ* 19 (1969) 123-124.

Herzliya

M[oshe] W. Prausnitz, F. Burian, E. Friedmann, and E. Wreschner, "Herzliya," *IEJ* 19 (1969) 236.

Heshbon (Tell Ḥesbân)

J. Starcky and C. M. Bennett, "Discoveries at Ancient Heshbon," *ADAJ* 12&13 (1967-68) 51-52.

Werner Vyhmeister, "The History of Heshbon from Literary Sources," *AUSS* 6 (1968) 158-177.

R. S. Boraas and S. H. Horn, "The First Campaign at *Tell Ḥesbân,*" *AUSS* 7 (1969) 97-117.

Dewey M. Beegle, "Area B," *AUSS* 7 (1969) 118-126.

Henry O. Thompson, "Area C," *AUSS* 7 (1969) 127-142.

Bastiaan Van Elderen, "Area A," *AUSS* 7 (1969) 142-165.

Phyllis A. Bird, "Area D," *AUSS* 7 (1969) 165-217.

R. S. Boraas and S. H. Horn, "The Results of the First Season's Work," *AUSS* 7 (1969) 217-222.

Siegfreid H. Horn, "The 1968 Heshbon Expedition," *BA* 32 (1969) 26-41. [Heshbon's History from Literary Sources; The Aims of the First Season; The Ruins of a Byzantine Church in Area A; Area B, a Deep Sounding Shaft; Area C: A Thick Layer of Debris; The Ascent to the Acropolis in Area D; Summary]

Tell el Hesy (See also: Lachish)

Anonymous, "Great Discoveries in Judea: An Amorite City Unearthed," *EN* 2 (1890) 503-504. *[Tel-el-Hesy]*

Camden Cobern, "The Work at Tell el Hesy, as Seen by an American Visitor," *PEFQS* 22 (1890) 166-170.

F[rederick] J[ones] Bliss, "Reports from Mr. F. J. Bliss," *PEFQS* 23 (1891) 207-211. 207-211. (Note by C. R. Conder, *PEFQS* 24 (1892) p. 46)

Frederick Jones Bliss, "Report of Excavations at Tell-el-Hesy During the Spring of 1891," *PEFQS* 23 (1891) 282-290.

Tell el Hesy concluded

Theodore F. Wright, "Excavations at Tell-Hesy. The Latest Work of the Palestine Exploration Fund," *AAOJ* 14 (1892) 105-106.

*Willam Hayes Ward, "The Latest Palestinian Discoveries," *HR* 24 (1892) 403-407. *[Tel-el-Hesy]*

Frederick Jones Bliss, "Notes from Tell el Hesy," *PEFQS* 24 (1892) 36-38.

Frederick Jones Bliss, "Report of the Excavations at Tell el Hesy, for the Autumn Season of the Year 1891," *PEFQS* 24 (1892) 95-114.

W. M. Flinders Petrie, "Notes on the Results at Tell el Hesy," *PEFQS* 24 (1892) 114-115. (Notes by C. R. Conder, pp. 205-206, 334)

F[rederick] J[ones] Bliss, "Notes from Tell el Hesy," *PEFQS* 24 (1892) 192-196.

Frederick Jones Bliss, "Report of the Excavations at Tell el Hesy," *PEFQS* 25 (1893) 9-20.

Frederick Jones Bliss, "Report of the Excavations at Tell el Hesy during the Autumn of 1892," *PEFQS* 25 (1893) 103-119. (Note by C. R. Conder, p. 254)

Anonymous, "Tell-el-Hesy," *MR* 76 (1894) 645-648.

Claude R. Conder, "Notes on Tell el Hesy," *PEFQS* 26 (1894) 203-205.

Anonymous, "Excavations at Tell el-Hesy, the Site of Ancient Lachish," *RP* 1 (1902) 107-112.

Hinnom

S. Beswick, "Valley of Hinnom," *PEFQS* 13 (1881) 102-104.

*W. F. Birch, "The Valley of Hinnom and Zion," *PEFQS* 14 (1882) 55-59.

Hinnom concluded

W. F. Birch, "The Valley of Hinnom," *PEFQS* 31 (1899) 65-67.

W. F. Birch, "Notes and Queries. (1.) *The Valley of Hinnom*," *PEFQS* 41 (1909) 229-230.

*Paul Haupt, "Hinnom and Kidron," *JBL* 38 (1919) 45-48.

Hippos

C. Clermont-Ganneau, "The Site of Hippos," *PEFQS* 7 (1875) 214-218.

Ḥolon

Tamar Yizraeli, "Ḥolon," *IEJ* 13 (1963) 137.

Tamar Yizraeli, "A Lower Palaeolithic Site at Ḥolon. Preliminary Report," *IEJ* 17 (1967) 144-152.

Mount Hor

*[Stephen D. Peet], "The Holy Land Pisgah and Mount Hor," *AAOJ* 20 (1898) 227-231.

George L. Robinson, "The True Mount Hor," *BW* 31 (1908) 86-100.

Cameron M. Mackay, "Mount Hor," *PEFQS* 65 (1933) 147-151.

Ḥorvat Beter (See also: Beersheba)

*M[oshe] Dothan, "Excavations at Ḥorvat Beter (Beersheba)," *'Atiqot* 2 (1959) 1-42.

Ḥorvat Dorban

*Y[ohanan] Aharoni, "Ḥorvat Dorban (Khirbet esh-Sheikh Ibrahim)," *IEJ* 13 (1963) 337.

(Lake) Huleh

*W. M. Thomson, "The Sources of the Jordan, the Lake el-Hûleh, and the Adjacent Country," *BS* 3 (1846) 184-214. (Communicated by E. Robinson) [Bâniâs; The Fountain; Lake Phiala; Castle of Bâniâs; Tell el-Kâdy; Region of Hûleh; Castle of Hûnîn; Region North of Hûnîn; Castle of esh-Shŭkîf]

P. L. O. Guy, "Prehistoric and Other Remains in the Huleh Basin. Preliminary Survey," *BSAJB* #6 (1924) 74-77.

Roger Washbourn, "The Percy Sladen Expedition to Lake Huleh, 1935," *PEFQS* 68 (1936) 204-210.

J. Neumann, "On the Water Balance of Lake Huleh and the Huleh Swamps 1942/43—1946/47," *IEJ* 5 (1955) 49-58.

Y. Karmon, "The Formation of the Huleh Plain," *BIES* 19 (1954-55) #1/2, III-IV.

Tell Ḥum

William Melville Christie, "Tell Ḥum the Site of Capernaum," *SSO* 1 (1920) 13-34.

Tell el-Husn (See also: Beth-Shan)

*Henry O. Thompson, "Tell el-Husn—Biblical Beth-Shan," *BA* 30 (1967) 110-135.

I

Ibleam

W. J. Phythian-Adams, "The Site of Ibleam," *PEFQS* 54 (1922) 142-147.

Idumea

Matthew Kingman, "Idumea," *BJ* 1 (1842) 80-84.

*M Gihon, "Idumean and the Herodian Limes," *IEJ* 17 (1967) 27-45.

(Valley of) 'Iron

Z. Vilnay, "The Valley of 'Iron," *BIES* 24 (1959-60) #1, V.

Tel Isdar

M[oshe] Kochavi, "Tel Isdar," *IEJ* 14 (1964) 111-112.

Ituraea

*J. L. Porter, "Bashan, Ituraea, Kenath," *BS* 13 (1856) 789-808.

J

Jabal el-Qusur

Anonymous, "Archaeological News. Amman—Jabal el-Qusur," *ADAJ* 11 (1966) 103.

Jabbul

R. Maxwell Hyslop, J. Du Plat Taylor, M. V. Seton-Williams, and J. D'A. Waechter, "An Archaeological Survey of the Plain of Jabbul, 1939," *PEQ* 74 (1942) 8-40.

Jabesh-Gilead

Nelson Glueck, "Jabesh-Gilead," *BASOR* #89 (1943) 2-6.

*M. Naor, "Jabesh-Gilead, Abel-Mehola and Zaretan," *BIES* 13 (1946-47) #3/4, III.

Jabneh (Jamnia)

*David M. Shohet, "Jabnea," *CJ* 7 (1950-51) #1, 8-14. *[Jamnia]*

Jacob's Well

S. Anderson, "Jacob's Well," *PEFQS* 9 (1877) 72-75.

James King, "Jacob's Well, Its History and Associations," *PEFQS* 11 (1879) 87-95.

G. Robinson Lees, "Jacob's Well," *PEFQS* 25 (1893) 255-256.

Anonymous, "Jacob's Well," *RP* 9 (1910) 284.

Jaffa

*J. E. Hanauer, "The Traditional 'Harbour of Solomon' and the Crusading Castle at Jaffa," *PEFQS* 35 (1903) 258-264.

*J. E. Hanauer, "The Traditional 'Harbour of Solomon' at Jaffa," *PEFQS* 35 (1903) 355-356.

J[acob] Kaplan, "The Third Excavation Campaign at Ancient Jaffa," *BIES* 24 (1959-60) #2/3, IV.

J[acob] Kaplan, "Jaffa," *IEJ* 11 (1961) 191-192; 12 (1962) 149-150; 14 (1964) 285-286.

J[acob] Kaplan, "The Fifth Season of the Excavation at Jaffa," *JQR, N.S.,* 54 (1963-64) 110-114.

J[acob] Kaplan, "Jaffa's History Revealed by the Spade," *Arch* 17 (1964) 270-276.

Jair

*W. Scott Watson, "The References in the Pentateuch to Jair and Havvoth Jair," *PRR* 6 (1895) 323-330.

Jamnia

*David M. Shohet, "Jabnea," *CJ* 7 (1950-51) #1, 8-14. *[Jamnia]*

El Jarba

*J[acob] Kaplan, "El-Jarba (Plain of Esdraelon)," *IEJ* 17 (1967) 269-270.

#J[acob] Kaplan, "Ein el Jarba. Chalcolithic Remains in the Plain of Esdraelon," *BASOR* #194 (1969) 2-39.

The Jaulân

G[ottieb] Schumacher, "The Jaulân," *PEFQS* 20 (1888) i-xi, 1-304. *[Paged separately; may also be bound separately]*

Jazer

L. Gruenhut, "Jazer and Its Site," *JQR, N.S.,* 2 (1911-12) 241-244.

George M. Landes, "The Fountain at Jazer," *BASOR* #144 (1956) 30-37.

Jebel 'Osha

*John P. Peters, "Palestinian Exploration. *Notes of a Vacation in Palestine in 1902,*" *JBL* 22 (1903) 15-31. [11. Jebel 'Osha, pp. 29-30]

Jebel Tor'an

Anonymous, "Panoramic View from Jebel Tor'an," *PEFQS* 10 (1878) 122-123.

Jehanah

*W[illiam] F[oxwell] Albright, "New Identifications of Ancient Towns," *BASOR* #9 (1923) 5-10. [The Site of Jehanah, pp. 7-8]

Jelemiye

*Anonymous, "Jelemiye, Beth-She'arim, Kafr Yasif," *IEJ* 16 (1966) 283-284.

Tell Jemmeh

W. J. Phythian-Adams, "Report on Soundings at Tell Jemmeh," *PEFQS* 55 (1923) 140-146.

Jerash

William Libbey, "Jerash," *RP* 4 (1905) 35-47.

Anonymous, "Note on Southern Theatre, Jerash," *BSAJB* #7 (1925) 98.

J[oan] W. Crowfoot, "Recent Work Round the Fountain Court at Jerash," *PEFQS* 63 (1931) 143-154.

John P. Naish, "The Excavations at Jerash," *PEFQS* 65 (1933) 90-96.

*Mary I. Hussey, "The Pompeii of Palestine," *A&A* 35 (1934) 3-17. *[Jerash, Gerasa]*

W. F. Stinespring, "Latest Excavations at Jerash," *AJA* 40 (1936) 125.

Nelson Glueck, "The Earliest History of Jerash," *BASOR* #75 (1939) 22-30.

Diana V. W. Kirkbride, "Notes on a Survey of Pre-Roman Archaeological Sites near Jerash," *ULBIA* 1 (1958) 9-20.

Diana V. W. Kirkbride, "A Brief Outline of the Restoration of the South Theatre at Jerash," *ADAJ* 4&5 (1960) 123-127.

Jericho (See also: Tell es-Sultân)

Anonymous, "Antiquities in the Plain of Jericho," *MR* 76 (1894) 966-967.

F[rederick] J[ones] Bliss, "Notes on the Plain of Jericho," *PEFQS* 26 (1894)175-185.

J. E. Hanauer, "The Ruins of the Herodian Jericho," *PEFQS* 31 (1899) 127-128.

*K. T. Frost, "The Siege of Jericho and the Strategy of the Exodus," *ET* 18 (1906-07) 464-467.

J. M. P. Smith, "The Excavations at Jericho," *BW* 31 (1908) 227-228.

Anonymous, "Excavations at Jericho," *RP* 8 (1909) 172-173.

Edgar de Knevett, "The German Excavations at Jericho," *ET* 21 (1909-10) 353-356. (Correction, p. 428)

Stanley A. Cook, "The German Excavations at Jericho," *PEFQS* 42 (1910) 54-68.

A. Forder, "Excavated Jericho," *RP* 9 (1910) 202-207.

Anonymous, "Professor Sellins at Jericho," *RP* 9 (1910) 283-284.

Anonymous, "Recent Excavation at Jericho," *MR* 93 (1911) 640.

Anonymous, "Jericho Through the Centuries," *HR* 75 (1918) 456.

John Garstang, "Jericho. Sir Charles Marston's Expedition of 1930," *PEFQS* 62 (1930) 123-134.

L. Hugues Vincent, "The Chronology of Jericho," *PEFQS* 63 (1931) 104-105.

John Garstang, "The Chonology of Jericho," *PEFQS* 63 (1931) 105-107.

J[ohn] Garstang, "The Walls of Jericho. The Marston-Melchett Expedition of 1931," *PEFQS* 63 (1931) 186-196.

Jericho cont.

John Garstang, "Jericho: City and Necropolis. *I. Late Stone Age. II. Early Bronze Age. III. Middle Bronze Age*," *AAA* 19 (1932) 3-22.

John Garstang, "Jericho: City and Necropolis. *II. Early Bronze Age (additional). III. Middle Bronze Age i (continued). IV. Middle Bronze Age ii.*," *AAA* 19 (1932) 35-54.

John Garstang, "A Third Season at Jericho. City and Necropolis," *PEFQS* 64 (1932) 149-153.

John Garstang, "Jericho: City and Necropolis," *AAA* 20 (1933) 3-42.

*John Garstang, "Jericho: City and Necropolis. Fourth Report," *AAA* 21 (1934) 99-136. (And a Note on an Inscribed Tablet and Fig. 2, by Sidney Smith, pp. 116-117)

John Garstang, J. P. Droop, and Joan Crowfoot, "Jericho: City and Necropolis. Fifth Report," *AAA* 22 (1935) 143-184.

John Garstang, "The Fall of Bronze Age Jericho," *PEFQS* 67 (1935) 61-68.

J[ohn] Gastang and G. M. FitzGerald, "Jericho: City and Necropolis. Report for Sixth and Concluding Season, 1936," *AAA* 23 (1936) 67-100.

*W. J. Phythian-Adams, "Jericho, Ai and the Occupation of Mount Ephriam," *PEFQS* 68 (1936) 141-149.

*William F. Stinespring, "Remarks on Biblical Archaeology," *DDSR* 2 (1937) 1-10. [Jericho, pp. 6-7]

*G. Ernest Wright, "Hebrew Origins in the Background of Near Eastern History," *BA* 3 (1940) 27-40. [The Fall of Jericho, pp. 32-36]

*William Ross, "Jericho and the Date of the Exodus," *HJ* 39 (1940-41) 299-308.

*J. W. Jack, "Recent Biblical Archaeology," *ET* 53 (1941-42) 208-212. [The Moabite Occupation of Jericho, pp. 208-209]

Jericho cont.

*H. H. Rowley, "Jericho and the Date of the Exodus: A Rejoinder," *HJ* 40 (1941-42) 207-208.

*G. Ernest Wright, "Two Misunderstood Items in the Exodus-Conquest Cycle," *BASOR* #86 (1942) 32-35. [1. The Problem of Jericho, pp. 32-34]

James L. Kelso, "The First Campaign of Excavation in New Testament Jericho," *BASOR* #120 (1950) 11-22.

*Auni Dajani, "Excavations in Jordan, 1949-1950," *ADAJ* 1 (1951) 44-48. [Jericho, pp. 44-45]

James B. Pritchard, "The 1951 Campaign At Herodian Jericho," *BASOR* #123 (1951) 8-17.

Anonymous, "Excavations at Jericho. Joint Expedition of the British School of Archaeology in Jerusalem and the Palestine Exploration Fund," *PEQ* 83 (1951) 88-89. (Letter by S. Yeivin, p. 175)

Kathleen M. Kenyon, "Some Notes on the History of Jericho in the 2nd Millennium B.C.," *PEQ* 83 (1951) 101-138.

Gurston Goldin, "Jericho; The Archaeological Problem," *HJ* 50 (1951-52) 130-137.

Kathleen M. Kenyon, "Early Jericho," *Antiq* 26 (1952) 116-122.

Lucetta Mowry, "Settlements in the Jericho Valley During the Roman Period (63 B.C. - A.D. 134)," *BA* 15 (1952) 26-42. [Geography and Climate; Roman Imperial Policy; The Towns of the Ara; Herodian Building at Jericho; Life at Jericho]

G. Ernest Wright, "New Excavations at Jericho," *BA* 15 (1952) 43-44.

A. Douglas Tushingham, "The Joint Excavations at Tell es-Sultân (Jericho)," *BASOR* #127 (1952) 5-16.

Kathleen M. Kenyon, "Excavations at Jericho, 1952. Interim Report," *PEQ* 84 (1952) 4-6.

Jericho cont.

Kathleen M. Kenyon, "Excavations at Jericho, 1952," *PEQ* 84 (1952) 62-82.

R. North, "The 1952 Jericho-Sultan Excavation," *B* 34 (1953) 1-12.

A. Douglas Tushingham, "Excavations at Old Testament Jericho," *BA* 16 (1953) 46-67. [The Garstang Expedition; The Kenyon Expedition, A. The Mesolithic, Neolithic and Chalcolithic Periods, B. The Early Bronze Age (roughly 3100-2100 B.C.), the transitional Early Bronze-Middle Bronze Period (2100-2900) and the Middle Bronze Age (1900-1550), C. The Late Bronze Age, D. The Iron Age]

*S. H. Horn, "Jericho in a Topographical List of Ramesses II," *JNES* 12 (1953) 201-203. (Comment by B. Maisler, p. 203)

Kathleen M. Kenyon, "Excavations at Jericho, 1953," *PEQ* 85 (1953) 81-96.

A. D[ouglas] Tushingham, "Excavations at Ancient Jericho, 1952 and 1953," *AJA* 58 (1954) 149.

Kathleen M. Kenyon, "Jericho: Oldest Walled Town," *Arch* 7 (1954) 2-8.

A. Douglas Tushingham, "Excavation at Old Testament Jericho," *BA* 17 (1954) 98-104.

G. E[rnest] Wright, "Additional Note On Excavations," *BA* 17 (1954) 104. *[Jericho]*

Kathleen M. Kenyon, "Excavations at Jericho, 1954," *PEQ* 86 (1954) 45-63.

F. E. Zeuner, "The Neolithic-Bronze Age Gap on the Tell of Jericho," *PEQ* 86 (1954) 64-68.

Kathleen M. Kenyon, "Some Archaeological Sites and the Old Testament. Jericho," *ET* 66 (1954-55) 355-358.

Kathleen M. Kenyon, "Excavations at Jericho, 1955," *PEQ* 87 (1955) 108-117.

Jericho cont.

*Anonymous, "Excavations in Jordan, 1953-1954," *ADAJ* 3 (1956) 74-87. [Jericho, pp. 74-75]

Kathleen M. Kenyon, "Jericho and its Setting in Near Eastern History," *Antiq* 30 (1956) 184-195.

F. E. Zeuner, "The Radioactive Age of Jericho," *Antiq* 30 (1956) 195-197.

Kathleen M. Kenyon, "Excavations at Jericho, 1956," *PEQ* 88 (1956) 67-82.

Anonymous, "Excavations at Jericho," *AT* 1 (1956-57) #1, 9.

Robert J. Braidwood, "Jericho and its Setting in Near Eastern History," *Anitq* 31 (1957) 73-81.

Kathleen M. Kenyon, "Reply to Professor Braidwood," *Antiq* 31 (1957) 82-84. *[Jericho]*

Norman Bentwich, "Jericho," *ContR* 192 (1957) 208-212.

Kathleen M. Kenyon, "Excavations at Jericho, 1957," *PEQ* 89 (1957) 101-107.

Mary Neely, "*The Exodus:* Recent Discoveries at Jericho," *AT* 2 (1957-58) #3, 11-14.

*Carl O. Saver, "Jericho and Composite Sickles," *Antiq* 32 (1958) 187-189.

*Edwin M. Good, "Two Notes on Aqhat," *JBL* 77 (1958) 72-74. [II. AQHT A. vi. 37 and Jericho, pp. 73-74]

Walter J. Beasley, "The Jericho Story. Part 1.," *AT* 3 (1958-59) #2, 15-18, 23.

Walter J. Beasley, "That Jericho Story. Part 2.," *AT* 3 (1958-59) #3, 4-7.

Kathleen M. Kenyon, "Earliest Jericho," *Antiq* 33 (1959) 5-9.

Jericho concluded

Kathleen M. Kenyon, "Excavations at Jericho, 1957-58," *PEQ* 92 (1960) 88-113.

Diana [V. W.] Kirkbride, "A Brief Report on the Pre-Pottery Flint Cultures of Jericho," *PEQ* 92 (1960) 114-119.

*Murray B. Nicol, "Archaeology and the Fall of Jericho," *R&E* 58 (1961) 173-180.

*Emmanuel Anati, "Prehistoric Trade and the Puzzle of Jericho," *BASOR* #167 (1962) 25-31.

*Eric F. F. Bishop, "'Down from Jerusalem to Jericho'," *EQ* 35 (1963) 97-102.

*H. J. Franken, "Tell es-Sultan and Old Testament Jericho," *OTS* 1 (1965) 189-200.

*Joseph Robinson, "Who Cares About Jericho?" *ET* 78 (1966-67) 83-86.

Kathleen M. Kenyon, "Jericho," *Arch* 20 (1967) 268-275.

*J[acob] Kaplan, "A Suggested Correlation Between Stratum IX, Jericho, and Stratum XXIV, Mersin," *JNES* 28 (1969) 197-199.

Jerusalem (includes Gates & Walls)

*Anonymous, "The History of the Reign of Bahman, and the Second Desolation of Jerusalem; by Persian and Oriental Writers," *MMBR* 28 (1809-10) 449-450.

Anonymous, "Remarkable Events Relating to Jerusalem," *CD* 2 (1814) 16-18.

Anonymous, "Jerusalem," *DUM* 26 (1845) 266-282. *(Review)*

E[dward] Robinson, "Topography of Jerusalem," *BS* 3 (1846) 431-461, 605-652.

Anonymous, "The Dome of the Rock," *DUM* 31 (1848) 411-429.

Jerusalem cont.

†Anonymous, "Dr. Barclay's City of the Great King," *TLJ* 10 (1857-58) 670-688. *(Review) [Jerusalem]*

†Anonymous, "Dr Barclay on the City of the Great King," *BFER* 7 (1858) 605-619. *(Review) [Jerusalem]*

Joseph P. Thompson, "Topography of Jerusalem," *BS* 15 (1858) 444-475.

Samuel Wolcott, "The Topography of Jerusalem," *BS* 23 (1866) 684-695; 24 (1867) 116-140.

W. T., "The Topography of Ancient Jerusalem, as Illustrated by Recent Excavations," *BFER* 17 (1868) 288-332. *(Review)*

Henry S. Burrage, "Ordnance Survey of Jerusalem," *BQ* 2 (1868) 156-171. *(Review)*

(   ) (D.), "Recent Researches in Jerusalem," *ThE* 5 (1868) 387-398.

Anonymous, "The Topography of Jerusalem," *PEFQS* 1 (1869) 3-5.

Rob Roy, "'Rob Roy' on the Works at Jerusalem," *PEFQS* 1 (1869) 17-23.

*W[illiam] Simpson, "Robinson's Arch," *PEFQS* 1 (1869) 46-48.

Edward L. Clark, "On Recent Explorations in Jerusalem," *JAOS* 9 (1869-71). l. *(Roman Numeral "fifty" - not page "one"!)*

*Charles Clermont-Ganneau, "The Stone of Zoheleth, En-Rogel and the King's Gardens," *PEFQS* 2 (1870) 251-253.

John Forbes, "The Topography of Jerusalem," *BS* 27 (1870) 191-196.

Anonymous, "The Haram Area," *PEFQS* 2 (1870) 368-370. *[Jerusalem]*

Charles Warren, "Discovery at the N.W. Angle," *PEFQS* 2 (1870) 370-372. *[Jerusalem - Haram Area]*

Jerusalem cont.

*William Simpson, "The Royal Caverns or Quarries, Jerusalem," *PEFQS* 2 (1870) 373-379.

Samuel Wolcott, "The Topography of Jerusalem," *BS* 27 (1870) 565-569.

C. Kegan Paul, "The Recovery of Jerusalem," *TR* 8 (1871) 407-414. *(Review)*

C. W. Wilson, "Recent Discoveries at Jerusalem," *PEFQS* 4 (1872) 47-51.

William Simpson, "Jerusalem, an Introduction to its Archaeology and Topography," *SBAT* 1 (1872) 310-327.

†Anonymous, "The Recovery of Jerusalem," *ERCJ* 137 (1873) 1-38. *(Review)*

C. W. Wilson, "Jerusalem," *PEFQS* 5 (1873) 36-38.

George St. Clair, "'Middle City'—'Second City'," *PEFQS* 5 (1873) 116-117.

Samuel Birch, "The Age of the Temple Wall," *PEFQS* 9 (1877) 75.

C. W. Wilson, "Recent Excavations at Jerusalem, by Herr C. Schick, K. K. Baurath," *PEFQS* 9 (1877) 9-10.

*W. F. Birch, "Nehemiah's Wall and David's Tomb," *PEFQS* 11 (1879) 176-179.

C[onrad] Schick, "New Discoveries in the North of Jerusalem," *PEFQS* 11 (1879) 198-200.

*C. W. Wilson, "The Masonry of the Haram Wall," *PEFQS* 12 (1880) 9-65, 195-196.

Claude R. Conder, "Register of Rock Levels, Jerusalem," *PEFQS* 12 (1880) 82-91.

*Claude R. Conder, "Note on Colonel Wilson's Paper on the Masonry of the Haram Wall," *PEFQS* 12 (1880) 91-97.

Jerusalem cont.

*Claude R. Conder, "Notes on Jerusalem," *PEFQS* 12 (1880) 101-103.
[The Stone hat T'aim, pp. 102-103]

*Charles Warren, "Notes on Colonel Wilson's Paper on the Masonry of
the Haram Wall," *PEFQS* 12 (1880) 159-166.

C[laude] R. Conder, "Supposed Cliff in the Haram," *PEFQS* 13 (1881)
56-60. *[Jerusalem]*

*W. F. Birch, "Varieties," *PEFQS* 14 (1882) 59-61. [The Dung Gate,
p. 60]

A. M. Mantell, "Jerusalem," *PEFQS* 14 (1882) 165-168. [The Bakoosh
Hill; Khurbet 'Adaseh]

A. M. Mantell, "Jerusalem. Newly opened Gate in the East Wall of
the Haram," *PEFQS* 14 (1882) 169-170.

C[onrad] Schick, "Newly Found Figure in the Haram Wall," *PEFQS* 14
(1882) 171.

A. H. Sayce, "The Topography of Prae*[sic]*-Exilic Jerusalem,"
PEFQS 15 (1883) 215-223.

Selah   Merrill,   "Jerusalem,"   *ONTS*   5   (1885-86)   97-103.

Selah Merrill, "Recent Discoveries at Jerusalem," *PEFQS* 18 (1886)
21-24.

*W. F. Birch, "Notes by Rev. W. F. Birch," *PEFQS* 18 (1886) 26-34.
[I. Acra South of the Temple; II. Professor Socin's Criticisms;
III. Captain Conder's Note on Jerusalem; IV. The Approximate
Position of the Castle of Zion]

Francis   Brown,   "Jerusalem,"   *AJA, O.S.,*   2   (1886)   428-430.

Lewis T. Hayter, "Notes from Jerusalem," *PEFQS* 18 (1886) 135-136.

(Mrs.) E. A. Finn, "The Second Wall of Jerusalem," *PEFQS* 18 (1886)
206-207.

Jerusalem cont.

C[onrad] Schick, "Notes from Jerusalem," *PEFQS* 19 (1887) 151-158, 213-221. [I. 1. Tomb in Wady Yasûl; 2. Second Wall; 3. Old Remains, &c., outside Jaffa Gate; 4. Triple Gate at Haram Esh Sherif; 5. Large Caves near Ramleh; 6. Mr. Luncz's Book; II. 1. The Tomb in Wâdy Yasûl with the Sarcophagus; 2. Old Channel near Jeremiah's Grotto; 3. *(untitled)*; 4. *(untitled)*; 5. Knankeh; 6. *(untitled)*; 7. The Second Wall]

Selah Merrill, "A Personal Explanation," *PEFQS* 20 (1888) 15-16. *[Wall at Jerusalem]*

C[onrad] Schick, "Jerusalem," *PEFQS* 20 (1888) 20-22.

C[onrad] Schick, "Line of the Second Wall. I," *PEFQS* 20 (1888) 62-63.

Selah Merrill, "Line of the Second Wall. II," *PEFQS* 20 (1888) 63-65.

*C[onrad] Schick, "Recent Discoveries in Jerusalem," *PEFQS* 21 (1889) 63-68. [I. Remains of Old Wall outside the present Northern Wall of the City; II. Remains of Old Wall near the North-east Corner of the City; III. Notes on the Plans and the Cave East of the Church of the Holy Sepulchre]

*George St. Clair, "Nehemiah's South Wall, and the Locality of the Royal Sepulchres," *PEFQS* 21 (1889) 90-102.

Anonymous, "Notes on the Plan of Jerusalem," *PEFQS* 21 (1889) 62-63. *(With Topographical map)*

C[laude] R. Conder, "Notes by Major Conder, D.C.L., R.E., IV. The South Wall of Jerusalem," *PEFQS* 21 (1889) 145.

(Mrs.) E. A. Finn, "Note on 'the Remains of Old Wall Outside the Present North Wall of Jerusalem'," *PEFQS* 21 (1889) 205.

W. F. Birch, "Nehemiah's Wall," *PEFQS* 21 (1889) 206-209.

C[onrad] Schick, "Rock Levels in Jerusalem," *PEFQS* 22 (1890) 20-21.

C[onrad] Schick, "Remains of the Old City Wall," *PEFQS* 22 (1890) 21.

Jerusalem cont.

C[onrad] Schick, "The Old Wall Outside Jerusalem," *PEFQS* 22 (1890) 39.

George St. Clair, "Nehemiah's Wall," *PEFQS* 22 (1890) 47-50.

W. F. Birch, "Nehemiah's Wall," *PEFQS* 22 (1890) 126-130.

George St. Clair, "Nehemiah's Wall and the Sepulchres of the Kings," *PEFQS* 22 (1890) 212.

W. M. Flinders Petrie, "Notes on Places Visited in Jerusalem. *Future Work required in Jerusalem*," *PEFQS* 22 (1890) 159.

(Mrs.) E. A. Finn, "Nehemiah's Wall," *PEFQS* 22 (1890) 194.

C[onrad] Schick, "Herr Schick's Reports from Jerusalem," *PEFQS* 22 (1890) 246-259. [I. The New Road North of the City; II. New Discoveries at the House of Caiaphas, on the so-called Mount of Zion; III. A newly-discovered Rock-cut Tomb at Aceldama; IV. Newly-discovered Rock-cut Tomb near Bethany; V. Another Rock-cut Chapel at Silwan; VI. Some Excavations on Mount of Olivet; VII. Recent Excavations at Siloah. 1. Searching for a second Aqueduct, 2. Searching for Gate of City of David]

C[onrad] Schick, "Reports from Jerusalem," *PEFQS* 22 (1890) 67-68. [Rock-cut Cave at Silwan; Excavations at Aceldama]

*C[onrad] Schick, "Reports from Jerusalem. Letters from Herr Schick," *PEFQS* 23 (1891) 198-204. [Discoveries in "Solomon's Stables"; Spring of an Ancient Arch; Various Notes; The Newly Discovered Arch in "Solomon's Stables"; Excavations at the Golden Gate; Tombs and Ossuaries at Rujm El Kahakir]

J. E. Hanauer, "Reports from Jerusalem. Letters from the Rev. J. E. Hanauer," *PEFQS* 23 (1891) 204-207. [A Subterranean Passage in Solomon's Stables; Cutting in the Rock in the Haram-Area]

*C[onrad] Schick, "Herr Schick's Reports. " *PEFQS* 23 (1891) 276-281. [1. *Foundation of the Present Wall*, pp. 276-277; 2. *Remains of Old Wall inside City*, pp. 277-278; *Some Innovations at Jerusalem*, pp. 280-281.]

Jerusalem cont.

*C[laude] R. Conder, "Notes by Major Conder, R.E. III. Notes on Herr Schick's Report, Tell el Hesy Inscriptions, and Dinhabah," *PEFQS* 24 (1892) 46. *[Nehemiah's Wall]*

C[onrad] Schick, "Letters from Herr Schick. II. The Gate Gennath, &c.," *PEFQS* 24 (1892) 186-188.

C[onrad] Schick, "Letters from Herr Schick. III. Discovery in Solomon's Stables, &c.," *PEFQS* 24 (1892) 188-190.

*H. B. Swete, "Requests and Replies," *ET* 3 (1891-92) 300. *[Alexander's visit to Jerusalem in Josephus & the Prophecies of Daniel]*

Selah Merrill, "Discoveries in Jerusalem," *PRR* 3 (1892) 630-650.

*W. F. Birch, "Ancient Jerusalem. *Zion or Acra, South not North, of the Temple*," *PEFQS* 25 (1893) 70-76, 164-166.

C[onrad] Schick, "Letters from Herr Baurath Schick. I. The Second Wall of Ancient Jerusalem," *PEFQS* 25 (1893) 191-193.

C[onrad] Schick, "Letters from Herr Baurath von Schick. I. Old Jerusalem, an Exceptional City," *PEFQS* 25 (1893) 282-283.

J. S. Riggs, "Studies in Palestinian Geography. III. Jerusalem," *BW* 4 (1894) 177-183.

C[laude] R. Conder, "Requests and Replies," *ET* 6 (1894-95) 25. *[Jerusalem]*

Anonymous, "Excavations in Jerusalem," *MR* 76 (1894) 964-966.

C[laude] R. Conder, "Jerusalem," *SRL* 24 (1894) 337-365.

George St. Clair, "Jerusalem Topography," *PEFQS* 26 (1894) 150-151.

Frederick Jones Bliss, "Excavations at Jerusalem," *PEFQS* 26 (1894) 169-175. (Notes by C. R. Conder, pp. 302-303)

F[rederick] J[ones] Bliss, "Second Report on the Excavations at Jerusalem," *PEFQS* 26 (1894) 243-257.

Jerusalem cont.

*W. F. Birch, "Ancient Jerusalem.—Zion, and Acra, South of the Temple," *PEFQS* 26 (1894) 282-284.

*C[onrad] Schick, "Jerusalem Notes," *PEFQS* 26 (1894) 261-266. [1. The Muristan; 2. A Colony of Bokhara Jews; 3. The English Hospital; 4. The Russian Orthodox Palestine Society; 5. Rock-cut Aqueduct on Skull Hill; 6. Muristan Inscription; 7. A Rock Scrap; 8. New Drains; 9. Tombs of the Judges; 10. Interesting Cisterns and Winepresses; 11. Alterations in the City; 12. *(untitled)* 13. *(untitled)*.

A. K. Parker, "Jerusalem and Thereabouts (Illustrated)," *BW* 7 (1895) 342-351.

F[rederick] J[ones] Bliss, "Third Report on the Excavations at Jerusalem," *PEFQS* 27 (1895) 9-25.

J. N. Dalton, "Note on the 'First Wall' of Ancient Jerusalem and the Present Excavations," *PEFQS* 27 (1895) 26-29.

*C[onrad] Schick, "Reports from Herr Baurath von Schick," *PEFQS* 27 (1895) 29-40. [1. Muristan; 2. A Stair and Postern in the Old Wall; 3. An Addition to the Report on the Recently-found Moasic outside the Damascus Gate; 4. Tombs, or Remainder of Third Wall? 5. Recent Discoveries on the Mount of Olives; 6. Bethzur; 7. Montefioreh]

C[laude] R. Conder, "Fourth Report on the Excavations at Jerusalem," *PEFQS* 27 (1895) 97-108.

*C[onrad] Schick, "Reports from Herr Baurath von Schick," *PEFQS* 27 (1895) 108-110. [1. Muristan; 2. Excavations inside the New Gate; 3. An old Pool west of the City; 4. Reckoning of time among the Armenians; 5. The Armenian Cross]

Archibald C. Dickie, "Fifth Report on the Excavations at Jerusalem," *PEFQS* 27 (1895) 235-248.

F[rederick] J[ones] Bliss, "Sixth Report on the Excavations at Jerusalem," *PEFQS* 27 (1895) 305-320. (Note by C. Clermont-Ganneau, *PEFQS* 28 (1896), p. 79; Note by C. R. Conder, *PEFQS* 28 (1896) p. 82)

Jerusalem cont.

*C[onrad] Schick, "Reports from Herr Baurath von Schick," *PEFQS* 27 (1895) 321-330. (Note by C. Clermont-Ganneau, *PEFQS* 28 (1896) p. 79) [4. Another Tomb at the Muristan; 5. Perpendicular Rock-cut Tomb and Stone Basin in it]

C[laude] R. Conder, "Notes on Dr. Bliss's Discoveries," *PEFQS* 27 (1895) 330-331. *[Nehemiah's Wall]*

*Cyrus Adler, "The Cotton Grotto, an Ancient Quarry in Jerusalem," *JQR* 8 (1895-96) 384-391.

F[rederick] J[ones] Bliss, "Seventh Report on the Excavations at Jerusalem," *PEFQS* 28 (1896) 9-22. (Note by C. R. Conder, pp. 169-170)

F[rederick] J[ones] Bliss, "Eighth Report on the Excavations at Jerusalem," *PEFQS* 28 (1896) 109-122.

F[rederick] J[ones] Bliss, "Ninth Report on the Excavations at Jerusalem," *PEFQS* 28 (1896) 208-213. (Note by C. R. Conder, pp. 340-341.

F[rederick] J[ones] Bliss, "Tenth Report on the Excavations at Jerusalem," *PEFQS* 28 (1896) 298-305.

Theodore F. Wright, "The Valley Gate and the Dung Gate," *PEFQS* 28 (1896) 342-343.

H. Porter, "A Visit to the Excavations at Jerusalem," *PEFQS* 28 (1896) 345-346.

F[rederick] J[ones] Bliss, "Eleventh Report on the Excavations at Jerusalem," *PEFQS* 29 (1897) 11-26.

George S. Clair, The Valley Gate and the Dung Gate," *PEFQS* 29 (1897) 69-70.

W. F. Birch, "Tophet and the King's Garden," *PEFQS* 29 (1897) 72-75. [Tophet; The Kings Garden; Note B. "Quarterly Statement," 1877, p. 204]

Jerusalem cont.

F[rederick] J[ones] Bliss, "Twelfth Report on the Excavations at Jerusalem," *PEFQS* 29 (1897) 91-102.

*C[onrad] Schick, "Reports and Papers by Dr. Conrad Schick," *PEFQS* 29 (1897) 103-122. (Notes by C. R. Conder, p. 211) [II. Newly-discovered Rock Block with Tombs; III. The West Wall of the Pool of Hezekiah; V. The Stone "Hat-Toîm"; VII. Bethpage and Bethany; VIII. Jeshimon of the Bible; IX. 1. *A Remarkable Stone in the Jewish Quarter, Jerusalem*, 2. *Jeremiah's Grotto Hill*, 3. *Kedron Valley*, 4. *Siloah Spring*]

F[rederick] J[ones] Bliss, "Thirteenth Report on the Excavations at Jerusalem," *PEFQS* 29 (1897) 173-181.

F[rederick] J[ones] Bliss, "Fourteenth Report on the Excavations at Jerusalem," *PEFQS* 29 (1897) 260-268.

*George Cormack, "The Holy City of Deuteronomy," *ET* 9 (1897-98) 439-442.

Selah Merrill, "Within Thy Gates, O Jerusalem," *BW* 12 (1898) 293-302.

*C[onrad] Schick, "Reports by Dr. Conrad Schick," *PEFQS* 30 (1898) 79-85. [III. *Remains of an Ancient City Wall*, pp. 82; IV. *untitled*]

W. F. Birch, "The Valley Gate," *PEFQS* 30 (1898) 168-169.

Theodore F. Wright, "The Valley Gate," *PEFQS* 30 (1898) 261-262.

A. Buchler, "The Nicanor Gate and the Brass Gate," *JQR* 11 (1898-99) 46-63. [(a) The Statements of the Mishna; (b) The Statements of Josephus on the Brass Gate]

Selah Merrill, "Jerusalem Explorations," *AAOJ* 21 (1899) 251-252.

George L. Robinson, "The Last Days of Old Jerusalem," *BW* 14 (1899) 112-119.

Selah Merrill, "An Archaeological Visit to Jerusalem," *BW* 14 (1899) 167-280.

Jerusalem cont.

Anonymous, "Jerusalem and the Monuments," *MR* 81 (1899) 967-970.

C[onrad] Schick, "Reports by Dr. Conrad Schick. II. Contribution to the Study of the Ancient City Walls of Jerusalem," *PEFQS* 31 (1899) 215-217.

*J. V. Prasek, "Sennacherib's Second Expedition to the West and the Siege of Jerusalem," *ET* 12 (1900-01) 225-229.

*J. V. Prasek, "Sennacherib's Second Expedition to the West, and the Date of His Siege of Jerusalem," *ET* 13 (1901-02) 326-328.

*John P. Peters, "Palestinian Exploration. *Notes of a Vacation in Palestine in 1902,*" *JBL* 22 (1903) 15-31. [10. Jerusalem, pp. 27-28]

Conrad Schick, "Notes to Accompany the Plan of Jeremiah's Grotto," *PEFQS* 34 (1902) 38-42.

*R. A. Stewart Macalister, "El-Edhemiyeh (Jeremiah's Grotto)," *PEFQS* 34 (1902) 129-132.

George A. Barton, "The Jerusalem of David and Solomon," *BW* 22 (1903) 8-21.

J. L. Leeper, "Voices from Underground Jerusalem," *BW* 22 (1903) 167-179.

G. A. Smith, "Studies in the History and Topography of Jerusalem," *Exp, 6th Ser.,* 7 (1903) 1-21, 122-135, 208-228, 298-315, 321-337. [I. A General View of the City; II. The Name Jerusalem and Other Names; III. The Waters of Jerusalem; IV. The Prelude; V. The Beginnings of the History]

*Hinckley G. Mitchell, "The Wall of Jerusalem according to the Book of Nehemiah," *JBL* 22 (1903) 85-163.

*J. E. Hanauer, "El-Edhemiyeh (Jeremiah's Grotto)," *PEFQS* 35 (1903) 86-90.

Jerusalem cont.

Lewis B. Paton, "Some Excavations on the Supposed Line of the Third Wall of Jerusalem," *AJA* 9 (1905) 81-82.

G. A. Smith, "Jerusalem under David and Solomon," *Exp, 6th Ser.,* 11 (1905) 81-102.

G. A. Smith, "Jerusalem from Rehoboam to Hezekiah," *Exp, 6th Ser.,* 11 (1905) 225-236, 306-320, 372-388.

G. A. Smith, "Manasseh's Jerusalem," *Exp, 6th Ser.,* 12 (1905) 303-320.

G. A. Smith, "Isaiah's Jerusalem," *Exp, 6th Ser.,* 12 (1905) 1-17.

*G. A. Smith, "Sennacherib and Jerusalem," *Exp, 6th Ser.,* 12 (1905) 215-233.

*G. A. Smith, "Jerusalem and Deuteronomy. Circa 638-608 B.C.," *Exp, 6th Ser.,* 12 (1905) 336-350.

Lewis B. Paton, "The Third Wall of Jerusalem and Some Excavations on Its Supposed Line," *JBL* 24 (1905) 196-211.

C. W. Wilson, "The Walls of Jerusalem," *PEFQS* 37 (1905) 231-243.

G. A. Smith, "Jeremiah's Jerusalem," *Exp, 7th Ser.,* 1 (1906) 61-77, 97-114.

*G. A. Smith, "The Desolate City," *Exp, 7th Ser.,* 1 (1906) 320-336. *[Jerusalem]*

G. A. Smith, "The Ideal City and the Real," *Exp, 7th Ser.,* 1 (1906) 435-452. *[Jerusalem]*

G. A. Smith, "Nehemiah's Jerusalem," *Exp, 7th Ser.,* 2 (1906) 121-134.

*Lewis Bayles Paton, "The Meaning of the Expression 'Between the Two Walls'," *JBL* 25 (1906) 1-13. *[Jerusalem]*

Jerusalem cont.

*J. C. Nevin, "Notes on the Topography of Jerusalem," *PEFQS* 38 (1906) 206-213, 278-286. [1. The Site of the Acra; 2. General Questions]

R. A. S. Macalister, "The Supposed Fragment of the First Wall of Jerusalem," *PEFQS* 38 (1906) 298-301.

*Lewis Bayles Paton, "Jerusalem in Bible Times: I. The Location of the Temple," *BW* 29 (1907) 7-22.

Lewis Bayles Paton, "Jerusalem in Bible Times: II. The Valleys of Ancient Jerusalem," *BW* 29 (1907) 86-96.

*Lewis Bayles Paton, "Jerusalem in Bible Times: III. The Springs and Pools of Ancient Jerusalem," *BW* 29 (1907) 168-182.

*Lewis Bayles Paton, "Jerusalem in Bible Times: IV. The City of David," *BW* 29 (1907) 247-259.

*Lewis Bayles Paton, "Jerusalem in Bible Times: V. Zion, Ophel, and Moriah," *BW* 29 (1907) 327-333.

Lewis Bayles Paton, "Jerusalem in Bible Times: VI. Jerusalem in the Earliest Times," *BW* 29 (1907) 409-419.

*Lewis Bayles Paton, "Jerusalem in Bible Times: VII. Solomon's Buildings," *BW* 30 (1907) 7-17.

*Lewis Bayles Paton, "Jerusalem in Bible Times: VIII. Solomon's Wall," *BW* 30 (1907) 88-100.

Lewis Bayles Paton, "Jerusalem in Bible Times: IX. Jerusalem under Hezekiah and Manasseh," *BW* 30 (1907) 167-178.

Lewis Bayles Paton, "Jerusalem in Bible Times: X. Nehemiah's Wall," *BW* 30 (1907) 248-257.

Lewis Bayles Paton, "Jerusalem in Bible Times: XI. Jerusalem in the Period between the Old and New Testaments," *BW* 30 (1907) 328-338.

Jerusalem cont.

C. K. Spyridonidis, "An Ancient Gate East of the Holy Sepulchre," *PEFQS* 39 (1907) 297-302.

Theodore F. Wright, "The Palestine Exploration Fund," *RP* 6 (1907) 215-216. *[Jerusalem]*

D. S. Margoliouth, "G. A. Smith and S. Merrill on Jerusalem," *Exp, 7th Ser.,* 6 (1908) 446-456. *(Review)*

D. S. Margoliouth, "Dr. G. A. Smith on Jerusalem," *Exp, 7th Ser.,* 6 (1908) 518-527.

Anonymous, "Jerusalem," *LQHR* 110 (1908) 123-126. *(Review)*

Anonymous, "Discovery of Ancient Gate at Jerusalem," *RP* 7 (1908) 170.

Thomas Nicol, "Jerusalem Ancient and Modern," *LQHR* 111 (1909) 258-274. *(Review)*

Anonymous, "Jerusalem," *MR* 91 (1909) 302-306.

*[Paul Carus], "The City of David," *OC* 23 (1909) 610-618.

W. O. E. Oesterley, "Jerusalem," *CQR* 69 (1909-10) 322-353.

[Paul Carus], "The Vicinity of Jerusalem," *OC* 24 (1910) 335-356.

C. F. Burney, "Ancient Jerusalem," *QRL* 212 (1910) 73-102. *(Review)*

*A. H. Sayce, "Yahweh and Jerusalem," *ET* 22 (1910-11) 226-229.

E. W. G. Masterman, "Recent Excavations in Jerusalem," *BW* 39 (1912) 295-306.

Hugh Pope, "Recent Light on Jeursalem Topography," *DR* 151 (1912) 277-298.

Anonymous, "Recent Explorations in Jerusalem," *MR* 94 (1912) 469-472.

Jerusalem cont.

Anonymous, "Explorations in Jerusalem," *MR* 95 (1913) 640-643.

J. D. Crace, "The Damascus Gate, Jerusalem," *PEFQS* 46 (1914) 29-33.

E. F. Beaumont, "Recent Discoveries in Jerusalem," *PEFQS* 46 (1914) 165-169.

Charles M. Watson, "Jerusalem, Past and Present," *JTVI* 46 (1914) 262-269.

Thomas à K. Reilly, "Sieges of Jerusalem. The First Two," *AER* 52 (1915) 13-28.

*Philip J. Baldensperger, "The Immovable East. *The General Characteristics of the Different Towns.* I. Jerusalem," *PEFQS* 48 (1916) 165-172.

George A. Barton, "Investigations Near the Damascus Gate," *A&A* 7 (1918) 212-214.

P[aul] Haupt, "The Tophet Gate," *JBL* 37 (1918) 232-233.

Anonymous, "Current Notes and News. The Archaeological Outlook for Jerusalem," *A&A* 9 (1920) 202.

E. W. G. Masterman, "The Walls of Jerusalem at Various Periods," *JTVI* 52 (1920) 125-137. (Discussion, pp. 137-141)

Frederick Jones Bliss, "Recent Excavations in Jerusalem," *AJSL* 38 (1921-22) 221-224. *(Review)*

*Gerald M. FitzGerald, "The City of David and the Excavations of 1913-14," *PEFQS* 54 (1922) 8-22.

R. A. S. Macalister, "First Quarterly Report on the Eastern Hill of Excavation of the Eastern Hill of Jerusalem," *PEFQS* 56 (1924) 9-23.

R. A. S. Macalister, "Second Quarterly Report of the excavation of the Eastern Hill of Jerusalem," *PEFQS* 56 (1924) 57-67.

Jerusalem cont.

J. Garrow Duncan, "Third Quarterly Report of the excavation of the Eastern Hill of Jerusalem," *PEFQS* 56 (1924) 124-136.

J. Garrow Duncan, "Fourth Quarterly Report of the excavation of the Eastern Hill of Jerusalem," *PEFQS* 56 (1924) 163-179.

W[illiam] F[oxwell] Albright, "The Third Wall of Jerusalem," *BASOR* #19 (1925) 19-21.

George W. Gilmore, "Jerusalem a City 5000 Years Old," *HR* 89 (1925) 49-50.

J. Garrow Duncan, "Fifth Quarterly Report of the excavation of the Eastern Hill of Jerusalem," *PEFQS* 57 (1925) 8-24.

J. Garrow Duncan, "Sixth Quarterly Report of the excavation of the Eastern Hill of Jerusalem," *PEFQS* 57 (1925) 134-139.

J. E. Hanauer and [J.] Garrow Duncan, "The Excavations of the Foundations of the Supposed Third Wall of Jerusalem," *PEFQS* 57 (1925) 172-182.

Anonymous, "An Interesting Discovery at the Jerusalem School," *BASOR* #25 (1927) 2-3. *[The Women's Towers]*

E. L. Sukenik, "Note on the North Wall of Jerusalem," *BASOR* #26 (1927) 8-9.

Julian Morgenstern, "The Gates of Righteousness," *HUCA* 6 (1929) 1-37.

*J. Garrow Duncan, "The Identification of the Site of Zion and Other Biblical Sites in and Around Jerusalem," *EQ* 2 (1930) 225-241.

C. Anne E. Moberly, "An Historical Place in Jerusalem," *ET* 41 (1929-30) 381. *[Tower of David]*

W. M. Christie, "The Wailing Wall at Jerusalem," *ET* 42 (1930-31) 176-180.

C. N. Johns, "Jerusalem: Ancient Street-Levels in the Tyropoeon Valley within the Walls," *QDAP* 1 (1932) 97-100.

Jerusalem cont.

‡L. A. Mayer and M[ichael] Avi-Yonah, "Concise Bibliography of Excavations in Palestine. Jerusalem," *QDAP* 1 (1932) 163-188.

(Mrs.) C. Agnes Boyd, "Jerusalem, According to Nehemiah," *JTVI* 65 (1933) 57-69. (Questions and Answers, pp. 69-70)

R. W. Hamilton, "Note on Excavations at Bishop Gobat School 1933," *PEFQS* 67 (1935) 141-143. *[Jerusalem]*

C. N. Johns, "Excavations at the Citadel, Jerusalem. *Interim Report*, 1935," *QDAP* 5 (1936) 127-131.

*C. C. McCown, "Two Years' Achievements in Palestinian Archaeology," *RL* 8 (1939) 97-108. [Jerusalem, pp. 102-103]

C. N. Johns, "Excavations at the Citadel, Jerusalem," *PEQ* 72 (1940) 36-58.

*J. W. Jack, "Recent Biblical Archaeology," *ET* 52 (1940-41) 229-233. [The Present North Wall of Jerusalem, pp. 232-233]

*Solomon Gandz, "The Hall of Reckonings in Jerusalem," *JQR, N.S.,* 31 (1940-41) 383-404.

W[illiam] F[oxwell] Albright, "New Light on the Walls of Jerusalem in the New Testament Age," *BASOR* #81 (1941) 6-10.

M. Solomiac, "The Towers and Cisterns of the Third Wall of Jerusalem," *BASOR* #84 (1941) 5-7.

Edward A. Cerny, "Archaeological Corner. The North Wall of Jerusalem," *CBQ* 3 (1941) 266-267.

W. F. Stinespring, "Some Archaeological Problems of Jerusalem," *JAAR* 9 (1941) 89-93.

William Ross, "The Four North Walls of Jerusalem," *PEQ* 74 (1942) 69-81.

*J. W. Jack, "Recent Biblical Archaeology," *ET* 54 (1942-43) 78-82. [3. Jerusalem, pp. 80-81]

Jerusalem cont.

J[oan] W. Crowfoot, "The Four North Walls of Jerusalem," *PEQ* 75 (1943) 58-60.

F. V. Filson, "Josephus' Second North Wall of Jerusalem," *JBL* 63 (1944) iv.

E. L. Sukenik and L. A. Mayer, "A New Section of the Third Wall, Jerusalem," *PEQ* 76 (1944) 145-151.

N. P. Clarke, "The Four North Walls of Jerusalem," *PEQ* 76 (1944) 199-212.

R. W. Hamilton, "Excavations against the North Wall of Jerusalem, 1937-8," *QDAP* 10 (1944) 1-54.

L. A. Mayer and E. L. Sukenik, "A New Sector of the Third Wall, Jerusalem," *KSJA* 2 (1945) V.

*Samuel Krauss, "Zion and Jerusalem. A Linguistic and Historical Study," *PEQ* 77 (1945) 15-33.

C. T. Norris, "New Reasoning Concerning the Fortifications of Jerusalem in the First Century A.D.," *PEQ* 78 (1946) 19-37.

*D. Winton Thomas, "Jerusalem in the Lachish Ostraca," *PEQ* 78 (1946) 86-91.

*Samuel Krauss, "Moriah-Ariel," *PEQ* 79 (1947) 45-55, 102-111. *[Jerusalem]*

*M[ichael] Avi-Yonah, "Excavations at Sheikh Bader, Jerusalem (1949)," *BIES* 15 (1949-50) #1/2, II.

J. Simons, "The Wall of Manasseh and the 'Mišneh' of Jerusalem," *OTS* 7 (1950) 179-200.

J. Simons, "Jerusalem-Exploration: Past and Future," *OTS* 8 (1950) 66-84.

C. N. Johns, "The Citadel, Jerusalem. A Summary of Work since 1934," *QDAP* 14 (1950) 121-190.

Jerusalem cont.

*B. Dinaburg, "Zion and Jerusalem: Their Role in the Historic Conciousness of Israel," *Zion* 16 (1951) #1/2, I-II.

J. W. Hirschberg, "The Sources of Moslem Traditions concerning Jerusalem," *RO* 17 (1951-52) 314-350.

*N[ahum] Avigad, "The Fortification of the City of David," *IEJ* 2 (1952) 230-236.

E. Wiesenberg, "The Nicanor Gate," *JJS* 3 (1952) 14-29.

*W. D. McHardy, "Religious Education. David and Jerusalem," *ET* 65 (1953-54) 123-125.

M[ichael] Avi-Yonah, "The Walls of Nehemiah—A Minimalist View," *IEJ* 4 (1954) 239-248.

Richard T. Murphy, "Arma Virumque Cano," *CBQ* 17 (1955) 233-247. [The Fourth Wall (of Jerusalem), pp. 237-242]

Eric F. F. Bishop, "The Damascus Gate of the Gate of the Pillar in Jerusalem," *CBQ* 17 (1955) 553-558.

*David Noel Freedman, "The Babylonian Chronicle," *BA* 19 (1956) 50-60. *[Background information on the Capture of Jerusalem by the Babylonians in 597 B.C.]*

Julian Morgenstern, "Jerusalem—485 B.C.," *HUCA* 27 (1956) 101-179; 28 (1957) 15-47; 31 (1960) 1-29.

E. Bammel, "Nicanor and His Gate," *JJS* 7 (1956) 77-78.

Anonymous, "The Capture of Jerusalem 597 B.C.," *AT* 1 (1956-57) #4, 14.

*Jack Finegan, "Nebuchadnezzar and Jerusalem," *JAAR* 25 (1957) 203-205.

Robert J. Marshall, "Sounding in the Grounds of the School in Jerusalem December, 1958—April, 1959," *BASOR* #156 (1959) 9-15.

Jerusalem cont.

Z. Vilnay, "Pictures of Jerusalem and Its Holy Places," *EI* 6 (1960) 37*.

*Kathleen [M.] Kenyon, "Excavations in Jordan 1960/1961. Excavations in Jerusalem," *ADAJ* 6&7 (1962) 114-117.

Kathleen M. Kenyon, "Excavations at Jerusalem, 1961," *Antiq* 36 (1962) 93-96.

Kathleen M. Kenyon, "Excavations in Jerusalem, 1961," *PEQ* 94 (1962) 72-89.

D. R. Ap-Thomas, "Excavations in Jerusalem (Jordan), 1962," *ZAW* 74 (1962) 321-322.

Sylvester Saller, "Jerusalem and its Surroundings in the Bronze Age," *SBFLA* 12 (1961-62) 146-176.

Kathleen M. Kenyon, "Biblical Jerusalem," *Exped* 5 (1962-63) #1, 32-35.

R. B. Y. Scott, "A Further Trace of the Sukenik Mayer 'Third Wall'?" *BASOR* #169 (1963) 61-62.

Kathleen M. Kenyon, "Excavations in Jerusalem, 1962," *PEQ* 95 (1963) 7-21.

S[ylvester] Saller, "Recent Archaeological Work in Palestine," *SBFLA* 14 (1963-64) 273-292. [Jerusalem; East of Jerusalem; South of Jerusalem; North of Jerusalem]

A. D. Tushingham, "New Excavations in Old Jerusalem," *AJA* 68 (1964) 203.

Kathleen M. Kenyon, "Excavations at Jerusalem," *BA* 27 (1964) 34-52.

Anonymous, "Jerusalem. The Australian Institute of Archaeology contributes to the current Excavation," *BH* 1 (1964) #2, 19-24.

*V. A. Tcherikover, "Was Jerusalem a 'Polis'?" *IEJ* 14 (1964) 61-78.

Jerusalem cont.

Kathleen M. Kenyon, "Excavations in Jerusalem, 1963," *PEQ* 96 (1964) 7-18.

Bruce T. Dahlberg, "Jerusalem," *BA* 38 (1965) 22-26.

Kathleen M. Kenyon, "Excavations in Jerusalem, 1964," *PEQ* 97 (1965) 9-20.

*M. Avnimelech, "Influence of Geological Conditions on the Development of Jerusalem," *BASOR* #181 (1966) 24-31.

E. W. Hamrick "New Excavations at Sukenik's 'Third Wall'," *BASOR* #183 (1966) 19-26.

*Julian Morgenstern, "Futher Light from the Book of Isaiah on the Catastrophe of 485 B.C.," *HUCA* 37 (1966) 1-28.

K[athleen] M. K[enyon], "Excavations in Jerusalem, 1965," *PEQ* 98 (1966) 73-88.

R. Pearce S. Hubbard, "The Topography of Ancient Jerusalem," *PEQ* 98 (1966) 130-154.

Kathleen M. Kenyon, "Jerusalem," *IEJ* 17 (1967) 275-277.

Harold Fisch, "Jerusalem, Jerusalem," *Jud* 16 (1967) 259-265.

Kathleen M. Kenyon, "Excavations in Jerusalem, 1966," *PEQ* 99 (1967) 65-73.

*Ronald F. Youngblood, "A Tale of Three Cities," *BSQ* 16 (1967-68) 67-78. [Jerusalem, pp. 71-74]

E. W. Hamrick, "Further Notes on the 'Third Wall'," *BASOR* #192 (1968) 21-25.

Norman Bentwich, "Rediscovering Ancient Jerusalem," *ContR* 213 (1968) 281-284.

M[ichael] Avi-Yonah, "The Third and Second Walls of Jerusalem," *IEJ* 18 (1968) 98-125.

Jerusalem concluded

*A[braham] Malamat, "The Last Kings of Judah and the Fall of Jerusalem," *IEJ* 18 (1968) 137-156.

*Walter Harrelson, "Guilt and Rites of Purification related to the Fall of Jerusalem in 587 B.C.," *Numen* 15 (1968) 218-221.

Kathleen M. Kenyon, "Excavations in Jerusalem, 1967," *PEQ* 100 (1968) 97-111.

*Peter R. Ackroyd, "Historians and Prophets," *SEÅ* 33 (1968) 18-54. [Jeremiah and the Fall of Jerusalem, pp. 37-54]

Ed. Janis, "'Jerusalem the Holy'," *Shekel* 1 (1968) #2, 25-28.

*Z. Kallai and H[ayim] Tadmor, "Bit Ninurta = Beth Horon—On the History of the Kingdom of Jerusalem in the Amarna Period," *EI* 9 (1969) 138. *[English Summary]*

J. H. Mankin, "Survey of the Old City of Jerusalem, 1865 and 1935," *PEQ* 101 (1969) 37-39.

*Alexander Guttmann, "Jerusalem in Tannaitic Law," *HUCA* 40&41 (1969-70) 251-275.

Jeshanah

C. Clermont-Ganneau, "The Site of Jeshanah," *PEFQS* 9 (1877) 206-207.

Jezreel

*Claude R. Conder, "New Identifications," *PEFQS* 12 (1880) 230-231. [Jezreel, p. 230]

N. Tzori, "An Ancient Site in Swamp Soil in the Emek (Valley of Jezreel)," *PEQ* 89 (1957) 82-83.

el-Jib

*James B. Pritchard, "Excavations in Jordon 1960/1961. Excavations at el-Jib, 1960," *ADAJ* 6&7 (1962) 121-122.

James B. Pritchard, "El-Jib Excavations," *ADAJ* 8&9 (1964) 86-87.

Joppa

[Marcus] Kalisch, "The Position and History of Joppa," *ONTS* 3 (1883-84) 256-258.

Hans Goedicke, "The Capture of Joppa," *CdÉ* 43 (1968) 219-232.

Jordan (the Country - General Studies)

*Auni Dajani, "Excavations in Jordan, 1949-1950," *ADAJ* 1 (1951) 44-48.

*Anonymous, "Excavations in Jordan, 1951-1952," *ADAJ* 2 (1953) 82-88. [Qumrân Caves; Bethany; Khirbet Qumran; Wady el Marabaat; Dhībān; Jerihco, 1952]

*Anonymous, "Excavations in Jordan, 1953-1954," *ADAJ* 3 (1956) 74-87.

F. E. Zeuner, "Stone Age Exploration in Jordan, I," *PEQ* 89 (1957) 17-54. (with the Cooperation of D. Kirkbridge and Barry C. Park)

G. Lankester Harding, "Recent Discoveries in Jordan," *PEQ* 90 (1958) 7-18.

Farah S. Ma'ayeh, "Recent Archaeological Discoveries in Jordan," *ADAJ* 4&5 (1960) 114-116. [Amman; Sweileh; Tell Safut (Sweileh); Umm el-Hanafieh; Jerash; Quailba (Irbid District); Umm Qeis; Madaba]

H. Donner, S. Herrmann, H. W. Huppenbauer, E. Kutsch, K. v. Rabenau, W. Schottroff, S. Wibbing, and Arnulf Kuschke, "New Contribution to the Topography of Jordan," *ADAJ* 6&7 (1962) 90-95.

Jordan (the Country) concluded

Farah S. Ma'ayeh, "Recent Archaeological Discoveries in Jordan," *ADAJ* 6&7 (1962) 104-113.

James B. Pritchard, "Reconnaissance in Jordan," *Exped* 6 (1963-64) #2, 3-9.

H.-U. Boesche, G. Morawe, K. Nandrasky, H. P. Ruger, P. Welten, and Herbert Donner, "Remarks and Observations on the Historical Topography of Jordan," *ADAJ* 8&9 (1964) 88-92.

Jordan (Plain of, River, & Valley)

Edward Robinson, "The Jordan and its Valley," *BRCR, N.S.,* 4 (1840) 265-277.

*W. M. Thomson, "The Sources of the Jordan, the Lake el-Hûleh, and the Adjacent Country," *BS* 3 (1846) 184-207. (Communicated by E. Robinson) [Bâniâs; The Fountain; Lake Phiala; Castle of Bâniâs; Tell el-Kâdy; Region of Hûleh; Castle of Hûnîn; Region North of Hûnîn; Castle of esh-Shükîf] (Notes to the preceding Article by E. Robinson, pp. 207-214)

*E[dward] Robinson, "Depression of the Dead Sea and the Jordan Valley," *BS* 5 (1848) 397-409.

*Anonymous, "The Jordan and the Dead Sea," *MR* 31 (1849) 633-653. *(Review)*

*†Anonymous, "The River Jordan and the Dead Sea," *NBR* 11 (1849) 494-527. *(Review)*

*†Anonymous, "The Dead Sea," *SPR* 3 (1849-50) 381-410. *(Review) [Narrative of the U.S. Expedition to the River Jordan and the Dead Sea]*

*†Anonymous, "United States Expedition to the Jordan and Dead Sea," *TLJ* 2 (1849-50) 288-301. *(Review)*

*T. H. F., "Narrative of the United States Expedition to the River Jordan and the Dead Sea," *MQR, 1st Ser.,* 4 (1850) 15-33. *(Review)*

Jordan (Plain of, River, & Valley) cont.

*Carl Ritter, "On the Explorations of the Jordan River and the Dead Sea," *JSL, 1st Ser.,* 7 (1851) 334-359.

*†Anonymous, "De Saulcy's Dead Sea and Bible Lands," *DR* 35 (1853) 139-172. *(Review) [Jordan River]*

*John Hogg, "On the Site of the Destroyed Cities of the Plain, and the Supposed Former Course of the Jordan into the Aelanitic Gulf," *JSL, 2nd Ser.,* 5 (1853-54) 510-516.

*(   ) Newbold, "On the Lake Phiala—the Jordan and its Sources," *JRAS* (1854) 8-31.

*Lyman Coleman, "The Great Crevasse of the Jordan and of the Red Sea," *BS* 24 (1867) 248-262.

J. L. Porter, "The Jordan Valley, in the Light of Biblical History and Scientific Research," *JTVI* 12 (1878-79) 372-387. (Discussion, pp. 387-392)

[Edward] Hull, "Did the Waters of the Jordan Originally flow into the Gulf of Akabah?" *PEFQS* 18 (1886) 145-148.

*J. S. Riggs, "Studies in Palestinian Geography. VI. The Jordan Valley and the Perea," *BW* 5 (1895) 36-44.

J. L. Leeper, "The Sources of the Jordan River," *BW* 16 (1900) 326-336.

R. L. Stewart, "Fords of the Jordan," *CFL, N.S.,* 2 (1900) 229-235.

J. L. Leeper, "The Upper Jordan," *BW* 17 (1901) 86-95.

J. L. Leeper, "The Jordan River Between the Seas," *BW* 20 (1902) 422-431.

*William Libbey, "Notes on the Jordan Valley and Petra," *PEFQS* 34 (1902) 411-413.

*[Edward] Hull, "Notes on Professor Libbey's Account of the Jordan Valley and Petra," *PEFQS* 35 (1903) 92-93.

Jordan (Plain of, River, & Valley) cont.

E. W. G. Masterman, "The Upper Jordan Valley," *BW* 32 (1908) 302-313.

M. G. Kyle, "A Research Journey to the 'Round' of the Jordan," *RP* 11 (1912) 247-252. *[Plain of Jordan]*

P. P. McKenna, "In the Jordan Valley," *IER, 5th Ser.,* 42 (1933) 384-398.

M[ichael] Avi-Yonah, "Two Notes on the Jordan Valley," *JPOS* 17 (1937) 252-254. [1. Psittatium; 2. Papyron]

B[enjamin] Maisler and S. Yeivin, "Provisional Report on an Exploration of the Northern Jordan Valley," *BIES* 10 (1942-44) #4, I-II.

M[oshe] Stekelis, "On the Prehistoric Stations Found in the Jordan Valley," *BIES* 10 (1942-44) #4, II.

Nelson Glueck, "The Jordan," *BA* 6 (1943) 62-67. *[The Jordan Valley]*

B[enjam] Maisler and S. Yeivin, "Second Provisional Report on the Exploration of the Northern Jordan Valley," *BIES* 11 (1944-45) #3/4, I.

Nelson Glueck, "A Chalcolithic Settlement in the Jordan Valley," *BASOR* #97 (1945) 10-22.

Nelson Glueck, "A Settlement of Middle Bronze I in the Jordan Valley," *BASOR* #100 (1945) 7-16.

W. C. Lowdermilk, "The Most Storied River in the World," *JAAR* 15 (1947) 53-54. *(Review) [The Jordan River]*

Nelson Glueck, "Some Biblical Sites in the Jordan Valley," *HUCA* 23 (1950-51) Part 1, 105-129.

I[saac] Schattner, "The Meanders of the Jordan," *BIES* 20 (1955-56) #3/4, II-III.

Jordan (Plain of, River, & Valley) concluded

I[saac] Schattner, "The Load of the Lower Jordan," *BIES* 23 (1959) #3/4, III-IV.

I[saac] Schattner, "The Load of the Lower Jordan," *SGEI* #1 (1959) III-IV.

*James Melleart/sic/, "Preliminary Report of the Archaeological Survey in the Yarmouk and Jordan Valley for the Point Four Irrigation Scheme," *ADAJ* 6&7 (1962) 126-157.

George Denzer, "The River Jordan," *BibT* #2 (1962) 71-76.

*Isaac Schattner, "The Lower Jordan Valley. A Study in the Fluviomorphology of an Arid Region," *SH* 11 (1962) 9-123.

*Henry/sic/ de Contenson, "The 1953 Survey in the Yarmuk and Jordan Valleys," *ADAJ* 8&9 (1964) 30-46.

Yehoshua Ben-Arieh, "The Changing Landscape of the Central Jordan Valley," *SH* 15 (1968) #3, 3-131.

Jotapata

*E. W. G. Masterman, "The Galilee of Josephus. The Positions of Gabara, Jotapata and Taricheae," *PEFQS* 42 (1910) 268-280.

Jubeiah

C[onrad] Schick, "Letters from Herr Baurath Schick. III. The Ruins of Jubeiah," *PEFQS* 25 (1893) 201-203. (Note by C. R. Conder, p. 323)

Judah

[W. M.] Flinders Petrie, "The South of Judah," *AEE* 13 (1928) 97-100.

*A. Saarisalo, "Sites and Roads in Asher and Western Judah," *SO* 28 (1964) #1, 1-30.

Judea

*Claude R. Conder, "Notes on Perrot and Chipiez's 'Histoire de l'Art'. Vol. IV.—Sardinia, Judea, and Asia Minor," *PEFQS* 19 (1887) 107-110.

A. H. Sayce, "Excavations in Judæa," *ContR* 58 (1890) 427-434.

J. S. Riggs, "Studies in Palestinian Geography. II. Judea," *BW* 4 (1894) 87-93.

*N. Shalem, "The Desert and the Sown in Judea," *Kobez* 4 (1945) X.

Anonymous, "Explorations Near the Wilderness of Judea," *AT* 1 (1956-57) #3, 15.

B. Kanael, The Partition of Judea by Gabinius," *IEJ* 7 (1957) 98-106.

*S. Safrai, "The Status of Provinicia Judaea after the Destruction of the Second Temple," *Zion* 27 (1962) #3/4, VII.

Tell ej-Judeideh

F[rederick] J[ones] Bliss, "First Report on the Excavations at Tell ej-Judeideh," *PEFQS* 32 (1900) 87-101.

F[rederick] J[ones] Bliss, "Second Report on the Excavations at Tell ej-Judeideh," *PEFQS* 32 (1900) 199-222.

Tell el-Jurn

*Anonymous, "En-gedi," *IEJ* 11 (1961) 76-77. *(Tell el-Jurn || Tel Goren)*

K

Kabri

M. W. Prausnitz, "The Excavations at Kabri," *EI* 9 (1969) 137. *[English Summary]*

Kadesh-Naphtali

*Julian Morgenstern, "Kadesh-Naphthali and Ta'anach," *JQR, N.S.,* 9 (1918-19) 359-369.

*Stanley A. Cook, "Kadesh-Napthali and Taanach: A Theory and Some Comments," *PEFQS* 51 (1919) 188-193.

Kefar Ḥebron

*J[acob] Kaplan, "Khirbet Ḥabra = Kefar Ḥebron," *BIES* 14 (1947-48) #3/4, II.

Kafr Yasif

*Anonymous, "Jelemiye, Beth-She'airm, Kafr Yasif," *IEJ* 16 (1966) 283-284.

Karm al-Shaikh

D. C. Baramki, "Note on a Cemetery at Karm al-Shaikh," *QDAP* 1 (1932) 3-9. [Additional note, *QDAP* 3 (1934) p. 48]

Kefer Gil'adi

J[acob] Kaplan, "Kefer Gil'adi," *IEJ* 16 (1966) 272-273.

Kefr Kenna

( ) Zeller, "Kefr Kenna," *PEFQS* 1 (1869) 71-73.

Kenath

*J. L. Porter, "Bashan, Ituraea, Kenath," *BS* 13 (1856) 789-808.

Kerazeh

*F. Turville Petre, "Dolmen Necropolis near Kerazeh, Galilee. Excavations of the British School of Archaeology in Jerusalem," *PEFQS* 63 (1931) 155-166.

Kerak

Theodore E. Dowling, "Kerak in 1896," *PEFQS* 28 (1896) 327-332.

*Charles Alexander Hornstein, "A Visit to Kerak and Petra," *PEFQS* 30 (1898) 94-103.

*B[enjamin] Maisler, M[oshe] Stekelis, and M[ichael] Avi-Yonah, "The Excavations at Beth Yerah (Khirbet el-Kerak), 1944-1946," *IEJ* 2 (1952) 165-173, 218-229.

Kfar Monash

Y[ohanan] Aharoni and Ruth Amiran, "Kfar Monash," *IEJ* 12 (1962) 144.

Khan Minyeh

*Edward A Wicher, "A New Argument for Locating Capernaum at Khan Minyeh," *AJA* 20 (1916) 90.

Tell el-Kheleifeh (See: Ezion-Geber ←)

el Khiam

Jaquin Gonzalez Echegary, "Excavation in el Khiam," *ADAJ* 8&9 (1964) 93-94.

Khirbet 'Adaseh

*W. F. Birch, "Notes and Queries. 2. *Kh. Adaseh and Gibeah of Saul,"* *PEFQS* 43 (1911) 161-162.

*E. W. G. Masterman, "Tell el-Ful and Khurbet 'Adaseh," *PEFQS* 45 (1913) 132-137.

Khirbet Delhamiyah

M[oshe] Stekelis, "Traces of Chalcolithic Culture," *EI* 8 (1967) 71*. *[Khirbet Delhamiyah]*

Khirbet Ḥabra

*J[acob] Kaplan, "Khirbet Ḥabra = Kefar Ḥebron," *BIES* 14 (1947-48) #3/4, II.

Khirbet Ḥaiyân

Joseph A. Callaway and Murray B. Nicol, "A Sounding at Khirbet Ḥaiyân," *BASOR* #183 (1966) 12-19.

Khirbet Iskander

*Anonymous, "Excavations in Jordan, 1953-1954," *ADAJ* 3 (1956) 74-87. [Khirbet Iskander—Ashmolean Museum Expedition under the direction of Peter Parr, p. 81]

Peter J. Parr, "Excavations at Khirbet Iskander," *ADAJ* 4&5 (1960) 128-133.

Khirbet Judeiyideh

F. J. Bliss, "Report by F. J. Bliss, Ph.D.," *PEFQS* 30 (1898) 223-224. *[Khurbet Judeiyideh]*

Khirbet Māsi

*Julius Jotham Rothschild, "Antiquities in the Mountains of Judah. I. The Khirbet Māsi," *PEQ* 88 (1956) 49-56. *[Beth Mëir]*

Khirbet Mazin

H[oward] E. Stutchbury and G. R. Nicholl, "Khirbet Mazin," *ADAJ* 6&7 (1962) 96-103.

Khirbet el Mefjer

D. C. Baramki, "Excavations at Khirbet el Mefjer," *QDAP* 5 (1936) 132-138; 6 (1938) 157-168; 8 (1939) 51-53; 10 (1944) 153-159.

Khirbet el-Muqanna'

*J. Naveh (Levy), "Khirbet el-Muqanna'—'Eqron," *BIES* 21 (1957) #3/4, III.

*J. Naveh (Levy), "Khirbat al-Muqanna'—Ekron," *IEJ* 8 (1958) 87-100, 165-170.

Khirbet 'Orma

J. E. Hanauer, "Khurbet 'Orma," *PEFQS* 18 (1886) 24-26. (Corrections, p. 161)

Khirbet esh-Sheikh Ibrahim

*Y[ohanan] Aharoni, "Ḥorvat Dorban (Khirbet esh-Sheikh Ibrahim)," *IEJ* 13 (1963) 337.

Khirbet Wadi Ez-Zaraniq

William R. Farmer, "Soundings at Khirbet Wadi Ez-Zaraniq," *BASOR* #147 (1957) 34-36.

Khirbet Yahuda

Y[igael] Yadin, "Aḥa of Jahud," *BIES* 16 (1951) #3/4, VII. *[Khirbet Yahuda]*

Kidron

*Paul Haupt, "Hinnom and Kidron," *JBL* 38 (1919) 45-48.

Howard E. Stutchbury, "Excavations in the Kidron Valley," *PEQ* 93 (1961) 101-113.

Kilwa

Nelson Glueck, "Kilwa: a Review," *Antiq* 13 (1939) 416-424.

Kirjath Jearim

Anonymous, "The Site of Kirjath Jearim," *PEFQS* 10 (1878) 114.

Archibald Henderson, "On the Site of Kirjath-Jerim," *PEFQS* 10 (1878) 196-199.

*Claude R. Conder, "Nephtoah and Kirjath-jearim," *PEFQS* 11 (1879) 95-99.

*W. F. Birch, "Varieties," *PEFQS* 14 (1882) 59-61. [Kirjath-Jearim]

C[laude] R. Conder, "Notes. *Kirjath Jearim,*" *PEFQS* 14 (1882) 157.

*Archibald Henderson, "Kirjath Jearim," *PEFQS* 14 (1882) 63-64.

*Walter Milner, "Kirjath-jearim and Eben-ezer,"*PEFQS* 19 (1887) 111.

Claude R. Conder, "Kirjath Jearim," *PEFQS* 20 (1888) 259.

Kirjath-Sepher (See also: Tell Beit Mirsim)

Anonymous, "Cable News of the Excavation at Kirjath-Sepher," *BASOR* #22 (1926) 12-13.

Melvin Grove Kyle, "Excavations at Kirjath Sepher," *BS* 83 (1926) 378-402.

Melvin Grove Kyle, "Summing Up Results at Kirjath-Sepher," *TTM* 10 (1926-27) 151-155.

M[elvin] G[rove] Kyle, "Excavations at Tell Beit Mirsim—Kirjath Sepher, Palestine, 1928," *BS* 85 (1928) 254-259.

M[elvin] G[rove] Kyle, "Excavations at Tell Beit Mirsim, The Ancient Kirjath Sepher," *BS* 85 (1928) 381-408.

Melvin Grove Kyle, "Excavations at Tell Beit Mirsim, the Ancient Kirjath-Sepher," *EQ* 2 (1930) 337-343.

I. O. Northstein, "Progress in the Excavation of Kirjath-sepher," *AugQ* 7 (1928) 267.

George St. Clair, "Kirjath-Sepher," *PEFQS* 20 (1888) 281-282.

A. H. Sayce, "The Site of Kirjath-Sepher," *PEFQS* 25 (1893) 33-35. (Note by C. R. Conder, p. 178)

Kishon

*N. Zimbalist, "Kishon and Kishyôn," *BIES* 13 (1946-47) #1/2, III.

Kishyôn

*N. Zimbalist, "Kishon and Kishyôn," *BIES* 13 (1946-47) #1/2, III.

Kourion-Bamboula

*S. S. Weinberg, "Kourion-Bamboula: The Late Bronze Age Architecture," *AJA* 56 (1952) 178.

Ksār 'Ā<u>k</u>il

*Alfred Ely Day, "The Rock Shelter of Ksār 'Ā<u>k</u>il Near the Cave of An<u>t</u>ilyas," *PEFQS* 58 (1926) 158-160.

J. F. Ewing, "Ksar 'Akil in 1948," *B* 29 (1948) 272-278.

Kurnub

S. Applebaum, "A Trial Excavation at Kurnub, 1956," *BIES* 23 (1959) #1/2, II.

el Kuseir

Ian Blake, "El Kuseir: A Hermitage in the Wilderness of Judaea," *PEQ* 101 (1969) 87-93.

Tell el Kussîs

Anonymous, "Tell el Kussîs," *BSAJB* #2 (1922) 16-17.

L

Lachish

*Anonymous, "Lachish and Eglon," *ONTS* 11 (1890) 313.

Anonymous, "The Site of Lachish," *ONTS* 11 (1890) 380.

*J. A. Paine, "Not Lachish, but Gath," *BS* 47 (1890) 682-691.

[Claude R. Conder], "Notes on the *Quarterly Statement,* July, 1890. *Lachish,*" *PEFQS* 22 (1890) 329-330.

C[laude] R. Conder, "Notes by Major Conder, R.E. II. The Lachish Ruins," *PEFQS* 23 (1891) 311.

Chas. F. Kent, "Excavations at Old Lachish," *ONTS* 15 (1892) 235-240.

*F. Vigouroux, "Recent Discoveries in Palestine," *AER* 8 (1893) 241-250. *[Lachish]*

Lachish cont.

*William Hayes Ward, "Light on Scriptural Texts from Recent Discoveries. The Siege of Lachish," *HR* 30 (1895) 27-29.

*David J. Gibson, "Correspondence," *PEFQS* 68 (1936) 102-103. *[Lachish]*

*W[illiam] F[oxwell] Albright, "Further Light on the History of Israel from Lachish and Megiddo," *BASOR* #68 (1937) 22-26.

J. L. Starkey, "'Lachish as Illustrating Bible History'," *PEQ* 69 (1937) 171-179.

G. Ernest Wright, "Lachish—Frontier Fortress of Judah," *BA* 1 (1938) 21-30.

*E. A. Cerny, "Archaeological Corner," *CBQ* 1 (1939) 166-168. [Lachis (Lachish), pp. 167-168]

*C. C. McCown, "Two Years' Achievements in Palestinian Archaeology," *RL* 8 (1939) 97-108. [Lachish, pp. 99-100]

*J. W. Jack, "Recent Biblical Archaeology," *ET* 52 (1940-41) 229-233. [Lachish, p. 232]

*H. F. D. Sparks, "Lachish and the Date of the Exodus," *JTS* 42 (1941) 178-179.

*H. F. D. Sparks, "The Lachish Excavations and Their Bearing upon Old Testament Study," *Theo* 43 (1941) 17-27.

C. H. Inge, "Lachish, city of Judah," *JMUEOS* #23 (1942) 1.

*David Diringer, "Sennacherib's Attack on Lachish: New Epigraphical Evidence," *VT* 1 (1951) 134-136.

G. Ernest Wright, "Judean Lachish," *BA* 18 (1955) 9-17.

Mary Neely, "*The Exodus:* The Fall of Lachish," *AT* 2 (1957-58) #4, 12-15.

*R. D. Barnett, "The Siege of Lachish," *IEJ* 8 (1958) 161-164.

Lachish concluded

*Olga Tufnell, "Hazor, Samaria and Lachish: A Synthesis," *PEQ* 91 (1959) 90-105.

Y[ohanan] Aharoni, "Lachish," *IEJ* 16 (1966) 280-281; 18 (1968) 254-255.

*Ronald F. Youngblood, "A Tale of Three Cities," *BSQ* 16 (1967-68) 67-78. [Lachish, pp. 67-71]

Y[ohanan] Aharoni, "Trial Excavation in the 'Solar Shrine' at Lachish. Preliminary Report," *IEJ* 18 (1968) 157-169.

Laish

*H. H. Rowley, "The Danite Migration to Laish," *ET* 51 (1939-40) 466-471.

Lebanon

J. L. Porter, "Lebanon," *JSL, 3rd Ser.*, 3 (1856) 337-342.

†Anonymous, "Lebanon," *LQHR* 15 (1860-61) 150-184. *(Review)*

Robert H. West, "Barometrical Determination of Heights in Lebanon and Anti-Lebanon," *PEFQS* 23 (1891) 147-151.

*Joseph Offord, "Archaeological Notes on Jewish Antiquities. LIV. *The Egyptian Name for Lebanon*," *PEFQS* 50 (1918) 183-185.

*Hugh G. Bévenot, "Ancient Lebanon and Byblos," *BS* 84 (1927) 203-224.

*G. Vermes, "The Symbolical Interpretation of *Lebanon* in the Targums: The Origin and Development of an Exegetical Tradition," *JTS, N.S.*, 9 (1958) 1-12.

*H. F. D. Sparks, "The Symbolical Interpretation of *Lebanon* in the Fathers," *JTS, N.S.*, 10 (1959) 264-279.

Mount Lebanon

T. Laurie, "Mount Lebanon," *BS* 26 (1869) 541-571, 673-713.

*W. M. Thompson, "Traces of Glacial Action on the Flank of Mt. Lebanon," *JAOS* 10 (1880) 185-188.

John A. Paine, "The True Mount Lebanon: The Name an Index to the Place," *JCP* 2 (1882-83) 365-379.

John A. Paine, "The True Mount Lebanon: Scriptural Testimony to the Place," *JCP* 2 (1882-83) 487-520.

Lebo Hamath

*B[enjamin] Maisler, "Topographical Researches," *BIES* 12 (1946) VIII-IX. [5. Lebo Hamath and the Northern boundary of Canaan]

Libnah

*Anonymous, "Libnah and Gath," *BASOR* #4 (1921) 6.

Charles Warren, "Site of Libnah," *PEFQS* 7 (1875) 181.

C[laude] R. Conder, "Libnah," *PEFQS* 29 (1897) 69.

M

Maacah

*B[enjamin] Mazar, "Gesher and Maacah," *JBL* 80 (1961) 16-28.

Machaerus

*G[eorge] A[dam] Smith, "Notes and Queries. 7. *Callirrhoe; Machaerus; 'Ataroth*," *PEFQS* 37 (1905) 170.

George Adam Smith, "Callirrhoe and Machaerus," *PEFQS* 37 (1905) 219-230.

Machaerus concluded

George Adam Smith, "From Machaerus to Aṭaroth," *PEFQS* 37 (1905) 357-363.

Machphelah

*Philip Schaff, "Disputed Scripture Localities," *PRev* 54 (1878) Part1, 851-884. [The Machphelah, pp. 868-871]

Madeba

*J. Cropper, "Madeba, M'kaur, and Callirrhoe," *PEFQS* 38 (1906) 292-298.

Madmenah

*H. H. Walker, "Where were Madmenah and the Gebim?" *JPOS* 13 (1933) 90-93.

Mahanaim

C[laude] R. Conder, "Mahanaim," *PEFQS* 23 (1891) 244-245.

M'kaur

*J. Cropper, "Madeba, M'kaur, and Callirrhoe," *PEFQS* 38 (1906) 292-298.

Makkedah

*Anonymous, "Makkedah and Shocoh," *BASOR* #4 (1921) 6-7.

Makmish

N[ahman] Avigad, "Excavations at Makmish (Preliminary Report)," *BIES* 23 (1959) #1/2, II-III.

N[ahman] Avigad, "Excavations at Makmish, 1960: Prelminary Report," *IEJ* 11 (1961) 97-100.

Tel Malḥata

M[oshe] Kokhavi, "Tel Malḥata," *IEJ* 17 (1967) 272-273.

Mamshath

H. L. Ginsberg, "The District of Mamshath," *JBL* 65 (1946) iv.

Mamshit

A[braham] Negev, "Mamshit (Kurnub)," *IEJ* 17 (1967) 121-123.

Mampsis

*A[braham] Negev, "Oboda, Mampsis and Provincia Arabia," *IEJ* 17 (1967) 46-55.

Manasseh

*M. H. Segal, "The Settlement of Manasseh East of the Jordan," *PEFQS* 50 (1918) 124-131.

*W[illiam] F[oxwell] Albright, "The Site of Tirzah and the Topography of Western Manasseh," *JPOS* 11 (1931) 241-251.

Patrick [P.] McKenna, "In the Territory of Manasses," *IER, 5th Ser.*, 46 (1935) 276-282; 47 (1935) 175-188.

Marissa

*M[ichael] Avi-Yonah, "Samaria and the 'Marissa' of Antiquities XIII, 275," *BIES* 16 (1951) #3/4, IV-V.

Masada

Frederick Bennett Wright, "The Fortress of Masada," *RP* 5 (1906) 368-372.

Christopher Hawkes, "The Roman Siege of Masada," *Antiq* 3 (1929) 195-213.

Masada concluded

S. Guttman, "Masada," *BIES* 18 (1953-54) #3/4, XI-XII.

M[ichael] Avi-Yonah, N[ahman] Avigad, Y[ohanan] Aharoni, I[manuel] Dunayevsky, and S[haryahu] Gutman, "The Archaeological Survey of Massada, 1955-1956," *IEJ* 7 (1957) 1-60.

Anonymous, "Masada—A Tragic Last Stand. A Review of a Current Excavation," *BH* 1 (1964) #3, 20-23.

*Solomon Zeitlin, "I. Masada and the Sicarii. The Occupants of Masada," *JQR, N.S.,* 55 (1964-65) 299-317.

Yigael Yadin, "Masada," *CNI* 16 (1965) #1/2, 23-30.

Y[igael] Yadin, "The Excavation of Masada 1963/64, Preliminary Report," *IEJ* 15 (1965) 1-120.

*Solomon Zeitlin, "The Sicarii and Masada," *JQR, N.S.,* 57 (1966-67) 251-270.

*Anonymous, "The Dead Sea Scrolls, and the New Book on Masada," *BH* 3 (1967) #1, 12-13. *(Review)*

Norman Bentwich, "The Masada Expedition and the Exhibition," *ContR* 210 (1967) 44-48.

Y[igael] Yadin, "Masada and the Limes," *IEJ* 17 (1967) 43-45.

Zalman Dimitrovsky, "Masada," *CJ* 22 (1967-68) #2, 36-47.

*Bernard Heller, "Masada and the Talmud," *Trad* 10 (1968-69) #2, 31-34.

Mashita

Gray Hill, "Mashita," *PEFQS* 22 (1890) 173-174.

Me'arat Shovakh

*Sally R. Binford, "Me'arat Shovakh (Mugharet esh-Subbabiq)," *IEJ* 16 (1966) 18-32, 96-103.

Medeba

Dean A. Walker, "Some Notes from Palestine," *BW* 2 (1893) 374-378. [Medeba, pp. 374-377]

Tel Megaddim

M[agen] Broshi, "Tel Megaddim," *IEJ* 17 (1967) 277-278.

Anonymous, "Tel Megaddim," *IEJ* 18 (1968) 256-257.

David Neiman, "Excavations at Tell Megadim, Second Season 1968: Preliminary Report," *AJA* 73 (1969) 243.

B[enjamin] Mazar, "Tel Megadim," *IEJ* 19 (1969) 248-250.

Megiddo

Claude R. Conder, "Megiddo," *PEFQS* 9 (1877) 13-20.

Trelawney Saunders and [Archibald] Henderson, "The Site of Megiddo," *PEFQS* 12 (1880) 223-224.

C[laude] R. Conder, "Notes on Disputed Points. *Megiddo*," *PEFQS* 13 (1881) 86-88.

W. F. Birch, "Megiddo," *PEFQS* 13 (1881) 232-235.

W. F. Birch, "Site of Megiddo," *PEFQS* 13 (1881) 319-322.

*Archibald Henderson, "Cana and Megiddo in Tatian's Diatessaron," *PEFQS* 26 (1894) 151.

*James Henry Breasted, "The Annals of Thutmose III, and the Location of Megiddo,"*SBAP* 22 (1900) 96-98.

Anonymous, "The Ancient City of Megiddo," *MQR, 3rd Ser.,* 30 (1904) 392-393.

Charles Wilson, 'Excavations of the German Palestine Exploration Society at Tell el-Mutesellim in 1903," *PEFQS* 37 (1905) 78-79. *[Megiddo]*

Megiddo cont.

*R. A. Stewart Macalister, "Gezer and Megiddo," *PEFQS* 38 (1906) 62-66.

*J[oan] W. Crowfoot, "Three Recent Excavations in Palestine," *PEFQS* 62 (1930) 172-177. [3. Megiddo, pp. 176-177]

*W[illiam] F[oxwell] Albright, "Further Light on the History of Israel from Lachish and Megiddo," *BASOR* #68 (1937) 22-26.

*William F. Stinespring, "Remarks on Biblical Archaeology," *DDSR* 2 (1937) 1-10. [Megiddo, pp. 4-6]

Edward A. Cerny, "Archaeological Corner. Tell el-Mutesellim (Mageedo, Megiddo)," *CBQ* 1 (1939) 369-371.

*C. C. McCown, "Two Years' Achievements in Palestine Archaeology," *RL* 8 (1939) 97-108. [Megiddo, pp. 101-102]

*M. Avnimelech, "On the Geology and Morphology of the Megiddo Area," *JPOS* 19 (1939-40) 18-37.

Robert M. Engberg, "Megiddo—Guardian of the Carmel Pass," *BA* 3 (1940) 41-51.

*Robert M. Engberg, "Historical Analysis of Archaeological Evidence: Megiddo and the Song of Deborah," *BASOR* #78 (1940) 4-7. (Reply by W. F. Albright, pp. 7-9)

J[oan] W. Crowfoot, "Megiddo: A Review," *PEQ* 72 (1940) 132-147.

*J. W. Jack, "Recent Biblical Archaeology," *ET* 52 (1940-41) 112-115. [Megiddo. Palatial Houses, Ablution, Altar, p. 114]

John A. Wilson, "The Egyptian Middle Kingdom at Megiddo," *AJSL* 58 (1941) 225-236.

Robert M. Engberg, "Megiddo—Guardian of the Carmel Pass Part II," *BA* 4 (1941) 11-16.

R. O. Faulkner, "The Battle of Megiddo," *JEA* 28 (1942) 2-15.

Megiddo cont.

J. Simons, "Caesurae in the History of Megiddo," *OTS* 1 (1942) 17-54.

*J. W. Jack, "Recent Biblical Archaeology," *ET* 54 (1942-43) 78-82. [2. Megiddo, pp. 79-80]

*B. D. Zaphrir (Frimorgen), "'Even Three Countries'," *BIES* 14 (1947-48) #3/4, II. *[Megiddo]*

G. Ernest Wright, "The Discoveries at Megiddo, 1935-39," *BA* 13 (1950) 28-46. [The Early History of the City; The Dark Age; Megiddo's Golden Age; Israel at Megiddo; Megiddo in the Time of David and Solomon]

*Robert North, "Beth-shan and Megiddo," *CBQ* 12 (1950) 84-89.

*R. Giveon, "'In the Valley of Megiddon' (Zech. xii: ii) (Notes on the Historical Geography of the Region East of Megiddo)," *JJS* 8 (1957) 155-164.

Kathleen M. Kenyon, "Some Notes on the Early and Middle Bronze Age Strata of Megiddo," *EI* 5 (1958) 51*-60*.

M[oshe] Dothan, "Some Problems of the Stratigraphy in Megiddo XX," *EI* 5 (1958) 85*.

*Anonymous, "Some Recent Activities in Israel," *AT* 4 (1959-60) #4, 15-16. *[Megiddo]*

Yagael Yadin, "New Light on Solomon's Megiddo," *BA* 23 (1960) 62-68.

*Yohanan Aharoni, "Some Geographical Remarks Concerning the Campaigns of Amenhotep II," *JNES* 19 (1960) 177-183. [B. Megiddo, pp. 181-183]

Herman Heupel, "A Summary of the Archaeological Discoveries at Megiddo," *Amb* 11 (1962-63) #4, 8-18.

*K[athleen] M. Kenyon, "Megiddo, Hazor, Samaria and Chronology," *ULBIA* 4 (1964) 143-156.

Megiddo concluded

Claire Epstein, "An Interpretation of the Megiddo Sacred Area During Middle Bronze II," *IEJ* 15 (1965) 204-221.

I[manuel] Dunayevski and A[haron] Kempinski, "Megiddo," *IEJ* 16 (1966) 142.

Y[igael] Yadin, "Megiddo," *IEJ* 16 (1966) 278-280; 17 (1967) 119-121.

Anonymous, "Further Excavations at Megiddo," *BH* 4 (1968) 16-18.

K[athleen] M. Kenyon, "The Middle and Late Bronze Age Strata at Megiddo," *L* 1 (1969) 25-60.

Merom

William Gover, "The Waters of Merom," *PEFQS* 22 (1890) 50-54.

(Mrs.) E. A. Finn, "The Waters of Merom," *PEFQS* 22 (1890) 195.

Mepha'ath

C. Clermont-Ganneau, "Archaeological and Epigraphic Notes on Palestine. 17. *The Site of Mepha'ath*," *PEFQS* 34 (1902) 260-261.

Meṣad Gozal

Y[ohanan] Aharoni, "Meṣad Gozal," *IEJ* 14 (1964) 112-113.

Meṣad Ḥashavyahu

J. Naveh, "The Excavations at Meṣad Ḥashavyahu—Preliminary Report," *IEJ* 12 (1962) 89-113.

Meṣad Yeruḥam

R. Cohen, "Meṣad Yeruḥam," *IEJ* 17 (1967) 123-124.

Meşer

M[oshe] Dothan, "Excavations at Meşer, 1956: Preliminary Report on the First Season," *IEJ* 7 (1957) 217-228.

M[oshe] Dothan, "Excavations at Meşer, 1957," *IEJ* 9 (1959) 13-29.

Mevasseret Yerushalayim

Ora Neghi, "Mevasseret Yerushalayim," *IEJ* 13 (1963) 145.

Mikhmoret

B. S. J. Isserlin, "Excavating in an Ancient Port in Israel," *ALUOS* 2 (1959-61) 3-5. *[Mikhmoret]*

Millo

*George St. Clair, "Millo, House of Millo, and Silla," *PEFQS* 23 (1891) 187-189. (Note by C. R. Conder, p. 254)

*Samuel Gergheim, "The Identification of the City of David—Zion and Millo," *PEFQS* 27 (1895) 120-123.

*W. F. Birch, "Zion (or Acra), Gihon, and Millo. *(All South of the Temple),*" *PEFQS* 25 (1893) 324-330.

*J. M. Tenz, "Notes and Queries. 3. *Millo, and the City of David,*" *PEFQS* 37 (1905) 165-167.

*F. Garrow Duncan, "Millo and the City of David," *ZAW* 42 (1924) 222-244.

(Mrs.) Ghosn-el-Howie, "The Mystery of Millo," *AJSL* 46 (1929-30) 52-53.

el Mird

G. R. H. Wright, "The Archaeological Remains at el Mird in the Wilderness of Judaea," *B* 42 (1961) 1-21.

Mizpah (Mizpeh)

W. F. Birch, "Mizpeh," *PEFQS* 13 (1881) 91-93; 14 (1882) 260-262.

Anonymous, "Mizpah," *EN* 1 (1889) 89-90.

*C[laude] R. Conder, "Note on Mezpeh and Shen," *PEFQS* 30 (1898) 169. (Note by C. Clermont-Ganneau, p. 251)

*G. A. Simcox, "IV.—Mispah," *SBAP* 20 (1898) 304-305.

*W. F. Birch, "Mizpeh and Gath," *PEFQS* 35 (1903) 276.

*Caleb Hauser, "Mizpeh and Mizpah," *PEFQS* 42 (1910) 126-131. [(1) The Valley of Mizpeh (Land of Mizpeh); (2) Mizpeh of Gilead (Jegar-Sahadutha); (3) Mipeh (of Benjamin); (4) Mizpeh (Neh. iii, 15)]

W[illiam] F[oxwell] Albright, "The Site of Mizpah in Benjamin," *JPOS* 3 (1923) 110-121.

James Muilenburg, "Mizpah of Benjamin," *ST* 8 (1954) 25-42.

*Ronald F. Youngblood, "A Tale of Three Cities," *BSQ* 16 (1967-68) 67-78. [Mizpah, pp. 74-78]

Moab

*E. H. Palmer, "The Desert of the Tih and the Country of Moab," *PEFQS* 3 (1871) 3-73. (Index, pp. 77-80)

C. Schick, "Journey into Moab," *PEFQS* 11 (1879) 187-192.

F. A. Klein, "Notes on a Journey to Moab," *PEFQS* 12 (1880) 249-255.

*†Anonymous, "Heth and Moab," *ERCJ* 159 (1884) 457-485. *(Review)*

*Charles W. Wilson, "Recent Investigations in Moab and Edom," *JTVI* 33 (1901) 242-248. (Discussion, pp. 248-252)

Moab concluded

*G. Buchanan Gray, "The 'Steppes of Moab'," *Exp, 6th Ser.*, 11 (1905) 68-76.

G[eorge] A[dam] Smith, "Herr Alois Musil on the Land of Moab," *Exp, 7th Ser.*, 6 (1908) 1-16, 131-150.

*Nelson Glueck, "Surface Finds in Edom and Moab," *PEQ* 71 (1939) 188-192.

Nelson Glueck, "Some Ancient Towns in the Plains of Moab," *BASOR* #91 (1943) 7-26.

*Roland E. Murphy, "Israel and Moab in the Ninth Century B.C.," *CBQ* 15 (1953) 409-417.

J. A. Thompson, "The History of Biblical Moab," *ABR* 5 (1956) 119-143.

A. Kuschke, "Horonaim and Qiryathaim. Remarks on a Recent Contribution to the Topography of Moab," *PEQ* 99 (1967) 104-105.

Tell Mor

M[oshe] Dothan, "Excavations at Tell Mor (1959 Season)," *BIES* 24 (1959-60) #2/3, II-III.

Anonymous, "Tell Mor, Israel," *AT* 5 (1960-61) #4, 15-16.

Moriah

Samuel Wolcott, "The Land of Moriah," *BS* 25 (1868) 765-778.

*Charles Warren, "The Comparative Holiness of Mounts Zion and Moriah," *PEFQS* 1 (1869) 76-88.

C. M. Mead, "El Mohrakah, or the Place of Elijah's Sacrifice," *BS* 30 (1873) 672-696.

Moriah concluded

*Claude R. Conder, "Notes on Disputed Points," *PEFQS* 12 (1880) 172-174. [Moriah, p. 173]

T. K. Cheyne, "Moriah," *AJLS* 1 (1884-85) 252.

Edward G. King, "Moriah," *AJSL* 2 (1885-86) 93-94.

Anonymous, "The Sakhrah," *PEFQS* 19 (1887) 74. *[Summit of Mount Moriah]*

*Lewis Bayles Paton, "Jerusalem in Bible Times: V. Zion, Ophel, and Moriah," *BW* 29 (1907) 327-333.

*Samuel Krauss, "Moriah-Ariel," *PEQ* 79 (1947) 45-55, 102-111.

Mughâret Abū Uṣba'

*W[illiam] F[oxwell] Albright, "Observations on the Date of the Pottery-Bearing Stratum of Mughârat Abū Uṣba'," *BASOR* #86 (1942) 10-14.

M[oshe] Stekelis, "Further Observations on the Chronology of Mughâret Abū Uṣba'," *BASOR* #89 (1943) 22-24.

Mughâret esh-Subbabiq

*Sally R. Binford, "Me'arat Shovakh (Mugharet esh-Subbabiq)," *IEJ* 16 (1966) 18-32, 96-103.

N

Naarath

*Claude R. Conder, "Notes on Disputed Points," *PEFQS* 12 (1880) 172-174. [Naarath, p. 174]

Tell Nagila

Ruth Amiran, "A Preliminary Note on the First Season of Excavations at Tell Nagila, 1962," *CNI* 13 (1962) #3/4, 24-26.

Richard A. Mitchell, "Tell Nagila Expedition," *AJA* 67 (1963) 215.

Ruth Amiran and A[braham] Eitan, "A Canaanite-Hyksos City at Tell Nagila," *Arch* 18 (1965) 113-123.

Nahal Amud

Anonymous, "Nahal Amud," *IEJ* 11 (1961) 189-191.

Nahal Oren

M[oshe] Stekelis and Tamar Yizraely, "Excavations at Nahal Oren. Preliminary Report," *IEJ* 13 (1963) 1-12.

Nahariya

*M. Avnimelech, "Contributions to the Geological History of the Palestinian Coastal Plain: Nahariya and its Vicinity," *BIES* 10 (1942-44) #2/3, I.

M[oshe] Dothan, "The Excavations at ☐ahariyah: Preliminary Report (Seasons 1954/55)," *IEJ* 6 (1956) 14-25.

Nahr Ruben

M[oshe] Dothan, "Archaeological Survey of the Nahr Ruben Area," *BIES* 16 (1951) #3/4, V-VI.

Tel Nagila

Ruth Amiran and A[braham] Eitan, "Tel Nagila," *IEJ* 13 (1963) 143-144, 333-334.

Tell en-Nasbeh

William Frederic Bade, "The Excavation of Tell en-Nasbeh," *BASOR* #26 (1927) 1-7.

William Frederic Bade, "The Excavations at Tell en-Nasbeh," *PEFQS* 59 (1927) 7-13.

Elihu Grant, "Tell en-Nasbeh Expedition of the Pacific School of Religion," *PEFQS* 59 (1927) 159-161.

Anonymous, "The Excavations at Tell en-Nasbeh," *BASOR* #35 (1929) 24-25.

E. W. G. Masterman, "Excavations at Tell en-Nasbeh," *PEFQS* 61 (1929) 56-57.

W[illiam] F[rederic] Bade, "The Tell en-Nasbeh Excavations of 1929," *PEFQS* 62 (1930) 8-19.

William Frederic Bade, "The Tell en-Nasbeh Excavations of 1929 — a preliminary report," *SIR* (1930) 483-494.

John P. Naish, "Tell en-Nasbeh," *PEFQS* 64 (1932) 204-209.

*Joseph Carson Wampler, "Three Cistern Groups from Tell en-Naṣbeh," *BASOR* #82 (1941) 25-43. *[Ataroth?]*

G. Ernest Wright, "Tell en-Nasbeh," *BA* 10 (1947) 69-77.

*K. Branigan, "The Four-Room Buildings of Tell En-Naṣbeh," *IEJ* 16 (1966) 206-208.

Naveh Yam

E[liezer] Wreschner and M[oshe] W. Prausnitz, "Naveh Yam," *IEJ* 18 (1968) 192.

Nazareth

Eberhard Nestle, "Nazareth," *OC* 24 (1910) 191-192.

Anonymous, "Nazareth," *IEJ* 13 (1963) 145.

Mount Nebo

H. B. Hackett, "Biblical Notes. 2. Glorious View from Nebo," *BS* 24 (1867) 179-181.

G. Buchanan Gray, "The View From Mount Nebo," *Exp, 6th Ser.*, 10 (1904) 321-341.

*J. Garrow Duncan, "Jebal Sawada: A probable Site for Mount Nebo," *PEFQS* 59 (1927) 197-201.

Sylvester Saller, "Hellenistic to Arabic Remains at Nebo, Jordan," *SBFLA* 17 (1967) 1-64.

E[ugene D.] Stockton, "Stone Age Culture in the Nebo Region, Jordan," *SBLFA* 17 (1967) 122-128.

Negeb (Negev)

*Claude R. Conder, "New Identifications," *PEFQS* 12 (1880) 230-231. [The Negeb]

*John P. Peters, "Palestinian Exploration. *Notes of a Vacation in Palestine in 1902*," *JBL* 22 (1903) 15-31. [6. Nejeb/sic/, pp. 19-20]

*Caleb Hauser, "Cities in the Negeb, and Tribal Boundaries," *PEFQS* 38 (1906) 213-221.

*Nathaniel Schmidt, "The 'Jerahmeel' Theory and the Historic Importance of the Negeb," *HJ* 6 (1907-08) 322-342.

Negeb (Negev) cont.

*W[illiam] F[oxwell] Albright, "Egypt and the Early History of the Negeb," *JPOS* 4 (1924) 131-161.

*D. Aschbel/*sic*/, "The Climate of the Judaean Desert," *BIES* 6 (1938-39) #2, I-II.

*D. Ashbel, "Rain and water conditions in the Negev," *BIES* 8 (1940-41) #2, I.

George Kirk, "The Negev, or Southern Desert of Palestine," *PEQ* 73 (1941) 57-71.

Naphtali Lewis, "New Light on the Negev in Ancient Times," *PEQ* 80 (1948) 102-117.

*D. H. Kallner-Amiran, "Geomorphology of the Central Negev Highlands," *IEJ* 1 (1950-51) 107-120.

*Nelson Glueck, "Explorations in Western Palestine," *BASOR* #131 (1953) 6-15. /*Negeb*/

M[ichael] Avi-Jonah /*sic*/, "Ancient Remains in the Negev," *CNI* 4 (1953) #1, 18-23.

G. E[rnest] Wright, "Explorations in the Negeb," *BA* 17 (1954) 48.

*Nelson Glueck, "The Age of Abraham in the Negeb," *BA* 18 (1955) 2-9.

Nelson Glueck, "Further Explorations in the Negeb," *BASOR* #137 (1955) 10-22.

Nelson Glueck, "The Third Season of Exploration in the Negeb," *BASOR* #138 (1955) 7-29.

E[mmanuel] Anati, "Subterranean Dwellings in the Central Negev," *IEJ* 5 (1955) 259-261.

*J. /*sic*/ Kedar, "The Problem of the Mounds or 'Tuleilat el 'Anab' and Their Relation to Ancient Agriculture in the Central Negev," *BIES* 20 (1955-56) #1/2, III.

Negeb (Negev) cont.

M[oshe] Stekelis, "The Negev in Prehistoric Times," *BIES* 20 (1955-56) #3/4, I.

*D. H. K. Amiran, "The Geography of the Negev and the Southern Border of Settlement in Israel," *BIES* 20 (1955-56) #3/4, I-II.

Nelson Glueck, "The Fourth Season of Exploration in the Negeb," *BASOR* #142 (1956) 17-35.

M[oshe] Stekelis, "Thirty Years of Research into the Prehistory of Negev Settlements of the Bronze Period," *EI* 4 (1956) II-III.

Nelson Glueck, "The Fifth Season of Exploration in the Negeb," *BASOR* #145 (1957) 11-25.

Philip Mayerson, "A Survey by Jeep of the Southern Desert of Palestine," *AJA* 62 (1958) 224-225. *[Negev]*

Nelson Glueck, "The Sixth Season of Archaeological Exploration in the Negeb," *BASOR* #149 (1958) 8-17.

Michael Evenari, "Note on a Recent Paper by Nelson Glueck," *BASOR* #150 (1958) 25-26. (with editorial note by W. F. Albright) *[Ref: Nelson Glueck, "The Sixth Season of Archaeological Exploration in the Negeb"]*

Nelson Glueck, "The Seventh Season of Archaeological Exploration in the Negeb," *BASOR* #152 (1958) 18-38.

Y[ohanan] Aharoni, "The Negeb of Judah," *IEJ* 8 (1958) 26-38.

Anonymous, "Discoveries in the Negeb," *AT* 3 (1958-59) #1, 10.

Anonymous, "Negeb Exploration," *AT* 3 (1958-59) #4, 6-7.

Nelson Glueck, "Archaeological Excavations in the Negev," *AJA* 63 (1959) 187-188.

Nelson Glueck, "The Negev," *BA* 22 (1959) 82-97.

*Philip Mayerson, "Ancient Agricultural Remains in the Central Negeb: The Teleilât el-'anab," *BASOR* #153 (1959) 19-31.

Negeb (Negev) concluded

Nelson Glueck, "An Aerial Reconnaissance of the Negeb," *BASOR* #155 (1959) 2-13.

Nelson Glueck, "Archaeological Exploration of the Negev in 1959," *BASOR* #159 (1960) 3-14.

*Philip Mayerson, "The Ancient Agricultural Remains of the Central Negeb: Methodology and Dating Criteria," *BASOR* #160 (1960) 27-37.

Nelson Glueck, "The Archaeological History of the Negev," *HUCA* 32 (1961) 11-18.

*N[ahman] Avigad, "The Expedition to the Judean Desert, 1961. Expedition A—Naḥal David," *IEJ* 12 (1962) 169-183.

*Y[ohanan] Aharoni, "The Expedition to the Judean Desert 1961. Expedition B—The Cave of Horror," *IEJ* 12 (1962) 186-199.

*P[esah] Bar-Adon, "The Expedition to the Judean Desert 1961. Expedition C—The Cave of Treasure," *IEJ* 12 (1962) 215-226.

*Y[igael] Yadin, The Expedition to the Judean Desert 1961. Expedition D—The Cave of Letters," *IEJ* 12 (1962) 227-257.

*Yehuda Kedar, "More About the Teleilât el-'Anab in the Negeb," *BASOR* #176 (1964) 47-49.

*Philip Mayerson, "The Issue of the Teleilât el-'Anab," *BASOR* #178 (1965) 69.

Nelson Glueck, "Further Explorations in the Negev," *BASOR* #179 (1965) 6-29.

*Y[ohanan] Aharoni, "Forerunners of the Limes: Iron Age Fortresses in the Negev," *IEJ* 17 (1967) 1-17.

A. Marks, "Prehistoric Sites in the Central Negev," *IEJ* 19 (1969) 118-121.

Nephtoah

*Claude R. Conder, "Nephtoah and Kirjath-jearim," *PEFQS* 11 (1879) 95-99.

Nob

*Claude R. Conder, "The Site of Nob and the High Places," *PEFQS* 7 (1875) 34-41.

C. W. Wilson, "Note on Lieut. Conder's Identification of Nob," *PEFQS* 7 (1875) 94-96.

Claude R. Conder, "Note on Nob," *PEFQS* 7 (1875) 183-184.

W. F. Birch, "Nob," *PEFQS* 9 (1877) 51-60. (Note by Claude R. Conder, p. 60)

W. F. Birch, "Note on Nob," *PEFQS* 9 (1877) 204-205.

W. F. Birch, "Varieties," *PEFQS* 14 (1882) 59-61. *[Nob]*

*Andrew J. Gregg, "Note on Gibeon, Nob, Bezek and the High-Level Aqueduct to Jerusalem," *PEFQS* 31 (1899) 128-129.

Edwin E. Voigt, "The Site of Nob," *JPOS* 3 (1923) 79-87.

Nysa-Scythopolis

Stella Ben-Dor, "Concerning the Era of Nysa-Scythopolis," *PEQ* 76 (1944) 152-156.

O

Oboda

*A[braham] Negev, "Oboda, Mampsis and Provincia Arabia," *IEJ* 17 (1967) 46-55.

Mount of Olives

C[onrad] Schick, "The Mount of Olives," *PEFQS* 21 (1889) 174-184.

*William Simpson, "The Temple and the Mount of Olives," *PEFQS* 29 (1897) 307-308.

*S. Yeivin, "Topographic Notes (annotations to S. Klein, *The Land of Judah*)," *BIES* 8 (1940-41) #2, II. [2. The Mount of Olives]

John Briggs Curtis, "An Investigation of the Mount of Olives in the Judaeo-Christian Tradition," *HUCA* 28 (1957) 137-180.

William Sanford LaSor, "The Sanctity of the Mount of Olives," *CNI* 13 (1962) #3/4, 16-23.

Ophel

*Lewis Bayles Paton, "Jerusalem in Bible Times: V. Zion, Ophel, and Moriah," *BW* 29 (1907) 327-333.

C. F. Burney, "The Meaning of the Name 'The Ophel'," *PEFQS* 43 (1911) 51-58.

*W. F. Birch, "The City and Tomb of David on Ophel (so called)," *PEFQS* 43 (1911) 187-189.

Charles Warren, "The Results of the Excavations on the Hill of Ophel (*Jerusalem sous Terre*), 1909-11," *PEFQS* 44 (1912) 68-74.

Hugues Vincent, "Recent Excavations on the Hill of Ophel. A Reply to General Sir Charles Warren, G.C.M.G.," *PEFQS* 44 (1912) 131-134. (Observations by Charles Warren, pp. 134-135)

E. W. G. Masterman, "The Ophel Hill," *PEFQS* 55 (1923) 37-45.

Ophel concluded

J. Garrow Duncan, "New Rock Chambers and Galleries on Ophel," *PEFQS* 58 (1926) 7-14.

H. Vincent, "The P.E.F. Map of Ophel," *PEFQS* 58 (1926) 160-162.

R. Weill, "The P.E.F. Map of Ophel," *PEFQS* 58 (1926) 171-175.

J[oan] W. Crowfoot, "First Report of the New Excavations on Ophel," *PEFQS* 59 (1927) 143-147.

J[oan] W. Crowfoot, "Ophel, 1928. Sixth Progress Report, covering the Period from December 3 to 22, 1928," *PEFQS* 61 (1929) 75-77.

J[oan] W. Crowfoot, "Excavations on Ophel, 1928," *PEFQS* 61 (1929) 150-166.

J[oan] W. Crowfoot, "Ophel Again," *PEQ* 77 (1945) 61-104.

Ophir

C[laude] R. Conder, "Notes on the 'Quarterly Statement'. *Ophir,*" *PEFQS* 28 (1896) 168-169.

P

Palmaḥim

R[am] Gophna, "Palmaḥim," *IEJ* 18 (1968) 132-133.

Pella (of Palestine)

E[dward] Robinson, "Excursion for the Identification of Pella," *BS* 12 (1855) 131-144.

C[laude] R. Conder, "Pella," *PEFQS* 22 (1890) 182.

Pella (of Palestine) concluded

*Selah Merrill, "Notes by Dr. Selah Merrill. Natural Bridge, Hot Spring, and Roman Road at Pella," *PEFQS* 23 (1891) 76.

*George A. Barton, "Pella in the El-Amarna Tablets," *ET* 47 (1935-36) 476-477.

R. W. Funk and N. H. Richardson, "The 1958 Sounding at Pella," *BA* 21 (1958) 82-96.

Robert H. Smith, "Pella of Decapolis, 1967," *Arch* 21 (1968) 134-137.

Pentapolis

*E. Power, "The site of Pentapolis," *B* 11 (1930) 23-62, 149-182.

*J. Simons, "Two Notes on the Problem of the Pentapolis," *OTS* 4 (1948) 92-117.

Penuel

*Selah Merrill, "Identification of Succoth and Penuel," *BS* 34 (1877) 742-754.

*J. A. Paine, "Succoth and Penuel Not Yet Identified," *BS* 35 (1878) 481-498.

*Selah Merrill, "The Identification of Succoth and Penuel," *PEFQS* 10 (1878) 81-88.

*Joseph Offord, "Archaeological Notes on Jewish Antiquities. LXII. *Peniel and a Hebrew Name at Elephantine*," *PEFQS* 52 (1920) 77-78.

*J. Garrow Duncan, "Notes on the Sites of Succoth and Penuel as bearing upon the Routes of Gideon and Jacob," *PEFQS* 59 (1927) 89-95, 188-191.

R. D. Middleton, "Penuel," *PEFQS* 60 (1928) 165.

Petra

*Anonymous, "Account of Newly-discovered Antiquities in Arabia Petræa, derived from the Personal Inspection of a recent British Traveler," *MMBR* 47 (1819) 481-485.

*†Anonymous, "Journey through Arabia Petræa to Mount Sinai and the Excavated City of Petra, the Edom of the Prophecies," *BCQTR, 4th Ser.,* 20 (1836) 446-474. *(Review)*

[B. B. Edwards], "Ruins of Ancient Petra," *BRCR* 9 (1837) 431-457.

[J. D. Knowles], "The Ancient City of Petra," *CRB* 3 (1838) 172-181.

*F. W. Holland, "A Journey on Foot Through Arabia Petraea," *PEFQS* 11 (1879) 59-72.

[Edward] Hull, "Petra, the Rock-Hewn Capital of Idumaea," *JTVI* 21 (1886-87) 139-149. (Discussion, pp. 149-154)

Gray Hill, "A Journey to Petra—1896," *PEFQS* 29 (1897) 35-44, 134-144.

*Charles W. Warren, "Notes on Arabia Petræa and the Country Lying between Egypt and Palestine," *PEFQS* 19 (1887) 38-46.

*Charles Alexander Hornstein, "A Visit to Kerak and Petra," *PEFQS* 30 (1898) 94-103.

*Samuel Ives Curtiss, "High Place and Altar at Petra," *PEFQS* 32 (1900) 350-355.

*George L. Robinson, "The 'High Place' at Petra in Edom," *AAOJ* 23 (1901) 229-241.

*George L. Robinson, "The Newly Discovered 'High Place' at Petra in Edom," *BW* 17 (1901) 6-16.

A. Forder, "Sela or Petra. 'The Strong City.' The Ruined Capital of Edom," *BW* 18 (1901) 328-337.

*W. Clarkson Wallis, "Note on the High Place at Petra," *PEFQS* 33 (1901) 65.

Petra cont.

*William Libbey, "Notes on the Jordan Valley and Petra," *PEFQS* 34 (1902) 411-413.

*F. E. Hoskins, "The Second High Place at Petra," *BW* 21 (1903) 167-174.

*[Edward] Hull, "Notes on Professor Libbey's Account of the Jordan Valley and Petra," *PEFQS* 35 (1903) 92-93.

Anonymous, "Petra, the Rock City of Seir," *MQR, 3rd Ser.,* 30 (1904) 598-600.

*F. E. Hoskins, "A Third 'High-Place' at Petra," *BW* 27 (1906) 385-390.

*George L. Robinson, "The Vaulted Chambers of Petra's High Places," *AAOJ* 30 (1908) 67-72.

*George L. Robinson, "The High Places of Petra," *BW* 31 (1908) 8-21.

A. H. Sayce, "The Exploration of Arabia Petraea," *ET* 20 (1908-09) 42-43.

Edward Hull, "A Recent Visit to Petra: A Lecture. By Mr. Arthur W. Sutton, F.L.S," *JTVI* 40 (1908) 112-114.

George L. Robinson, "The Ancient City of Petra, Wonder of the Desert," *A&A* 4 (1916) 101-109.

E. Herman, "A Rose-Red City of the East," *HR* 80 (1920) 282. *[Petra]*

James A. Kelso, "A Pilgrimage to Petra," *A&A* 19 (1925) 21-35.

R. A. MacLean, "The Vanished Cities of Arabia, Petra," *AJA* 30 (1926) 88.

*H. J. Orr-Ewing, "The Lion and the Cavern of Bones at Petra," *PEFQS* 59 (1927) 155-156.

A. H. Sayce, "Petra," *PEFQS* 59 (1927) 214-215.

Petra cont.

*T. Canaan, "Studies in the Topography and Folklore of Petra," *JPOS* 9 (1929) 136-218. [I. Phonology of the Arabic Dialect of Petra and Method of Work; II. Monuments with Arabic Names and Bedouin Stories of the Monuments; III. Topography; IV. Comparative Lists of Place-names; V. The *Liâṭneh:* 'the Bedouin of Petra']

George Horsfield, "The Gorge of Petra," *Antiq* 4 (1930) 225-228.

A. W. Webster, "'The Rose Red City. Half as Old as Time'," *BS* 87 (1930) 298-318. *[Petra]*

T. Canaan, "Additions to 'Studies in the Topography and Folklore of Petra'," *JPOS* 10 (1930) 178-180.

Ditlef Nielsen, "The Mountain Sanctuaries in Petra and its Environs," *JPOS* 11 (1931) 222-240; 13 (1933) 185-208.

*W[illiam] F[oxwell] Albright, "The Excavation of the Conway High Place at Petra," *BASOR* #57 (1935) 18-26.

G. Horsfield and A. Horsfield, "Sela-Petra, the Rock, of Edom and Nabatene," *QDAP* 7 (1938) 1-42; 8 (1939) 87-115; 9 (1942) 105-204. *[Numerous Plates]*

Peter J. Parr, "Recent Discoveries at Petra," *PEQ* 89 (1957) 5-16.

*William L. Reed, "Caravan Cities of the Near East," *CollBQ* 35 (1958) #3, 1-16. [Petra-The Rose Red City, pp. 12-16]

Diana Kirkbride, "A Short Account of the Excavations at Petra in 1955-1956," *ADAJ* 4&5 (1960) 117-122.

Philip C. Hammond, "The Excavations of Petra, 1959," *AJA* 64 (1960) 185.

Philip C. Hammond Jr. *[sic]*, "Petra," *BA* 23 (1960) 29-32.

Philip C. Hammond, "Excavations at Petra in 1959," *BASOR* #159 (1960) 26-31.

Petra concluded

P[eter] J. Parr, "Excavations at Petra, 1958-59," *PEQ* 92 (1960) 124-135.

*G. R. H. Wright, "Structure of the Sasr Bint Far'un. A Preliminary Report," *PEQ* 93 (1961) 8-37.

*G. R. H. Wright, "Petra—The Arched Gate," *PEQ* 93 (1961) 124-135.

*Peter J. Parr, "Nabataean Sanctuary Near Petra: A Preliminary Notice," *ADAJ* 6&7 (1962) 21-23.

*G. R. H. Wright, "The Khazne at Petra: A Review," *ADAJ* 6&7 (1962) 24-54.

*Crystal M. Bennett, "The Nabataeans in Petra," *Arch* 15 (1962) 233-243.

Philip C. Hammond, "The Excavation of the Main Theater, Petra: 1962," *AJA* 67 (1963) 211-212.

Philip C. Hammond, "The Excavation of the Main Theater at Petra," *ADAJ* 8&9 (1964) 81-85.

Philip C. Hammond, "The Excavation of the Main Theater, Petra," *AJA* 68 (1964) 195.

Philip C. Hammond, "The Excavation of the Main Theater at Petra," *BASOR* #174 (1964) 59-66.

Peter J. Parr, "The Investigation of Some 'Inaccessible' Rock-Cut Chambers at Petra," *PEQ* 100 (1968) 5-15.

*Eugene D. Stockton, "Petra Revisited: A Review of a Semitic Cult Complex," *AJBA* 1 (1968-71) #4, 51-73.

Lake Phiala

*(   ) Newbold, "On the Lake Phiala—the Jordan and its Sources," *JRAS* (1854) 8-31.

Philoteria (See also: Beth Yeraḥ)

*L. Sukenik, "The Ancient City of Philoteria (*Beth Yeraḥ*)," *JPOS* 2 (1922) 101-109.

Philistia

Charles Warren, "The Plain of Philistia," *PEFQS* 3 (1871) 82-96.

*Charles Warren, "Approximate Latitudes, Longitudes, and Altitudes Above Mean Sea Level of Points in the Plain of Philistia," *PEFQS* 3 (1871) 162-164.

Charles Warren, "Philistia," *PEFQS* 7 (1875) 180-181.

*Duncan Mackenzie, "The Port of Gaza and Excavations in Philistia," *PEFQS* 50 (1918) 72-87.

Anonymous, "Sites in Philistia," *BASOR* #4 (1921) 6.

Ḥayim Tadmor, "Philistia Under Assyrian Rule," *BA* 29 (1966) 86-102.

Piatane

*C. Clermont-Ganneau, "Archaeological and Epigraphic Notes on Palestine. 25. *Platanos and Piatane,*" *PEFQS* 36 (1904) 42-49.

(Mount) Pisgah

Thomas Laurie, "Review of the 'Identification of Mount Pisgah," *BS* 33 (1876) 132-153.

*[Stephen D. Peet], "The Holy Land Pisgah and Mount Hor," *AAOJ* 20 (1898) 227-231.

*W. F. Birch, "The Prospect from Pisgah," *PEFQS* 30 (1898) 110-120. (Remarks by C. R. Conder, pp. 120-121) [Zoar; The Hinder Sea; Dan; Dan and Baal-gad; Pisgah; *Addenda*]

W. F. Birch, "Pisgah," *PEFQS* 31 (1899) 67-69.

Platanos

*C. Clermont-Ganneau, "Archaeological and Epigraphic Notes on Palestine. 25. *Platanos and Piatane*," *PEFQS* 36 (1904) 42-49.

Tel Poleg

R[am] Gophna, "Tel Poleg," *IEJ* 14 (1964) 109-111.

Q

Tell Qasîle

B[enjamin] Maisler, "Excavations at Tell Qasîle (1948-49)," *BIES* 15 (1949-50) #1/2, I.

B[enjamin] Maisler, "Excavations at Tell Qasîle: Preliminary Report I," *IEJ* 1 (1950-51) 61-76.

B[enjamin] Maisler, "Excavations at Tell Qasîle: Preliminary Report II," *IEJ* 1 (1950-51) 125-140.

B[enjamin] Maisler, "Excavations at Tell Qasîle: Preliminary Report III," *IEJ* 1 (1950-51) 194-218.

B[enjamin] Maisler, "The Excavation of Tell Qasile," *BA* 14 (1951) 43-49.

Tel Qedesh

E. Stern, "Tel Qedesh," *IEJ* 18 (1968) 193-194.

R

Rabbah

W. F. Birch, "Rabbah of the Children of Ammon," *PEFQS* 10 (1878) 189-190.

*W. F. Birch, "Varieties," *PEFQS* 14 (1882) 59-61. *[Rabbah]*

Ramah

*Edward Robinson, "Notes on Biblical Geography," *BS* (1843) 563-566. [Arimathea or Ramah, pp. 565-566]

Joseph Horner, The Ramah of Samuel and Rachel's Lament," *MR* 57 (1875) 50-67.

*Lucien Gautier, "The Home of Samuel," *PEFQS* 30 (1898) 135-137. *[Ramah, i.e., Ramathaim-zophim]*

Harold M. Wiener, "The Ramah of Samuel," *JPOS* 7 (1927) 109-111.

Rāmallāh

Elihu Grant, "Rāmallāh. Signs of the Early Occupation of this and other Sites," *PEFQS* 58 (1926) 186-195.

Ramathaim-zophim

*D. K., "Ramathïm Zophim and Rachel's Sepulchre," *JSL, 1st Ser.,* 6 (1850) 403-410.

*C[onrad] Schick, "Ramathaim-Zophim—The Home of Samuel the Prophet," *PEFQS* 30 (1898) 7-20.

*Lucien Gautier, "The Home of Samuel," *PEFQS* 30 (1898) 135-137. *[Ramah, i.e., Ramathaim-zophim]*

Ramat Maṭred

*Y[ohanan] Aharoni, M.. Evenari, L. Shanan, and N. H. Tadmor, "The Ancient Desert Agriculture of the Negev, V: An Israelite Agricultural Settlement at Ramat Maṭred," *IEJ* 10 (1960) 23-36, 97-111.

Ramat Raḥel

Anonymous, "Excavation of Ramat Rahel," *AT* 1 (1956-57) #3, 14.

Anonymous, "A Recent Excavation in Israel. The Mound of Ramat Rahel," *BH* 2 (1965) #3, 10-14.

Y[ohanan] Aharoni, "The Excavations at Ramath-Rachel (Preliminary Report)," *BIES* 19 (1955) #3/4, i.

Y[ohanan] Aharoni, "The Excavations at Ramath Raḥel, 1954: Preliminary Report," *IEJ* 6 (1956) 102-111, 137-157.

Y[ohanan] Aharoni, "The Second Season of Excavations at Ramat Raḥel," *BIES* 24 (1959-60) II-III.

Yohanan Aharoni, "Excavations at Ramat Raḥel," *BA* 24 (1961) 98-118.

Y[ohanan] Aharoni, "Ramat Raḥel," *IEJ* 11 (1961) 193-195.

Yohanan Aharoni, "The Citadel of Ramat Rahel," *Arch* 18 (1965) 15-25.

Ramoth-Gilead

Nelson Glueck, "Ramoth-Gilead," *BASOR* #92 (1943) 10-16.

Rās el 'Ain

J. Ory, "Excavations at Rās el 'Ain," *QDAP* 5 (1936) 111-112; 6 (1938) 99-120.

Tell-er-Ras

*H. C. Kee, "Tell-er-Ras and the Samaritan Temple," *NTS* 13 (1966-67) 401-402.

Tell er Reesh

J. E. Hanauer, "Tell er Reesh, &c.," *PEFQS* 30 (1898) 244-246.

Rephaim

John Gray, "The Rephaim," *PEQ* 81 (1949) 127-139.

Rephaim Baqa

Moshe Stekelis, "Rephaim Baqa, a palaeolithic station in Jerusalem," *JPOS* 21 (1948) 80-97. (Appendix by P. Solomonica)

The Rock Rimmon

H. B. Rawnsley, "The Rock of the Pomegranate," *PEFQS* 11 (1879) 118-126. (Note by C. R. Conder, pp. 126-127; Observations by W. F. Birch, pp. 127-129)

Claude R. Conder, "Rimmon," *PEFQS* 11 (1879) 170-171.

W. F. Birch, "The Rock of Rimmon or the Pomeganate," *PEFQS* 12 (1880) 106-107.

*Claude R. Conder, "Notes on Disputed Points," *PEFQS* 12 (1880) 172-174. [Rock Rimmon, p. 173]

*W. F. Birch, "The Rock Rimmon and Gibeah," *PEFQS* 12 (1880) 236-237.

W. F. Birch, "The Rock Rimmon," *PEFQS* 14 (1882) 50-55.

C[laude] R. Conder, "Notes. *Rock Rimmon*," *PEFQS* 14 (1882) 156; 15 (1883) 102.

The Rock Rimmon concluded

H. D./sic/ Rawnsley, "The Rock Rimmon," *PEFQS* 14 (1882) 177.

W. F. Birch, "Hiding Places in Canaan. IV. The Rock Rimmon," *PEFQS* 14 (1882) 265.

Rosh Hanniqra

Miriam Tadmor and M. Prausnitz, "Excavations at Rosh Hanniqra," *'Atiqot* 2 (1959) 72-88.

Rubin River

M[oshe] Dothan, "An Archaeological Survey of the Lower Rubin River," *IEJ* 2 (1952) 104-117.

S

Safed

E. W. G. Masterman, "Safed," *PEFQS* 46 (1914) 169-179.

Tell es-Safi

*C. W. Votaw, "Present Excavations in Palestine," *BW* 14 (1899) 434-443. [II. Tell-es-Safî, pp. 441-443]

F. J. Bliss, "First Report on the Excavations at Tell-es-Safi," *PEFQS* 31 (1899) 183-199. (Notes by C. Clermont-Ganneau, pp. 354-355; L. Gautier, pp. 355-356)

F. J. Bliss, "Second Report on the Excavations at Tell es-Safi," *PEFQS* 31 (1899) 317-333. [Note by C. R. Conder, pp. 77-78; C. Clermont-Ganneau, *PEFQS* 32 (1900) p. 79]

*A[ngus] C[rawford], "Notes—Archæological, Etc.," *PER* 13 (1899-1900) 48-50. [Tell-es-Sâfi, pp. 48-49]

*A[ngus] C[rawford], "Notes—Critical, Etc.," *PER* 13 (1899-1900) 279-282. [Tell-es-Sâfi, pp. 280-281]

Tell es-Safi concluded

F. J. Bliss, "Third Report on the Excavations at Tell Es-Safi," *PEFQS* 32 (1900) 16-29.

R. A. Stewart Macalister, "The Rock-Cuttings of Tell Es-Safi," *PEFQS* 32 (1900) 29-39.

Saida

Anonymous, "The Recent Excavations at Saida," *PEFQS* 19 (1887) 201-212.

Tell es-Sa'idiyeh

E. T. Rogers, "Excavation of the Tell Salahiyeh," *PEFQS* 1 (1896) 43-44.

Henri de Contenson, "Three Soundings in the Jordan Valley," *ADAJ* 4&5 (1960) 12-98. [III. Tell es-Saidiyeh el Tahta, pp. 49-57]

James B. Pritchard, "Excavation at Tell es-Sa'ideyeh (Preliminary Report)," *ADAJ* 8&9 (1964) 95-98.

John Huesman, "A Report on Tell es-Sa'idiyeh," *CBQ* 26 (1964) 242-243.

James B. Pritchard, "The First Excavations at Tell es-Sa'idiyeh," *BA* 28 (1965) 10-17.

John Huesman, "Tell es-Sa'idiyeh," *BibT* #16 (1965) 1051-1060.

James B. Pritchard, "A Cosmopolitan Culture of the Late Bronze Age," *Exped* 7 (1964-65) #4, 26-33. *[Tell es-Sa'idiyeh]*

James B. Pritchard, "The Palace of Tell es-Sa'idiyeh," *Exped* 11 (1968-69) #1, 20-22.

Tell Salahiyeh

E. T. Rogers, "Excavation of the Tell Salahiyeh," *PEFQS* 1 (1896) 43-44.

Salem

Cameron Mackay, "Salem," *PEQ* 80 (1948) 121-130.

Salihi

*Diana V. W. Kirkbride, "Short Notes on Some Hitherto Unrecorded Prehistoric Sites in Transjordan," *PEQ* 91 (1959) 52-54. [Salihi, p. 53]

Samaria

*Claude R. Conder, "Samaritan Topography," *PEFQS* 8 (1876) 182-197.

Willis J. Beecher, "The Date of downfall of Samaria," *JBL* 11 (1892) 211-213.

Anonymous, "Samaria," *ONTS* 15 (1892) 269.

J. S. Riggs, "Studies in Palestinian Geography. IV. Samaria," *BW* 4 (1894) 279-286.

A. T. Olmstead, "The Fall of Samaria," *AJSL* 21 (1904-05) 179-182.

Anonymous, "Excavations at Samaria," *HTR* 1 (1908) 518-519.

David G. Lyon, "The Harvard Expedition to Samaria," *HTR* 2 (1909) 102-113; 3 (1910) 136-138, 248-263.

Anonymous, "The Harvard Expedition to Samaria," *RP* 8 (1909) 175-176.

David G. Lyon, "The Harvard Excavations at Samaria," *AJA* 14 (1910) 76-77.

Anonymous, "The Harvard Expedition to Samaria," *MR* 92 (1910) 1007-1010.

Anonymous, "The Excavations at Samaria," *MR* 94 (1912) 134-137.

Samaria cont.

Anonymous, "Another Voice from the Past," *TZTM* 3 (1913) 174-177. *[Samaria]*

David G. Lyon, "The Harvard Excavations at Samaria," *A&A* 7 (1918) 197-205.

I. G. Matthews, "The Harvard Excavations at Samaria," *CQ* 1 (1924) 445-447.

E. W. G. Masterman, "The Harvard Excavations at Samaria," *PEFQS* 57 (1925) 25-30.

J. W. Jack, "Samaria in Ahab's Time: Havard Excavations and Their Results," *ET* 38 (1926-27) 264-269.

J[oan] W. Crowfoot, "Work of the Joint Expedition to Samaria-Sebustiya, April and May, 1931," *PEFQS* 63 (1931) 139-142.

J[oan] W. Crowfoot, "Excavations at Samaria, 1931," *PEFQS* 64 (1932) 8-34.

J[oan] W. Crowfoot, "The Expedition to Samaria-Sebustiya," *PEFQS* 64 (1932) 63-70.

J[oan] W. Crowfoot, "Recent Discoveries of the Joint Expedition to Samaria," *PEFQS* 64 (1932) 132-133.

J[oan] W. Crowfoot, "The Joint Samaria Expedition. Proposals of 1933," *PEFQS* 64 (1932) 134-137.

J[oan] W. Crowfoot, "Samaria Excavations: The Stadium," *PEFQS* 65 (1933) 62-73.

*Kathleen Kenyon, "Excavations at Samaria. The Forecourt of the Augusteum," *PEFQS* 65 (1933) 74-87.

J[oan] W. Crowfoot, "Samaria: Interim Report on the Work in 1933," *PEFQS* 65 (1933) 129-136.

J[oan] W. Crowfoot, "Report of the 1935 Samaria Excavations," *PEFQS* 67 (1935) 182-194.

Samaria concluded

P[atrick] P. McKenna, "Some Ancient Cities and Sites of Samaria," *IER, 5th Ser.,* 52 (1938) 602-614.

E. L. Sukenik, "City-Gates of Samaria," *KSJA* 1 (1942) IX.

*M[ichael] Avi-Yonah, "Samaria and the 'Marissa' of Antiquities XIII, 275," *BIES* 16 (1951) #3/4, IV-V.

*W[illiam] F[oxwell] Albright, "Recent Progress in Palestinian Archaeology: Samaria-Sebaste III and Hazor I," *BASOR* #150 (1958) 21-25.

G. Ernest Wright, "Samaria," *BA* 22 (1959) 67-78.

*G. Ernest Wright, "Israelites, Samaria and Iron Age Chronology," *BASOR* #155 (1959) 13-29.

*Olga Tufnell, "Hazor, Samaria and Lachish: A Synthesis," *PEQ* 91 (1959) 90-105.

*W[illiam] F[oxwell] Albright, "The Original Account of the Fall of Samaria in II Kings," *BASOR* #174 (1964) 66-67.

*K[athleen] M. Kenyon, "Megiddo, Hazor, Samaria and Chronology," *ULBIA* 4 (1964) 143-156.

C[lifford] A. W[ilson], "Your Questions Answered. Who Captured Samaria?" *BH* 3 (1967) #4, 21-23.

Frwzi Zayadine, "Samaria-Sebaste. Clearance and Excavations (October 1965 - June 1967)," *ADAJ* 12&13 (1967-68) 77-80.

*S[tephanie] Page, "Joash and Samaria in a New Stela Excavated at Tell el Rimah," *VT* 19 (1969) 483-484.

Samieh

David G. Lyon, "The Necropolis of Samieh," *AJA* 12 (1908) 66-67.

Tell Sandahannah

F. J. Bliss, "Report on the Excavations at Tell Sandahannah," *PEFQS* 32 (1900) 319-338.

R. A. Stewart Macalister, "Preliminary Observations on the Rock-cuttings of Tell Sandahannah," *PEFQS* 32 (1900) 338-341.

R. A. Stewart Macalister, "Reports by R. A. Stewart Macalister, M. A., I. 'es-Suk,' Tell Sandahannah," *PEFQS* 33 (1901) 11-19.

*John P. Peters, "Palestinian Exploration. *Notes of a Vacation in Palestine in 1902.*," *JBL* 22 (1903) 15-31. [7. Sandahannah, pp. 21-23]

*E. W. G. Masterman, "Beit Jibrin and Tell Sandahannah," *PEFQS* 58 (1926) 176-185.

S'baita

Colin Baly, "S'baita," *PEFQS* 67 (1935) 171-181.

Scopus

Claude R. Conder, "On the Identification of Scopus," *PEFQS* 6 (1874) 111-114.

Scythopolis

M[ichael] Avi-Yonah, "Scythopolis," *IEJ* 12 (1962) 123-134.

*Andrew Miles, "Beth-Shan—Scythopolis: Part I," *BibT* #41 (1969) 2825-2831.

*Eugene A. LaVerdiere, "Beth-Shan—Scythopolis: Part II," *BibT* #42 (1969) 2926-2931.

Seb'a Rujum

C[onrad] Schick, "Letters from Herr Baurath Schick. V. The Seb'a Rujum," *PEFQS* 25 (1893) 133.

Segor

*C. Clermont-Ganneau, "Segor, Gomorrah, and Sodom," *PEFQS* 18 (1886) 19-21.

Seilun (See also: Shiloh)

*W[illiam] F[oxwell] Albright, "The Danish Excavations at Seilun—a Correction," *PEFQS* 59 (1927) 157-158.

Seir

*J. R. Bartlett, "The Land of Seir and the Brotherhood of Edom," *JTS, N.S.,* 20 (1969) 1-20.

Seirath

*W. F. Birch, "Seirath (Judg. iii, 26)," *PEFQS* 13 (1881) 102.

Sephar

*C[laude] R. Conder, "Notes on Bible Geography. V. *Sephar,*" *PEFQS* 37 (1905) 74.

Shaaraim

C. Clermont-Ganneau, "Note on Shaaraim," *PEFQS* 7 (1875) 182.

*Claude R. Conder, "David and Goliath," *PEFQS* 7 (1875) 191-195. [Shaaraim, p. 194]

Shamash-Edom

*Yohanan Aharoni, "Some Geographical Remarks Concerning the Campaigns of Amenhotep II," *JNES* 19 (1960) 177-183. [A. Shamash-Edom, pp. 177-181]

Shamir (Tel Anafa)

*S[aul] S. Weinberg, "Tel Anafa (Shamir)," *IEJ* 18 (1968) 195-196;
19 (1969) 250-252.

The Plain of Sharon

J. Waitz, "Is the Plain of Sharon on the Coast?" *BIES* 6 (1938-39)
#3, III.

A. J. Brawer, "The Sharon on the Sea—Coast," *BIES* 7 (1939-40) #1,
III-IV.

*Y. Karmon, "Geographical Conditions in the Sharon Plain and Their
Impact on Its Settlement," *BIES* 23 (1959) #3/4, I-III.

*Y. Karmon, "Geographical Conditions in the Sharon Plain and Their
Impact on Its Settlement," *SGEI* #1 (1959) I-III.

R[am] Gophna and M. Kokhavi, "An Archaeological Survey of the
Plain of Sharon," *IEJ* 16 (1966) 143-144.

Shechem

*H. Vogelstein, "Shechem and Bethel," *JQR* 4 (1891-92) 513-532.

R. L. Stewart, "Shechem and its Environs," *CFL, N.S.,* 1 (1900)
101-107.

*Howard Tillman Kuist, "Shechem and the Bones of Joseph," *BR* 11
(1926) 412-420.

*H. M. Du Bose, "Shechem and the Primeval Monotheism," *BR* 12
(1927) 171-188.

*H. M. Du Bose, "Shechem and the Historicity of Jacob," *BR* 13
(1928) 528-548.

C. Ryder Smith, "The Stories of Shechem, Three Questions," *JTS* 47
(1946) 33-38.

A. M. Honeyman, "The Salting of Shechem," *VT* 3 (1953) 192-195.

Shechem cont.

J. Gutman, "The Jewish-Hellenistic Epic of Shechem," *EI* 3 (1954) X.

Lawrence E. Toombs, "Drew at Shechem," *DG* 26 (1955-56) 195-203.

G. Ernest Wright, "The First Campaign at Tell Balâṭah (Shechem)," *BASOR* #144 (1956) 9-20.

Walter Harrelson, "Shechem, the 'Navel of the Land,' Part I. Shechem in Extra-Biblical References," *BA* 20 (1957) 2-10. [Egyptian References; Shechem in the Amarna Period; Shechem in Later Extra-Biblical Sources]

Bernard W. Anderson, "Shechem, 'Navel of the Land,' Part II. The Place of Shechem in the Bible," *BA* 20 (1957) 10-19. [The Navel of the Land; The Attack Against Shechem; The Shechem Assembly; Abimelech's Kingdom; The Revolt of Northern Israel; Shechem in Deuteronomic Tradition; The Later History of Shechem]

G. Ernest Wright, "Shechem, 'Navel of the Land,' Part III. The Archaeology of the City," *BA* 20 (1957) 19-32. [First Excavations; The Sellin Discoveries in 1926-1927; Final German Work at Shechem; The First Campaign of the Drew-McCormick Expedition]

*H. C. Kee and L[awrence] E. Toombs, "The Second Season of Excavation at Shechem," *BA* 20 (1957) 82-105. [Part I. What Goes On At A Dig? Part II. The Archaeological Results; General Impressions; The Temple Area; The Eastern Fortifications; The Hellenistic Period]

G. Ernest Wright, "The Second Campaign at Tell Balâṭah (Shechem)," *BASOR* #148 (1957) 11-28.

G. Ernest Wright, "McCormick at Shechem, 1957," *McQ* 11 (1957-58) #2, 3-6.

Anonymous, "Shechem," *AT* 3 (1958-59) #2, 6.

Edward F. Campbell Jr., "Excavations at Shechem, 1960," *BA* 23 (1960) 102-110.

Shechem cont.

G. R. H. Wright, "The Architectural Recording of the Shechem Excavation," *BA* 23 (1960) 120-126.

Edward F. Campbell [Jr.], "Shechem, Mound of Many Digs," *McQ* 14 (1960-61) #2, 3-8.

James F. Ross and Lawrence E. Toombs, "Three Campaigns at Biblical Shechem," *Arch* 14 (1961) 171-179.

Lawrence E. Toombs and G. Ernest Wright, "The Third Campaign at Balâṭah (Shechem)," *BASOR* #161 (1961) 11-54.

Bernhard W. Anderson, "The Drew-McCormick Archaeological Expedition," *DG* 32 (1961-62) 127-134. *[Shechem]*

G. Ernest Wright, "Shechem: The City and Its Excavation," *DG* 32 (1961-62) 135-148.

*James R. Ross, "What We Do When We Dig," *DG* 32 (1961-62) 149-155. *[Shechem]*

*Lawrence E. Toombs, "Daily Life in Ancient Shechem," *DG* 32 (1961-62) 166-172.

*Edward J. Campbell Jr. and James F. Ross, "The Excavation of Shechem and the Biblical Tradition," *BA* 26 (1963) 2-27.

Lawrence E. Toombs and G. Ernest Wright, "The Fourth Campaign at Balâṭah (Shechem)," *BASOR* #169 (1963) 1-60.

H. Reviv, "Regarding the History of the Territory of Shekhem in the El-Amarna Period," *Tarbiz* 33 (1963-64) #1, I.

Edward F. Campbell Jr., "Dispatch from Jordan," *McQ* 18 (1964-65) #3, 25-31. *[Shechem]*

Siegfried H. Horn, "Shechem. History and Excavations of a Palestinian City," *JEOL* #18 (1964) 284-306.

Edward F. Campbell Jr., "Shechem," *BA* 28 (1965) 18-22.

Shechem concluded

Robert J. Bull, Joseph A. Callaway, Edward F. Campbell Jr., James F. Ross, and G. Ernest Wright, "The Fifth Campaign at Balâṭah (Shechem)," *BASOR* #180 (1965) 7-41.

*Anonymous, "Some Archaeological Notes," *BH* 2 (1965) #3, 16-18. [Shechem—Mt. Gerizim Temple]

*H. Reviv, "The Government of Shechem in the El-Amarna Period and in the Days of Abimelech," *IEJ* 16 (1966) 252-257.

D. Larrimore Holland, "Report from Shechem, 1966," *McQ* 20 (1966-67) 45-50.

*G. R. H. Wright, "The Place Name Balâṭah and the Excavations at Shechem," *ZDPV* 83 (1967) 199-202.

Robert J. Bull and Edward F. Campbell Jr., "The Sixth Campaign at Balâṭah (Shechem)," *BASOR* #190 (1968) 2-41.

*E. D. Stockton, "The Fortress Temple of Shechem and Joshua's Covenant," *AJBA* 1 (1968-71) #1, 24-28.

E[dward] F. Cambell/*sic*/ [Jr.], "Shechem," *IEJ* 18 (1968) 192-193.

Siegfried H. Horn, "Shechem in the Light of Archeological Evidence," *ASW* 23 (1969) #3, 9-19.

Sheikh Bader

*M[ichael] Avi-Yonah, "Excavations at Sheikh Bader, Jerusalem (1949)," *BIES* 15 (1949-50) #1/2, II.

Shen

*C[laude] R. Conder, "Note on Mezpeh and Shen," *PEFQS* 30 (1898) 169. (Note by C. Clermont-Ganneau, p. 251)

Shephelah

*C[harles] F. Tyrwhitt Drake, "Mr. Tyrwhitt Drake's Reports. II," *PEFQS* 4 (1872) 43-47. [The Shephelah]

Shephelah concluded

*Anonymous, "The Shephelah," *ONTS* 14 (1892) 374.

Aapeli Saarisalo, "Topographical Researches in the Shephelah," *JPOS* 11 (1931) 98-104. *[Pages misnumbered 14-20]*

S. Kallai-Kleinmann, "The Judaean Shefelah/sic/*," *BIES* 19 (1955) #3/4, iv. *[Title page reads: "The Shephelah of Judeah]*

*Eliezer Oren, "The Caves of the Palestinian Shephelah," *Arch* 18 (1965) 218-224.

Shihor

*Joseph Offord, "Archaeological Notes. *III. The Sites of Shihor and of Zoar*," *PEFQS* 45 (1913) 148-149.

Shiloah

*Anonymous, "Shiloah—A Lesson Ignored," *BH* 2 (1965) #4, 20-24.

Shiloh

W[illiam] F[oxwell] Albright, "The Danish Excavations at Shiloh," *BASOR* #9 (1923) 10-11.

A. T. Richardson, "The site of Shiloh," *PEFQS* 57 (1925) 162-163.

A. T. Richardson, "The Site of Shiloh," *PEFQS* 59 (1927) 85-88.

*W[illiam] F[oxwell] Albright, "The Danish Excavations at Seilun—a Correction," *PEFQS* 59 (1927) 157-158. *[Shiloh]*

Hans Kjaer, "The Danish Excavation of Shiloh," *PEFQS* 59 (1927) 202-213.

Hans Kjær, "The Excavation of Shiloh 1929. Preliminary Report," *JPOS* 10 (1930) 87-174.

Hans Kjaer, "Shiloh. A Summary Report of the Second Danish Expedition, 1929," *PEFQS* 63 (1931) 71-88.

Shiqmona

J. Elgavish, "Shiqmona," *IEJ* 19 (1969) 247-248.

Shishak

*Richard St. Barbe Baker, "The Lost Cities of Judah," *A&A* 33 (1932) 253-258. *[Tell Fara = Shishak]*

Shittim Plain

*Selah Merrill, "Modern Researches in Palestine," *PEFQS* 11 (1879) 138-154. [The Shittim Plain, pp. 143-144]

Selah Merrill, "Notes by Dr. Selah Merrill. Pits in the Shittim Plain," *PEFQS* 23 (1891) 74-75.

James Neil, "Pits in the Shittim Plain," *PEFQS* 23 (1891) 161-163.

Tell esh-Shuna

*Henri de Contenson, "Three Soundings in the Jordan Valley," *ADAJ* 4&5 (1960) 12-98. [I. Tell esh-Shuna, pp. 12-31]

Valley of Siddim

James Neil, "Ruins on the 'Slime Pits' in the Vale of Siddim," *PEFQS* 22 (1890) 130-132.

*James Neil, "Site of the Cities of the Plain and the 'Pits' of the Vale of Siddim," *TML* 3 (1890) 289-307.

Silla

*George St. Clair, "Millo, House of Millo, and Silla," *PEFQS* 23 (1891) 187-189. (Note by C. R. Conder, p. 254)

Silwan

*C[onrad] Schick, "Reports from Herr Baurath von Schick," *PEFQS* 27 (1895) 321-330. (Note by C. Clermont-Ganneau, *PEFQS* 28 (1896) p. 79) [3. Silwan, pp. 328-329]

Sion (See: Zion)

Sidon

Charles Warren, "Notes on A Visit to Saida in July, 1869," *PEFQS* 1 (1869) 136-141. *[Sidon]*

W. K. Eddy, "Letter from Sidon, Phœnicia," *AJA, O.S.,* 3 (1887) 97-101.

*John P. Peters, "Palestinian Exploration. *Notes of a Vacation in Palestine in 1902*," *JBL* 22 (1903) 15-31. [3. Sidon, pp. 16-17]

Ghosu el Howie, "Excavations at Sidon," *AAOJ* 27 (1905) 223-225.

Sinabri

*P. Bar-Adon, "Sinabri and Beth Yerah in the Light of the Literary Sources and Archaeological Finds," *EI* 4 (1956) V-VI.

Tell Şippor

A. Biran and Ora Negbi, "Tel Şippor," *IEJ* 13 (1963) 338-340; 14 (1964) 284-285; 15 (1965) 255-256.

Lake Sirbonis (Sabkhat el-Bardawil)

M[oshe] Dothan, "Lake Sirbonis (Sabkhat el-Bardawil)," *IEJ* 17 (1967) 279-280; 18 (1968) 255-256.

Skifta

J. Prip-Moller, "A Rock-cut Place at Skifta," *PEFQS* 61 (1929) 223-227.

Socoh (Shoco, Shocho, Shochoh)

*Claude R. Conder, "David and Goliath," *PEFQS* 7 (1875) 191-195. [Shochoh, p. 191]

*Anonymous, "Makkedah and Shocoh," *BASOR* #4 (1921) 6-7.

Sodom (and Gomorrah)

*Edward Robinson, "On the Dead Sea, and the Destruction of Sodom and Gomorrah," *BRCR, N.S.,* 3 (1840) 24-39. [Letter from Leopold de Buch and extract from his writings, pp. 31-36; Extract from a paper by N. Hugent, pp. 36-39]

*Charles A. Lee, "On the Geology of Palestine, and the Destruction of Sodom and Gomorrah," *BRCR, N.S.,* 3 (1840) 324-352.

G. S. Faber, "On the Site of the Destroyed Cities of the Plain," *DUM* 42 (1853) 491-494.

*John Hogg, "On the Site of the Destroyed Cities of the Plain, and the Supposed Former Course of the Jordan into the Aelanitic Gulf," *JSL, 2nd Ser.,* 5 (1853-54) 510-516.

G. S. Faber, "The Rev. G. S. Faber and the Site of the Cities of the Plain," *JSL, 2nd Ser.,* 6 (1854) 241-242.

*George Warington, "The Site of Sodom and Gomorrah," *JSL, 4th Ser.,* 9 (1866) 36-57.

*John Hogg, "On the Site of Sodom and Gomorrah," *JSL, 4th Ser.,* 10 (1866-67) 185-186.

Samuel Wolcott, "The Site of Sodom," *BS* 25 (1868) 112-151.

W. F. Birch, "Sodom," *PEFQS* 13 (1881) 101.

*J. W. Dawson, "The Probable Physical Causes of the Destruction of the Cities of the Plain," *Exp, 3rd Ser.,* 3 (1886) 69-77.

*C. Clermont-Ganneau, "Segor, Gomorrah, and Sodom," *PEFQS* 18 (1886) 19-21.

Sodom (and Gomorrah) cont.

*H. B. S. W., "Zoar and the Doomed 'Cities of the Plain," *PEFQS* 18 (1886) 113-114.

*James Neil, "The Site of the Cities of the Plain and the 'Pits' of the Vale of Siddim," *TML* 3 (1890) 289-307.

*T. K. Cheyne, "The Origin and Meaning of the Story of Sodom," *NW* 1 (1892) 236-245.

*Edward Hull, "Requests and Replies," *ET* 6 (1894-95) 420. *[Location of Sodom and Gomorrah]*

W. W. Moore, "A Question of Biblical Topography," *USR* 7 (1895-96) 269-280. *[Sodom and Gomorrah]*

Geo. H. Schodde, "Biblical Research Notes. A Geologist on the Destruction of Sodom," *ColTM* 18 (1898) 126-128.

*G. Frederick Wright, "Physical Preparation for Israel in Palestine," *BS* 58 (1901) 360-369. *[Sodom and Gomorrah]*

*G. Frederick Wright, "Geological Confirmations of the Biblical History of Israel from Abraham to the Exodus," *CFL, 3rd Ser.,* 2 (1905) 423-430. [Destruction of Sodom and Gomorrah, pp. 426-430]

Ellsworth Huntington, "Facts Bearing on the Bible Story of Sodom and Gomorrah," *CFL, 3rd Ser.,* 13 (1910) 7-9.

Melvin Grove Kyle, "The Story of Ancient Sodom in the Light of Modern Science—The Xenia Seminary Expedition to the Cities of the Plain—The Reports of the Various Members of the Staff. Introductory Narrative," *BS* 81 (1924) 262-263.

*Alfred Ely Day, "Geology of the Dead Sea," *BS* 81 (1924) 264-270.

*Pere Alois Mallon, "Flint Implements and Megalitic Monuments," *BS* 81 (1924) 271-275. *(Trans. by W. F. Albright)*

Sodom (and Gomorrah) cont.

*M[elvin] G[rove] Kyle and W[illiam] F[oxwell] Albright, "Results of the Archaeological Survey of the Ghor in Search for the Cities of the Plain," *BS* 81 (1924) 276-291. [I. Searching the Ghor; II. The Sanctuary and Settlement at Bab ed-Dra'; III. The Great Catastrophe; IV. Site of the Cities of the Plain; V. Description of the Natural Conditions of Life on the Plain; VI. Researches in the Mountains of Moab; VII. Summary]

Melvin Grove Kyle, "Ancient Sodom in the Light of Modern Science," *JTVI* 59 (1927) 217-231. (Discussion and Communication, pp. 231-235)

I. O. Nothstein, "Explorations at Sodom," *AugQ* 7 (1928) 175-176.

*E. Power, "The site of Pentapolis," *B* 11 (1930) 23-62, 149-182.

*Frederick G. Clapp, "The Site of Sodom and Gomorrah," *AJA* 40 (1936) 323-344.

*P. E. Kretzmann, "The Site of Sodom and Gomorrah," *CTM* 8 (1937) 132-133.

*E. W. G. Masterman, "The Dead Sea and the Lost Cities of the Plain," *JTVI* 69 (1937) 212-223, 228-229. (Discussion, pp. 223-228)

*J. Penrose Harland, "Sodom and Gomorrah: The Location of the Cities of the Plain," *BA* 5 (1942) 17-32. [Evidence from the Bible; Evidence from Greek and Latin Writers; The Pillar of Salt; Water Supply; Evidence from Archaeology; The Rise in Water-Level; The Roman Road; The Location of the Cities of the Plain]

*J. Penrose Harland, "Sodom and Gomorrah: II. The Destruction of the Cities of the Plain," *BA* 6 (1943) 41-54. [The Biblical Evidence; Evidence of Later Writers; Fire and Brimstone and Geology; The Apple of Sodom; Notes on the Later History of the Plain; Oil in Palestine]

*Parray Marshall, "Life from the Dead Sea," *ContR* 169 (1946) 296-299. *[Sodom and Gomorrah]*

Sodom (and Gomorrah) concluded

*J. Simons, "Two Notes on the Problem of the Pentapolis," *OTS* 5 (1948) 92-117.

*Anonymous, "Some Recent Activities in Israel," *AT* 4 (1959-60) #4, 15-16. [Sodom and Gomorrah, p. 16]

*Hugh Ross Williamson, "Sodom and Homosexuality," *CIR* 48 (1963) 507-514.

Anonymous, "A Comment on Sodom and Gomorrah," *BH* 3 (1967) #1, 14-16.

Succoth

*Selah Merrill, "Identification of Succoth and Penuel," *BS* 34 (1877) 742-754.

*Selah Merrill, "The Identification of Succoth and Penuel," *PEFQS* 10 (1878) 81-88.

*J. A. Paine, "Succoth and Penuel Not Yet Identified," *BS* 35 (1878) 481-498.

*J. Garrow Duncan, "Notes on the Sites of Succoth and Penuel as bearing upon the Routes of Gideon and Jacob," *PEFQS* 59 (1927) 89-95, 188-191.

*Nelson Glueck, "Three Israelite Towns in the Jordan Valley: Zarethan, Succoth, Zaphon," *BASOR* #90 (1943) 2-23.

Tell es-Sultan

*H. J. Franken, "Tell es-Sultan and Old Testament Jericho," *OTS* 14 (1965) 189-200.

Suwwanet eth-Thaniya

G. M. Landes, "Suwwanet eth-Thaniya," *IEJ* 18 (1968) 131-132.

T

(Tell) Ta'anach

G. Schumacher, "Recent Discoveries near Galilee," *PEFQS* 34 (1902) 301-304. *[Tell Ta'annek]*

*John P. Peters, "Palestinian Exploration. *Notes of a Vacation in Palestine in 1902*," *JBL* 22 (1903) 15-31. [5. Ta'anuk, ancient Ta'anach, on the Plain of Megiddo, pp. 17-19]

Charles Wilson, "Austrian Excavations at Taanach," *PEFQS* 36 (1904) 388-391.

*R. A. Stewart Macalister, "Gezer and Taanach," *PEFQS* 38 (1906) 115-120.

*Julian Morgenstern, "Kedesh-Naphtali and Ta'anach," *JQR, N.S.,* 9 (1918-19) 395-369.

*Stanley A. Cook, "Kedesh-Naphtali and Taanach: A Theory and Some Comments," *PEFQS* 51 (1919) 188-193.

*B. D. Zaphrir (Frimorgen), "'Even Three Countries'," *BIES* 14 (1947-48) #3/4, II. *[Ta'anach]*

Paul W. Lapp, "The 1963 Excavations at Tell Ta'annek," *BASOR* #173 (1964) 4-44.

Paul W. Lapp, "Taanach by the Waters of Megiddo," *BA* 30 (1967) 2-27.

Paul W. Lapp, "The 1966 Excavations at Tell Ta'annek," *BASOR* #185 (1967) 2-39.

Paul W. Lapp, "The 1968 Excavations at Tell Ta'annek," *BASOR* #195 (1969) 2-49.

et Tabghah

Stanislao Loffreda, "The First Season of Excavations at Tabgha (near Capharnaum)," *SBFLA* 18 (1968) 238-243.

et Tabghah concluded

F. T[urville]-P[etre], "Pre-Historic Remains in the Vicinity of et Tabghah, Lake of Tiberias," *BSAJB* #3 (1923) 32-33.

et-Tabūn

A. J. Jelinek, "Et-Tabūn," *IEJ* 19 (1969) 114-115.

Mount Tabor

S. D. Phelps, "Mount Tabor from the Southwest," *OBJ* 1 (1880) 83-84.

*Julius Lewy, "Tabor, Tibar, Atabyros," *HUCA* 23 (1950-51) Part 1, 357-386. *[Etymological Study of the Name Tabor]*

*D. Winton Thomas, "Mount Tabor: The Meaning of the Name," *VT* 1 (1951) 229-230.

Eugene D. Stockton, "Prehistory of Mount Tabor," *SBFLA* 15 (1964-65) 131-136.

Tamar

*Y[ohanan] Aharoni, "Tamar and the Roads to Elath," *EI* 5 (1958) 91*.

*Y[ohanan] Aharoni, "Tamar and the Roads to Elath," *IEJ* 13 (1963) 30-42.

Tanturah (Dora)

Anonymous, "Tanturah (Dora). Part I.—Historical Notes," *BSAJB* #4 (1924) 35-40.

Anonymous, "Tanturah (Dora). Part II.—Archaeological Results," *BSAJB* #4 (1924) 40-45.

Anonymous, "Tanturah (Dora). Part III.—The Site," *BSAJB* #6 (1924) 65.

Tanturah (Dora) concluded

Anonymous, "Tanturah (Dora). Part IV.—Excavations, 1924,"
BSAJB #6 (1924) 65-73.

Tarichea

*C. W. Wilson, "The Site of Tarichea and Bethesda," *PEFQS* 9 (1877)
10-13.

H. H. Kitchener, "Note on Tarichaea*/sic/*," *PEFQS* 10 (1878) 79.

C[laude] R. Conder, "Notes on the Position of Tarichea," *PEFQS* 10
(1878) 190-192.

*E. W. G. Masterman, "The Galilee of Josephus. The Positions of
Gabara, Jotapata and Taricheae," *PEFQS* 42 (1910) 268-280.

Teima

*John Dayton, "The City of Teima and the Land of Edom,"
ULBIA 8&9 (1968-69) 253-256.

Tekoa

Thomas Whitelaw, "The Story of an Ancient Battle-field," *TML* 3
(1890) 217-230. */Theko/Tekoa/*

Martin H. Heicksen, "Tekoa: Excavations in 1968," *GJ* 10 (1969) #2,
3-10.

Tel - See names alphabetized under last word, disregarding *ed, ej, el, en* or *es* [Eg. Tell ed-Duweir *under* Duwier]

Tel Aviv

J. Kaplan, "A Cemetery of the Bronze Age Discovered near Tel Aviv
Harbour," *'Atiqot* 1 (1955) 1-12.

*J[acob] Kaplan, "Tel Aviv-Yafo," *IEJ* 16 (1966) 282-283.

Teleilât el-'Anab

*Philip Mayerson, "Ancient Agricultural Remains in the Central Negeb: The Teleilât el-'Anab," *BASOR* #153 (1959) 19-31.

*Yehuda Kedar, "More about the Teleilât el-'Anab in the Negeb," *BASOR* #176 (1964) 47-49.

*Philip Mayerson, "The Issue of the Teleilât el-'Anab," *BASOR* #178 (1965) 69.

Teluliot Batashi

J[acob] Kaplan, "Excavations at Teluliot Batashi in the Vale of Sorek," *EI* 5 (1958) 83*-84*.

Tiberias

G. Schumacher, "Recent Discoveries. *Tiberias,*" *PEFQS* 20 (1888) 105.

R. D. Middleton, "Tiberias," *PEFQS* 58 (1926) 162-163.

M[ichael] Avi-Yonah, "The Foundation of Tiberias," *IEJ* 1 (1950-51) 160-169.

V. Tzaferis, "A Middle Bronze Age I Cemetery in Tiberias," *IEJ* 18 (1968) 15-19.

Tiberias (Sea of/Lake)

M. Th. Barrois, "On the Depth and Temperature of the Lake of Tiberias," *PEFQS* 26 (1894) 211-220.

J. Garrow Duncan, "The Sea of Tiberias and its Environs," *PEFQS* 58 (1926) 15-22, 65-73.

Y[ehoshua] Ben-Arieh, "Fluctuations in the Level of Lake Tiberias," *IEJ* 15 (1965) 160-168.

Yehoshua Ben-Arieh, "The Shift in the Outlet of the Jordan at the Southern Shore of Lake Tiberias," *PEQ* 97 (1965) 54-65.

Timnah

*Anonymous, "Researches of the Circle for Historical Geography,"
BIES 16 (1951) #3/4, VI. *[Timnah]*

*S. Kallai-Kleinmann, "Notes on Eltekeh, Ekron and Timnah," *BIES* 17
(1952-53) #1/2, IV.

Ṭirat Yehudah

Z. Yeivin, "Ṭirat Yehudah," *IEJ* 12 (1962) 150.

Tirzah

*W[illiam] F[oxwell] Albright, "The Site of Tirzah and the Topography
of Western Manasseh," *JPOS* 11 (1931) 241-251.

Anonymous, "Excavations at Tirzah," *AT* 1 (1956-57) #1, 9.

Trans-Jordan

L. W. B. Rees, "The Transjordan Desert," *Antiq* 3 (1928) 389-407.

P[atrick] P. McKenna, "The Transjordan Highlands," *IER, 5th Ser.*, 37
(1931) 368-378.

*Millar Burrows, "Palestinian and Syrian Archaeology in 1931,"
AJA 36 (1932) 64-73. [II. Transjordan, pp. 70-71]

*P[atrick] P. McKenna, "Transjordania and its Rulers after the Birth
of Christ," *IER, 5th Ser.*, 41 (1933) 277-288.

Nelson Glueck, "Newly Discovered Nabataean Sites in Transjordan,"
AJA 38 (1934) 185.

*W[illiam] F[oxwell] Albright and Nelson Glueck, "Archaeological
Exploration and Excavation in Palestine, Transjordan and Syria,
during 1936," *AJA* 41 (1937) 146-153.

*‡Anonymous, "Bibliography of Excavations in Palestine and
Trans-Jordan, 1936-7," *QDAP* 7 (1938) 61-62.

Transjordan concluded

*C. C. McCown, "Two Years' Achievements in Palestinian Archaeology," *RL* 8 (1939) 97-108. [Transjordan, pp. 104-107]

*J. W. Jack, "Recent Biblical Archaeology," *ET* 52 (1940-41) 229-233. [Transjordan, pp. 231-232]

Nelson Glueck, "Transjordan," *BA* 9 (1946) 45-61. [The Eastern Desert; The Highlands of Transjordan]

Tsinnor (See: The Gutter)

Tel Turmus

Y. Dayan, "Tel Turmus in the Ḥuleh Valley," *IEJ* 19 (1969) 65-78.

Tyre

*G. A. Simcox, "Tyre," *SBAP* 12 (1889-90) 457-459.

E. D. Morris, "Tyre: A Lesson in Prophecy," *HR* 23 (1892) 489-498.

*J. A. Selbie, "Was Tyre Taken by Nebuchadrezzar?" *ET* 10 (1898-99) 378-379.

*A. H. Sayce, "The Capture of Tyre by Nebuchadrezzar," *ET* 10 (1898-99) 430.

*J. A. Selbie, "Nebuchadrezzar and the Siege of Tyre," *ET* 10 (1898-99) 475.

*Fritz Hommel, "Was Tyre Taken by Nebuchadrezzar?" *ET* 10 (1898-99) 520.

Emily DeNyse Wright, "News About Old Tyre," *BA* 2 (1939) 20-22.

*W[illiam] F[oxwell] Albright, "The New Assyro-Tyrian Synchronism and the Chronology of Tyre," *AIPHOS* 13 (1953) 1-9.

Tyre concluded

*J. Liver, "The Chronology of Tyre at the Beginning of the First Millennium B.C.," *IEJ* 3 (1953) 113-120.

*B[enjamin] Mazar, "The Philistines and the Rise of Israel and Tyre," *PIASH* 1 (1967) #7, 1-22.

(Miss) M. E. Martin, "The Destruction of Tyre," *BH* 4 (1968) 121-122.

*R. D. Barnett, "Ezekiel and Tyre," *EI* 9 (1969) 6-13. *[Non-Hebrew Section]*

Tyropoeon Valley

Claude R. Conder, "The Tyropoeon Valley," *PEFQS* 12 (1880) 77-81.

C[laude] R. Conder, "Notes. *Tyrophoeon,*" *PEFQS* 14 (1882) 156-157.

J[oan] W. Crowfoot, "Second Report of the Excavations in the Tyropoeon Valley," *PEFQS* 59 (1927) 178-183.

J[oan] W. Crowfoot, "Excavations in the Tyropoeon Valley," *PEFQS* 60 (1928) 9-27.

R. W. Hamilton, "Street Levels in the Tyropoeon Valley," *QDAP* 1 (1932) 105-110; 2 (1933) 34-40.

U

'Ubeidiya

O. Bar-Yosef and E. Tchernov, "'Ubeidiya," *IEJ* 19 (1969) 234-235.

Um el Jemal

*Selah Merrill, "The American Expedition. Um el Jemal—the Beth Gamul of Jeremiah?" *PEFQS* 8 (1876) 51-55.

Umm-Juni

N. Zimbalist, "Umm-Juni," *BIES* 10 (1942-44) #4, III.

Uzzen-Sherah

*Anonymous, "Uzzen-Sherah; and Israel's Right to Canaan," *CongR* 1 (1861) 472-489.

W

Wady 'Arrub

*Conrad Schick, "Wady 'Arrub, the Aruboth of Scripture," *PEFQS* 30 (1898) 238-241.

Wadi Dhobaian

*J. d'A Waechter, V. M. Seton-Williams, Dorothea M. A. Bate, and L. Pichard, "The Excavations at Wadi Dhobai, 1937-1938 and the Dhobaian Industry," *JPOS* 18 (1938) 127-186.

Wady Kelt

*Anonymous, "Wady Kelt," *PEFQS* 10 (1878) 119-120. [Brook Cherith]

Wadi Kufrein

*Robert Raikes, "Sites in Wadi Shu'eib and Wadi Kufrein, Jordan," *PEQ* 97 (1965) 161-168.

Wady el-Mughara

(Miss) Dorothy [A. E.] Garrod, "Excavations in the Wady el-Mughara, 1931," *PEFQS* 64 (1932) 46-51.

(Miss) D[orothy] A. E. Garrod, "Excavations at the Wady el-Mughara, 1932-3," *PEFQS* 66 (1934) 85-89.

Wadi Murabba'at

Anonymous, "Wadi Murabba'at," *BA* 16 (1953) 18-20.

R[am] Gophna, "Ma'abart," *IEJ* 17 (1967) 119.

Wadi Rabah

J[acob] Kaplan, "Excavations at Wadi Rabah," *IEJ* 8 (1958) 149-160.

Wadi Shu'eib

*Robert Raikes, "Sites in Wadi Shu'eib and Wadi Kufrein, Jordan," *PEQ* 97 (1965) 161-168.

Wadi Suweil

*Nathaniel Schmidt, "The East Shore of the Dead Sea and the Ruins in Wadi Suweil," *JBL* 25 (1906) 82-96.

Wadi el Yabis

D[iana] V. W. Kirkbride, "A Neolithic Site at Wadi el Yabis," *ADAJ* 3 (1956) 56-60.

Y

Yafo

*J[acob] Kaplan, "Tel Aviv-Yafo," *IEJ* 16 (1966) 282-283.

Yakron Valley

*M. Avnimelech, "Notes on the Geological History of the Yakron Valley and its Influence on Ancient Settlements," *IEJ* 1 (1950-51) 77-83.

Yannay Line

J[acob] Kaplan, "Excavations in the Yannay Line," *BIES* 16 (1951) #1/2, I-II.

Yarmuk

'Henry /*sic*/ de Contenson, "The 1953 Survey in the Yarmuk and Jordan Valleys," *ADAJ* 8&9 (1964) 30-46.

*James Melleart, "Preliminary Report of the Archaeological Survey in the Yarmouk and Jordan Valley for a Point Four Irrigation Scheme," *ADAJ* 6&8 (1962) 126-157.

Yas'ur

M. Prausnitz, "Tell Bir el-Gharbi (Yas'ur)," *IEJ* 12 (1962) 143.

Yavneh-Yam

*J[acob] Kaplan, "Yavneh-Yam and Ashdod-Yam," *IEJ* 17 (1967) 268-269.

J[acob] Kaplan, "Yavne-Yam," *IEJ* 19 (1969) 120-121.

J[acob] Kaplan, "An Archaeological Survey of the Yevneh Region," *BIES* 21 (1957) #3/4, II.

Tell Yunis

C[onrad] Schick, "'Tell Yunis'," *PEFQS* 21 (1889) 7-8.

Yurza (Tell Jemmeh)

B[enjamin] Maisler, "Yurza—Tell Jemmeh," *BIES* 16 (1951) #1/2, II.

B[enjamin] Maisler, "Yurza: The Identification of Tell Jemmeh," *PEQ* 84 (1952) 48-51.

Z

ez-Ẓâherîyeh

*Sylvester J. Saller, "Ez-Zahiriyye in the light of Ancient Pottery," *SBFLA* 7 (1956-57) 53-63.

Tell Zakarîya

*C. W. V[otaw], "Present Excavations in Palestine," *BW* 14 (1899) 434-443. [I. Tell Zakarîya, pp. 434-441]

F. J. Bliss, "First Report on the Excavations at Tell Zakarîya," *PEFQS* 31 (1899) 10-25.

R. A. Stewart Macalister, "The Rock-Cuttings of Tell Zakarîya," *PEFQS* 31 (1899) 25-36.

Tell Zakariya concluded

F. J. Bliss, "Second Report on the Excavations at Tell Zakarîya," *PEFQS* 31 (1899) 89-111. (Note by C. R. Conder, pp. 269-270)

F. J. Bliss, "Third Report on the Excavations at Tell Zakarîya," *PEFQS* 31 (1899) 170-187.

Charles W. Wilson, "A Visit to Tell Zakarîya," *PEFQS* 31 (1899) 334-338.

F. J. Bliss, "Fourth Report on the Excavations at Tell Zakarîya," *PEFQS* 32 (1900) 7-16.

*A[ngus] C[rawford, "Notes — Archæological, Etc.," *PER* 13 (1899-1900) 48-50. [Tell Zakarîya, pp. 48-49]

*A[ngus] C[rawford, "Notes — Critical, Etc.," *PER* 13 (1899-1900) 279-282. [Tell Zakarîya, pp. 279-281]

R. A. Stewart Macalister, "Further Notes on the Rock-Cuttings of Tell Zakarîya," *PEFQS* 32 (1900) 39-53.

C[laude] R. Conder, "Notes on the October 'Quarterly Statement.' P. 289. *Tell Zakarîya*," *PEFQS* 32 (1900) 77.

Zaphon

*Nelson Glueck, "Three Israelite Towns in the Jordan Valley: Zarethan, Succoth, Zaphon," *BASOR* #90 (1943) 2-23.

Zarefat

*Jehuda Rosenthal, "Ashkenaz, Sefarad, and Zarefat," *HJud* 5 (1943) 58-62.

Zaretan

C[laude] R. Conder, "Notes on Bible Geography.   II. Zaretan," *PEFQS* 37 (1905) 69-72.

Zarethan-Ṣarṭabeh

*George F. Moore, Conjectanea Talmudica: Notes on Rev. 13:18; Matt. 23:35f.; 28:1; 2 Cor. 2:14-16; Jubilees 34:4, 7; 7:4," *JAOS* 26 (1905) 315-333. [Zarethan-Ṣarṭabeh, pp. 331-333]

Zerethan

*Nelson Glueck, "Three Israelite Towns in the Jordan Valley: Zarethan, Succoth, Zaphon," *BASOR* #90 (1943) 2-23.

*M. Naor, "Jabesh-Gilead, Abel-Mehola and Zeretan," *BIES* 13 (1946-47) #3/4, III.

*James B. Pritchard, "Two Tombs and a Tunnel in the Jordan Valley: Discoveries at the Biblical Zarethan," *Exped* 6 (1963-64) #4, 2-9.

Zeboim

W. F. Birch, "Zeboim," *PEFQS* 11 (1879) 101-103.

W. F. Birch, "Varieties," *PEFQS* 14 (1882) 59-61. *[Zebiom]*

Zelzah

W. F. Birch, "Zelzah," *PEFQS* 12 (1880) 239-240.

Zephath

Y[ohanan] Aharoni, "Zephath *(ṣft)* of Thutmose III," *BIES* 22 (1958) #3/4, n.p.n.

Y[ohanan] Aharoni, "Zephath of Thutmose," *IEJ* 9 (1959) 110-122.

Zephathah

*C[laude] R. Conder, "New Identifications," *PEFQS* 13 (1881) 89. *[Zephathah]*

Zephathah concluded

E. Flecker, "'The Valley of Zephathah at Mareshah'," *PEFQS* 18 (1886) 148-151.

C[laude] R. Conder, "Notes on Quarterly Statement, January 1886, *Zephathah*," *PEFQS* 18 (1886) 83.

Tel Zeror

K. Ohata and M[oshe] Kochavi, "Tel Zeror," *IEJ* 14 (1964) 283-284; 16 (1966) 274-276.

M[oshe] Kokhavi, "Tel Zeror," *IEJ* 15 (1965) 253-255.

Wilderness of Zin

D. G. Hogarth, "The Wilderness of Zin," *PEFQS* 47 (1915) 61-63.

Anonymous, "Research in the Wilderness of Zin," *AT* 1 (1956-57) #1, 16.

Zion (Sion)

*Charles Warren, "The Comparative Holiness of Mounts Zion and Moriah," *PEFQS* 1 (1869) 76-88.

*W. F. Brich, "The City of David. Zion not at 'Goliath's Castle'," *PEFQS* 27 (1895) 263-264.

*W. F. Birch, "Zion, the City of David. Where was it? How did Joab make his way in to it? and who helped him?" *PEFQS* 10 (1878) 129-132, 178-189.

*W. F. Birch, "Zion, the City of David'," *PEFQS* 11 (1879) 104.

*W. F. Birch, "The Tomb of David, Zion, and Josephus," *PEFQS* 12 (1880) 167-170.

*W. F. Birch, "The Valley of Hinnom and Zion," *PEFQS* 14 (1882) 55-59.

Zion (Sion) cont.

C[laude] R. Conder, "Notes. *Sion,*" *PEFQS* 14 (1882) 156.

*W. F. Birch, "Zion, the City of David, or Acra, South of the Temple—*continued,*" *PEFQS* 18 (1886) 151-154.

*W. F. Birch, "Reply to Captain Conder's Notes on Zion," *PEFQS* 20 (1888) 42-44.

C[onrad] Schick, "Excavations on the Eastern Brow of 'Zion'," *PEFQS* 22 (1890) 12-15.

*W. F. Birch, "Ancient Jerusalem. *Zion or Acra, South not North, of the Temple,*" *PEFQS* 25 (1893) 70-76, 164-166.

*W. F. Birch, "Zion (or Acra), Gihon, and Millo. *(All South of the Temple),*" *PEFQS* 25 (1893) 324-330.

*W. F. Birch, "Ancient Jerusalem.—Zion, and Acra, South of the Temple," *PEFQS* 26 (1894) 282-284.

*Samuel Gergheim, "The Identification of the City of David—Zion and Millo," *PEFQS* 27 (1895) 120-123.

*W. F. Brich, "The City of David. Zion not at 'Goliath's Castle'," *PEFQS* 27 (1895) 263-264.

Joseph Bruneau, "Biblical Research. I. Biblical Archaeology and Discoveries. *The Location of Sion,*" *AER* 19 (1898) 46-48.

G. A. Smith, "Sion: The City of David," *Exp, 6th Ser.,* 11 (1905) 1-15.

W. F. Birch, "Notes and Queries. 1. *Mount Zion,*" *PEFQS* 37 (1905) 86-87.

Anonymous, "Notes and Queries. 2. *The true site of Zion,*" *PEFQS* 39 (1907) 162-163.

*Lewis Bayles Paton, "Jerusalem in Bible Times: V. Zion, Ophel, and Moriah," *BW* 29 (1907) 327-333.

Armand Lipman, "Notes and Queries. (2) *Zion,*" *PEFQS* 39 (1907) 317-318.

Zion (Sion) concluded

C. M. Watson, "The Traditional Sites of Sion," *PEFQS* 42 (1910) 196-220.

Cornelius Roberts, "The Lost City of Sion," *ACR* 3 (1926) 312-315.

*J. Garrow Duncan, "The Identification of the Site of Zion and Other Biblical Sites in and Around Jerusalem," *EQ* 2 (1930) 225-241.

*Samuel Krauss, "Zion and Jerusalem. A Linguistic and Historical Study," *PEQ* 77 (1945) 15-33.

*B. Dinaburg, "Zion and Jerusalem: Their Role in the Historic Consciousness of Israel," *Zion* 16 (1951) #1/2, I-II.

Zoar

W. F. Birch, "Zoar," *PEFFQS* 11 (1879) 15-18, 99-101.

*Selah Merrill, "Modern Researches in Palestine," *PEFQS* 11 (1879) 138-154. [The Site of Zoar, pp. 145-154]

*H. B. S. W., "Zoar and the Doomed 'Cities of the Plain," *PEFQS* 18 (1886) 113-114.

J. H. Cardew, "Zoar," *PEFQS* 22 (1890) 266.

W. F. Birch, "Notes and Queries. 1. *The Site of Zoar*," *PEFQS* 38 (1906) 81-84.

*E. Naville, "Hebraeo-Aegyptiaca," *SBAP* 34 (1912) 308-315. [II. The City of Zoar]

*Joseph Offord, "Archaeological Notes. *III. The Sites of Shihor and of Zoar*," *PEFQS* 45 (1913) 148-149.

*E. Power, "The site of Pentapolis," *B* 11 (1930) 23-62, 149-182. *[Zoar]*

Zobah

*G.   A.   Simcox,   "III.—Zobah,"   *SBAP* 20   (1898)   303-304.

Zoheleth

C[laude] R. Conder, "Notes by Major Conder, R.E.   V. The Stone Zoheleth," *PEFQS* 21 (1889) 90.

E. A. Finn, "The Stone (Eben) of Zoheleth," *PEFQS* 22 (1890) 199.